PEOPLE

Under the Editorship of H. Philip Zeigler

PEOPLE

An introduction to psychology

JOSEPH LYONS

University of California, Davis

JAMES J. BARRELL

Stanford Research Institute International

Harper & Row, Publishers

New York   Hagerstown   Philadelphia   San Francisco   London

Sponsoring Editor: Bhagan Narine
Book Production: Greg Hubit Bookworks
Designer: Albert Burkhardt
Illustrator: Judi McCarty
Photo Researcher: Sally Thompson
Compositor: Computer Typesetting Services Inc.
Printer and Binder: Murray Printing Company

People: An introduction to psychology

Library of Congress Cataloging in Publication Data

Lyons, Joseph, 1918–
    People: an introduction to psychology.

    Bibliography: p.
    Includes indexes.
    1. Psychology. I. Barrell, James J., joint author.
II. Title.
BF38.L9   150   78-25797
ISBN 0-06-044142-9

Contents
In brief

Contents

In detail

The past few decades have been among the most exciting and productive times in the hundred-year history of modern psychology. In this introductory textbook, we have tried to convey some of that excitement as well as what has been accomplished. However, from the outset we were faced with a number of problems. How we solved them has determined the format of this book.

A first problem is that the field of psychology, while constantly changing, retains a great deal of traditional material that should be included within a comprehensive survey, even at the introductory level. It would be just as unfair to students to imply that psychology consists only of new directions as to tell them that nothing new has happened in recent years. Yet, at the same time, we did not want to give the impression that nothing is stable or reasonably certain in this field nor that everything is constantly in flux. We have tried to solve this problem of combining the new and the old by, first, retaining the framework and organization that is familiar to psychology instructors. All the major divisions and subdivisions will be found in successive chapters, in the order in which they most frequently appear—biologically oriented material, then basic psychological topics, followed by developmental chapters, and concluding with the interpersonal and social. Second, we have included, within this overall framework, separate chapters on all the important topics, new as well as old, and in addition minichapters, which we call *excursions*, on smaller topics—emotions, time, death, and sex. These represent areas of current interest that cut across traditional categories, and that can be included in any way that the instructor sees fit. Finally, within each chapter our strategy has been to present a review of established or traditional material and then, wherever possible, to conclude with newer developments and alternative views.

A second, and perhaps more serious, problem in writing an introductory text is that although the interests of students and those of the instructor overlap to some degree—they would not be in the same classroom if this were not so—there is also a considerable divergence of interests and needs. Teachers of introductory courses are fond of saying that the hardest thing to get across is not some particular content but rather a way of thinking about the content of psychology. The divergence is reflected as well in the single demand most frequently heard from students: that the psychology they are taught be *relevant*. It is our feeling that a textbook that responds too superficially to this demand will end up as a review of fads and of the more sensational aspects of a "pop" psychology. On the other hand, we think that the demand is legitimate and that it can be answered without sacrifice of rigor or level in presenting psychology. To do so requires that one understand the serious, often unarticulated meaning behind the students' demand for relevance.

The term *relevance*, as we understand it, refers to a concordance with students' own life experiences. We think that in using this term they are asking that the material of psychology, perhaps more so than in any other science, conform to people's everyday experiences—to how and what they think and feel and want and know. This means that students will ask that certain topics be included that in fact occupy the "inner world" of most people—attitudes toward death, variations in states of consciousness, perceptions of oneself and one's body, and attitudes toward other persons. In addition, students will also ask that the methods and approaches in psychology take some account of individuals' "inner" experience, that little understood source of the most personally relevant data in psychology.

Until the past decade or so, it might have seemed an impossible task to combine this sort of relevance with an acceptable treatment of more traditional content and methods. But our sense of the recent history of psychology is that it has been undergoing a significant series of shifts during these years. One such shift has been reflected in the emergence of a new emphasis—almost a new subdiscipline—called *cognitive psychology*. Not only are new areas of interest being explored—sleep and dreams, other "inner" states, the world of the infant, the self—but a cognitive emphasis is also being applied systematically in the development of new views of established areas, for example, in recent work on memory, on learning, and on language development. In addition, the "inner" world of experience is being opened to experimental study in such approaches as that of Barber on hypnosis, Schacter on emotion, Singer on daydreaming, Fantz on infant perception, the Braginskys on adjustment among psychotics, and Schaie and others on functional changes with aging. We think that one part of what students ask for, in using the term *relevance*, is beginning to be satisfied through the new cognitive emphasis in psychology. Our book has therefore been built in major part around this new direction. We have tried to cover the new developments, and in addition we have within each chapter devoted some space to exploring topics from what we call *inside* views—that is, views which give the perspective of an individual in given situations. (Our use of this method is discussed fully in the Message to students, which follows this Preface.) In this way, we think that we have answered much of the students' legitimate demands for relevance while presenting an introductory survey that satisfies the equally legitimate needs of instructors.

As additional aids to student learning, each chapter begins with a statement of its objectives and ends with a summary of its major points. Sequentially numbered headings appear at regular intervals throughout each chapter, summarizing in advance what is about to be presented. Many of the illustrations have several parts, and, with their captions, are to be used as teaching devices. New or difficult terms are set off in the text and defined on the same page; and the definitions are then gathered in the Glossary, which is combined with the Subject Index. References are extensively used, but they are identified by superscript numbers referring to the Chapter Notes, so that they do not interfere with the flow of the text. The introductory Message tells the student what the book is, how the topics are arranged, and in addition, gives the reader what we call the *inside* viewpoint. Finally, the Epilogue contains brief essays from a number of the world's leading psychologists, to provide students with some trustworthy thoughts about the future of psychology—just in case their introductory course should have motivated any of them to become psychology majors.

For the benefit of instructors, we have also prepared a teaching manual, which we have called *Instructor's Notebook*, available for use with the text. It is intended to be a supplement and aid in teaching the introductory course, and contains the following special features: (1) An outline and summary of the contents of the chapter; (2) a brief class exercise for student practice in using the *inside viewpoint*; (3) a selection of material, keyed to appropriate passages in the text, which is difficult or technical enough to require exposition by the instructor, including basic statistical concepts, "backup" material such as basic neurology and signal detection theory, and significant research studies (where necessary, these materials are accompanied by full-page graphic or tabular presentations suitable for presenting on an opaque projector); (4) additional material, such as very recent work, "exotic" material, and some things left out of the text for reasons of space; (5) class exercises and projects, to be done in class or outside of class; (6) annotated references, for further reading or book reports; (7) examination questions, in a number of forms: objective, essay, "thought" questions, crossword puzzles based on the glossary, and questions or topics for reports.

We wish to acknowledge the reviewers who provided detailed criticism of the chapters. Moreover, special thanks are due to Madeline Iverson for preparation of the glossary, Donald Price for cartoons, and Celeste Barrell for general assistance with the manuscript. Finally, we are especially grateful to the patient and efficient staff of our publishers.

We hope that you will find this book as useful and enjoyable in the teaching as we did in the writing of it.

Joseph Lyons
James J. Barrell

T his opening message is addressed to you, the student and reader. In it, we, the authors, would like to tell you what this book is about, including some of its special features, and give you some advice as to how you can make the best use of it.

What this book contains

You may have heard the term *information explosion*. It refers to the fact that during the past twenty years or so, the amount of information that has been discovered and published by scientists has increased so fast that its growth has been like an explosion. In psychology alone, more than 20,000 separate books and articles are published every year—and this has been going on for at least ten years. And, of course, for seventy-five years before the information explosion began, psychology had been a flourishing field, with books and articles being published all the time.

Therefore, you may well wonder how one book, such as the one you are now holding, could possibly survey the whole field of psychology. It would have to either leave out much that was important or else skim everything very superficially. Fortunately, neither of these extremes is necessary. We have been able to include in this one book most of the important topics that are needed in order to survey the field—for two reasons:

Agreement on topics First, and luckily, psychologists generally agree on the most important topics in psychology and even on how these topics are to be divided up and organized. It is generally agreed that psychology consists of four main kinds of problems and topics. The first of these is related to biology—that is, answers to questions about how people's bodies, and their bodily processes, work. The material here will be found in Part One of this book, in the first four chapters. Second, there are questions concerning how people's minds work—that is, how they think and learn and remember and attend to things, and so on. This material is in Part Two, in Chapters 5 through 9. Third, there are questions concerning how people develop, from birth to death, particularly in regard to characteristics that make one person different from another. These kinds of topics are dealt with in Part Three, in Chapters 10 through 14. Finally, there are questions concerning how people get along with each other, either on a one-to-one basis or in groups, and how things sometimes go wrong in relations between people. These topics are dealt with in the final Part Four of the book, in Chapters 15 through 19.

In this way, by dividing up the vast amount of material in psychology into segments that psychologists agree on, the important topics can be covered in a single book. We have added some other material as well. There are some topics that are either new or do not fit into the usual organization, so we have reserved them for special "minichapters" that we call *excursions*. They are placed between the major parts of the book and cover such issues as feelings and emotions, time, death and dying, and sex.

Organization of topics A second reason that we have been able to provide a coverage of the field of psychology is that we, as authors, have thought about it in terms of four general statements about people. Each of these statements has helped us to organize one of the four major parts. They are as follows:

Part One. People are always embodied. Every creature, both human and animal, has a body. How that creature behaves and whatever it experiences will be determined in many important ways by what kind of body it has and how the body works.

Part Two. People are always engaged in making their own meanings. All

But first, this message...

1

creatures—certainly humans and probably most animals as well—keep trying to make sense out of what happens to them. In addition, every creature acts in ways that make the best sense to it—even though other creatures may have a different view of the matter or may make a different meaning out of it.

Part Three. People grow and change. Every creature, both human and animal, starts out in one condition at birth, develops through its own natural process of growth, and finally dies. A great deal of what each creature does can be understood in terms of where it is in its own cycle of growth and development.

Part Four. People are always in situations. Every creature, both human and animal, is somewhere at every moment. Among humans, that "somewhere" usually includes other people; among other animals, it usually includes others of its kind. What each creature does from moment to moment will depend in many ways on the kind of situation it finds itself in and on who else is in it.

As you can see from looking at the table of contents for this book, these four propositions describe the kinds of topics that are discussed in each of the four main parts of the book. To bring all this to a conclusion, we asked a number of the leading psychologists in the world to tell us, in a brief message, what they thought was missing in present-day psychology and what they thought might happen in psychology in the course of the next ten years. Their replies, plus some identification so that you will know who they are, will be found in the Epilogue.

How to use this book

Here we offer some advice on how this book is organized and how you, as the reader, might make the best use of it.

You will find that each chapter will begin with an introduction, in the form of a statement about what we plan to cover. This introduction will also give you an idea of how the material in that chapter connects with other chapters. When you begin the chapter, then, you will have some idea of the most important things to be learned, and you may then keep checking this expectation against what you read in the chapter. In addition, a summary at the end of the chapter will give you the chance to check out how well you have mastered the essential content.

Within each chapter, you will also find some aids to learning. The illustrations, in particular, have been planned to be an important part of the text. They will often consist of more than one picture, and they may have fairly lengthy captions or even questions addressed to you. We present some of our material in this way because we believe that some ideas are best offered and some questions best raised through pictures, just as other ideas are best presented through an extended verbal discussion. You should therefore study the illustrations and their captions in the same way that you might study a paragraph of the text.

We have also tried to define all the new or difficult terms at the place where they occur, by putting the definition on the same page as the term. You will find it helpful to spend a moment looking at the definition, even reading it aloud, when you come across it. (We learn by hearing as well as by looking, and it pays to take advantage of both methods.)

Finally, we have included special headings that are numbered in sequence throughout each chapter. They will provide you with a little summary in advance, so that you will know what is going to be discussed in the following few pages. These headings, plus the chapter introductions and summaries, will be useful when you review for a test.

In the remainder of this Message, we want to introduce you to this book, first by describing one of its special features, and then by using this special feature to discuss the topic of the self. Welcome to the study of *People.*

A special feature

Imagine the following situation. There is a person, X, who is fast asleep, and there are two other persons in the same room who are wide awake and talking to each other. They are talking about X and, not having very positive feelings, they take the opportunity to trade a lot of insulting remarks about X — who is, of course, fast asleep and therefore does not make any response. If awake, we can be sure that X would be greatly distressed.

Notice that this scene contains not one, but at least two situations. On the one hand, there is the situation as we just described: two persons who are awake and in the same room with a third person who is asleep, and the two are engaged in insulting the third. This is, as we usually say, what is "really" going on — and, unless there is something wrong with the two persons who are awake, they would probably agree with this description of the situation. But notice that there is at least one other situation here. It consists of the scene *from the point of view of the sleeper.* From this person's point of view, the situation does not consist of these three people; how many it does consist of, we cannot be sure, unless we were to awaken the sleeper and ask. In addition, from the sleeper's point of view, there is no insulting going on; many other things might be going on, but again, we would not know about them unless we asked.

Now notice that all three people in this scene are acting quite sensibly in terms of how the scene appears to them — that is, in terms of the situation from their own point of view. The two awake persons are having an enjoyable time insulting someone who, perhaps, might not permit it if awake. The sleeper, on the other hand, continues sleeping peacefully, for in the situation of sleeping and dreaming no insults are being made. Yet because the sleeper has a different point of view than the two awake persons, their behavior is quite different.

We would like to suggest that in any scene in which people are present — and perhaps many kinds of animals as well — you will find more than one situation. There will be, first of all, the situation in general, just as an observer might describe it — that is, the situation as it "really" is, as we usually say. But in addition, there will also be, at the very same time, one or more situations from the points of view of the persons who are present. Each person will have their individual point of view; each will be, from that point of view, in a different situation. If the scene consists of two persons talking, we will find, first, the situation as it "really" is, or the situation as it might be described by an observer. In addition, there will be two other situations in this scene, one the situation from the point of view of Person A, the other the situation from the point of view of Person B. Whether the "A" situation and the "B" situation are alike or whether they resemble the "observer" situation could not be determined unless we asked each of the participants, or more specifically, unless the participants were able to tell us.

In this book, we are going to talk about many different kinds of behavior, by both humans and animals, from the point of view of an observer. We will refer to this as the *outside view*. This is the view psychologists as well as other scientists take when they want to study some kind of behavior. They try to make the most accurate possible observations, arranging circumstances so that their own personal viewpoints are eliminated as far as possible. In other words, they do their best to stick to the *outside* view. This is because the outside view is the general view, and that is what scientists are trying to achieve: a general, agreed-on set of observations that they can then try to explain by means of a theory. Psychologists, like other scientists, have therefore been committed to emphasizing the outside view in their research.

But it has also been apparent to some psychologists, for at least a hundred

4

Fig. 1. Ernst Mach looks out through his eyes, over his mustache, and past his nose to his lap and his legs. This is what we call the *inside* view. (From Mach, 1897).

years, that for every situation described by an observer, there could be found a different situation that might be described by a participant. Look at Figure 1. It appeared in a book by Ernst Mach, an Austrian physicist and psychologist, almost a century ago, as part of his discussion of the difference between the two sciences. Physics, he said, dealt with the view of the scene that might be taken by an observer—the outside view, as we have called it—whereas psychology dealt with the kind of view shown in Figure 1. We will be referring to this other view, which we will call the *inside* view, in many of the discussions that follow.

Psychology differs from the other sciences in this one important respect: that every bit of behavior that it studies can be looked at from either an outside or an inside view. Or, to put it another way: Every bit of behavior that the psychologist studies can be described in two ways—either from the viewpoint of an outside observer, or from the viewpoint of the creature that is engaged in the behavior. However, although we may be sure that both views, the outside and the inside, are available, it is the outside that is usually easier to obtain. Inside views are hidden and private. Indeed, in some instances, such as the inside views held by very young children, or mentally retarded adults, or any other animals than humans, a great deal of ingenuity is required in order to find out what their inside views might be. And even intelligent adults have some difficulty providing complete and accurate reports of their personal experiences.

For these reasons, most of the data collected by psychologists consist of observations made from the outside view. The inside view has been rather neglected as a source of information. It is our hope, as authors, that this book will help to correct the imbalance and to restore inside views to the respectable position that Mach thought they should have, a century ago. Within each chapter, as you will see, we will make some place for considering the topic from an inside point of view.

My self

In order to introduce you to our use of the inside view, we will devote the remainder of this Message to discussing a single topic, the self. We have chosen it because this is a topic that can be considered from many different points of view, outside as well as inside and various "mixes" of the two.

We will have to admit at the beginning that this is not an easy topic to discuss. We do not, for example, have an adequate definition of the self. As a start, then, we make some general statements, hoping that as we go along, we can achieve a little more precision.

We think that if you asked a lot of people about their selves, many of them would say something like, "I think there is some central element in me, or in my personality, that defines me as an individual." One writer put it in these words:

"What shall I compare it to, this fantastic thing I call my Mind? To a wastepaper basket, to a sieve choked with sediment, or to a barrel full of floating froth and refuse? No, what it is really most like is a spider's web, insecurely hung on leaves and twigs, quivering in every wind, and sprinkled with dewdrops and dead flies. And at its geometric center, pondering forever the problem of Existence, sits motionless and spiderlike the uncanny Soul."[1]*

Some people might use the word *soul*, some might use the more technical term *ego*, and still others would simply say I, but we think they would all be referring to much the same thing. We will call it the self—meaning the sense of one's own individuality that resides at one's very center.

---

*Numbers like this will appear all through the book. They are meant to refer you to the Chapter Notes, which begin on page 487, immediately following the Epilogue. The Chapter Note will tell you the source of this quotation, and you may then refer to the References to find the complete name of the book or article.

The first curious aspect of the self that we must mention is that we are talking about it here as though it were present within each person—yet of course it is not an object or a thing. The self that we are discussing here is certainly not an identifiable structure in the body. We would dissect the brain in vain to find its location. Like the little man in the cartoon (Figure 2), we would be rather surprised to have its location pinpointed exactly.

Because it is not a thing, some ways of talking about the self are inappropriate. If I say that I know I "have" a self, I am using the verb in an unusual way. I might say, for example, that I "have" two arms, or that I "have" some Elton John records, or that I "have" a parent or two, or even that I "have" a bad case of sunburn. These are all forms of possession, although they may differ in permanence or importance.

These items—the arms, the parents, the sunburn, the records—are all possessions, and this is why I can say that I "have" them. Curiously, however, I can only say that I have them because they are *not* me. My self, on the other hand, *is* me, or at least a very important part of me—and so it is not quite correct to say that I "have" it. It is so central a part of me that I cannot "lose" it without ceasing in some way to be me; and so I do not say that I *have* my self, but that I *am* my self.

What might it be like to feel the Self being lost? It would be an unbearable moment, as we see in these words, spoken by a very disturbed and anxious five-year-old child to her psychiatrist: "Are you the bogey man? Are you going to fight my mother? Are you the same mother? Are you the same father? Are you going to be another mother?" And then, screaming—"I am afraid I am going to be someone else!"[2] We may guess that for this child the very sense of personal identity is sometimes in doubt.

We have just looked at a number of characteristics of the self. One conclusion from our brief review might be that it is so elusive a notion that it cannot be pinned down for study. But as we shall see, the self has in fact been the subject of many studies, and even more surprisingly, from both the outside and the inside viewpoints. We will now examine some representative kinds of research.

Fig. 2

1. The self has been studied from the outside, in animals and children, by observing responses to mirror images, and in adults by exploring what they are willing to disclose about themselves.

Self-concepts*© *and how they develop. If the self is a part of the personality, then it probably comes into being and develops just as do the other aspects of the personality. This development has been studied in young children, but of course not from an inside view. That is, one could not ask children who do not yet talk whether they are aware of some central element in their personality. Instead, psychologists have to devise some technique that will produce the same information, but from the outside. One of the most ingenious of such techniques was devised independently for chimpanzees and for infants. It consists of placing a spot of chalk or rouge on the nose of the animal or child, placing the animal or child in front of a mirror, and then observing what happens. When this was done by Gallup, using chimpanzees as subjects, the animals did not reach up to the mirror but to their own faces to rub off the spot. From this, he drew the conclusion that they realized the image was of their own faces. It can then be inferred that these animals had a sense of their own selves.[3]

In a more elaborate study, which independently used a similar procedure,

self-concept. The whole image of self, including ideas, attitudes, and feelings persons have about themselves from infancy onward.

Beulah Amsterdam[4] tested a series of children ranging in age from three to twenty-four months. In her procedure, the child was placed in a playpen that had a mirror on one side, and the mother then put a spot of rouge on the side of the child's nose. She positioned the child facing the mirror, saying "See, see, see," and then pointed at the child's face and said "Who's that?" The child's behavior was now observed after the mother sat down.

Although they showed some individual variability, the children in this study tended to go through a common sequence of stages, as shown in Figure 3. Beginning as early as three months, the child shows a definite interest in the mirror, reacting to it as a bright and fascinating new toy. By the fifth month, the child has started to play with the mirror image, as though it were a friendly playmate. Between seven and thirteen months, movements are directed toward the image, such as pushing, patting, and kissing or mouthing. Occasionally at the seventh month, but more often between nine and thirteen months, the child searches for the "person" seen in the mirror—looking behind the mirror or feeling around it. (Cats and dogs often show this stage of response, although they rapidly lose interest when they find nothing there.)

At about eleven months, fear first appears as the child begins to react negatively to its own mirror image. This is followed by a withdrawal phase, at times accompanied by crying, between the thirteenth and seventeenth months. As early as fourteen months in some children, but almost always by twenty months, the child begins to show self-consciousness before the mirror, acting in ways that adults can appreciate—preening, showing embarrassment or shyness, or acting coy. Clear evidence of self-recognition, as shown by a definite reaction to the spot of rouge, appears in some children as early as eighteen months and in at least two-thirds of the children by twenty-four months. Thus we can say with some confidence that at some time toward the end of the second year children develop this aspect of the self, but that this occurs only after a fairly well-defined succession of earlier stages that include interest, fear, and pleasure.

What people will disclose of themselves. Using the mirror is a technique that will work with young children and animals, but other approaches are necessary if adults are being studied from the outside view. One possibility would be to reason as follows: If people do have some special sense of themselves that refers to a self at the core of their personality, then they should talk about it or report it differently than they talk about more impersonal matters. In other words, the way that people disclose themselves, compared to the way they talk about impersonal

Fig. 3. Stages in the development of one aspect of the self-concept in children. The placement of the horizontal bars indicates the time during which each type of behavior was displayed (see text). (Based on data from Amsterdam, 1972)

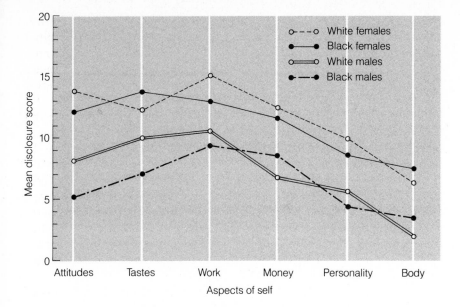

Fig. 4. Average of self-disclosure scores toward one's own father. (Adapted from Jourard, 1971)

matters, should tell us something about how they either reveal or protect the self.

However, in pursuing this line of investigation, we have to bear in mind that disclosure can be quite complex. A lot of skill and practice is needed in order to talk precisely about one's own self. To talk freely about oneself, on the other hand, may require a lack of concern about being precise. Equally, concealing aspects of the self, such as we do when we lie, is not easy to do well. Young children are often poor liars and only learn it by repeated practice in interaction with older persons who have more skill at it. It is not certain whether dogs and cats are capable of lying; the evidence we have is mostly anecdotal, since no one seems yet to have devised an experiment that might give a firm answer. Among the higher apes, however, deception has been observed that is very nearly the equivalent of lying—for example, a caged chimpanzee that seems to ignore human visitors, "pretending" innocence, until they are close enough to be hit suddenly with dirt or feces from a hand hidden behind its back.[5]

It can also be argued that lying, being a verbal skill among humans, enters into most of our social activities. In this connection, one student of communication and language remarks, "The ability to say that which may not be so (lies, fictions, errors, superstitions, religions, hypotheses, science, delusions, and ambitions) lays the foundations for some of man's greatest achievements, as well as for some of his basest acts, and much of his mental illnesses."[6]

The topic of self-disclosure© was extensively studied by Sidney Jourard.[7] Using a simple questionnaire, he asked people what kinds of information they would reveal about themselves to specific other persons such as mother, father, male friend, female friend, or spouse. Typical responses for some groups of subjects are shown in Figure 4. It appears that on the average people will disclose impersonal information—about work or tastes or attitudes—more easily than they will disclose more personal information about finances, personality, or their own bodies. Jourard also found that college students in America, England, Lebanon, or Puerto Rico respond in about the same way, but that there are important differences between the sexes. In general, adult women were willing to disclose more to their fathers than were adult men. Jourard concluded that women disclosed more or less depending on how they felt about the topic and the questioner, while men varied their disclosure in terms of how they defined the situation.

self-disclosure. Jourard's term for the act of communicating one's experiences to others through words and actions.

2. Self-reports often mix up the person's own inside and outside view of the matter.

At this point, we must add one complication to what we have said so far about inside and outside reports. We said that an outside view is what is taken by an observer, who is usually relatively neutral. For example, if you look out the window of your house and see someone on the sidewalk who appears to be screaming angrily at another person, you can observe the situation calmly, with some interest and without any anger on your own part. This is an outside view of the situation. For an inside view, we would have to go to one of the two participants, whose reports would probably differ from yours and also from each other.

The complication is that when people make reports about themselves, they can take an inside view, or an outside view, or just about any mix of the two. People are often able to be quite objective and neutral about themselves, just as though they were taking a completely outside view. Indeed, athletes and other performers probably need to be able to do this in order to improve their skills. Some persons may even strike us as being remarkably objective about themselves, so much so that we look in vain for some expression of feeling that might indicate they are taking a personal, private, inside view of their own selves.

Most of the time, however, our own view of ourselves is more like that of an insider than an outsider. Our self-reports will lean more toward inside than outside views, although usually with some mix of the two. This may lead to some interesting results, as was once shown in an experiment by Werner Wolff.[8] It is a complicated experiment that requires some explaining.

Wolff was interested in whether people could make accurate judgments of others on the basis of limited information about them. To find this out, he set up an elaborate experiment, in the course of which he made an unexpected discovery about people's reports of their selves. His procedure consisted in recruiting twenty people, whom he then told that he wanted samples of their behavior for his studies in learning. He had each of them do various tasks, but as they were doing them he obtained, without their knowledge, other samples of their behavior and expression. For example, he would ask them to read an eye chart, but at the same time he would obtain a silhouette photograph of their face; or he would ask them to take a test in English composition, although his real interest was in getting a sample of their handwriting. He also recorded their voices, took motion pictures of their gaits, and obtained photographs of their hands, for a total of twenty samples that they did not know had been obtained. Wolff then contacted the closest personal friend of each subject and obtained a capsule description of that person's personality. Finally, he waited until some months had passed, called his twenty subjects individually, and asked if they would like to serve as judges in a different set of experiments on personality.

When they returned to the laboratory, assuming that this was to be a different experiment, they were presented with all the behavior samples, their own as well as that of the others, and asked to describe the personality of the individuals concerned. The criterion,$^\odot$ or standard for how well they did, was the set of descriptions that had been given by the best friends. Surprisingly, Wolff's twenty subjects did very well by comparison with the best friends, even when he tested them on only a few samples from an individual—for example, even when they had nothing to go on but a sample of handwriting and a photograph of a hand. More surprising, and quite unexpected, were the results when they judged their own samples. The first finding was that they almost never recognized that it was their own, not even their handwriting or the sound of their own voice. The second

criterion. The level of performance at which learning is defined as being completed for a certain task.

finding, which is significant for the topic of the self, was that when they judged the samples that were their own, their descriptions usually differed. They were much more strongly expressed or more emotionally charged, either positively or negatively.

These results certainly suggest that when judging expressions produced by one's own self (even when there is no conscious recognition of the identity), one can hardly avoid mixing in a personal, inside view. In other words, when I pass judgment on myself, I may try to maintain an outside, observer's view and I may even think that I am successfully doing so, but the chances are that to some extent my own personal, inside view of myself will enter and color my judgment.

3. Examples of primarily inside views of the self are found in studies of self-esteem and in the personality theory of Carl Rogers.

Studies of self-esteem.[○] The most direct way to find out what people personally and individually feel about their own selves is to ask them. As Wolff's experiment shows, the answers that people give to such a question will usually be very *evaluative*. They will take the form of judgments of good versus bad, and, as we might suspect, they will be quite personal. They may or may not correspond with what other persons, taking an outside view, might say.

As might be expected, one's self-esteem is deeply influenced by circumstances of early life. During the years prior to the emergence of feelings of pride and unity among American blacks, it was often found that black schoolchildren were low in self-esteem, quite probably as a consequence of their treatment by whites. When kindergarten children were shown two dolls, one black and one white, and asked for their preference, two-thirds of the black children picked the white doll as "nicer" and one-third of them even picked the white doll as looking like them.[9] In extensive studies of self-esteem among fifth-grade children, Coopersmith has found that higher levels of self-esteem occur when children have had parents who acted in these ways: They accepted their children unreservedly but set and enforced definite limits, and they made clear that this was done out of respect for the children. On retesting a sample of fifth graders after an interval of three years, to determine whether level of self-esteem was a stable characteristic of the personality, Coopersmith found that their scores had not changed significantly.[10]

Carl Rogers' self-theory. The concept of self figures prominently in the theory of the personality developed by Carl Rogers.[11] He begins by assuming that each individual personality is organized around a central element, the self. This means that people's behavior, including most of what they think, feel, and do, will be determined in important ways by the self that is theirs. It also means that in order to understand another person well enough to be of help to them, as a counselor or a therapist, one has to empathize[○] with that person's self. One has to "hook in" to the person's inside view of themselves and their world.

For Rogers, these are not mere words or labels but very real parts of the personality, determining how each person sees the world. In the course of growing up, the powerful influences of one's parents and other significant adults lead to some acts and thoughts that one does getting valued as good and others as bad. In effect, people connect themselves with good and bad acts and thoughts. The totality of all these connections becomes the anchor around which all new actions are

self-esteem. A person's self-respect, or one's concept of one's own worth.

empathy. Literally, "in-feeling" or "in-suffering." Taking another person's point of view, especially to the extent of feeling what the other person is feeling.

organized. If the result is a rigid self that is defended at all costs, or an isolated self that is closed off from others, the person may then need counseling. The starting point of such counseling, in Rogers' system, has to be a complete, unconditional acceptance by some other person, a guarantee that one's beleaguered self, in all its strengths and weaknesses, is accepted for what it is. Then the way is open to change in the self, leading to change in the whole personality.

4. In exceptional cases, we may see a breakdown of the self, leading to disturbances of the personality.

We have been talking about the self as though it is usually coherent and whole. Yet certain unusual cases provide evidence that this is not always so, and that some people can develop either a self that is split into parts or perhaps a personality made up of a number of different selves. This condition is called *multiple personality*.[◎] It was first documented in the 1890s, when the first attempts were being made at systematic theories of the personality. One of the best known such cases in modern times received wide publicity as a book and then as a movie, under the title *The Three Faces of Eve*.[12] It concerned a woman who was known in her "first" personality as Eve White, a sweet, conforming, and traditionally feminine woman. During one session of her psychotherapy, which she had undertaken for help with her headaches and blackout spells, she suddenly changed into Eve Black, a playful and seductive vixen. Eve Black knew about Eve White, but Eve White seemed to be unaware of Eve Black. As the treatment proceeded, the two personalities alternated, until Eve's problem was resolved with the emergence of a more mature form of Eve White, named Jane. With Jane's appearance came the dramatic breakthrough of repressed childhood memories, followed by the development of a new, integrated personality.

A still more elaborate drama was played out in the recent case of Sybil, also published as a novel and made into a movie for TV. Here the number of separate personalities reached sixteen.[13] Under hypnosis, the many personalities, male and female, were able to talk to each other and finally, after more than 2,300 therapy sessions, to resolve their split by forming a new, integrated seventeenth personality. Although the separate development of so many seemingly complete personalities might appear to be a remarkable achievement, it resulted in this case from a lifelong tendency to withdraw from stress and to deny the reality of the neglect and brutality she experienced from a psychotic mother. Sybil had apparently resorted to the first defense of the self, to limit the world of experience in which it was engaged. Only after years of support and guidance in therapy was she able to give up this defense, to face what the various selves had blocked out of her own history, and to form a mature self that could accept and deal with the world as it was.

In Oscar Wilde's remarkable novel *Dorian Gray*, on the other hand, there is presented, not only a number of selves in conflict but also a tension between them so intense that it can only be resolved in death. The plot of the novel is well known. A very handsome young man has his portrait painted and then has the mad desire that he should stay forever young, while his portrait ages. His wish is granted, but in excess, for not only are the normal marks of aging imprinted on the painting but every change in his social self as well—signs of dissipation, moral decay, and finally ruin. But Dorian himself, meanwhile, remains as fresh, youthful, and innocent in appearance as the day the portrait was painted. Each day he creeps up to a hidden room of his house to stand in horror before the painting. Like

multiple personality. An extreme form of a dissociative personality in which an individual has two or more separate and distinctive personalities alternating and often conflicting with one another. The personalities are not usually known to each other.

our own changes in the social self, however, only the results are visible; the process of change itself is never seen.

What Wilde presents, masterfully if somewhat overdramatically, is thus the self as it confronts one's ever-changing social selves. In the author's view, when *I* and *me* are so badly at odds as here, they can no longer be joined in life. And so, when Dorian can no longer stand the image of his own self, he stabs the portrait in the heart. The next morning his servants come on the scene: "When they entered, they found hanging upon the wall a splendid portrait of their master as they had last seen him, in all the wonder of his exquisite youth and beauty. Lying on the floor was a dead man, in evening dress, with a knife in his heart. He was withered, wrinkled, and loathsome of visage. It was not till they had examined the rings that they recognized who it was."[14]

A concluding word on the self. In this section, we have tried to spell out two ideas—first, that even a concept as elusive and intangible as the self can be studied, discussed, and made use of in many different ways. Second, we have used the topic of the self as a demonstration project, to exemplify the various viewpoints that can be taken in psychological studies—inside, outside, and mixes of the two.

We do not mean to imply that a person's self can be pinned down easily for study, either by that person or by observers. We suggest, rather, that each of us keeps some sort of contact with the individual self, and may even be organized around it or guided by it. But we probably do not ever "know" it in the sense that we clearly know other things about ourselves. It may even be that as we go through our individual lives, we learn more and more, in many different ways, about this self that is always with us.

In James Agee's provocative novel of childhood, *A Death in the Family*, he writes, "sleep, soft smiling, draws me unto her; and those receive me, who quietly treat me as one familiar and well beloved in that home: but will not, oh, will not, not now, not ever; but will not ever tell me who I am."[15] They will not, as the boy who speaks these lines learns; no one will, for life may be nothing but a continuing voyage, through significant choices, to discover the self.

Part one

BODIES
The psychobiology
of individuals

This book tells about people's behavior, or what they do, and people's experience, or what they think and feel and want. Neither behavior nor experience begins at birth. The roots of both are to be found in the prenatal period, and they extend back beyond that to earlier generations.

This is why we begin this book on psychology with a chapter on genetics and inheritance.

This chapter will help you to think about inheritance as more than the simple matter of passing bits of genetic material from one generation to the next. It will give you an idea of the complexities involved in this process and also of the mechanisms by which inheritance is accomplished.

Specifically, this chapter will show you that what happens in the course of inheritance is something like this: Living creatures inherit the physical structures that belong to their species, but they also inherit the natural settings in which they live. The structure and the setting, fitting together, make an individual's appropriate behavior possible.

Notice that the statement just made is very different from a statement that says: behavior is inherited. You will see that this is the main point of Chapter 1, that behavior is not inherited, only structures and settings that fit together. At the end of the chapter, this will be spelled out in detail, using sexuality as an example.

1

Genetics and inheritance

Each one of us begins life as the individual union of two cells, an ovum that is about 1/120 of an inch in size and a sperm cell that is even smaller. After weeks of furious growth, the human embryo may have multiplied to as much as 10,000 times its original size, but even at seven weeks it is barely an inch long and weighs less than 1/30 of an ounce (Figure 1.1). Within this tiny organism, however, there is already a distinguishable face with its eyes, nose, lips, ears, and tongue, a pair of hands with thumbs, and a working liver, stomach, and kidneys. From the moment of conception, a schedule of development has taken over and started to produce a functioning creature according to the plan of its species. The schedule is in the form of a genetic blueprint, passed on from one generation to the next, in every kind of living thing, whether tree or insect or animal or human. Much of what the living being is and does are determined in important ways by its genetic blueprint. Our question in this chapter is, "How does this come about?"

1. The question of what is inherited is more complex than it seems. It is a matter of both genetics and setting.

If we were to ask most persons a question about what we inherit genetically, they might point to an example such as skin color or perhaps pigmentation of the eye. In explanation, they might add that what is passed on from parents to child are certain genes, which in turn determine individual characteristics, such as eye

15

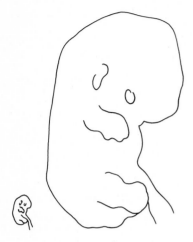

Fig. 1.1. The human embryo at seven weeks of age. The larger view shows the development in detail. The smaller view (in the lower lefthand corner) shows the actual size of an embryo at this stage of development.

chromosome. The chainlike structures, found in all body cells, that carry the genes, which are the genetic determiners that are transmitted from parent to child.

DNA. Deoxyribonucleic acid; large molecules that are responsible for genetic coding and are found in the nuclei of all body cells.

gene. The basic element by which heredity is transmitted. They are located within the chromosomes and contain DNA.

genetic engineering. The control and manipulation of hereditary factors by scientists to achieve certain desired characteristics.

color; other physical characteristics, such as height; and perhaps even musical ability or excitable temperament. But all that can be transmitted, as far as we know, are the chemical molecules contained in the original pair of ovum and sperm. What can we mean when we say that one or more of these molecules "determines" a person's eye color, or even more remarkable, that some molecules "determine" the skill and artistry with which someone will later play the violin?

There are two different questions here. The first has to do with the mechanics of the genetic process, or more precisely: What is the process by which the genetic material is transmitted from one generation to the next? We will discuss this genetic mechanism in the next section. A second question, larger and more important for psychology, concerns the nature of inheritance. Again, stating it more precisely: in what way are the structure and behavior of living creatures related to their genetic makeup? This is not simply a biochemical question, so we will discuss it first under the heading of *Behavioral Settings* and then under the heading of *Behavioral Genetics*.

The genetic mechanism

Thanks to recent advances in molecular biology and in particular the advent of the electron microscope, we now know in some detail how the mechanism works.[1] Each human ovum and spermatozoon contain, inside their nuclei, bits of material called **chromosomes.**⊙(Much of this knowledge, incidentally, is surprisingly new. It was not until 1956 that we had definite proof that in humans there are twenty-three pairs of chromosomes.) The chromosomes, themselves about 1/2000 of an inch in size, contain in turn molecules that measure barely one 50-millionth of an inch. Some of these molecules are composed of a chemical called DNA⊙ — and it is the particular arrangement of the DNA molecules that carries an individual's inheritance. An arrangement of DNA molecules, coiled in the form of strands and joined by other chemical bonds, is called a *gene,*⊙ the basic unit of the genetic mechanism (Figure 1.2). All of these structures occur, of course, at the molecular level, and the amounts of substance involved are almost unimaginably minute. The total amount of the chemical DNA, at birth, in all the humans who have ever been born would total less than 1/100 of an ounce. Yet this droplet has determined the different genetic programs for every individual of our species for more than two million years. Such is the delicate balance of our biological inheritance.

2. Genetic engineering⊙ is approaching a working possibility. Should it be pursued, and if so, should it be controlled?

Discovery always leads to further discovery. As the history of research on atomic nuclei showed, pure science may be carried on for its own sake but often leads to practical results, which can be either advantageous (as in the use of radioactive particles in medicine) or dangerous to humanity (as in the case of nuclear weapons) or a mix of good and bad (as in the development of atomic power). With the lessons of recent history behind them, geneticists have become concerned about the outcome of current research, in which some of the genes of one creature are transferred into another creature. So far the procedures are in their infancy, but no one doubts that the possibilities are, in principle, almost unlimited. At present, such transfers have been done successfully from one strain of bacteria to another, and even from the cells of a human donor to the chromosomes of a bacterium recipient. It is also known that DNA transfers occur spontaneously in nature, especially at the bacterial level.

Perhaps the human genetic constitution is far too complex to be very much altered by introducing some bits of DNA from another species or another kind of creature—and so this kind of biogenetic engineering poses very little risk. But there is always the possibility that altering one gene, or only a few, by such methods may produce a strain of human monsters or deadly bacteria. Such possibilities are no longer mere science fiction.

A serious argument is now underway over ethical issues, between those who say that science should go wherever the search for knowledge leads and those who claim that scientists and other citizens have no moral right to destroy or profoundly alter the pattern of nature just because they have the capability of doing so. This argument surely lies behind our every discussion of the achievements of a science of genetics.

The phenotype and the genotype. As the human organism grows, from a single fertilized cell at conception to the more than 200 billion cells that make up a newborn infant, the way it develops is determined largely by the organization of its genes. The particular makeup and organization of genes in an individual is called its *genotype*.[○] It is similar but not precisely the same in all the members of a species. But even given this genetic mechanism, the transmission of characteristics from one generation to the next is far from simple. The set of observable characteristics to which the genotype gives rise is called the *phenotype*.[○]

3. The relation between genotype and phenotype in an individual may be simple or complex and can be studied in cases of chromosomal "error."

In the simplest case, phenotype is the expression of the genotype, and the direct connection can be traced, as has been done repeatedly with the tiny fruit fly *Drosophila*. In humans, this direct connection is well established in characteristics such as the color of one's eyes or whether one's earwax will be more dry than wet. The connection also seems to be direct in regard to characteristics that are not simply structural but functional as well. An example of such genotype-phenotype linkage is given in Table 1.1, together with some experimental data to support it. The crystals of phenylthiocarbamide, or PTC, taste bitter to some persons but not to others. It has been known for some time that the "ability" to taste PTC seems to run in families. There is a simple mathematical procedure, the foundation of what

Table 1.1. The bitter taste of PTC. (Modified from Cotterman and Snyder, 1939, p. 514)

If the parents were	The predicted percentage of tasters among their children would be	And the actual (observed) percentage of tasters was
Both nontasters	0.0	2.24
One taster and one nontaster	64.68	63.47
Both tasters	87.53	87.72

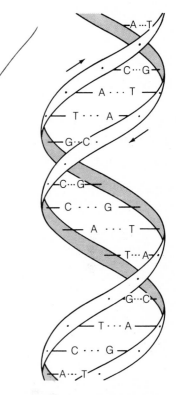

Fig. 1.2. The structure of a gene, according to Watson and Crick. The twisted strands consist of sugar and phosphate. Linking the strands are different sequences of either cytosine and guanine (labeled CG) or adenine and thymine (labeled AT). The particular sequence of CG and AT links forms an informational code that determines the individual's genetic inheritance. (From Watson, 1968, p. 202)

genotype. The genetic makeup of the individual, which is transmitted to descendants through dominant and recessive genes.

phenotype. In genetics, the observable characteristics of an organism, such as hair color or intelligence. It is distinct from the genotype, which is not displayed.

is known as *classical* or Mendelian genetics, by which one can predict the inheritance of certain simply determined traits. It was first worked out, using as data the characteristics of varieties of garden peas, by an Austrian monk, Gregor Mendel. He published his results in 1868, but, as so often happens, it was largely ignored. Then, in 1900, Hugo de Vries, a Dutch scientist, independently did similar work — and, incidentally, coined the term *mutation*[☉] to refer to sudden or traumatic changes in genetic makeup. Table 1.1 presents the results of a study of 800 families of tasters and nontasters of PTC. As you can see, the observed percentages agree almost perfectly with what would be predicted by Mendelian formulas.

"Errors" in the chromosomes. Genetic errors (or, as they are called, *anomalies*) may also appear at the level of entire chromosomes. As we have noted, the chromosomes are small bodies contained within the nuclei of an individual's cells. Of the twenty-three pairs of chromosomes that each human being carries within every cell of the body, one of the pairs, called *sex chromosomes*,[☉] determines whether the individual will be male or female. If both are shaped like an *X*, the individual will be female; if one is shaped like an *X* and one more like a *Y*, the individual will be a male.

In a small percentage of cases among humans, for reasons that are not presently known, the individual is born with an excess of either X or Y sex chromosomes. For example, in addition to a forty-fifth and forty-sixth sex chromosome both being X, as in the normal female, there will be a forty-seventh, also X, and even a forty-eighth and a forty-ninth. Studies of such conditions of "chromosomal error" indicate that in addition to many kinds of physical and mental defect accompanying this situation, which usually requires hospitalization, the more extra X chromosomes there are, the more severe the mental defect. Among males, similar conditions involving extra Y sex chromosomes are also found.

The most extensively studied such condition among males is known as "47 XYY," because the individual has a forty-seventh sex chromosome, which is Y-shaped. In the 1960s, it was suggested that the presence of the extra Y chromosome was associated with three characteristics of personality: borderline intelligence, extreme height, and periodic aggressiveness of a dangerous nature. The evidence came from chromosomal studies of a group of mentally retarded criminals, in whom seven XYY cases were found in 197 subjects. This percentage far exceeds what would be discovered in the normal, nonprison population. The finding precipitated extensive studies of the chromosomal makeup of large populations of males, for here seemed to be the first instance in which a clearly identifiable genetic structure could be linked to a socially important type of behavior.

The results of some ten years of studies are now in, and they are far from conclusive. First, not all XYY males are tall, nor are all of them of borderline intelligence. Further, many XYY males are sober citizens, leading exemplary lives. A recent summary of the data shows that whereas only about one or two in a thousand adult males who are law-abiding citizens have the XYY makeup, it is found in more than one per hundred in mental hospitals and in more than two per hundred in jails. The authors of this survey suggest that since the Y chromosome is what determines male sex and since males are strongly suspected of being innately more aggressive than females, there may be a genetic connection between "maleness" and the number of Y chromosomes and aggression. Thus, as they say, "the XYY genotype may be seen as highlighting the association between maleness and violence," making the person more male, so to speak. Under particular environmental conditions, this may appear as antisocial violence.[2] Equally, some very "male" men who happen to be large and tall may have found it easier to commit crimes of violence.

mutation. A change in the chemical makeup of a gene that causes an altering of the characteristics carried by that gene.

sex chromosomes. The chromosomes that determine the sex of an individual. Females have two X chromosomes, and males have an X and a Y chromosome.

Other studies in a number of different countries, however, have cast some doubt on these conclusions. One recent review of all the evidence suggests that there is no relation at all between the XYY pattern and antisocial behavior as long as one takes into account the individual's background and social class.[3] As we will see in the rest of this chapter and in a later chapter on the measurement of intelligence, the issue is partly a technical question concerning the connection between genotype and phenotype. However, it is also partly a larger question concerning the interaction of genetic and environmental factors.

To the question of what is transmitted by way of the genetic mechanism, we may now answer, "Parents pass on to the next generation of their species some molecules located in specific arrangements within the chromosomes of the children, and this in turn leads to, although it may not completely determine, a set of active, functioning structures."

Genetic inheritance: The setting

As we have seen, the question of transmission between generations can be answered by referring to active chemical structures. But this is not enough to explain *inheritance*, as distinct from mere transmission of characteristics. Parents transmit characteristics to their offspring, to be sure, but the offspring inherit more than these characteristics. One of the additional elements that must be included, if we are to understand inheritance, is the *setting* or environment in which structures are active.

4. The individual's given structure serves as a starting point that must be located within an appropriate setting.

What was implied but not sufficiently emphasized up to this point is that every living organism, from the one-celled amoeba to the multibillion-cell mammal, exists somewhere in the world (see Figure 1.3). All behavior is nothing but a means for getting along in the world. It must therefore always occur in a setting—a fact so obvious that we tend to ignore it. Particularly in humans, the settings are likely to be extremely variable, ranging from isolated mountain tops to crowded city streets, from mothers' laps to lovers' arms, from swimming pools to space capsules.

The case of the trained raccoon. Two American psychologists, Keller and Marian Breland, some years ago developed a thriving business of training animals for commercial displays (Figure 1.4). One of their cleverest notions was a live behavioral display to be presented in shop windows as an inducement to customers to deposit their savings in a specific bank. Instead of using trained pigs (which would have been quite feasible) to drop coins into a large piggy bank, they decided to work with a raccoon, since it is known to be very skilled at manipulating small objects. After some difficulty, they trained a raccoon to drop a coin into a slot in a metal box in order to receive a food reward. Then came the next step: The raccoon had to learn to pick up two coins in sequence and drop them in before being rewarded. Here is the Brelands' description of what happened:

Now the raccoon really had problems (and so did we). Not only could he not let go of the coins, but he spent seconds, even minutes, rubbing them together in a most miserly fashion, and dipping them into the container. He carried on this behavior to such an

Fig. 1.3. Is this a monster? If so, it is a monster only on our planet, where it is out of its natural setting. If it were in its own setting (whatever that might be), it would not be a monster, but an inhabitant. What is "normal" in one setting may be "monstrous" in another. (Drawing by Dean, 1975)

Fig. 1.4. If a pigeon is trained to peck at a disc for food, and if both a button and a star are available as targets within the disc, it will always choose to make its "food peck" at the button, as shown. In addition, if it is trained to peck at one disc for food and at an identical disc for water, it will always make its "food peck" at the food disc and quite a different kind of peck at the water disc. The behavior of most animals toward specific targets is quite precisely organized and is often very difficult to alter. (From Garcia, Clarke, and Hankins, 1973, Fig. 3)

extent that the practical application we had in mind . . . simply was not feasible. The rubbing behavior became worse and worse as time went on, in spite of nonreinforcement [The term *nonreinforcement* here refers to the fact that the animal did not get rewarded for the behavior].[4]

The raccoon was not simply being miserly, although that term may be appropriate from our human point of view. Rather, we have to keep in mind that in their natural state, living in the forest and searching for food under logs and in streams, racoons often need to "wash" their food or, if it consists of crayfish, to crack and shell it. Part of the normal activity of a raccoon is to hold and manipulate objects in this way rather than to pick them up and drop them. The behavior is thus "normal" in the sense that it belongs in the raccoon's natural setting. If we remove the raccoon to a store window, it will now go through the same behavior. From the inside viewpoint of the raccoon, it brings along its setting and is behaving normally. From the outside viewpoint of the human observer, the raccoon is bringing behavior that is appropriate only to another setting.

5. The term *instinct*, which was once widely used to explain such behavior, is not very useful and leaves out the factor of setting.

Because such seemingly fixed behavior is very common in animals and perhaps even to some degree in humans, a term was introduced to refer to it. The term

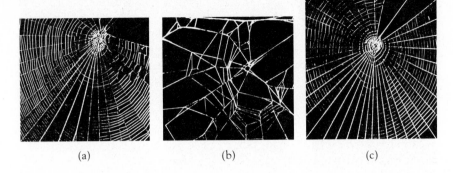

Fig. 1.5. (a) A normal web for one species of spider, (b) a web made by a spider of the same species when under the influence of caffeine, and (c) a web by a spider when under the influence of LSD-25. Note that the LSD results in an almost artificially perfect web structure.

(a)   (b)   (c)

was *instinct*.[☉] Scientists who used it implied that the animal was genetically "programmed" in such a way that, unless one interfered with it, the animal would act in certain fixed and predictable ways. The cuckoo, for example, even though it often happens to be hatched and reared by a different kind of bird, will at the appropriate point in development begin to sing its cuckoo song and will carry out an elaborate courting ritual so as to mate with another cuckoo. Surely, or so these scientists reasoned, the only explanation for such unlearned behavior was that it was inherited, and, specifically, what was inherited was an instinct to behave in this way.

A major objection to the idea of instinct is that it leaves out of account the very important factor of setting. Behavior that used to be called *instinctive* had two major characteristics: that it did not appear to be learned from or taught by another member of the species and that it was carried out in the same way by every member of the species. In attempting to find an explanation, biologists were struck with the fact that all members of the same species have in common a set of genotypes; that is, that they all share the same heredity. It was therefore concluded that the behavior, which is typical for the species, must be caused by the genetic inheritance, which is also species-typical. What was forgotten in all this, however, is that the setting in which a species lives is as common to all its members as its genetic makeup. Species-typical environments are as typical and as fixed as species-typical genotypes. Behavior that is called *instinctive* is therefore just as much a function of regularities and similarities in the environment as in the genes (Figure 1.5).

Indeed, without this environment that is typical for the species, an individual member would be unable to function as a member of the species. The loss would be as disastrous as being born with an "error" in the chromosomal arrangement. Thus, the raccoon's behavior in persisting in "washing" its coins rather than depositing them in a slot is not blind and instinctive at all. It is the animal's transplanted response to the demands of its natural setting, demands that include the requirement that objects be fingered and rubbed before being used in any way. As one psychologist has put it, "Pick any animal species at random, study its behavior in its normal habitat throughout its life cycle, and you will discover an intricate set of behaviors, many of them of almost incredible matching relationships to demands of the environment, like a lock and key."[5]

A more appropriate term than *instinct* for such phenomena would be *species-typical behavior*,[☉] recognizing that what is typical is both the genetic background and the behavioral setting. In the course of evolution, certain structures have evolved in each species. The structures, on their part, have evolved as successful adaptations within specific environments. In a real sense, nature has developed creatures that are each fitted to an environmental niche. Some niches, of course,

instinct. A complex, inborn pattern of behavior that is supposed to be unlearned and common to all members within a species.

species-typical behavior. Also, *species-specific* behavior. Characteristics found in one species of animals but not in other species. It is sometimes linked to instinctive behavior.

are so small that almost any disruption of the environment threatens the existence of the species. This was seen recently in the discovery of a species of fish, the snail darter, whose ecological niche was restricted to one ledge on the bank of one river in Tennessee. Change the course of this river, and the species would be wiped out. Other species, such as the cockroach, the American crow, and the common field rat, appear to be able to survive and even flourish in an amazingly wide range of settings, to a degree equaled, perhaps, only by humans.

6. Settings change, and so the creatures adapted to them also change. The result is history.

Only under the most ideal circumstances, which probably occur rarely, will an individual run off a genetic "program" in completely rigid fashion. In fact, this may be the essential difference between a living creature and a mechanical device. A machine that is, let us say, programmed to stamp things flat will keep doing this as long as energy is available to run it—even if nothing is there to be stamped or even if the wrong thing, like someone's foot, happens to be in the way. In order for the machine to refrain from stamping someone's foot or to discontinue its stamping under special circumstances (such as a humid afternoon, when sparks from the stamping might create a hazard), special and additional instructions for just such possibilities have to be included in its programming.

But living creatures seem to be different. In addition to whatever functions are built into them, they all seem to be equipped to make whatever *general* variations may be necessary to accommodate themselves to a changing or unpredictable environment. That is, they appear to operate by flexible rules rather than by strict instructions. This difference is exemplified in the instructions, "Put the large objects on top of the small objects," as distinct from the rule, "Make as neat a pile as you can." Even the lowly and simple amoeba has its defenses, limited though they are. Under many different kinds of threat, it will draw away, change its shape, and alter its boundaries—not in a fixed way but in terms of the specific threat of the moment. Thus it is capable of an almost infinite variety of reactions to threat.

From light moth to dark moth. What happens when the setting changes at a pace more rapid than usually occurs in the course of evolution? An answer can be given from extensive studies of species of common moths in England that are the normal food of birds. One of the ways that such moths protect themselves from predators is by blending into the natural color of tree trunks. As a result, until about a century ago most such moths were fairly light in color, since the tree trunks in daytime were also light colored. Then, beginning during the last half of the nineteenth century, airborne particles of coal and other contaminants began to darken the tree trunks in industrial areas. As more and more trees changed in color from light to dark, the natural resting places of the moths disappeared; and if they did seek refuge on these tree trunks they were immediately spotted by birds and eaten.

Under such environmental pressures, these species of moths began to change in coloring. The result was that they adapted by blending into tree trunks. No single moth changed its color, of course. Rather, careful studies have indicated that a process of natural selection⊙ has occurred. Lighter colored moths have died out, or have been eaten in greater quantities by birds, and darker colored moths have survived to pass on their protective coloring to their offspring. In this way, over a

natural selection. In evolution, the process of selection in nature by which those within a species whose genetic makeup is most adaptive to their environment continue to survive and transmit these characteristics. Those that are less fit tend to die off.

rather short period of time, significant changes in a species' color have occurred under the direct influence of a changed environment.[6]

Genetic inheritance: Behavior

We have distinguished, first, between the genetic mechanism itself, which serves to transmit certain arrangements of molecules, and the process of inheritance. In the preceding section, we maintained that one cannot properly speak of genetic inheritance without including, as part of the picture, the setting in which the inheritance works itself out or is displayed. In the present section, we will discuss additional elements to increase our understanding of how the process of inheritance results in an individual's behavior.

7. The individual's given structure is also a starting point in time—that is, it is at the origin of a network of possibilities of behavior.

The structures that individuals possess and the settings in which they act are not two separated things but rather two closely interlinked elements in the individual's total existence. Through the course of generations of inheritance, setting and structure affect each other in a continuing process that we call an individual's *behavior*. Since the behavior is a part of the continuing genetic process, it would not be stretching the term too much to say that the individual's behavior is also selected in the course of generations (see Table 1.2). Behavioral patterns have their own course of evolution: Those that work get selected *in*, and those that do not work get selected *out*. In the extreme case, the individual fails to survive, but in the majority of instances the behavior undergoes shifting and adaptation.

As a result, if we look closely at instances of animal behavior in its natural, nonlaboratory state, we find that it represents the end result of a process of selecting structures to fit settings. For example, at first sight it seems rather puzzling that rats in a laboratory can easily learn to choose alternate paths to a maze—that is, first Path A, then Path B, and A again, and so on—if their reward is food, but not if their reward is water. The puzzle is solved, however, when we learn that in the natural setting, which is where wild Norway rats must survive, food is likely to vary in its location, while water is not. They have therefore developed a kind of behavior, which can then be tested as an ability, that enables them to survive under the particular conditions of the natural setting. The question of whether or not a rat can learn an alternating maze is thus less sensible than it seems, for it does

Table 1.2 Some examples of behavior that, for some creatures, are possible, but that are a limit that other creatures cannot achieve. Every living creature has its own repertoire of both possibilities and limits.

Some creatures can	Creatures for which this is either		
	a possibility	or	a limit
Live 100 years	human		dog
See ultraviolet light	bee		human
Answer to their name	horse		snake
Come when their name is called	dog		horse
Learn by means of punishment	dog		cat
Get up off their back	human		turtle

not take into account the naturally occurring restrictions on what the animal *can* learn. Similarly, the question of whether a horse can learn to answer to its name is more complex than it seems. Studies have shown that horses easily learn their names and will prick up their ears and whinny when called by the appropriate person. A horse can even be trained to come when called — but not if it is in the company of other horses.[7] The reason, of course, is that a horse is a herd animal, selected over thousands of generations to place the highest priority on remaining with the herd as a matter of survival; so, under these conditions of setting, the horse is unable to "learn" a simple trick that it is certainly capable of mastering.

8. Inheritance in the full sense helps to ensure that each form of behavior develops in its setting at the appropriate time.

As the individual now develops, it may even happen that patterns of behavior appear, play their part, and then disappear, fitting into an appropriate segment in time. This is what happens in the case of what is called *imprinting*.° Young fowl reach a point in time at which for a brief period they are acutely sensitized to the presence of a large moving object. Normally this is the mother, and so normally they zero in on this visual target and follow it faithfully, often for years afterward. But if the young are kept isolated during this period — it ranges from a few days to a few weeks in different species — they may never "learn" to follow the mother or, indeed, any large moving object.[8]

Full development requires that critical events occur and at the "right" time. Thus, disadvantaged children in modern society are compelled to live in impoverished settings during critical periods of childhood and then may grow up to appear retarded on mental tests. In a similar development of its possibilities in time, the human infant begins life with a specific reflex action of the toes: A light touch or scratch on the sole of the infant's foot causes the toes to fan out. Toward the end of the first year of life, however, this reflex changes, and almost certainly the structures in the central nervous system that are associated with the reflex also change. The pattern is replaced by one precisely its opposite: Pressure on the sole of the foot causes it to curl up. This new reflex — and the nervous system structures that underlie it — is just what the young child needs at this point in development, an ability to curl the foot to get a grip on the ground as it learns to walk. Each structure fits its setting within the unfolding context of its development in time.

The fine adjustment of structure-setting-behavior-time, changing subtly in the course of the individual's life span, is often marvelous to behold. One of the most critical moments of development, in many species of animals, occurs just at birth. Thrust into the world and forced to exist on its own, the individual creature must adjust its behavior with absolute precision at this point; very few mistakes can be tolerated. The inheritance of many animals, therefore, appears to be concentrated at birth, in the form of abilities so delicately attuned to the setting that they can be hard to believe. For example, in many species of birds, such as gulls, nesting sites are extremely crowded. Thousands of nest sites will be packed together on a stretch of beach. Under these circumstances, a fledgling that wanders even a few feet away from its nest and mother will very soon be lost among others of its kind or possibly be killed by waiting predators. In the interests of survival, the young of such species as Antarctic penguins must be able to make a sound that can be recognized by an individual mother and the mother in turn must be capable of making a sound that is recognized by the individual fledgling.

imprinting. Relatively fixed learning that occurs within a critical period of development in response to a stimulus and is later difficult to modify.

The balance of existence of many members of a species thus depends on this sensory structure, in this setting, displayed as this mode of behavior, at a point in time no later than the first few days of life. The total pattern is closely related to its setting, for in a species of gull whose nesting habits are different (they build isolated nests high on cliffs) and whose members therefore do not need such a specialized skill for survival, neither the making nor the hearing of such sounds has been developed. Members of these latter species cannot even be trained to respond to such sounds.[9]

The cycle of the ring dove. An American psychologist, Daniel Lehrman,[10] studied one developmental pattern that is so elaborate and so little dependent on training that it is tempting to apply to it such terms as "instinctive pattern" or "innately determined behavior" or even "maternal drive." It is the sequence of feeding behaviors that occur between a mother ring dove and its squabs in the nest, from birth to weaning (Figure 1.6).

After the dove's eggs are hatched, two hormones are automatically produced in the mother's body. One of the hormones apparently leads her to sitting very close to the newborn squabs, perhaps even on them, and remaining there when prodded. The other hormone causes her to produce a secretion called *cropmilk*, so called because it is stored in pouches at the throat called *crops*. No more than the production of these hormones is required to start off a complex cycle of behavior in the setting of a crowded nest. The mother dove, in some discomfort as the crop becomes distended with stored milk, crouches among the squabs. They thrash around, still very weak and helpless, until—as very probably will happen sooner or later—one of them brushes its beak against the mother's crop. She turns at the touch and pecks at the source of the irritation, just as she might do in other circumstances—but at this moment her pecking just may result in the squab's bill ending up inside her mouth.

If this should happen, the squab's immediate movements cause the mother to

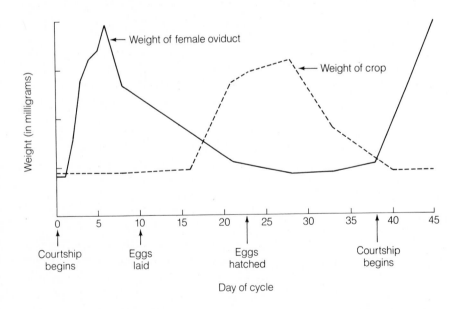

Fig. 1.6. Lehrman's studies of the reproductive cycle of the ring dove (see text) showed that the weight of the parent's crop as well as the weight of the female oviduct (or fallopian tube), changed in accordance with the situation from day to day. The birds were supplied with hay for nest building and with a small glass dish for a nest, as in the drawing on the right. (From Lehrman, 1964, pp. 48, 54)

regurgitate her cropmilk—just as you or I might do if a beak were stuck down our throat—and so feeding can take place. In this way, the sequence occurs for the first time, by a series of prepared for but fortuitous "accidents." The second time the sequence may occur more rapidly, for it is now, as psychologists say, more probable. In addition, the fact that it occurs with one squab increases the probability that it will happen with one or more of the others, for they all have now started to learn that the parent, and in particular the parent's beak, is a source of food. Very shortly, and seemingly without any previous training, they are all engaged in a complicated ritual of feeding.

The process of weaning, too, is accomplished as part of the cycle. The parent's own food has been grains, which up to the time of weaning are directed to the bird's stomach, bypassing the crop. At the appropriate time in the sequence, the parent's supply of cropmilk begins to decline and is mixed in with grain in a proportion that finally becomes all grain and no milk. As the growing young birds learn to feed on a diet that is closer and closer to that of adult birds, they gradually become equipped to forage for themselves when they finally leave the nest. The entire complex process of interlinked behavior has been started by minimal structural changes in the parent's body that are genetically determined. They lead to action and reaction, on the part of the young, which fit their setting like a key in a lock. From the point of view of an observer, it might appear that these birds are "instinctively" directed toward the desired end. From the point of view of a contemporary ethologist,° however, the pattern is an understandable sequence unfolding in time. Finally, from the point of view of the individual squabs (if we may use such a phrasing), a situation has been presented, some learning has taken place, and some greatly desired rewards have been obtained. Thus we see that in one sense, learning is the individual's "inner" view of the unfolding of its own behavioral possibilities.

What is inherited? We are now in a position to make a summary statement in answer to the apparently simple question of what is inherited. There is surely no question that much of the behavior of living creatures is related to their genetic makeup and inheritance. But it would hardly be correct to say that for this reason the individual inherits its way of life. For one thing, there are no "behavioral genes," no genetic structures that determine behavior in any direct mechanical way. The full statement has to be somewhat more elaborate.

As we have seen, all that is transmitted between generations is the biochemical basis for specific structures and bodily processes. These structures interact with some setting that is appropriate for the species, changing the setting and also being changed by it, in a pattern that develops in time. This end result, experienced by the individual and observed by others, is itself the product of a very long process of evolutionary selection within the species.

The genetics of sexuality

In earlier sections of this chapter, we distinguished between genetic mechanisms and the process of inheritance. As we noted there, some of the traits and characteristics that are transmitted between generations are linked directly to the presence or absence of certain genes. For example, whether an individual shows the trait of color blindness depends on whether the parents possessed a specific combination of genes for the trait. On the other hand, a characteristic such as being female or male (that is, one's gender) is not determined by the presence or absence of any genes but by whether the individual's makeup of chromosomes contains twenty-two pairs plus a pair of X chromosomes, or twenty-two pairs plus an X and a Y chromosome. The differentiation occurs at the moment of fertilization. if at this moment the X chromosome produced by the mother links up with a father's

ethologist. A scientist who studies animal behavior under natural conditions, particularly behavior that is instinctive or specific to a certain species.

sperm cell bearing an X chromosome, the result will be an XX offspring, which will then become female. If the mother's X chromosome links up with a sperm cell containing a Y chromosome from the father, the result will be an XY offspring, which will then become male.

The combination produced at fertilization, whether XX or XY, immediately affects all the cells that are subsequently produced by the development of the fertilized ovum. If the fertilization had produced an XX combination, all the cells of the body produced thereafter will contain the twenty-two human pairs of chromosomes plus an XX pair. If an XY combination had been produced at fertilization, all the body's cells will contain twenty-two pairs of chromosomes plus an XY pair.

The X and Y chromosomes. The field of molecular genetics has been very actively developed during this century, so that a great deal is now known about the way the molecular arrangements that we call *genes* are distributed along the various chromosomes.[11] A picture of such a distribution is called a *gene map.* Two kinds of data are involved in gene mapping. On the one hand, it is possible by various methods to trace an observable trait to the presence or absence of specific genes—even though one might not know to what particular chromosome that particular gene belonged. On the other hand, by means of specialized investigations at the molecular level, using electron microscopes, one can find evidence of just where on a particular chromosome a known gene is located.

Out of the approximately 50,000 genes that are estimated to exist in the human chromosomal makeup, approximately 1,200 have been connected with known traits. However, to date only about 210 of these genes have been mapped to specific locations on chromosomes in humans. As examples, the genetic locations for the ABO blood group are found on Chromosome 9, and that for the Rh blood group on Chromosome 1.

The X and Y chromosomes have been found to differ remarkably in their genetic material. More than a hundred genes have been traced to the X chromosome, but only two with some certainty, and possibly a third, to the Y chromosome. The one that is merely probable on the Y chromosome is that for excessive height in males, as seen in many XYY males—but microscopic evidence for this is scanty. Of the other two genes traced to the Y chromosome, one appears to determine the male's acceptance or rejection of tissues, as, for example, occurs during transplant operations. The other, known as TDF (testis-determining factor) controls for the presence or absence of the testes (the sperm-producing organ). Aside from these, it seems from present evidence that most other traits that are carried in the genes and transmitted through the sex chromosomes are found on the X chromosome.

Recall that the female bears two X chromosomes and the male only one (plus a Y chromosome). Since the X chromosomes are the major bearers of genetic transmission, it has been seriously suggested that the female XX configuration is genetically "basic." According to this thesis, just about everything that can be carried genetically in the sex chromosomes is supplied by the female. The purpose of male chromosomes, then, is not to transmit characteristics but to increase variation through bisexual breeding.

9. Sexuality is a species-specific patterning of behavior that is controlled by genetic, chromosomal, structural, environmental, and finally cultural factors.

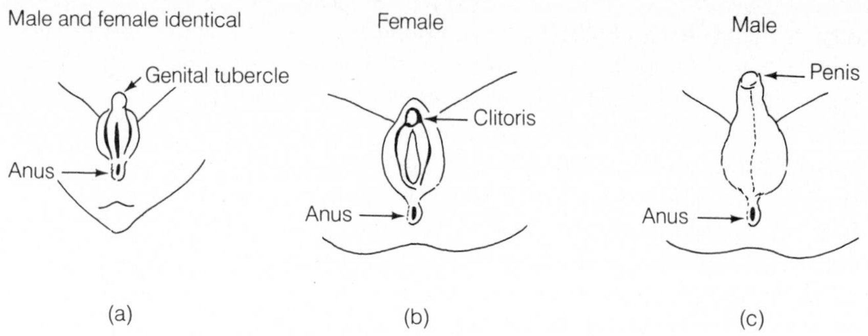

Male and female identical   Female   Male

(a)   (b)   (c)

Fig. 1.7. Although the external genital apparatus of the two sexes is identical before the third month of pregnancy, as shown in (a), it has differentiated into two quite different structures by the time of birth—(b) and (c). (From J. Money, 1965, p. 5)

Sexuality—that is, whether the individual is female or male and the consequences that result from this—is not determined at the gene but at the chromosomal level. Sexuality is not a genetically transmitted trait like eye color or color blindness. Rather, it is an inherited pattern of behavior-in-a-setting, which is profoundly influenced, as all such patterns are, by a complex mix of psychological and social factors. To understand this, we must look first at the structures of sexuality, at the anatomical and biochemical arrangements through which sexuality occurs. In Excursion V, at the end of the book, we will take up the topic of how sexual behavior is related to its setting and to the influences of culture and society.

Sexual structure and sexual hormones. Until about the third month of fetal development in the human embryo, it is very difficult to detect any structural difference in the sexual apparatus of the male and female, either internally or externally (Figure 1.7). The fetus in either case has, externally, a minimal groove where the vagina may later be and a small, rounded mass that may later become the penis. Internally, there is both a male and a female structure plus an organ that will eventually become either ovaries or testes.[12] The determination as to which occurs has already been decided, by the union of XX or XY chromosomes at conception. When this structure begins to function as a sex gland, as ovaries or testes, it controls everything that happens subsequently in sexual development.

These sex glands, or gonads,° accomplish this by means of the specific hormones that they secrete under the influence of the master hormonal gland of the body, the pituitary. Normally the ovaries secrete the female hormones, and the testes secrete the male hormones. The hormones in turn determine the development of other sexual characteristics through childhood and into adulthood, when they are finally responsible for effecting the production of either egg cells in the female or sperm cells in the male.

In both male and female, the sex hormones are compounds of a number of different substances, and their intermixture, as well as their effect on each other and on behavior, is not completely understood. It might appear that because the hormones are necessary for sexual development and functioning, removing them or adding them to the individual would produce predictable effects, but this is not so. The results obtained depend in part on the size and complexity of the individual creature in an evolutionary sense. For example, if the gonads are surgically removed in laboratory rats, the effect in both sexes is quick and drastic: The female ceases to have a regular estrus cycle and is no longer sexually receptive. The male stops all sex-related behavior. In dogs, although the same result is obtained in the female, the male's reaction is much slower (see Figure 1.8). In some male dogs observed under laboratory conditions, complete sexual performance persisted for years following castration.[13]

The situation is even more complex if the procedure is reversed and the animals are given sexual hormones, either following surgery or in addition to their

gonads. The sex glands of either males (testicles) or females (ovaries) that determine secondary sex characteristics.

own normal supply. Under these circumstances, sexual behavior is always rein-stated in the rat and often in the dog but not necessarily to the same degree in the male and female. At the human level, ovariectomy or castration may or may not affect sexual behavior, depending on the individual. Injecting artificial hormones appears to affect only the intensity of the sexual drive rather than the object or the timing of sexual behavior. For example, the use of artificial male hormones as a form of medical therapy for male homosexuals does not change their sexual pref-erence but merely increases the intensity of their sexual preference for males. For all these reasons, the generalization has been offered that as one goes up the evolutionary scale, with increasing complexity of nervous systems and with in-creasing dominance by certain parts of the brain, sexual behavior comes to be less and less controlled entirely by the presence or amount of sexual hormones.

Fig. 1.8. Some effects of castration on the copulatory performance of dogs. (From Beach, 1969)

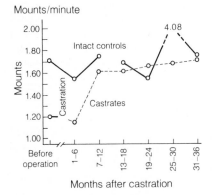

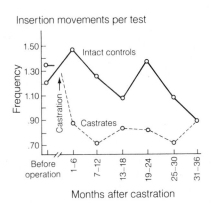

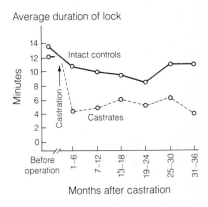

The control of sexuality. This conclusion may be stated in another way. At the most primitive level of sexuality, the formula "1 + 1 = conception" seems to apply. That is, under certain regular conditions that are always related to timing, one female and one male when brought together will result in starting off a process that results in conception and then the birth of the next generation. But as the individuals of a species and their behavior become more complex, capable of being influenced by more and more factors in themselves and in the environment, the simple formula no longer applies. Sexual behavior becomes increasingly more complex and less predictable. As Frank Beach has shown, female beagles, even when in heat, show clearcut and reliable preferences for certain male dogs and will even completely reject some (see Figure 1.8). Other factors, such as territory, be-come equally important, and often competing, imperatives in the individual's existence.

Genetic, chromosomal, and structural factors thus become only one of a number of controlling influences in sexuality. To state the matter in summary fashion, we may say that, to some degree in most species but to a maximal degree in humans, the following factors beyond the genetic play a part in determining sexual behavior:

- Chromosomal makeup, specifically the presence of XX or XY sex chromo-somes, which determines sex structure and gender
- Hormonal° production, specifically of estrogens (female) or androgens (male sex hormones), determining sexual development, many sex characteristics, and the production of eggs or sperm
- Reproductive structure, or the presence and functioning of the full internal set of reproductive organs

hormone. Chemical secreted by the endocrine glands that affects behavior and body functions.

- Physical structure, or the presence of the full external set of genital organs and characteristics appropriate to each sex
- Assigned sex, or the gender that adults say the child is
- Psychological sex, or the specific masculine or feminine identification that the individual develops in the course of socialization. This may or may not be identical with the individual's preference for sexual acts and partners.

In humans, where all of these factors come into play, the weight of each factor will vary from one individual to another. To relate the specifics of sexual behavior to only one of the factors, then, is to ignore the full complexity of an act as fundamental for all living creatures as is the sexual.

10. The appearance of fully unrestricted breeding in humans shifts control over sexual selection to cultural rather than biological factors.

A distinguishing characteristic of species that are "higher" on the evolutionary scale is that, while the female tends to preserve a restricted breeding season, the male's sexually motivated behavior is unrestricted. Thus the male of such species as the dog or cat is constantly on the prowl or at least constantly available for sex. However, the female's interest and receptivity is limited to relatively brief periods of heat known as *estrus*.© The biological advantages of this kind of arrangement are evident: It permits each one of the pair to exercise in individual ways a choice of characteristics that may then be transmitted between generations. At the lower phylogenetic levels, we usually find restricted breeding on the part of both males and females, the more or less random mating of an individual male and female, and very large numbers of offspring. This shotgun approach maintains the high probability that most of the characteristics of the species will be passed on and preserved.

One of the most remarkable distinctions between humans and other species of mammals is that neither male nor female humans have a restricted breeding season. In this respect, we are unique. As a result, it is at least biologically possible for mating and production of children to occur as a consequence of all sorts of factors—a chance meeting, casual acquaintance, political or economic arrangements, or rape (Figure 1.9). The control over sexual choices, exercised at the level of most animal species by biologically fixed patterns of courtship and mating, disappears; people are, at least in principle, free to mate at random. But, as we know, this does not happen in any human group that has been studied. In fact, humans have developed a substitute set of arrangements to take the place of the biologically patterned mating procedures that are found in other animals.

At the human level, uniquely among all species, patterns of social organization take the place of patterns of biological organization in determining who mates with whom. We cannot ever know, of course, whether human families and societies originally arose so as to serve as controls over random mating. Nonetheless, whatever their origins, this is the purpose that they came to serve. By means of family groupings whose members were forbidden to mate with one another (based on the well known incest taboo that is found in every known human group), provision was made for variability of inheritance. Mating outside the family guaranteed that new traits would be introduced. Then, by various forms of courtship and approved or disapproved mating bonds, a society was able to exercise control over sexual selection. What is achieved in nonhuman species by mating dances or

estrus. A recurring state in which female mammals are sexually receptive, or in heat.

Fig. 1.9. Who is doing the choosing here, the female or the male?

by fights between males during the rutting season, is accomplished among humans by means of traditions that become part of the group's culture.

At the most basic level, then, humans utilize their biological inheritance in ways that differ significantly from those of any other species. Humans are not locked into specific periods of time for mating, nor are they linked to specific or fixed settings. Rather, their breeding time is spaced out through the year, and their biological settings are transformed into the demands imposed by culture. It is because of these differences that human psychology, although it is just as firmly grounded in biology as that of any other species, encompasses areas of concern that are largely closed off to nonhuman creatures—as we shall see in detail in the remaining chapters of this book.

Summary

1. Living creatures inherit both their structure and the settings in which they act. The basic units of the mechanism by which the inheritance of structure is accomplished are the *genes*, consisting of arrangements of DNA molecules.

2. The transfer of DNA material from one creature to another, even between species, is now technically feasible. This raises the possibility of "engineering" new life forms.

3. Genetic potentiality, or genotype, is expressed, directly or indirectly, in structures called *phenotypes*.

4. The term *instinct*, formerly used to refer to the genetic transmission of behavior, fails to take into account the setting in which behavior takes place. A more appropriate term is *species-specific behavior*.

5. Introducing the notion of setting enables us to understand changes in species and the development of new species. Settings change, and individuals that fit their structure and behavior to the new demands will survive. The process is known as *adaptation*.

6. Through inheritance, behavior as well as structure is selected. What is selected then fits the new settings, which in turn determines new behavior. This sequence changes and unrolls through time.

7. There is a most appropriate time in an individual's development for each kind of behavior in its setting. This is particularly evident in behavior that appears very soon after birth.

8. Human sexuality is determined at the chromosomal level by whether the twenty-third pair of chromosomes is XX or XY.

9. The X chromosomes of the twenty-third pair carry most of the species characteristics.

10. Patterns of sexual behavior in the human result from a number of factors: whether the chromosomal arrangement is XX or XY, the specific anatomical structures that develop in embryos as a result of sex hormones, and the influences of the environment that begin at birth.

11. As we go from "lower" species to humans, we can trace a change in how mating and breeding occur: from restricted breeding periods and random mating to unrestricted breeding seasons and highly selective mating.

In this chapter, we consider in some detail the body that each individual inherits. It is appropriate to consider the body at this point, following our chapter on genetics and inheritance, because all the behavior and experience that occurs in an individual's life is done through the body. It is the carrier of what is inherited and is the means by which this inheritance develops and shows itself.

A body is, of course, a structure, and a very complex one at that. It is also an apparatus—that is, a structure with its own potential for behavior. In this chapter, you will learn about the body as a working whole, with an emphasis on the fact that the body works together as a fairly well unified whole.

You will also learn about the major parts of the body. Although it can be divided up anatomically in many different ways, it is convenient to think of the body as consisting of two major functional aspects. The first of these is a system of action that is expressed through the musculature. The second is a pair of information networks that are called *nervous systems*.

Finally, you will see some of the ways in which an individual's body comes to be used as a social instrument. Each person "carves out" space in a unique way, but all persons seem to carve out directions of space in terms of certain common distinctions, such as those based on left and right and those based on the differences between the sexes.

"These pieces of moral prose have been written, dear Reader, by a large Carnivorous Mammal, belonging to that suborder of the Animal Kingdom, which includes also the Orang-outang, the tusked Gorilla, the Baboon with his bright and scarlet bottom, and the gentle Chimpanzee."[1]

2

The human body

Denying the body

What would your schooling have been like if the facts of your bodily existence had been placed at the very center of the school curriculum? The body's wondrous structures and its miraculous functions, its intricate behavior, as well as your own lived experience of it, would have been the core subject, perhaps called *Me*. It would have been concerned with each one of us—how we feel from hour to hour, from day to day, from time to time, where we itch and why, what goes on inside us and what we think and do about it, and all the other ways that we use our bodies to move and want and do and grow.

1. Culture and education have served as major instruments for the denial of the body.

However, the view of the whole person that we have just described is almost nonexistent. Feiffer's cartoon (Figure 2.1) expresses the view that is prevalent, the commonsense view implicit in everyday thinking and expressed in our educational system as well as in the institutions of society. The view can be stated very succinctly: We largely deny our bodies.

Fig. 2.1

The consequences for socialization. In his theory of child development, Sigmund Freud described three stages of the preschool years—the oral, the anal, and the phallic, referring respectively to the areas of the body whose activities largely determine the child's experience and behavior at that stage (regarding boys, not girls, for Freud was never certain nor confident about what happened with little girls). We will consider in a later chapter the details of these developmental stages, but here we can note that in at least one respect Freud's insight was sound. Until children are plunged into the process of being socialized at school and of coming to terms with the impersonal authority of the adult world, their personality development centers primarily around their own bodies. As studies of child temperament have shown, preschool children express their problems primarily in bodily terms—by hiding, by striking out, or by temper tantrums. After they enter school and begin to be socialized in one way or another, these same children will express their problems in more "mental" ways, such as poor self-concepts, negativistic or self-defeating attitudes, extensive fantasies, and depression.[2] Their parents, of course, may have already helped them to begin denying the body.

With the first year of culture shock on entering school, like the shock experienced on diving into the cold water of a swimming pool, the life of the body is put aside. Freud called the next five years the latency period,° a time when sexual impulses, as he thought, were held in abeyance, not to be revived until puberty. Freud may not have been correct about sexuality but his insight was sound concerning socialization. The early school years are the time in which we adults do our best to force the child's interest and energy out of the body, and into the head and the abstract world of letters and numbers.

This seems to be especially true of the children of both sexes who become the successes in our academic system and later in our society. They are the ones who end up living in their heads, and specifically in their brains. For them, as with some idealized science fiction character, the person is essentially a nervous system dominated by the brain. Somewhere down below this can be found, in descending order, some mechanical contrivances called *muscles*, which carry out the executive orders coming from on high, and some automatic and usually cyclic functions done by a set of vague internal organs. There are, in addition, occasional urges and drives that upset the orderly process of executive activity by their demands for release of dammed-up tension. Finally, there are specific parts—our feet, our buttocks, our lower backs—that we know nothing and care less about, and would prefer to rule out of awareness.

This portrait, supposedly of the whole human being, is a reasonably accurate summary of how many people function. It is also a summary of the "whole" human being as described in many textbooks of psychology. If a Martian were to imagine the adult human being on the basis of how that creature is described by contemporary psychology, this would be its picture: an asexual behaver consisting of a nervous system for carrying messages and directing actions, plus a set of processes called *drives* or *motives* that well up mysteriously from down below.

A new orientation. However, over the past ten years a new orientation toward the body seems to be appearing, at least in the United States. A number of reasons can be found for this turnabout in attitude. The most sacred of all our attitudes that have served to hide the body, the sexual, has undergone vast changes in the period since World War II. The youth culture has had a special impact on views of the self and of people's experiences of themselves and others. The worldwide interest in ecological causes parallels a renewed interest in what is natural, including the animal body of the human being. Years of economic affluence have helped to make possible our freedom from the extremes of climate and a consequent widespread pleasure in using the body freely in outdoor activities.

Professional interests have also changed, because they are products of a culture. A set of disciplines have become popular that are concerned with learning about the body for purposes of training and guidance; for example, yoga, forms of massage, Rolfing, and body therapies. What has been aptly called a "movement movement," marked by an interest in the study of body movement and body and facial expression, has developed out of a fusion of dance therapy, communication, and cultural anthropology.

The whole body

Nothing is so much taken for granted as our bodies. It is as though they did not matter. Yet the life of the individual, the personality we know so well, and the behavior that we observe and try to understand are all tied closely to the effective functioning of the body. It works within surprisingly narrow limits. An increase of body temperature — that is, the temperature of the major internal organs — of no more than 9° Fahrenheit (5°Celsius) will cause death; and so will a loss of no more than 8½ quarts of one's body water through dehydration. At the same time, the body is unbelievably adaptable. It functions unfailingly, and usually without our conscious intervention, on a twenty-four-hour a day basis — the heart pumping more than 3,000 gallons of blood in twenty-four hours, the internal regulators accommodating to sudden or marked changes in temperature, humidity, noise, oxygen, or gravitational position, the sensors telling us when and how to breathe and how to move and position ourselves. Rhythms of internal chemical production, of digestion and excretion, of repair, of response to infection, of control over many bodily functions, of heat and metabolism,° go on regularly in appropriate synchrony with the day-night cycle of our normal lives.[3]

2. Although our experience is that the body functions as an assemblage of parts, in fact the body functions as a whole.

Because we have so many ways to analyze the functions of the body, we are strongly tempted to believe that its work consists in fact of many little part-processes all somehow meshing together — and then we may even spend a lot of time

metabolism. The continual physical and chemical processes going on within a living organism. Some of these processes build up food into protoplasm, and some break down protoplasm into simpler units and waste, releasing energy.

Fig. 2.2. Acupuncture, a system of medical diagnosis and treatment that is more than 2,000 years old, is based on a holistic view of bodily functioning. (From Veith, 1949)

larynx. Commonly known as the "voice box," the muscle and cartilage in the upper trachea containing the vocal cords through which sound is emitted.

trying to find out the secret of their unity. But it is just the opposite that is closer to the truth (Figure 2.2). The body *always* works as a whole. The robot appears mechanical precisely because its parts seem to move separately.

This is easy enough to demonstrate. Bend your right arm at the elbow, as though you were gripping someone around the head in a wrestling hold—that is, with your elbow held away from the body. Now bring your elbow down close to your side and repeat the movement. You will find that you have a lot more power in the gripping movement of your forearm if your elbow is held at your side—that is, if your upper arm is also brought into play. Now do the same thing with your hand. Hold your arm straight out, with your wrist level, and clench your fist as hard as you can. Compare this with the greater power in your grip when you flex your hand upward at the elbow, when your forearm is also brought in to help.

The point is that we can muster one level of strength when the arm is straight and away from the body, and we can muster a greater level of strength when the arm is held close to the body. The same arm muscles are used in both cases, but when we bend the arm we also bring into play the powerful muscles of the torso. We are not usually aware of this at a conscious level, and it takes a little demonstration, such as we just tried, to bring it to our awareness. But at another bodily level we are always aware of how our total body is positioned and what we are doing with its parts, and this is why we spontaneously bring the arm closer to the trunk if we want to exert maximum force.

In general, the normal tendency of the body is to engage every part of it in each movement, no matter how small. The smaller, finer, and more precise the movement becomes, the greater the requirements for holding in check the parts of the body that are not needed. When children are first learning to walk, they show that they have not yet mastered the trick of holding the nonwalking parts of the body in check. They use their whole bodies, clearly demonstrating that walking is what Erwin Straus once called "movement on credit," involving the use of every muscle in a continuous, balanced interchange with a moving environment. (From the point of view of the walker, we must remember, the environment is in motion.) If you find it hard to believe that even the simple act of standing still is a total bodily performance, integrated from eyebrows to toenails with a demanding and reciprocating environment, see how your own stance comes alive when you stand for 30 seconds with your eyes closed.

One of the most interesting kinds of evidence in support of the notion that the body functions as a whole comes from animal researchers who have studied what happens when some normal function is interfered with. Ordinarily breathing is done by means of the muscles around the rib cage, but if the nerves to these muscles are cut, an animal will immediately learn to breathe by means of the muscles of the larynx.[⊙] If a rat has learned to run through a maze for food and its spinal cord is then cut so that its legs are paralyzed, it will immediately switch to rolling over and over to reach its goal. These examples suggest that the original movement or action was not simply the activity of certain parts of the body but an organized function of the whole body. When the normal means of achieving the effect was interfered with, a substitute was quickly brought into play.[4]

Muscles and movements. The structures of the body alone cannot get things done. What is needed is a system to lead to movement, to get things done. This is what is done by means of our muscles.

Even a simple bending of the arm calls for different muscle roles, for different sets of muscles to take up the roles, and for a smooth and continuous changing of roles as the movement proceeds. Try it again: Rest your elbow on the table, with your arm bent at the elbow so that your hand is held up, and then let your hand fall down to the table. If you really concentrate, it may be possible to begin—but just to begin—to become aware of the continuing, delicate play of changes between extending and holding back, falling and flexing, giving and going. You may, if you are lucky and pay attention, also get to be aware of how this movement in your arm was accompanied by movements in your trunk and even in your legs.

3. There are two kinds of muscles, smooth and striped, each kind forming an action system that is interconnected throughout the body so that each part influences every other part.

We need to do two different things with our muscles: to act fairly rapidly and precisely and to build up to and maintain certain states. Just as might be expected, the body has two different kinds of muscles, each kind specialized for one of these general functions.

Smooth muscles and striped muscles. The smooth muscles,[○] which get their name because they are unstriped in appearance, make up the walls of the visceral organs[○] and the blood vessels. They respond rather slowly. They are mainly stimulated by nervous system activity inside the body. They do their work more or less automatically and rhythmically. In short, they are specialized so as to function slowly and repetitiously. Thus they allow the stability that the internal organs of the body require.

The striped muscles,[○] on the other hand, consist of fibers that are arranged so that they appear striated when seen under the microscope. These muscles form our primary social system, the action system with which we are familiar. It is attached to the skeleton, and can be exercised to enlarge so as to produce an appearance of muscularity. It is involved in all of our observable movements.

Individual muscle cells do only one thing: They contract, usually to about half their length, when they are stimulated by the release of chemicals where they are in contact with the outgoing fibers of a cell in the central nervous system. The striped muscle system is therefore a part of that whole information-and-action network that includes the brain, the spinal cord, and the central nervous system. We make our voluntary movements by bringing this network into play.

Normally, muscle tissue is in a state of continuous, mild, vibrating contraction (Figure 2.3). The condition is referred to as *muscle tonus,*[○] and it is the mark of healthy tissue. Its absence can be felt and even seen in such abnormal states as paralysis, in which the affected limb may look and feel as though it is not quite alive. Normal tonus is associated with a normal level of warmth at the skin and a normal degree of color in the skin. But, in at least some parts of their bodies, most persons also set up and sustain states of increased contraction in groups of muscles. In effect, their striped, voluntary muscle system assumes chronic states that resemble those of the smooth, involuntary muscle system. When this occurs, we are displaying what is called *muscle tension*, a condition with which most of us are quite familiar.

If we try to tense one arm and then keep it tensed, we discover that we very soon tire. Curiously enough, however, similar chronic muscle tensions, which many persons sustain throughout their bodies, appear to be maintained for years with little experience of fatigue or strain. Indeed, most of us are quite surprised to discover (often with the help of a trained professional) that we have been holding one group of muscles in a state of chronic contraction. The fact that this can occur, and the additional fact that it can continue without our being aware of it, has

smooth muscles. Muscles found in blood vessels, intestines, and some internal organs. They exhibit no stripes.

visceral organs. The internal organs of the body, especially those from the neck down to and including the abdomen.

striped muscles. Muscles found on the skeleton such as those that move limbs and torso. They appear to be striped.

muscle tonus. A healthy muscle's normal tension or resistance to stretching.

Fig. 2.3. The term *muscle tension* is sometimes used, inappropriately, to refer to one's state of muscular contraction. Yet most situations require specific arrangements of muscle tension, contraction, and vibration. We are always in a state of muscle "tension." For examples, what muscles are you holding right now?

Fig. 2.4. An individually expressive muscular "holding pattern."

suggested to many clinicians that muscles can, so to speak, learn to act in certain habitual ways. Once the learning has taken place, we may be no more aware that we are acting in a learned way in our muscles than we are normally aware that we act in learned ways when we walk or speak our native language.

Muscles and posture. Consider now what was noted above about the framework of your body. It is made up of bone and, as we said, of the groups of muscles and the tissues that tie the framework together. When you stand, you are held erect in part by your backbone and in part by the backbone's firm attachment at the joints to your pelvis. The greater part of the work of holding you upright against gravity, as well as the additional work of lowering your torso when you bend at the waist, is done by the powerful muscles of your back, abdomen, and thighs.

We seem to be implying here that your top half helps to hold up your bottom half. A physical construction, or a robot, is so made that the top half rests on top of the bottom half, and, if necessary, the bottom half can stand by itself. The foundation of a building will not collapse if the roof or the top floor is removed. But, in the case of the human body, it can be shown that the legs and pelvis will not stand by themselves. In the living human being, the top half is needed in order to keep the bottom half erect. This is why we cannot sleep standing up, as a horse, for example, can.

What this means is that the human upright stance is a condition of activity, not of rest. Whatever we do, stand or walk or bend, is a total activity involving our whole bodies, with each part participating in whatever ways the muscles of that part have "learned." Thus, we express our individual histories in every movement we make. An individualized "holding pattern" of muscles, once adopted, influences every other part of the body to make adjustments as a compensation. One example is shown in Figure 2.4. Suppose I once learned to walk, not in an atmosphere of trusting but in a climate of uncaring or neglect. My walking stance may be stiff and held back rather than loose and freely falling forward. In such a world of potential danger, the muscles of my thighs may be stretched in front and shortened in back. My pelvis may then become carried, not freely swinging and tilted a little forward, but held tightly and tucked under. My back muscles may then compensate by shortening at the lower back and holding my shoulders and arms back, thus forcing my neck and head to thrust forward. The stance we have just described is easy to assume. If you try it, you may well find that it "fits" an attitude of fear and uncertain aggressiveness. The body, the personality, and even the behavior may thus collaborate in a lifetime synthesis that has its roots in muscular adaptations in early childhood.

Stanley Keleman, a leading teacher and therapist in work with the body, has described this process very well: "If I chronically contract my chest, I feel unloving and unlovable, and I believe that life has ill-treated me. . . . If I constantly restrain my crying and clench my fists to keep from striking out, I smoulder with unexpressed vexation and offer the tight lipped opinion that it's a dog-eat-dog world."[5]

4. The whole body also participates in the action of every key part—for example, the stomach, or the breathing apparatus—and they in turn reflect the whole of one's experience.

The stomach is not an internal organ in the same sense that, say, the large intestine is. As we have said, the stomach is simply an "intruded" or invaginated continuation of your skin. What is in your stomach is not yet inside your body, not yet in your digestive system—which may be why the stomach can be surgically removed with no particular results on your digestive apparatus. Your stomach can change its position more than any other visceral organ. The familiar expression about your heart sinking in fear or anxiety properly refers to the stomach, which can drop as much as 12 inches under emotional stress. In addition, like the skin, its wall can change appearance under the influence of emotion. One of the most famous studies in the history of the biological sciences, published by an American surgeon, William Beaumont, in 1833, was based on observations made directly on the stomach of a trapper named Alexis St. Martin. Through a permanent opening in St. Martin's stomach left after a healed gunshot wound, Beaumont was able to insert and remove food and observe the process of digestion as well as the relation of emotional states to St. Martin's stomach lining.

The stomach, like the skin, also serves as boundary between inner and outer. Like so much of what happens in the body, this function may not always be present in awareness, but such awareness is easy enough to bring about. We have only to find ourselves in the situation of half-accepting and half-rejecting some nourishment that has reached the stomach. At this uneasy point, when the body seems almost to be asking itself whether to keep the nourishment out or to incorporate it, our typical feeling is nausea. If we choose to reject the nourishment, first the stomach and then the walls of the tract leading upward reverse their usual downward action waves. We vomit. Once this has happened, our immediate feeling is one of exhilaration, arousal, and relief.

Even though the socialization we undergo in our culture keeps most of us from an acceptance of vomiting, we may still be open to recognizing that the stomach and its mechanisms of intake and rejection are of profound significance for our sense of our bodily selves. Nausea may mark the boundary of our sense of self, and we may be very close to a fundamental truth when we refer to something we cannot accept with the phrase, "I can't stomach it."

Breathing: automatic and voluntary. Breathing is the newborn infant's first act in the world and the dying person's last. Between that first inhalation at birth and the final exhalation on one's deathbed, we pass our lives in a series of

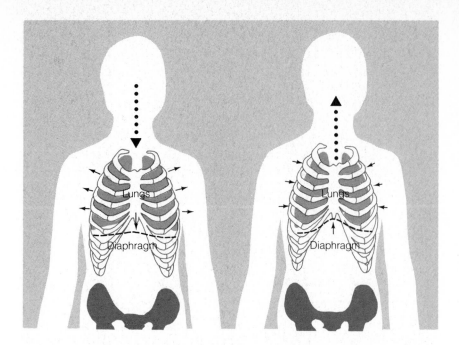

Fig. 2.5. Inhalation in breathing is accomplished by dropping the diaphragm to its lower position, which permits the chest and rib cage to be expanded and air to fill the lungs. The diaphragm is connected to both the lower ribs and the spinal column and thus reflects your entire posture and attitude—which in turn is reflected in your pattern of breathing.

respiratory cycles that reflect with unfailing accuracy our changes in mood and feeling. For this is a most remarkable characteristic of our respiratory systems, which should make us suspect that it is the most basic of our body systems. It keeps working in a completely automatic way, at each moment reflecting perfectly the state of our awareness and attitude, yet any time that we choose we can override its automatic action and deliberately breathe in any way that we want (Figure 2.5). It is both automatic and voluntary. No other system of the body can make that claim—for those that are involuntary, such as digestion or the orgasmic reflex in sex, are not usually brought under voluntary control, at least without special training, and those that are voluntary, such as movement, can only in a limited way be made involuntary.

The breathing apparatus is formed out of the alimentary tract and remains connected with many parts of our digestive system. In addition, our breathing is closely linked with the position and movements of the pelvis through muscular ties to the diaphragm, which we move in order to inhale. Thus the body as a whole takes part in our breathing. The respiratory system reflects the total voluntary and involuntary state of the person—the moods, the feelings, the state of health, the automatic responses, the nonconscious reactions and stances—while at the same time it just as aptly mirrors the nature and extent of one's deliberate actions and the field of one's awareness. It is for this reason, as many current psychotherapists have begun to realize, that breathing patterns are a simple yet fundamental diagnostic tool but also a simple and basic way to affect the personality. One teaches the client how to breathe differently.

One more point about breathing. It is also a basic way in which the person interacts with the world. Sighing, for example, is not a momentary defect in breathing, but a deliberate form of communication; it is the use of the breath to say what cannot be said in words. The breath has always been recognized as having this role in human life. For most civilizations, it is the carrier of life itself, the very seat of the soul.

Organization: the central nervous system

We have said that the body can be thought of as a framework, held together by various kinds of connective tissue, covered inside and outside with a skin and housing a number of interrelated systems. Three major systems have already been briefly discussed: one serving the functions of intake and excretion, the respiratory, and the "movement system" of muscles and their connections. We now have to consider the system of pathways and connectors by which internal communications are carried out — the nervous system.

5. Uniquely, the central nervous system makes it possible for the body to act as a whole.

Most of us think of the nervous system as an arrangement to carry messages from one place in the body to another. Like any message system, there is a control center, called the *brain*, connected directly with a subcenter below, called the *spinal cord*. From the spinal cord, many fibers run out to the extremities. What passes along the fibers, both in and out, are messages, and what takes place between the parts of the body is communication of information.

So runs the layperson's picture. Its weakness is that it does not tell us how the system can cause the body to act as a whole. The picture consists only of an assemblage of parts, linked briefly when a message from one part reaches another part.

The discontinuous nervous system. There is one major problem with whole systems that process information. They tend toward a democratic sharing of whatever information they generate; or, in other terms, they tend toward a steady state. As an example, suppose that there were a closed system containing energy in the form of heat, with the heat unevenly distributed throughout the system and no way for any heat to escape the system. Under these circumstances, it would inevitably happen that after a certain period of time — depending on conditions — the entire system would be at the same temperature. At the start of the process, when the heat was unevenly distributed, the system would be able to offer information; that is, statements about relevant conditions inside the system. By the end of the process of sharing or running down toward a steady state (the degree of uniformity is called *entropy*), the total information in the system is zero.

If the central nervous system of the body is to generate information, its parts must be interconnected within the whole. Yet if it is interconnected in this way, the system would tend to run down toward a steady state with zero information level. How to resolve this dilemma? The solution is an example of the often marvelous ways that living creatures have found, through evolutionary selection, to solve apparently unsolvable problems.

The solution is to organize the central nervous system as a discontinuous yet connected series of elements (Figure 2.6). The discontinuity occurs at special junctions between nerve cells, called *synapses*.$^{\odot}$ The "output" fiber of a nerve cell, varying in length from a full meter down to a few millionths of a meter, does not physically contact the "input" fiber of an adjacent nerve cell. Between the two is a gap large enough to be seen under the electron microscope. Thus, when an electrical charge appears at one side of the synaptic gap, a complex electrochemical process is started. One of two substances, acetylcholine$^{\odot}$ or noradrenaline,$^{\odot}$ is produced; and the presence of one of these substances kicks off a burst of electrical energy across the gap, in the next fiber. If the point where this occurs is not at the synapse but at the "end of the line", for example, at a muscle, the release of the chemical substance energizes the muscle cell into contraction.

One consequence of this arrangement is that the entire central nervous system can act as an information processor yet not tend toward a zero state. Another

synapse. The place where two nerve cells make electrochemical (but not physical) contact.

acetylcholine. A chemical that acts in the transmission of nerve impulses across the synapse from one neuron to another.

noradrenaline. Also, *norepinephrine.* A hormone secreted by the adrenal medulla during strong emotion. It is believed to be a transmitter in some sympathetic synapses, bringing about many changes, including constriction of the blood vessels near the body's surface.

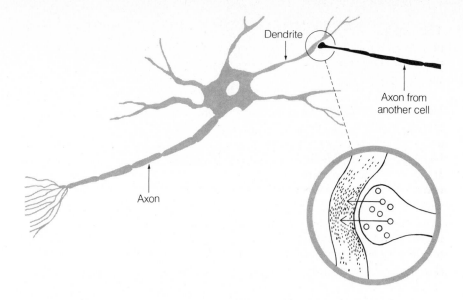

Fig. 2.6. The cells of the central nervous system are connected (at the synaptic junctions), yet are still discontinuous.

consequence is that the whole system can be at different levels at the same time. This is what makes it possible for us to maintain one part of the body in a state of rigid tension while allowing another part of the body to move rapidly or gracefully—as dancers do, or as we do if we whisper softly while standing stiffly at attention. This latter consequence is brought about chiefly by what is called *neural inhibition* or restraint. Remove the inhibition, as can be done with a drug such as strychnine, and the organism will immediately express itself, all at once and totally, in the form of convulsions.

6. The autonomic nervous system$^\circ$ provides the internal setting from which voluntary action can take place.

In addition to having developed a central nervous system as highly refined as we have described, human beings are also the recipients of many other evolutionary developments. One of these is a system that is related to the central nervous system but differs in two ways: It is less specialized for information processing, and it is not immediately connected to "where the action is." This system is called the *autonomic nervous system* (ANS), a name originally given because it was thought to be independent of the central nervous system. It is, in fact, not autonomous, or independent; nor is it completely involuntary (which is another of its names). Rather, it provides information about the world inside the body, just as other nervous system components provide information about the outside world. The function of the ANS, then, is not to organize the organism in regard to action in the environment but to maintain internal conditions as they are or else to change them as needed.

We can understand this basic function of the ANS if we consider the needs of a mobile creature. Such a creature must be equipped to take in nutriment and excrete the waste products, to be able to move around, to make sensory contact with its environment, and to reproduce in some fashion. But, more fundamentally, it must be able to respond to changes in its environment, particularly those that arise suddenly as emergencies. It has to be able to fight or flee as necessary.

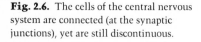

autonomic nervous system (ANS).
The group of nerve cells and nerve fibers that regulate glandular and smooth muscle activities. It is composed of the *sympathetic* and *parasympathetic* divisions.

This requires, in turn, that it be able to mobilize far more rapidly than it might ordinarily move. Once the emergency, large or small, has been successfully met, the creature must then have some way of settling itself down, in a "demobilization" process.

Ups and downs. It is to satisfy these two needs that the ANS consists of two interdependent parts, one to arouse (called the *sympathetic*)° and one to settle down (called the *parasympathetic*)° (Figure 2.7). The chemical substances that both parts use, acetylcholine and noradrenaline, are the same as those that are used at the synapses of the central nervous system—but now we can see the reason for two substances rather than one. Their effects, when they are brought into contact with the muscles that form the walls of our internal organs, are exactly opposite. In general, noradrenaline works to arouse or energize the muscles, and so it is used largely by the sympathetic branch of the ANS. It speeds up the heart, widens the pupils of the eyes, constricts small blood vessels (thus forcing blood away from the skin and to the brain), slows down the regular work of many internal organs, and "excites" the skin by producing sweat and causing the hair to stand on end. Acetylcholine has in general an opposite effect, so it serves the tranquilizing needs of the parasympathetic system.

All of this is not to say that this primitive "internal" behavior is ever completely disconnected from what goes on in the central nervous system. The brain, too, has its part in the process—particularly those areas of the brain that are older in an evolutionary sense. Thus the "executive control" of such basic functions as breathing, heartbeat, or swallowing is housed in an area called the *brain stem*, which is at the very base of the brain in back, just where it joins the spinal cord. And the brain centers for control of eating or body temperature are found mainly in the *hypothalamus*, another structure deep in the lower recesses of the brain. Many of these brain areas do their work by operating through the *glandular system* in the body. This is a network of chemical factories where very small portions of chemical substances are manufactured and then released as needed. These serve as specialized informational inputs to control the starting and stopping and the rate of operation of bodily processes such as bone growth, nest building, or eating. The case of the ring dove that was described in Chapter 1 is an example of the glandular system at work: Two hormones, produced after the young are hatched, organize the parent bird to initiate the feeding cycle.

Again, we emphasize that all the parts of the body, although we describe them separately, work together at every moment. Your body's state is thus always an elaborate and delicate balance of forces, as many kinds of information are developed and processed at any one time. This may be why, and how, you are able to accomplish the miracle of doing a dozen things at once: standing, breathing, digesting, thinking, relaxing the left buttock and tensing the right, seeing, hearing, smelling, sulking, blinking, and scratching. The central and autonomic nervous systems are not like two separate companies within a conglomerate but more like two aspects of the same performance—like the soloists and chorus of a ballet company. Similarly, the sympathetic and parasympathetic nervous systems are not two systems at all but two interdependent aspects of the same network, always adjusting to each other for the most appropriate effect.

The body in the world

What we have left out of our account of the body is that the actions for which it is the instrument take place in the world. The body is not just an assemblage of parts, as we said, but a coherent whole, and, equally, it is not simply a machine that happens to be in a certain place at a certain time, but part of your ongoing, vital

Fig. 2.7. Two versions of the "autonomic" cat: (a) the "sympathetic" cat and (b) the "parasympathetic" cat.

sympathetic nervous system. A subdivision of the autonomous nervous system that is active in emergency situations and states of fear, anger, or other arousal.

parasympathetic nervous system. A subdivision of the autonomous nervous system that is active in the restful state of the organism. It is primarily concerned with the recuperative, restorative, and nutritive functions of the body.

interchange with a specific environment. As the environment changes, the bodies that are active in them change as well. Boys' voices mature and lower in pitch at the onset of their bodily changes in adolescence, but, whereas two centuries ago this usually happened at the age of seventeen or eighteen, today it usually occurs at the age of thirteen or fourteen. In girls, the onset of menstruation is occurring at progressively earlier ages. We cannot say with certainty which is cause and which is effect, the bodily changes or the environmental changes, but it is clear that they change together, just as though they were demonstrating their interdependence.

7. The body as a social instrument is not bounded by its skin but exists as a body space—a body in its own personal space.

It should take only a little consideration and reflection about yourself to reveal that you do not experience space in exactly the same way in all directions around you. If you stand still, concentrate on your ongoing experience, and then call up the image of any action, you will discover that it belongs more to one side of you than to the other, or to the upper part of you rather than the lower part. If you are right-handed, try to summon up the image of yourself throwing a ball with your left hand. Now switch to imagining yourself throwing it with your right hand. The difference is evident, not only in what you imagined but also in where you felt the action belonged. For right-handed persons, the space on the right side is a space of sensible action, and the space on the left is experienced as more vague, less articulated, an arena for being rather than doing.

Right and wrong sides. In former ages, when people's lives were much more intimately tied to the way they used their bodies than is true today, it was strongly felt by the majority that there is a right side (the right) and a wrong side (the left) of the body. The Latin word *sinister* meant "left." Death was over the left shoulder, and many of the words for correct or proper actions—such as *rectitude*—were derived from the word for "right" (see Figure 2.8). As recently as a generation ago, parents and schoolteachers in some small communities, disturbed by the prospect that a child might develop a "sinister" pattern of behavior, would tie the child's left hand behind the back to enforce right-handed writing. (If they were going to be this authoritarian, they should have done the job earlier, in kindergarten or preschool, because handedness is firmly established by the age of six.)

As a result, the conditions of modern culture are arranged almost entirely for right-handed persons: knives, forks, tools, automobile controls, doorknobs, school desks, notebooks, playing cards, instructions for doing almost anything, sporting equipment, gadgets, wristwatches, and of course scissors.[6] Some interesting inferences might be drawn from the fact that the overwhelming majority of left-handed persons have learned to use, in clumsy fashion, a right-handed pair of scissors but have never thought of finding a pair that is more comfortable for them. Most lefties have also learned, often with great difficulty, to write upside down and in a direction that is backward for them.

The ability that most persons have to accommodate in this fashion seems to have convinced both righties and lefties that handedness is a minor aspect of motor behavior, to be ignored or else overcome with a little effort. But there is some evidence that this is not so. Animals are also organized so as to act asymmetrically in space; most elephants, for example, are right-footed, and laboratory rats are well known for their tendencies to make right turns or left turns, depending on their inborn preference, at choice points in a maze. Evidence gathered from prehistoric

Fig. 2.8. Left and right have had many meanings in the symbols of various religions.

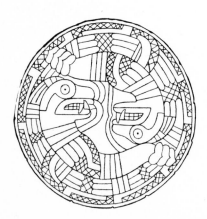

caves in northern Spain, where hundreds of stenciled hands were drawn by Paleolithic hunters, is also suggestive. These drawings, made between 25,000 and 15,000 B.C., were done by placing one hand against the wall, making an outline by using the other hand, which had been dipped in paint, and then filling in the outline with more paint; or, alternatively, by holding one hand against the wall and then blowing through a tube a mixture of ground pigment and a sticky base such as honey. A count of these stencils reveals that about 85 percent are of the left hand—indicating that, just as we find today, about 85 percent of adults spontaneously choose to use their right hand for fine work.

Our unequal sides. But the disparity between right and left sides as spaces for action is even more fundamental than this. Consider your own posture at this precise moment: Are you in a position that is exactly equal on the right and left sides; that is, a position that is bilaterally symmetrical? Unless you are sitting upright, head stiff and pointed straight ahead, arms and hands precisely the same, weight exactly equal on both buttocks, legs and feet side by side and arranged the same way—unless this describes your posture, then it is not bilaterally *a*symmetrical. Indeed, if you try it out you will soon discover that it is simply not possible to assume any natural pose or to initiate any natural action without being bilaterally asymmetrical. A robot, or Frankenstein's monster, might be able to do so, but not a living creature exhibiting natural movement.

What this means is that asymmetry, far from being simply a matter of the relative emphasis we put on the right or the left hand, is in fact the very basis for sensible movement in the world. An infant starts its action career in a position that is almost bilaterally symmetrical—on its back, with its arms in equivalent positions on the two sides, with its head flopped accidentally to one side or the other and with legs akimbo and similarly placed. Its very first movements are toward asymmetry of position and action, within which context it soon develops its own preferences. Some children start crawling with one side rather than another, some are more attentive on one side rather than the other, and all finally become left-handed or right-handed.

Societies in all ages seem to have recognized the close link between bilaterality and action (Figure 2.9). In a surprising number of independent instances, the position that is ritually prescribed to denote "no action" is one that is bilaterally symmetrical. The position in which the dead were placed, with arms crossed on the chest, is a familiar example in Western culture; the full lotus position is its equally familiar counterpart in Eastern cultures. Prayer, which is a position in which the penitent is not going to initiate a worldly action, requires in every culture some form of bilaterally symmetrical positioning of the body, as does the military pose called attention.

On ball throwing. If, as we are suggesting here, the way in which we occupy our personal space of action is a fundamental aspect of our lives, we should expect that it will show up in some differences between the sexes. Developmental studies on these aspects of motor activity are only just beginning—countering a long-term and pervasive denial of the body in our culture—but some evidence is at hand.[7] In reviewing a large number of studies on sex differences in childhood, Elinor Maccoby and Carol Jacklin find that one of the few distinctions that holds up is that boys are more aggressive than girls. Most of this difference arises out of the fact that boys are more aggressive with other boys than they are with girls or than girls are with either sex. These authors suggest that boys seem to "trigger" each other more easily than girls trigger girls.[8] Observation of the way children of both sexes move, of how they take up space, supports this suggestion, for boys appear to take up more space. The way they move their arms, in particular, is observably dif-

Fig. 2.9. "The Thinker," by Auguste Rodin. Notice that the right arm is unexpectedly crossed over to rest on the left knee—a form of postural asymmetry that may imply that even thinking is a kind of action.

ferent than similar movements on the part of girls. This is not a difference that can be attributed to differences in size or personality or bodily structures.

That boys and girls differ at a very early age in this regard suggests that even before they enter school, the two sexes have learned different ways of moving in the world. A clear indication of the consequences is given in the way that adults throw a ball. The differences between the sexes, although recently less obvious than they were in former generations, can still be observed. In adults who are not professionally skilled, the female will throw a ball with her elbow rather close to her side so that the ball will be pushed, the wrist being kept almost stiff. The male, on the other hand, will whip the ball forward, releasing it at the end of a descending arc of the hand, with the elbow marking out a circle in space away from the body and with the wrist providing the final impetus. The difference can be summed up as follows: The two sexes occupy different amounts of space at the side of their bodies—just as they have done since early childhood. That the difference is one of cultural adaptation is indicated by the changes that take place in both sexes when they are given training in ball throwing. In that case, both females and males learn to throw a ball in the efficient way that is prescribed for males in a male-dominated society.

Summary

1. Freud's developmental theory suggests that, from the time of birth to the time of entering school, the individual's development is determined by successive developments in the life of the body.

2. Beginning with the entrance to school, individuals are socialized primarily through deemphasizing the experience of the body in favor of the life of the mind.

3. Every part of the body is structurally as well as functionally connected with every other part, so that the body normally functions as a whole.

4. There are two muscle systems: a system of smooth muscles, for slow and rhythmic responses and for maintaining existing conditions; and a system of striated muscles, for rapid response, behavioral movements, and postural adjustment.

5. The stomach uniquely expresses both inner experience and outer behavior because it is situated midway between one's inner and outer structures. Breathing also represents the entire organism, because it is uniquely able to be both voluntary and involuntary, as we wish.

6. The central nervous system is an interconnected yet discontinuous network that enables the flow of information by which the body functions as a whole. It is centralized through the "higher" brain structures such as the cortex.

7. The autonomic nervous system functions in regard to the interior of the body, to produce the most appropriate balance of arousal and maintenance, of "ups" and "downs." It is centralized through the "lower" brain structures and the body's glandular system.

8. The two sides of the body are both experienced and used differently, a phenomenon that is called *handedness*. In general, all meaningful action takes place in terms of asymmetry of right and left.

W e now turn to the systems in the body that interface between the body and its action settings. They are called *sensory systems*, because each consists of an arrangement of structures organized to carry out certain functions.

In this chapter, we will review five sensory systems, which correspond fairly closely to the senses with which we are all familiar. We will have space enough only to present an overview of these systems: gravity, touch, smell and taste, hearing, and seeing.

You will be able to become acquainted with the general structure of each of the sensory systems and with how their major characteristics differ and enable the system to carry out its tasks. You will also review what each system accomplishes in the life of living creatures and, in particular, what kind of information the system selects, processes, and furnishes. This will provide you with a basis for understanding what kind of "world" may be found by the use of each kind of sensory system.

Every kind of living creature appears to have one or more systems by means of which it makes contact with the world around it. In this chapter, we consider the systems in humans — which they share with many animals — that enable all of us to "make sense": to contact the sea of energy in the world, to receive and process some of this energy, and to make use of it as information (Figure 3.1).

These functions of contact and processing are biological: They are vital sensory interfaces between body and surround. We emphasize this point at the outset because the biological functions that we discuss in this chapter are not the same as the related psychological functions that we discuss in Chapter 5. The latter are called *perception*. The distinction between sensing and perception may be illustrated by means of an example.

When we *look* at something, we usually *see* it. However, these are two different activities, as shown by our use of two different verbs. Looking is a matter of directing our attention so that the appropriate information will be selectively received. Seeing is a different process. To appreciate the difference, try looking at something with a gaze that is completely and passively relaxed. It is not an easy thing to do, but if you relax your seeing activity so that you do not impose any organization or meaning on what you look at, and if what you are looking at comes toward you without effort on your part, you will achieve it: a kind of two-dimensional seeing merely "at your eyeball," a looking without seeing or sensation without perception. A very similar effect can be achieved in the auditory mode by allowing one word to be said "at you," over and over and over — for example, the word "lookingglass" repeated over and over on a tape loop, until it finally loses all meaning. Sometimes, when we drive through an unchanging scene, we allow ourselves to drift into this mode of visual sensing, as when we pass through a snowstorm or through a seemingly endless avenue of identical trees.

The sea of energy surrounding us and impinging on us can be said to have three major characteristics. It reaches us, not in a steady stream, but in cycles or waves that have a certain *frequency*. It impinges on us with a certain intensity, or *amplitude*. And it lasts for some period of time; that is, it has some *duration*. Although we receive energy of many different kinds and although we have a number of different sensing systems to tune in to the varieties of energy, these three characteristics are usually evident.

3

Making sense: the five sensory systems

Fig. 3.1. Once out of his normal sensory setting, the astronaut can easily leap many feet into the air. But notice that here, on the moon, it is his total sensory environment, not just gravity, that has changed: visually, the shadows are much deeper and sharper, touching is eliminated, and the near vacuum makes both hearing and smelling impossible.

The sensory systems

In this chapter, we will be discussing the various systems by which sensing occurs; in Chapter 5 we will discuss the varieties and results of perception.

1. What we call our "senses" are better called "sensory systems,"[1] or arrangements to respond to gravity, contact, airborne molecules, sound, and light.

We usually think of ourselves as having five senses, but in fact the number of sensory systems that we have will depend on how many different kinds of energy we are able to process. There are five such systems that we certainly share with most other living creatures.

- *Responses to gravity.* In effect, this is the system that tells the organism which way is up and is a response to the gravitational field that is ever-present on earth. Gravity does not reach the organism as a specific kind of energy—at least, as far as we now know—and for this reason the systems for processing its effect vary widely from one species to another.
- *Responses to physical contact, which are referred to generally as touch.* Contact can take many forms, and so its effect is processed in different ways—as a blow, a pinch, a tap, a caress, a scratch, a prick, a tickle, or a rub; as sharp or diffuse. A touch sensation can be pleasant or unpleasant, hot or cold, pleasurable or painful. We cannot know, of course, to what extent other species can distinguish all these contacts, although most animals will respond differently to a light touch or tap than to a blow, and chimpanzees will delight in being tickled as opposed to being rubbed or simply touched. Even a one-celled organism, floating on the surface of water, will contract if touched with a fine probe. One of the unique aspects of the touch system is that it has two aspects, the active and the passive, which we experience as touching and as being touched. They are not experienced the same way, and they may not even be organized through the same physical structures.

- *Responses to certain airborne molecules.* If these are processed as gas, we call the resulting effect a *smell*; if they are processed in a liquid medium in the mouth, in contact with the buds on the tongue, we call the resulting effect a *taste.* Among humans, smell and taste are not very finely developed and are often even confused. Thus, we often refer to the *taste* of a substance when we are really getting most of our information about it by way of smell. Although humans have almost identical sensory systems for seeing, hearing, and touching as do other animals, particularly the higher apes, we may be less well equipped than other species in regard to smelling and tasting.

- *Responses to low-frequency vibrations.* These vibrations are what we usually sense as sounds and usually receive through a vibrating medium such as air. Most of the sounds with which we are familiar are produced by causing a compressible medium to vibrate—a gas such as air, or a liquid such as water, or a solid object such as a violin string or the membrane on the face of a loudspeaker or someone's vocal cords. The organ that picks up the vibrations will usually be itself a structure that can vibrate in resonance, such as our eardrum or the hair cells in the inner ear.

- *Responses to high-frequency electromagnetic energy.* Humans cannot process the entire range of such energy but only a small portion in the middle of the range. We call this part *light,* and, as with other creatures, our processing is usually accomplished by means of a number of chemicals that change structure under the influence of light, as do the chemicals used in making photographic prints. It may be that some birds that can navigate over long stretches of open sea can process energy at the upper end of the electromagnetic spectrum, outside of the range of human capability; and it may also be that persons who are able to locate water beneath the ground—so-called dowsers—also process high-frequency electromagnetic energy. This would also be "visual sensing," but by means of different kinds of energy.

Beyond the interface. In the simplest creature, such as a one-celled organism, any energy to which it is sensitive that reaches the outer boundary will usually affect the entire cell. There is not much such a creature can do about this energy. It must act as a whole—either to withdraw or contract if the energy "means" a negative signal or to expand or move toward if the energy "means" a positive signal.

But as we go up the evolutionary scale, with increasing complexity we find increasing specialization. One part of the organism becomes specialized for picking up the energy. Another part takes over the job of processing the energy in the form of a signal. A third part may get the job of doing something about what is now a signal. We can therefore distinguish three stages in the operation of sensory systems, as shown in Figure 3.2. They are as follows:

- *The receptor.* This is a specialized cell or combination of cells, usually near the surface of the organism. Our skin serves as the major receptor organ for the various modes of contact to which we are sensitive, just as the eardrum is our receptor for auditory sensation and the retina of the eye is the receptor involved in seeing. The "design" of receptors in different species is often a remarkable solution to the problem of picking up and transmitting a specific kind of energy; for example, eyes that see in very dim light or at great distances.

- *The transmitter.* This is a pathway by which signals or information are sent from the receptor to some area where it can then be made use of by the organism. When the receptor is affected by the kind of energy to which it is sensitive—electromagnetic, or contact, or whatever—it builds up a charge. When the charge is strong enough, the cell discharges and affects a neighbor-

Fig. 3.2. The parts of an informational system. In this picture, the energy at the green light (receptor) is passed through the motorist (transmitter), resulting in the mechanical operation of the car (processor).

ing cell along the line, which in turn builds up and then discharges. If we could get a look at a string of such cells, from receptor all the way back to their terminus, we might see a succession of bursts appearing to travel along the line. Each one would look like this:

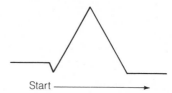

The importance of these discharges, or "spikes," is that no matter what kind of energy is involved at the receptor, and, no matter what kind of receptor starts off the process, all that ever gets transmitted is a succession of such spikes or bursts.

■ *The processor.* At the end of the line of cells, from receptor back to some terminus, the most complex creatures have some organ by which the successive bursts of electrical activity are received and then used in some way. In an earthworm, for example, there are a series of processors, called *ganglia*,⊙ which are spaced along segments of the worm's body. In humans, there is a central processor, the brain, with different processing stations at different brain levels.

The gravity system

The sensory system that is most widely found among living creatures is the one related to gravity. Its basic function appears to be to orient the organism in terms of up and down. In our own case, the fact that we possess such a system may escape our notice, for the field of gravity is approximately constant and ever present. We are in it from birth to death, and so, like a fish in relation to water, we are not always aware of its existence. But there are evidences wherever we look that moving is nothing but a silent struggle against gravity; for example, the dark meat of a chicken's legs, resulting from its unending "push" to remain erect, as compared with the white meat of its breast, where no such effort is needed.

ganglia. A group of nerve cell bodies lying outside of the central nervous system.

2. Sensors in our muscles, joints, and inner ear canals provide information to orient us in the gravitational field.

From one species to another and from one level of complexity to another, organisms vary widely in the structures they have developed to orient them in relation to gravity. Plants that grow upward, in contrast with creepers, orient themselves in this direction by means of tubes in their stems. In certain simple, waterborne organisms, tiny grains of sand are absorbed, float (internally) to one side of the creature, and thus keep it oriented in a kind of upright posture. The commonest device in more complex organisms is a system of canals or small tubes filled with liquid. The pressure of the liquid when a tilt occurs in relation to gravity provides a signal to the organism to bring itself back to a level stance. The system is particularly rapid and effective in the cat.

In addition, humans and many other mammals receive a continuing flow of information from all parts of the body to the brain. This serves a number of purposes, one of the most important being to indicate that the joints of the body are being influenced by gravity in their "normal" way. Again, we are usually unaware of the fact that by this means we always "know" (perhaps below a threshold of awareness) how the parts of our bodies are positioned. But, even if we are not usually aware of the continuous monitoring of our gravitational alignment, we have only to reduce the effect of gravity in our bodies to bring it into awareness. The simplest way to do this is to allow ourselves to float in water; the contrast brings home a realization that ordinarily we are surprisingly weighted down by gravity. It is this weighting that is continuously sensed in our joints and muscles and relayed as information to the brain.

Life without gravity. In his remarkable essay on human size, F. W. Went[2] has pointed out that there are really two categories of living things—those below about 1 millimeter in size, and those above. The distinction between the two categories has to do with their relation to gravity. Gravity is only one of the physical forces that draw things together; another force is molecular attraction, or cohesion.[©] In the world of humans, cohesion is irrelevant because it is enormously overshadowed by the force of gravity. But, as a physical object is made smaller, the gravitational force acting on it decreases faster than forces of cohesion. For example, if we cut a perfectly smooth cube of wood that is 1 centimeter on a side, the gravitational force acting on it would be fifty times as great as the cohesive force; therefore, if we tried to make it stick to the wall, it would fall down. If the cube were just as smooth but only 1 millimeter on a side, then the two forces would just about balance, and it would be hard to predict whether the cube would stick to the wall or not. Now, if we make the cube still smaller, 1/10 of a millimeter on a side, the cohesive forces (between the molecules of the cube and the molecules of the wall) would be fifty times greater than the force of gravity, and the cube would stick to any surface. It would act as does a particle of dust, which will also stick anywhere it lands.

The significance of this is that if a living creature is small enough or has a small enough mass, the cohesive forces between it and a surface would be greater than the gravitational force between it and the earth. It could therefore stick to any surface—as, in fact, the common housefly does or as most other insects do, not because their feet are sticky but simply because of their size and weight. In effect, such a creature would exist in a "gravity-free" environment, just as astronauts do

cohesion. Hanging together in some way or being mutually attractive. The term is used in reference to social groups, learning theory, and perceptual phenomena.

Fig. 3.3. An orphaned baby hippopotamus, only twelve days old, follows its keeper around "like a dog," keeping in constant physical contact. When the keeper is gone, a larger rubber dish has to be left in the hippo's pond as a tactile substitute. In Harry Harlow's words (1958, pp. 677–678),

> "This is the skin some babies feel
> Replete with hippo love appeal.
> Each contact, cuddle, push, and shove
> Elicits tons of baby love."

free nerve ending. Nerve endings that are not associated with any particular receptors. They are found in blood vessels, skin, and other parts of the body and may be the sense organs for pain.

who go into orbit or fly to the moon. Went has suggested some of the more interesting consequences in the life of an ant, which we may put in the form of some questions.

- *Could an ant read a book?* No, because it would not be possible to make a book whose pages could be turned by an ant. Even the thinnest possible pages, supposing they were then light enough to be lifted by an ant, would stick together by cohesion; if they were thick enough to be affected by gravity rather than cohesion, the ant could never move them.
- *Could an ant find out the weight of anything?* No, for two reasons: first, because if something were of a size and weight to be moved by an ant, it would stick to the scales; second, because in a world without gravity, the notion of weight simply has no meaning. (Recall that what we mean by weight is the relation between the mass of the earth and the mass of an object.)
- *Could an ant win a weight-lifting contest?* Easily, for it has only to overcome the cohesive bond between an object and its surface. Once free of the surface, an object as much as ten times its own weight can be "lifted" — although the more appropriate term might be "floated."
- *Could an ant hurt itself by falling?* Not at all. It simply floats down, much as a dust particle might.
- *Could an ant dry itself with a towel?* No, because the fibers of the towel have a very large surface area (which is why a towel will dry us off) that will suck the ant against it. An ant can only clean itself off by a process of drycleaning; that is, by rubbing itself clean against another surface.

These questions and answers are more than fanciful. They remind us that in our human world we walk around and sit in chairs and read books and dry ourselves with towels, but we do not stick to surfaces and we do not let ourselves fall from great heights. Just about everything we do, or do not do, is determined by the fixed and unconquerable force of gravity, against which our bodies are in a constant, changing adjustment.

The contact system

No single name is adequate to cover all the forms of physical contact that are processed by this system. Touch, temperature, pressure, and perhaps pain, as well as a variety of feelings associated with them, are all to be found in the ways that this system provides us with our basic being-in-touch with the world.

3. The contact system, largely mediated through the skin, is also a basic affectional system.

The major structural part of this system is, of course, the skin. We do not ordinarily think of this as an organ of the body, like brain or heart, but it is in fact an elaborate, eight-layered, multipurpose organ that is crowded with all sorts of receptor cells. The skin therefore serves as the first, receptor stage of the mechanical-contact sensory system (Figure 3.3).

Unfortunately, it is not known with certainty what cells in the skin serve as receptors for the different contact experiences, with the possible exception of pain. It is agreed that the receptors for pain are the extremely numerous tips of nerve fibers that are found all through the skin and are called *free nerve endings*.[○] The fibers with which they connect, then, are probably the transmitters for pain. These consist of more than one type, but just how they function is not known.

Whatever the precise structural arrangement, the sensory system involving the skin is fairly crude as compared with other systems in the body. It accepts many different kinds of input — electrical, chemical, mechanical, thermal, or electromagnetic. It passes on this information in gross and perhaps mixed-up ways. Above all, it is remarkably insensitive; for example, the skin requires 100 million times as much energy as the eye to be stimulated.

On the other hand, the use that living creatures are able to make of this crude system is often marvelous to behold. Frank Geldard, in his survey of the human senses, remarks,

> We commonly make entirely correct judgments, on the basis of "feel" alone, concerning hardness or softness, roughness or smoothness, wetness or dryness, stickiness, oiliness, and a host of other object qualities. Even with auditory cues excluded, tapping with a fingernail is often sufficient to determine whether an object is made of wood, metal, or plastic. . . . A brief tap, lasting no more than 1/300 of a second, has been found in some experiments to be enough for complete identification of the material touched. . . . A lightly etched piece of glass having eminences no higher than .001 mm can be successfully discriminated from an entirely smooth one.[3]

That figure of .001 mm is the equivalent of no more than 1/26,000 of an inch.

Love and touch. A great deal of evidence, both clinical and experimental, has now begun to accumulate, all testifying to what any human or animal mother could have said for the past 100,000 or more years: Infants need warm, loving physical contact just as much as they need food or air. Indeed, there is specific evidence to show that it is through the medium of such contact, at the earliest ages, that animals may learn the "meaning" of love. (Of course, it is equally true that infants "need" continuing stimulation through all the other senses as well.)

The most famous studies in this regard have been carried out by Harry Harlow and his colleagues at the University of Wisconsin over the past two decades. They worked with monkeys rather than humans, because one cannot ethically experiment on deprivation in infants. Their studies addressed such questions as whether it made any difference to an infant monkey whether its mother was a live monkey or merely a manufactured substitute of the same general shape; if monkeys could become attached to such substitute "mothers"; if they could, what characteristics of the substitutes made any difference to the infants; and, finally, how the different characteristics of the substitute were related.

The results were as clear-cut as one could have wished. Monkeys do prefer monkeys, as we might expect, but in the absence of real, live mothers infant monkeys will (if we can judge by their behavior) come to love and need the substitutes with as much intensity as they might show toward genuine monkey mothers. Any kind of mother will do in a pinch, it appears, but there is a definite hierarchy of preference — and this is where we begin to learn what is important for monkey babies. The technique used was to rear the infants in cages where substitutes of various sorts were available, such as one equipped with a nipple for feeding, one covered with terrycloth, one covered with chicken wire, and so on. The infants were observed, and the amount of time they spent clinging to one or another of the substitutes was charted. Figure 3.4 shows one of the more important sets of results. If monkeys are reared with one terrycloth "mother" and one chicken-wire "mother" in the cage, it makes no difference where the nipple for feeding is located. The infant monkeys will always spend more time clinging to the terrycloth figure, from which (we suppose) they receive contact comfort. Further, when an air jet is built into the terrycloth figure, the infants will cling to it

BODIES
*The psychobiology
of individuals*

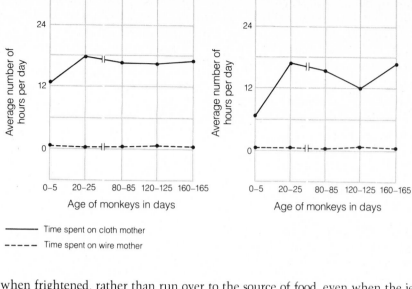

Fig. 3.4. A comparison of the amount of time that Harlow's infant monkeys spent on two kinds of mother substitutes. (From Harlow, 1958, p. 676)

when frightened, rather than run over to the source of food, even when the jet almost blasts them across the cage. Food does not seem to be the only basic need; physical contact is a basic need, too.

Smell and taste

Smell and taste may be considered as one system or two, depending on whether one emphasizes their structure or their function. They share a receptor location, in the front part of the head, but their structures are otherwise separate. On the other hand, they are usually so closely interrelated in their functioning, at least in humans, that most taste sensations are largely made up of smell.

4. The interface between smell or taste and their targets is not direct, but referential and qualifying.

An important characteristic that the systems of smell and taste have in common is that in humans—but probably not in any other species—they serve as ways of qualifying what we already know. They rarely provide us with hard facts, and we would be in some trouble if we had to depend mainly on smell or taste to tell us the facts about what is "out there." The best that most people are usually able to do, even if they are particularly gifted or practiced, is to make such statements as "It tastes as if it had vanilla flavoring in it." These are really primitive achievements when compared with the exquisitely detailed and elaborate knowledge we can gain from only a moment's looking or listening (Figure 3.5).

Humans get most of their information about the world by means of the two senses of hearing and seeing. Smell and taste are usually used primarily as qualifiers, to add adjectives to the nouns that are gathered through seeing and hearing. As we will see in a moment, this arrangement is peculiar to our species; many other kinds of arrangements are possible and in fact are found in other species. But in our case, probably uniquely among species, smell and taste do not always add to our store of facts but usually enrich the facts that we have already gathered by other means. The word *taste*, in fact, has this meaning in human

Fig. 3.5. If you stick your tongue out, someone can see all your zones of primary taste: SW = sweet, SA = salt, SO = sour, and B = bitter.

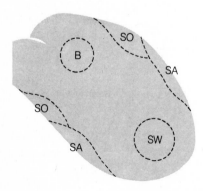

affairs. It refers to an esthetic sensibility, the ability to appreciate fine distinctions or nuances in what is already factually known. This is essentially what professional winetasters and tea tasters do. They are not paid to tell us whether the liquid they taste is wine rather than whiskey, or tea rather than coffee, but rather to detect and compare the most subtle qualities of the wine and tea.

The sense of smell. In regard to the sense of smell, and perhaps in regard to tasting also, the difference between humans and other species is more marked than in regard to any other sense. There are some differences of structure and sensitivity. It is reported, for example, that a polar bear can sniff out the presence of food across five miles of ice. Most animals also have more taste buds on the tongue than do humans—the pig, for example, has 15,000 to the human's mere 9,000. But these are not the only differences, and they may not even be the basic ones. A more important distinction is that animals other than human appear to use their senses of smell and taste as a means of gathering hard facts about the world. Their use of these two senses—smell in particular—appears to serve primarily to answer the question, "What is it?", just as we do mostly by means of seeing and hearing. Once we have thus answered for ourselves what *it* might be, we then usually go on to use our sense of smell to answer the further question, "What is it like?" Thus, the cartoon about the bloodhounds (Figure 3.6) may be funny, but it is probably wrong. There is no evidence at all that animals will object to any odor except one that is accompanied by a chemically noxious vapor. (This may explain why your family dog will usually shy away from the smoke of a cigarette or the scent of a cocktail.) Even highly domesticated dogs or cats will eat decayed meat; and, far from objecting, as we do, to the odors of urine or feces, animals are quite attracted to them, are interested in them, and depend on them for marking off individual territories. The dog that sniffs for minutes on end at the base of a tree is sorting out, much as we do when we read a newspaper, a whole series of related facts imprinted thereon; such as who passed by and what the passersby were like in regard to breed and age and familiarity.

"To be perfectly frank about it, with a scent like that I don't care if we never find him."

Fig. 3.6

The dog that sniffs at the anus of a strange animal in its neighborhood (perhaps to assign it a "dog tag") and the laboratory rat that rises on its hind legs to sniff out what its poor eyesight cannot detect are both doing just what humans ordinarily accomplish by means of vision—or sometimes by cupping the ear and leaning toward a sound to listen intently. The animals are engaged in surveying a target or examining it so as to identify it. They are using their sense of smell in just the way we use our senses of sight or hearing.

Structures for smell and taste. In spite of the obvious differences between the way humans and other animals use the senses of smell and taste, the physical structures involved appear to be very similar. That portion of the cortex in other animals where olfactory signals are processed is proportionately much larger than in humans, but we do not know which is cause and which effect—whether the more acute sense of smell is the result of having more brain capacity for it or whether the larger brain capacity results from a more developed use of the sense of smell. Much of the olfactory system in humans appears to be unused, so it may be this, rather than its size, that explains our lesser sensitivity.

All that is known with certainty about the structure of the olfactory° system is that a volatile substance—in the form of a gas or vapor—must be inhaled over a patch of nerve endings high up in the nasal cavity. The nerve fibers are gathered from here into a bundle, the olfactory nerve, which proceeds to the olfactory bulb in the cortex.° But how the system works is still obscure. The major problem is how a creature is able to distinguish one smell from another. The most recent, and most attractive, of the theories is that the size and shape of specific molecules in the

olfactory. Pertaining to the sense of smell.

cortex. Also called *gray matter* of the brain. A rind of tissue consisting of neurons and connectors covering the cerebrum. It is thought to be active in conscious experiences and higher mental processes.

stimulating gas trigger off sensitive receptor cells; for this reason, it is known as the "stereochemical" theory.[4]

The structures for tasting, on the other hand, are not anatomically related to those of smelling, but rather to the touching and skin system. In addition, as Zeigler has recently shown,[5] there is an anatomical link (at least in pigeons and rats, and possibly in other animals as well) between the hunger-eating mechanism and the mechanism that gives us most of our oral sensations. The link is in a network of nerves called the *trigeminal system*,⊙ which runs from mouth and face back to the brain and carries information about touch and similar sensations. Damage this nerve system, even without damage to any part of the brain, and the animal's appetite drops. This suggests that basic information required for the sense of taste is obtained by this route. To state it in humanlike terms, oral sensations play a major part in the experiences of hunger and tasting.

The receptors for tasting are, as we all know, the taste buds,⊙ most of which are located on the top and sides of the tongue, except for a strange little area in the middle of the top surface of the tongue that completely lacks taste buds. They are apparently quite sensitive and delicate, usually existing only a few days before they degenerate and are replaced. Four kinds of tastes are usually identified, each approximately localized on the tongue—sweetness toward the front tip, bitterness toward the back (although many substances can taste sweet or bitter if moved from front to back), sour (acid) along the sides, and salty on the rest of the tongue. The number of taste buds decreases with age, which may be why older persons prefer more strongly flavored foods. But all these statements are either vague or approximate, for the fact is that we do not know how the cells embedded in the sides of the taste buds do their work or what it is they are sensitive to—especially considering the fact that many taste buds will respond to more than one of the four taste qualities.

The auditory system

With the auditory system, we come, at least in humans, to a level of complexity and sensitivity of sensing that is not even approached by the systems we have discussed thus far.

5. Our hearing system, which has extraordinary sensitivity, provides us with a special kind of information, not of places or things, but of events.

The energy that is processed by the auditory system is in the form of relatively low-frequency vibrations. The essential characteristic of a series of vibrations is that it is spread out in time. As a result, what is sensed and transmitted in hearing is almost never a momentary "sound" but rather some pattern of sounds that takes place through time. Figure 3.7 presents some examples. The exception to this is the sudden, sharp sound, lasting only a moment, such as a pistol shot—and it is significant that practically all species react in a special way to such an auditory stimulus. The response is, in fact, so unique that it has its own name: the *startle response*.⊙[6] It consists of freezing one's action and contracting all one's muscles, and it can be produced in most animals simply by a sudden loud noise near them.

Pure and mixed noises. In our normal use of our auditory systems, brief, objectlike sounds do not occur very often. If such a sound does occur, we try to

Fig. 3.7. Two different sound "events."

trigeminal system. The system of facial and cranial nerves containing both motor and sensory fibers.

taste bud. The sense organs for taste. These clusters of cells are located at the base of the papillae of the tongue.

startle response. A sudden response to a quick, unexpected stimulus such as a loud noise. It is characterized often by opening the mouth, closing the eyes, and thrusting the head forward. It is fairly consistent from one person to another.

avoid it, or we adopt a special stance toward it such as the startle or, at a lower level, the "orienting reflex." The latter can be seen in almost any mammal. It consists of a sudden pinpointing of attention to any brief sound that is strange; for example, a click. In the course of our ordinary behavior, however, we much prefer ongoing auditory events to such clipped and localized signals.

Similarly, our auditory stimulation is made up very largely of "impure" rather than pure tones.[○] This is partly a matter of preference, as shown, for example, in the universal preference among singers and musicians for the "irregular regularity" of a vibrato. It is also a result of the fact that pure tones, such as those made by a tuning fork or an oscillator, are rarely heard in ordinary life. They are as infrequent in nature as a straight line, which is another of our human abstractions. Because our experience has been with impure tones, we are quite accustomed to impurities and mixes and are perfectly able to pull out of them the meaning that we need. We can listen to a choir made up of dozens of different voices, each clearly different from all the others even when the members all sing the same note, and what we hear is one complex note. A swarm of bees, its noise made up of hundreds of different sounds (as we could easily tell if we heard them individually) is heard as one harmonically rich hum, like the rumble of traffic we often sense. It is only when we begin to sustain a hearing loss, especially in the upper frequencies, or if our attention really lapses, that ordinary conversation starts to sound like the ongoing mumble that it "really" is. Persons who are in this situation report an experience much like that of the person in a foreign country, hearing a strange language for the first time and being unable to separate words out of what seems like a continuing blur of sound that goes by too fast.

From this we can learn that the auditory event that we experience as normal, that we have no difficulty making sense out of and processing, is usually a very complex and impure mix that is spread out in a kind of blur over time, like a dozen superimposed movies shown a little too fast. The perfect, pure voice, like that of the robot, sounds to us very unreal. Unfortunately, many experiments on audition, in a misguided attempt to simplify the conditions, present "pure" sounds that are more fitted to the receptors of robots than to the normal experience of living animals.

Sounds. We hear sounds because the vibrations of the molecules of the air, in regular waves, are causing our eardrums to move. The eardrum, together with the external ear (which is movable in most other animals), collects the sounds. Behind the eardrum, a linked set of small bones amplifies the sounds—that is, it makes them thirty to sixty times louder. Behind that, a complex arrangement changes these vibrations to bursts of electrical energy that are fed to appropriate parts of the cortex.

Why do we, and most other hearing animals, have such a complicated arrangement? To answer this question, we look first at the nature of the energy we call *sound*. In any substance, no matter whether it is solid, liquid, or a gas, its molecules are in a state of constant vibration, called *Brownian movement*,[○] to a degree that depends on the temperature. If anything presses against part of the substance—against the surface of a solid, or in the form of a wiggling stick inserted in a liquid—the molecules will be pushed away from that point. If the pressure is repeated regularly, the molecules will be alternately compressed and released, and they in turn will push and release others, thus causing information to be transmitted through the substance. Generally speaking, the denser the substance the farther the impulse will travel with the same amount of initial input of energy. For example, as many children have discovered, sounds travel along a wire or string better than through the air.

There are two aspects of this traveling "wave" (which you can see most clearly by dropping a stone in some water) that are important to note. One is how

pure tone. The tone achieved from the simplest kind of sound wave energy, consisting of one or a very few frequencies.

Brownian movement. Random thermal motion of particles.

rapidly the pattern of compression and release takes place; this is called its *fre-quency*. The other is how powerful the vibrations are, how "strong" the waves; this aspect of the sound wave is called its *amplitude*. In general, the higher the frequency of a sound wave, the higher is its tone, or pitch, and the greater the amplitude of a sound wave the stronger or louder is the sound. However, this is by no means a simple, straightforward relation—for what we experience never corresponds in any simple way to the physical energy involved. Add the sound of one voice to the noise of a cheering crowd and the increase will hardly be sensed at all. Add the same voice to a silent room, and the increase will be sensed as very great.

The outer ear. The part of the hearing system known as the outer ear works a little bit like a drum turned inside out; its resonating chamber is on the outside, and its vibrating membrane is farther in. The outer ear and its associated cavities serve as a complex resonating chamber. The principle of such a chamber was apparently known to prehistoric cave dwellers, as is shown in Figure 3.8.

The outer, visible part of the ear, having collected the sounds and begun to resonate, now leads back through a tube—about 1.25 inches long and the thickness of a knitting needle—to the eardrum. If all the cavities are set into resonance at one time, as by a sudden or sharp sound, our ears may "ring." Otherwise, a harmony of different sound waves strikes the eardrum and sets it into its own complex pattern of vibrations. Like a drumhead or a bell (which is really a specially curved membrane), the eardrum can sustain many kinds of vibrations at the same time.

The middle ear. The three small bones of the middle ear are attached at one end to the eardrum and at the other end to the oval window,° which is the entrance to

Fig. 3.8. This tangle of engravings, shown very much enlarged, was probably done about 12,000 B.C. by members of a nomadic hunting culture (Magdalenian IV), in southern France, that had not yet domesticated animals nor discovered agriculture. Yet, if we can judge from the humanlike figure (perhaps of a medicine man) in the lower right center, they apparently knew the principle of the mouth bow, in which the mouth is used as a resonating chamber.

oval window. The oval opening between the middle and inner ear through which sound vibrations pass.

the inner ear. The linkage of these bones is such that they do some amplifying of the sound, but that is not their main purpose. Their function should help us to appreciate how this structure had developed in the course of evolution.

Bear in mind that any structure will vibrate, as long as it is not rigid. The perfect sound insulator would simply be a substance that is perfectly rigid. Most structures, then, will vibrate according to their own characteristics—but, since there will be a loss of energy as we go from one substance to another as their characteristics change, another way to make an insulator would be to use layers of different substances. Some millions of years ago, when all creatures lived in the sea, the ear must have functioned very well, because sound came through the dense liquid medium.

But then some creatures moved out of the water, and their auditory system must have suffered an immediate loss in efficiency. Vibrations through the medium of the air now had to pass through the eardrum and then the fluid of the inner ear, with a consequent loss of energy. The device that was developed to make up for this loss was the little, bony amplifier of the middle ear. In the form in which it appears in vertebrates, hearing is therefore the most recently developed of the senses. It is rarely found in insects; it exists in much simpler form in fishes; and as regards amphibians the evidence is mixed. Salamanders, frogs, and toads can probably hear, and perhaps alligators and lizards, among the reptiles, but most snakes cannot, and it is uncertain whether turtles can.[7] However, functioning parts of the whole system can still be found in all these species, so it may be that the system was once operative but fell into disuse over millions of years.

The inner ear. This is the most complex part of the structure of the auditory system, and the hardest to understand. Only recently have its workings been made clear, due primarily to the researches of Georg von Békésy,[8] who in 1962 was awarded the Nobel Prize for his work—the first award for research related to psychology since that given to Pavlov in 1904.

The inner ear is a tube within a tube, a coiled unit called the *cochlea.*° To picture it, imagine it uncoiled: It will then resemble a tube that is divided along its length by a shelf, part bone and part membrane, on which some 24,000 fine fibers are planted. The fibers are connected in turn to extensions of cells in the auditory nerve, from which information is passed along to the thalamus,° a part of the brain that serves as a relay station, and thence to the temporal lobes° of the cortex.

There have been many years of controversy over how the cochlea is able to turn complex patterns of sound waves into some form of electrical discharge to be carried by the auditory nerve. In 1930 a great deal of excitement was generated when two experimenters, Wever and Bray, showed that a recording pickup placed on the cochlea of a cat, very close to where it joins the auditory nerve, will perfectly reproduce even complex sounds.[9] The cochlea, they concluded, acted like a good microphone, probably through stimulation of its fibers. However, the matter turned out to be much more complicated, and according to von Békésy's studies, the sounds we hear depend on many aspects of the cochlea working at once. We hear high frequencies because certain places on the cochlea are most sensitive to them; we hear lower frequencies because some of the nerve fibers are also stimulated to discharge. And we hear sounds as loud or soft partly depending on how many fibers in the auditory nerve are set into activity and partly depending on which fibers are activated, and this in turn is partly caused by patterns of bending in the fine fibers within the cochlea.

Our sensitive ears. This complex arrangement helps to explain that we are able to hear with such sensitivity and that some animals are able to hear over such a wide range of frequency. The latter is usually stated in hertz (Hz),° or cycles per

cochlea. The coiled, shell-shaped bone cavity of the inner ear containing the hearing receptors.

thalamus. The part of the forebrain that is a relay station for emotion and for nervous impulses from the body's senses to the cerebral cortex.

temporal lobe. The part of the cerebral cortex that controls speech and language processing as well as other auditory functions. It is located on the side of the head below the lateral fissure.

hertz (Hz). A term meaning "cycles per second."

second — that is, the number of times per second that a wave of compression and release occurs. Human hearing covers the range from about 50 Hz (so low that what we hear is a mixture of sound and throb) to about 15,000 Hz. Cats are able to hear in a greater range, from 30 Hz to 70,000 Hz. The ability of some animals that use reflected sound waves for navigational purposes — bats and porpoises, for example — seems to be a combination of facilities to produce pulses as high as 100,000 Hz and specialized systems to process the echoes.

If our hearing apparatus is normal, the amount that we hear will depend on the amount of energy we receive. Humans do not by any means have the most sensitive hearing apparatus among mammals, but our sensitivity is still amazing. The human voice in ordinary conversation has an energy output of only .000024 watts, so that it would take the energy in five million voices, talking at once, to light a 50-watt lightbulb; yet even this is five million times as much energy as the ear needs to detect a sound. We can hear something when our eardrum moves as little as one-tenth the diameter of an atom. Some persons, if they are in a perfectly quiet, echo-free room, are actually able to hear the Brownian movement of molecules in the air.

Most remarkable of all, given this sensitivity, is the range of sound intensity to which we can adjust. This is usually stated in decibels (db),[☉] which is a scale in which entries can be expressed as multiples of some minimal value. In Table 3.1 the scale on the left is expressed in decibels. Each entry is a certain number of times as intense as the zero point, which is the point of minimum audibility of a note two octaves above middle *C*. Thus, the noise in a quiet garden is rated at 20 db, meaning that it is 100 times as intense as the threshold sound, whereas the noise on an ordinary street, at 80 db, is 100 million times as intense as the threshold. Sustained noises much above this level may produce damage to the auditory system, although as we all know, relatively brief exposures to loud rock music, at 120 db, are not at all uncommon and seem to be enjoyed by some persons. The value of a chart such as Table 3.1 is to remind us of the extraordinary range of intensities that we process every day of our lives, usually without being particularly aware of the great differences between one situation and another.

The visual system

In humans, as in many other species and particularly among the primates, seeing is informationally the most important of the senses, although our basic test for whether something is "real" is probably our sense of touch. Perhaps for this reason, most of the research that has been done in the past hundred years on the experimental psychology of sensation and perception has been concerned with vision.

---

6. The visual system provides us with information about objects arrayed in a three-dimensional space.

There is some practical justification for this emphasis on vision. Like the other carnivores[☉] and hunters and like the more highly developed species, we get most of our useful information by means of vision. In addition, we use vision more than any other sense for our learning. If for some reason our visual information conflicts with information conveyed by another system, as in an experiment done by Rock and Victor, people depend on the visual information. Given the opportunity to see something as well as touch it, when the results from the two channels

decibel (db). The unit by which the intensity of a sound is measured.

carnivore. An animal (or plant) whose diet is mainly meat.

Table 3.1 The amount of energy in some sounds, expressed in decibels and in multiples of threshold energy.

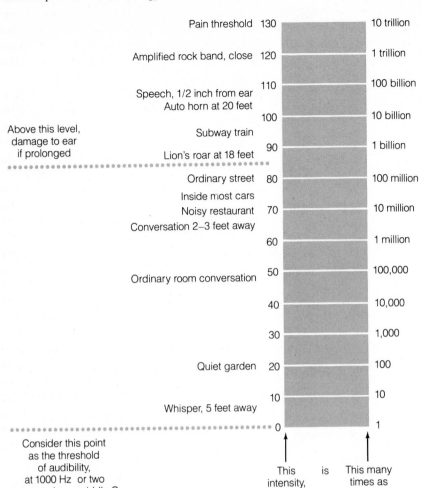

Sound	Intensity (decibels)	Times as intense as threshold
Pain threshold	130	10 trillion
Amplified rock band, close	120	1 trillion
Speech, 1/2 inch from ear Auto horn at 20 feet	110	100 billion
	100	10 billion
Subway train	90	1 billion
Lion's roar at 18 feet		
Ordinary street	80	100 million
Inside most cars Noisy restaurant	70	10 million
Conversation 2–3 feet away		
	60	1 million
Ordinary room conversation	50	100,000
	40	10,000
	30	1,000
Quiet garden	20	100
	10	10
Whisper, 5 feet away	0	1

Above this level, damage to ear if prolonged

Consider this point as the threshold of audibility, at 1000 Hz or two octaves above middle C

This intensity, in decibels   is   This many times as intense as the threshold

are not the same, subjects reported that they relied on their vision. Further, once they had made the decision in favor of the visual system, seeing it in a certain way actually made it feel different.[10]

Three-dimensional seeing. It is often maintained, incorrectly, that the reason we are able to take the two-dimensional "picture" from our retina and turn it into a three-dimensional picture of the world is that we have two eyes to work with. Since these give us two different views, we are able to "construct" a third dimension. But it is now certain that three-dimensionality is done by the whole visual system, from the lens of both eyes back to the visual cortex. However, how it is accomplished is not clear. We can only say, with one writer, "A remarkable thing about the visual system is its ability to synthesize the two somewhat different images into a single perception of solid objects lying in three-dimensional space."[11] The most popular, and plausible, explanation that we have was offered a century ago by the great German physiologist Helmholtz: Although all one has is two-dimensional information, one somehow learns in the course of development to make "inferences" at an unconscious level, inferring from experience that space is three-dimensional.

A different point of view would be that it is three-dimensional vision that is basic. Supporting this view (which seems to run counter to common sense) is experimental work that showed that if people are given no distance clues at all (for example, if they view a flat, perfectly homogeneous, painted wall extending across their field of view), they report, not a two-dimensional plane, but a foggy, three-dimensional "mist of light" in which they are "swimming."[12] Further, many different animals behave from birth, without any training, as though the world were three-dimensional. Newborn chicks will begin to peck at the correct distance to the ground as soon as their eyes open, and the laboratory rat, with no previous jumping experience, will leap the correct distance across a gap to land in a net.[13] Apparently, these animals do not have to learn or be taught that space stretches away from them in all directions. However, how they "know" this, or how they process the visual information, is not known.

Seeing objects. So far we have not mentioned one of the most important "tasks" of the visual system—to pick out forms from their background and to identify them as objects. The ability of the human visual system to do this—and it is far from the most sensitive one among mammals—is quite remarkable: We can adjust over a range of light intensity of the order of 1 to 10 billion, and within this range we can detect a target as minimal as a river viewed from more than a hundred miles away.

The trick of adapting to great differences in intensity is accomplished, at least in the vertebrates, by having the equivalent of two functioning retinas.⊙ On the surface of our retinas, there are scattered two kinds of cells, which get their names from the shape of their tips. They are as follows:

- The cones,⊙ about 6 million in each eye, are packed densely at one spot on the retina, with each connected to its own fiber in the optic nerve. They are clearly specialized, "higher-order" receptors whose function is to respond to color and to take over during the first five minutes or so of adapting to bright light.
- The rods,⊙ about 100 million of them, are scattered out toward the edge of the retina, with many cells connected to each fiber. They respond to dimmer, colorless light, as in twilight, and can take over from the cones to adapt, over about thirty minutes, to a level 100,000 times as sensitive as when they began.

Picking out and identifying the shape of objects, on the other hand, is done by specialized cells—in lower animals such as the frog, by cells at the retina, and in higher animals, such as the mammals, by cells further along in the system, in the visual cortex. This arrangement would seem to give the higher animals a great deal more flexibility and "choice" as to what they identify. Two kinds of arrangements, one in the frog and the other in the cat, will give us some indication of how object vision works. The data were obtained by inserting microelectrodes (a probe so fine it can be inserted into a single cell) at different points in the visual system and determining how and when the cells fire at various visual stimuli.

- Testing the frog in this way[14] reveals, first, that the overall level of illumination is usually ignored; the frog couldn't care less how bright it is outdoors. What it does "care" about, or automatically respond to, is, first, a sudden, reasonably large reduction in illumination (perhaps a shadow or an enemy?); second, a reasonably sharp edge, especially if it is moving; and third, a reasonably dark object, between ½ and 1 inch in diameter, preferably if its movement is jerky (ahah! a live fly). The important thing here is that the frog can respond selectively toward these complex objects even though it may have neither awareness nor a thought process; it is simply built to act this way. The

retina. The photosensitive part of the eye at the back of the eyeball, containing rods and cones on which images are projected.

cone. Photosensitive receptors found in the retina of the eye, predominantly around the fovea. They are responsible for both chromatic (color) and achromatic (without color) vision.

rod. Part of the eye's retina, shaped like a rod, sensitive to light but not color. Rods are particularly important for both peripheral and night vision.

Fig. 3.9. Two views of the "same" scene: (a) the hawk sees the large objects (the house and the trees) almost as part of the background; what stands out is the streak caused by the movement of a small animal. (b) the human might see from the same height the house and trees in all their details, but not the small animal.

monkey, too, has its built-in "object scanner" — in this case, special cells in the brain that respond only to a form resembling the monkey's hand.

■ Testing the cat,[15] on the other hand, reveals that fibers in the optic nerve are active (discharging) all the time, even in the dark or without external stimulation. Visually, the cat is always at the ready. But, unlike the frog, the cat's cortex is not equipped for straightforward responses to specific shapes or movements. Many different sizes and shapes will trigger off the cells; the most important aspects appear to be, first, the location of the visual stimulus, and second, the orientation or slant of an edge. Another critical factor may be the way the available light energy changes from moment to moment.[16]

■ One other important difference between frog and cat is that the latter's cortex is apparently capable of "learning," or at least of structural change as a result of past experience. Normally, certain cells in the visual cortex of the cat are lined up horizontally, like this: ——— . However, if the cat is reared in a specially constructed visual environment in which there are only vertical stripes, like this: , the cells will change to a vertical alignment.

Many creatures are able to "see," as is indicated in Figure 3.9. We place this word in quotes in order to emphasize the fact that the meaning of the word, as we can now guess, is not at all simple. Humans cannot "see" through brick walls — which means that our visual systems are not equipped to be stimulated by X rays. The frog cannot "see" a fly that is not moving — and so it will starve to death if it is surrounded by recently killed flies, just as we might starve to death in the "presence" of food on the other side of a brick wall. What we can sense, with any of our systems, is just what we are equipped to sense, no more. The nature of the sensing equipment, and even how it functions, will differ from one species to another and from one individual to another as well.

Summary

1. Sensory systems consist of structural arrangements by which selected kinds of energy are processed.

2. There are five commonly recognized sensory systems, responding in turn to the ever-present gravitational field; physical contact; certain airborne molecules, in the form of either gas or liquid; sound vibrations; and light.

3. The three parts of a sensory system are a receptor, for picking up energy; a transmitter, for conveying information about the energy; and a processor, for converting the energy into usable information.

4. The gravity system consists of sensors in muscles and joints, plus canals in the inner ear. Gravity is normally ever-present and is therefore a foundation and background for all action.

5. The contact system is mediated largely through structures in the skin. It serves both to provide information and to express feelings of love.

6. The smell and taste system is used by nonhuman animals to gain factual information but by humans primarily to gain information that qualifies what is already known as fact.

7. The receptors for smell are probably receptor cells in the nasal cavity, and the receptors for taste, in the form of buds, are on the surface of the tongue.

8. The auditory system provides information in the form of events that take place in time.

9. The structures for hearing consist of an external receiver (the ear) to capture and channel sound; an eardrum to resonate with the sound; an amplifying system, the middle ear; and structures in the inner ear that change vibrations into bursts of electrical impulses.

10. Species differ markedly in auditory sensitivity. Humans are sensitive over an intensity range of 10 trillion to one and are sensitive to a frequency range of about 50 to 15,000 cycles per second.

11. The visual system provides information about three-dimensional space and about the objects and distances within it.

12. In vertebrates, discriminating intensity of light is accomplished by the functioning of two kinds of cells in the retina. These are the cones, for initial adaptation over a small range, and the rods, for more extended adaptation over a much larger range.

13. Visual sensing of objects is accomplished differently in different species, depending on the species' survival needs. The general rule appears to be that the "higher" the species the closer to the cortex lies the major center for processing information about identity of objects.

14. In all species, visual systems are limited, in the sense that they do not enable the individual to see everything.

Now that we have discussed the physical structures and the sensory systems that people inherit and develop, we are prepared to raise some questions concerned with understanding and explaining people's behavior. The first such question is, "Why do people do what they do?"

In this chapter, you will be introduced to this basic question in the form in which it has usually been asked in psychology. That form has been, "What are the motives and drives 'inside' people that impel them to experience and act in the ways that they do?" You will survey the first answer to this question, called *traditional drive theory*, according to which certain biologically based, primary needs arise in the person, find satisfaction, and then die down in regularly recurring cycles of tension increase and tension reduction.

Typical of such primary drives is hunger, although we will also discuss others that seem equally basic, such as the curiosity motive and "life-or-death" drives, as well as certain "transitional" motives that are concerned with relations with other persons.

You will then learn about some other, more recently proposed ways of understanding and explaining motivation. In place of a traditional theory that describes people as being driven or incited to reduce their tensions, you will be offered some arguments and evidence leading to a quite different view of motives. It is based on the idea that very often people are not pushed by tensions but are pulled by their needs and expectations, not induced by their drives but incited by their wishes. Both these views, as you will see, may be necessary in order to understand the full range of motivated behavior in animals and humans.

Our example, again, will be hunger, but you will have an opportunity to explore this drive as a process of organizing information rather than of reducing tension. You will also learn about the experience of wanting from an inside viewpoint, particularly in its relation to feelings of certainty.

Wanting: the story of basic motives

In one of James Thurber's stories, a scientist, interviewing a lemming, remarks that the behavior of these animals has always puzzled him. Why, he asks, do they periodically rush down to the sea and drown themselves in large numbers? To which the lemming replies, "That's funny. I've always wondered why you humans don't."[1]

It is the behavior of others that often puzzles us, for we all know, or at least think we know, about our own behavior and what makes us act the way we do. However, even when we are puzzled by what others do, we take for granted that there must be some reason for it. We take for granted that there must be something that "makes" others do what they do. Our conviction seems to be that if there were no such something, we might all just sit around like inanimate objects until pushed into action by an outside force. Since it is obvious that we do not sit around like this, it is taken for granted that our activity, our striving, our goal seeking, are the results of inner forces. It is these forces that, as we say, *motivate* us even in extreme situations (as in Figure 4.1).

Now, this is a very recent notion in history. Like so many other ideas that we

"Love, work, and knowledge are the well-springs of life. They should also govern it." — Wilhelm Reich

BODIES
*The psychobiology
of individuals*

"I've got an idea..."

Fig. 4.1

unconscious processes. Mental
processes of which the individual is
unaware and that may require
considerable effort to bring to awareness.

take for granted, the idea that living creatures are driven, or motivated, by some
forces inside them is only a few centuries old. Neither Plato, the Greek philosopher of 2,000 years ago, nor Aquinas, the great theologian of the Catholic Church
during the Middle Ages, had any need to explain behavior in terms of drives or
motives or even important wants. In the view of these thinkers, it was the *will* that
determined people's actions (they were not at all concerned with other animals,
and so had even less need for a theory about animal motivation). "If I act in an evil
manner," they said, "it is because this is what I choose to do, out of my own God-
given free will." All human beings, it was thought, come equipped with this free
will from the time of birth, even the youngest person who does wrong. For example, even a starving child who steals food deserves to be punished. The punishment is not simply for the child's evil deed, but, more importantly, for the evil will
that led the child to do the deed.

These people of ancient and medieval times were not being cruel when they
executed babies for thievery. They even expressed great sorrow that the child had
been thus invaded by evil. Basically, they acted just as we do today. They were in
general agreement on what made people act the way they did, and so they collectively rewarded and punished people for doing so. This view seemed to these
people, in those far-off days, absolutely self-evident—just as self-evident as it seems
to us today to explain people's behavior as the result of their inner motives and
drives.

We no longer talk much about the will, just as in earlier times no one thought
of talking about one's motives. The most important influence in bringing about
this historic change in our attitudes concerning motivation was the work of Sigmund Freud, in the first two decades of this century.[2] Before that, the closest idea
one can find to a theory of motivation was the generally held belief that most
living creatures act so as to gain pleasure or avoid pain. Such a belief, although it
seems to make some sense, does not contain the notion of an inner drive or motive.
It was not really until the seventeenth century, in Western culture, that writers
began to seriously entertain the idea that an individual's behavior occurred as a
consequence of some pressure within the organism.

But theories about human behavior were still very closely tied to the medieval notions of will and reason. Humans, by virtue of their immortal souls, were
believed to be reasoning creatures who acted in terms of will. Then Freud came
along, to blow apart this comfortable, rational view of human nature. He popularized the notion of *unconscious processes*© of the mind—with the strong and
frightening implication that our deepest and most fundamental motivation stems
from those dark recesses of our mind that are hidden even from ourselves. In the
face of such a theory, the older picture of human beings as rational creatures,
ennobled and organized by use of the will, simply collapsed.

The ordinary person today might not follow all the details of Freud's theory,
for most persons do not have a personal "theory" of motivation so much as a
general set of beliefs that seem to them self-evident. However, one common belief
derives directly from Freud's thinking. It is that the basic cause of human behavior
is to be found in the inner drives that motivate us. In this view, we are all a bit like
the boilers of steam locomotives: containers for potentially explosive, driving
forces that impel us to do what we do.

This kind of belief appears in the form of traditional drive theory in psychology. It may therefore sound familiar and even self-evident to you, the reader, even
though it is dressed up in elaborate terminology. In this chapter we will first
examine this theory—but we want to go beyond it to discuss the criticisms that
have been leveled against it and some alternatives that have been proposed. Finally, we want to conclude by presenting a quite different understanding of what
is called *drive* or *motive*. We will suggest an alternative way of considering moti-

vation, based on an inside viewpoint and expressed in terms of the distinction between being *pushed* and being *pulled*.

Traditional drive theory

The most widely studied of the basic motives is hunger. Like other basic motives such as thirst or sex, hunger appears to arise out of the fundamental "tissue needs" of an organism. It appears to be completely physiological in its origin. It is required for the survival of the individual, just as the sex drive is required for the survival of the species. And it appears in a regular cycle, regardless of circumstance or personal choice, demanding satisfaction and then disappearing until the cycle reappears.

These three basic drives are not, however, the sum total of a living creature's needs. In addition to food, water, and sexual satisfaction, every living creature (with the exception of anaerobic bacteria) needs oxygen, needs to be free of pain, needs an environment within an appropriate temperature range. But these needs are not the same as drives, for they are usually neither rhythmic nor cyclic, and they do not give rise to certain specific forms of behavior.

---

1. Experimental research, especially in regard to hunger, has traced out a cycle of need arousal, instrumental behavior, and need reduction.

Consider the familiar phenomenon of becoming hungry. At one time, let us say, we are not hungry; we neither feel hungry nor act in our usual "hungry" way. Then something happens inside our bodies, some sort of tissue need,⊙ which causes us to feel hungry and also to start to do something to satisfy our hunger. That is, our behavior now becomes both *energized* and *directed* so as to satisfy the aroused need (Figure 4.2). In the ordinary course of events, we now behave in such a way as to satisfy our hunger. When this happens, the drive subsides, and, as far as our experience and our behavior are concerned, we are no longer hungry—until the next time the tissue need is aroused, when the sequence begins all over again.

What we have just described here has the form of a cycle. Like all cycles, it recurs on a regular basis, and it usually follows the same general pattern, returning each time to the condition that started it off. Thus, as we know from much

Fig. 4.2. These animals were probably behaving peacefully until the threat of a forest fire aroused them. Their high level of drive (in this case, fear) has led to the nearly disorganized behavior you see here. If they escape the fire, the threat will lessen and they will probably resume their former drive level.

tissue need. A term referring to the basic need of tissues for food, oxygen, and so on.

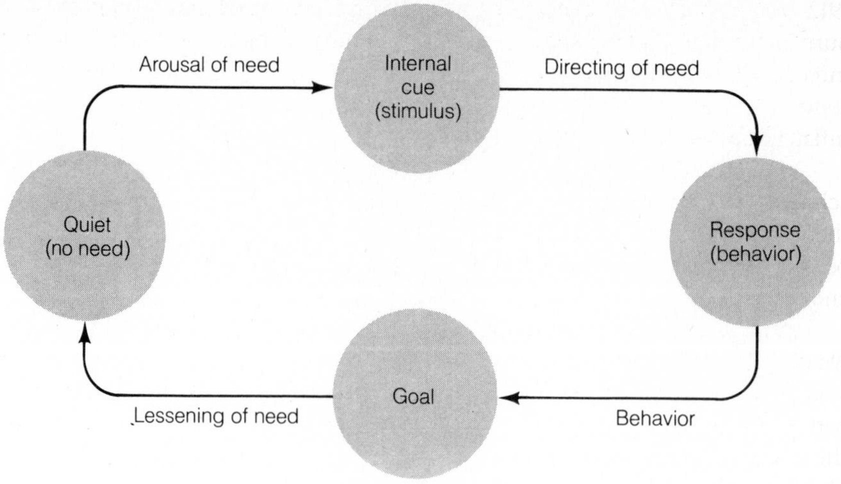

Fig. 4.3. A cycle of motivation and drive reduction.

experience, our hunger recurs on a very regular basis. It builds up until we find a way to satisfy it. This in turn makes it subside until we are again in a state of no hunger, just as though the cycle had never happened.

Such a very simple model, however, will not do as a complete explanation in science. Many generations of careful work have been devoted to spelling out the details of this cycle. Much of the work has been in regard to hunger, because this is the easiest of all tissue needs to manipulate in a laboratory situation. But, whether in regard to hunger, or thirst, or sex, the picture that emerged was about the same. The sequence by which these needs are regularly satisfied is generally described in these, more elaborate terms — still in the form of a cycle, but with more stages, as in Figure 4.3.

In this sequence, the arousal of a need kicks off some internal "cue" that serves as a stimulus — for example, my increasing hunger need changes my internal organization in such a way that I am made aware of my hunger and impelled to do something about it. This may take the form of a feeling of emptiness in my stomach, or a mild restlessness and irritability, or even a slight headache. I now am stimulated to direct my need — that is, my behavior is the kind that is instrumental[○] in satisfying my hunger. Again, in the ordinary course of events, such behavior will lead me to an appropriate goal. Gaining this goal, in the form of food to be eaten, will then serve to lessen or reduce my need. This puts me back in the quiescent state from which I started out.

A more complete picture. Presenting the picture in this more complete way has a major advantage for research, in that it provides many more opportunities for experimental testing than does the simpler cycle we described. There are three different aspects of the cycle in Figure 4.3 that can be controlled, or *manipulated*, in laboratory experiments: the internal cue,[○] the behavioral response and the goal by which the original need is satisfied. Consider, for example, how much is learned about the hunger drive when one simply keeps asking more and more precise questions concerning one of the three aspects, the internal cue.

One first asks the obvious question, "What is the internal cue for hunger? That is, what is it inside of us that tells us when we are hungry?" The most immediate answer, and the one that accords most closely with our common experience, is that we usually know we are hungry because we feel certain changes in our stomach; it rumbles, it feels empty, it even seems to undergo rhythmic contractions. In a set of classic experiments, these changes were in fact verified. In

instrumental behavior. Often referred to as *operant behavior.* Behavior that generally accomplishes a purpose, such as the satisfaction of a need.

cue. A function of motivation whose purpose is to trigger specific responses from a subject in a given direction.

1912, Walter B. Cannon, a physiologist at Harvard, persuaded his assistant, Washburn, to swallow a balloon that was fixed to the end of a long tube so that it could be inflated while in the assistant's stomach. Just as expected, Washburn's stomach contractions, which could be detected by means of changes in pressure on the inflated balloon, usually signaled the onset of his hunger pangs.[3]

However, things are not quite this simple. Although it is clear that the stomach plays some part in the process of providing internal cues for hunger, it is not the source of the cues, and it may not even be a necessary step. We know this because persons whose stomachs have been surgically removed can still experience hunger pangs in the ordinary way.

We can now begin to see that when we speak of an internal cue for hunger, we do not mean a specific, single event, but a set of events that are significant in varying degrees. Researchers in this area have known for a long time that certain parts of the brain can affect one's hunger and one's appetite. The specific organ of the mammalian brain that has been pinpointed is the hypothalamus;○ this is a part of the brain (actually situated just above the roof of the mouth) that has a great deal to do with control over the endocrine glands. If certain parts of the hypothalamus are injured or removed, the animal will overeat to a serious degree.

The switch for eating. The hypothalamus, then serves as one link in the chain of events that provide an internal cue for hunger. We can now ask, "How does the hypothalamus function in this way?" (Notice how precise a question this is, compared to the more general one we began with a few paragraphs back.) Elaborate "mapping" studies of the parts of the hypothalamus have shown that it contains an off switch for eating, an area that seems to trigger a command to stop eating when the animal has had enough. Damage this area, and the animal will not be able to stop eating; stimulate the damaged switch electrically, so that the switch works again, and the animal will now stop eating.[4]

Every switch should have two positions—on and off. Thus, just as we might expect, the hypothalamus contains still another area that appears to serve as an on switch. If this area is damaged so that the switch does not function, the animal will stop eating, in spite of the presence of food, and will thus starve to death. The entire system within the hypothalamus, then, requires that eating start when required and stop when appropriate. Although we cannot know what animals other than humans actually experience, it is a safe guess that the hypothalamic switches, when properly activated, make the animal feel hungry and then at a later time make it feel full.

Other basic drives

The discussion of traditional drive theory just given was stated in terms of the most familiar and the most widely studied of basic motives, hunger. A similar analysis of other basic motives, such as thirst and sex, could be offered. In the case of thirst, a similarly complex chain of events, again with the hypothalamus playing an important role, results in the set of feelings and sensations that we call "being thirsty." In the case of the sex drive, the chain of events is simpler in lower animals, such as the rat, but is proportionately more complex as one proceeds up the evolutionary chain toward more complex creatures. In rats, sexual drive and behavior is largely controlled by the production of hormones, from the ovaries in the female and from the testes in the male; but the hypothalamus, too, has been shown to play a part. In higher-order mammals, sexuality becomes increasingly more complex, more variable, and more strongly affected by factors of opportunity, past experience, emotional state, and social influence.

hypothalamus. A region of the forebrain that plays an important role for regulation of temperature, thirst, sex, sleep, hunger, emotion, and endocrine gland functions.

Fig. 4.4. Behavior for its own sake may be pursued (a) at some expense or (b) at the risk of danger to oneself.

motivational systems. A set of behaviors organized around a single motive.

2. There may be more than the three basic biological drives just discussed—specifically, there may be exploration-curiosity and life-death drives.

It is clear that hunger, thirst, and sex do not exhaust the phenomenon of motivation. At every level of complexity, living creatures seem to be driven in ways other than being hungry or thirsty or sexually aroused. What such activity seems to have in common is that it is triggered by its own kind of situation and is then usually pursued even in the face of odds (Figure 4.4).

Behavior for its own sake. An everyday example will serve to describe behavior for its own sake. Consider what often happens when you are presented with a puzzle to be solved. Try this one, for example: SECURA. This is an anagram, so you have to unscramble it or change the letters around, so as to make a common English word.[5] Most persons who are presented with this kind of puzzle immediately try to solve it—a response that we can easily understand in terms of the notion of a challenge. But what is not at all easy to understand is why most persons will also continue at this rather frustrating task (it is quite a difficult anagram) for a surprisingly long time. Indeed, if they had been asked to do the same thing but not in the guise of solving a puzzle, such as switching the letters around in as many different combinations as possible, they would very soon have become bored with the task. When it is presented as a puzzle, however, they continue at it for many minutes on end. Even more surprisingly, if they are asked whether they would like the answer supplied to them, they will usually refuse with great vehemence.

In short, when challenged to begin working on such a puzzle, most persons act as if they were motivated by the doing of the problem itself. It is hard to believe that there is any strong need that motivates them to devote so much effort to an essentially boring task. Rather, they seem to have become involved in what can best be called "behavior for its own sake." It satisfies no tissue needs, such as hunger; it does not lead toward a very desirable goal, as happens in the case of a sexual drive. It is simply pursued for its own sake. (The correct answer to the anagram, incidentally, is the common English word *saucer.*)

Behaviors such as these are often called *motivational systems,*° to indicate their connection with motivation yet to distinguish them from the basic motives, or drives, such as hunger, thirst, and sex. Two such systems have been studied in detail—*contact-comfort*, discussed in Chapter 3, and *exploration*—and you will note how closely they are both tied to the activities of young animals.

- *Exploration.* Exploration is a key element in the cycle shown in Figure 4.3, a few pages back; there it is labeled "Directing of need." This refers to the portion of a drive reduction cycle in which the animal, aroused by a need, begins to explore the environment for ways to satisfy the need. The hungry lion in the zoo, with no place to go, paces in its cage, just as the hungry lion in the wild rouses itself to hunt for game. The reason for this connection between need arousal and exploration is, of course, that very seldom is the goal or satisfaction of a need found immediately at hand.

But, interestingly enough, exploration also appears under circumstances in which, apparently, no physiological need has been aroused. In many different creatures, under a wide range of conditions, exploratory behavior occurs, seemingly for its own sake. All that is required is that there be something to explore—that is, that the environment contain some aspect that is novel for the animal. Laboratory mice can easily be trained to turn on a light, apparently just for the sake of turning it on, or to step on a platform so as to produce nothing but clicks. Monkeys in cages will work very hard to open latches that provide no other "reward" than to open a door on an empty room. Practically all animals will engage in extensive exploratory behavior when placed in new surroundings. And, as parents have often discovered to their distress, the young child's drive to explore is almost inexhaustible.

The term that suggests itself in this connection is *curiosity*, and some psychologists have even claimed that curiosity deserves to be called a *motive* in its own right, as unlearned yet as compelling as are hunger and thirst. Observations and experiments have confirmed repeatedly that the kind of exploratory behavior we call *curiosity* plays a very important part in many creatures, particularly in the young. In a series of ingenious studies using monkeys, it has been shown that these animals quickly learn to open only the door that gives them a chance to "satisfy their curiosity"—for example, a view of a complex scene or something that is moving or another animal. With humans, too, the more complicated or unusual a visual target is (within reasonable limits), the more time people will spend looking at it (Figure 4.5). Even infants follow this pattern. It would seem that most creatures actively seek out ways to satisfy curiosity, to deal with novelty, to discover complexity slightly greater than they are used to—in short, to explore and so to extend their working environments. And it seems to be done with no other reward than the doing of it, not to satisfy any goal or to lessen any need.[6]

■ *To Live or to Die.* Not as well studied, but perhaps of equal importance, is another kind of basic motive that also seems to operate for its own sake. If we observe a chick in the process of breaking out of its shell at the moment of hatching, we see a remarkable frenzy of effort that mobilizes the creature totally. Similarly, infant monkeys cling for comfort to their terrycloth "mothers," just as though their very lives depended on it (see Chapter 3). The absence of such a "will to live" is equally striking. The biologist Curt Richter found that, in situations in which there was no way at all to escape, healthy

Fig. 4.5. The kinds of patterns that seem to be preferred by humans. (Based on data in Berlyne, 1966)

Irregular

Complicated

Filled

Odd

and vigorous rats, whether wild or laboratory bred, simply gave up and died. If the slightest hope for escape was offered them, however, they then recovered rapidly and struggled vigorously again.

The British psychiatrist John Bowlby has described a similar phenomenon in human infants, which he calls a "separation syndrome." Its first stage, when infants are first separated from their caretakers, is one of protest. If the separation continues, there occurs a phase of "mourning" for what is no longer there, for what Bowlby calls "what is lost but still regainable." Finally, there is a stage of "detachment" for what the infant seems to feel is "no longer regainable."[7]

"Transitional" views of motive. A number of psychologists have argued that there may be many basic human motives that are not simply biological. On the other hand, they are not the kind of basic "social" motives that we will be discussing in the next chapter. We are therefore referring to these views as "transitional." A summary of the motives suggested by two psychologists is presented in Table 4.1. Erich Fromm[8] is a psychoanalyst and social philosopher who has written widely on social problems, the ideal society, psychoanalytic theory, dreams, love, and aggression. Abraham Maslow[9] is the founder of the movement known as *humanistic psychology.*⊙

These lists of motives have been arranged so that they approximately correspond. Thus, Fromm's motive of identity corresponds approximately to what Maslow would call a need for self-esteem, and so on. The two lists are similar in that they both include motives that go beyond basic biological satisfactions, and in that they both consist entirely of positive motives. For instance, neither Maslow nor Fromm would agree with Freud that human beings have a basic drive toward destructiveness or aggression. The difference between the two lists is chiefly that Maslow's is more organized and includes motives at all levels of functioning.

In Maslow's view, basic physiological drives such as hunger, thirst, and sex are absolutely necessary, and in fact if they are not satisfied they will dominate one's thinking and behavior. However, once they have been satisfied, they recede into the background and allow other, "higher" motives to take over and direct one's behavior. Thus satisfaction occurs progressively through the list; the satisfying of one level of motive opens the way for seeking out satisfaction of the next level. Some persons, in Maslow's view, are fortunate enough to be able to devote their energies largely to actualizing,⊙ or living out, their own highest possibilities. These are the persons that he would consider the healthiest personalities.

humanistic psychology. A contemporary branch of psychology in which Maslow and others accent the positive features of humans. Maslow's psychology takes human life as it is, with all its potentials and aspirations toward personal growth and self-actualization.

actualize (or self-actualize). A humanistic term popularized by Maslow, by which he means that persons strive toward maximum realization of their potential. It is the fundamental need in Maslow's hierarchy of human needs.

Table 4.1. The basic human motives, according to Fromm and Maslow

Fromm	Maslow
	Physiological
	Affectional (need for safety and security)
Relatedness (need to relate to others)	Interpersonal (need for love and belonging)
Rootedness (need to belong with others)	
Identity (need for uniqueness)	Psychological-Personal (need for self-esteem)
Transcendance (creative needs)	Transpersonal (need for self-actualization)
Orientation (need for a frame of reference to perceive the world)	

3. Once energized, an organism, if motivated, is directed toward satisfying needs, on the basis either of past learning or of the progressive organization of information.

We have been considering what we have called "traditional drive theory." In this explanation, we do what we do because we are driven by some forces or motives within us. Some of these forces, as we saw, are biological or physiological. Others are on a "higher" psychological or even spiritual level.

But no matter what the level, the basic motives that we have discussed so far had this one characteristic in common: They were all assumed to be in the form of forces that drive or push the animal. Once aroused, these forces are assumed to drive the creature into action so as to satisfy the drive. But, when we state it in this way, we can see immediately that there is a flaw in such a view. Just because an animal is aroused by a hunger drive is no reason to assume that it will do anything *organized* or sensible to satisfy the drive. Such drives certainly arouse or *energize* the animal, but they do not necessarily *direct* it. We can see this easily if we consider the analogous problem of pushing a stalled car. If the car is merely pushed from behind in an undirected way—as, for example, by a very strong wind—it is likely to go anywhere. In order for a push to be effective, someone should be at the wheel, giving the car direction as well as motion.

Just the same thing seems to happen in the case of strong, impelling motives when they are aroused in living creatures. The motive, by itself, produces merely movement; if no organization or direction occurs, the creature would simply move wildly, restlessly, or at random (see Figure 4.6). In short, it appears that motivated behavior cannot be understood entirely in terms of what *pushes* or drives the creature; an additional element is needed.

Considerations of this sort have led some theorists to make a distinction between what pushes a motivated creature and what pulls it; or, to put it in another pair of terms, between what *incites* a creature to do something and what *induces* it to do something. Traditional drive theory, which emphasizes the push rather than the pull, the incitement rather than the inducement, is built around the notion of deprivation and its consequences; whereas motivational theory developed more recently is built around the notion of incentives. We will consider briefly two different but related forms of incentive theory.⊙

The "reinforcement" approach.[10] The basis of this view is the observation that traditional drive theory explains only the start of the cycle; an additional explanation of its end results is also needed. In such a cycle, the end result—that is, reaching the goal or satisfying the need—occurs because it serves as a reinforcement.⊙ This term, which is a fundamental one in the psychological literature, refers to anything that helps to "stamp in" some kind of behavior and make it a little more probable that the behavior will happen again under the same circumstances. Another term for positive reinforcement is reward.

There is little disagreement with the fact that many living creatures are energized, or aroused into action, by their own inner drives. But these drives, or urges, may serve as triggers rather than as motives for the whole cycle. One reason for some confusion in these matters is that certain basic life urges, such as hunger or thirst, are taken as the model for all other kinds of drives, big and small. Another

(a)

(b)

Fig 4.6. The difference between being pushed and being pulled by a high level of drive. In (a) the man is driven by thirst, but, as his track shows, he is only being energized, not directed. In (b), however, he is being drawn toward the mirage, and so, rightly or wrongly, he is now directed as well as energized.

incentive theory. A theory of motivation that stresses the importance of rewards or threats in determining behavior. It is opposed to the theory that internal drives instigate activity.

reinforcement. Stimulation that increases or decreases the strength of a response and the conditioning process.

reason may be that, because drives such as hunger or thirst are easy to manipulate in laboratory experiments, the picture that they present is taken as typical of all cases. In the case of hunger, the picture is that of a deprived animal whose situation is restricted to ways of alleviating the symptoms of deprivation. Under such unusual and artificial constraints, most animals will display behavior that overly stresses the importance of the original energizing drive. What happens will then be understood in terms of the start of the cycle rather than in terms of how the animal finds ways to finish the cycle. The conditions of deprivation will be emphasized at the expense of the conditions of reinforcement.

An alternative view would also stress the ways that the cycle is ended. A motivational theory derived in this way, then, would explain behavior in terms of how it is reinforced rather than how it is driven. The pull on the animal would be emphasized, not the push; the inducement, not the incitement.

Such a view, stressing the reinforcement at the end of the cycle rather than the drive at the start of the cycle as the "cause" of behavior, might help to explain an important set of facts. This set concerns the well-known finding that it makes a great deal of difference whether an animal has already had some experience in satisfying its drives in specific ways. The hungry laboratory rat, dropped into a strange and difficult maze, not knowing how or even whether it will satisfy its need, is quite likely to act as though it is being driven from behind by a strong wind; its movements will be disorganized, hurried, even jerky, and it will hardly act very "intelligently." But place the same animal in a maze in which it has already been reinforced for learning the correct path, and its behavior will be smooth, purposeful, seemingly planned, and involving a minimum of effort. In the first case, the animal will be "pushed" blindly from behind; in the latter case, it will be "pulled" ahead sensibly by the consequences of the reinforcements it has already experienced. The first case might seem to prove a traditional theory of motivation, but it does so only by forcing the animal into as "stupid" a mode of behavior as possible.

The organism information approach. On the basis of an extensive review of the experimental literature on motivation, John Garcia and his colleagues have recently proposed an alternative approach to understanding motivated behavior.[11] Their explanation also falls into a cycle—or, as they put it, a "patterned sequence"—but of a different sort than the ones we have considered above.

There are four major phases to this cycle, shown in Figure 4.7. The first phase, arousal, is similar to the opening stages of the cycles we showed earlier in Figure 4.3. In the second phase, orientation, the animal begins the specific kind of searching, directed behavior called for by the specific arousal. A hungry animal does not "search" in the same way as it might if sexually aroused; the lion on the prowl for game behaves differently than the same lion running down some game that has been sighted. If it is hunger that has been aroused, orientation will consist of salivating, a sharpened sense of smell, and a change in attitude so that edible things begin to smell good—all of which we are familiar with from our own experiences of hunger.

Orientation,° as it is meant here, is part of the survival equipment that is specific to each species. Like the other behavioral patterns that we discussed in Chapter 1, orientation enables a moment-to-moment fitting of an organism to its environment, like a key in a lock. Its major element is a focused attention and sensing. Thus, if a laboratory rat hears a click, it will immediately attend to the source of the sound, showing a focused and sharpened seeing and hearing. Repeat the click a moment later, and the rat will attend again. If the click is repeated often enough, the rat will appear to lose interest in it—unless it changes in some way, or

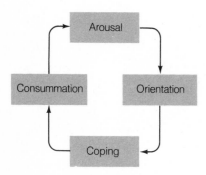

Fig. 4.7. The phases of an information-based motivational cycle of arousal and drive reduction.

orientation. Attention focused on something in the environment.

unless it resumes after a pause. In these cases, the orientation phase will begin all over again.

Behavior during the orientation phase is thus behavior that once triggered is continued (like your persistence in working on the anagram) until fatigue or boredom sets in. It is important to note that orienting behavior can occur only in an environment where novelty is possible. This happens very often in the natural state of most animals, but relatively seldom when animals are caged or placed in familiar mazes for laboratory experiments. Indeed, one of the precautions that is usually taken when laboratory animals are used as subjects for research is that they are first made very familiar with the experimental setting, so that no element of shock or surprise will detract from their performance. The result is, inevitably, that they then never show the very important phase of orientation; it is short-circuited, and our consequent understanding of the animals' motivated behavior is lessened.

In the "appetitive coping" phase that follows, the animal demonstrates adaptive behavior that is related to some appetite, motive, or drive. It is in this phase that the motivated animal is able to learn, for here it picks up and uses whatever information is available in order to reach its goal and satisfy its drive. In the preceding phase, the animal might have quieted down once it became oriented; but in the appetitive phase it can never become "coped" until the goal is reached, and so it will continue moving, coping, learning, figuring out, and searching as long as is necessary. What it learns in this phase, and how well it learns, seems to depend on how close to the final phase the learning occurred. However, if the animal is in this phase but has not been able to reach its goal—for example, if the food is taken away just as the animal finds it—it will engage in what is called *displacement*° behavior. The caged lion will pace and roar; the hungry rat will drink water even though what it wants is food.

One important, and novel, feature of the view we are describing here is that it emphasizes *information* rather than rewards, satisfactions, or punishments. It states that living creatures operate in terms of the kinds of information they are able to gather and that the way they achieve their goals is to get as much organized information as possible rather than simply to seek out rewards or try to avoid punishments. As an example, in an experiment done by D. P. Hendry,[12] pigeons were trained to peck at a key in their cages in order to receive food—but the food was delivered only occasionally, rather than at every peck. Next to the food key, another key was available that could serve as a signal: If it turned red when it was pecked, then that meant the food key would deliver food when *it* was pecked; but if the second key turned green that meant no food would be received at the food key. The pigeons quite easily learned, not to peck away at the food key, but to peck at the "signal" key, even though it did not give them a reward but only information about a reward.

The final phase of this cycle consists of the consummatory behavior, as it is called, by which a drive is satisfied. For example, the hungry animal eats, or the sexually aroused individual engages in sexual behavior. The specific form of behavior that occurs at this phase is usually genetically programmed for the species, particularly in nonhuman animals. Even among humans, consummatory behavior is often surprisingly unchanging for the individual. Consider, for example, the eating habits of yourself or of people you know and of how little they change regardless of your degree of hunger or what it is you are eating. Consummatory behavior usually follows a fixed routine and cannot easily be "turned off" once it has started. Interfering with it thus results in an immediate and often negative reaction, as can be seen if you try to take your dog's food dish away in the middle of a feeding. In all these respects behavior is the least flexible in this phase of the motivational cycle.

displacement behavior. In the "informational" model of motivation, the specific behavior displayed by an animal in the "coping" phase which is prevented from reaching its goal.

An alternative approach

Thus far we have discussed a traditional drive theory, which quite closely resembles the viewpoint that most persons would offer as their explanation of what makes people do what they do. But it turns out to be a limited theory, even when it is elaborated into a more detailed cycle. In answer to its major difficulties, we then said, two major alternatives have been offered. The first of these claims that, through the process of learning and reinforcement, organisms gain their own store of meanings and that these meanings determine how they will be motivated to act in a situation. What is implied by this theory—although we left it unstated a few pages back—is that, in order to know what the organism will do in any situation, one must know the meaning that it has learned. If we know that this child has learned that the little brown objects held out by the experimenter and called M&M's are really good to eat, then we can predict how the child will be motivated to act when M&M's are offered as a reward. Our prediction, the test of our understanding and our theory, depends on two prior facts: that the M&M's have come to have this meaning for the child and that we know that this is so.

The second alternative to traditional drive theory that we discussed, an informational approach, likewise depends on the organism evolving new meanings by which to cope with situations. In this theory, however, much more emphasis is placed on the organism's active role in seeking out and, so to speak, finding new knowledge. The theory says that whenever the organism is aroused it will immediately begin to organize its own situation for whatever meaning can be created in it. Again, in order to make use of the theory, we would have to have some idea of the old and new meanings by which an organism has made sense out of its situation. We would have to know how a situation is organized for an individual before being able to understand or predict its motivated behavior.

What is suggested in regard to both these theories is that at the heart of an individual's behavior is the individual's experience. The question "How do things seem to this individual in this situation?" may well be the central question for understanding motivation. The approach to motivation that we will now be offering will therefore start with this question. We will attempt to explore motivation, not as a special kind of behavior, but as a special kind of experience. We will discuss it from the inside viewpoint.

4. An inside view emphasizes the experience of wanting and its relation to the experience of uncertainty.

Being hungry. One advantage of an approach based on the individual's experience is that the data are always at hand for each one of us. In this case, we have only to recollect or imagine that most familiar of personal experiences, being hungry. Bear in mind that the description that follows will necessarily be both too general (because it is meant to apply to most persons) and too specific (because it comes out of the thought processes of two individuals, the authors). You, as a different individual reading our description, will have to compare it with your own.

If I were only mildly hungry, I would probably experience the state as a pleasant kind of arousal, in which I might enjoy the anticipation of food. If I were at home, I would be interested in all the sights and sounds that signal a meal in the early stages of preparation. My senses would be slightly sharpened; I would notice more sights, sounds, and smells connected with the meal.

We sense what we are primed to sense; our needs direct our sensing. Thus the anxious mother hears the slightest whimper of her newborn baby, although some-one else sleeping in the same room may sleep soundly through the baby's awakening. Thirsty wanderers in the desert see the mirage of an oasis when it is not there. The phenomenon can even be demonstrated in the psychologist's laboratory, as was repeatedly done during the 1950s when the topic of motivated needs was something of a fad. In the simplest version of the experiment, a slide is flashed on a screen, much too rapidly for people actually to tell what was shown. The hungrier they are — that is, the more their seeing is motivated by a need for food — the more food-related objects they report.[13]

Now suppose that as I wait around for a meal to be prepared, my hunger begins to increase. Very soon I would discover that my pleasantly anticipatory state gives way to slight impatience and perhaps irritability. My need now begins to prime me in another way and may even begin to interfere with my activity as it increases. As wanting changes from an instigator of my behavior to its antagonist, I have the experience of being focused, almost without my wishing it, more and more narrowly. I try to read, but my attention keeps wandering back to ways that my hunger can be satisfied. My behavior becomes a little disorganized, a little less tied to longer-term goals. I begin to move restlessly, almost at random. And time seems to move with surprising slowness.

If my hunger were to increase in this way without prospect of immediate satisfaction, I would become more and more preoccupied with my wanting, unable to distract myself from it, trapped in it to the exclusion of other needs or goals. We are all familiar with behavioral expressions of this subjective situation — in the noise one can hear in the zoo just before feeding time, in the baby's restless crying for its bottle, in the random irritability many persons show if a meal is delayed. These are examples of what one may call the "buzzing fly" situation: behavior that expresses the experience of being trapped up against a goal that cannot be either reached or given up (as in Figure 4.8). The wanting is now no longer tempered by one's ability to delay or be distracted. It is now a kind of *pure wanting*, just as though one were being pushed inexorably from behind.

Wanting and certainty. The preceding description does not do full justice to the normal experience of wanting. The fact is, we very rarely reach the stage of "pure wanting" that was described in the preceding paragraph. Our wants are rarely this demanding and are not usually permitted to proceed to such a state of near desperation. The more normal course of events is that our wanting occurs in a situation that is more or less familiar to us and in which there is some reasonable prospect of our getting satisfaction.

Fig 4.8. For this child, everything is now collapsed into one moment of wanting. There is no distance, no ability to wait, no selectivity. Space and time are lost — just as they often are for very tired and hungry children who ask repeatedly, at the end of a long ride, "Are we there yet?"

In order to adequately describe the everyday experience of wanting, then, we will have to include an element that was left out of the preceding description. It will turn out, in fact, that this second element, our degree of *certainty*, will enable us to comprehend a much greater range of wanting situations. By the term *certainty* we mean the individual's expectation that the want will be satisfied.

Consider again the situation that we described earlier. If I have not eaten for a number of hours, I might become mildly hungry—and this hunger might normally increase as time goes on. But now we have to ask, "Does it make any difference at this point whether or not food is available in the refrigerator?" We would say that it makes a great deal of difference. If I have ready access to food, then my hunger will be less than if no food is available to me. In other words—it is not simply my biological state, or the amount of time since I have last eaten, that will determine how hungry I *feel*, but the way in which this biological state interacts with my certainty about getting food.

There is a difference between being hungry and feeling hungry or, in other words, between the state of hunger and the experience of hunger. In the normal range of being hungry, which is what most of us experience most of the time, the degree of wanting that we experience will depend as much on our feeling of certainty as on the state of our stomach or our blood-sugar level. It is only as the biological condition increases and then passes a certain critical point that I am likely to experience a desperate wanting that is not relieved by the knowledge that food is definitely on its way to me. If I am starving, I will probably feel starving. At most stages short of starvation, however, my expectation and my confidence as to whether food is available will play the major role in my wanting. This is why I can put up with a great deal of deprivation if I am on a diet—because being on a diet means that I fully expect food to be available if my will should weaken. In the expectation that I can get food whenever I really go after it, my wanting changes; I feel the deprivation less than if it had occurred because, let us say, I were shipwrecked. It is not that, as many writers put it, I want what I cannot have, but rather that I experience my wanting more keenly *if* I cannot have what I want.

We are referring here to a set of personal experiences that take place within the biological context. The process begins and will probably end in biological and physiological terms: food deprivation, hunger, and finally satiation. Therefore whatever experiences I have can be overridden by a great enough increase in the biological drive itself. No matter what I may think or feel about the possibility of getting food, if I am kept from eating long enough I will begin to feel that "pure wanting" that we described earlier. If this should happen, then my associated experiences—of knowing, of expecting, of preferring and choosing—all go by the wayside. Hungry enough, I will eat anything; I am bound completely by the push that drives me, and all possible targets fade into a single, simple meaning.

5. Overeating is seen to be related to one's experiencing of "distancing" in regard to food.

Some persons overeat; some are overweight. Overeating and being overweight do not always coincide in an individual, because many overweight people eat surprisingly little for their size, and many overeaters manage to remain surprisingly thin for their level of consumption. But if overeating and being overweight do coincide the person usually attributes the weight to the eating—although the reverse is just as likely to be true.

Our concern here is with those cases in which the calculation was correct and in which the overweight was in fact caused by the overeating. A great deal of

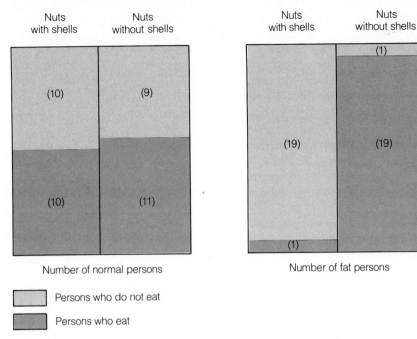

Fig. 4.9. The effects of work on the eating behavior of normal and fat persons. In one condition, participants were offered nuts with the shells on, to munch on while filling out questionnaires; in the other condition, the nuts had no shells on. (From Schacter, 1971b, p. 135)

laboratory research has been carried out, undoubtedly sparked by continuing public concern, by an awareness of the medical problems involved in obesity, and by individuals' desire to lose weight. The most general conclusion that can be drawn from this research is that obese persons are sensitive to external rather than internal cues in regard to hunger, whereas persons of normal weight are usually more sensitive to internal cues (Figure 4.9). That is, nonobese persons time their eating and regulate the amount they eat on the basis of cues from inside their bodies, such as feelings of emptiness or fullness in the stomach. Obese persons, on the other hand, seem to be regulated much more by cues in the environment, such as the time that a clock or wristwatch might show or the color or flavor of the food to be eaten.[14]

This conclusion is based on a number of very ingenious experiments, the results of which can hardly be faulted. Our objection here is, rather, with the notion of *cue* when it is used loosely as part of an explanation. From the point of view of an experimenter, or a theorist, or indeed any external observer, a cue is simply some signal that helps to bring about a change in behavior when it comes to the attention of the individual. Taken in this sense, the contractions I feel in my stomach are, or can be, a cue for me, and so can the bitter, quinine taste of some food. The first of these cues would then impel me to start eating, and the second would lead me to stop eating.

Another puzzling issue arises in regard to some experiments originally done by Nisbett, who showed that obese persons were apparently more sensitive than normals to the taste and smell of the food they were eating.[15] If this were changed, as by putting them on a bland diet, their food consumption would drop markedly. This finding seems to fit in with the notion of external cues having greater value. But, as many obese persons will testify, their eating habits are not at all as discriminatory as those of normals. They often eat very fast, shoveling in the food with little concern for its taste, particularly when they are on "eating binges." How can these conflicting facts be reconciled?

In answer to this question, consider the all-too-familiar scene of stuffing oneself. Obese persons who report that this is what they do, especially when they feel unhappy or anxious, also report that they tend to eat quickly and steadily, in a kind of monotonous rhythm. They eat without thinking about what they are eating, often to the accompaniment of reading or watching TV. They choose edibles that can be consumed with a minimum of preparation or utensils. These edibles, too, are often the "gloppy" kind—syrupy, a little sweet, endlessly the same at each mouthful, with substance but without much structure, and usually not requiring much chewing nor much effort to make them available. What can we now say about a situation that overeaters seek out that has these characteristics?

It can be said that this situation must almost guarantee a specific kind of eating experience. The experience to which it closely corresponds is that of the infant at the breast. Suckling infants nurse most comfortably when they can maintain a mild but constant level of pleasurable sensation, when nothing interferes with their total absorption in the food intake, when they can fall into a rhythm of mindless yet harmonious bodily activity. Think of how this differs from practically every other kind of activity that we carry out as adults. The mark of our adult activity is that we are almost never totally and immediately absorbed in our ongoing experience but rather keep ourselves at a little distance from it. We know what we are doing, for example, and could talk or think about it. We work at what we are doing, rather than having it flow automatically. We are aware of ups and downs and of changes in levels of sensation, as we do what we are doing. By contrast, the suckling infant—and the overeating person who seems to try to approximate the infant's situation—incorporates desire and goal and activity in one ongoing, harmonious whole.

The term that personality theorists since Freud have used for this sort of activity is *oral*, because its first instance is in what the nursing infant does—but the essence of this experience is not the particular channel that is used. It is the attitude or stance that one takes toward one's present situation. An oral stance, which is what we are describing here, is one that mouths the world—as indeed the infant does, given a chance. It is a stance in which one gives up the customary

Table 4.2. Some hints for overeaters

---

1 Work hard at eating:
    a. Divide the eating procedure into tasks, such as three or four portions rather than one big one. Take some trouble to be absolutely sure the portions are the same. Be quite compulsive about it.
    b. Choose foods that require some effort—foods that need to be peeled, or cut, or buttered, or sliced; or foods that crumble if not handled properly.
    c. Use utensils as often and in as many ways as possible. Use chopsticks instead of Western-style utensils. Eat meat with a spoon or peas with a knife.
    d. Sit a few more inches away from the table. Always eat at the table, in the setting of a meal. Never eat on the run, nor in an easy chair.
2 Heighten and focus your attention on the process of eating:
    a. Never be perceptually distracted during eating. No TV, no book. Use all your senses, as deliberately and as fully as possible.
    b. Attend deliberately to what you are doing and to the elements of your eating situation. Count the number of beans left on your plate. Rearrange the food left on your plate.
    c. If you are with others, don't just listen. Take part actively. Start an argument.
    d. Anything you can do with your mouth is good: If with others, talk; if alone, talk to yourself, or sing.
    e. Overseason your food slightly.
3 Keep your expectations high:
    a. Don't let yourself get in a situation in which you have less food available than you might need. Always be sure that food is available.
4 Increase your knowledge:
    a. Try to become a gourmet. Study up on how foods are prepared and cooked. Learn to identify specific seasonings or learn about wines. Read a book about the anatomy and physiology of the digestive system. Try to apply your knowledge as you eat.

distance from situations and arranges things so as to become totally absorbed in the situation, incorporating it and being incorporated by it.

If this analysis of the eating experience of overeaters has any value, it should suggest some ways to change the experience. We have summarized these, in the form of some hints, in Table 4.2. They consist of ways that overeaters might reconstruct their eating situation so as to create as great a psychological distance as possible between their selves and their experience.

6. As a systematic approach to the experience of wanting, we distinguish between being pushed and being pulled.

In order to compare two experiences, we may consider two situations in which the experiences typically occur. In this case, there is, on the one hand, the experience of increasing hunger that is finally satisfied by eating, and, on the other hand, the experience of wanting to attain a goal such as a European vacation or graduation from college. Let us try to summarize and compare the different experiences in a tabular listing.

	Being Pushed	*versus*	**Being Pulled**
1.	Incitement.		Inducement.
2.	I feel that I am being pushed by a want.		I feel that I am being drawn toward a goal.
3.	The want is imposed on me; I do not seek it out; it arrives cyclically.		The goal arises naturally out of my present state and often out of my conscious planning.
4.	I feel the presence of bodily needs.		I feel the presence of externally defined incentives.
5.	The want is familiar; it feels like what most people want; I can talk about it in ordinary terms.		The goal feels more new than familiar; it feels individually unique; I would have to explain it to others.
6.	I feel that the conditions for satisfying the want are fixed, but not by me.		The ways of reaching the goal seem varied, with many possibilities, but the choice is under my control.
7.	The end to which I am pushed is clear to me and becomes more clear and specified as time passes.		The goal can take many different forms; it may change as time passes, and it does not become clear until I am very close to it.
8.	The way that I reach satisfaction is not meaningfully but only habitually related to the satisfaction.		The path to the goal is an intrinsic aspect of the goal, and in fact I achieve the goal only by a deepening understanding of the path.
9.	The cycle ends with a decrease of tension, a settling down; the goal itself is of no value except to end the wanting.		Reaching the goal is experienced as an achievement; I feel that I have grown; the achievement itself is memorable in its own right.
10.	Once satisfaction is attained, I am simply back where I was, and subsequent wants are experienced as though they had never happened before.		Setting up a new goal is experienced as being related to other goals that I have known and either achieved or not.

7. The limitations of some traditional experimental approaches are contrasted with an approach based on ordinary experience.

If we now return to the situation with which we began this discussion—a situation in which I find myself getting increasingly hungry—we may be able to formulate some first principles for an overall account of the experience of wanting. We suggest that we examine motivation from the point of view of the person who is motivated, rather than observe nothing but the person's behavior. We must allow a situation in which the wanting is naturally connected with the activity rather than disconnected and in which the intensity of wanting increases at a natural and gradual rate.

When a situation of wanting, such as being hungry, begins its ordinary cycle, my state is mostly one of anticipation. I feel myself attracted toward the goal; I can visualize it and enjoy the visualizing; I can think about the goal, picture it, or imagine how the eating will be. But, as I get more and more hungry and thus as I get closer and closer to a state of pure wanting, I begin to get taken over by the need. I no longer experience the goal as something up ahead, beckoning me, but rather as an immediate and pressing aspect of my experience right now, an obstacle that I must burst through. So, when I finally do get to satisfy my hunger, my experience is not so much pleasure as the slacking of greed. I am likely to gobble up the food, absorbing it hurriedly and hungrily, wolfing my food rather than enjoying it. And when I am finished, all I will have done is reduce my need and returned to my initial state of minimal hunger. I will not have had any experience more memorable than the satisfying of a drive.

When we describe the experience of this kind of wanting, we can see that it resembles in many respects the motivational cycle that is usually described for the basic physiological drives of hunger, thirst, and sex. And in fact this is very much what seems to happen in the case of many animals and perhaps occasionally with humans as well. A need is aroused. It increases without satisfaction until the animal is totally consumed with it, and then it is satisfied and the tension reduced, thus returning the animal to the starting point of the cycle.

As we know, this is not usually the way it is with humans and perhaps not even with most other animals. Quite rarely does the wanting reach this level, even with such basic drives as hunger or thirst. In addition, most of the wanting that we experience as humans seems to have different qualities and to furnish different kinds of satisfactions. It would seem, then, that there may be two different *experiences* of wanting and that one can shade into the other under conditions of biological stress. Notice that we are not saying here that there are two different kinds of motives or two kinds of motivational cycles, but rather that, no matter what the motive, humans are capable of having two different kinds of wanting experiences.

Summary

1. The present-day view of human motives is that people do what they do because of drives or motive forces "inside" them. This view is actually only a few centuries old.

2. Sigmund Freud, with his emphasis on the importance of unconscious mental processes, was the theorist most responsible for the widespread acceptance of this view of motivation.

3. Typical of so-called basic or primary motives is hunger—physiological in its origin, required for survival, and appearing regularly on a cyclic basis.

4. The basic motivational cycle, in its simplest form, consists of, first, the arousal of a need or drive; this evokes behavior that is aimed at satisfying the drive; and when it is satisfied the need subsides.

5. A more elaborate form of this cycle consists of, first, a stage of need arousal that elicits some internal cue or signal. Directed behavior then responds to the signal and leads to a goal that constitutes satisfaction of the need. The need then subsides.

6. The internal cue for hunger seems to be a set of events in the hypothalamus, triggering a neurological on-off "switch."

7. Aside from hunger, thirst, and the sex drive, other basic motives are those related to curiosity or exploration, to physical contact, and to the "will to live." Their relation to physiological events is not clear, but they are basic to survival.

8. Fromm and Maslow have identified still other needs that may also be necessary for survival. They include needs to relate to others for identity and security.

9. The preceding views of basic motives describe them as inducing or "pushing" the organism. An alternative view would see basic motives as inciting or "pulling" the organism.

10. A "reinforcement" approach to basic motivation suggests that a drive cycle ends, not when deprivation is satisfied, but when the organism is reinforced or rewarded for achieving a goal.

11. An "informational" approach to basic motivation suggests that the drive cycle has four phases: arousal; orientation, which is specific to the drive; adaptive, coping behavior, again specific to the drive; and consummation.

12. We suggest still another way of viewing the cycle of basic motivation, emphasizing the importance of the inside view of an individual's experience. Key elements here are the meaning of the ongoing situation for the individual and the degree of certainty concerning possible satisfaction of the need.

13. Overeating may be considered as the prototype of a drive situation in which the person becomes trapped in a situation of "pure wanting," unable to achieve any cognitive "distancing" from the act of eating.

14. Studies of the behavior of obese persons indicate that they are regulated more by perception of cues in the environment than by internal cues. Their situation is psychologically similar to that of the nursing infant.

15. Humans are able to experience their basic motivational cycle in either of two ways: being pushed or being pulled toward a goal. The distinction is apparent in both their behavior and their experience.

Excursion 1

The feelings: pleasure and pain

We now present the first of the "minichapters" that we call *excursions*. We chose this name because they consist of explorations across a number of related areas rather than (as in the full chapters) a coverage of one well-defined area.

In Chapters 1 through 4, we surveyed the ways in which people are embodied in their lives and in their actions. But this discussion left out a major aspect of living, the feelings that accompany all our behavior. Feelings are only partly ways of being embodied. They are also ways of knowing and ways of perceiving the world. They seem to be positioned, so to speak, between our bodies and our minds.

In Excursion 1, you will follow the application of both the outside and the inside view to the general topic of feelings. The remainder of this excursion will then be devoted to a discussion of one basic dimension of feeling, the dimension that we call pleasure *versus* pain.

You will first learn about the roles played by the neurological and physical structures of the body in the experience of pleasure or pain. You will then review the related roles played by social and cultural factors in influencing these experiences.

Our discussion of one's personal experience of pain will emphasize the factor of set, or attitude, especially the attitude of "distance" that one may assume. You should be able to compare this formulation with what you know about yourself, based on your own experience. Then you will be able to evaluate, again in terms of your own experience, our suggestion that one's pleasure and pain experiences depend on some combination of safety and novelty and on some match between your expectations and your accomplishments.

A life without feeling is inconceivable. True, some states may be described as *feelingless*; for example, the numbed state that sometimes follows a personal tragedy or the state of perfect control over feeling that is claimed to accompany rational thinking. However, closer examination of these states will usually reveal that they are hardly devoid of feeling and may even be identified by their overriding emotional coloring.

Our feelings accompany us during every moment, but where do they come from? At times they come from the circumstances of our daily lives, as when an interchange with a stranger makes you angry (and may leave in its wake a lingering feeling of irritability) or a piece of good news leaves you feeling pleased for the rest of the day. But other feelings cannot so easily be traced to their sources. They seem to well up out of our insides, and in some persons they may do so on a fairly regular schedule. Feelings can rarely be produced at will, although we may to some extent control their expression. Are they, then, just the outpourings or overflow of our autonomic nervous systems? Partly, yes, for feelings arise in part out of our being *embodied*, out of the life of our bodies. But only partly, for, as we shall see, feelings also arise out of our perceptions, wishes, and memories, even out of the attitudes that we assume toward our ongoing situations.

Because feelings are positioned so as to be expressions of both our bodies and our minds, they are almost always both externally observable and privately experienced, and usually at the same time. They are therefore especially open to study from both inside and outside viewpoints. In most instances of feeling, these parallel viewpoints are both available. On the one hand, an individual will report something like, "I feel angry"—or else "sad," or "hopeful," or "nostalgic," or "guilty," or "afraid," or perhaps even some mixture of these and other feelings. On the other hand, the individual will also present an appearance that an observer would describe as "emotionally aroused." This appearance is usually distinctive for each kind of feeling (but see Fig. E1.1). It is also associated with quite specific indications such as excitement, tension, blushing, change in posture, change in tempo and character of movements, crying, blanching, running away, striking out, and so on.

1. The example of laughing and crying suggests the difference between the expression of an inside experience and the behavior resulting from an outside influence.

Laughing and crying, among the most familiar of emotional events, provide an excellent example for exploring some of the complexities of feelings and their expression. Laughing and crying are, of course, forms of behavior. Are they also expressions of feeling? We might be tempted to say that of course they are, that laughing is the "natural" expression of the feeling state of joy and that crying is just as much a "natural" expression of the feeling state of sadness. But if this is so, why is it that most animals, which are often quite capable of showing other signs that they are either happy or sad, do not either laugh or cry? The higher apes can cry, and perhaps they produce a sound like a laugh, but even these two forms of behavior, so primitive and requiring so little in the way of a speech mechanism, seem to be beyond the capacity of other animals.

There are other difficulties as well. Expressions of feeling are usually specific to that feeling. The glowering look, the snarl, the raised fist of anger are not easily confused with the open smile of friendliness, the terror-stricken eyes of fear, or the downtrodden posture of resignation. But laughing and crying are not that easy to distinguish. If you hear laughter but do not know the source, you will have a hard time deciding whether it stems from fear or joy or even pain. If you see tears, you cannot easily tell whether they come from anger or sorrow. Many people cry when they laugh or laugh until they cry. The strangled sound, and even the facial expression, of some states might be either laughing or crying. In short, the two are mixed up—and even when they are distinctively different they do not reveal the feeling behind them but rather seem to conceal it.

Inner states, such as feelings, usually show themselves outwardly, and we call the result an *expression*. Thus, we speak of the "expression" of joy or reverence. We all have some ability to perceive the expression and then make a good guess as to the feeling that led to it, although how we do this, and how well, are problems that need further study. (See Chapter 12.) There are also kinds of *behavior* that do not arise as the expression of inner feelings, but as the result of other influences. For example, someone who is struck by a car and is knocked down and injured displays behavior stemming from an external influence; someone running from an angry bull shows behavior, although they may also display emotional expression. If we see an expression, we can often make a good guess as to the feeling that led to it, but it is very difficult to do the same in regard to behavior. Behavior is neutral in regard to its antecedents. If I see someone limping down the street, I may accurately perceive the behavior, yet be unable to tell whether its antecedent was a

Fig. E1.1. Pleasure and pain.

stone in the person's shoe, a childhood injury or illness, a requirement for initiation into a club, the instructions in a psychology experiment, or the person's decision to see what it felt like to limp down the street.

2. Four aspects of the feeling event can be distinguished: its external influences, its observable behavior and expression, its inner experience, and its underlying physiological structure.

These four aspects can be treated separately, for purposes of discussion, but it must be kept in mind that in any feeling event they are always interrelated. An external influence has an effect only in the way that I experience it and then respond to it. My response as behavior affects my experience; my experience of the influences and of my own response in turn affects my behavior, emotional expression, and perhaps even my physiological structure, and so on.

Structures for pleasure and pain

3. There do not appear to be distinctive structures for pleasure versus pain below the level of the brain.

Although we might consider pleasure and pain as occupying the opposite ends of a major dimension of feeling and therefore as different in every important respect, the fact is that their similarities are as evident as their differences. Judged on the basis of how they appear to an observer, the signs of pleasure and pain may be hard to distinguish—particularly when they are intense. This may be because the structures and mechanisms that subserve them are indistinguishable, as we shall see.

Neurological structures. The structures involved in pleasure and pain begin at the skin, are connected to others in the spinal cord, and terminate in various centers of the brain (Figure E1.2). At the level of the skin, there are no receptors that appear to be specific for pleasure, although there is some evidence that fibers in the skin conduct pain sensations. A number of different kinds of cells within the skin do appear to be specifically sensitive to pressure or to temperature, but on the basis of skin structures alone it would not be possible for the individual to "have" the experience of pleasure as distinct from pain. The same structure, at this level, can give rise to pleasurable or to painful sensations. If a distinction is felt at all, it is created primarily by the nature of the stimulus.

If a stimulus is moving, if it is brought into contact with the skin, if it is in light contact only, and/or if it is repeated rapidly (as in stroking or rubbing), the sensation is likely to be felt as pleasurable. But if the stimulus does not move but stays in one spot or if its contact increases along some dimension, either in intensity or in time, then it may be felt as painful. Thus, stroking the skin in one area may produce feelings of pleasure; low-level stimulation in the same area may produce a feeling of warmth. But a high-level stimulation, especially if it is prolonged, will be felt as painful heat.

When nerve fibers are traced from the skin, up the spinal cord, into various parts of the brain, and then back down the spinal cord to the muscular system, it

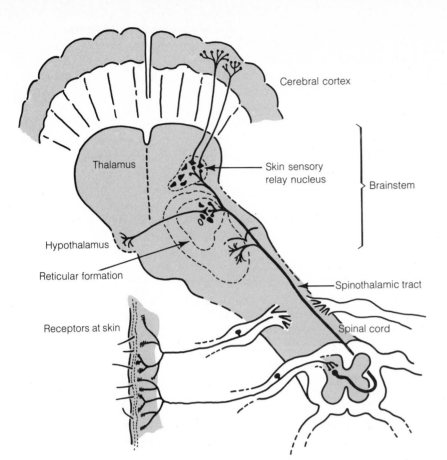

Fig. E1.2. The probable connections in the nervous system by which pleasure and pain sensations are transmitted from our external organs to the brain.

appears that the impulses going up the spinal cord are constantly interacting with other impulses coming down. It is possible that, by this arrangement, the brain centers exercise a continuing control of incoming impulses. This cannot be known for certain, but what does seem indicated by recent research is that fibers from receptors in the skin that are related to sensations of pain and pleasure both excite the same neurons in the tracts between spinal cord and thalamus.

Some of this evidence comes from the results of surgical procedures on patients who suffer from intractable pain,° which cannot be eased by usual means. In one surgical technique, the tracts are severed on the affected side of the body, on the theory that "messages" of pain can then no longer go to the brain. If it is the left tract that is cut, the pain becomes lessened on the right side of the body, with the further consequence that the patient becomes insensitive to other painful stimulation in this area. However, with the loss in pain there is also found a deficit in sensations that are related to pleasure, such as tickle, itch, or sexual stimulation; and, in addition, they may become less capable of experiencing the full sensory qualities of a sexual orgasm. It appears that the same structures may carry sensations as different as acute pain and exquisite pleasure and that the distinctions of which we are all aware are made only at the level of the brain, where the sensory information is processed.[1]

Brain centers. During the 1950s, as a result of advances in instrumentation, a number of laboratories were engaged in stimulation of points in the brain in order

intractable pain. Pain that is difficult to treat or alleviate.

to produce a map of the brain's functions. The pioneering work had been done by a Swiss physiologist, W. R. Hess, almost thirty years before. He had suggested that "centers" existed in the brain that controlled groups of related functions. For example, the control centers for hunger, for autonomic arousal, for eating, for eliminating, and even for assuming hunting postures were all positioned in one area in the upper part of the brain stem.

An almost accidental discovery by James Olds, working at McGill University, revealed that a very small area in the rat's brain, close to the hypothalamus, was a control center for pleasure sensations. The evidence for this was clear-cut and dramatic. A fine wire was inserted into this area, so that a tiny electric current would be delivered to the area every time a switch was pressed. The switch was placed in the rat's cage, in the form of a little bar that it could press. Under these conditions, the animals soon learned to press the bar to get the surge of current to this area. They would then sit there pressing the bar endlessly, ignoring food even when they were hungry, until they collapsed from exhaustion. Some animals pressed the bar as often as 7,000 times an hour. One may assume that for the rat, this was either pleasure or the next best thing to it.[2]

Similar work with other animals has resulted in the discovery of pleasure centers for cats and for monkeys, although not in exactly the same brain locations as in the rat. Among humans, the findings are mixed. Some subjects who are stimulated in the appropriate centers of the brain report a pleasurable sensation. Other persons report either no sensation at all or even some mild discomfort. But among the smaller laboratory animals, with less complex brain structures, distinct pleasure centers appear to exist for specific forms of pleasure — eating, for example, as opposed to sex. What these animals experience, of course — or even whether that term is applicable to them — cannot be known. One can only draw inferences on the basis of their behavior. The most plausible inference is that normally, when a rat eats, certain brain areas are stimulated so as to produce saliva, induce the flow of digestive juices, and so on. If these same areas are stimulated when the animal is not engaged in eating, it has the "experience" of an eating process, which is both pleasurable and biologically adaptive. Therefore it presses the bar so as to continue the "experience." (But see Figure E1.3.)

More recently, exploration of other brain areas in rats and cats has revealed that there are "pain centers" as well — although this may not be the most appropriate term. Stimulation of some centers in the brain of the rat or cat will produce a violent and extreme reaction of shock, fear, and pain. The animal acts as though it is being attacked in a life-or-death struggle, and it will become completely mobilized in an effort to fight its way out. It will also very quickly learn to turn *off* a current that produces this "experience." Again, one cannot be certain just what is going on in the animal under these conditions, but it seems clear that the stimulation in a specific area produces an extremely negative reaction that is the opposite

Fig. E1.3. On heaven and hell: an alternative view. It may be that the rat's pleasure is not simply in pressing the bar (a) but in letting up on the bar (b). Continuous stimulation (as in c) might very well produce pain, not pleasure. As someone once said, heaven and hell are very close together in the hypothalamus. In human experience at least, heaven is achieved by getting out of hell; only angels could stand being unendingly in heaven.

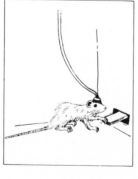
(a)

(b)

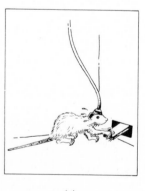
(c)

Table E1.1. Some ways of testing for either threshold or tolerance to pain.

Tests for threshold	Tests for tolerance
Stimulation of tooth pulp Application of radiant heat to the skin (dolorimeter) Squeezing the finger (algometer)	Cold pressor test (how long one can tolerate a hand or foot in ice water) Electrical stimulation (level of intensity of shock) Pressure, as from a head band slowly tightened or from an arm cuff (ischemic pain)

of pleasure. In fact, when an animal has become exhausted by turning off the current so as to avoid the "pain" stimulation, only a few surges of current to its pleasure center are sufficient to restore its composure. Pain and pleasure, then, seem to be clearly distinguished at the brain level.[3]

Psychological controls. The neurological structures for handling and distinguishing impulses related to pain and pleasure tell only a part of the story. In addition, we find evidence for important psychological influences. They act either at the brain level or at various, descending points to affect input of impulses for pain and pleasure. A major theory concerning this kind of control is the gating theory° of Melzack and Wall.[4] They propose that mechanisms (probably located in the spine) serve to open or close the "gate" to impulses of pain passing up to the brain. Thus feelings of pain can be influenced by many associated variables, indicating that being in pain or feeling some pleasure is not a passive but a very active state.

For example, the threshold° for pleasure, the level at which pleasure will first be felt as the sensations increase in intensity, is usually lowered when we are relaxed. That is, we can be made to feel good with less input when we are relaxed. On the other hand, if we are fatigued, tense, or distracted, it is much harder for us to feel something as pleasurable. Pain, too, is felt only at a higher threshold level if we are distracted; hence the old frontier technique of biting a bullet or squeezing a tree trunk in order to stand the pain of surgery without anesthetics. The use of hypnosis is well known as a technique for markedly altering one's psychological state and hence one's use of psychological controls. For this reason, hypnosis has been used for more than a century as an anesthetic procedure in medicine and dentistry.

However, it should be added here that one's threshold, especially for pain, is not a certain indicator of one's tolerance for pain. The two functions of threshold and tolerance° may even work in opposition. A person with a low threshold (who will say "ouch" at a low level of stimulation) may be able to tolerate a high level of pain or a long continued pain (see Table E1.1).

Social influences on pleasure and pain

4. Responses in pleasure and pain situations, and perhaps also the experiences, can be influenced by social and cultural factors.

gating theory. Postulates that information about noxious stimuli (pain) is modulated by peripheral and central control at the first synapse.

threshold. The point at which a stimulus is just perceivably recognized or able to produce a response.

tolerance. The point at which one will no longer accept subsequent increases in the intensity of a specific stimulus.

Behavior in pleasure and in pain is, like any other behavior, influenced by all the factors that make up the person's world of social and cultural reality. As we might expect, children and adults express their pleasures and pains differently, and so do women and men, and people of different ethnic groups or different social classes. This pattern keeps changing from one era in history to another.

This is not to say that the experiences of pleasure and pain that are had by people are different in the same way that their behavior differs. Adults, for example, are heavily influenced by their social environments to restrain their expressions of pleasure, in comparison with the relative freedom permitted children under the same circumstances. Does this mean that adults therefore experience less pleasure than children do? This is a more complex matter than it seems and not at all easy to answer definitively. One problem is that—as we can each verify from our own experience—the way I act influences, in turn, the way I experience. If I feel constrained to control my exuberance and to act "like a grownup," this constraint itself may put a damper on the degree of pleasure that I feel. It is difficult to feel wild enthusiasm while displaying only polite approval—just as difficult as the reverse.

Judging only on the basis of what people do, it can be said that people can be categorized just as easily by their responses to pleasure and pain as by any other form of behavior, and that the kind of response prescribed for each group aptly summarizes the major social characteristics of the group. Adult males, for example, are supposed to be characterized by their status as controllers, in contemporary society; and so, as we might expect, they are also defined as controllers of their pleasure-pain behavior.

Pain in history. Some of the most striking evidence in regard to the influence of social factors on behavior in pleasure and pain is given in accounts of earlier centuries. For example, in the histories of military campaigns and in the memoirs of battlefield surgeons, we find very frequent references to injuries and wounds that, by our modern standards, would cause unbearable pain. Yet in a surprising number of instances, ordinary soldiers put up with these situations with a minimum of outward signs of discomfort. Nor did they appear to respond as we might today to crude battlefield medicine and surgery, practiced with no form of anesthesia. The hypodermic needle and a useful painkiller (morphine) were not introduced into surgery until the Civil War, yet many accounts of earlier campaigns describe the treatment of casualties without complaint from the victims.[5]

The experience of pleasure and pain

The varieties of pleasure and pain, of joy and suffering, are almost infinite, and probably encompass the range of human experience. Suffering, for example, may be experienced on a continuum of intensity. In its mild form, it is an unpleasant experience that more or less interferes with life's activities, as when we have a bad cold. In slightly more intense form, it is a strong sensation that has to be endured, as in the pain-filled situation of having a toothache. In its most extreme form, it may be the experience of possible annihilation, as in the situation of terminal cancer. Pain and suffering need not coincide at every point on this dimension of intensity but may occur and alter independently.

Equally, the experience of joy or pleasure may range from the mild to the ecstatic; it may refer to one's present, one's past, or one's future, as Wilhelm Reich pointed out.[6] It may also involve almost any combination of those "fast" pleasures we call *excitement* and the "slowed-down" pleasures we call *enjoyment*. Like pain and suffering, the forms of pleasure and joy can occupy us in only a corner of our activities or at the margin of our lives, as when we experience some pleasure almost as a by-product of an activity. Alternatively, they can overcome our existence and fill our lives, as in the various kinds of ecstasy and bliss reported in some forms of bodily and religious practices. One significant dimension for many persons appears to be the degree of control or freedom that is experienced in the situation of pleasure. There are persons whose greatest joy is to experience an "out-of-control" situation, as in riding a rollercoaster, whereas for others this situation leads only to panic or nausea. Their pleasure, in turn, is gained in situations where they fully experience control, as in maneuvering a racing car.[7]

5. Experiences of pain will change as a function of one's felt "distance" from the situation.

In one study, subjects were put into a situation in which they expected to receive a painful shock. They were then divided into three groups, and each group was given different instructions concerning the attitude, or *set* that they should assume toward the expected shock.

- Group A was given a set toward the past. They were told to place themselves psychologically in some previous situation or experience that was free of any strong emotional tone.
- Group B was given a set toward the present. They were told to try to become fully occupied with the foot that was going to be shocked, and to stay with the sensations of this foot.
- Group C was given a set toward the future. They were told to concentrate on the shock that was going to happen very soon.

The subjects reported experiences, when the shock actually arrived, that differed according to the set induced in them. Those who had received the "past" set reported that the shock was experienced as a sensation without pain. Their experience was of "knowing" that something happened, but then it was gone. This is, of course, the way we now experience the pains that belong to our own past: We "know" about them, at this moment, but we do not experience the pain at this time. The subjects who assumed the "present" set reported a painful or noxious sensation, but in two parts. First there was an early sensation, followed by a burning or throbbing a second later. In addition, all of them showed a marked jerk or startle response in the affected foot. The third group, who had assumed a "future" set, also reported a painful sensation, but they experienced only the first and not the second one. They too showed a startle response, and in addition they reported this as a major aspect of the total experience.[8]

The experience of pain, then, will change in quality, in intensity, in its components, and even in the way it is felt as localized in the body—all as a consequence of the kind of "distance" one feels from the pain situation. These findings certainly fit with much common knowledge. It is known that persons who are able to dissociate themselves from their immediate psychological situation will experience less pain or pleasure.

Methods of altering the suffering state that are more deliberate include

1. Reinterpreting the situation—for example, gaining control over the experience by the use of visual imagination or attending primarily to what one senses rather than what the sensation means.
2. Distracting oneself from the source of the pain or pleasure. This has been widely used by dentists in the form of a distracting auditory stimulus such as soft, meaningless noise or some kinds of music. It has also been demonstrated

experimentally, by having subjects lessen their experienced pain through the distraction involved in concentrating on a test.

3. Practices derived from or related to meditative practices, such as holding one's breath, or gazing fixedly at a single point or target in space,[9] or grasping the "essence" of a pain in the form of its sensation while bypassing its meaning to oneself.[10]

6. The degree of pleasure that is experienced is a function of the combination of two factors: safety and novelty.

A number of writers, beginning with Freud,[11] have pointed out that we tend to strive toward opening up our worlds or toward closing them down; toward the objects of our drives, in what Freud called the *pleasure principle*, or toward the objects of our knowledge, in what he called the *reality principle*; toward sensation, with its risks, or toward security, with its inhibitions.[12]

Extensive evidence from studies on infants suggests very strongly that what attracts their attention and engages their willing and interested observation is what is different or novel. We may then say that one major dimension in pleasurable striving is *novelty*. What is predictable soon leads to boredom. That which lacks internal novelty, in the sense that it is too regular or too formularized, soon loses its attractiveness even if it was novel at first glance.

In the more intensely pleasurable states of excitement, this is even more evident. Nothing can remain exciting for long if it is simply a repeat or if it is known in advance. Here the distinction between our behavior and our experience comes out very clearly. Many things that we do have the pleasurableness of excitement—for example, sexual activity, rollercoaster rides, or playing tennis. It may indeed appear that each time we have these pleasures we are going through just about the same behavior as before, and therefore the excitement does not have the element of novelty. The behavior might very well be the same, but most certainly that is not how we experience it. As any of us can verify from our own experience, an act that we enjoy very much is always anticipated by us just as though it were completely novel, as though we had never done it before. And in fact, this is exactly the point at which we can no longer experience pleasure based on excitement: the moment when we say to ourselves that it is no longer new, but just one more repetition of what we have done before. Thus, whether the act is novel is based on how we experience it, not just on how we behave in it.

Important as is the dimension of novelty, however, it should be clear also that sheer novelty does not by itself determine what we experience as pleasure. Suppose a child sees a scary movie on TV. Cuddled in a familiar chair, at home with known people, the child may well enjoy the delicious thrill of being frightened in this safe setting. The resulting combination of *novelty* and *safety* might produce a high level of pleasure. But if the child goes to sleep and dreams about the movie, the result might well be a nightmare—all terror and no pleasure at all. The difference, of course, is that in sleep one is usually so caught up in one's own dream material that it is not possible to feel safely removed from the content of the dream.

To some degree in enjoyment and to a greater degree in excitement, pleasure is experienced only when there is the appropriate combination of novelty and safety (Figure E1.4). This helps to explain the most curious of all kinds of pleasure that one finds in excitement seekers such as adventurers and children: the pleasure of risk and challenge and danger. Some personality theorists have proposed

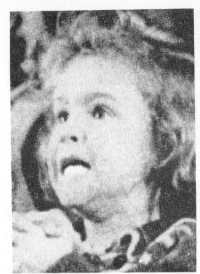

Fig. E1.4. Feelings of safety, novelty, and danger are deliciously mixed at this moment, as the children watch the hero in a perilous situation at a puppet show.

that what happens in these instances is a hidden desire for death. A much more likely explanation, one that is consistent with all of the evidence presented so far, is that certain risks offer just the right mix of what is novel, at a high level of excitement, and what is safe: the rollercoaster ride, or the mountain-scaling expedition (at least, when we feel competent), and many athletic contests. Again we emphasize that this is primarily a matter of our experience, not our behavior. For some persons, a rollercoaster is a perfectly balanced "safe thrill," and so they will even pay money to take the ride. These same people might very well refuse to hunt lions, on the grounds that it is neither a thrill nor a pleasure but simply a danger, the safety factor for them being much too low.

7. Experiences of pleasure and pain can also be understood as a consequence of one's "match" of desire and fulfillment.

We have stressed a number of times that states of pain and pleasure, of joy and suffering, can be understood better in terms of our ongoing experience than in terms of our ongoing behavior. But to this we must now add that our experience is not some abstract and unreal event that occurs with no connection with the real world. Experiencing something is just as much a real act as is doing something — it simply occurs in different ways, by different processes, and is known to the person and others by different kinds of evidence.

We can therefore say that joy and suffering, although they are essentially ways of experiencing, are linked to the world around us. The state of pleasure, we would suggest, occurs when there is a match between what we want and what we expect will happen. If I have a desire and if this is followed by my obtaining or knowing that I will obtain what I desire, my state will be pleasurable. Desire without this expectation is, of course, felt as unpleasurable, because one is thwarted. Expectation that I will get or do something, but without an accompanying desire, is, of course, equally lacking in pleasure; it is just neutral knowledge. Ordinarily, the highest pleasure occurs when desire and expectation are maximal and simultaneous, as it is for children on Christmas day.

But the match that defines joy extends even deeper into our experience. We are always experiencing in relation to how we perceive the world around us. A prominent undercurrent of that experiencing is our ongoing sense of our own state, in particular our total bodily state. There are occasions when we feel that the way we are at the moment is somehow aligned with, or fitting to, the way the world is—and this is the state that we usually call *joy*. The match here is between self and world; it is the ongoing moment when things just seem right—when, as we say, everything is going for us.

By contrast, the experience of suffering represents, in varying degrees, our sense of a mismatch between self and world, and, more specifically, a sharp mismatch between desire and expectation. If I really want something but know very clearly that I will not get it—high desire and low expectation—my state is bound to be one of distress or even suffering. And, again, the mismatch extends even deeper. If I can somehow join my experience of self with my sense of the world, I can often thereby lessen even physical pain. When I am wholly caught up in my own action, I may not even know that I am hurt—as occurs often in the course of heroic rescues or even thrilling athletic activities. This helps us to understand the cases, quoted earlier, of apparent absence of pain—perhaps because in former times many persons felt a "match" between themselves and their worlds. And quite possibly these persons could also do what some people do in regard to pain or any other feeling: Simply pay attention to it and in this way make it lessen.

Summary

1. Feelings appear to be a fundamental aspect of living. Their sources may be in the body's autonomic functioning or in the circumstances of our lives. They can be studied from both inside and outside viewpoints.

2. Feeling states produce their characteristic outward expressions, which in turn are often different from behavior resulting from an external influence.

3. Pleasure and pain are distinct in terms of their associated experiences, their outward expression, and their behavior. However, they are not clearly distinct in regard to their underlying neurological structures, at least below the level of the brain.

4. At the level of the (skin) receptors, pleasure and pain are discriminated primarily in terms of differences in the stimulus. The same fibers apparently carry both pleasure and pain messages from skin to spinal cord.

5. Control centers for distinct forms of pleasure have been located in the brain, based on work initiated by James Olds. Located near the hypothalamus, they appear to function dramatically for laboratory animals, but less clearly so for humans.

6. Pain centers have also been found in the brain, stimulation of which produces negative reactions in laboratory animals.

7. The "gating" theory of Melzack and Wall postulates spinal mechanisms that open or close pathways for impulses related to pain.

8. Experiences of both pleasure and pain are influenced by a wide variety of cognitive and motivational factors. Both threshold and tolerance for pain are therefore under some control by psychological mechanisms.

9. Responses to situations calling for pleasure and pain will also vary according to many social, cultural, and developmental factors, as shown, for example, in historical accounts of responses to pain.

10. Experiences of pain and pleasure vary along such dimensions as intensity, speed, time, scope, and degree of control.

11. Experimental evidence indicates that the set a person adapts toward pain will significantly influence their experience and their expression.

12. The experience of pleasure appears to be a function of two interacting cognitive factors: the degree of safety or security, as opposed to risk, and the degree of novelty. The greatest pleasure is experienced under the most appropriate combination of safety and novelty and will therefore differ between individuals.

13. Experiences of pleasure and pain also appear to be related to one's individual "match" between what is desired and what is experienced as fulfilled.

The feelings: varieties of emotion

In this excursion, we conclude our treatment of the topic of feelings by discussing, first, a dimension that is applicable to all emotional states: their degree of arousal or intensity. You will learn about the neurological structures that appear to subserve such arousal in humans, and also about the general adaptation syndrome, which results when the body's defenses against stress and heightened arousal are strained. From the inside viewpoint, we then present a model of the experience of arousal.

You will be able to consider some alternative explanations of two characteristics of emotional states. The first characteristic is their universality — that is, within each species and often even between species, specific states are experienced or perceived by others in the same way. The second characteristic is that these states have their sources in both biological and psychological functioning. You will then briefly review a number of theories of emotion, leading up to currently held views that place a great deal of emphasis on the importance of cognitive and psychological factors.

To conclude this excursion, three basic emotions will be discussed, each from both the inner and the outer viewpoints. These emotions are fear, a future-oriented state; sadness, a past-oriented state; and anger, a present-oriented state.

No other topic in psychology shows us as clearly as does emotion the two major *sources* of every psychological event, its biological and its experiential source. That is to say,

- Emotions and feelings arise out of the biological reality of our lives. We are animals, and we are embodied. From this given wellspring, as Darwin[1] was the first to show, there constantly arise in us the forms of energy that move us and color our existence from within, in rich and complex ways (Figure E2.1).
- Equally, emotions and feelings arise out of the psychological reality of our experience. We are persons, constantly engaged in creating and developing individually significant worlds of experience. Out of this activity are formed the modes of experience by which our worlds are enriched beyond the merely cognitive.

Our theme here will be the interplay between the biological and psychological sources of our emotional lives.

Emotional intensity

1. The most general characteristic of a feeling is its level of arousal—felt as intensity and experienced as significance.

Emotional states are varied, so much so that no single, comprehensive theory seems possible. Some feelings may be so complex as to be almost indescribable. But

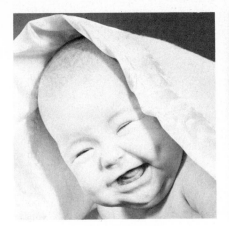

EXCURSION II
*The feelings:
varieties of emotion*

Fig. E2.1. Emotion, and its expression, is found everywhere and appears to be universally understood.

however the various emotions may differ, they resemble each other in one respect: They can be placed somewhere on a dimension of arousal or excitement. The angry animal is aroused; it is in a heightened state compared to its normal, relaxed, nonangered condition. Fear may not resemble anger, but the frightened animal is also aroused. The phenomenon of arousal appears to be related to a set of physiological events in the body. These do their work through specific structures of the nervous system—which we now need to consider briefly.

The hypothalamus. If you were able to poke straight up through the roof of your mouth, you would encounter some structures buried deep in the center of your brain. One of these, the hypothalamus, appears to have important connections with both (1) the oldest and most primitive parts of the brain, those parts inherited through millions of years of evolution and concerned with basic patterns of survival and (2) the newer, more evolutionarily developed parts of the brain, concerned with control and organization of more primitive reactions. This position in the middle may be what enables the hypothalamus to work with the pituitary,⊙ the master gland for scheduling the body's supply of many different hormones, as well as for integrating the separate elements involved in any emotional pattern. When the hypothalamus triggers off such a pattern, it also relays a set of signals from the pituitary that make for autonomic arousal. This pattern of heightened responsiveness and readiness is familiar to all of us. It consists of most of the following: increased heart rate, sweating, flushing, muscle tension, trembling, pupils widening, stomach contractions lessening, and mouth drying.

In addition to its contribution to the general state of physiological arousal that accompanies most emotional states, the hypothalamus also contains the centers that are directly related to pleasure and pain. Its role may therefore be both general and more or less specific, contributing both to the dimension of arousal-excitement and to the specific way the arousal is directed.

Arousal. There is a pattern of physiological response that appears to be closely related to—and may even be the basis for—the intensity of emotional states. The different levels are shown in Figure E2.2.

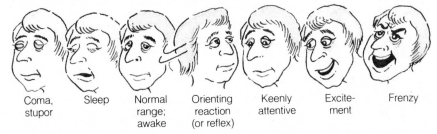

| Coma, stupor | Sleep | Normal range; awake | Orienting reaction (or reflex) | Keenly attentive | Excitement | Frenzy |

Fig. E2.2. A scale of arousal.

pituitary gland. An endocrine gland located beneath the hypothalamus that secretes hormones that control growth and activates other endocrine glands.

The normal waking state is one of mild arousal, but just above it is the point at which most creatures can be alerted in a reaction that Pavlov called the *orienting reaction*.[2] Clap your hands near a dozing cat, and it will perk up, ears pointed, and turn in the direction of the sound. As careful studies have shown, its response will also include specific changes in heartbeat, blood pressure, breathing, and the patterning of the dominant brain waves.

Much recent evidence suggests that certain structures in the brain, close to the area where the hypothalamus lies, play a major part in arousal reactions. One of these called the *septal area*,[○] has been studied by damaging or removing it in animals. When this area is tampered with, docile animals become vicious. Conversely, when the area is left intact and electrically stimulated, formerly vicious animals become calm. Evidence of this sort suggests that the septal area acts as a kind of gateway: When it is undamaged and active, it inhibits patterns of attack and the rage states accompanying them. Similarly, a nearby network of cells and fibers, called the *reticular formation*,[○] appears to serve as a way station or gateway through which alerting and arousing signals pass on their way to the cerebral cortex (the "higher" centers of the brain). It can therefore be considered the major brain structure for attentional arousal. If it is destroyed, the animal falls into a stupor from which it cannot be awakened. On the other hand, if it is stimulated, as was shown in an ingenious experiment by Fuster,[3] the performance of monkeys on a difficult perceptual task is improved. He required the animals to select one of two geometrical figures on the basis of exposures of only 4/100 of a second. They did better if they were given a brief electrical stimulation to the reticular formation just before making a choice.

The general adaptation syndrome. For more than three decades a distinguished Canadian scientist, Hans Selye, has been studying what happens when living creatures are subjected to chronic states of stress.[4] His conclusions are summed up in his concept of the general adaptation syndrome.[○] The term refers to the fact that the response involves the entire organism generally, that it becomes a mode of adaptation for the creature, and that it forms a generally similar pattern of reactions, called a *syndrome*.[○] Subjects typically pass through three stages in developing this syndrome: There is, first, an alarm stage, very similar to mild attentional arousal; second, there is a resistance stage if the stress is continued, decreasing the arousal symptoms through adaptation to the stress, but paying a price that leads to the third stage; and, third, there appears an exhaustion stage that may culminate in severe, chronic illness or death.

Stress, as Selye conceives it, is not the same as hardship. Most animals have available a usable response to conditions of deprivation or hardship; for example, rats raised in a temperature cooler than is normal for them will grow up plumper and with heavier coats, thus exposing less skin to the air and protecting what they do expose. They will be perfectly healthy, but by contrast, rats raised with their legs tied together will go through Selye's three stages and die, even if they are fed and watered. It is a matter of whether the animal has a response pattern available that is within its normal range of adaptation (Figure E2.3).

We can understand the factors involved in stress-related conditions by comparing three typical experiments:

- Brady and his colleagues[5] gave shock every few seconds to two groups of monkeys. One group, which could press a lever to avoid the shock, developed ulcers. The other group, which could do nothing to avoid the shock, did not develop ulcers.
- Sawrey and Weisz[6] electrified the food and water sources in rats' cages for 47 hours out of each 48-hour period. The animals developed ulcers—but other

orienting reaction. The physiological reaction that allows an organism to pay attention to a novel stimulus. It includes changes in viscera, muscles, and brain waves, increasing the organism's sensitivity and preparing it for action.

septal area. A part of the limbic system of the forebrain that appears to be involved in emotional expression and aggression.

reticular formation. An important arousal mechanism in the brain stem composed of a mass of nuclei and fibers. It is also important in controlling attention and in discriminating processes in perception.

General Adaptation Syndrome. A term for Selye's theoretical approach to the body's reaction to continual stress. He defines three stages as (1) the alarm reaction (the body recharges); (2) resistance to stress (coping through further adrenal secretions); (3) exhaustion.

syndrome. A number of symptoms occurring together. Also the personality characteristics and underlying causes in a person's life history.

Fig. E2.3. These concentration camp inmates managed to endure, not simply hardship, but severe stress—yet they survived. Perhaps they managed it by not trying to "tough it out," by giving in, by managing a form of surrender that was close to but not quite at the breaking point. Rather than give up, they gave in. Thus they became, as the picture shows, the living dead, with all desire gone.

animals who were also fed 1 hour out of 48, but without shock, did not develop ulcers.

■ Seligman[7] shocked rats without warning in an experimental box, and most of them developed ulcers. However, other rats, under the same circumstances but with the addition of a warning light or tone that came on three minutes before the shock, did not develop ulcers.

The common element in these studies appears to be whether the environment is predictable from the animals' point of view. No ulcers result if shock appears regularly or inescapably, even if the animals have to wait for it for three minutes. If the shock is presented randomly, or if its occurrence depends not on the environment but on their own decision, or if their relation to a feeding place is disturbed by shock for an excessively long period of time, then chronic anxiety is added to their normal distress. Under these circumstances, apparently, the body overworks its hormonal system, and some form of breakdown, such as ulcers, results.

A model of emotional arousal. The material we have just reviewed certainly supports the notion of a level of intensity or arousal as a fundamental characteristic of emotional states. However, feelings and emotions are a part of our lived experience. They are not simply physiological conditions that impersonally happen to us. Therefore, in addition to such questions as the source of arousal and its effects on behavior, we must also ask about the way that arousal enters our experience of emotions. We suggest that intensity of feeling can be appropriately described in terms of two major factors: the importance or significance of a desired goal and the degree of expectation that it will be fulfilled.[7a] Neither of these factors appears to be specifically emotional, yet much of what we recognize in ourselves as the particular feeling tone of an emotional state can be understood as a variation in these two factors and their interrelations.

To consider first an extreme case, suppose that our feeling for a goal has a high degree of intensity—for example, we feel that it is extremely important or significant for us. Under these circumstances, if the fulfillment of the wish is likely and still in the future, our emotional state will be one of excitement. If we are able to fulfill the wish, our feeling will be one of satisfaction. If fulfillment is more or less possible but not certain, we experience anxiety. If fulfillment is at first possible and then turns to become impossible, we may experience anger. Finally, if the wish is still present but it is clear that fulfillment is impossible, our experience will be one of depression. Thus, a wide and seemingly varied array of emotional states can be organized along the interplay of two general dimensions of experience, significance and fulfillment.

Emotional universals

2. A second general characteristic of emotion is that its varieties appear to be universal, across species, in both display and in perception.

Although the variety and complexity of emotional states may seem so great as to defy any orderly description,[8] much less an explanation or theory about them, some aspects of emotions are universal. Most creatures at the level of mammals seem to possess about the same basic repertoire of emotions; they all get angry, or afraid, or happy, or excited, or sad—and they seem to do so in response to the same kinds of situations. No creature that can show both fear and joy ever seems to get the two mixed up, being happy in a situation where others of its kind normally show fear, or vice versa. In addition, no creature seems to need any training in order to recognize these universal displays in another creature, even across species. The young puppy can correctly identify a human's angry voice, and distinguish it from a tender voice, just as the young child can recognize when a cat is angry rather than afraid. There has probably never been an instance in human history in which a normal adult, on meeting another adult who was smiling broadly and whose arms were spread wide, spontaneously perceived this display as anger or grief.[9]

Because of this universality of both display and perception in regard to at least basic emotional states, it has seemed to many theorists that they are biologically "built in" for each species. One famous theory, that of Freud, is built on such a notion of biologically based instinctual drives. In Freud's view, emotion enters into every experience that we can have, since the very basis of our experience is the motive force coming from the basic drives, of sex and aggression. Thus, the feeling of anger would be the experience accompanying a direct outpouring of the aggressive drive, without cover-up or elaboration. Sadness or depression, on the other hand, would be this same drive when it is turned inward against oneself, in its extreme form leading to self-destruction. In a related view, an American psychologist, Elizabeth Duffy,[10] has suggested that an emotional state is a form of behavior like any other, differing essentially in that in emotion the person's energy level changes very rapidly or goes to extreme heights or depths.

Biologically based views of emotion often sound plausible, since they seem to explain the universality of display and perception of basic states. And in fact, such biologically given programs of response may well exist in many species, serving as organized ways to respond to emergency situations. The flaws in these views are, first, that they do not explain the enormous complexity to be found in emotional life, especially among humans, and they do not take into account the cognitive element that is so central a part of human emotional experience.

Biological and experiential influences

Is an emotional state mostly the result of our ongoing experience, or is it primarily the result of physiological changes in the body? Do physiological events

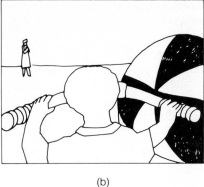

(a)   (b)

Fig. E2.4. The same scene, as viewed by an observer (a) and by its participant (b).

occur first, followed by experiences that we know as feelings, or is it the reverse? If one kind of event precedes the other, where in the sequence can it be said that the emotion occurs? Or, in crude but familiar terms, are the causes and antecedents of emotional states essentially mental or physical? (See Figure E2.4.)

3. Given a degree of biological arousal, the specific emotional experience seems to be more a consequence of psychological than of physiological factors.

The case of the menstrual blues. In a pioneering study, Karen Paige[11] tested the interrelations as well as the relative importance of psychological and physiological factors. Her study concerned a phenomenon, familiar to many women, that is often called "menstrual blues" — feelings of anxiety, irritability, and depression before and during the menstrual period. The hormones that significantly influence the occurrence and timing of a woman's menstrual cycle are at their high point in midcycle and at their low point during menstruation. So a plausible hypothesis is that the change in hormonal levels is the major cause of observed changes in emotional state. On the other hand, it is also known that in many women menstruating is associated with strong feelings of guilt, resentment, self-pity, and lack of self-control. These feelings and attitudes may be the result of widespread social influences, because menstruation is, more than any other bodily phenomenon, connected with enduring superstitions and taboos. Understandably, women may reflect these social influences in their own attitudes, leading to regularly occurring states of anxiety, depression, and irritability. The question is whether it is attitudes or hormones that play a dominant role.

Paige's study was based on the fact that birth control pills balance the level of hormones in a woman's body by supplying daily, fixed dosages of estrogen and progesterone. However, they may or may not interfere with the woman's normal amount of menstrual bleeding. Paige therefore questioned three groups of women: (1) those who were not using the pill, who maintained their usual changes in hormonal level and also experienced the same level of menstrual flow; (2) those on the pill and whose volume and duration of menstrual flow had not been lessened, thereby eliminating the hormonal influence but keeping unchanged the basis for their attitudes and feelings; and (3) those on the pill whose menstrual bleeding was decreased, thereby eliminating both the hormonal and cognitive factors in their state. Of the three groups, only the third showed a significant decrease in indications of menstrual blues, thereby clearly indicating that the emotional state associated with menstruation is also a consequence of socially influenced attitudes rather than only of hormonal or physiological influences.

The cognitive element. The first major attempt to develop a theory of emotions that took some account of the cognitive element was the contribution of William James.[12] In 1884, he offered a theory of emotion that was also independently published a few months later by a Danish psychologist, C. G. Lange; the view is therefore known as the James-Lange theory. Its essential feature is that it reverses our commonsense notion about how the elements of an emotional state are related.

Our commonsense view is that we feel sad, so we cry; we feel happy, so we laugh. In the James-Lange theory, however, we cry, and this makes us feel sad; we laugh, we become aware of what our body is doing, and so we feel happy. The theory says that once we are aware of a situation our whole body responds first, and this is followed by our becoming aware of the situation and our response to it. It is this final awareness that we identify as a feeling. James was a very persuasive writer and urged his readers to try it out for themselves: Go around with downcast shoulders and a dejected expression, and, sure enough, you will start to feel sad; lift your shoulders and smile at the world, and you will feel better.

This was an ingenious attempt at explaining how cognition did its work in influencing an emotional experience. Its weakness, as we can now see, was that it assumed an almost complete split between what happens in your body and what you are then aware of. Indeed, the theory holds true only for a rather extreme case, in which your body can develop an emotional state that is outside of your awareness and that comes over you almost as a surprise to you. This may have been true for James himself—we have no way of knowing—but it does not conform with what most persons will report about themselves and their feelings. But James was so influential a psychologist that this criticism was not made of his theory. As a result, for thirty years it remained essentially unchallenged—and when the major attack on it came the source was not in the work of another psychologist but of the leading American physiologist, Walter B. Cannon.

Cannon's experimental evidence mainly concerned the results of surgical intervention in the viscera, and so it was not directly relevant to the claims of the James-Lange theory.[13] But some points he made were very telling—that precisely the same visceral and other physiological changes occurred under different emotional states and even under some nonemotional states, such as colds or insulin overdose. Cannon pointed out that if this were so, it would be hard to understand how one ever knew, cognitively, which emotion to be aware of.

More recent theoretical formulations have tried to take into account the objections made to earlier theories and the experimental evidence such as that of Paige. It is now generally agreed that emotional states are neither simple physiological conditions, nor biologically programmed autonomic patterns, but complex modes of experience. As such, they are determined to a great extent by the mixture of attitudes, images, thoughts, memories, expectations, and perceptions that people have, in an ongoing stream, concerning their own current and prospective situations. An adequate experimental test of this position would require that subjects have their physiological states altered independently of the situation they are in and also independently of what they think or know about their physiological states and their situation.

In a well-known experiment in which just this was attempted, Schacter and Singer[14] used different drugs, different instructions to the participants, and different situations and influences to determine how they were interrelated. The results showed that first, some sort of bodily arousal is necessary in order for someone to know or think or feel that they are in an emotional state. Second, once a general arousal does occur, a specific emotional state will be experienced only if the person can connect their own arousal with an appropriate situation. If, for example, the person is told that their shaking and trembling is caused by a drug they have taken, they will not have the experience of being in an emotionally charged state. But if they are given no information, or incorrect information, then cognitive operations of perception, thinking, knowing, guessing, and anticipating will come into play. They will then experience the situation in terms of some meaning that seems appropriate to them. If it seems appropriate to them to be happy, they will feel happy (and act happy as well); or, if the situation seems to them to have the meaning of anger, they will feel anger. Thus, in general there seems to be a basal state of arousal, but what happens after that, or the specific emotional state that is experienced and reported, depends on the meaning and the significance that one attributes to the situation. The specific form of the emotion, in short, is largely determined by cognition.

Varieties of emotional experience

Some emotional states are apparently basic—fear, anger, and sadness, certainly. In addition, there are many others, often with their own shadings and variations, so that it is probable that no comprehensive system has yet been devised for arranging all the varieties of emotion.

In this section, we will not attempt a thorough review, only a summary statement about some of the major emotional states. We will deal with anger, fear, sadness, and joy.

Fear, anxiety, and the future. The emotional state called *fear* is familiar to most of us. It appears very early in life, it is seemingly universal among humans, and its appearance and appropriate antecedents are approximately similar among most species of animals. Yet it is by no means simply a mechanical reaction to fixed types of external events. On the contrary—at least at the human level—fear is tied quite closely, not to what is evident now, but to what the person thinks is going to happen. I may be afraid, for example, that I will slip and fall over a cliff—but then, if I do in fact start to fall, my feelings at that moment will turn into a mixture of fear (of what *will* now happen) and shock, disorganization, excitement, or perhaps even release or ecstasy or serenity.

Given this future-pointing aspect of fear as an experience, one would think that people can be taught or their behavior changed by playing on their fear of what might happen. Even laboratory rats will learn if they are motivated solely by fear of what might happen if they do not do a certain thing.[15] But what about humans? Will graphically unpleasant information about lung cancer cause people to change their smoking habits? Do scare techniques in high school driving classes decrease the chances of the students driving carelessly?

The results of many years of research on this question are so mixed as to defy a clear-cut answer for or against such "hellfire and damnation" tactics. If the listener is already disposed toward such an appeal, understands its consequences well, believes what is being taught, and can put the teaching into effect quickly, then scare tactics have an effect. Otherwise, people and their motivations seem to be too complex to expect that significant learning can be brought about solely by instilling fear.

Fear has its externally observable signs—the widened or fixed eye, the tension, the perspiration, the cold skin, the blanching, just as though all one's vital energy were withdrawn from an endangered surface toward the center of the body. So does that form of vague and seemingly objectless fear that is called *anxiety*. When it is specific to a situation, it is called *state anxiety;*[○] or it may be a

state anxiety. A condition of anxiety that is transitory and a result of a specific situation.

chronic condition of the person, usually called *trait anxiety*.$^\odot$ Its signs are nervousness, irritability, autonomic arousal, edginess, inability to concentrate, and self-reports of vaguely directed unhappiness and confusion. A great deal of research on anxiety, particularly in its relation to learning, seems to have resulted in only one stable finding: Anxiety in small degree is necessary for learning, perhaps because it leads to arousal, but as anxiety increases in intensity its effect reverses, so that at moderate and high levels it is a hindrance to learning.[16] Many students have discovered this in preparing for examinations.

Sadness, depression, and the past. Sadness is most commonly associated with one's past. We may in extreme instances feel hopeless about the present or the future, but in general our sadness has to do with what has happened, what is now gone, or with what might have been. If our feelings are a mixture of positive and negative, as happens when elderly people think back on their lives, we may experience nostalgia or pleasant regret about what is now gone or even that idealized longing that colors the past romantically. If our negative feelings are directed to ourselves as cause, the result may be that bittersweet quality that we call guilt; but if another person is the target, our sadness may mix with anger and come out as resentment. Too often we seem to confuse ourselves and others as sources to blame, being resentful of others for what is our own responsibility, or else feeling guilty because we are unable to be angry at others. In this way, guilt and resentment often get traded off, covertly substituting for each other.

The observable behavior that is the outer face of sadness is called *depression*. It is so common a condition, whether in the form of a brief episode or as a chronic condition, mild or severe, that it has aptly been called "the common cold of psychopathology." Depression may also be a central character trait. In studies carried out in foundling homes, Spitz[17] showed that infants who received insufficient mothering and contact often developed long-standing conditions resembling severe depression.

More recently, research and theory on depression have emphasized that it is a pattern of behavior that can be learned. Seligman[18] has induced states of helplessness in laboratory animals by applying unavoidable electric shock; after the animals had exhausted their available responses, to no avail, they sank into a chronic state of resignation resembling human depression. Seligman theorizes that this condition, which he calls *learned helplessness*,$^\odot$ may be in humans the forerunner of observable depression—as can be seen, for example, in instances of voodoo deaths or among condemned prisoners or some inmates of homes for the aged. On the basis of this argument, he has shown that depressed persons can be dramatically helped by retraining so that they no longer feel helpless. He has also suggested that by proper training in self-control, children may be given a legitimate sense of their own power and so immunized, as it were, against the possibility of depressive reactions in later life.

Anger, aggression, and the present. The experience of anger is as familiar as anything in our lives and is probably little changed from very early childhood. It is what we feel when we are charged up from within, ready to burst out or to strike back, in voice or action or sometimes just in "looks that could kill." We learn at a very young age to recognize and name this experience, although we may not always be in touch with all its bodily indicators. Almost as soon as we can talk, we can tell someone whether we are angry. What we do about our anger, however, is highly individualized, sex determined, and socially influenced.

The outer, or behavioral aspect of anger is, in its commonest form, what we call *aggression*. This is not to say that the inside and outside forms of the emotional state always occur together. Even in animals, as Konrad Lorenz[19] has noted, ag-

---

trait anxiety. A condition of anxiety that dominates and is an enduring characteristic of the person.

learned helplessness. A feeling of helplessness an organism has, because of prior experiences, when it realizes that it cannot change a situation to avoid hurt. It is often manifested as depression in humans.

gressivelike behavior may occur in hunting for food, which is emotionally quite different from the similar aroused behavior seen in fighting for a mate. The relation between the inside state of anger and the outside behavior of aggression is complex and as yet not too well understood, in spite of decades of theorizing and experimenting. For many years, the most popular theory in psychology was that aggression occurs when someone's goal-directed behavior or desire is blocked. This causes frustration, which in turn leads to anger. The result is the striking-back or striking-out behavior we call *aggression*. This theory can sometimes be supported, in a simple form, with experiments on young children,[20] and it seems to gain additional support from the behavior of animals under extreme conditions such as overcrowding.

But such views are oversimplified, as we see when we consider the developmental aspects of anger and aggression. In infants, for whom emotional states and behavior are usually directly linked, to be angry is to act angrily; the connection is direct and immediate. But as children grow up and learn about themselves, especially about what they should and should not do, the connection becomes more and more complex. For some persons, or at some times, the major complexity in the connection is control. In place of a direct and immediate behavior that expresses the feeling, the person may experience the feeling but control the behavior. Other persons may show the behavior but state that they do not have the experience, as for example occurs with someone who is clearly and evidently angry but says, in all sincerity, "Not me. I never get angry."

Another possibility consists of redirecting the behavior so that it appears in a socially acceptable form — as we do when we talk sarcastically or bitingly instead of starting a fight. Whatever may be the kind of connection in adults between expression and behavior, an important influence will usually be the person's own sense of the social and personal significance of his or her own acts.

In general, studies have shown that anger and frustration lead to aggression only if the person is sufficiently aroused or prone to such behavior or if the person views the frustration as unjustified.[21] Whether frustration leads to aggression in a particular case will depend on many situational and personal factors — rewards and punishments available, feelings of self-liking, social constraints and aids, the presence of others, and so on. And, even if the person does become aroused, his or her behavior may be flight, collapse, determination, increased control, or insight rather than anger-related behavior such as aggression. Most current thinking, then, supports the view that both inside and outside factors must be taken into account, in the form of a two-stage sequence: People must first be *aroused*, and then some appropriate *trigger* is required, under the appropriate situation, in order for aggression to occur.

Summary

1. Emotions and feelings have their sources in both our biological and psychological functioning.

2. All emotional states can be placed on a dimension of arousal, from stupor to frenzy. The neurological basis of autonomic arousal is the hypothalamus, which controls the degree of arousal as well as how it is directed.

3. The septal area of the brain serves as a "gateway" for attacklike states of emotion. The reticular formation serves as a "gateway" for attentional arousal.

4. Hans Selye has described the general adaptation syndrome, a pattern of reaction to stress in three stages: alarm, resistance, and exhaustion.

5. Studies of stress reaction in animals indicate that the critical element in their response is whether noxious input from the environment is predictable by the animal.

6. A proposed model of emotional arousal suggests two factors: the significance of the desired goal and the expectation of fulfillment of this goal.

7. Emotional states are displayed and perceived in much the same way by all members of a species. This similarity extends to a great degree across species as well.

8. Study of the "menstrual blues" has helped answer the question of whether the primary cause of emotional states is psychological change or physiological change. The evidence suggests that the psychological change is primary.

9. The James-Lange theory of emotion postulates that a change in one's bodily state produces the emotional experience, rather than vice versa. The theory probably holds true only for extreme states.

10. Emotional states are neither biological nor physiological patterns but complex conditions with significant cognitive elements.

11. Experimental studies in which physiological, cognitive, and situational cues have been controlled suggest that, following a general state of minimal arousal, the specific feeling that is experienced and expressed depends on the person's perception of his or her situation.

12. Fear is directed mainly toward what *might* happen. In its "objectless" form, it appears as anxiety, either specific (trait anxiety) or chronic (state anxiety).

13. Sadness is directed mainly toward the past. Its behavioral manifestation is depression. According to Seligman, depression is a form of helplessness that is learned.

14. Anger is directed mainly toward what is present, and its behavioral aspect is aggression. Anger and aggression are related in complex, indirect, and individual ways. Some form of arousal to anger is followed by situationally influenced aggressive behavior.

Part two

MINDS

The cognitive psychology of individuals

We now turn from the study of the biological basis of human behavior to the study of its psychological and social sources. In this chapter, you will continue a survey of human motives, or of what impels people to do what they do, but here concentrating on secondary rather than primary motivation. Secondary motives are psychological and social rather than purely biological or physiological.

Secondary motives are in the service of human choice rather than in the service of biological needs. You will therefore find that the discussion is now more relevant to the needs and values by which you, as an individual, more or less consciously conduct your own life. You will be learning about your own life of experience and choice.

One of these highly valued needs is for self-acceptance, which, as you will see, is experienced in such secondary motives as needing attention, affiliation, and approval from others. A related need that has been very extensively studied is that for personal achievement, whose variations you will explore in relation to family background, sex, and social influences.

A second basic need is for personal freedom, expressed through specific needs for personal competence. You will learn the relation of this set of secondary motives to the human activities of work and play and to the behavior of consumers in the marketplace.

A third basic need is to find a continuing purpose in one's life. You will see how this may be gained in the course of competing with others and also in the process of self-actualizing or realizing one's own highest potential. You will then learn how each individual's purposes seem to be maintained through cognitive activities that are aimed at resolving dissonance.

Finally, we suggest that personally significant behavior may be motivated not just by pushes and not even by pulls but by the continuing effort to organize your individually meaningful world of experience.

5

Secondary motives: the story of needs and values

Not long ago, one of the last fighting survivors of the Japanese Imperial Army of World War II, a lieutenant named Hiroo Onoda, was persuaded to come back to the outside world after thirty years of hiding in the jungles of a Philippine island. His former superior officer had once ordered him to take up intelligence duties on the island and to stay alive at all costs without surrendering. This the lieutenant did, in the face of determined efforts to bring him out. He refused to give in until the officer, now the owner of a bookstore, was brought to him and personally rescinded the thirty-year-old order. Onoda's statement to the press was a marvel of motivation: "I am a soldier. I have to follow orders. Without an order, I cannot come out." Arrived home, he answered the questions *how* and *why*—the questions that we all feel must be answered—by saying simply, "I'm happy to have devoted the most important period of my life to what I believed in. My parents told me that you should do your best at any moment. I never thought of surrendering without orders."[1]

The lieutenant's motivation in acting in this way was clearly not biological, yet it was as powerful and enduring as any biological impulse. It falls into the class of what is called *secondary motivation*.

Fig. 5.1. The baby's motivation here is hunger, a primary motive; the mother is offering approval, a secondary motive. It is in this way that the secondary motive may be "learned" by association with the primary.

primary motivation. A term for the primary motives based on physical conditions that drive an individual to action. Also called *physiological motives*.

secondary motivation. Motives that a person acquires during his or her life as a result of experience. Motives such as affiliation and imitation are secondary.

deprivation needs. Maslow's deficiency needs, which he believes arise from a lack of something and are basic. They include hunger, thirst, sex, security, and so on.

metaneed. Maslow's needs, beyond the basic ones, that he believes must be filled if one is to become a completely developed human being. These needs include justice, beauty, order, and so on.

The meaning of secondary motivation

We have used the term *primary motivation*[○] to refer to states that are influenced by biological drives. Secondary motivation,[○] on the other hand, has more complex origins and consequences:

- It may be both biological and social in origin; for example, aggression, sometimes considered a secondary motive, may be innate in the human species and may also be a product of social conditioning.
- It may have social and personal as well as biological goals, as can be seen in the altruism shown in the life of Albert Schweitzer.
- It may lead to rewards that are known only to the person concerned (as when someone writes a poem that is never published) or that is known worldwide (as when someone builds a huge business empire).
- It may be learned or unlearned. This question arises whenever we compare females and males, whose secondary motives are often very different. It is not clear whether the difference is caused by genetic differences or by differences in the way they are reared.
- It may vary from one occasion to another in how much delay is tolerated before a goal is reached. For example, secondary motives may impel a child to demand a toy immediately, because a playmate has one, but another secondary motive may permit someone to work for years to obtain a professional degree.
- It may be found more often in mature adults than in children, and perhaps not at all in other animals. This suggests that it is related to the way the individual develops and learns.
- It will not usually become active until primary motives are satisfied. Maslow pointed out that basic biological needs, which he called *deprivation needs*,[○] usually have to be satisfied before secondary needs, or metaneeds,[○] are entertained.[2] For example, someone who is starving is not likely to feel needs for fame or social approval.
- It may even operate to oppose or interfere with satisfying one's biological needs. This can be seen in the prisoner who goes on a starvation diet as a matter of principle or in soldiers who sacrifice their lives for a cause.

These distinctions are also shown in Figure 5.1.

111

*Secondary
motives:
the story of
needs and values*

1. We will distinguish between primary motives in the service of biological needs and secondary motives in the service of human freedom and choice.

In this chapter, we will review the major forms in which secondary motives appear. Our listing will be in accordance with what we consider the three major ways in which such motives operate to enhance our freedom. For convenience, we will state these three ways to freedom in the first-person singular.

- *Self-acceptance.* I have a need to see myself as a good person. This may be the most basic of the wants through which I organize myself and my life in the service of freedom. It may also be the most difficult to achieve. It has often been noted that the extent to which people do *not* accept themselves can be so great as to exceed belief. Some clinicians will put the matter very bluntly, because it is applicable even to persons who seem to be normally adjusted: "Suppose you had an acquaintance who was as hard on you as you are on yourself. How long would you keep such a person as a friend?" It may be suggested that the self-torturing games that many persons play with themselves indicate both how difficult it is to satisfy this need and how deeply the need is felt.

- *Personal freedom.* I have a need to feel that I can do what I want to do. We can sometimes find in children, before they are otherwise channeled by our educational systems, the indications of this need in quite direct form. Some educators, such as A. S. Neill, have in fact argued that all children would be self-directing if the interference of adults were removed.[3] But, like the need to see oneself as a good person, we may settle for less in regard to the need to be free.

- *Reality and meaning.* I have a need to feel that my life and my doings have meaning and significance. This may be the most pervasive of our wants, closest to all that we do, yet the most difficult to pin down specifically. It is an enduring need for our experience to be justified. We attain this, or come to know about it, by seeing that our world of experience is consistent, sensible, and permanent. We satisfy this need to the degree that we have a continuing feeling of doing what we do in circumstances that we know about and can trust, with some ongoing expectation that things fit together, that we know how they fit, and that the world we manage to construct has both an order and a purpose.

With this broad outline of major types, we will now turn to the more specific secondary motives that have been most studied in psychology.

Self-acceptance

2. A fundamental set of human needs centers on acting in such a way that acceptance is achieved from others.

A major set of secondary motives are social in their operation. That is, they appear to motivate activities that are social in nature (see Figure 5.2).

Fig 5.2. Attention is nice, belonging is
better, but approval is best.

stimulus augmenter. Petrie's term for
a person who tends to intensify a constant
and repeated sensory input.

stimulus reducer. Petrie's term for a
person who tends to attenuate a constant
and repeated sensory input.

Attention. This social motive often takes the form of a need for positive attention. It is then difficult to distinguish from a need for approval. However, the
distinction is clear in the case of hyperactive children, whose demand for attention
has been observed to be so great that it does not seem to matter to them whether
the attention is positive or negative. One investigator, Asenath Petrie,[4] points out
that most persons are able to increase the amount of stimulation they are getting
by slowing down and so increasing their own sensitivity. These stimulus augmen-
ters[○] can be distinguished from other persons, called stimulus reducers,[○] whose
activity level is high, who are therefore relatively insensitive, and who thus need
to seek more attention and stimulation from others because they cannot furnish it
for themselves. In school settings, the difference between the two groups is often
evident: on the one hand, we see sensitive and withdrawn children who seldom
seek attention and, on the other hand, overly active and insensitive children who
constantly demand attention.

Among adults as well, attention serves as a powerful motive. A dramatic
confirmation of its strength occurred in the course of one of the most remarkable
series of studies in the history of industrial psychology. In the 1920s, some engineers at the Hawthorne plant of the Western Electric Company attempted to
study the effect of illumination on work efficiency among its women employes.[5]
To do this, the experimenters first measured their output under existing conditions and then increased the illumination at regular intervals during a month. At
each increase in lighting, they determined the new level of output. To their surprise, the engineers discovered that a change in illumination seemed to have no
effect on output. One group's output "bobbed up and down" unpredictably, the
output of a second group rose steadily during the experiment, and the output of a
third group rose at the beginning and remained at a high level.

In a follow-up study, one group with constant intensity was compared with
another for whom the intensity level was regularly *decreased*. But now the output
of both groups steadily rose, until finally the workers in the "decrease" group
complained that they could barely see what they were doing, although their work

113

*Secondary
motives:
the story of
needs and values*

had not suffered at all! To test out this rather startling result, the investigators compared the carefully monitored output of two operators who worked alone under careful control of illumination. Both maintained their efficiency even when the amount of light was decreased to approximately that of "an ordinary moon-light night," stating that working under lower illumination made them "less tired."

It became clear in these studies that hours of work, degree of fatigue, monot-ony, amount of money, and even type of supervision were all less important (within reasonable limits, of course) than one unsuspected factor, the amount of attention being received by the workers. It was the actual doing of the experiment that was producing the most powerful effect. No wonder, then, that the experi-menters could not initially control the effect. The term *Hawthorne effect*° has since been used to refer to the impact of attention resulting from the fact that an experiment is being carried out. It is now widely recognized that in schools, facto-ries, and mental hospitals Hawthorne effects may be as powerful as those of any other condition in an experiment. In addition, they may be much harder to con-trol or eliminate, because they rest on the continuing expression of the powerful need for attention (Figure 5.3).

Affiliation.° The affiliation motive, in the form of the need to experience con-tinuing contact with others persons, is experienced both as a desire for others and as anxiety that one may be an isolate. It is most probable that from our earliest years we gain a sense of ourselves, and of much of the meaning in our lives, out of continuing affiliation with others. In some degree, too, we may even come to depend on the presence and the attention of others to experience fully our own possibilities. This is particularly evident to us when our usual, inner-based sup-ports weaken, as was shown in a series of studies by Schacter.[6] He put groups of female undergraduates through a stress situation by convincing them that they were about to be subjects in a psychological experiment in which they would be given electrical shock. Compared to another group of subjects not made to feel anxious in this way, twice as many girls chose to wait in a group for the experi-menter. Misery, at least in the form of fear and anxiety, clearly loves company. These results also suggest that the affiliation motive may serve, for some persons, as a way of forestalling or expressing the anxiety that might occur if one were left along.

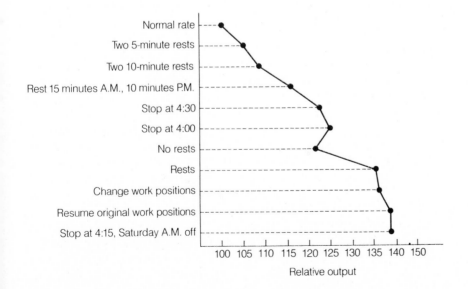

Relative output

Fig. 5.3. When the participants in the Hawthorne experiments were given a sequence of working conditions, some good and some bad, their output rose steadily (see text).

Hawthorne effect. The (positive) effect on the performance of experimental subjects who know they are being used as subjects or being treated in a special manner.

affiliation. The need or desire to be with other people; a basic social need.

Affiliation does not appear to be directly linked to any single biological drive or impulse. It is adaptive, of course, in the sense that the members of any species are probably better protected if they stay with one another. This may be especially true in regard to the young. In fact, certain kinds of fowl, such as ducks, at a very early age show a strong tendency to pick out a larger creature (usually the mother) and to stay close to it no matter what happens. Mammals that nurse their young can thus usually be sure that the newborn will stay close and be assured of a food supply. (See Chapter 18 for a discussion of affiliation.)

Social approval. Closely linked to affiliation is the need to have others think well of one. Just as we all seem to prefer to share one another's physical presence, in affiliation we need to share a community of judgments and values. In addition, the two motives are usually found together in an individual, for those whose need for approval is high, often in order to bolster their own self-esteem, will also need the company of others in order to continue feeling approved. Approval, however, has been studied and even measured separately, in a series of investigations by two social psychologists, Crowne and Marlowe.[7] The scale that they developed for assessing the strength of this motive has been very useful in interpreting the results of some personality tests. The reason is as follows: When people answer questions about themselves on a paper-and-pencil test of personality, they (quite understandably) shade their answers so as to put themselves in as good a light as possible. Because the higher their need for social approval, the greater their tendency to color their answers in this way, a separate score on the Crowne and Marlowe scale can be used to correct for their answers on the personality test.

In the year 1900, an advertisement appeared in the Help Wanted columns of some London newspapers. It read, "Men wanted for hazardous journey. Small wages, bitter cold, long months of complete darkness, constant danger, safe return doubtful. Honor and recognition in case of success." The advertisement had been inserted by Sir Ernest Shackleton, one of the leaders of Robert Scott's proposed expedition to the South Pole. Shackleton had no difficulty in recruiting volunteers by appealing solely to the motive of gaining the approval of society. Apparently he had even calculated—correctly, as it turned out—that this motive is strong enough in many men to overcome the negative effects of possible discomfort and risk.

Need achievement

The most extensively studied of all secondary motives is the need to achieve, abbreviated as *n Ach*© and defined by its major investigator, David McClelland, as the need to do something better than it has been done before.

The study of n Ach grew out of earlier work on the relation of primary needs to behavior. Initially, the investigators thought of n Ach as a motive very much like hunger: a mode of expression that anyone could develop if the circumstances were right. It was not a characteristic peculiar to some persons but a state of arousal that could be produced in just about everyone. Their method was to treat n Ach just as though it were a form of hunger. They aroused the need by persuading their participants that the tests they would take were measures of their ability, skills, and intelligence. They had the participants make up stories to ambiguous pictures. Then they put the participants in a state of deprivation of the need, by having them experience failure through the use of false instructions. Finally, they retested the participants in the writing of new stories.[8] As predicted, and, just as one might find in the case of experimentally manipulated hunger states, subjects who experienced increased deprivation told stories that dealt more directly with depri-

n Ach (need Achievement).
McClelland's term for the learned tendency to want to do something better than it has been done before.

115

*Secondary
motives:
the story of
needs and values*

vation. Their story characters also gave vent to more expressions of wanting goals, and they described more events showing how people could achieve their goals. One way to describe these results is to say that the subjects made up in their fantasy what they lacked in realistic satisfaction—just as we do when we dream of what we are deprived of.

Expressions of n Ach will vary according to a person's sex, background, training, family, socioeconomic status, and society. McClelland's research has led to the conclusion that in some families there can be found a continuing, if subtle, form of training of children. Some growing persons take to this training and consequently develop easily aroused needs to achieve. These persons may then become successful and exercise influence in their own society, especially in regard to economic affairs. The picture is clearly representative of those individuals, almost all male, who dominate the economic growth of industrial societies. As they influence the development of their own children and provide models for other parents, the n Ach "syndrome" comes to spread through a society—particularly as those male children who develop in this way find it easier to gain the society's rewards.[9]

N Ach and society. Tests of n Ach consist simply of stories that subjects make up to ambiguous pictures, which are then scored according to a standardized scheme. They have been used in literally thousands of experimental studies in laboratories, classrooms, and various settings in other countries. Interestingly, the test has also been turned around to become a tool for training rather than assessing, thus putting the theory to work in real-life contexts.[10] On the assumption that persons who show high n Ach usually have a great deal of fantasy associated with the need, people are deliberately trained in having such fantasies. In effect, they are trained to think, feel, and plan like persons who show high n Ach. The result is that many such people can be taught a kind of achievement motivation that we associate with citizens of industralized countries. The behavior of businesspersons in underdeveloped countries can change significantly to become more like that of their American counterparts, with sometimes remarkable effects on their productivity and efficiency. Similarly, schoolchildren who are spotted as potential dropouts can be taught to think, talk, and finally even behave like other children who initially score high on tests of n Ach. In effect, they are trained to model their lives on those who are academically successful. In this way, they come to fit the role to which they have been trained. As the old saying has it, nothing succeeds like success, whether in school grades or occupational mobility.

McClelland's work has been criticized by learning theorists who claim that he stresses "learned inner drives" and ignores the "situational contexts" that may affect achievement.[11] It has also been criticized by psychologists with differing national backgrounds. Durganand Sinha, a social psychologist in India, has presented data showing that the achievement motive is socially useful if a country's resources are unlimited but may even be detrimental to members of a society if their country has limited resources—as is true of most underdeveloped nations.[12]

N Ach and sex roles. From the beginning of work on n Ach, it had been evident that the motive to achieve was related to how one views oneself—for example, as a success or as a failure in life. Self-image and achievement needs seem to be related in a circular arrangement, an image of oneself as successful helping to evoke n Ach fantasy and action, which in turn develops in one a more positive self-image (Figure 5.4).

It should follow from this that women and men will respond differently to tests of n Ach as well as to training in achievement motivation. Curiously, however, this sensible inference was not seriously entertained even by 1965, when

Fig. 5.4. The consequences of n Ach.

Lesser reported that studies of achievement motivation in women were so limited that the area was virtually unexplored.[13] One problem, as he discovered in his own research, was that n Ach is aroused differently in female and male subjects, so that tests of the aroused or deprived need produce different results. When he and his coworkers tested both high-achieving and low-achieving adolescent girls, they found that in a high school with high standards, the high-achieving girls responded to experimental arousal of n Ach but only when the task consisted of writing stories to pictures of men. The low-achieving girls in the same school showed arousal of n Ach, but only when the pictures presented were of women. From this it was concluded that high-achievers had self-images involving achievement motivation but primarily in roles similar to that of men. In a society in which males are encouraged and even expected to be achievers in their own gender roles, no such disparity in self-image is required in them in order to develop high achievement motivation.

It might be expected, then, that if women permit themselves to become highly motivated toward achievement, in a "typical" male kind of performance, they might experience a conflict of motives. Such conflicts show increased anxiety, indecisiveness, self-critical attitudes, and a strong tendency to "leave the field"—that is, to deny one's motives and to repress the experience related to them. Particularly in the younger years, n Ach is linked to being socially accepted for girls, whereas in the case of boys it is more often related to goals that are valued or socially useful in their own right.

A straightforward test of some of these sex differences was carried out by Matilda Horner, in an experiment in which she simply asked ninety female students to make up the endings to achievement-related stories.[14] A typical beginning for a story would be: "After first-term finals, Anne finds herself at the top of her medical school class." Male subjects were also given stories, similar in every respect except that the character described was a male. The results clearly indicated a powerful "motive to avoid success" in the female subjects. Their stories suggested that if a woman experienced success, the consequences would be largely negative, in the form of rejection by her peers and by society as well as becoming aggressive or being seen as aggressive. A motive to do well would thus inevitably lead in women either to a serious conflict of motives or to continuing anxiety if the achievement motive won out. When male and female test subjects were compared, less than 10 percent of the males, but more than 65 percent of the females showed such "fear of success" imagery in the stories they composed. Most disquieting of all were the results for the female subjects who also showed independent evidence of high ability. The greater their ability, the stronger their achievement motives, and the greater their objective success in college, the more powerful was their motive to avoid success!

N Ach and uncertainty. One factor influencing a person's measured n Ach seems to be one's expectancy of success. It is possible to measure this independently, by a technique called *level of aspiration.*[15] People are presented tasks that can only be performed well with a fair amount of practice—for example, tossing rings around a post at distances of 10 or 15 feet. At the start of each series of tosses, they are asked how well they think they will do, and this estimate is then compared to their actual performance.

Achievement motivation, we have noted, is not to be understood as a trait of character. It is an oversimplification to say that some persons possess more n Ach and others less. Rather, n Ach is a construct referring to behavior-in-a-situation: in this case, to the situation of doing something well. However, the character trait that may be related to n Ach is suggested by the work of a British psychologist, John Cohen.[16] It is the degree of confidence that the person typically displays under conditions of uncertainty. Persons who typically show high confidence under uncertainty need not necessarily prefer high-risk situations in order to demonstrate high n Ach. In fact, Cohen's evidence shows that they are more likely to prefer situations of intermediate risk, so that they will avoid low-risk situations that gain them nothing as well as high-risk situations where they are unlikely to succeed. On the other hand, people who are low in personal confidence and responsibility for their own successes are just as likely to prefer high-risk as low-risk situations.[17]

Freedom

3. A second set of human needs centers on being able to "do one's thing," whether for the pleasure of so doing or in order to produce some effect.

Recently, the term *intrinsic motivation*[18] has been introduced to refer to doing things because this is what one wants to do rather than because one expects a reward for getting them done. Whenever there is energy to spare beyond what is natural and necessary, there seems to come into being a range of behaviors that are chosen entirely because that is what seems right and interesting to do, because that is what constitutes making one's mark, being one's own self, doing one's thing, organizing and developing one's individual world (see Figure 5.5).

Competence. These ideas were first formulated by Robert White of Harvard University in 1959.[19] He noted that conceptions of animal behavior as largely drive-directed are simply inadequate to explain even commonly observable behavior, let alone unique or peak experiences. Ordinary behavior among many animals is marked by a great deal of exploratory activity, curiosity, and an excess of energy expressed in play, challenge, and risk. Asked why they choose to walk along the narrow ledge above rather than the safe sidewalk below, the average child would simply look at the questioner in astonishment. To explain these and similar phenomena, White proposed another kind of motivation. It appears, for example, in the persistent and moderate urging that operates primarily during the developmental periods of most animals. It is what leads them to work actively, to engage constructively and energetically and often playfully with their environments, to

level of aspiration. The level at which an individual sets goals.

intrinsic motivation. A type of personal motivation based on behaving for the sake of doing rather than for an external reward to be gained.

Fig. 5.5. Motivated behavior may produce the same results but not always for the same reasons.

interact effectively with their surroundings—in short, to display what White would call *competence*.[©] If animals did not act like this, they would resemble insects, repeating in mechanical fashion the built-in patterns that define them as units of a species. (It may be no accident that insects wear their skeletons on the outside, and so are trapped within their own, preformed structures.)

Competence is therefore both similar to and different from n Ach. It is similar, in that both kinds of motives refer to ways of fulfilling one's life, of demonstrating accomplishment, and of succeeding at living. But the differences between competence and achievement are perhaps more important. The difference has to do with whether one's goals are generated out of one's own action or whether they are found in external and socially determined standards. N Ach, as McClelland defined it, refers to doing something better than it has been done before, whereas competence has to do with displaying the best of oneself. The former is based on society's standards, the latter on one's own inner standards (although it may have been learned from society). The difference shows up clearly in the distinction between being aggressive as a consequence of one's self-generated needs, and being aggressive in reaction to situations or pressures from the outside; that is, between fighting and fighting back.

Work and play. In his provocative novel, *The Woman in the Dunes*, the Japanese novelist KōBō Abe[20] presents us with a couple who live in a deep hollow in the sand dunes. Sand flows into their hollow every night, so they must spend most of the day shoveling it out. At one point, the man stops his shoveling to ask, "Do we shovel in order to sleep, or do we sleep in order to shovel?" Their lives having been reduced to only two modes, each mode now serves as both means and end, and need and goal are tragically intertwined.

But this extreme case is not true for the rest of us. We eat, and we work; and the relation between the two may take many forms. It may be interdependence, as in Abe's novel, or the dependence of eating on working, as in the case of draft animals or an experimenter's rats, who must literally work to eat. Eating is a primary motive, aroused and then satisfied in a biologically determined cycle. Working, however, is a form of goal-directed activity that may sometimes satisfy physiological needs, but only indirectly.

Can we, then, speak of a motive to work? And if we do, are we also entitled to speak of a motive to play? To put the question in familiar terms, "Do you believe that people would continue working if their paychecks were mailed to them

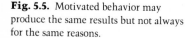

competence. The ability or skill that enables one to interact effectively with one's environment.

119

*Secondary
motives:
the story of
needs and values*

whether they worked or not?" Here we turn to evidence from animals to help answer the question.

In a series of ingenious experiments with rats, Allen Neuringer[21] set two animals a series of conditions:

1. Under the usual conditions of hunger, the animals were trained to press a lever to obtain food, at the rate of one pellet per press.
2. For fifteen days, they were allowed to obtain food in this way—but, meanwhile, "free" food was always available in another cup nearby. Results: Rat No. 1 obtained 200 pellets per day from the bar, Rat No. 2 about 200 pellets.
3. For the next ten days, the levers were disconnected, so that pressing them resulted in a click but no food. Both rats stopped pressing the bars, their rate dropping to about ten per day.
4. The conditions of Item 2 above were restored for six days. The rats resumed their bar-pressing behavior, with the result that Rat No. 1 obtained about 350 pellets per day and Rat No. 2 about 160.
5. Now for the first time the second food cup was emptied. Results: Rat No. 1 pressed the bar about 430 times per day, Rat No. 2 about 380 times.

Rats, it appears, will "work" for food in the presence of enough free food to keep them well fed.

It appears that the age-old notion that work is an evil and that humans and other animals will do anything to avoid it may be applicable only under certain circumstances. An alternative view is suggested by these findings and also fits the activity of creative adults. This is that work, when carried out under the proper circumstances, is not a burden but a creative challenge, and that doing it fulfills certain needs.

Consumer motivation. Under some circumstances, work may be considered a burden; under others, work may be pursued for its own sake. There is a third possibility, that people engage in work simply to get the money to buy the things they want. Their basic motive, then, would be to purchase and own—in a word, to be consumers.

However widespread it may be, the wanting of consumer goods is not as simple as it seems. Most such products do not satisfy any obvious needs—certainly not any of the biological needs. Rather, they satisfy motives that may in turn be related to observable needs. For example, a more expensive car may be desired because possessing it would, in turn, enable the consumer to feel superior to other persons. In the case of children, the advertised product is then desired because the wanting has been imposed in connection with a TV program or by means of an idealized situation depicted in a commercial.

It is interesting that commercially induced wanting, artificial and nonbiological though it may seem, has much in common with biological drives. When such wanting is consummated—for example, when the latest fad has run its course—the consumers have simply been sated, no more. Nothing memorable been contributed to their histories. They have simply returned to their earlier state and are now receptive victims of the next push from outside, caught in a timeless cycle of tension and release. In the case of children who have become addicted to wanting the endless flood of goodies shown to them via television, the most recent need to buy this item or to see that program may be forgotten as soon as the occasion is over. It may well be that our encouragement as citizens or parents in continuing this situation for children will help to make their growth as mature individuals more difficult than it might otherwise have been.

Behavioral economics. The major part of our systematic knowledge of the field of consumer motivation, which is sometimes known as *behavioral econom-*

ics,⊙ is owed to the work of an economist, journalist, and learning theorist named George Katona. Trained as an economist and psychologist in Europe, he developed a view of consumer behavior that ran counter to prevailing doctrine in economics. According to the thinking of John Maynard Keynes,[22] the most influential economic theorist of the period just before World War II, consumer spending is largely a function of two factors, personal income and the state of the market. Equations can be derived that are then used to predict the relative rise and fall of consumer income, or consumption, and industrial prices, or production.

Katona, however, argued that in a society that was reasonably affluent people have more money than they need for necessities.[23] He called it *discretionary income.*⊙ What they spend of this income cannot be predicted solely from statistics of income distribution but must take into account as well the changing tastes, attitudes, and expectations of the consumer (see Figure 5.6). And, because their discretionary income may amount to an appreciable amount of money, it becomes a "third force" (added to government and business spending) that must be taken into account if we are to understand the economics as well as the psychology of consumerism.

One of the more important outgrowths of work on consumer motivation, originally sparked by Katona's ideas, was the development of techniques for surveying large groups of people in order to determine their wants and preferences. Over the years, these techniques have become highly refined. They are now a familiar part of the business and political scene, under the name of public opinion polls.⊙ The Gallup and Roper polls are perhaps the best-known national efforts of this type, in which a small number of persons, usually less than 2,000, is selected so as to represent the population of the entire United States. Their answers to questions of current interest are then taken to represent the thinking of all American adults.

Many kinds of businesses depend on public opinion surveys when making decisions concerning the introduction of a new product or a sales campaign in a new market. Such marketing research is almost a day-to-day necessity for businesses that rely heavily on information about daily changes in consumer response. The well-known Neilsen report in the television industry is a good example of

Fig. 5.6. How much of what we purchase is meant to satisfy important primary or secondary motives, and how much is simply our expenditure of discretionary income?

behavioral economics. The study of consumer behavior in relation to prices and personal income. It is based on the theories of George Katona.

discretionary income. Katona's term for that portion of one's income that is not needed for necessities and so can be spent for whatever one wants.

public opinion poll (or survey). A technique of measuring the attitudes or opinions of the population, by asking questions of a selected portion (or *sample)* of the population.

data gathered on almost a continuous basis. It is part of a research effort that in the United States alone now amounts to more than $600 million a year.

Reality and meaning

4. A third set of human needs centers on feeling that one's life and one's doings have purpose. They enable one to develop and maintain a consistent reality in the presence of others.

One of the most important ways that we have of experiencing a full social reality is by comparing ourselves with others. For many persons, comparison is not a neutral activity; they are involved in its significance for themselves and for their own place in the world. Comparison and competitiveness may be two aspects of the same phenomenon, two interrelated motives that arise out of the same need to have things be real and meaningful. We will treat competition first, and then the more personal motives through which we also achieve and maintain our own worlds of reality and meaning—realizing our own possibilities and preserving our inner consistency.

Competition. One problem for all of us is that in an organized society the number of rewards available is less than the number of people who want those rewards. Could a society be run effectively in which there were always enough rewards to go around? The question is probably not answerable, given the present state of our knowledge, but one thing at least is clear: Such an arrangement would run directly counter to our current standards. Thus, what would be your own honest answer to this question: "would you have any objection to everyone, in all your classes, receiving an *A* for every course?"

The all-*A* arrangement is not impossible, but it would almost certainly run into opposition from all concerned—teachers, parents, and, most of all, students. School, we would insist, is a preparation for living, and we all know that in the real world there is always a relative scarcity of rewards. Competition may be in some ways immoral, and perhaps it exacts a great price, but it may also be a practical necessity. And, indeed, this helps to explain why our school system serves as a training ground in developing and encouraging the social motive of competitiveness. It is only serving its purpose of training effective citizens. Families play their part in this too, particularly in the additional pressures they put on boys over girls, and in their support of what we appropriately term *competitive sports*, such as Little League baseball. The result of all this unremitting pressure is that competition is firmly implanted in most persons. Furthermore, competitiveness, the striving itself, is taken as a valuable attribute of one's character. Notice that this does not mean simply that one should strive or work hard, but rather that one ought to gain one's rewards at the expense of other persons. The competitively gained reward is the one that is socially the most justifiable.

Fig. 5.7. The competitor and his options.

But, unlike the exercise of so many other learned motives, the exercise of competitiveness appears to take a toll, first in the body and later in other aspects of living. It is as though the person spent a lifetime in efforts to break the tape in a series of races with close competitors (Figure 5.7). The effects are seen primarily in the circulatory system.

A great deal of laboratory and other medical evidence has recently been brought together to support the hypothesis: coronary heart disease will not occur before the age of seventy, regardless of one's diet or exercise, unless the individual shows a typical behavior pattern. The behavior pattern is called *Type A behavior*○ by the two physicians, Meyer Friedman and Ray H. Rosenman, who have studied it. It is a pattern of personality characteristics and associated behavior that is marked by impatient aggressiveness, a constant sense of urgency, and extreme competitiveness.[24] Their evidence comes from case studies of successful, hard-driving achievers in the intensely competitive settings of industry and government. However, it should be noted that their evidence is not conclusive. What is still needed would be a long-term study of a random sample of adults, some Type A and some not, to determine the percentage of each group that develops some form of heart disease. Only then could one legitimately conclude that the heart disease is *caused* by the pattern of living.

Self-actualization. There is a point of view in psychology that is closely associated with the name of Abraham Maslow. In friendly contrast with what he considered the two dominant forces in modern psychology, psychoanalysis and behaviorism, he proposed a "third force."○ This was to be a humanistic approach that focused on healthy and "normal" persons, as distinct from the neurotic or unhealthy persons who are usually the concern of psychoanalysis. It would stress values and subjective experiences as much as the impersonal facts that are emphasized by behaviorism. And it would emphasize the positive and creative aspects of human striving as much as neutral and habitual aspects of behavior. Humanistic psychology has never became a formal school of thought but has remained an orientation within psychology.

Maslow's early research interest was in the related areas of motivation and personality. Faced with evidence concerning what we have called *primary* and *secondary* drives, he proposed that human motives were organized in a hierarchy.[25] At the basic level, where survival is at stake, one finds primary motives, such as hunger, thirst, sexuality, and maternal drives, which operate so as to keep creatures and their species alive. Ordinarily, these motives are satisfied in the course of normal living. When they are, other motives may emerge that have to do with security—motives to seek safety from dangers, to be free of fear, and to associate with other members of the species (as herd animals do). When these motives are satisfied in turn by the normal social arrangements of the group—by herds, by couples, by the family—then it is possible for the person to seek expression of even more highly evolved needs. From a prominent German neurologist and social philosopher, Kurt Goldstein, Maslow had taken the notion of a single, general human motive at this level, which Goldstein called the drive for *self-actualization*—the drive to live up to and to fulfill one's own best potential, to actualize one's self to the fullest degree.

Maslow pointed to an evolutionary, developmental pattern in his hierarchy of needs, in the sense that the primary survival needs were restricted to creatures at a lower level of development and the more advanced needs were available only to the more highly developed species. Self-actualization, as well as related spiritual needs, were to be found only in humans, and specifically, only in a few persons to any appreciable degree. These are persons who are like the rest of us in that they always have some energy left over beyond what is needed to satisfy biological urges or to react to influences from the environment. But they are unique in that they are capable of growing to the fullest and in that they may achieve what Maslow called *peak experiences.*○

Self-actualization, you will note, does not consist of reaching a goal that is outside of oneself. Indeed, the goal is nothing other than the fulfillment of oneself. Evidence for it, therefore, is hardly to be found in "ordinary" forms of behavior. Quite the contrary. The evidence is best obtained from reports by those who have attained this level of experience, usually in the form of a peak experience. Other

Type A behavior. A behavior pattern of some individuals who overreact to their environment. Such persons may be predisposed to stress and cardiovascular problems.

"third force" psychology. Another name for *humanistic psychology*, in contrast to the first two "forces," behaviorism and psychoanalysis.

peak experience. Maslow's term for a rare moment of self-actualization. This experience is one of happiness and fulfillment characterized by a state of being in which the individual feels at one with the world.

123

*Secondary
motives:
the story of
needs and values*

evidence is found, although perhaps in less certain fashion, in the empathic observation and understanding of the state reached by the self-actualized person.

Consistency. When one event follows another, we usually see a connection between them that we call the *cause*. If a billiard ball moves across the table and comes into contact with another and the second one then moves off, we say that the first one hit the second and caused it to move. Or, if someone raises a tennis racket and brings it into contact with a ball, and the ball then flies across a net, we say the person has hit the ball and caused it to move in this way. How we make such judgments was first studied as far back as the 1920s by a brilliant Belgian psychologist, Albert Michotte,[26] and the problem was then brought to the United States by another transplanted European, the social psychologist Fritz Heider.

Heider offered a simple and elegant formulation of the problem. We tend to observe and to think in causal units, he said, each unit usually consisting of a person (P), an object (X), and often another person (O).[27] Our thinking about the world of social relations is thus made up of such little units, each one a variant of P and O and X who are linked by some relation. The commonest kind of relation is one involving feeling, such as "P *likes* O." The major rule determining how these units are composed is simply that we prefer that the feelings expressed in them be in balance. For example, if we have positive feelings toward some person, we will tend to see that person's acts as positive.[28] If a person we like is seen to do an act that we dislike, the imbalance between P and P's act bothers us, and our impulse is usually to change our view of one or the other (see Figure 5.8).

Heider's contribution is to have compressed into one tidy formulation a world of diverse human actions and motives. Consider the following example, to

Fig. 5.8. Above, a Vietnamese police official in the performance of his duty. Your attitude toward him is probably neutral. Now look at the picture below. This is the man that the official was shooting, in the performance of his "duty." Did your attitude toward the official change as a consequence of knowing the nature of his act?

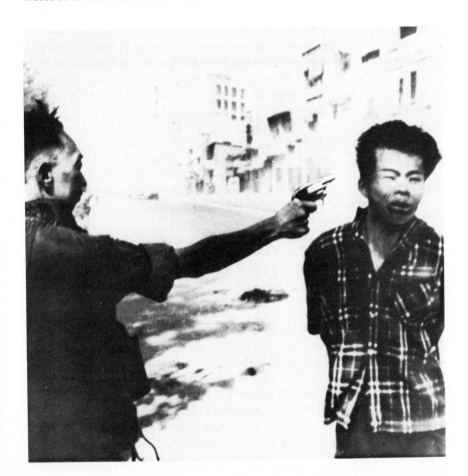

show what the formulation can encompass. Suppose that your very best friend, who is the president of the local bank, has just absconded with the bank's funds and also with his secretary. In this case, P is your friend, whom, of course, you like (+). His act, without doubt, is despicable (–); and up to this point your feelings toward the secretary are neutral (0). You are disturbed by what has happened — because the bank has been robbed, but also because you are confronted with a situation that for you is not in balance. (It is for this reason that Heider's approach to these problems is known as balance theory.⊙) How can you go about reconciling the imbalance? The alternatives are few and can easily be summarized in terms of our symbols:

P	O	Act	Your Reaction
+	0	–	This is the event as you first hear about it: P (+) and a neutral secretary (0) have committed an act that you do not like (–). There is an imbalance.
+	–	–	This is your first reaction: You now dislike (–) the secretary, but there is still an imbalance in the unit.
(+)	–	–	One possible resolution: You "disconnect" your friend from the secretary and the act, saying "I don't believe he did it" or "He wasn't himself when he did it" or even "She somehow made him do it."
+	+	+	You redefine the act, and the secretary along with it, thus: "So what's so bad about what he did? The bank can afford the loss. Besides, he and his wife never got along, so he'll be happier with the secretary."
–	–	–	Most difficult of all, you change your perception of your friend, and probably of the secretary as well: "Well, he certainly had me fooled all these years. I always thought they were both honest."

However the imbalance is righted, you will probably not feel comfortable until you do so. It is this commonplace phenomenon that has led a number of theorists to claim that there is a genuinely powerful motive that might be called *consistency* or *stability*, which operates in our ongoing view of ourselves and other persons.

Cognitive dissonance. It was this widespread phenomenon of consistency that attracted another social psychologist, Leon Festinger, to adapt Heider's formulation to a line of experimental research.[29] Festinger used the term *cognitive dissonance*⊙ to refer to what Heider would have called a *lack of balance* — that is, the state of imbalance that is aroused whenever you find yourself operating with two cognitions that conflict.

In a classic study of real-life dissonance, Festinger and his colleagues observed the behavior of a group of persons who, following their religious leader, were preparing themselves for a forthcoming day of world destruction that the leader had predicted. On the crucial day, the chosen few, who were convinced they would be transported to heaven as the world was destroyed, waited all day and night for the event that never came to pass. Their resolution of the consequent dissonance was a tribute to their faith: They became convinced that only the faith and purity of their own small group had prevented the rest of the world from being destroyed. The event X, originally felt by them to be (–), was thus transformed to a (+) event, for they now saw it as a test of themselves and their beliefs.[30]

In a line of research that has given rise to many studies, Festinger's group used a technique they called *forced compliance*.⊙ Typically, participants would be asked, or persuaded, or perhaps even bribed, to do something in support of a political position or candidate that it was known they disagreed with. Once this (–) act had been done, the subjects' attitudes were measured again to see if they had

balance theory. Heider's consistency theory, which indicates that people prefer consistency and harmony among their own attitudes and feelings and will try to effect a change to achieve such a balanced state toward an object.

cognitive dissonance. Festinger's principle that when an individual has beliefs or actions that conflict or disagree with one another, a state of tension is present. One therefore acts to reduce this dissonance through changes in thought or behavior.

forced compliance. An experimental arrangement in which persons are induced to do or say something that they do not necessarily believe.

125

*Secondary
motives:
the story of
needs and values*

been changed to conform to the act. According to the theory, people would change their view of the position or candidate to conform to their own (+) expressed support. The results of these studies, although often suggestive, are not always clear-cut, largely because it turns out to be very difficult to present a situation in which alternatives are neatly divided and easily measurable. As a result, Festinger's position has occasioned a good deal of discussion, pro and con, and, as we shall see in a later chapter where we discuss attitudes, other models for explaining these phenomena have also been proposed.

An inside view of motives

The material that we have discussed in this chapter, particularly in its later sections, suggests a general approach to viewing human motives. We might summarize this approach as follows: Our significant actions, those that we feel are meaningful to our lives and that are marked by a sense of decision and commitment, seem to arise out of our most personal interests and potentialities. They are actions that in each case seem to represent us and even to fulfill us. They are not simply responses to a push that is felt as outside of ourselves, nor even to a pull that is ahead of us.

Meaningful and motivated actions, we are saying, seem to go beyond both the push and the pull. They are done in the process of expressing ourselves and toward the goal of organizing, unifying, and developing our individually meaningful worlds. Some such view of directed and motivated behavior is implied in balance theory, for example, and in what has been called *intrinsic motivation*.

The center of such a view is our individual experience — the way that things appear to each of us, individually, at any moment. Experience is really all that any of us has; everything else is not what we have but what we know about. From the point of view of each one of us as an individual, the world consists of whatever experience we happen to be having. This is the case even though we may be troubled by the fact that what we know does not fit this experience, or may be buoyed by the fact that what we expect or remember will support this experience. Thus, I may be absolutely convinced of the fact that I have a biologically based hunger drive — but I do not experience this drive itself. All that I can find, if I should ask myself what is going on with me at this moment, is a mix of sensations, feelings, and perceptions. This is not to deny the truth of my hunger drive. It is well established as a fact, but experience is more than facts. It is made up of bits of knowing and bits of feeling, in whatever way they appear to me as an individual. As my experience changes, I express myself differently in regard to my wants.

Summary

1. Secondary motives differ from primary motives in their sources, their goals, their rewards, and their relation to learning, to maturity, and to survival needs.

2. Maslow distinguished deprivation (biological) needs from metaneeds, the former having to be satisfied before the latter can come into play.

3. Secondary motives operate in three major ways: in terms of self-acceptance, of personal freedom, and of the need to find meaning in one's life.

4. Secondary motives that help to direct our social behavior include needs for attention, affiliation, and social approval.

5. The need for attention may be for positive or negative attention. The Hawthorne effect, named after a famous series of studies in industrial psychology, refers to the fact that participants in an experiment improve their performance simply because of the attention paid to them by the experimenters.

6. The need for affiliation, or for contact and company with other persons, may provide a means for forestalling anxiety.

7. Social approval serves as an important motive in social encounters and is also a significant determinant of responses on personality tests.

8. The most widely studied of secondary motives is need achievement (n Ach), defined by McClelland as the need to do something better than it has been done before. It varies measurably among individuals, groups and social classes, and even societies, and is probably inculcated by parents in family settings.

9. Persons can be trained to behave as though they had high n Ach, thereby leading them to act in ways that are academically or socially more productive.

10. The sexes differ in regard to n Ach, males showing it to a higher degree. Horner's study indicated that high-n Ach females may experience serious conflict of motives and even a motive to avoid success.

11. The character traits related to n Ach have to do with one's typical expectancy patterns in situations of uncertainty.

12. Another set of secondary motives arises from one's "intrinsic motivation," or the need to be and act at one's best. This set includes such needs as competence and work–play and helps us also to understand some of the motivation of consumers.

13. The competence motive, as described by White, is a basis for curiosity, exploration, and constructive and challenging behavior beyond the requirements of built-in patterns.

14. Laboratory animals will work for food even when this is unnecessary, apparently in response to a basic need for work as a challenge.

15. The fact of discretionary income in affluent societies leads consumers to make a variety of spending choices with significant impact on their economies.

16. Because there are always fewer rewards available than people who want them, society tends to justify competition or gaining rewards at others' expense.

17. Maslow proposed a theory in which motives were effective in a hierarchy: Survival needs come first, then more evolved social and personal needs, with the drive for self-actualization as a peak.

18. Heider's formulation of balance theory and Festinger's later studies of cognitive dissonance are based on the proposition that we prefer that our social environment appear in balance, with persons, acts, and events matched in terms of our feelings about them. We correct perceived imbalances by altering our perceptions and cognitions.

This chapter will introduce you to the topic of *perception*, certainly the most intensively studied area of experimental psychology. In Chapter 3, we discussed the various sensory systems, those arrangements of receptors and transmitters that serve as interfaces to accept and process different kinds of physical energy. Perception, as we study it in this chapter, consists of additional processes. Their function is to organize the energy into an individual "world" that appears coherent and meaningful. The result is that what we see (or hear, touch, taste, or smell) seems to each of us to "make sense," to be ordered and familiar and appropriate.

In this introduction to perception, you will review the four major psychological processes that are always involved: attention, motivation, learning, and organization. As you will see, some of what happens in perception is "given;" that is, it is wired into the organism so that the perceptual behavior appears at birth. Just what is given and what is developed are not easy questions to answer, and some of the answers may therefore be unexpected.

You will also review the four major modes of perception, corresponding to the basic sensory systems: touching, perceived mainly through the skin; tasting and smelling, with their significant dependence on cultural and social factors; hearing, the most personal mode and the one that is basic to human communication; and the noble mode of seeing, the source of most of our information about space and the objects in it. You will then learn about the organizing effects of figure *versus* ground, of context, of color, and of the factors of stability and change. In turn, this will lead you to a discussion of our concluding topic: the still unsettled problem of whether we do perceive what is "really" there.

6

Perception and attention: the creating of meaning

A few years ago three educators, Donald Naftulin, Frank Donley, and John E. Ware, Jr., invited one Dr. Myron L. Fox to deliver a lecture to a group of eleven professional persons. The topic he chose was "mathematical game theory as applied to physician education." As feedback on his skill as a lecturer, the listeners filled out an eight-item questionnaire, dealing with such matters as Fox's interest in his subject, whether he put across the material in an interesting way, and whether he stimulated their thinking. The responses to Dr. Fox were so uniformly positive that the three educators videotaped a repeat performance of his talk and showed it to another forty-four professional persons, with equally favorable results. Perhaps the most negative comment received was that it seemed just like a "typical conference lecture."

Introducing Dr. Fox

All this would hardly be worth mentioning except for the fact that the lecturer, although introduced as an expert named Dr. Myron L. Fox, was really an actor named Michael Fox who was very skilled at playing medical roles. He had not really delivered the lecture promised by his title. Rather, his presentation had consisted of a string of invented terms, double-talk phrases, jokes, irrelevant facts and comments, meaningless references, and internal contradictions, all spiced with pleasingly seductive gestures and mannerisms. And, although "Dr. Fox" talked at them for an hour, not one of his professionally trained listeners caught on.[1]

The results were unexpected, even to the three experimenters. A more elaborate study was therefore carried out by Ware and Reed Williams. Michael Fox was videotaped in the delivery of six different lectures on "the biochemistry of memory." For three of these lectures his presentation was "highly seductive," as it had been in the first experiment—that is, pleasant, with many jokes, the kind of performance that makes listening a pleasure. For the other three lectures his presentation was "low seductive"—that is, as dull and boring as it could be made. Each of the two types of presentation was done with either a lot of factual content (a total of twenty-six substantive points to be remembered), with a medium amount of content (fourteen substantive points), or with low content (only four substantive points)—making in all six different lectures of about twenty minutes each. Students at Southern Illinois University served as participants, with a different class viewing each videotape. They were then given two tests, one a nineteen-item test covering their responses to the lecturer's style and manner, and the other a twenty-six-item multiple-choice test on the substance of the lecture.

As might be expected, on the first test the high seductive style won out over the low seductive style, hands down (Figure 6.1). No matter what the content of the lecture, a more pleasing presentation was scored higher than one that was dull and boring. But unexpectedly, when the scores for recall of content were compared, it turned out that students who had heard only four substantive items, under the high seduction condition, did just as well as those who had heard twenty-six items under the low seduction condition. And again the listeners did not see through Michael Fox's guise.[2]

This experiment is certainly worth pondering for its lessons in higher education—but at this point we want to consider it, instead, as an example of what this chapter is about: perception. The participants in the experiments heard and saw patterns that were familiar, such as words and sentences, gestures and expressions.

Fig. 6.1. How different groups of students rated lectures by Dr. Fox that differed in content or in level of "seductiveness." (From Ware and Williams, 1975, p. 153)

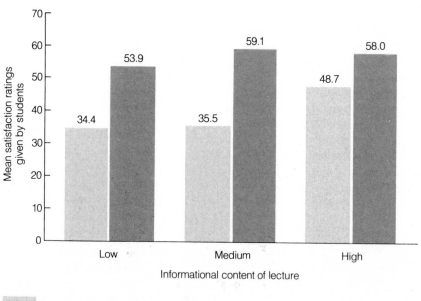

However, many of the patterns were irrelevant, out of place, or even clearly wrong, given the setting in which they occurred.

Yet for some reason the viewers did not seem to see or hear these irrelevant and meaningless patterns. Instead, they *perceived* an enjoyable or a dull lecture about a serious topic in higher education—and apparently a significant number of them also managed to learn something from the lecture. How can we explain this curious fact, that the majority of the students did not seem to see nor hear what in fact they saw and heard? Our answer in this chapter will be that perceivers are not simply instruments taking in sensory input, but that perception takes place through the individual actively making and organizing a "world" of shared meanings.

Our sense organs are always receiving impulses of energy, such as patterns of light rays, sequences of sound waves, puffs of odor, and so on. We can experience this "pure" sensory input if, for example, we stare blankly, concentrating on nothing in particular. However, our sense organs rarely absorb stimulation in this passive way. Even the cells of the retina are actively engaged in selecting, arranging, and organizing the light that reaches them. We have to deliberately put ourselves in a state of "pure" sensing, concentrating on nothing in particular, if we even want to approximate a state of passive reception of stimulation.

1. Perception may be defined as using what we have learned, in a motivated way, to focus attention so as to organize sensory stimulation meaningfully.

This definition, although complex because it includes a number of key terms, is meant to describe our ongoing processing or organizing of sensory information so that it is experienced in an individually meaningful way. We will be discussing its four key terms—attention, motivation, learning, and organization—in the rest of this chapter.

Attention

When we start to pay attention, what we do is orient selectively to some situational demand, that is, to something that attracts us in the situation. We seem to do this in two stages, most often one after the other and more rarely at the same time. In the first stage, we come in touch with the situation or with some aspect of it, and in the second stage, we zero in, select, or organize the data for our immediate purposes.

The first stage is very well exemplified by the orienting reflex.[3] Here the perceiver switches over from an attitude of passive, nonprecise perception to an attitude that is more active, alert, directed, and charged. This kind of attentional shift, which occurs most clearly in hearing, has recently been taken advantage of in a nearly foolproof test for hearing defects that is applicable to subjects of any age and condition. It works as follows. In many animals, the entire body responds involuntarily whenever a sound is heard. This response can easily be detected as a sudden change in the breathing pattern. By means of a simple sensing apparatus strapped around the body, it is then possible to find out whether the human subject hears various tones, even when subjects are too young to indicate their perception in any way, or too incapacitated by age or physical condition, or are trying to fake a hearing loss.[4]

The mechanics of selectivity. Two different approaches have been used in order to explore how attention works in perception. In the first of these, investigators make use of the fact that whenever there is any perceptual input through the sense organs, parts of the cortex of the brain are triggered into electrical activity. This is known as a *cortical-evoked response.*© In order to detect it, one places fine wires on different points on the scalp, picks up the minute electrical signals, and amplifies them through an apparatus known as the *electroencephalograph*, or EEG.© In one such study, investigators at the Brain Research Laboratory at UCLA presented people with tasks requiring their attention to either a visual or an auditory stimulus.[5] For example, in one task they were required to attend to a series of light flashes, count them, and press a key after every fiftieth flash — thus ensuring their attention — while at the same time deliberately ignoring an ongoing series of clicks. In another task, they would be required to attend to and count the clicks while deliberately ignoring the light flashes. The EEG tracings of their cortical evoked responses were then examined. These showed that when the people were attending to the visual input and ignoring the auditory input, they produced electrical response in the occipital (or visual) lobe of the brain, which is at the back of the head. When they were attending to the auditory input, their response was in the temporal (or auditory) lobe, which is just over the temple. Apparently different parts of the cortex each have their specific roles to play in this process of selecting.

A second line of approach, which was initiated by E. Colin Cherry[6] in Great Britain during the 1950s, takes off from what he called the "cocktail party phenomenon."© In any gathering where many different kinds of sounds compete for your attention, you would probably have no difficulty in simultaneously listening to one person while tuning in on another conversation just over your right shoulder and perhaps occasionally noticing a voice with a distinctive accent somewhere in the crush to your left.

In order to study the way that this is accomplished and what factors affect it, Cherry devised an ingenious technique based on dichotic,© or two-eared, listening. He had people listen to and repeat out loud a message that was fed into one ear while a different message was fed into the other ear. They had no difficulty attending in such a way that the unwanted message was "subordinated" to the wanted one — although we should not conclude from this that what people do is simply attend to one ear rather than the other. They are just as capable of subordinating a message of one level of intensity to another, or a message heard in one direction to a message heard in another, or even a message of one frequency to a message of another. What seems to happen here is much like what you do when you turn up the volume in one stereo speaker and turn down the volume in another: It is a matter of emphasizing one channel at the expense of another.

How is this done? Interestingly enough, the subordinate channel (or ear) is never tuned out completely. While repeating the preferred message without error, people can still report whether the unwanted message is being spoken by a female voice or a male voice, or whether the language of the unwanted message is changed, or whether their own name is mentioned at the start of the unwanted message. They can do this even if the unwanted message is delayed by as much as 4.5 seconds behind the preferred message.[7] It has been suggested that attending involves setting up perceptual "filters" that assure that only certain kinds of material get through. On the basis of the evidence, it seems likely that this filtering takes place in two stages.[8] At the first stage, you screen things in or out almost automatically, requiring very little in the way of conscious decision making. Thus, you are able to "accept" the mention of your name, or "notice" that the voice speaking the unwanted message is one sex or another or is speaking your native tongue. These are operations that can be carried out almost without think-

cortical evoked response. (also *cortical evoked potential*). The term for neural impulses that have been evoked by a stimulus and are then recorded as electrical potential in the brain.

EEG (electroencephalograph). A record of brain waves made by attaching electrodes to the head and measuring fluctuations in voltage.

"cocktail party phenomenon." The phenomenon by which one registers stimuli to which one is not directly attending until something makes it important to notice the stimulus.

dichotic listening. Stumpf's term for presenting different auditory stimuli to each ear simultaneously; a procedure now used in studies of how individuals process auditory information.

ing. Once the input has passed this passive test, however, it can only be passed on to be fully perceived if you do some *active* work on it, organizing it into a meaning that makes sense and is useful to you.

Motivation

Some of our perceiving takes place because we are, in a way, forced into it—for example, if we react to a sudden clap of thunder. But if our behavior is spontaneous, and as long as the stimulus does not suddenly overwhelm us, then it is probably closer to the facts to say that we usually perceive what we want to or need to. We are motivated to perceive certain things and are motivated also in regard to when and how we perceive (see Figure 6.2).

2. The more ambiguous the situation for the perceiver, the greater the influence of the perceiver's motivation.

If we meet for the first time a person we do not know well—as is often the case in social situations—our perceptions may be strongly influenced by our own needs and feelings. Similarly, when the situation is unfamiliar and strong motives are aroused, **perception** may become remarkably creative. A young child, alone in a room at night, may experience uncertainty and fear that lead to seeing clearly a

Fig. 6.2. Which one of these captions do you think fits this picture: (1) "An example of overreacting for the benefit of photographers"; (2) "Wasted lives, wasted tears"; or (3) "A young woman weeps for her fallen friends." How do you suppose your own motivation entered into your choice of caption?

Table 6.1. Percentages of liked and disliked performers judged as correct or incorrect.

| | | ... the following percentages were judged as | |
		Correct	Incorrect
When the liked			
girls were in	Right	81.2	18.8
fact ...	Wrong	54.6	45.4
When the disliked			
girls were in	Right	62.7	37.3
fact ...	Wrong	20.8	79.2

Source: Data from Zillig, 1928, table 5.

growling figure flit past the window, although in fact nothing has happened but the scraping of tree branches on the glass.

In a series of experiments with fourth-grade schoolgirls in Germany, the five best-liked and the five least-liked girls in one class, as previously selected in a secret ballot, were rehearsed in exercises to do in front of the class. For some exercises, the liked girls were trained to perform without error and for others they were trained to do poorly. Equally, for some exercises the disliked girls were trained to perfection, and for others they were trained to make errors. After each group of exercises, the other girls in the class were asked to recall which of the performers had been correct and which had made errors. If the factor of liking–disliking had no effect, liked and disliked girls would have been judged in the same way. They were not, as Table 6.1 shows. When they were in fact correct, liked girls were more often judged as correct; but when they were in fact incorrect, liked girls were less often judged as incorrect. That these judgments were not simply errors on the part of the other girls was shown when the experiments were repeated, with identical results. That the judgments were not simply rigid prejudices is shown by the fact that with many repetitions, the perceptions of the other girls began to come closer to objective truth.[9]

Motives may be influential in changing the way things seem to be or even in distorting things to fit our feelings. A charming example of the latter occurred in the course of a series of demonstrations by the group working with Adelbert Ames at Princeton during the 1950s. The approach of this group was based on the notion that perception is a *transaction* between person and environment—that is, what you do in perceiving is take all the evidence into account and then arrive at some "best bet" that fits with your own past experience.[10] One of their better-known demonstrations consisted of a room that was distorted in shape. However, when viewed with one eye from a position on one side, it appeared to be normal. The reason is that the viewer's perceptual "best bet," based on a lifetime of experience, would be that rooms are "square." So, even at the expense of some perceptual distortion of the people in it, the room is seen as "square" and the people in it as distorted or as changing in size.

At this point, however, a powerful motive can enter the picture. In one series of studies, viewers of all ages reported the same perceptual result, that the room looked normal but that someone walking across it appeared to be changing size. All the viewers, that is, with one exception. The exception was a woman whose husband was asked to walk across the distorted room. Under these circumstances, she "chose" another perceptual alternative and reported that it was the room that appeared to change size and shape as he walked across it. This intriguing result was studied further and came to be called the *Honi effect*© (based on the nickname of

Honi effect. In experiments using the Ames distorted room, a subject fails to perceive a familiar person in a distorted size or manner, although everything else appears distorted.

the woman who first reported it). What the evidence showed was that in general the effect could be found during approximately the first year of marriage but not afterward—at which point, we must assume on the basis of experimental evidence, for most couples the honeymoon is over.[11]

How motivation affects perception. Motives and feelings exert the greatest influence on perception when the situation is not clear or when the individual does not have dependable, objective standards for judgment. This effect is strong enough to be demonstrable under laboratory conditions, as was shown repeatedly in studies some years ago. In this research, often called the "new look in perceptual theory" (because for the first time the effects of motivation were taken seriously), people were presented with an ambiguous situation and then motivated to perceive it in one way or another. The first such study, by Gardner Murphy and Roy Schafer, presented viewers with an ambiguous figure that can be seen either as two profiles or as two vases.[12] Subjects who were given money for making one perceptual choice reported seeing that choice more often. In a similar series of experiments, by McClelland and Atkinson, subjects reported seeing more food-related objects on a series of rapidly flashed slides when they were hungry than when they were not hungry.[13] Clearly, motivation can have important influences on perception.

Learning

3. The results of learning affect perception when the learning leads to a change in the perceiver's situation.

The major difficulty in determining how learning and perception are related is that the term *learning* may mean two different things: either a process of changing or the results of that process, as shown in one's performance. The process of learning, or changing, is, of course, always accompanied by perceiving. It is not possible to go through a period in one's life, while changing, without also being involved in perceiving. All that can be said is that the *results* of learning may or may not affect one's perception. It is this proposition that we will examine here.

An impressive study of the way the processes of learning and perception are interlinked was done by Held and Hein.[14] It involved an ingenious arrangement in which pairs of kittens were restricted to a total of three hours a day of visual experience for the first ten days of their lives, all of it in a specially constructed apparatus whose walls were painted in vertical stripes of black and white. One of each pair of kittens was restrained within a box riding on the end of an arm, so that it could see where and how it was moving but had no experience at physically making the movements. The other kitten of the pair did all the moving. It was harnessed to the other end of the arm so that its movements affected the box in which its partner was riding (Figure 6.3). When the kittens were later tested, it was found that those which had had both visual and motor experience were essentially normal, but that those which had been restrained and so lacked the motor experience now acted as though they were almost blind, particularly in regard to perception of depth. Thus, for cats at least, the implication is clear. The process of learning is a developmental matter that involves both perceiving and acting. One caution should be mentioned here, however. If we were to come across an adult cat that lacked some perceptual ability, we could not tell from the performance alone

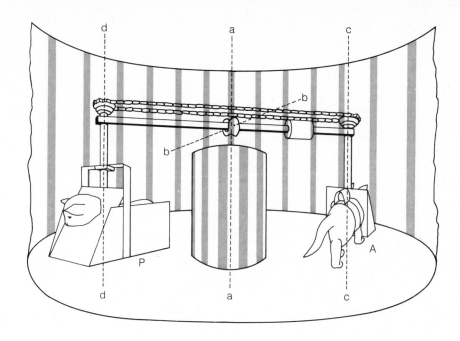

Fig. 6.3. The apparatus used by Held and Hein to train kittens in either active or passive viewing. The two kittens received the same amount of visual stimulation. (From Held and Hein, 1963, p. 873)

whether the animal had suffered a failure in a visual or a motor aspect of development, or both.

What is given in perception. Under normal conditions of development, newborn chicks will peck accurately and from the proper distance at certain objects that are biologically appropriate for them. They do not seem to need to learn not to peck at objects that are much bigger or much smaller than those grains that are their normal diet. Nor do most species of animals, from rats to human, seem to require learning in order to see the world three-dimensionally (in depth). Rats will jump across a gap quite accurately, appearing to be able to judge the distance, when they are only a few days old and lack any prior experience in this perception or behavior.[15]

Similarly, human infants no more than two weeks of age react appropriately as objects are brought toward them.[16] Using an ingenious arrangement called a "visual cliff"—in which various subjects are given a choice between a level floor and a sharp drop in the floor, both quite safely covered by a heavy pane of glass—it can be shown that any animal that is old enough to be capable of moving around, from rat to human, will avoid the part that looks like it might be dangerous.[17] In short, many perceptual skills appear to be "built in."

Almost 300 years ago, there was first suggested a way of experimentally testing whether such performances are really "built-in" or are learned very rapidly when needed. Find someone who has been blind from birth and who then has had surgery to recover sight. As soon as the person's eyes are uncovered, ask, "What do you see?"

Interestingly enough, a fair number of such cases have been reported, most of them instances in which cataracts prevented any functional use of the eyes prior to surgery.[18] However, very few of these cases provide trustworthy data on which a conclusion can be based. The most thoroughly studied subject, reported by Gregory and Wallace, was that of a fifty-two-year old man whose cataracts had kept him from seeing since the age of ten months.[19] The answer that he might have given to the question we just posed is "A blur." Like other such patients, his initial report was that he saw blurs or blotches in color, somewhere away from him in space and appearing to stand out against the background. From this we may conclude that some primitive organization of visual perception is given: It includes color, figure-ground, and depth perception, and at least the beginnings of object perception.

The difficulties that the Gregory and Wallace's patient had are of equal significance. When shown slides, he had great difficulty in grasping relations of depth in what they showed. He remained genuinely puzzled by facial expressions and by reflections in mirrors. And he could never really understand how the same object could look different when viewed from different aspects. All of these difficulties, you will note, relate to what might be called the "illusions" that we manage to create. A facial expression is simply a certain arrangement of muscles—yet in it we see profundities of depth and human significance. A reflection in a mirror, like the space that we perceive in a slide projected on a screen, is very much a matter of what we create. And the permanence of objects, a fact of which we are quite certain even though we may never perceive them the same way twice, is surely an aspect of the world that is as much our creation as our genetic program.

Some basic aspects of perception do indeed appear to be innately given, and quite probably we would never be able to arrive at more developed stages if we did not have these aspects to build on. But much of our perception beyond this level seems to be a product of our continuing, creative series of transactions in situations that are presented to us. How much work we put into this perceptual production may be seen in the fact that many patients like the one just described do not welcome the gift of vision. They soon give up the attempt to learn how to see and spend their lives as blind persons. Apparently it is by no means easy to see. It just seems easy because this active process, like our unthinking use of our native tongue, is learned very early by most of us and has become a part of everything we do.

Experience and perception

Attention, motivation, and learning all play important roles in our ongoing perception. However, they do not in themselves provide an explanation for perception itself, particularly for the basic question, "How is sensory stimulation continually processed into meaningfully organized perception?"

Two points need to be kept in mind in this connection. First, some sort of "coding" seems to take place between the point where energy is received and the end result. Thus, we never perceive our own sensations but rather a coded representation of them. This representation is never simply an unchanged copy of the stream of impulses. The second point is that perception is always in the form of our individual experience. We are individually and personally learned and motivated and attentive in a way that leads each one of us to organize the world in our own somewhat unique way.

4. Psychophysics is the study of the relations between sensory energy and perceptual experience.

Given these two points, what remains as a problem in perception is that sensations reach us in one form but that perception takes place in another. We receive wavelengths of light, but we see colors; we receive sound waves of different frequencies, but we hear high and low notes. In short, there is on the one hand a set of physical dimensions, and on the other a set of dimensions of experience. For more than a century in psychology, the field of study known as *psycho-*

Fig. 6.4. If someone is asked to squeeze a hand-held instrument so as to indicate the intensity of shock that is being experienced, a number of different measurements can be taken at the same time: (a) the objective level of shock being administered, (b) the perceived level of shock and (c) a self-report of the experience. Psychophysics is concerned with the relations between (a) and (b) or (a) and (c).

physics has been concerned with the relations between these two sets of dimensions (Figure 6.4).

The basic problem that psychophysics deals with is that perceptual dimensions do not coincide with physical dimensions. Consider an example from music. If we listen to a sequence of ten notes and if each note is exactly double the frequency of the one before (50 cycles per second, 100 cps, 200 cps, 400 cps, and so on), what does a person with normal hearing report if asked how the notes seem in relation to each other? Does the listener report what is physically true, that the second seems twice as high as the first, the third twice as high as the second, and so on? No. Usually the listener reports that the second seems about one third higher than the first, the third one about one third higher than the second, and so on. A physical range of, say, eight to one is experienced as a psychological range of about three to one.

In addition, our experience of a *change* in stimulation differs from the physical change in that it is not always directly related to the physical intensity of the stimulation. A familiar example is as follows: If the lighting in a room is very dim and a small light is then turned on, we experience a marked change in illumination; but if the room is already brightly lit and exactly the same small light is added we experience it as a very small change. Again, the experience of the change does not correspond precisely with the physical facts of the change.

However, we may well suspect that our experience is related in some regular way to what goes on "out there." It would be hard to believe that perception and reality go on independently, with only random relations between them. If they are related in some regular way, there ought to be a logical statement, such as a formula, that summarizes that relationship. One long-term investigator in this area, the late S. S. Stevens of Harvard, developed such a formula, which he called the *power law*.[20] It may be expressed as follows:

Sensory experience = [(some constant) × (the physical energy)]ᵃ power

That is to say, the rating that we might give a stimulus (how bright or how loud it seems) will equal the measured physical energy (in watts or in photons) multiplied by some factor that is constant for each sensory system, with the product raised to some power. Investigations on many different kinds of perceptual operations, covering all the various sensory systems, give surprising support to this rather simple formulation. They suggest that the regularities of our dimensions of experience are indeed sensibly related to the regularities of the physical world.

5. We can distinguish four major modes of meaning that we share through the senses—touching, tasting and smelling, hearing, and seeing.

The dimensions of experience, as we have said, are sensibly related to the dimensions of physical energy. Our perceptual activity consists of working with the incoming sea of energy and organizing it into what is for us a meaningful world. Four different modes can be distinguished for purposes of discussion, although in practice they constantly interweave and affect one another. The four modes are related to four of our major sensory systems, as described in Chapter 3.

Touching. One of the peculiarities of Howard Hughes, the late billionaire industrialist, was that he had a curious fear of being contaminated by germs. For example, when one of his aides went out to buy the day's paper, the required ritual consisted of buying three copies and presenting them all to Hughes, who would carefully, with hand protected by Kleenex, pull out the middle one and order the other two destroyed. This ritualistic behavior, centering on a desperate need to avoid contamination by dirt and germs, is a common symptom among certain kinds of severely neurotic persons. It is significant to the specialist in abnormal behavior, but it is also of some interest in its own right, for it provides some clues to the psychological meaning of touch.

It is through the skin that we make our first and perhaps most important contact with our environment—beginning with the way that we are bathed in the amniotic fluid of the womb and continuing almost without interruption in the swaddling and holding and nursing that is our situation as infants. In the usual sense of the word, at least as many adults conceive it, the perceptual information that we gain and give through the touching system is quite crude and primitive. At most, we are able to sense or to say something like "Ah—good," or perhaps "No good." Sensory information through touch, however, can be very precise, and in another kind of language, the language of basic feeling, to touch or be touched is a very complex kind of act. We can gain some sense of the great complexity of touching as a perceptual act if we consider how many of its instances are weighted with significance: the laying on of hands, the handshake, the caress, the tickle, the hands of the healer, the contamination by touch, and the meaning conveyed by such phrases as "to be deeply touched."

If we had only the sense of touch, our detailed factual information about the world would be rather limited. Quite likely we would only be able to note the presence of some target, perceived as a separate object with its own boundaries. Touching is in this sense the most primitive of the familiar perceptual systems. It seems to serve as a basic link with the world, as we imply in such expressions as "keeping in touch." With touching, we begin our contact with the world, as infants do, and in the last resort this is what we always have to fall back on, that something is *tangible* (see Figure 6.5).

Tasting and smelling. Whether tasting and smelling are one system or two depends on how one divides up the information-processing capacity of living creatures. In any case, the fact that we raise such a question at all indicates how

Fig. 6.5. There is a world of difference between being touched (a) and touching (b) (See also Figure 6.6.)

(a)

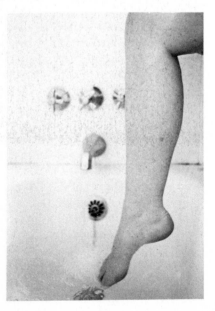

(b)

Olfactory perception without olfactory sensation

Dear Ann Landers:

I have a terrible problem, and it is ruining my life. I've been sitting here for half an hour trying to word it delicately so you can print it in the paper, but there seems to be no nice way to say it, and I'll just have to be vulgar.

I am a girl, twenty years of age, who hates to be around people because I have an offensive odor. I take a shower every morning and every night. I change underwear daily. If I have an evening date I will change again. I have tried every kind of deodorant, antiperspirant, mouthwash, breath sweetener, cologne, dusting powder—all the intimate feminine products advertised in the magazines—but still I have this embarrassing odor.

No one has ever mentioned it to me, but I am aware it is there. It has made me very self-conscious, and I try to keep my distance from people. Is there any medication that will relieve me of this condition? Do I have a chemical imbalance in my system that the doctors cannot identify? I have been to four doctors (two skin specialists and two gynecologists), and they say there is nothing wrong with me. They also say they cannot detect the odor that plagues me night and day. Please help me, Ann.

Not Nice to Be Around

arbitrary our classifying may be. In everyday behavior, tasting and smelling are intermingled beyond any hope of untangling them. This is true at least for humans, in whom both tasting and smelling are usually underdeveloped, except perhaps in the cases of tea tasters and wine judges. However, in a recent experiment, ordinary adults showed themselves capable of distinguishing by smell alone a T-shirt worn by a male from one worn by a female.[21]

However, in the case of tasting to some extent and in the case of smelling to a great degree, the information handled by the system is as much social as perceptual. For example, the very mention of the topic of smelling is enough to evoke an amused or slightly offended reaction. In contemporary Western culture, smell is simply not a "nice" topic. Natural smells relating to persons are taboo as a topic of conversation, although, interestingly enough, artificial odors that one puts on an otherwise odor-free body may be freely discussed. But to keep the distinction quite clear, a different term is used: The socially acceptable, unnatural, nice odor is not a *smell* but a *fragrance*.

One consequence of all this is that humans do not usually react markedly to all the information that might be conveyed in olfactory perceptions. Our environment of smells has changed markedly over the past few centuries, yet we do not act as though very much change has taken place. Less than a century ago, smells were omnipresent in social life, but people simply took them for granted. Occasionally, smells served some purpose, as when the perceptive stagecoach traveler could easily identify the next town over the hill by its unique combination of smells from dirt, garbage, animals, and excreta. But no matter what the level of society, personal smells were ignored. Louis XIV, the eighteenth-century king of France, could remark quite casually that the odor from his armpit would knock down a pig at ten paces. It was an age in which bedpans, filled during the night, remained in closed-in bedrooms until they were emptied into the street the next morning. On the American frontier, the man of the house was sewed into his long underwear for the winter and was unsewed for a bath only with the advent of warm weather in the spring.

Hearing. More than any other perceptual mode, hearing possesses characteristics that are unique to it. Because we organize our auditory perception primarily as events spread out in time (even though we describe these events as "taking place"), we are able to form the events into a language. The naturally occurring sequences of smells, tastes, or touches that we encounter do not easily form into language—although, as Frank Geldard has shown, with special training one can develop a communicatory system based on sequences of touches or taps on the skin.[22]

Hearing is unique in another way as well. Each of our perceptual modes has its appropriate locus of action. If we were to ask where the action is in regard to touching, we would, of course, say that it is at the point of contact between one skin and another. For smelling or tasting, the point of action is at the point of sensory contact. Thus, we taste something when we touch it with our tongue, or the dog smells something by bringing its nose into direct contact. Seeing, too, has an action space: It is always located by us at the place of the target. If I see a moving object, then both the object and the movement are at the perceived distance of the object. But with hearing the case is different. We place what is heard somewhere in the space between the origin and the reception, and in fact we often perceive what is heard as actually filling this space. There is no experience in the other senses corresponding to what we call "volume" in hearing.

Related to this characteristic of hearing is the fact that much of what we hear is heard on two levels: as straightforward input or information, relatively neutral and impersonal, and also as unique tone and expression, a kind of "inner meaning" to which we respond personally and judgmentally. Music, for example, is certainly more expression than information, whereas the words spoken by a human voice combine elements of both. Different kinds of sounds have their own unique emotional qualities, too; for example, the whisper as distinct from the shout, or the sob as compared to the shriek. The way that we go about perceiving through the hearing system may often emphasize the personal rather than the informational quality of what is heard. In hearing, we receive what comes to us, rather than reaching out to sniff at it, as in smelling, or to peer at it, as in looking. Animals other than humans may cock their ears, but that is only to improve the reception; the perceptual act of hearing makes no place for reaching out toward the source. In hearing, rather, we are caught by sounds. It is interesting to note that in every known language, the word for "obey" (in English it comes from the Latin *ob-audio*) has the same root as the word for "hear" (as in the English *audible*), as suggested in the expression, "To hear is to obey."

Seeing. Seeing is generally considered the most "noble" of the perceptual systems. It is certainly the channel by which we gain most of our information, and thus it serves as the model for one of our proudest achievements, science. As we know, science concerns itself with the accumulation, organization, and utilization of facts, all done objectively, impersonally, and rationally. No other perceptual system is equipped to accomplish this better than the visual, which may help to explain why most of our words referring to forms of knowing are "vision" words—as when we "take a closer look" or "take the long view of things" or "see what someone is talking about" or achieve "insight."

Vision, more than any of the other perceptual systems, can serve both actively and passively. I can direct a "piercing gaze" toward you, or I can become uncomfortable "under your gaze." Similarly, certain personality problems can take the form of either *exhibitionism* or *voyeurism*—although almost never both in the same person, because they are each a preferred way of acting (Figure 6.6).

Visual perception is unique in another way as well. It is the only system by which we are able to grasp an array of separate and distinguishable objects, all at

Our word *science* is derived from the Latin *scire*, meaning "to know." The word *conscious* comes from the same root. Its origin is probably a Sanskrit term, *chyati*, which refers to the act of cutting. The link to seeing is very clear here and in fact is still preserved in the expression, "a piercing glance."

Fig. 6.6. The experience of seeing is not at all the same as the experience of being seen.

once. Hearing presents us mostly with patterns in time, smell with vaguely sensed indicators of one or two things, and touching with no more than a few things at a time. But by means of vision we grasp, all at once, a field spread before us in the form of a varied array of differentiated objects, each separately bounded, at different distances, and often against an encompassing background. More than any other system, then, the visual presents us with what looks like an entire world in which we can act and react. And how we act in this world depends in large part on the distance that we, as individuals, choose to assume from our visual array. We may choose to keep our distance, to see it whole, to survey it, to look it over, and in a real sense to command it. Or we may prefer to see it rather than look at it, to accept it rather than control it. We may stare persons down or gaze at them in awe or love. Traditionally, some persons possess an Evil Eye, whereas who ever heard of an Evil Ear? These are some of the choices available in visual perception.

We are accustomed to thinking that two eyes must be better than one, yet in a wide range of cultural traditions there may also be found a belief in the "third eye," the single eye of wisdom and knowledge. In Eastern cultures, one is asked to turn this insightful third eye toward the inner self, where all truth is presumed to reside, whereas in the West, since the time of the ancient Greeks, it has been assumed that the breakthrough must be in the outer world. But in any case, only in the noble system of seeing are these choices possible — looking and seeing, inner and outer, single- and dual-eyed.

Organization in perception

6. We perceive a world that appears to be organized in space and time.

The most evident characteristic of what we perceive is that it seems organized. In order to appreciate what this means, try for a moment to imagine a world that is not organized. What would it seem like? It would be the world that might be described by someone who is in a state of total confusion or in a delirium — although it is doubtful that someone in such a state could make a coherent report about their perception. A better approximation might be obtained if we suppose the following, more likely situation: You walk down a hall toward a large door. Opening the door, you are unexpectedly confronted with a huge, brilliantly lighted, noisy, busy room. For a second or two, all that appears to you, perceptually, is an unorganized field of light, color, sound, and activity. You are dazzled, taken aback; but within a few seconds you recover your senses (the more adequate phrase would be, "recover your perceptions"), and you see what is "really" there. But, of course, you saw what was really there when you first opened the door. The difference is not that the room has changed but that you have arranged your sensory input into a perceptual organization. This is what we accomplish easily and automatically, every moment of our waking lives.

Things. The commonest form of perceptual organization is of objects or things. In vision, we see separate things, each one different from the next. Equally, in hearing, we hear auditory events in the form of separate sounds or groups of sounds. In touching, we are in contact with felt objects; in olfaction, we smell something before the smell dies away; and so on. Object organization would seem to be the most basic of all perceptual characteristics, if we are to believe the reports from the adults described by Von Senden. When they gained vision for the first time, after surgery for cataracts, they reported spontaneously that they first saw

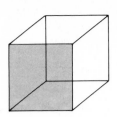 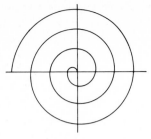 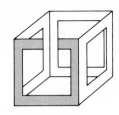

(a) The Necker cube   (b) The Archimedes spiral   (c) The "impossible" figure

Fig. 6.7. Some figures (a and b) are reversible as well as possible. Other figures (c) are reversible even though they are not "possible."

vague, colored blotches—hardly what we would consider fully defined objects but certainly shapes that were diffusely organized in objectlike ways.

Living creatures appear to be naturally equipped so as to perceive things or at least whatever constitutes things for each species. In some cases, object perception is simply of the edges—for example, the leading edge of a sound that alerts an animal; the edge of a dark shadow, to which a frog will respond; or the line drawing, to which even human infants will respond appropriately.

Recent experimental studies with animals as well as human infants suggest that they prefer to look at forms and patterns that are reasonably novel, reasonably complex, and of rather high redundancy.[⊙23] The latter term refers to a pattern in which the same information is repeated a number of times. That such preferences exist in the auditory mode as well is shown in the universal use of simple, repetitive sounds that seem to attract babies, as in words such as *Mama* and *bye-bye*.

Painters and art critics have long known that in perception an object is not necessarily a solid thing. What we see when we organize some sensory input into an object is apparently a boundary enclosing some space. This is why humans as well as the other primates have no difficulty understanding a line drawing as an object, even though no "inside" is shown. Here is certainly an instance of the miracle of everyday perception. Bear in mind that in purely physical terms an object is some solid matter of a certain size and shape. Its boundary does not exist separately. If our perception were identical with what the target is physically, we would see the matter but not a distinguishable boundary. Instead, we perceive the edge and are able to organize this into the object. Thus, when only the edge is shown, as in a line drawing, we "see" the object that it bounds. We do the same thing when we look at a picture with a frame around it. Instead of seeing the contents of the picture plus a line that belongs to the space around the contents, we spontaneously perceive the frame as belonging to the picture and as determining its limits.

These terms lead us to another important way in which space is organized in perception. As we saw in Chapter 3, experimental evidence indicates that if a creature can move around it acts as though space had depth—and so, for example, it will avoid the seemingly sharp drop of the "visual cliff." Within this extended space, objects and things appear to us as organized in terms of figure and ground.[⊙] That is, what we attend to as objects of perception always seem to stand out against a background to which we are not at the moment attending. This fundamental perceptual fact was once put in the form of this teasing question: "Why is it that I see that building against the sky rather than the sky against the building?"

The phenomenon of figure-ground distinctions seems to be basic to perception. If a slide is flashed so rapidly that we cannot see any of its details, we may still report whether it contains an object against a background.[24] Even a meaningless blot of ink, as in the Rorschach ink blot test, is spontaneously seen as some sort of figure against the rest of the card. However, in most cases, no matter how hard we try, we cannot attend to both the figure and its ground at the same time. This provides the basis for many familiar "illusions" of reversibility, such as those shown in Figure 6.7. Because either possibility permits organizing the pattern as

redundancy. The repetition of the same information within a pattern.

figure-ground. The Gestalt principle of perceptual organization whereby objects or figures stand out distinctly from a background. This principle holds even when objects are ambiguous or when the foreground and background are reversed.

figure against ground, we usually have no difficulty in voluntarily switching back and forth between them. The simple pattern of Figure 6.7b has been of some value in indicating gross brain damage, because some brain-damaged persons are unable to make the switch at the same rate as normals. This suggests that figure–ground organization may be a function of the brain mechanisms involved in visual perception.

Context. Every act of perception takes place within some context. The experience of this context then influences the way the perception is organized. For example, if you hold one weight in each hand and attempt to compare them, your kinesthetic perception⊙ will take place within a context consisting of your physical size and strength, your previous experience in such judgments, your estimate of how much the weights ought to weigh, your role as an experimental participant, and how many weights you have already compared in this series. Any perception that is part of our judging behavior—and this includes most of the decisions that we make—will therefore be organized in complex ways that can depend in part on the context in which they occur.

The effects of judgment on perception, and vice versa, have been extensively studied, because they are evident in even the simplest acts. If you observe a snow-covered lawn at dusk and compare the perceived brightness of the snow with a standard such as a piece of white paper, your judgment will not be "correct" in terms of the physical stimulation reaching your retina. Rather, your perception will occur within a context made up of your past experience, your present situation, and your knowledge about snow and afternoon light at this particular time of year. You will probably judge the snow as being brighter than it "really" is. Similarly, your perception of a lump of coal in direct sunlight will result in a judgement that it is duller than it "really" is.

Colors. How are we able to distinguish literally thousands of shades and hues of color? We know that every true color (not including black, brown, silver, and gold, which may not be colors in the same sense) can be produced by appropriately mixing three "primary" colors: blue-violet, green, and red. The simplest answer to the question of how the visual system does this is that the system is in some way sensitive to these three colors and "mixes" its response appropriately. This, as we shall see, is the major theory of color vision. However, it does not account for all the facts, chiefly the facts of defects in color vision, and therefore it has always been in conflict with an alternative theory. The latter theory says that the visual system responds not to individual primary colors but to "categories" of colors or to opposing pairs of colors. Both theories, as it turns out, are partly correct.

■ At the beginning of the nineteenth century, Thomas Young, a brilliant British gentleman scientist, proposed that the retina contains three kinds of receptors, each sensitive to one of the primary colors, blue, green, and red. The great German scientist Helmholtz improved and extended the theory, and it has recently been strikingly supported by the discovery—made by means of very delicate experiments—that the retina does indeed contain three kinds of pigments, each of which is maximally sensitive to one of the three wavelengths.[25]

■ Another nineteenth-century German physiologist, Ewald Hering, proposed an alternative theory: that the retinal elements were sensitive not to colors but to "categories" that were arranged in opposing pairs. Some elements were sensitive to the pair of colors black–white, some to red–green, and some to blue–yellow. Again, recent experimental work on humans[26] and on rhesus monkeys[27] (whose color-vision mechanism is very much like ours) has

kinesthetic perception. Sensing or perceiving one's own muscles.

shown that this theory is also partly true. However, it turns out that the elements that code the input in terms of these pairs are not in the cones of the retina but are in two other places along the line: in the banks of cells deeper in the retina (which in many ways functions like a "little brain" of its own) and in special cells in one of the relay stations, the thalamus.

Even these elaborate explanations in terms of photochemical and neurological activity, however, do not account for all the phenomena of color perception. Edwin Land, the inventor of polaroid glass and of the Polaroid or Land camera, has shown, in striking demonstrations, that colored objects can be photographed with black-and-white film and then projected in such a way that they will appear in full color. Apparently the viewer can "make" color out of black and white. Again, our perception is a constant organizing process. This is seen even more clearly in the fact that "where" we perceive the color depends very much on what we are perceiving. This phenomenon, first pointed out by David Katz in a classic work on color many years ago,[28] can be demonstrated by a simple experiment. Chickens are first trained to peck at white grains of rice and to avoid grains that are stained blue. The chickens are then placed in a room containing white grains that are lit by a blue light shining on them. Will they accept or avoid the rice?

The answer is that they accept the rice, treating it as though it were white. Apparently chickens can distinguish between a color that is "inside" a target and a color that is "at" the surface of the target. Katz referred to these as "film color" and "surface color," and he pointed out that we are constantly called on to make this distinction. In fact, the distinction is at the basis of our ability to perceive an object's color as constant although the ambient light that hits it may vary from reddish to blueish or from bright to almost dark. As Rudolf Arnheim has shown in his work on the perceptual basis of the arts, artists such as Rembrandt have been very effective in producing the impression of "glow" by placing bright objects against a dark background and by leaving the surface relatively undefined. Thus the viewer has the impression of seeing into the depths of the object, and the colors thus appear to be glowing out of the object's depths.[29]

Stability and change. Perception is also organized in terms of constant change—which in turn interacts with stability, an equally basic characteristic of our perceptual world. If things do not change but merely repeat unchangingly, perception breaks down. For example, listen to a tape loop on which a single familiar word *(lookingglass* is a good example) is repeated over and over. Very soon the familiarly organized pattern will begin to break up, and either meaningless sounds or else some newly perceived sounds, not present in the original, will begin to be heard.

A series of ingenious studies by psychologists in Canada demonstrated the same phenomenon in the visual system. Normally the eye moves constantly in little jumps, even when it is seemingly fixated on a target. These movements, occurring at the rate of 50–100 per minute, make it impossible to fixate your own eyes in a mirror (although you may think you are doing so) or to scan a line smoothly in reading. Now, suppose the viewer is fitted with a contact lens to which a tiny projector is attached and that the viewer then looks at the image thrown by the projector. What will be seen is an image that faithfully follows the eyeball's movements. The visual image will, of course, appear absolutely stable to the viewer. Under these conditions, people report that geometric figures quickly fragment and disappear by parts. Some parts, or even the whole figure, might reappear briefly, and corner angles tend to hold up better than straight lines, but unless some change occurs in the viewing conditions, such as the light flickering or the screen jiggling, the viewer is not able to keep the stimulus organized as a perception. The stimulus is now stable and unchanging, and therefore it breaks down. The reason is that for stable perception one needs constant change in the stimulus.[30]

Both stability and change appear to be necessary, in perception as well as the organization of behavior; and we might even suppose that if an organism is reduced to only one of these two it will die—although the mode of dying might differ in the two cases. Most change in the environment is perceived as movement, although what the visual system picks up is not usually movement but more properly changes in a target's position. This was first shown by researchers who set up two lights and arranged the timing so that first the left one and then the right one flashed. As all of us know who have ever observed a "moving" neon display, the sequence of flashes produced a clear perception of one light moving. It is now known as the *phi phenomenon*© and has been shown to depend on the pattern of timing as well as the distance between the lights.

Perceiving and reality

In the definition of perception offered at the start of this chapter, we referred to the experience of focusing attention so as to organize sensory stimulation into meaningful targets. Thus far, the chapter has been devoted to spelling out the factors that affect this experience, the different modes of perceptual experience in animals and humans, and some of the results of that experience.

However, although this definition of perception has helped us to arrange much of our material for orderly presentation, it bypasses some important questions that might be raised. We will deal with these issues briefly in the concluding section.

The issues have to do chiefly with the relations between our perceptions and the physical world "out there." There is indeed something out there, as we would all agree. The world exists, and it will go on existing whether or not it is perceived by you or me or any other perceivers. But the only access that any of us has to the world is by means of our perceptions. We are all in the position of someone who must depend on letters written by one parent to tell about the health of the other parent—in which case the truth of the matter, or the answer to a question about what is really going on with the sick parent, depends entirely on the accuracy of the letters.

But the matter is even more complex than this. Our analogy of the sick parent does not correspond entirely to the perceptual process, for the reason that we have been emphasizing throughout this chapter. Perception is a continuously working process by which we keep organizing our sensory input into our individually meaningful worlds of things and events and sequences and all their interrelations. Our question, then, must be "How accurate are the results of our active perceptual processes? To what degree do these results correspond to what is, we suppose, really out there?"

The shape of tables. Consider the everyday experience of perceiving a table. We all know that the top of an ordinary table is "really" rectangular in shape. (At this point we must put that term of certainty, "really," in quote marks, because it is our certainty that we are here calling into question.) If we view the table from directly above, its shape would be perceived as in Figure 6.8a, where the *X*'s are meant to denote the positions of the legs underneath. Now, the curious fact is that probably none of us has ever seen a table in this "correct" rectangular shape. To do so, we would have to be suspended somewhere above the middle of the table, but not too close, because then we could not see all of it. Not too far away, either,

phi phenomenon. The apparent movement of light from one place to another when, in fact, two stationary lights are being flashed on and off in succession.

because then we might perceive it as shaped like a diamond. Rather, what all of us have seen, all our lives, is a series of trapezoids, as in Figure 6.8b or perhaps Figure 6.8c. Our sensory perception of trapezoids has somehow resulted in our perception, and thus our knowledge, of rectangles. But then how did we come to know that tables were "really" rectangular?

To make matters still more difficult, we find that the first drawings that children make of tables are usually not trapezoidal at all, but rectangular as in Figure 6.8d. It is as though the child begins by knowing, and drawing, what the table is "really" like, and only later learns to perceive it, and draw it, as trapezoidal. This is just the reverse of the way that things ought to be in development.

The British psychologist Richard Gregory[31] points out that any shape can in fact represent one object from one viewing position "or any of an infinite set of somewhat different objects seen in some other orientations." He illustrates this with a drawing, as in Figure 6.8e, of one of those rolling hoops with which children used to play. By itself, this drawing might be a hoop standing on edge, or it might be an elliptical object such as an egg. And the answer to the question, "How do we ever know which is correct?" is given by Gregory as "When we know what the object is, then we know how it must be lying to give the projection given by the artist."

But this is no help at all. Gregory is saying that in order to know what an object *really* is, we have to know what it is. But the point is, how did we ever find out what and how things "really" are, if we could not learn from our perceptions? Did we ask our parents if dishes were really round and tables really rectangular? Or did we, rather, learn directly in and through our perceiving? And, if so, how was this accomplished?

Fortunately, an answer is at hand, once we give up the conviction that we perceive as instruments do, merely taking in one kind of information and putting out another. The lesson to be gained from the Held and Hein studies of kittens is that perception develops through working out one's world through self-directed and organized behavior. Thus, if the growing child moves around the table, viewing it in a constantly changing series of partial perceptions and also feeling it, bumping against it, hitting it, rubbing it, even biting it, then all sorts of informational contacts are made. The child's resulting conviction will be that surely something is there—not the infinite number of things that Gregory implied, but one thing that can appear in a marvelous variety of guises. And out of all these different guises, it appears that the child discovers a central core, an essence that represents the real thing; for example, the circularity of the hoop or the rectangularity of the table. Then, later in development, one is able to recognize the "true" character of someone's face, or the essential sound of a word no matter how it is pronounced. This in turn is probably brought about because to an increasing degree the child lives in a shared world of experiences, a perceptual community.

We are constantly at work at constructing a meaningful, personal world around the core essences that we have learned. Out of a universe in flux, we create stability; out of a fixed universe, we create change and movement. Out of the energy that is present for us only at our bodily surface, we make a world that seems

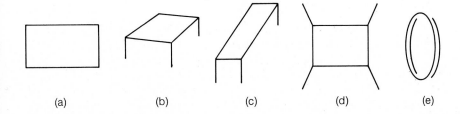

(a)   (b)   (c)   (d)   (e)

Fig. 6.8. The perceived shapes of some common objects (see text).

to us spread out in space away from us. Out of unceasing change in our viewing position, we create constancies of shape, color, and distance. Yet we do all this not by means of a fixed, mechanically determined program but as part of our work of behaving in the world. Therefore, the results that we produce at *any moment* may not correspond to a version based on instruments nor on the consensus of other perceivers.

Summary

1. There is a difference between "pure" sensation, as when we passively absorb sensory energy, and the many forms of perception, all of which involve some activity by the individual.

2. Perception involves four kinds of cognitive processes, all usually working at once: attention, motivation, learning, and organization.

3. Perceptual attention occurs in two stages: first, an orienting or alerting stage and, second, various levels of selection and organization of stimulus information.

4. Perceptual selectivity has been studied by means of the cortical-evoked response and by means of dichotic listening. Both kinds of studies suggest that a filtering mechanism in two stages may be responsible, the first stage working automatically and the second more actively.

5. Motivational factors in perception function in inverse relation to information. That is, the more information or the clearer is the information, the less influence is apparent from attitudes or motives; and, the more ambiguous the situation appears to be, the more powerful are motivational effects on perception.

6. Processes of learning and perception are necessarily intertwined from birth onward. What is perceived affects what is learned, and what is then learned affects what is later perceived.

7. Visual perception of depth appears to be built in for most animals at birth. Studies of humans who first gain vision in adulthood suggest that color, figure—ground, and depth perception are given but that other perceptual abilities are difficult to learn.

8. Psychophysics is the study of the relations between measured physical dimensions of energy and experienced perceptual dimensions. One simple formula, Stevens' "power law," may summarize such relations.

9. Tactile perception, accomplished by way of the skin, provides basic and usually general information that is often experienced as personally significant.

10. Perception of tastes and smells may be more developed in humans than our culture allows us to admit. In general, contemporary societies restrict such perceptions to either the niceties or the realm of the unmentionable.

11. Perception of auditory events consists of organization in time rather than space and can therefore serve as a basis for language understanding and use.

12. Vision is, in humans and probably the higher apes, the most "informational" of the perceptual systems. Like touching, visual perception functions in both active and passive modes.

13. By means of perception, we are able to organize for ourselves a world of things or objects, arrayed in space and time and with their own boundaries so as to constitute figures against a ground.

14. A major organizing factor in perception is the context in which a target is perceived.

15. Two major theoretical approaches to color vision are that the visual system is responsive to three "primary" colors or that it is responsive to three pairs of opposing colors. Both views find experimental and anatomical support, and each may be partly correct.

16. Color perception may, however, also be a complex organizing process in which context plays an important role.

17. Adequate perception requires a continually changing input, resulting in the stability that is achieved via perception.

18. Developmental evidence indicates that perception is not simply a copy of what is "really" there but is rather the result of active learning through which reality becomes sensibly organized for the individual.

In this chapter, we survey the area of learning, a topic in research and theory that has long been central to experimental psychology. You will first learn about the origins of the scientific approach to learning, in the process of classical conditioning devised by Pavlov, and then about a major alternative, the process of instrumental conditioning, an American development owed to the work of Thorndike and, later, of B. F. Skinner.

You will learn how, by using these two basic methods, modern learning theory based on experimental research has studied the process of behavioral change. As one result, a host of practical applications have been produced, in education as well as in clinical work. In connection with this development, you will review some criticism of conditioning and of its limits, some stemming from advances in biological observations and some from consideration of differences between voluntary and involuntary actions.

You will then survey some of the more recent work in learning, centering on the meanings, values, and expectancies that an individual finds in the learning situation. In this work, emphasis is placed on the importance of cognitive processes in both animals and humans, an emphasis particularly evident in the approach known as *social learning theory*. You will be able to see some significant practical consequences of this approach in new understandings of phenomena such as helplessness and depression.

As you will see, experimental work on learning in animals appears to have arrived at a position very similar to that taken by social psychologists in regard to humans (the latter discussed in Chapter 18).

7

Learning: the new and the old

A living creature that added nothing to its behavioral repertoire beyond its fixed genetic program would be nothing more than a machine. Even the lowliest of living creatures, such as tiny flatworms or insects, seem to be able to take this one great step beyond the machine level. They adapt to a changing and often unpredictable environment by appropriately changing their behavior, and then they retain the change so that they do not have to learn it all over again. Ants, for example, can learn to make the correct turn in a maze that will reward them with food. They retain the learning from one day to the next, and they even show observable individual differences.[1]

This is not to say that what is learned is necessarily the most appropriate or adaptive way to behave. Animals as well as humans can learn habits that are against their own best interests or that persist long after their original usefulness has passed. As we shall see in Chapter 15, this is one way of understanding what are called *neuroses*, namely that they are maladaptive habits that persist long after circumstances have changed and they are no longer useful.

Because the field of learning has been a central interest of psychologists for nearly a century, the literature on it is vast. In this chapter, we will not be able to do more than survey some of the major forms of learning and conditioning, touch on some major problems, and suggest a few important recent developments.[2] As we shall see, what started out as a set of techniques for bringing about learning under laboratory conditions has become a major field of study on changes in behavior and cognition.

1. There are two major forms of conditioning, similar in many ways: classical conditioning, based on Pavlov's work, and instrumental conditioning, currently based on Skinner's work.

Pavlov's discovery

Suppose it could be shown that an animal can learn, under the controlled conditions of a scientific laboratory, behavior that was not in its original, genetic repertoire but that had been chosen by an experimenter. Suppose, in addition, this learning could be demonstrated to appear and then to disappear under the strict control of the experimenter. Would this not be strong support for the experimenter's theory of how such learning takes place?

This was essentially what was accomplished around the beginning of this century when Ivan Pavlov first succeeded in conditioning dogs in his laboratory. In the course of laboratory studies of the digestive process (for which he was awarded the Nobel Prize in medicine in 1904), Pavlov had noticed that the animals often salivated profusely even before they began eating. The smell of their food in the next room, or the fact of being brought into their feeding place, or even a change in the laboratory's activity in preparation for feeding were enough to bring on salivation.

An ordinary observation, surely. Probably thousands of owners of animals had made it before. But to Pavlov's creative mind it suggested an intriguing theoretical possibility.[3] Dogs come equipped, so to speak, to salivate at the taste of a meal. This is their natural device for assuring that the food will be properly digested. But no dog begins life prepared to salivate at the sight or smell of a certain laboratory assistant or at such events as the cessation of some laboratory activity. *This* salivation must have been learned, that is, added to the dogs' natural repertoire.

The significance of this discovery may not be apparent to someone in our day. But to a scientist such as Pavlov it was of great importance. At that time, there was no science of psychology, no theory to explain human or animal *behavior*. Darwin's contributions had indicated how, in general, the characteristics of a particular species might have developed over millions of years of evolutionary change. However, this would not enable one to explain or predict the behavior of an individual member of a species. This Pavlov saw as the important element in his laboratory discovery: If the scientist could explain how learning in an individual takes place and could reproduce that learning at will in the laboratory, the way would be clear for an objective scientific explanation of individual behavior. Conditioning, as he viewed it, was the fundamental mechanism by which the individual built its own learning history. And, as he reasoned, such a theory made biological sense as well, for it seemed clear that a creature that could become conditioned was thereby capable of adaptive behavior and had an evolutionary advantage over creatures that could not learn in this way.[4]

According to Pavlov's interpretation, which became the foundation for what is known as *classical conditioning*, an original (genetic) connection existed in the dog's nervous system. The smell and taste of food automatically brought about the activation of the animal's salivary glands. Now, under the controlled conditions of the laboratory, a new connection was formed, or more precisely, a new relation between stimulus (food) and response (salivation). The sequence is shown in Figure 7.1a and 7.1b. The new relation was between, for example, a bell and salivation. Any new stimulus might do, as long as it was obvious enough to catch the animal's

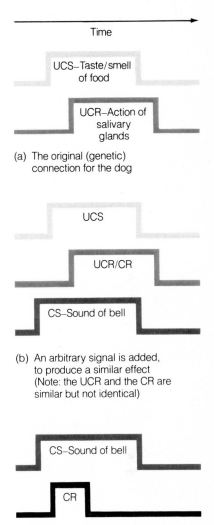

(a) The original (genetic) connection for the dog

(b) An arbitrary signal is added, to produce a similar effect (Note: the UCR and the CR are similar but not identical)

(c) The new, learned relationship

Fig. 7.1. The development of a Pavlovian conditioned response in a dog. UCS = unconditioned stimulus, UCR = unconditioned response, CS = conditioned stimulus, CR = conditioned response. In his writings, Pavlov referred to the original (genetic) components as "unconditional," meaning that they were not dependent on training; other components were "conditional," or dependent on training. When they were translated into English, the terms were changed to "unconditioned" and "conditioned"; hence our current usage. The diagrams are meant to show the relationships in time as well.

attention. Once it did, the animal displayed a typical orienting response and there-after would salivate at the new stimulus, as shown in Figure 7.1c.

Classical conditioning ⊙

Pavlov's method is sometimes called *Pavlovian* conditioning in his honor, but more commonly (because it was the initial method devised) it is known as *classical* conditioning. It is simple in essence. All that is required is that the animal be equipped with some original, unlearned connection between stimulus and response. For example, dogs salivate when presented with food or when a weak acid solution is placed in their mouths. Humans blink if a puff of air is directed at their eyes. If a new conditioned stimulus (the CS) is now presented and then followed by the original, unconditioned stimulus (UCS), and if this pairing is done a number of times, the animal will begin to produce a conditioned response (CR) that is retained even after the UCS is withdrawn. It will not be identical with the original, unlearned, unconditioned response (UCR), but it will be sufficiently similar to support the inference that learning has occurred.

In the course of much laboratory research in Soviet and later in British and American universities, a number of basic terms were introduced.

Extinction.⊙ If a dog has been conditioned to salivate at the sound of a bell and is then brought into the laboratory, day after day, and allowed to hear the bell without receiving any food, its conditioned salivary response will disappear. It will then behave no differently than a dog that was never trained — that is, until it is retrained, when its conditioning history will affect its rate of re-learning. The process of extinction appears to be simply the opposite of conditioning, but it has turned out to be a complex phenomenon that is still not completely understood. How long extinction takes will depend on many factors, including the nature of the original training, the individual animal or human, and the time intervals involved.

Aversive conditioning.⊙ Pavlov's countryman, Bekterev, very soon began a program of research on a related form of conditioning that used punishment instead of reward as the reinforcer.⊙ Like other animals, dogs do not have to be trained to withdraw a paw when it is stimulated with an electric shock. In this case, the shock is the UCS, and the withdrawal is the UCR. If the sound of a bell is now paired with the shock, the dog will learn to withdraw its foot when the bell sounds. The bell is now the CS and the withdrawal is the CR. One important distinction must be mentioned here, however, between an *avoidance* response and an *escape* response. The experimental arrangement may be such that the shock is always presented together with the bell, and the best that the dog can then do is terminate the shock by withdrawing its paw; this would be an escape response. On the other hand, the experiment may be arranged so that withdrawal prevents the shock from ever occurring at all; this would be an avoidance response. In the latter case, the dog's process of learning would determine whether the shock is ever presented, for if it learned to respond without error, it would never feel the shock. This distinction, trivial though it may seem, has raised a number of important theoretical questions in the field of learning.

Higher-order conditioning.⊙ It could easily be shown that an animal can learn a second conditioned response built on a first one. For example, once conditioned to salivate to the sound of a bell, a dog can be presented with a flashing light just before the bell sounds. It might then begin to salivate to the light — a kind of conditioning to its own conditioning. This became a matter of some importance in Pavlov's thinking, for if such chains of conditioning could be

classical conditioning. Learning in which a stimulus paired with a desired or meaningful stimulus becomes a substitute for the meaningful stimulus itself. Pavlov, the originator of the concept, paired the sound of a bell with food, and his dogs learned to respond by salivating to just the bell ringing.

extinction. A procedure of both classical and operant conditioning in which a learned behavior disappears when the reinforcement for behavior is removed.

aversive conditioning. A technique that pairs a stimulus one is trying to alter with a painful stimulus, thus extinguishing the undesirable element.

higher-order conditioning. A process whereby a new conditioned stimulus may function as a substitute for the original conditioned stimulus and produce the conditioned response itself. (We see this same kind of response after taking pets to the veterinarian a couple of times. The smell of the office terrifies the animals.)

shown to occur in humans, it might be possible to argue that this was how our complex learning histories develop.[5]

A related problem has become an important issue among contemporary learning theorists. It rests on the distinction between a primary reinforcer[⊙] and a secondary reinforcer.[⊙] The classical conditioning process consists of forming relationships with secondary in place of primary reinforcers. In higher-order conditioning, still other secondary reinforcers may be added. The problem that is raised by such processes is this: What are the relevant characteristics of *any* secondary reinforcer that make it work for the individual? As we will see in a later section, evidence favoring a cognitive theory of learning rests on studies of the role of secondary reinforcers.

Generalization and discrimination. Pavlov was convinced that the process of conditioning was an advantage in evolution. One of the phenomena that helped to persuade him was called *generalization.*[⊙] Clearly, an animal that could become conditioned to a range of similar or related environmental events would learn faster and more effectively under the conditions in which most animals live. Nature does not always offer precisely identified, laboratory-pure events for one's learning. Recognition of generalization was soon followed by work on its opposite number, discrimination.[⊙] The latter would turn out to be of great value in animal experiments, particularly in the field of sensation and perception. The reason was that by training test animals to discriminate among presented stimuli it was possible to discover what the animal sensed or perceived. For example, if a pigeon can be trained to peck at a blue disk but avoid a red disk while a dog (presumably of equal intelligence) cannot be trained to make this discrimination, one would conclude that the dog does not perceive the difference between the colors.

Instrumental conditioning

Almost ten years before Pavlov's discoveries in his Russian laboratory, the American psychologist Edward L. Thorndike was attempting to build his own version of an objective science of animal behavior. Like Pavlov, he wanted to show that the learning of new behavior could be explained as a kind of mechanical process of "stamping in" new connections in the brain. To test this out, he experimented with cats, placing them in boxlike cages and observing their escape behavior.[6] The cages were secured with latches which the cats were usually able to open only after much frantic clawing. Their behavior seemed to Thorndike to demonstrate trial-and-error learning.[⊙] That is, many trials, accompanied by many errors, finally led to success; and, once achieved, success was later gained in shorter and shorter periods of time through the successive elimination of errors. It was as though a mechanical stamping process had done its work, producing connections that resulted in effective behavior.

Some years later, Thorndike generalized his findings to what he called the *law of effect.*[⊙] Its relevance for learning is that what gets stamped in, or learned, produces an effect, usually in the form of a reward. Out of all the possible behaviors that an individual shows in a lifetime, only those that have such an effect remain as learned and therefore are likely to be repeated.

In the 1930s, B. F. Skinner took up the study of learning and conditioning. His major inspiration was Thorndike's work, particularly the law of effect, which he restated in a form that was experimentally more usable. It became the basis for the approach to conditioning that he developed: if a behavior, once emitted, is rewarded, the probability increases that it will be emitted again.[7] This formulation, in Skinner's view, is sufficient as a basis for learning theory. In addition, he was concerned to link his explanation of learning to the demands of evolution, but he

primary reinforcer. The unconditioned stimulus presented right after the conditioned stimulus.

secondary reinforcer. A situation in which a stimulus is rewarding because of previous association with a reinforcing stimulus.

generalization. In conditioning, the process of an organism responding to a stimulus because it is similar to one to which the organism has been previously conditioned.

discrimination. The ability to separate stimuli and thus to respond to the relevant stimulus and avoid the irrelevant stimulus.

trial-and-error learning. Learning involving multiple choices that are either rewarded or punished until the proper choices are made.

law of effect. Thorndike's principle that the outcome of an activity will determine whether it is learned or repeated. He postulated that reward would tend to increase learning and discomfort would tend to inhibit learning.

was unsatisfied with the implications of Pavlov's theory. Classical conditioning, according to Pavlov, explained the complex network of behavior patterns that are learned by each individual by assuming chains of high-order conditioning. This is a very unlikely, even an inefficient, possibility.

Skinner offered an alternative explanation, one that not only served as a more plausible explanation of individual learning histories but that also profoundly changed the course of learning theory. He noted that in classical conditioning the CR is not made until *after* a UCS-UCR link has been shown. That is, first the experimenter notes that the dog salivates (UCR) to the smell of food (UCS); and only then does the experimenter give the dog a chance to do something else, such as salivate (CR) to another event (CS) such as the sound of a bell. The dog's behavior is thus a response to the new arrangement. In Skinner's terminology, it is *respondent* behavior. As an alternative, Skinner proceeded to study the conditioning process of the behavior that the animal shows. In such an arrangement, it is the animal's behavior that produces the rewards. In Skinner's terms, the behavior is *operant,*⊙ or as it has also been called, *instrumental.*⊙ Hence the name that we use in this section for the second major form of conditioning.

Instrumental applications. The instrumental approach in conditioning has led to extensive use of a procedure known as *shaping.*⊙ To envision what is involved in shaping, imagine a pigeon placed in a sealed, air-conditioned box containing nothing but a lighted panel on one wall and a small tray beneath it. In this unnatural (for a pigeon) environment, the bird cannot at first be expected to do anything but display its nervousness. However, in the course of the necessarily random behavior that it exhibits, there is bound to occur a movement that brings the bird to face the panel. Immediately on seeing this behavior, the experimenter (who is observing through an aperture in the top of the box) drops some grain in the tray. It will take the pigeon very little time to learn this behavior, and thereafter each time it is placed in the box it will quickly assume its "reward position" facing the panel.

Further movements are just as easily trained. As a second step, the pigeon is no longer rewarded for simply facing the panel unless it also takes a step closer to the panel. Once this behavior has been learned, the pigeon is successively rewarded for a series of movements that finally bring it directly in front of the panel. In a final stage, it is then trained in a similar way to peck at the panel, or any part of it, on any schedule that the experimenter desires. If we were to take time-lapse photography of the pigeon's successive movements, it would be clearly evident that its behavior has been shaped by the use of appropriate schedules of rewards. A very similar method was used in the work by the Brelands, described in Chapter 1 (Pages 19–20).

Because control over the presentation of rewards (or punishments) is in the hands of the experimenter, it becomes possible to study the effect of different reward schedules. This topic is at the heart of Skinner's work, not only for theoretical reasons but for practical reasons as well. If it can be shown that behavior is related to its consequences in a regular manner, through the action of rewards and punishments, then a strong case is made for the theory as a comprehensive explanation of learned behavior. Further, a thorough knowledge of the workings of rewards and punishments might be of great value in predicting and controlling behavior of both humans and animals.

The scheduling of rewards has been exhaustively studied by Skinner and his colleagues,[8] with impressive results. Each type of schedule appears to produce its own pattern of behavior, lending support to the idea that these are lawfully occurring processes. To take one example, a pigeon may easily be taught to peck at a disk in order to produce reward in the form of grain; and the relation between the

operant conditioning (also instrumental conditioning). A type of behavior conditioning in which a subject learns to make a particular response in order to secure positive reinforcement or avoid negative reinforcement.

shaping. An operant conditioning technique in which a desired response is learned by rewarding all close responses initially and by then decreasing rewards until only the desired response is elicited.

amount and rate of pecking and the delivery of the food can be strictly controlled. Now, does it make any difference whether reinforcement is given to every peck or only to, let us say, 70 percent of the pecks? It turns out to make a lot of difference. *Partial reinforcement,* as it is called, produces learning that is more resistant to extinction. If the reward is occasionally withheld, the pigeon will go on pecking for a longer time without reward if it has been conditioned under conditions of partial reinforcement. (Some interesting consequences for training children arise from this.)

Comparing the two approaches

Two major kinds of conditioning have been developed, each with a number of different names. On the one hand, there is Pavlovian, classical, or respondent conditioning; and on the other hand there is Skinnerian, instrumental, or operant conditioning. Their similarities as well as their differences are important to note.

---

2. The classical and instrumental approaches to conditioning are alike in most major respects; the differences center on the structure and timing of the CR.

A great deal of thought and research by learning theorists has gone into the question of whether the two major kinds of conditioning really represent two distinct forms of learning. Some distinctions that are useful can be made between the two, but the question is still unsettled as to whether we have two biologically different kinds of learning (Figure 7.2).

As approaches to conditioning, however, the two methods of training are alike in many ways. Just about every significant element of conditioning that is found in one system is found in the other—conditioned and unconditioned stimuli and responses, extinction, primary and secondary reinforcement, generalization, scheduling and its effects, and even limits on what can be done. In addition, the methods are alike in what they accomplish. Under both procedures, a creature can be trained to change its pattern of response, from behavior that is originally "natural" for it under certain circumstances to behavior that is only arbitrarily connected with those circumstances. For example, dogs will "naturally" sit at certain times, just as pigeons will peck. The usual circumstances for this behavior are that the dog is resting or waiting and the pigeon is eating. By means of conditioning, the dog can easily be trained to sit when middle *C* is sounded on a piano, and the pigeon can be trained to peck at a green plastic disk when a blue light flashes above the disk.

Fig. 7.2. From the point of view of the dog, the master is being classically conditioned. From the point of view of the master, the dog is undergoing operant conditioning.

These are arbitrary behaviors, in the sense that they have no "natural" connection with the animal's biological structures, or needs, or life patterns. The behaviors have been chosen by human experimenters, who not only are able to instill the behaviors but also can control their timing, their rate, their appearance or inhibition, and to some degree their intensity. Thus, the learning pattern of an animal can be programmed and then put into effect. It is understandable that the prospect of such control as applied to humans raises questions of great significance. Skinner has dealt with such questions in both fiction and essays.[9]

Some of the differences between the two forms of conditioning may be just as important. Consider again the case of the salivating dog in Pavlov's laboratory. The purpose of the training procedure was to get the animal to salivate to some other, arbitrarily chosen stimulus, thus changing the UCS to a CS and in the course of this changing the UCR to a CR. The two responses of salivation were, as we have said, usually very much alike, although there were also differences of quantity and perhaps even in the chemical composition of the saliva. In the instrumental conditioning procedure, however, the CR and the UCR are less likely to be similar. Pigions peck, but normally at food grains rather than at green disks on the wall of a cage. The still more common technique of training a rat to press a bar in its Skinner box° in order to receive food, which is the CR in many animal studies, is again clearly different than the rat's normal behavior in relation to food. And related to this is the fact that in instrumental conditioning the reinforcement is presented after the behavior occurs, so that partial reinforcement is possible, as it is not in classical conditioning.

The most significant distinction between the two methods is emphasized by Skinner. The behavior that is conditioned, usually by shaping, in instrumental procedures did not obviously occur in response to a stimulus. In classical conditioning the UCS is known: food, for example, or an acid solution, which causes the dog to salivate. But if one wants to shape a pigeon's twirling movements by instrumental methods one does so by shaping whatever turning occurs—and the UCS for the bird's turning movements is not usually known. Skinner recognizes, of course, that the turning behavior does not arise out of nowhere. It does indeed have its stimulus, somewhere in the bird's functioning, but the UCS does not have to be known by the experimenter in order for the behavior to come under control. For this reason, in Skinner's view, instrumental conditioning opens up the possibility of training animals and humans in a very wide range of behaviors.

The limits of conditioning

As we saw in Chapter 1, particularly in the discussion of the Brelands' work, there appear to be built-in constraints on what some animals can do or can be trained to do. We will discuss first this kind of limit on conditioning, and then a related distinction, between voluntary and involuntary behavior.

---

3. As emphasized especially by ethologists, there may be genetically fixed constraints on animal behavior and learning.

Side by side with laboratory approaches to the study of human and animal learning, there has developed over the past few decades a biological discipline called *ethology*. It is based primarily on field studies of animal behavior. Its theory consists of a combination of evolutionary principles and inferences that are drawn from observations and controlled studies in the animals' natural habitats.

In one important series of studies, Tinbergen[10] has described the behavior shown by a little fish, the three-spined stickleback. Some of its courtship and mating behavior is fixed—the female's approach to the male when she produces eggs; the male's construction of a small nest of stones; an approach–retreat pattern between female and male until she deposits the eggs in the nest; the male's fertilizing of the eggs; and the separation of female and male as soon as this phase is completed. But subsequent aspects of the sequence are less fixed. The male now has responsibility for guarding the nest with its eggs until they hatch. Under these circumstances, the male's behavior must be more flexible, for there is no way to determine precisely what the danger will be or from where it will come. The

Skinner box. A simple box designed by Skinner that has a bar or other device at one end that, if manipulated by the subject (usually some small animal), produces reinforcement.

major danger is that another male stickleback will appropriate the nest and its eggs or at least try to take over that spot of territory for its own nest. During this phase of their annual cycle, male sticklebacks display a red belly, and this stimulus serves as a trigger, or releaser,⊙ for the homeowner's fiercest display of possessiveness. Experimental studies have shown that in this situation the male stickleback will attack almost any small, moving object that is painted red on its underside.

One may ask whether the flexibility of behavior shown by the stickleback shows learning or simply a process of discrimination. Here the evolutionary emphasis found in ethology becomes evident. One of its major theorists, Konrad Lorenz,[11] describes two kinds of learning. On the level of the species, there is a kind of evolutionary "learning" that has taken place through millennia of time. In this form of "learning," the process of natural selection plays the role that personal experience usually plays in the life of the individual. On the level of the individual, conditioning may take place during normal behavior, depending on the ongoing circumstances. In the case of individual behavior, however, major forms of behavior are only released, or triggered, by appropriate stimuli. They were there waiting, so to speak, as in the case of the male stickleback's response to a red-bellied "intruder," rather than being newly acquired, as in laboratory instances of conditioning. The ethological approach, in short, describes behavior with a very great emphasis on genetically fixed components, although allowing some room for alterations and variations based on individual learning within the limits imposed by instincts.

In support of their approach, ethologists point to studies on a wide range of animal species. This work suggests very strongly that in naturally occurring situations there are usually limits to the relations between a reinforcer and a response. Not all reinforcers reinforce, even when there is no obvious reason why they do not. Thus, many animals simply cannot be conditioned to do certain things that as far as we know they are physically capable of doing. Thorndike discovered this very early in his work: He was not able to condition cats to lick, although of course they are capable of the behavior itself (Figure 7.3).

The discovery of such limits on conditioning was perhaps a blow to early conditioning enthusiasts such as Pavlov, for the first successes in this field seemed to suggest that universal principles of animal behavior had been discovered. However, as the problem of limits is further explored, what seemed to be a setback to theories of learning has turned into a source of enrichment. As an example, in a study by Garcia and Koelling[12] rats were easily trained to associate electric shock with the flavor of specially sweetened water. They learned that if their drinking water tasted sweet they had better run into another compartment to avoid being shocked. However, they were unable to learn what seems to be a discrimination

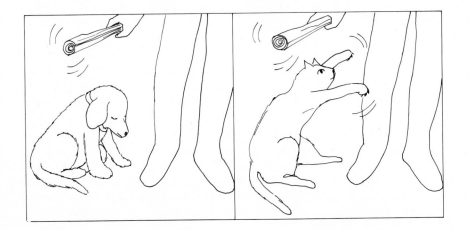

Fig. 7.3. Most dogs can be trained by means of punishment. If you try to train a cat by punishment, however, it will either strike back or run away. It is not that one animal is "smarter" than the other but that one is genetically equipped to be a pack animal and the other to be a lone hunter.

releaser. In ethology, a term used for a stimulus that triggers a cycle of instinctive behavior.

that is no more difficult: to associate the electric shock with an external, visual characteristic of the drinking situation — for example, the presence of flashing lights. They could not learn that if lights flashed while they were drinking they had better escape to avoid being shocked.

The explanation offered for this curious state of affairs is as follows. Rats are nocturnal animals with poor vision. Nature has simply not equipped them to be warned by visual means, although they are very well equipped indeed to attend to cues that come from their "internal" sources, such as taste. In fact, they even display a behavioral facility that is not as yet completely understood. If they should eat food that makes them ill, such as poisoned bait, they will thereafter avoid the food (or even the place) that caused the illness — although in this case the punishment may have occurred as much as twelve hours after the eating. It is hard to understand this in terms of conditioning, for here the UCS (food) and the UCR (illness) are quite separated in time.

4. There are two observably distinct kinds of behavior, one based on the musculature and largely voluntary, the other based on the autonomic system and seemingly involuntary. How they are related to conditioning is not yet clear.

The distinction between voluntary and involuntary behavior is very old. It has usually been assumed that some behavior, especially in humans, is fixed — by heredity, or by anatomical structure, for example — while other behavior is voluntary, or free. Learning theorists have done much to weaken this distinction by their emphasis on the universality of learning. The seemingly free act, they have argued, is only an act whose learning history is not fully known. If we knew its antecedents in the history of the individual, we would then see that it is no more (and no less) determined than those behaviors that we show as a result of our heredity.

However, in spite of these claims, there still seemed to be important distinctions between behavior that is carried out by the muscular-skeletal system (such as raising an arm) and other behavior carried out by the autonomic system (such as blushing). The development of two forms of conditioning, one seeming to be based on the organism's passive, involuntary response to the unconditioned stimulus and the other arising out of acts freely emitted, only emphasized again that behavior seemed to be of two kinds. It was discovered very early that classical conditioning worked very well on the autonomic nervous system, whereas for many years it was thought that autonomic responses were not subject to operant conditioning.

Thus a tradition arose. It was assumed that classical or respondent conditioning was applicable to involuntary acts, primarily of the autonomic variety and also including other kinds of fixed behavior, in which a specific unconditioned stimulus was keyed to a specific unconditioned response. Operant conditioning, on the other hand, appeared to apply to voluntary or freely emitted acts of the skeletal musculature, in which the relation between unconditioned stimulus and response was more variable. The distinction seemed so clear-cut and so basic that one prominent theorist, O. H. Mowrer, wrote it into an elaborate two-factor learning theory.[13]

There the matter rested until a series of experimental studies, followed by the procedure known as *biofeedback*,° cast some doubt on the neat distinction. Ac-

biofeedback. A process by which an individual can voluntarily regulate bodily processes such as brain waves or blood pressure by observing physiological processes one is normally unaware of.

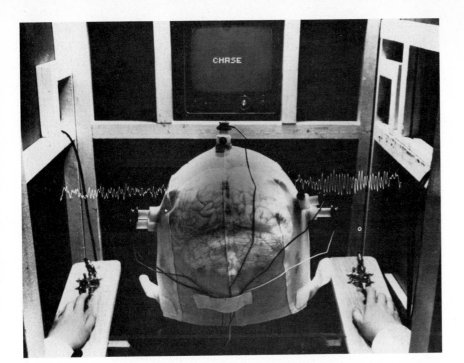

Fig. 7.4. The two hemispheres (or halves) of the cortex of the brain can produce different brain waves at the same time, as shown in this specially constructed photograph. Here a participant in an experiment is shown from the rear; the fissures of his cortex have been drawn on the cap he is wearing. He is asked to perform a difficult task involving verbal and perceptual discrimination. This kind of task involves primarily the left hemisphere (in right-handed persons.) The brain waves superimposed on the photograph show this distinction: in his left hemisphere, *beta* waves for a condition of alertness and problem solving, and in his right hemisphere *alpha* waves for a condition of relaxation. (Data from Rebert and Mahoney, 1978)

cording to a recent survey, nearly a hundred experimental studies have demonstrated autonomic conditioning by the use of operant procedures.[14] Biofeedback instruments, which were largely a spinoff of the technology developed in the American space program, made it rather simple to monitor most autonomic functions on a continuous basis (Figure 7.4). It was then easily shown that many autonomic functions, including heartbeat, blood pressure, skin temperature, and brain waves, could be conditioned by operant means. For example, Elmer and Alyce Green, while investigating migraine headaches, found that the pain experienced in this condition could be greatly alleviated if people were trained to lower their blood pressure at the first warning symptom of the headache.[15]

If there are two types of behavior, then, the voluntary and the involuntary, they are clearly not related in any simple way to the two major forms of conditioning. It has been suggested, as one way out of the puzzle, that there is really no such thing as voluntary behavior. Or, stated in another way, it is sometimes said that a science of psychology does not need a notion such as "voluntary." According to this view, both classical and operant conditioning are mechanistic or automatic processes in which individual will never appears. For example, if I become frightened when I see a snake, that is my "automatic" response, caused by certain events that occurred in my life. Similarly, if I "voluntarily" raise my arm because I feel like doing it, that behavior too is the "automatic" result of my past history. The only reason we call the first of these acts *involuntary* and the second *voluntary* is that we know the antecedents and causes of one but not of the other. If we knew in complete detail the antecedent history of any organism, we would see clearly that all behavior is determined, just as much as is the behavior of the pigeon that we have conditioned. This view has been argued most convincingly by Skinner.[16]

The significance of the distinction between voluntary and involuntary behavior is that the question is still unsettled. Even the terms are still in dispute, as we have seen. What is suggested by the present nature of the problem is that there are evident limits on what is known about the process of conditioning and perhaps about what it can accomplish.

Contiguity and conditioning

We have now presented, rather sketchily, an introduction to the basic concepts and procedures in conditioning. But this is by no means the whole of the field of learning. It has turned out that the conditioning procedure is not simply a training method (although it is certainly that) but is also a very fertile ground for raising and exploring important questions of *theory*. One of the major developments in modern learning theory has to do with the concept of contiguity and, alternatively, with the concept of information.

The term *contiguity*© refers to a basic and apparently necessary element in conditioning. This procedure seems to require that the learner be able to make a series of associations. In Pavlov's arrangement, the dog has to be equipped to associate, without training, the smell of food (UCS) and the action of the salivary glands (UCR). Then, an association has to be made between the UCS and the CS (a bell). Finally, and as a consequence, a link is formed between the CS and the CR (salivating). In order for these links to be formed, the elements must be presented together (or contiguously), either spatially or temporally and preferably both. A similar argument can be made for instrumental conditioning—that contiguity of the different elements is required in order for the procedure to be effective. This issue is now in question.

5. An issue of current importance is whether learning in conditioning takes place via contiguity or via access to information.

Consider a seemingly simple conditioning experiment, reported by Garcia, Kovner, and Green.[17] Their apparatus consists of a box divided into two compartments, with an opening in the wall between them. Within each compartment, there is nothing but a floor grid, wired so that the animal can be shocked when standing on it, and a little bottle for the animal to drink out of. Rats used as subjects in this experiment were deprived of water until they were quite thirsty, and in this condition they were dropped into one of the compartments for training. One compartment's water bottle had water flavored to taste sweet, and the other had water flavored so as to be slightly salty, an easy discrimination for rats to learn. In the training, the two kinds of water were varied from one compartment to the other, but no matter which compartment it was in one of the flavors was always paired with shock. Within two seconds of the rat's attempt to drink water of that flavor, the shock was applied to the floor. The animal, of course, immediately scurried into the other compartment, where it was permitted to drink peacefully for two minutes.

Here was a straightforward instance of classical conditioning. Shock is a "natural," or unconditioned stimulus (UCS) for a shock-avoidance response (UCR). When shock was paired with one of the two flavors, that flavor became the signal (CS) for the response of avoidance (CR). The animals would thus take one tentative lick at the water bottle, determine if it was a "safe" flavor or a "shock" flavor, and then either stay to drink or run into the other compartment to drink (and to avoid being shocked).

In the language of classical conditioning, we would say that the taste of one flavor had become a CS for avoidance. Just as a dog was trained to salivate at the sound of a bell, so the rat would now turn away when offered a drink of the "shock" flavor. Now for the key question: What if the rat is later offered this

contiguity. The occurrence of stimulus-response elements close together in time in order for the learning process to be facilitated.

"shock" flavor of water, not in the training box but back in its home cage? It turns out, quite surprisingly, that the animal has no objection to the water but drinks it as though the training had never occurred.

The explanation for these results that has been offered by some psychologists is this. Apparently the animals did not learn to associate flavor with shock. The phenomenon has been termed *blocking*, referring to an associative block in the course of the animals' learning. The rats did learn when to stay and drink or when to run into the other compartment, but the association(s) responsible for the learning may have been other than "flavor = shock." Other stimuli in the situation, it is suggested, do the job, thus blocking the effect of shock as a stimulus.

It is apparent that this explanation preserves all the elements of standard conditioning, including in particular the notion of contiguity. Now we turn to an alternative explanation that has been offered of the same kind of experimental result, this one in effect deemphasizing the importance of contiguity.

The role of information. In a series of studies and some theoretical papers, Rescorla[18] has reexamined the elements of the conditioning situation. A typical experiment is arranged as follows.[19] First, a rat is taught to press a bar, in a Skinner box, in order to receive food. Next, the rat is trained by instrumental procedures to press the bar only when a tone is sounded (CS), in order to receive food. In a third step, the experimenter pairs shock (UCS) with the tone, with the result that the rat very soon learns *not* to press the bar when the tone is sounded. Under these circumstances, referred to as *conditioned suppression*, the rat shows many signs of fear and, of course, no longer displays its learned ability at bar pressing to get food.

On the basis of these preparatory stages, it is now possible to make a crucial test. As we have just described, the usual procedure consists of pairing the shock with the tone; each time the tone sounds, it is followed very shortly by the shock. But suppose that instead of this regular pairing, the tone and the shock are programmed to appear on different schedules: The tone appears regularly, as before, but the shock appears both together with the tone and at random intervals between tones as well. The result is that the shock loses its value as UCS, and conditioned suppression no longer occurs. The rat now learns to press the bar when a tone sounds, just as though no shock were used at all.

Rescorla argues that if it were simply a matter of contiguity his arrangement provides this: The shock still appears together with the tone. The result should be the same as in the usual experiment, and conditioned suppression should occur. But apparently this is not what happens. Now that the shock appears both with the tone and without the tone, tones have lost their ability to serve as a signal that shock is coming. What has been changed in the new arrangement is the *informational* value of the tone-and-shock combination. The rat can no longer predict when the shock will appear, because the information that was previously carried in the tone is no longer available (see Figure 7.5).

This new element, the amount of information available to the rat, is the basis for important developments in the field of learning. To interpret learning experiments with rats and pigeons in terms of their search for information or their ability to predict what will happen is to emphasize *cognitive* processes that had very little place in more traditional theories. In order to see how far such an interpretation can be extended, we may consider Restle's explanation of the Rescorla experiment.

Restle[20] notes that there may be more than one kind of information that is available to the rat in Rescorla's arrangement. There is information about the "content" of the situation—in this case, about the relation between a stimulus and its context. But there is also information available about the "time segments" of the procedure. One characteristic of every procedure is that there are time periods

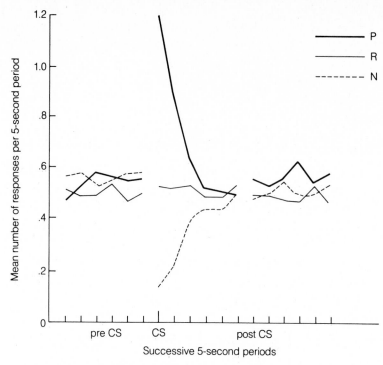

Fig. 7.5. The average number of
responses given by three groups of dogs, in
Rescorla's experiment (see text). (From
Rescorla, 1966, p. 384)

when something is happening, but there are also time periods when nothing is
happening. Silence may present as much information as activity. In a conditioning
experiment, one usually pays attention to the time period when the UCS and CS
occur but ignores the time period when no-UCS and no-CS also occur together.
Restle would say that the animal learns as much from the latter as from the
former, for both contain information.

Thus, in Rescorla's experiment, the UCS (shock) occurs together with the CS
(tone), as is known. But equally, in this experiment UCS (shock) occurs together
with no-CS (no-tone), and no-UCS (no-shock) sometimes occurs together with no-
CS (no-tone). A rat trying to extract as much informational value as possible from
this situation is not likely to discover much that refers to the links between tone
and shock—and so the rat will not "learn" that tone means shock. Therefore the
presence of the shock will not suppress the rat's conditioned behavior of bar pressing at the tone to get food.

In spite of its apparent complexities, this analysis is straightforward in its
implications. It suggests that what may be happening even in the case of the lowly
laboratory rat is not a process of "thoughtless" stamping in of connections in the
brain. Rather, the rat may be actively involved in its own form of problem solving,
decision making, and information evaluating—all cognitive processes that had
formerly been deemphasized in learning theory.

Helplessness and control

6. Unpredictable situations, like unavoidable
punishments, can have severe negative consequences in
both animals and humans.

We have referred to the laboratory animal's ability to predict (on the basis of
the information available) what is going to happen or how one event is related to

another. Now, to state that an animal such as a rat is involved in a cognitive activity such as prediction is to imply that it is able to make some connection between its own response and the consequences of that response. One way to test whether the animal is capable of making such a connection is to put it in a situation in which no connection of this kind can possibly be made — and then to test out the consequences.

Reasoning along these lines has led to a very productive area of research. What is usually shown is that if the animal experiences a situation of unpredictability, it then appears to become unable even to use its normal capacities for figuring out what is happening. Specifically, if you subject a laboratory animal to shock that is not only unavoidable but also unpredictable, it will become so demoralized or disorganized that it will not avoid shock even when this possibility is presented. The consequences of the nonpredictable–nonavoidable situation are devastating. One test of what happens to the animal, under these circumstances, was Lockard's[21] experiment, in which it was shown that rats who were going to receive shock anyway much preferred to receive it in a compartment in which it came on a regular basis. This is understandable, because it is probable that if shock is at least predictable the animal will be able to make some preparatory adjustments so as to lessen the punishment.

In a series of studies, Seligman has used this experimental situation to develop a theory of what he termed *learned helplessness*. Dogs are used as experimental animals. They are first subjected to unavoidable and unpredictable shock, and then they are tested on the consequences for their adaptive behavior.[22] The results show clearly the central importance of the dog's cognitive processes even under these extreme conditions. If the circumstances are such that the dog "becomes convinced" that no control or predictability is possible, it becomes disorganized and is unable to show adaptive behavior even under neutral conditions. But if it is permitted to learn any means of controlling the events, even though it still receives as much shock as before, its later behavior is more organized and adaptive.

Seligman has extended these studies to human behavior as well. He and his colleagues[23] have shown that if the affected animal is in some way induced or even forced to make some adaptive response (for example, by pulling it on a leash out of the shock compartment and into a "safe" compartment) it will then begin to recover its adaptive behavior. The implication for human behavior is its relation to instances of severe depression. People who are severely depressed act in many ways like the dogs in Seligman's studies. They often cannot be induced to make any adaptive responses to events that are clearly nonthreatening. It is suggested that the background of their condition may have been a period of time in which, from their own point of view, unpredictable and unavoidable punishment was inflicted on them. The consequence would have been a state of disorganization. Treatment might then consist of pulling them through "safe" areas of conduct, so to speak, so that they begin to relearn modes of adaptive behavior.[24]

On rewards and expectancies. Much of what we have just been discussing consists of looking at the learning process from an inside viewpoint. We have taken the point of view of the rat, or the dog, who is being conditioned. Recent trends in what may be called a *cognitive approach* to learning theory have emphasized factors that can best be understood from this inside view — factors such as prediction, problem solving, and expectancies. It will now be useful to extend this line of thought.

One way of describing expectancy, from the point of view of the individual, is that it consists of some changing balance between two sets of observed circumstances: on the one hand, the way things are now, and on the other hand, the way things actually turn out. Thus, one might refer to a continuing and changing *expectancy balance*. We suggest that, in the course of learning, reinforcements

Table 7.1. Determinants of the expectancy balance. The four major possibilities relating expectancy and reward: In Condition 1 ($+/+$), you expect to get the reward, and then you do—expectancy balance is good. In Condition 2 ($+/-$), you expect to get the reward, and then you do not—expectancy balance is poor. In Condition 3 ($-/+$), you do not expect the reward, but you get it. In Condition 4 ($-/-$), you do not expect to get the reward, and you do not.

		Receiving the reward	
		Yes	No
Expecting the reward	Yes	(1) $+/+$	(2) $+/-$
	No	(3) $-/+$	(4) $-/-$

have their effects primarily by the way they affect the expectancy balance. When we state the situation in this way, we can formulate the major possibilities, as in Table 7.1. Expectancy can be relatively high or relatively low, and the reward obtained can be relatively good or relatively poor; hence the four possibilities shown.

The first possibility, in which the reward is expected and it is then received, covers the cases that are explained in terms of the law of effect. What usually happens is that at the outset of the learning, expectancy is relatively low (the animal surely does not know it will be rewarded), but the reward shows up anyway. Learning then proceeds—but as expectancy rises and we have the arrangement shown in Condition 1, the pace of learning levels off. Finally, when expectancy is as high as it will get (certainty regarding the reward), nothing more can happen. At this point, too, satisfaction is likely to decrease, for one does not usually get much pleasure out of receiving something that one was certain to receive anyway.

We can see, from a comparison of Conditions 1 and 3, how partial reinforcement is related to the learning process. As we have mentioned, it has long been known that if learning takes place under conditions of partial reinforcement what was learned is more difficult to extinguish. In terms of Table 7.1 partial reinforcement constitutes a case in which the learner cannot have too high an expectation. The situation is somewhere between Conditions 1 and 3. It is probable that under these circumstances, learning is more effective than under Condition 1, which is more like 100 percent reinforcement. A human analogy suggests itself here: When I sit down to the table for dinner, I expect food, and I always get it. Under these conditions, I am not likely to learn, only to be satisfied.

An equally important possibility is shown in Condition 3, in which expectation is low or minimal, but the reward occurs anyway. For example, animals that have been led to expect punishment, or that are suddenly switched from a no-reward to a reward condition, and are then given the reward for some behavior, learn very rapidly. Similarly, the reverse situation, shown in Condition 2, produces very rapid and often longlasting effects. For example, if a monkey is presented with food and prepares to eat (high expectation of reward) but is then unexpectedly given what amounts to a punishment (shown a snake while eating), the result is immediate, severe, and permanent. Monkeys treated in this way, or cats who are shocked while eating, may be reduced to a situation in which they will refuse to eat and will starve in the presence of available food.

Examination of our own experience suggests that we usually attempt to understand what is happening, or the behavior of ourselves or others, by figuring out the causes. (The process of attributing causes will be discussed at length in Chapter 18, as a major topic of experimental study in social psychology.) The evidence we have been reviewing in this chapter suggests that similar processes may also occur in the case of animals other than human. It appears that much of our behavior in general, and in particular our learning behavior, depends on the nature of our expectancies (for example, if I fully expect failure in a situation, I am unlikely to begin) and, equally, that our response is related to our perception of the control we have over some reinforcement. Thus, an event that is unpredictable (meaning that I do not perceive myself as having control over its occurrence) will be experienced as more stressful than an equally unpleasant event whose occurrence I can predict. This was shown in the studies of "executive monkeys," reported in Excursion 2.

An interpretation of learning that stresses the elements of expectancy and personal control has been offered under the general concept of *locus of control.*[25] For example, if I see no connection between my success in a task and my own efforts, perhaps because I view my success as purely a chance matter, reinforcement of my behavior may have little effect on my skill; I will not learn easily nor quickly. But, if I am convinced that my skill enters into my success, which implies that some of the control may be found in my own efforts, then reinforcement will influence what I do, and I can be shown to learn.

If one believes that the locus of control in a situation is external rather than the result of one's own efforts, a gap is immediately created between reinforcement and behavior. For example, if you try to condition me to raise my arm to the sound of a bell but you do it forcibly, by raising my arm each time the bell sounds, I will perceive the locus of control as in your action rather than in mine. My actual behavior, raising my arm, might be the same as though I had raised it on my own account, but my behavior will not become conditioned to the sound of the bell. In general, the law of effect does not predict when conditioning will occur if the individual perceives the locus of control as being external. This is one reason why not all reinforced behaviors will be learned.

In summarizing, we may say that recent developments in animal learning theory, as well as consideration of the human learning situation from the inside viewpoint, converge in emphasizing what we have called *cognitive elements.* These include the individual's expectancies, processes such as problem solving, hypothesis making, decision making, planning, and predicting, and the individual's sense of control over events. It has been shown repeatedly that, when given a choice, animals prefer signaling conditions that are reliable—that is, signals that each contain the maximum amount of information. Like humans (who stop watching the thermometer if it gives no new information, as when the weather is always the same), laboratory animals make use of signals, or choose signals, to the degree that they help predict whether something will or will not occur. Both humans and animals, then, appear to seek out information in order to increase the predictability of their environments and thus extend their control over their own behavior.

Social learning theory

A cognitive emphasis in learning is not completely recent. Scattered evidence has always been available to suggest that the learning process as it was studied in the laboratory may have made the test animals seem more like machines and less like cognitive information processors than they really were. (A good example is Thorndike's work with cats: He placed them in the one kind of situation calculated to make them act inefficiently and therefore become frantic.) A major figure in learning studies before World War II, Edward Tolman, once went so far as to suggest that even the rat learned a maze by generating a "cognitive map" in its

locus of control. Rotter's term for where the individual places causation and life consequences. Persons with an *internal locus* see causation as part of their own destiny. Persons with an *external locus* are more apt to look outside themselves for causation.

Fig. 7.6. Which of these children is more likely to learn—the one staring out the window, the one fearful of the teacher's punishment, or the one seemingly interested in working? We suggest that the first child is not in the situation at all and therefore will not learn anything; that the second is in the situation of "If I don't do this work, I'll get hit" and so will probably learn to do the lesson but will not learn the lesson; but that the third, who is in the situation of learning, will learn. It is a matter of the learner's psychological situation.

brain. Learning, he said, was less a matter of stamping in some brain connections than of expectancies, hypothesis making, and even mental imagery.[26]

Some criticisms of contemporary learning theory have also rested on taking cognitive processes into account. Typical of these is the criticism leveled by Levine and Fasnacht[27] in regard to what is called *token learning*.[○] Suppose that by threatening you, I force you to mark *X*'s on a sheet all day long. If you were asked whether this labor is worth doing, you would probably reply, "Of course not. I'm only doing it because I have to." Normally, however, this is not the case. If someone asks us whether what we are doing right now is worth doing, we would usually say that it is. Now, under these normal circumstances what happens if someone rewards you for it anyway?

Evidence from many studies indicates that when unnecessary reward is given, the person's attitude changes. One begins to lean toward the view that the activity was not worth doing without the reward. And if the reward is *then* withdrawn, the person may well stop doing it—even though there would have been no problem in continuing if no reward had been given in the first place. This is very like what happens when children are given rewards for doing chores around the house. Without the reward, they might have learned that the chore had to be done anyway and was even worth doing. But once the reward is given for what they have been doing anyway, the task loses meaning and they learn to work only for the reward. Token rewards, it has been said, may therefore lead only to token learning (see Figure 7.6).

token learning. In operant conditioning, an arrangement whereby a token of some sort (a secondary reinforcer) is exchanged for a primary reinforcer, such as food.

7. Social learning theory emphasizes individual values and expectancies as a basis for the continuous process of learning in real life.

An important recent attempt to emphasize cognitive processes and thus to take account of some of the issues we have discussed, is *social learning theory*.[☉] The term was introduced by Neal Miller, an experimental psychologist, and John Dollard, a sociologist, in a work in which they tried to restate Freud's psychoanalytic theory in terms of a learning theory.[28] Some years later, Julian Rotter and his colleagues,[29] also combining a clinical and an experimentalist approach, developed a general theory of development under the same name. Most recently, in the productive years following the impact of Skinner's formulations, Albert Bandura has been among the most influential in elaborating the social learning approach as a general theory of human behavior.[30]

The original formulation by Rotter was as follows. An individual's behavior is determined primarily by the value of the goals that are sought and the individual's expectancy of achieving those goals. According to this view, we exert our efforts only in regard to goals that we perceive as worth striving for and that either offer us some challenge in the effort or show some reasonable possibility that they can be achieved. The amount of our effort will depend on the value of the goal, as we perceive it, and on our expectation of reaching the goal—although these relationships may be quite complex in real life. Both the value and the expectancy are developed by each individual on the basis of past experience, which becomes increasingly refined as the individual accumulates more experience. This process of learning, now understood more broadly than as mere conditioning, includes cognitive processes as major elements. Automatic, "accidental" instances of conditioning and learning are therefore not typical but rather unusual, often caused by restricted circumstances.

To the question of how learning occurs, Bandura has offered a similar but in some ways more elaborate answer. He emphasizes, first, that whatever learning takes place in the course of someone's life is an ongoing process. Learning is only rarely a one-shot, all-or-none affair. What happens in real life, instead, is that conditioning may occur and lead to a change in someone's behavior, but their behavior in turn then changes the circumstances of their environment. This now leads to the possibility of further conditioning, which again produces environmental changes, in a continuing, cyclic process. Neither the individual nor the environment is the cause of learning and change, but rather both are, in an endless and productive interchange.

A second major element in Bandura's view is that human learning need not depend on the individual having a direct contact with a stimulus situation. More often, particularly in the learning that takes place in childhood, the major process is modeling.[☉] As Bandura and others have shown in many experimental studies, children learn rapidly and thoroughly simply by having the opportunity to observe another person do something (Figure 7.7). If the behavior is something they feel positive about doing and if the other person is liked or admired or perceived as significant, they will imitate the behavior. Thus, the incredibly complex array of

Fig. 7.7. These still pictures, from film showing the effects of modeling, indicate how well children may learn to act aggressively. (From Bandura, Ross, and Ross, 1963, p. 8)

social learning theory. Rotter's extension of learning theory to involve social standards, social behavior, and expectancies.

modeling. A behavior modification technique, developed by Bandura, that stresses imitation and observation.

behaviors that seem to be learned so quickly by the growing child need not be attributed to specific instances of conditioning but to a more general process of learning by modeling.

A number of very important consequences follow from this conception. The first is the logical consequence that persons who can observe others can also observe themselves. The way is then open to including in social learning theory the spectrum of self-observational and self-regulatory processes by which people organize, control, and even change their *own* behavior. As we shall see in Chapter 17, where we discuss the various behavioral therapies, many effective clinical techniques have been built on this development in theory. A second consequence stemming from the conception of observation and modeling is that it leads to a more complete picture of humans than is offered by traditional conditioning theory. People can only learn through observing and modeling on others if they are capable of perceiving their social environment in special ways. They must be able to understand the causes of another's behavior, to separate the essential from the irrelevant, and to infer with reasonable accuracy the other's motives. Learning, even the modeling that begins to occur in early childhood, implies that the learner already possesses and uses a range of developed cognitive abilities.

Summary

1. In classical conditioning, a genetically given response relationship is changed to a new relationship between the response and an arbitrary stimulus.

2. In instrumental conditioning, spontaneously emitted behavior comes under the control of an arbitrarily selected stimulus.

3. The law of effect states that what gets learned is that which produces an effect, most often in the form of a reward.

4. Partial reinforcement results in learning that is more resistant to extinction than learning under 100 percent reinforcement.

5. Compared to classical conditioning, the CR and the UCR are less likely to be similar under instrumental conditioning.

6. The two major forms of conditioning are first, classical, respondent, or Pavlovian and, second, instrumental, operant, or Skinnerian.

7. The UCS is known in classical conditioning and is usually unknown in instrumental conditioning.

8. Under natural conditions, there are usually some limits to the possible relations between a reinforcer and a response; not every response can be reinforced nor can every response be conditioned.

9. After much controversy, it is now accepted that autonomic functions can be modified by both classical and instrumental procedures.

10. Traditional learning theory explained conditioning in terms of contiguity — that is, the occurrence together (in time and/or space) of two events so that an association was formed between them.

11. An important current trend in learning theory explains conditioning in terms of the informational value that one event has for another.

12. Situations that are either unpredictable or involve unavoidable punishment often have severe negative consequences, for both animals and humans.

13. Severely "depressed" animals can be retrained in modes of adaptive behavior by compelling them to go through the feared and avoided behavior. A similar consequence is implied for humans.

14. In general, human learning depends largely on the nature of our expectations and the control we experience over our reinforcements.

15. Animals as well as humans prefer signals that enable them to predict the course of events, presumably to allow them to make preparations.

16. Rotter's form of social learning theory suggests that an individual's behavior is determined by the value of the goals that are sought and the individual's expectancies of achieving the goals.

17. Bandura has shown that children learn rapidly and effectively through the process of modeling, based on observation of another person performing the act.

To begin to understand memory, we will consider three processes: retrieval, storage, and encoding. Traditional studies in memory will be reviewed, and the concept of the memory trace will be elaborated. It will be indicated that remembering and forgetting are two sides of the same event. Since the process of encoding starts off the remembering sequence, we will offer some practical advice on encoding to improve remembering and reduce forgetting. Finally, we will present arguments against the concept of the memory trace and indicate how it might be absorbed into the notion of encoding.

In this chapter, you will learn that there are two ways to experience retrieval, through recall and through recognition, and two major stages of storage, short term and long term. Moreover, the significance of a target will be shown to be a major determinant for how well you remember or forget.

Toward the end of the chapter, we will reconsider traditional conceptions of memory. A case will be made for dropping the stage of storage from a theory of remembering. In its place, you will be introduced to the notion that retrieval depends primarily on the way that one encodes. In conclusion, we will point out that the effectiveness of encoding depends, in turn, on relative degrees of one's distancing, participation, and grasp of the significance of remembered material.

8

Remembering: the old and the new

The two pictures on Page 169, Figures 8.1a and 8.1b, were done by William Blake, the great British artist and poet. The top portrait was drawn when Blake was a fourteen-year-old apprentice engraver, learning his trade by copying monuments. The portrait below it was done forty-nine years later, when Blake was sixty-three years old and used to amuse himself and his friend John Varley by calling up what he called "visionary heads." These were visual images of persons who "sat" for him at his wish—and in this case the subject of the portrait represented a visual memory that had persisted with remarkably little change for almost half a century.

We are likely to be a little astonished at Blake's ability to maintain this image and then to summon it forth at will. However, we are not likely to think that there are any difficult or important theoretical problems hidden in this dramatic instance of remembering. Of all the topics in psychology, it is probable that nothing seems to us so obvious, so free of unanswered questions, as memory. There is a well-known Zen Buddhist tale that nicely sums up this commonsense view of memory while containing significance as well. It concerns two monks who, while walking in the rain, came across a beautiful girl who was unable to ford the river. One of the monks, Tan-Zan, immediately picked her up and carried her across, then accepted her thanks and caught up with his fellow monk, Eki-Do. The latter, however, was silent and remained so until late at night, when they found lodging. Finally Tan-Zan asked him what was bothering him. Eki-Do said, "You would touch a woman, especially a young one." "Ah," said Tan-Zan. "Now I see. But I left the girl back at the river. Why are you still carrying her?"

This is the usual, commonsense theory of memory. At a point in time I take in some details of an event and I carry this with me as a recollection, much as the

Fig. 8.1. Are these two portraits similar? (See the discussion in the text.)

monk in our story "carried" the young girl all day. Then, at a later time, I reach back into my store of memories and bring some portion into my awareness as a memory. The process does not always work perfectly, as we well know. Thus, we may forget something completely or remember it only hazily or in part or even incorrectly. These lapses seem to be related to many factors, such as our age, the significance of the original event, the time that has elapsed, and perhaps our individual ability to remember. In general, however, the commonsense scheme just described would seem to explain the process of remembering. As a convincing demonstration, we have only to offer the example of your mother's maiden name: If you were now asked for it, you would have no difficulty recalling it, although you have probably not been thinking of it during the last few minutes. Clearly, it was "stored away," as one of your many remembered details, ready to be recalled on demand.

But is the matter really this simple and straightforward? In this chapter, we will try to show that the process of remembering and recalling is almost miraculously complex. Thus, our treatment of the topic will require a shift away from the straightforward, commonsense view that was just outlined, but, as we will try to show, the shift is worth the effort. It makes possible a broader understanding of other topics in cognition, and even of the process of development and growth.

To pursue this argument, we need first of all to agree on some terms. In this chapter, then, we will be using three central terms:

- *Retrieval.*⊙ The process by which material is recalled
- *Storage.*⊙ The process by which material is retained
- *Encoding.*⊙ The process by which material is originally taken in

In commonsense terms, these can be stated thus: You take something in, you keep it but put it aside, and you bring it back out. We will use these terms, as defined, even though it will be evident that they are not independent, either in theory or in practice. Encoding is the necessary condition for retrieval, and, equally, retrieval is the only way an experimenter can test whether encoding has occurred. It is not possible to retrieve material unless it has previously been encoded, and it is not possible to determine whether material has been encoded unless one retrieves it.

We will begin by summarizing the major trends in the history of traditional experimental studies of memory and forgetting. We will then be in a position to consider the problem of memory in the light of recent thinking and research. Finally, in our analysis of remembering, we will discuss the importance of one's experimental method. That is, we will examine the notion that how you study a set of problems often determines in large part what you will discover.

retrieval. The means of locating items in the memory and bringing them out.

storage. A stage of remembering in which material is stored for later retrieval.

encoding. The process of transforming input from the senses into a system that the memory can more easily process; for example, grouping numbers.

Fig. 8.2. The three major forms of
retrieval. The police lineup requires the
operation of recognition; the quiz show
demands recall; and the experience of
looking through an album of family
pictures often involves redintegration.

nonsense syllable. A syllable, usually
consisting of three letters (consonant,
vowel, and consonant), that has no
meaning in familiar languages.
Ebbinghaus developed this device for the
study of rote memorization.

savings method. A technique of
measuring retention in which the subject
relearns something previously learned.
The difference between the time it takes
to learn the material the first and second
times represents the savings.

We will do one other thing in this chapter. In order to bring home some of the
major points as they are made, we will present some memory experiments in the
page margins. They are easy to do and helpful in learning about remembering.
When you try them, you will notice that the instructions and material are given
on one page and the answers and discussion on one of the pages following, either in
the margin or in the text. The experiments will be clearly identified in each case.

Retrieval

**1. The two ways in which we experience
remembering (retrieving) something are from the
"inside," or recall, and from the object, or
recognition.**

How we retrieve memories depends on the circumstances surrounding our
remembering as well as on what we choose to do. Many memories simply pop into
mind unannounced, either as a part of the flux of thoughts and images that occupy
us all the time or as a result of being triggered by some detail of our environment.
In fact, if we simply let our mind wander, whatever then passes through our
thinking might properly be called *memory*. Thus, the most elementary distinction that can be made between kinds of retrieval is between *reproduction*, in
which we simply recover what is there in the "stream of thought," without
particular effort on our part, and *production*, in which we actively produce a
memory as a result of searching for it or deliberately reconstructing it. Psychologists have, in addition, described three distinct modes of retrieval: recall, redintegration, and recognition (Figure 8.2).

Recall. The most familiar mode of retrieval is recall and is the one that is used
most often in laboratory experiments on memory. It is the process that we go
through when we try to remember something, to bring it back to mind. How we
do this will depend on our aim at the moment—for example, whether we ask
ourselves for an item of trivia ("Who was the pianist in Rick's Bar in *Casablanca?*")
or recall a list of words *(free recall)*.

The experimental study of memory began with work on recall by Hermann
Ebbinghaus,[1] a German teacher and amateur scientist. In the 1880s, he began to
apply what was called the *new psychology* to elucidating the higher mental
processes. Untutored in scientific work or even in academic pursuits, Ebbinghaus
boldly and ingeniously developed his own methods, invented units of measurement, and produced results on which theories of memory rested for many decades.

The stimulus that Ebbinghaus invented is known as the *nonsense syllable.*⊙
Examples of nonsense syllables would be *noz, tek,* and *xad,* using two consonants
and one vowel; and *jowin, risab,* and *henut,* using double-syllable combinations.
Ebbinghaus coined 2,300 one-syllable units and used them as the material to be
memorized in his studies on himself.

Ebbinghaus' studies are remarkable for their elegance. His basic method was
to determine how many trials it took him to learn a list of his nonsense syllables to
some criterion; for example, to be able to recite it through twice without error. He
would then wait for some interval, which might be anywhere from 10 seconds to a
month, and then attempt to relearn the list. If any part of the original list had been
retained in memory, he would now need fewer trials to memorize the list to the
same criterion. This is called the *savings method*⊙ and provides a simple but effective method of quantifying the memory process.

With this technique, Ebbinghaus soon answered his basic question: Is there a usual rate at which memory lapses; that is, a rate at which forgetting usually occurs? If so, how does this rate relate to the passage of time? The answer is given in the so-called curve of forgetting, shown schematically in Figure 8.3. There we see that forgetting takes place most rapidly at the onset but less and less rapidly thereafter, until it bottoms out at a level where little forgetting occurs.

Ebbinghaus was also the first to notice, and measure, what has come to be

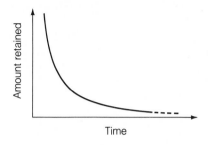

Fig. 8.3. Schematic rendering of the typical course of forgetting nonsense syllables over time. If you experience your school assignments as "nonsense," you may forget much of the material in the period immediately after memorizing it.

known as the *serial position effect.*⊙ This term refers to the fact that, in any organized sequence of items to be remembered, the most recent (or the last) material is remembered best, the material at the beginning next best, and the material in the middle least. In Memory Experiment A, this should have been the result that you obtained. It has been shown that as long as the items on a list are approximately equal in ease of remembering the serial position effect is remarkably powerful. Whether the material to be remembered is entirely high or low in meaningfulness, whether it is presented through vision or hearing, or whether it is composed of words or numbers, all seem to make no difference to this effect.[2]

Redintegration. This, the second major mode of retrieval, is really the noun *reintegrate* with the letter *d* inserted for ease of pronunciation. It refers to a familiar retrieval phenomenon in which we recover the memory of some whole on the basis of stimulation by some part or aspect of it. The most famous example in literature occurs in Marcel Proust's novel *Remembrance of Things Past*, in which the smell of a cookie evokes in the narrator a flood of vivid and detailed memories of his childhood.

Redintegration is spontaneous rather than deliberate, and so it cannot be brought about by any specific method. For this reason, it is not usually used as a technique in experimental studies of memory. Redintegration is also the most personal of the retrieval methods, in the sense that only you yourself, possessed of your individual store of memories, can have any of them evoked by a specific detail. What may be a powerful cue for one person, such as a song that was popular when you were a sophomore in high school, may be either a different kind of cue or no cue at all for another. Because it is both uncontrolled and individually determined, the process of redintegration is not well understood. It may be more convenient to consider it not as a separate process but rather as a quality or characteristic of all our remembering. In general, this is what we seem to do whenever we remember, using a limited set of cues to remind us of a larger store of memories.

The closest we can get to controlled redintegration may be in the dramatic phenomenon known as *eidetic imagery* (or memory).⊙ This is a form of retrieval in which the person, having scanned a picture or drawing for 30 seconds or so, is able at a later time to call up the image, inspect it at will, and answer detailed questions about it. Eidetic imagery is not at all common. Fewer than 10 percent of young children have the capacity, and far fewer adults. Nor is it a process that resembles normal recollection and recall, for those who are capable of it go about it in an unusual way:

Memory experiment A: the serial position effect

For this experiment, you will need a 3-X 5-inch index card, a sheet of paper, and a pencil. On the sheet of paper, write down "List Number 1" and below that the numbers 1 to 10 in a column. Then write down "List Number 2" and below that the numbers 1 to 10 in a column. You are now ready.

Look at List No. 1, below. Memorize this list by reading it slowly, three times. Read the items out loud, at the rate of about one per second.

List No. 1. WOC — NER — KOV — QUG — FYM — FEP — DIB — KES — TEB — JID

Now, count up to 20, slowly. Then take your index card, turn over to Page 172, and immediately cover up List No. 1 in the margin. Read the instructions at the top of the margin, above List No. 1.

* * *

Now memorize List No. 2, below, in the same way that you previously memorized the first list.

List No. 2. BAZ — MEP — LUJ — VUS — JOF — NIZ — DOP — QEC — XAD — FID

Count up to 20, slowly. Now turn over again to Page 172, and with your index card cover up List No. 2 on that page. Again, follow the instructions at the top of the margin, above List No. 1.

serial position effect. The effect of position on learning a series of items. Items at the beginning and end of the series are easier to remember than the middle ones.

eidetic imagery (or memory). The ability to retain a sharp and detailed image or memory of something once seen and to call it up and scan it at will.

**Memory experiment A
(continued)**

With the list covered up by your index card, guess what the first item on the list is. *After* you make your guess, uncover the first item only and see if you were right. If you were right, make a check mark on your paper, under "List No. 1" next to 1. Then guess what the second item is, uncover that item only, check to see if you were right. If you were, make a check mark on your paper next to 2. Go through the List No. 1 in this way, one item at a time.

List 1. WOC — NER — KOV — QUG — FYM — FEP — DIB — KES — TEB — JID

Now, turn back to Page 171 and follow the instructions there, below the asterisks.

List 2. BAZ — MEP — LUJ — VUS — JOF — NIZ — DOP — QEC — XAD — FID

These are the results you should have obtained: You *should* have recalled the last item in each list, and you *may* have recalled the first item in each list, but you probably made errors in recalling the items in the middle of each list. This is known as the *serial position effect*.

1. They must scan the picture rather than stare at it, as we might, for example, if we want to produce an afterimage.
2. They can only encode it visually, and so their imaging is interfered with if they are asked to talk about the picture. This is unlike the ordinary processes of memory, in which encoding is aided by describing or otherwise organizing the material to be remembered (which is what good learners often do while studying — whisper some main points to themselves as they go along).
3. When they call back the image, they seem to go through a process of projecting it on a screen in front of their eyes, after which they rescan the screen to see things they had not noticed before.[3]

It is possible to test for eidetic imaging just as we might test for ordinary perceiving and recalling. However, a strict test to distinguish the two kinds of processes requires very careful control of the situation. One such set of experiments is reported by two researchers at Harvard, Stromeyer and Psotka,[4] who enlisted the services of a woman with apparently remarkable eidetic ability. She was able to maintain and "reproduce" vivid eidetic images, in varied colors, after a lapse of as much as twenty-four hours. To test her, the experimenters used materials originally developed by Edwin Land (the inventor of the Polaroid camera and polaroid glass). He had previously shown that if a 3- × 3-inch card of randomly placed gray dots is projected on a screen with red light and if there is superimposed on it another 3 × 3 card in green light, the resulting image on the screen contains colors that were not in the projecting lights. This was the task set to the eidetiker. On one day she was shown one card in a red light, the next day she was shown the other card in a green light, and later she was asked to call back the two images, superimpose them, and report what she could see. Her report of the resulting colors was precisely the same as the normal viewer might give if seeing the two at the same time, superimposed on a screen. It appears that some persons do have a special gift for redintegrative imaging that can depend on processes different from those used in ordinary retrieval.

Recognition. This third mode of retrieval may be the most familiar. It can be tested simply by asking the person to select a remembered target out of a number of choices. What the person then requires is to be able to recognize the correct target rather than call it up completely out of memory.

It is not always simple, however, to distinguish between a test of learning and a test of remembering. If someone once tried to learn something and is tested at a later time to see whether the learning took place, it might be difficult to distinguish between two different possibilities: On the one hand, the person might never have learned it in the first place; on the other hand, the person might have learned it once and then forgotten it. The most sensitive test of whether learning occurred in the first place is one that was used by Ebbinghaus. It consists of seeing how long it takes the person to relearn the material. If there was some learning originally, the relearning will go faster than it ordinarily might. The most sensitive test of remembering, on the other hand, is recognition. For example, if you learn a list of nonsense syllables and are later tested by a number of different methods, you will score higher if you are asked whether you recognize the syllables than if you are asked to reproduce them from memory. (This is the result you should have obtained in Memory Experiment B.)

Our ability to recall by way of recognition is quite remarkable. We recognize a face as familiar after a lapse of as much as twenty years. We recognize a very large number of details of our everyday environment as familiar or known. Or, as experimenters have shown, we correctly identify a thousand or more pictures as ones we have seen in a very long list that was previously shown. Other animals can perform equally prodigious feats of retrieval through recognition.

Recognition is a very common phenomenon, yet the ways in which it differs from other modes of retrieval are not easily understood in terms of traditional theories of memory. If memory consists of three processes operating one after the other—putting it in, keeping it there, and taking it back out—why should a memory be easier to retrieve if we are first shown what is wanted than if we are simply asked about it?

We suggest that the difference between recognition and other modes of retrieval can best be understood if we consider it from the inside, or from the point of view of the rememberer. Unlike other modes of retrieval, when something is recognized the act is accompanied by a feeling of familiarity. We have this feeling first, and then we recapture the memory. On the other hand, when we are asked to recall something, we recapture it first and only then may recognize it as familiar. Indeed, it is even possible to experience the feeling of familiarity but not to be able to carry it on to the next step, of recapturing the memory. This is what happens in the curious phenomenon known as *déjà vu,*[○] when we have the feeling that we have seen this before but cannot recapture the memory sufficiently to pin down how or where we have seen it. It is a kind of "half-recognition."

Equally curious is the fact that déjà vu is primarily a visual phenomenon. What happens in hearing is in some ways similar but it is accompanied by a quite different kind of feeling. When we hear an "old familiar tune" that we know we have heard before but cannot quite identify, our experience is not the rather uncomfortable one of déjà vu but rather the slightly frustrating one of *Name That Tune.* This has its own name, the "tip-of-the-tongue" phenomenon (which we will discuss more fully in a later section of this chapter), in which the central aspect of the experience concerns the recapture rather than the familiarity. In recognition, such as in cases of déjà vu, our experience of remembering is centered on the object; whereas in recall, as in instances of tip-of-the-tongue, our experience of remembering is centered on our remembering process.

Another important difference between recognition and recall as modes of retrieval is that recognition can only occur spontaneously. I can actively and deliberately recall something, but I can only hope or expect that recognition will occur. Trying to recognize something will usually not help at all. On the other hand, recognition requires less active "triggering" than does recall, and for this reason it may be more effective as a retrieval mechanism even though it cannot be brought into action at will.

Storage

2. A traditional view of how memories are stored calls on the notion of memory traces[○] and how they affect each other.

Perhaps it now begins to be apparent that many problems are hidden in what seems to be the straightforward process of remembering and recalling something. One problem has to do with the relation between the stages of retrieval and storage. During the period from about 1900 to 1950, theories of memory in American psychology were dominated by the ideas of Edward L. Thorndike. He taught that remembering was nothing but one automatically occurring stage in the process of learning. Whenever one was influenced by some stimulus, one or more "connections" were made in the brain if that stimulus was followed by a pleasant effect. Memory thus consisted essentially of the storage portion of the learning process.

Memory experiment B: recall and recognition

In this experiment, you will need a 3-×5-inch index card, a sheet of paper, and a pencil.

First, read List No. 1 below. Read it through *once only,* out loud, at the rate of about one word a second. When you are finished, close your eyes and count to 20, slowly.

List No. 1: girl—porch—car—pillow—hill—tree—pen—dog—window—shoe—pipe—cup—house—pencil

Cover up List No. 1 with your index card. Now write down all the words you remember from this list, in any order you like. Before you check your results, do the second part of the experiment.

For this part, read List No. 2, the same way that you read the first list. Read it through *once only,* out loud, about one word a second. When you are finished, close your eyes and count to 20, slowly.

List No. 2: door—dish—man—yard—shirt—table—cat—shade—paper—chair—box—pin—book—key

Now turn to Page 174 and follow the instructions there.

déjà vu. An illusion that a new situation or experience has happened before.

memory trace. A physical representation of memory on tissue of the brain. Also called *engram.*

**Memory experiment B
(continued)**

Look at the list of words below. If you see any words that appeared in the list you just read (List No. 2 on Page 173), check them.

When you have finished, turn back to List No. 2 on Page 173 to see how many you got right.

yard — sock — book — door — horse — table — pin — floor — boy — cat — key — sink — paper — chair — box — hair — dish — shirt — lamp — man

* * *

These are the results you should have obtained: On the basis of one reading, you should have been able to recall seven to ten of the items in List No. 1. However, on the basis of the same reading, using the method of recognition, you should have been able to remember ten or more of the items in List No. 2. This is due to the superiority of recognition over recall in remembering.

Some reports by patients when their brains were stimulated electrically (Penfield, 1959):

"There was a piano over there and someone playing. I could hear the song, you know."

"Something brings back a memory. I can see Seven-Up Bottling Company . . . Harrison Bakery."

"My mother is telling my brother he has got his coat on backward. I can just hear them."

"Yes, 'Oh, Marie, Oh, Marie!' Someone is singing it."

"Now I hear people laughing — my friends in South Africa!"

"Someone is speaking to another. He mentioned a name, but I could not understand it . . . It was like a dream."

engram. The memory trace that is supposedly imprinted in the brain.

The other two stages, encoding and retrieval, were ignored, as far as a theory of memory was concerned.

More recently, however, it has been shown that at least two of these stages, storage and retrieval, can be studied separately. It now appears that storage is not an automatic process, a kind of mechanical by-product of the input involved in learning, but a phenomenon in its own right that takes a measurable amount of time to occur. McGaugh[5] demonstrated this by the use of convulsive electric shock (similar to what is administered to some mental patients) on rats, a procedure that is known to destroy memory for recent events. The shock was administered at various intervals after the animals had learned a task, with the result that the greater a delay between learning and shock, the more of the learning was retained. A logical inference from these results is that the storage process, or the consolidation of some "trace" of what is learned, takes a measurable time to accomplish. Shock given immediately prevents any such imprinting of a storage trace, and the longer the shock is delayed the more of the event can be stored or the more firmly the storage is consolidated.

Traces. Clearly, the central notion regarding the stage that is called *storage* is the memory trace, or as it is also called, the *engram*© (literally "a marking upon"). If remembering involves some kind of storage, then there must be some form in which memories are stored. And, because we are all sure that processes such as these take place primarily in the parts of the central nervous system (not, let us say, in the endocrine glands or on the eardrum), the memory trace is usually pictured as some kind of imprint on the structure or the organization of the brain or the nervous system.

The notion of a trace seems so obvious and, indeed, so necessary a part of the memory process that it can be found as far back as there exist any writings on the subject of remembering. More than 2,000 years ago, Aristotle discussed the well-known fact that adults recall very little of their early childhood and the equally well-known fact that elderly persons may recall the events of their youth better than they recall what happened yesterday. Aristotle invoked the idea of traces as an explanation. In early childhood, he said, the material of the brain is too soft, so traces imprinted on it easily disappear. In old age, the brain material is too hard, so new traces are unlikely to be made. We may no longer accept his primitive notion of brain structure, but we still usually agree with Aristotle's conception of an imprint.

One of the most interesting kinds of evidence regarding memory traces comes from the work of a Canadian neurologist, Wilder Penfield,[6] who some years ago reported the results of mild electrical stimulation of specific brain areas in some of his patients. Originally undertaken in order to develop surgical procedures for the relief of epilepsy, Penfield's work took an unexpected turn when he found that the effect of an electrical probe on certain areas of the brain was to elicit sudden, unexpected flashbacks of early childhood experiences. The experience reported by the patients was quite dramatic. Almost as though a tape recorder had been switched on and off, their recalled experiences began and stopped with the presence or absence of stimulation by the surgeon's probe. In many instances, the patients reported that they seemed to be reliving the earlier experiences, and at other times they reported a kind of dual awareness in which they were simultaneously aware of themselves in the present and of their own memories being "replayed." In either case, it appears that neurologically active places, perhaps the seats of the memory traces of former events, were here being reactivated.

Storage theories. The major question in regard to the storage of memories is what happens to them. As we all know, we do not store everything that we could.

For example, you probably cannot recall every detail of every scene that you saw and heard during all of yesterday. But we do not even seem to retain everything that we do store. Traces may be made, but something seems to happen to them with the passage of time.

Common sense will explain this by telling us that the trace simply fades out. This view, known as the *decay theory*,⊙ has had its supporters through the centuries, but unfortunately the evidence against it is almost overwhelming. The decay theory contains two notions: first, the assumption that the mere passage of time will weaken traces and, second, the conclusion that less recent traces will therefore be either less vivid or totally gone. As regards the first assumption, we can be sure that memories are not necessarily obliterated just because they refer to events that took place many years ago. If we knew nothing about a memory except that it referred to a much earlier event, we would never be able to predict whether it would be remembered or not. Obviously other factors must play an important part in determining why, for example, you no longer recall the material you crammed for examinations in high school yet you can recall very well your tenth birthday party. As regards the second assumption, concerning the lessening vivid-

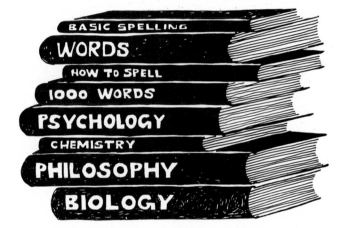

Fig. 8.4. In studying for an exam, if your aim is only rote memorizing, you should not study the books in sequence from the top. They are so much alike that they will produce both retroactive and proactive inhibition and thus interfere with remembering. Rather, you should study the books in the bottom half of the stack, or else skip around. But if your aim is understanding you would do better to start from the top, studying at one time the books that are alike.

ness of memories in direct relation to the passage of time, we know that this too is not supported. Most of our memories, in fact, are experienced at about the same degree of "vividness," regardless of how old they may be.

A much more plausible theory of what happens to traces is that they keep getting mixed up with other, newer traces. This view, often known as the *inter- ference theory*,⊙ has some good experimental evidence to support it. In a classic piece of research during the early days of American psychology, Jenkins and Dallenbach[7] reasoned that being awake provided more interference with traces than being asleep. They arranged to have two people learn tasks and then try to recall them after varying periods up to eight hours when they had been either asleep or awake. As predicted, forgetting was about the same for sleepers and nonsleepers during the two-hour period following learning. But for longer periods being awake markedly interfered with retention of the learned material.

Two kinds of interference are possible, and they have been given separate names. *Retroactive inhibition*⊙ refers to interference from some activity that occurs after something is taken in; for example, learning something and then subsequently learning something else. *Proactive inhibition*⊙ refers to inter- ference from some activity that occurred before something was taken in; for exam- ple, learning a Task A and then trying to memorize Task B (Figure 8.4). Whether the inhibition works forward or backward in time, the same general rule has been

decay theory. A theory of forgetting that hypothesizes that learned material fades away if unused.

interference theory. In learning, the theory that forgetting is caused by interference from other material.

retroactive inhibition. The process in which earlier learning is hampered by subsequent material that is learned.

proactive inhibition. The process in which the recall of new learning is interfered with by previously learned material.

Memory experiment C: the von Restorff effect

For this experiment, you will need only a sheet of paper and a pencil.

First, look at List No. 1, below. Read the list out loud, once and then again, at the rate of about one item a second. Then close your eyes and count to 20, slowly.

List No. 1: 19 — 92 — rin — 67 — 38 — 45 — dap — 74 — 21

Now close the book and write down all the items you remember from List No. 1, in any order you like. Then wait for about ten minutes before doing the next part.

* * *

For the next part, look at List No. 2, below. Just as you did before, read this list out loud, once and then again, at the rate of about one item a second. Then close your eyes and count to 20, slowly.

List No. 2: lat — 26 — sig — mol — 51 — lis — zum — feg — kas

Again, close the book and write down all the items you remember from List No. 2, in any order you like. Then wait for about ten minutes before doing the next part.

* * *

For the last part, look at List No. 3, below. Again, read the list through twice, out loud, one item per second. Then close your eyes and count to 20, slowly.

List No. 3: 13 — thirty-seven — 65 — eighteen — 78 — 24 — 31 — 82 — 49

Close the book and write down all the items you remember from List No. 3, in any order you like. Then turn to Page 178 for a statement about the results of this experiment.

von Restorff effect. The tendency of atypical items in a learning list to stand out and be learned more easily than the common items.

sensory register. Atkinson's and Shiffrin's term for the first stage in memory, which receives the visual stimuli and decays almost momentarily.

suggested: The more similar the interfering material is to the material to be remembered, the more interference it generates.[8] However, this should not be taken to imply that we are all condemned to go around in a state of perpetual confusion, for the studies from which these generalizations have been taken were mostly done using materials such as nonsense syllables. When more meaningful material is used, such as the kinds of verbal material that we are likely to encounter in everyday situations (such as something your best friend told you last week), similarity does not have an inhibiting but rather a neutral or even a facilitating effect. One practical consequence for academic learning is that if in your studying you experience the material as relatively meaningless, as something that you simply have to memorize in a rote fashion, you would be well advised to avoid interference by dividing it up into segments that are as diverse as possible.

Interference, whether in the form of retroactive or proactive inhibition, is a negative phenomenon in which the learning or memorizing of one thing interferes with that of another. But the phenomenon of interference may also be positive in its effects. This is what happens when one item or detail out of a sequence stands out so as to catch the rememberer's attention rather than to interfere with it. The result, which is known as the *von Restorff effect*,⊙ after the psychologist who first studied it, should be what you obtained in Memory Experiment C: You should have recalled best the items that stood out because they were different. It may very well be that much of our personal store of memories is organized in terms of multiple von Restorff effects. New material may be remembered because it stands out for us either perceptually or logically when we experience it. And, conversely, what does not stand out or what sinks into the background of our notice is not likely to be perceived or remembered. A clever propagandist will influence us, not with one or a few big lies, but with many small ones.

Encoding

---

3. Experimental evidence suggests that encoding is a process with two distinct stages—short term and long term.

Remembering, or so our common sense tells us, is a process of retrieving, of pulling something out of our personal storage. It is not a process of putting something into that storage. Thus, as common sense might dictate, earlier theories of remembering emphasized retrieval rather than encoding. It is only in more recent views of memory that encoding is seen as an important process that deserves to be studied.

The sensory register.⊙ The first step in encoding occurs at the point where information is processed by the different sensory systems. Their operation is apparently not instantaneous but consists of "holding" the input for some very brief but measurable period of time. In vision, for example, what we see does not completely disappear for nearly a tenth of a second. This may seem like a very brief period, but in fact it is what makes possible the phenomenon of motion pictures. Each successive frame of the movie replaces the one before it so rapidly that the earlier one has not yet faded out of perception, with the result that we perceive a continuous flow of movement rather than a series of different frames.

The first step of the encoding stage of memory is thus tied closely to all our other cognitive processes—attention, perception, selection, organization, and orienting. This holistic character of human functioning is important to keep in mind, because the necessity for breaking it up into chapters and sections, for purposes of a textbook, often gives the impression that the different processes go on independently. Keeping in mind that all behavior is a meaningful whole also reminds us that it takes place within the person's total, ongoing situation.

Most experimental work on memory is based on arrangements that simplify the situation. This is done by the use of nonsense syllables, for example, or by carrying out the experiments in the nondistracting conditions of a laboratory where strict control can be exercised over what it is that the person is asked to remember. Yet, as we know, most of the remembering of our lives does not occur as a result of what we memorize but as an unintended by-product of what we experience and do. If I know my wife's favorite color, it is not because I heard it and then made sure that I committed it to memory. If you remember what your home looks like, it is not because you went about trying to memorize its appearance but because you got to know it.

The difference between the two has been neatly tested in an ingenious study by Russian experimenters.[9] They observed children on a school playground and noted some of the things they did. Later, they brought the children into the laboratory and tested their memory for these things. Another group of children, from the same class as the first group, were now required to memorize in the laboratory the things the first group had done. They were then taken out on the playground and tested, after the same lapse of time, for what they remembered. As predicted, the first group recalled more, although their remembering had occurred apparently without any deliberate effort at it.

Short-term memory (STM). Suppose you look up a number in the phone book in order to make a call. If you are unable to write it down, you will probably repeat it a number of times to "keep it in mind." If anything interferes with this concentration, such as someone asking you something or your hearing other numbers, you may well lose it and have to look it up again. Then, by the time your call is finished, it is almost certain that you will have again forgotten the number.

This seems like a very inefficient system of memory. If our remembering process works this haltingly, how is it that we ever learn anything, much less remember it for long periods of time? Yet it is really a more effective mechanism than we might think. What is at work here is your short-term memory,[⊙] a kind of entryway into your memory that serves as a preliminary processor for whatever passes through your sensory register. How long it will retain incoming material depends on how significant the material is, the circumstances under which it was received, and what happens in the moments immediately following the input. But in any case your STM span is probably limited to less than a minute. In addition, it is also limited in capacity, as you can easily demonstrate for yourself by reading one telephone number, repeating it once, reading a second number, repeating both, then reading a third and repeating all three, and so on. Very soon the new input will start displacing the old, just as though there were a fixed limit to your STM capacity.

The phenomenon of retrograde amnesia[⊙] provides some everyday evidence for STM. In this form of amnesia, a shocking event that results in injury and an unpleasant memory (for example, an automobile accident) usually results in a loss of memory for the few moments immediately preceding the accident. It is as though the input related to those moments was still being processed when the accident occurred, resulting in these STM contents being lost (Figure 8.5). This interpretation of retrograde amnesia suggests that all encoding requires some time in STM before it becomes more or less permanently available in some longer-term storage. Much of our ongoing input, of course, never proceeds past this point. We conduct our conversations by keeping in mind the last sentence or two that the participants have uttered, but then that is lost (usually permanently), and we

Fig. 8.5. If an accident happens at (b), we may block out (forget) not only the events and the few moments following it (b through c), but also the few moments before the event (a through b). The latter phenomenon is known as *retrograde amnesia.*

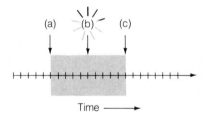

Time ⟶

short-term memory (STM). Memory storage in which items do not stay long but are easily accessible.

retrograde amnesia. A memory defect characterized by the inability of an individual to recall events just prior to the occurrence of forgetting (caused by shock, a blow, or illness), even though the person can recall earlier experiences.

MINDS
*The cognitive psychology
of individuals*

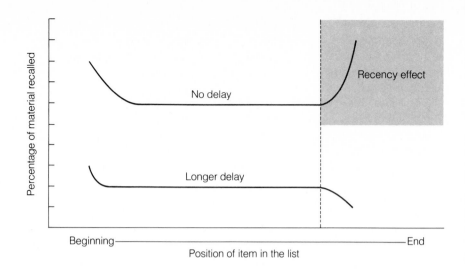

Fig. 8.6. How recall varies with different amounts of delay (see text).

**Memory experiment C
(continued)**

In this experiment, you should have recalled all of the "isolated" items—that is, items that in some way stood out for you. In List No. 1, these would have been the nonsense syllables, in List No. 2 the numbers, and in List No. 3 the numbers that were spelled out. The recall for these isolated items should have been better than for the other items in each list.

long-term memory (LTM). The component of the memory's storage system characterized by its relative permanence.

Korsakoff's syndrome. A chronic brain syndrome characterized by severe disorientation, confusion, and loss of immediate memory. It is found in some cases of chronic alcoholism.

recency effect. The tendency for the last thing presented—word, object, number, or idea—to be remembered more readily than previous ones.

retain only an approximate outline of what has been said. In this way, the apparently inefficient system of STM suffices perfectly for our everyday needs, enabling us to keep in touch with what is going on without being burdened by the long-term remembering of everything that happens.

Long-term memory (LTM).⊙ In the familiar, more dramatic form of amnesia, as when the person loses track of identity, sometimes for years at a time, a new and quite different identity may be assumed. The person then carries on from day to day, not remembering the old life but certainly not without a memory system for ongoing events. What has happened here is that LTM content has been lost but STM ability has been retained. Just the reverse seems to occur in the form of brain damage known as *Korsakoff's syndrome,*⊙ in which the person is still capable of recalling and acting on the memories of a lifetime but cannot seem to keep in mind what happened only a minute ago. Here LTM content is preserved but STM ability is gone. Elderly people who are thought to have severe memory loss are more likely to have lost *either* LTM or STM rather than both. If they keep reasonably alert and active, STM will be preserved even if LTM is lost, but if they reduced to a wheelchair existence with no stimulation or variety, they are more likely to preserve LTM and lose STM[10]. They will recall their childhood but not the attendant's name.

The presence of all these variations provides strong evidence that the encoding system of memory functions through at least two steps, STM and LTM. Even more persuasive evidence comes from laboratory studies of immediate and delayed recall of lists of nonsense syllables. (Typical results are shown in Figure 8.6). We mentioned in an earlier section that recall of such a list produces a serial position effect. That is, items at the beginning and ending of the list are recalled better than is the material in the middle. Superior recall for the material at the end of the list, we said, is known as the *recency effect.*⊙ It can be seen in the part of the upper curve in Figure 8.6 that is shaded.

But the results shown here are a little more complicated. Notice the difference in the two curves of Figure 8.6. One result is not surprising, that the "no delay" curve shows more material recalled. In general, the longer the delay, the smaller the percentage of the material that will be recalled. The upturn at the start of each curve, denoting that material at the beginning of a list is recalled better, is also to be expected. However, one other feature of the results is unexpected, that we do not get a recency effect under conditions of longer delay. The lower curve turns down rather than up at the end. How can this be explained?

Here we introduce the idea of two stages of memory, STM and LTM, to explain our results. We said that material coming into STM stays there for a measurable amount of time and is then displaced by new material coming in. If the person is trying to memorize a list, they will probably do what most of us do— rehearse the items as they are heard. It is assumed that if no rehearsal takes place, material in STM will be displaced and simply drop away (as happens when you forget a telephone number soon after you have used it). But if rehearsal does take place, material that is crowded out of STM will then move to LTM.[11] Now, does this help to explain the results shown in Figure 8.6? Under conditions of no-delay (the upper curve), items that first enter STM are rehearsed and move to LTM. The closer they are to the beginning of the list, the more rehearsal they will get and therefore the better they will be remembered. Items at the end of the list are still in STM by the time the person is asked for recall, so they too will be easily recalled. As a consequence, we get the familiar result shown in the (upper) no-delay curve.

But if there is a longer delay before the person is asked for recall, the results will depend entirely on rehearsal. The closer an item is to the end of the list, the less rehearsal it will have had. It will then have had little chance to be stored in LTM, so that if recall is asked for at a later time the material will have faded away. Hence the shape of the (lower) curve for longer delay, showing increased retention for earlier items but lower retention for items at the end of the list.

Remembering and forgetting

4. Encoding depends on the significance of the target, and so how well you encode determines how well you remember and how soon you forget.

As a result of recent interest in the encoding process, a great deal is now understood about the ways that remembering can be improved, even taught. There are many kinds of "memory systems," and the history of the subject goes back many thousands of years. On examination, it appears that all of them consist of systems for improving the process of encoding.

Improving memory. For any relatively neutral material to be retained longer than it will stay in STM, it clearly must be rehearsed. If, in addition, you do not stop rehearsing at once but repeat the rehearsal, the effect may well be the same as learning the same material over and over. This appears to be essentially what happens in the course of the most familiar of all methods for improving memory, by overlearning.○ Other and better methods for improving memory, however, rest primarily on more effective systems of coding the material. The most common method, and perhaps the most basic, would be to try to do deliberately what our memory processes seem best equipped to do—that is, to organize the material into manageable parts, or "chunks" as they are usually called, and to make sure that these chunks form some "natural" or meaningful units. Almost any device that forms a familiar code will help to arrange the material in terms of such chunks; for example, the old technique of using rhymes as cues for remembering.

Finally, there are a number of variants of systems which are particularly effective in memorizing lists of unrelated items. The problem with such a list is that there is no way to "chunk" it, no way to organize it into meaningful parts, and no way to assign the items to categories. Memory systems that work with such lists, then, have to offer some way for the person to link the separate items with

overlearning. A method of improving memory that involves extra practice after the basic mastery is completed.

Memory experiment D: tip-of-the-tongue

For this experiment, you will need some paper and a pen or pencil. Below, you will find a list of dictionary definitions of some rather uncommon words. You are to read each definition and then write down your guess as to the word.

Because these are not common words, the task will not be easy. Therefore, if you cannot think of the word, try to get at least some part of it. For example, try to make guesses in the following order: first, the word itself; then, its first letter; then its last letter; and then, the number of syllables you think it has. After you have done this, try putting down a word that you think might rhyme with the target word.

Write down all of this material—any guesses you make about the word, the first and last letters, the number of syllables, and other words that might rhyme with it. Do this for each word before going on to the next one.

Here are the definitions:

1. A small, one-oared boat used in China and Japan.
2. Someone who collects stamps.
3. A substance produced by sperm whales, used to make perfume.
4. The emblem of the medical profession, in the form of a wand with a snake coiled around it.
5. Favoritism or patronage to one's relative by an officeholder.
6. A navigational instrument, used to measure the height of celestial targets.

* * *

Now turn to Page 182 for a discussion of the results.

individual parts of some other, more memorable kind of sequence. The Russian psychologist Aleksandr Luria[12] recently published a full-scale study of a newspaperman who was particularly gifted in the use of such a system, which he had apparently devised on his own. He used a kind of map to plot the items of a list, based on the well-remembered visual images that he might get in walking down a certain street. These images were so familiar, and their sequence so well known to him that he had them automatically at his command whenever he needed them. He then had only to link each item of a sequence to the successive images of the familiar sequence, and he could then learn and remember astonishingly long lists.

The key to success in the system was in the links between the two sequences, the one familiar and the other to be learned. Each link was, in effect, a small learning–remembering task in itself. How could it be accomplished? The simplest way might be to overlearn the links. For example, if the first item of a list to be learned was *cabbage* and if the image with which it was to be linked was the stoplight at a corner of this street, he might repeat over and over to himself, "Cabbage—stoplight, Cabbage—stoplight. . . ." But this is hardly an efficient procedure, especially when one wants to memorize a list rather rapidly. A far more effective device would consist of taking advantage of the Von Restorff effect. He would then arrange that for each pair of items to be linked, the thought or mental image connected with the pairing would be very striking, or as we usually say, *memorable.* If the thought or idea in connection with the link were striking enough, it would serve to guarantee that this linked pair would be stored in LTM as a pair. Then, in the course of recall, the pair would be retrieved together in the correct sequence, giving the impression that he had memorized the list of unrelated items. What he would have "memorized," however—or, rather, *encoded*—would have been a linked pair such as "a cabbage in the shape and with the colors of a stoplight."

Such memory systems are impressive as demonstrations but are useful only when the material to be retrieved cannot be organized into other, more meaningfully integrated categories. Unfortunately, this may often be true of material that students have to cram for exams. Effective learning, however, should depend on other approaches that both rest on and take advantage of the naturally occurring processes in memory. We know, for example, that we "naturally" encode in terms of sensible categories. Therefore we should try to organize material to be learned so that it falls into a sensible set of clusters, topics, and subtopics. The emphasis in memorizing would then be on the stage of encoding rather than on the stage of retrieval.

Some important additional hints may be gained from your results in Memory Experiment D, which repeats a part of a well-known *tip-of-the-tongue* (TOT) experiment by Brown and McNeill.[13] On at least some of the words in this list, you may have had the familiar experience of knowing that you knew the word yet not quite being able to think of it or say it. What is of interest here is the incorrect words that you did put down as best guesses. These should have been somewhat similar to the words you were really reaching for. If so, we may ask, In what ways were they similar? For example, were your best (but wrong) guesses more like the target word in meaning or in sound? Brown and McNeill's participants produced guesses that were usually more like the target word in sound. This suggests that what is encoded is more likely to be the sound of a word than its meaning. In addition, the Brown and McNeill study showed that guesses resembled the target words in number of syllables, in the initial letter, and to a lesser degree in the nature of the final sound.

From these results, we may draw some tentative ideas as to how encoding takes place and therefore as to the encoding processes that one might try to use in the course of learning, say, a list of words. Here are some hints: Say the key words out loud, and listen to yourself say them, so that you will become familiar with their sound. Then, when the time for retrieval is at hand, whisper your guesses to yourself until you feel that you have recaptured the sound. Further, in saying the words aloud during encoding, attend to the length of the words, emphasize their initial sound, and listen to their final sound as well. In short, try to grasp the full sound and rhythm of words to be remembered. Then repeat this process during retrieval. In all this, you will be taking advantage of encoding processes that seem to occur "naturally."

Forgetting. It may have occurred to you that we have left out of our discussion of memory one of its most important aspects, forgetting. In fact, we have been discussing forgetting all along. Forgetting can be viewed as another term for the fact that not everything is remembered. If we were able to retain everything to which we attend, forgetting would never occur, or, rather, the concept of forgetting would have no meaning. Because this does not happen, it is useful to have a separate term, *forgetting*, for those instances in which we do not remember. It follows, then, that stages or types of forgetting are equally stages or types of remembering. It also follows that theories of forgetting are connected with major aspects of remembering.

Remembering and forgetting are both significant phenomena, for they are two sides of the same event. We can see the consequences of ignoring one of the two sides if we look at a claim that is often made concerning a computer's "memory." The difficulty in using a term such as *memory* in connection with the operations of a computer is that it is only partially appropriate. True, there is built into a computer a set of systems for receiving input, often for coding it, for storing it, and then for retrieving it as ordered. One might even build into a computer an additional system such that when it is overloaded additional input into the storage will displace certain kinds of material already stored there, much like what happens with the STM of humans.

But the difference is that a computer, like other inanimate mechanisms, cannot forget. In this sense, the computer is no different from the side of your house, which "remembers" last year's hard winter and stores that information in the decay of its coat of paint. But the house, and the computer, cannot help thus "remembering." Either they encode and store, or they do not. What they cannot do is encode, store, and then "forget." Forgetting may be nothing but the other face of memory, but it is a necessary other face for the memory process as we mean it in this chapter.

Theories of forgetting. The three major theories of forgetting are, as we might expect, simply alternate ways of referring to the relative inefficiency of the three stages of remembering—encoding, storage, and retrieval. Two of the theories of forgetting, in fact, have already been discussed and will be dealt with only briefly here. The first, the *decay* theory, states that we forget because traces in storage fade away with time. As we noted earlier, the evidence for this is either poor or contradictory. The second theory, concerning various forms of *interference*, has also been called *trace-dependent* forgetting, because it assumes that the result of interference in encoding is to weaken or eliminate traces. A good deal of experimental evidence supports the theory that various forms of interference, whether or not connected with the forming of traces, prevent learning, or, alternatively, they increase forgetting.

A third theory of forgetting remains to be mentioned. It is less obvious than the two just mentioned, and so it may be more difficult to understand, but it is in some ways more interesting. It is called *cue-dependent forgetting*.[○]

This term refers to the fact that sometimes one attends to something and then

cue-dependent forgetting. The inability to retrieve material in long-term memory unless the individual has the appropriate cues to facilitate retrieval; or the inability to remember because appropriate cues have been detached.

Fig. 8.7. What is remembered or forgotten at such a moment is very largely a matter of one's motives and feelings.

**Memory experiment D
(continued)**

One result of your attempt to find words for the definitions might have been the familiar "tip-of-the-tongue" phenomenon, in which you are sure you know what a word is but cannot quite say it. If something like this happened to you, you might also have found that you were able to recapture many characteristics of the word but not the word itself—how long it was, how it began or ended, or how it sounded. These were the results obtained by Brown and McNeill, as discussed in the text.

Here are the words for which the definitions were given: *sampan, philatelist, ambergris, caduceus, nepotism,* and *sextant.*

stores it away as memory, along with certain cues. For example, in the TOT experiment just discussed, one of the cues that is stored away along with a word seems to be the number of syllables it has. Retrieval of this cue usually helps people to recall a word that may be on the tip of the tongue. However, if retrieval of the word depends to some degree on retrieval of the cue, then mistakes can happen. One might, for example, call up the wrong cue, which would lead in turn to retrieving the wrong word. Lacking the correct cue, the right word would not be recalled, and so one would say that the word was forgotten. The theory of cue-dependent forgetting says that the word has not simply been forgotten. Rather, the needed cue has been detached or misplaced, so that it is not available.

This theory of forgetting has two unique aspects. One is that it refers to what happens in retrieval rather than what happens in encoding or storage. In this respect, it differs from other theories of forgetting. A second unique aspect is that it helps to explain one of the most interesting characteristics of remembering and forgetting. This is that these processes seem to be connected with our motives (Figure 8.7). Justifiably or not, most of us suspect that our motives, particularly our hidden or unconscious motives, may have a great deal to do with what we remember and forget. For example, you encounter someone whom you had met before and had disliked at sight; you might even have hoped, at the first meeting, that you would never see the person again. Now, at a second meeting, you find that you have "conveniently" forgotten the person's name. (Using a term lifted from Freud's theory, we often say that in this instance we have *repressed* the person's name. We will discuss this idea at greater length in Chapter 13.)

The theory of cue-dependent forgetting suggests that the motive (of liking or disliking) that is attached to the memory of that first meeting serves as a cue for later retrieval. If the person had been someone we liked and perhaps hoped to meet again, we might then keep the memory in mind, alive and recalled, for a long period of time. But if it had been someone we wanted to forget as soon as possible, as in the preceding example, we would forget the person's name or fail to remember it. In either case, according to this theory, the motive to like or to dislike would have served as a cue that determines how well our retrieval works.

Reconsidering memory

Thus far we have discussed the major traditional views of memory, including some evidence for and against a number of competing theories. What has not yet been mentioned is that these views are in many ways seriously flawed. As a result they have recently come under attack from many within the field of psychology. In the present section, we reconsider the ideas presented earlier, this time on the basis of recent attacks on them. Again, we will divide the discussion into three parts, but this time we will take them up in the order in which they are currently being reevaluated in experimental psychology: that is, first storage, then encoding, and finally retrieval.

5. The case against the idea of a storage system for memory comprises at least three arguments, referring to interindividual transfer, brain models, and memory traces.

Transfer. If we accept the idea that memories are stored in some way, or in some place, within a creature's anatomy — which seems an acceptable way of stating the notion of storage — it would follow that the specific part of the anatomy affected might be able to be transferred from one body to another. This idea remained a science-fiction conjecture until in the 1960s a great deal became known about molecules that can mediate such transfers. The chief of these is DNA, which serves to carry the individual's genetic code (see Chapter 1). If the entire code can be thus transferred from parents to offspring, why not the much easier transfer of individual memories from one mature individual to another, by injection or by surgery? The molecular substance chosen was RNA, the "messenger" of DNA, which controls the functions of cells.

An initial demonstration, by Babich and colleagues,[14] raised high hopes, for it appeared that RNA from the brain cells of maze-trained rats, when given to naive (untrained) rats, helped the performance of the latter on similar mazes. The promise of transfer of stored memories (for what else could have been transferred?) seemed even more probable when similar studies supported the original finding. And finally, in a dramatic flourish, it appeared that tiny flatworms, conditioned to react to light when it was paired with electric shock, could pass on their stored memories if they were ground up and fed to other flatworms.[15]

Since that earlier series of promising studies, however, the strong case has gradually evaporated. It has been very difficult to replicate the findings — that is, to repeat the experiments and obtain the same results. In addition, a very careful study, examining a number of possible explanations of the transfer phenomenon, has cast much doubt on the hypothesis that stored memories of some learning are being transferred. In this study, rats were given three kinds of training, with and without electric shock and with nonshock stress (the latter by rolling them over and over inside a small container). The trained rats were killed, and then their brain substance was injected into one group of naive rats and their liver substance injected into another group. Both groups of recipients were then tested. Injection of liver seemed to have as much effect as injection of brain, and in addition the greatest effect came from injection from rats that had sustained nonshock stress that was quite unrelated to the performance tested. The authors conclude that results that seem to be caused by the transfer of memories are better explained on the basis of two factors. First, some animals are more susceptible to stresses of all sorts. Second, a general stress factor may be created in the body as a result of training, which then can be transferred by injection but which can hardly be viewed as the transfer of specific memories.[16] In short, the notion of memory transfer between individuals, which if supported might lend great weight to the concept of storage systems, remains very much in doubt.

Brain models. The idea of a memory storage with identifiable locations in the brain rests on a certain conception, or model, of what happens when we remember something. Penfield's work, previously discussed, is a good example of evidence that rests on a specific model. In this case, the model of the tape recorder, perhaps even the model of the telephone switchboard. In this conception, memories are received, appropriately coded, and filed away where they belong, so that to retrieve them one need only know the code. As one recent survey of the field puts it, "This theory conceives of the memory process as analogous to other storage problems, like operating a warehouse or a library. . . . Information-processing theory conceives of memory as analogous to running a library."[17]

This analogy is rarely pushed too far, for it requires that the rememberer be, at the same time, the librarian, the client, and the author of all the library's books. But it still serves, in one form or another, as the implicit structure for much theorizing. This is somewhat surprising, for it was all but demolished many years ago by Karl Lashley. He spent many years of experiments "in search of the engram," as he called it.[18] In a long series of experiments with rats, he trained them on all sorts of tasks, then surgically removed parts of their brains, and determined if loss of brain substance interfered with their memory of what they had learned. The results were clear-cut, and they were devastating for any theory of anatomical traces. No matter what parts of the animals' brains were cut out by surgery, some memory of the original learning persisted, so that it became clear that memories were not stored in any specific part of the brain. All that really mattered was how much brain tissue was cut out, not where the cut took place. Lashley then formulated two general principles to explain how learning was stored and thus to answer his own question about the engram. The first principle he called *equipotentiality*, that all parts of the brain were approximately equal in their ability to take over in case of damage to one part. The second principle he called *mass action*, that the brain either before or after surgery tended to act as a whole rather than in terms of localization of memories.

The cortex does not, apparently, work like a tape recorder, with specific locations energized in some way to produce an imprint. Indeed, this should have been apparent much earlier, for simple consideration will indicate that a tape recorder does not remember, but only repeats. Nor, as we have noted, can it forget; it only forgets when someone remembers to erase it.

Some lessons in method. One of the most important conclusions to be drawn from experimental work on remembering is that the kinds of experiments used to study it have largely determined the results obtained and thus the conclusions drawn.

Now, this is an unusual situation in a science. Experiments are supposed to be neutral. Their purpose is to test one explanation against another or else to test whether an explanation holds up under examination. The experiment itself is not supposed to influence one outcome rather than another. Yet a review of studies of memory shows that this is just what has often occurred. The experiments, as it turned out, were not neutral at all. They had a theory hidden in them, with the result that only certain outcomes were possible.

This is not to say, of course, that the experimenters were in any way dishonest. They were not. They do seem, however, to have been limited in their outlook. It simply did not occur to them that the very *way* they asked their questions, or the very methods they used to answer their questions, already loaded the experiments in favor of a limited set of answers. What they did seemed to them self-evident—which suggests that the greatest stumbling block in the way of an adequate theory may be one's own "self-evident" ideas.

For example, studies of memory have from the very beginning been based on these assumptions: (1) requiring a person to memorize something is an adequate test of the everyday process of spontaneous remembering; (2) using material that is essentially nonsense gives results that are comparable with our everyday remembering of what is meaningful to us;[19] (3) what goes into our memory storage is not processed at this point but is simply filed, like a book being placed on a library shelf; and (4) what is stored in memory is in the form of traces. All of these assumptions seem to make sense, but all of them should have been questioned and tested, for it turns out that none are completely correct.

Very direct evidence on this point comes from an experiment by Hyde and Jenkins.[20] Using lists of words that people heard and then recalled, three groups of listeners were tested: (1) those who simply heard the lists of words and were tested later for recall; (2) those who heard the material with instructions to do something with it that required a grasp of its meaning—for example, to rate it as pleasant or unpleasant; and (3) those who heard the material with instructions to do something with it that impeded grasping its meaning—for example, to note whether it was spelled with a certain letter. The recall of the third group was poor compared to that of the second group. This indicates that when one encodes through the grasp of meaning memories are better organized for recall. But the recall of the first group was also superior, which suggests that in the absence of instructions people will spontaneously encode in terms of meaning.

Notice, however, that this experimental result could have been obtained only in a study in which some of the subjects were permitted to remember in a "meaningful" way. In more traditional memory experiments, none of the experimental conditions would have compared a meaningful method of encoding with a "meaningless" method. Rather, the material was likely to have been nonsense syllables, chosen because they suggested very little meaning. The experimental method, rather than a theory, would then have been an important influence in what was supposed to have been a neutral experiment.

6. The concept of the memory trace can be considered as part of the encoding process.

The central idea supporting the theories we are discussing is the idea of a memory trace. It is the most durable of all concepts in psychology, having been around for more than twenty centuries in essentially the same form. Aristotle would most likely have had no difficulty recognizing Penfield's theory of memory storage. Yet a close analysis reveals that the concept of memory trace has no reasonable basis, either in logic or in psychology. In support of this rather extreme claim, we offer a summary of the arguments presented by Erwin Straus, in a classic paper on the problem of memory traces.[21] The arguments are subtle but worth rereading and pondering.

The input that produced the trace is gone at the moment the trace is made, like a mother who dies in giving birth. Therefore whatever useful information the trace can contain must be completely within it, to be read off later. Can this occur?

It cannot, for any number of reasons. Consider a typical "trace," such as a footprint in the sand (see Figure 8.8). It is fragmentary, not whole, for it is only one part of a lengthy sequence. It is not an event, as the original was, but a static sign that can only be understood within its context—yet the context is not contained in the trace. And it is the negative image of a positive imprint. For all these reasons, the trace, like the footprint in the sand, makes sense only if it can be read. Traces do

Fig. 8.8. A trace can be "read" only if someone is there to read it (see text).

not read themselves, but require readers in order to be useful when they are retrieved.

However, because the trace is different from the matrix that receives it, the "reader" must be able to separate the two. This implies the ability to understand the trace as a figure against a ground. Indeed, amateur woodsmen miss many traces for just this reason, that for them the trace does not "stand out." And a trace can make only a limited impression, not a total transformation (which is why you cannot leave traces in water). A "reader" of the trace must also be able to utilize such limited information.

A sequence of traces has to be read by the reader backward in time, not in the direction in which one comes across them. For example, to understand that a person walked across the sand, we must be able, first, to see the set of tracks as a whole, and then to reconstruct the original sequence backward. One trace at a time would not be read but simply reacted to. But in order to read the trace in this way, the "reader" must be capable of spanning time, of having some sense of the past. In short, the "reader" must *already* be capable of memory. In order for me to "read" my own memory traces, I must already be capable of remembering.

Traces cannot read themselves; that would be like asking the footprint to reproduce the person who made it. Nor can traces simply be reactivated, or run off, for the reasons already given. What is required, then, is a "reader" who is already possessed of just that memory that traces are supposed to supply.

The notion of a trace as a kind of imprint in the brain, in the sense implied by Penfield's work or in the sense implied by the analogy of a library, is simply not possible. It defeats itself, because it requires a rememberer in order to explain remembering.

But if the notion of a memory storage, in the sense of footprintlike traces on some brain substance, has to be abandoned, what can take its place? Recent experimental work and theorizing, centered on the problems of encoding, has furnished at least preliminary answers. In effect, the notion of storage has begun to be absorbed into the notion of encoding. In place of a separate storage stage, there is now a more elaborate stage of encoding.

Specifics of encoding. This development has been demonstrated most clearly in the work of Endel Tulving and his associates,[22] leading to a modern theory of memory. In one series of studies, they begin with a problem similar to that shown in our Memory Experiment C. There, you will recall, we demonstrated that the "natural" process of encoding appears to take place in what has been called *associative clusters*—material that naturally or logically belongs together being linked together in the process of memorizing it. A similar process can be shown in most memory studies involving the recall of lists of words. For example, if the word *chair* was on an original list to be remembered, but not the word *table*, the word *table* will still serve later as an effective cue for the subject to recall *chair*.

Many explanations have been offered of how these "extra-list" cues work, but carefully designed experiments appear to rule out any except those referring to encoding. What this means is that the reason we recall in terms of clusters, and the reason that certain related words serve as cues to help recall, is that we originally *encode* in just these ways. The theory says that what we do with material when we first receive it determines how we will remember it later. The conditions under which encoding takes place are what counts.

This general notion is not at all obvious or easy to grasp. On the contrary, if we do not think too seriously about it we are likely to assume that in remembering something we just take it in, store it away appropriately, and then search for it as needed in recall. But the new emphasis on the important role played by encoding processes suggests that the simpler view should be superseded, in two ways. In the first place, encoding is now viewed as an active, organizing process, even when it seems to go on as a casual by-product of our ongoing activity. We are always encoding, in elaborate and organized ways. Second, the notion of the trace can now be, if not eliminated, at least restated: "The trace itself is simply the link between encoding conditions and the retrieval environment."[23]

What is encoded. With the emphasis now shifted to the process of encoding, it is possible to make some important distinctions in regard to *what* is encoded. We do not take in, as input, everything that comes to us—or, if we do, it does not seem to stay with us. In perceiving and attending, it appears, we actively select, choose, and organize, and only the result of these processes gets "remembered."

But we are also constantly in some meaningful situation. So, our ongoing relation to situations also must be considered when we emphasize encoding, particularly because almost all of the remembering that takes place in everyday life is involuntary rather than deliberate, schoolroom-type memorizing. The Soviet experimenters mentioned earlier base their work on a general principle: "that everything an individual experiences should be remembered to the extent that the materials perceived are related to organized activities in progress."[24]

The conclusion we can draw is that, as we experience our constantly changing situation, we take in what is happening, encoding it in sensible and meaningful ways. But unless we are specifically primed for the purpose, we do not deliberately encode or retain details of what we experience. Thus, what we are likely to recall of an event or an experience is not necessarily the completely detailed picture but simply the fact *that* we did this or that, heard this or that, or felt this or that. It is this general knowledge that is usually retained and that can then be retrieved.

You can verify this quite easily, if you try to recollect a dozen different situations in which you took part today. You may remember, for example, *that* you brushed your teeth, or *that* you felt grumpy at breakfast. What you are not likely to recall is the specific sequence of thoughts that went through your mind as you brushed your teeth, or all the things you muttered as you looked for that sock, or the different words that others might have directed at you during breakfast.

7. Retrieval depends primarily on the way that encoding took place, which rests in turn on relative degrees of distancing and participation and of significance.

A point of view that emphasizes a person's experience of the quality of an event, in its context, as a basis for encoding has been termed by Jenkins a *contextualist* theory of memory.[25] It may be contrasted with two others that we have already discussed, as shown in Table 8.1, which compares the three views in terms of how they deal with the major aspects of remembering. In the contextualist theory, memory is conceived as an actively organizing by-product of normal behavior and experience that leads to specific modes of encoding and thus results in specific kinds of retrieval. In the most practical sense, how and how well you encode can determine how and how well you recall—for example, by the use of such encoding methods as imagery, self-recitation, elaborate organization, and overlearning.

Retrieval, then, involves forming links between the encoding and retrieval situations. Sometimes this is only partially successful, as in our incomplete recall of dreams or our failure to recall them. On other occasions, the encoding and retrieval situations are so different that what is encoded in one remains lost to the other. This phenomenon is known as *state-dependent learning*.[○] It can be seen in the case of someone who, while intoxicated, does something that is completely forgotten later, when the person is sober. In many cases, it is possible for a subject to learn something while in one (drug-induced) state, to be unable to recall it or perform it when in another (normal) state, and then to be quite capable of demonstrating the learning again when reintroduced into the original (drug-induced) state.[26]

On distancing and participation. A major condition for forming links between encoding and retrieval is that the person be able to maintain some "distance" in experiencing the event at both encoding and retrieval. The term *distancing* refers to a kind of attention that can best be understood if we contrast it with its alternative, *participation*. Most activity in childhood, most intimate, personal, or emotional experience and also most physical activity is highly participative. When engaged in such activity, we do not usually distance ourselves from the situation to confront, judge, or think about it. As a result, we are not likely to remember it, at least not in any detail. Participative behavior and experience are like habits. We can be so totally caught up in the doing of them that we do not usually step back to contemplate or register the fact of their occurrence. To remem-

Table 8.1. Stages of memory, according to three theoretical approaches.

	Associationist	Information processing	Contextualist
Encoding	ignored	deemphasized	emphasized as active
Storage	central element; the heart of learning	automatic; deemphasized	eliminated
Retrieval	automatic; deemphasized	emphasized as active	emphasized as key element

state-dependent learning. A characteristic of learning in which material learned in one state of consciousness can only later be recalled in the same state.

ber something that someone else did, it must stand out for us. To remember something that we ourselves did, it must also stand out. That is, we must be able to take some distance from it rather than be totally caught up in it. Thus, I may not recall any of the single breaths I took yesterday, but I will surely remember the one that was associated with a sharp pain in my chest.

Aristotle once put this very well: "For, whenever one exercises the faculty of remembering, he must say within himself, 'I formerly heard this' or 'I formerly had this thought.' "[27] We might restate this in current terminology as "When I recall something, I *now* perceive that I *did* perceive something then." Each of the parts of this miraculously complex operation requires a distancing. I must hold off on my ongoing participation in the immediate present in order to start the remembering process expressed in "I now perceive." I must get in touch with my own personal history in order to continue the remembering process expressed in "that I did perceive." Finally, I must scan my own history and then zero in on a specific point in it in order to carry out the remembering process expressed in the final word "then."

The problem of infantile amnesia.

In the phenomenon of infantile amnesia is contained the essence of the problems of memory, and so it will serve as a fitting topic with which to close our chapter on remembering. The term *infantile amnesia*© refers to the well-known fact that for almost all persons the first few years of life are largely a closed book. There are, of course, many instances, more or less well authenticated, in which individual events or details of infancy (or even earlier) may later be recaptured in adulthood. However, these are so rare, in comparison with the vast amount of infantile experience that is utterly beyond our recall, that we may consider infantile amnesia as the state of normal occurrence (Figure 8.9).

Fig. 8.9. How can all this be completely forgotten?

Such forgetting, or loss, of infantile experience raises a very serious problem for any theory of development. If there is amnesia for all important events that occurred before, let us say, the age of two, how is it that we can be so profoundly influenced by what happened to us during those early years? One way that this can be reconciled is to assume two quite unrelated processes, learning and memory; but such a step would raise serious problems for theories of learning.

For example, if my father walked with a very heavy, stolid gait and if I now, as an adult, show the same kind of gait, then the conclusion will probably be drawn that I learned my style of walking in early childhood by imitation of my father. Can we, then, properly say that I now, as an adult, *remember* the style of walking that I learned many years ago? Somehow this phrasing does not seem correct. How does such remembering, if it is that, differ from the recall that we all can exercise in regard to events of our later childhood?

The essential difference, it would seem, is between conscious *cognitive* learning, which is what I experience in later childhood, and *body* learning, which is what happens to me in infancy and which I then demonstrate by performance at a later time. Cognitive learning-and-remembering (for it is all one process) is what we have been discussing in this and the previous chapter. It depends on interrelated processes of encoding and retrieval. It requires distancing at the time of encoding and then distancing again at the time of retrieval. It may be directed at total experiences or events, but it may also, if the person so wills it, be directed at details and units abstracted out of a total event.

Body learning, on the other hand, occurs when the person participates in some situation, both bodily and in terms of feeling, and in which some change in their physical structure probably takes place. The changed person can then demonstrate the change in subsequent performances, and this serves as a continuing "memory" of the original learning. My style of walking is not something I once

infantile amnesia. The normal forgetting of early childhood experiences, particularly of the first three years of life.

experienced by means of distancing myself from a situation, but something I fully participated in. My present, unchanged style of walking is not a "memory" of that original learning but a performance based on the way that I participated in my original learning.

Memory is a cognitive process, as is learning. Body learning, however, is a central aspect of quite a different set of processes, which we call *growth* or *development;* and this will be taken up in the separate chapters of Part Three.

Summary

1. How we retrieve our memories depends on our situation as well as on our choice of method.

2. There are three major modes of retrieval: recall, redintegration, and recognition.

3. Forgetting occurs most rapidly at the onset of a period of time and decreases in rate until the curve levels off.

4. With respect to an organized sequence of items to be remembered, the most recent (or the last) material presented is remembered best, the material at the beginning next best, and the material in the middle least.

5. Recognition is the most sensitive test of remembering.

6. Memory storage takes a measurable amount of time to occur, both in the initial "sensory buffer" and in the later "short-term memory" stage.

7. Compared to being asleep, being awake can markedly interfere with the retention (remembering) of learned material.

8. The more similar the interfering material is to the material to be remembered, the more interference it generates.

9. Most of our everyday remembering occurs not as memorizing but as an unintended by-product of what we experience and do.

10. What is encoded appears to remain for a measurable space of time in short-term memory before passing to more or less permanent "storage" in long-term memory.

11. Material that is relatively neutral to the person must be rehearsed in order to be retained in storage.

12. Evidence indicates that we "naturally" encode in terms of sensible categories.

13. Different forms of interference that prevent learning also increase forgetting.

14. The possibility of memory transfer between individual organisms remains in doubt.

15. It appears that the human cortex does not work like a tape recorder, with specific locations energized in some way to produce an imprint.

16. Memories are better organized for recall when one encodes intentionally (or spontaneously) through the grasp of meaning.

17. Recent views of the process of remembering, particularly the "contextualist" theory of Jenkins, absorb the storage process into the encoding process. Thus, what counts in remembering is what we do with material when we first receive it (encoding).

18. As a rule, we encode or retain general knowledge about a phenomenon or event rather than the details of the event as an experience.

19. The term *state-dependent learning* refers to a phenomenon in which material learned in one state is forgotten when the individual is in another state but can then be recalled if the individual returns to the original state.

I n this chapter, we will consider the many states of consciousness. They will be seen to fall into two chief categories, induced or natural. Their definitions can be based on behavior, on instruments, or on reports of experience.

Within this framework, you will see how sleep and dreams can be distinguished and will learn about the use of the EEG in making these distinctions. Different interpretations and uses of the dream state will be pointed out, and factors of both theoretical and cultural importance will be elaborated.

Then you will learn about some of the interesting effects that induced states may have on bodily sensations and responses. For example, it will be shown how pain perception and physiological responses may be modified through the use of hypnosis or meditation. In concluding, we will raise the important question of whether there are in fact different states of consciousness, and we will emphasize that different answers are possible from inside and from outside viewpoints. On this basis, you will see that the viewpoint one takes to study these states largely determines the kind of information that is gathered.

9

Consciousness: normal and altered states of mind

"One conclusion was forced upon my mind at that time, and my impression of its truth has ever since remained unshaken. It is that our normal waking consciousness, rational consciousness as we call it, is but one special type of consciousness, whilst all about it, parted from it by the filmiest of screens, there lie potential forms of consciousness entirely different. We may go through life without suspecting their existence, but apply the requisite stimulus, and at a touch they are there in all their completeness. . . . No account of the universe in its totality can be final which leaves these other forms of consciousness quite disregarded."[1]

Thus William James asserted in 1902, in a book that he called *Varieties of Religious Experience*, because seventy-five years ago right-thinking people were convinced that altered states of consciousness had to be religious in nature. Today we are not so sure. Are there "potential forms of consciousness" that lie all about us? And, if so, do they seem to be separated from the normal waking state by only "the filmiest of screens"?

---

1. A very common "prejudice" is that our normal state of mind is primary and that all other states are inferior or secondary.

Whether or not you share James' position, one thing will probably seem as certain to you as it did to him. It is that each of us has a primary state of mind, which James called "our normal waking consciousness." In Western cultures, all other states seem secondary to it, or alterations of it. Because they seem to be secondary, these other states are often considered to be inferior and the information they furnish not quite "real."

Sleeping and dreaming, the most common of our altered states, are good examples of how we "put down" states while recognizing their special virtues. Dreams have always exercised a special fascination, and all sorts of special powers have been imputed to them. Yet even as the dream state is accorded special privilege, it is also characterized as strange, distorted, and always needing interpretation to fit it into the proper mode of thinking that goes with our "normal" state. The more socially useless the dream is considered by a social group, the more distorted and illogical does it seem; and the more useful it appears, to the group or the individual, the clearer is its message.[2]

It is a prejudice so universal that it seems self-evident—that there is one "natural" state to be in, and that we are in it when we act our parts as normal adults during the waking part of the day. The prejudice is owed in large measure, as are so many of our very contemporary notions about ourselves, to the work of Sigmund Freud. He taught that the human personality was made up of more than positive aspects such as reason and reality orientation. There was in each of us a "dark side" of which we were not aware and usually could not be aware. Thus, if we are playful, childish, make jokes, or express our fantasies, these are really the erupting of unconscious repressed impulses into our primary, normal, conscious state. Our artistic and creative lives, if we are gifted enough to have them, are really only the breakthrough of unconscious impulses in disguised form. The fairytales and myths that circulate in a society are nothing but disguised messages from unconscious thinking that everyone shares. And, of course, our dream state is a period of revolutionary takeover by the dark forces. Threatened by the possible expression of these unconscious impulses, we "allow" it to happen at night, dreaming so that we may continue our sleep.

It is hard to accept the view that every state other than our normal one represents a failure of our waking lives in exactly the same way. Altered states are too many, too varied, too much (as William James put it) "all about us." They may be induced by too much or too little stimulation, by chemical means such as an almost infinite variety of drugs (as well as by the lack of them in some cases), or by psychological means such as hypnosis. They result in evident changes in our time sense, our body image, our emotional states, our sense of self, and our experience of our surroundings. Their variety, as rich as is our "normal" experience, suggests that their source is not simply in one kind of disturbance but in the very nature of human experience and behavior. In the discussion that follows, we will ask that you try to put aside the prejudice that affects us all and consider the different "altered" states as equally primary rather than as secondary or inferior (Figure 9.1).

Natural states. We define natural states as states that seem to occur "naturally," in the normal course of living. They usually begin and end according to one's "natural" schedule, without imposition from without. We experience them as a part of our biological and social existence. They may be divided into two major groups:

1. Those that occur during our waking state(s)—being normally awake, various emotional states, and daydreaming or reverie.
2. Those that occur in connection with sleep—the different stages, or depths, of sleeping, REM and non-REM states (defined and discussed later), and dreaming.

Induced states. We define induced states as states that usually require special training, special outside influence, special devices, or intervention by a specific other person, to be brought about. They do not usually begin or end by themselves without such imposition. They include the following:

1. *Delirium,* as is seen in conditions of physiological extremity such as sickness, pain, starvation, sensory or perceptual strain, lack of sleep, or extreme danger or isolation.

MINDS
The cognitive psychology
of individuals

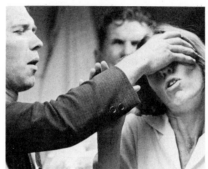

Fig. 9.1. There are very many possible states of consciousness.

2. *Amnesia*, that is, conditions in which for some period of time the individual loses or alters the ongoing sense of self and personal history.
3. *Hypnosis*, induced either by another person or by oneself (autohypnosis).
4. *Meditation*, a very broad term in which we include states brought on by established meditative techniques and also apparently similar states of relaxation or ecstasy brought on by any of a wide variety of physical, physiological, or mystical approaches.

2. The awake, normal state is public and consensual, the state from which we collectively judge our other states of mind.

The most important distinction between the awake state and all the other states in our list is that the awake state is communal, or consensual, rather than individual. The awake state is that state in which we all usually meet in order to share information about other states and about the nature of our agreement. By contrast, the other states on our list are always more or less individual. That is, they are known and experienced first of all, or primarily, by the individual concerned and only later, or secondarily, by other persons.

One consequence of the fact that other states are essentially individual ones is that it is very difficult to gather objective, consensual data on them. Because they are known primarily to the person experiencing them, the method for identifying them, or for verifying that they are occurring, takes the form of a subjective, personal report. Surprisingly, even the most careful external investigation, using the best available objective methods, can produce some evidence about whether the state is occurring but says little about what it is like to the experiencing individual.

For example, until the dreamer gives us a report there would be no way of knowing, by external and objective means, what was occurring in a dream. Simply by observation of behavior, there is as yet no sure way of determining that a person is in a delirious state, much less what might have brought it about. The many kinds of objective psychological tests are not of much help in this regard. There are no foolproof indicators to tell us that a person is in a hypnotic trance—and as a result there is a continuing controversy in the field of hypnosis as to whether there even is such a state. On a more everyday level, classroom teachers will admit, if pressed, that there is really no method for deciding whether the students facing them are daydreaming, half asleep, awake but in a reverie, alert but thinking about something far from the classroom, hallucinating, in a meditative trance, or thoughtfully attending.

In regard to all these states, the necessary information to determine with certainty what the state is and what it is like can come only from the individual who is having the experience. This information will, of course, be some form of subjective and personal report.

The study of altered states

Until fairly recently the study of the various altered states has remained relatively undeveloped or has been considered as at best a set of concerns that are marginal to the interests of a behavioral science. However, within the last fifteen years or so, a major shift has been occurring in regard to the study of these phenomena, with the result that they are now considered not only "respectable" but even exciting and challenging problems from which we may learn a great deal.

The change has come about for two reasons. First, an increasing number of investigators have become interested, often for personal reasons, in the practice of disciplines that consist of inducing states of altered consciousness. This is undoubtedly a reflection of major shifts in public awareness that took place during the decade of the 1960's.[3] With the publication of Charles Tart's pioneering book *Altered States of Consciousness* in 1969,[4] the term itself entered the psychological literature. Second, as a result of a number of discoveries regarding sleep and dreams and discoveries concerning biofeedback and self-control of internal states, it now seems quite feasible to study most altered states by objective scientific methods. In turn, the methods used have been very much aided by the development of new and more sensitive electronic instruments.

The EEG. The methods and machines available for measurement may play an important role in psychological investigations. Without an adequate measurement device, an event is not of much practical use, except (and perhaps crucially) to the one who experiences it. On the other hand, if a device is available, it often helps to determine significant lines of investigation. One such measuring device is the electroencephalograph, or EEG for short. It is a very sensitive instrument for picking up and amplifying the faint electrical currents that normally sweep across the surface of the skull. These currents are indicators of the electrical activity that is always taking place in the cortex of the brain. It must be emphasized, however, that these EEG currents, or "brain waves," are rather crude indicators, the average activity of millions of cells. They give us only the barest minimum of information about what is actually going on, electrically, within the skull. (This is why brain waves could probably not transmit thoughts, as is suggested to occur in telepathy.)

For convenience, the types of waves that can be recorded on an EEG apparatus have been divided into four kinds, differing normally in both frequency (how many occur every second) as well as amplitude (how powerful they are, as measured in millionths of a volt). They are shown in Figure 9.2a in more or less ideal form and in Figure 9.2b as they might actually appear on an EEG tracing. Notice

(a)

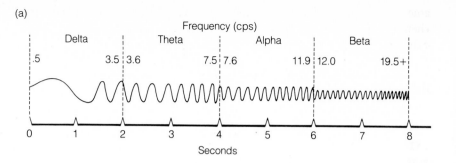

Fig. 9.2. The four major kinds of brain waves, and their approximate frequencies in cycles per second (cps). Each kind of wave includes a range of frequencies, from slower to faster, and the dividing lines between them are largely a matter of convention.

These waves are shown in (a) in their ideal form; in fact, brain waves almost never look this regular. In (b) we can see the way that typical brain waves actually look; they are tracings from the EEG records of normal subjects.

(b)

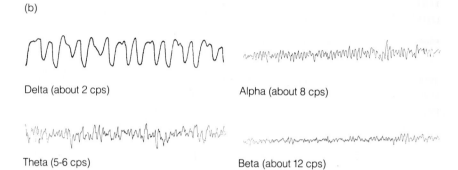

Delta (about 2 cps)

Alpha (about 8 cps)

Theta (5-6 cps)

Beta (about 12 cps)

that, generally, the slower the waves, or the lower their frequency, the greater their amplitude.

Because it is the only instrument normally available for use in recording information from inside the human skull (although internal probes of various kinds are used with laboratory animals such as rats and monkeys) the EEG has become the most important source of data in many psychophysiological studies.[5] A related kind of instrument, the electromyograph (EMG), performs a similar function for detecting and amplifying the minute electrical currents that are generated whenever a muscle goes into action. Placed on the skin, the EMG pickup is sensitive to changes in muscular activity even when the person is unaware that these are occurring. It is thus an important instrument in psychophysiological studies in which the event to be studied is the degree of muscular tension.

Set. A psychological set$^\odot$ is a readiness to respond. There are two types: The first is implicit set,$^\odot$ which refers to the subject's psychological state; this is what predisposes people to act in a certain way in an experiment; for example, being highly motivated, or being suspicious of the experimenter's motives, or being bored after waiting too long for the experiment to begin. The second type of set is explicit set,$^\odot$ which refers to the state that the experimenter tries to induce by means of the instructions. Examples are asking the person to relax, warning the person that a flashing light will indicate that electric shock is imminent, or telling the person to fall asleep in his or her normal way.

In an experiment, explicit set is known to both subject and experimenter, but implicit set only to the subject and perhaps not even to that person. The two kinds of set may or may not coincide in an experiment. It has always been known that implicit set may have important effects in an experiment. As an example, someone's increasing tension will alter the measurements made of blood pressure or breathing pattern. What was less well known, but is now established, is that the

psychological set. The total attitudes, feelings, ideas, and perceptions that an individual brings to a new experience.

implicit set. The beliefs and attitudes with which a subject enters in an experiment or new project.

explicit set. The attitudes and beliefs that have been dictated by the experimenter in an experiment.

same physiological variables can often be affected by changes in explicit set, as when the examiner delivers a pep talk to the people about the historic significance of this research.

Sleeping

---

3. Sleep has three definitions, based on behavior, instrument readings, or experiential report. These may not match, because sleep is both an individual and a significant social act.

Like most other phenomena that can be studied in psychology, sleep can be viewed from both inside and outside viewpoints. The report can be made on the basis of information gained by an outside observer, with or without the use of special instruments. As a result, we can distinguish three ways to define sleep:

Behavioral definition. If we see someone get undressed and put on pajamas, spend some time in the bathroom, get into bed, turn out the light, and then lie fairly quietly for the next seven or eight hours, we would probably say the person was sleeping. But the flaws in this kind of evidence are rather obvious. Are there any more rigorous behavioral tests to help us define just when a person is in fact sleeping? The one most commonly used in sleep studies is to have the person hold a card between the fingers. When the card slips out, the person is said to be asleep. Other tests would include reports of the difficulty in making someone wake up or respond. One might also deprive people of sleep until they collapse in exhaustion, at which point we can reasonably infer that they are sleeping.

Instrument definition. To get around possible attempts to pretend or to fake sleep, one can introduce instruments whose results are presumably not under the person's control. The most commonly used instrument is the EEG, with sleep being defined in terms of the type of brain wave that is dominant. As we will see later, the EEG is like any other instrument: Originally introduced to gather data on a state that had already been defined by other means, the instrument soon "takes over" and determines how the state shall be defined. Thus, as a result of using the EEG to gather data on sleeping, we now distinguish five different stages of the waking and sleeping cycle.

Experiential definition. Subjects can be asked to report on their own experience of being asleep—in retrospect, of course. If awakened and questioned, most persons can report what the experience of awakening was like, how disoriented or bewildered they feel, and what they recall of the sleep experience. They can usually tell whether or not they were dreaming, what the dream was about and what its emotional quality was. Studies of sleepers who are awakened at various times and immediately questioned indicate that the defining characteristic of the sleep experience, or the way that adults generally describe having been asleep rather than awake, is in terms of their sense of "being present." That is, people know they have been asleep because for some period of time they have not felt themselves "present" to themselves.[6] This definition is by no means completely satisfactory, but as we will see below, it is useful in exploring the experience of sleeping.

Although it may seem helpful to be able to define sleep in three ways rather than one, the fact is that the initial result is one of confusion. The problem is that

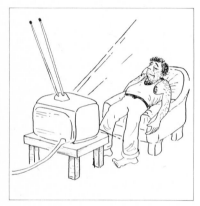

Fig. 9.3. Sleeping requires that one surrender to the situation—but it may not occur as easily, nor in the same way, for everyone.

rapid eye movements (REMs). Eye movements that usually occur during dreaming periods in sleep.

results obtained by the three definitions are not necessarily identical. Persons who appear to be dozing may well say, with some indignation, "I heard every word you said," and the curious thing is that, if properly motivated, many persons can discriminate both familiar and unfamiliar sounds in all EEG stages of sleep.[7] What is suggested by a comparison of results from the three definitions is that sleep is not a single nor simple phenomenon but an extremely complex and variable state that may be influenced by personal, physiological, biological, cultural, and even sociohistorical factors (see Figure 9.3).

Personal and social sleeping. Sleep is not only a highly individualized experience and behavior, but a significant social act as well. Like every important social act, how we sleep and how we feel about the sleep of ourselves and others will be influenced by our roles as social beings. We are trained to sleep for certain periods, at certain times, and for certain lengths of time. In fact, the stages of our development through childhood as well as our positions as older persons may often be defined entirely in terms of what time we go to bed. Society arranges for us to become sleepy during the evening, to sleep uninterruptedly for some seven or eight hours, and then to wake up in the morning and go about our business.

However, there are wide individual differences in how this established schedule is enjoyed or disliked, adhered to or not. We differ as well in how we experience the time of sleeping, whether or not it seemed like a moment or a longer period, and whether or not we recall what we did during sleep, such as dreaming. We differ in our sleep activities, some of us lying quietly or with little movement, others tossing, turning, walking, talking, or snoring. We differ even more in how we fall asleep and the ways in which we wake up. We differ by age, society, and historical era in the place for sleeping, the time for sleeping, and the position for sleeping. At the two ends of the life cycle, in early years and in late years, social restrictions on time, place, and position are greatly relaxed: Infants and old folks are permitted to nap almost anywhere. Some persons are larks in their sleep habits, some are owls; and this may be related to individual roles and preferences as well as to social demands. Work seems to be related to the day, fun and play to the night. Thus the hard worker gets up early, stays awake, and retires at an early hour, whereas the entertainer sleeps late and stays awake until the early morning hours.

In short, sleep is one of our most significant and central kinds of behavior. So, rather than refer to it as simply an act or a state, it might more properly be described as an institution, like marriage.

4. EEG sleep records indicate two different "awake" stages and four successively deeper "sleep" stages.

As we have just seen, individual reports of the experience of sleep can lead us to viewing the phenomenon in new ways. What such reports do not tell us, however, is what happens over the course of a period of sleep, and in particular what are the common characteristics of the course of sleep among people in general. On the other hand, external evidence, either from observation or from instruments, has always been difficult to obtain without awakening the sleeper. Two breakthroughs in sleep research have changed all this. The first is the use of the EEG to indicate stages, or depth, of sleep. The second is the discovery of REM's, or rapid eye movements,⊙ and their relation to dreaming. The full story has resulted in an unexpected and complicated set of findings that are not as yet fully understood.

The EEG sleep record. Through the centuries of intense interest in sleeping, many hints had appeared to suggest that various bodily activities did not cease but either changed or even increased when one fell asleep. The brain, the eyes, and the autonomic nervous system, in particular, had attracted the attention of investigators. When Hans Berger introduced the use of the EEG in the late 1920s, it became possible to record moment-to-moment changes in the general pattern of brain activity. One of the pioneers in sleep research, using the EEG as well as other approaches, was Nathaniel Kleitman, of the University of Chicago. He made the first studies of the sleep patterns of normal adults in such settings as underground caves, where environmental cues were completely absent.[8] William Dement, then a medical student with an interest in sleep research, joined Kleitman in the 1950s, and soon the two investigators began using the EEG to chart progressive changes in brain waves in the course of a night's sleep.[9]

The stages of sleep that are now agreed on by investigators, and the characteristics associated with each stage, are shown in summary form in Figure 9.4. Individuals differ in their sleep patterns, of course, and one individual may vary from one sleep session to the next. The figure is meant only to indicate the characteristics most generally found among the healthy college students who usually serve as participants in such studies.

It is apparent from this kind of data that brain activity does not decrease during sleep, as might be expected, but rather changes its form. Sleeping is in its own way a very active experience, but because muscular movement is blocked (probably by a heightened level of activity in the portion of the brain called the *reticular activating system*) the activity takes place in different ways than it does when we are awake.

Sleep is also an activity that changes as the person's bodily condition changes for better or worse. For example, normal sleep patterns and stages have been found

Questioned about their normal sleeping habits, a number of adults reported that they could not fall asleep unless they went through one of the following rituals:

- The right foot was sticking out of the covers.
- The blanket was exactly halfway up the middle of the back.
- The head was lying flat without a pillow.
- The arms were stretched above the head.
- Earphones from a radio were delivering loud music.
- Light was coming in from outside the room.
- They were holding some familiar object, such as a stuffed toy.
- They were wearing pajamas; or no pajamas; or half pajamas.
- The room was completely dark and silent.
- The head was between two pillows, in a "pillow sandwich."
- The blanket was wrapped around the head.

Stage		Condition	EEG waveform (idealized)	EEG wave type and frequency (cps)
Awake 1		Alert, quiet, awake		Beta 12+
Awake 2		Drowsy, relaxed, falling asleep		Alpha 8–12
Sleep 1	(REM)	Lightly asleep, dreaming	 X X	Mostly 2–7, mixed; sawtooth at X
	(NREM)	Lightly asleep, not dreaming	 X X	Mostly 2–7, mixed; spike at X
Sleep 2		Moderate sleep	 X X	12–14; K-complex at X
Sleep 3		Deep sleep		20–50% Delta, 1–2
Sleep 4		Very deep sleep		More than 50% Delta, 1–2

Fig. 9.4. Sleep stages, and some of the characteristics of sleep, according to the EEG record.

to be markedly disturbed during the period following major surgery, even when the patient seemed otherwise to be progressing well. Further, sleep gives rise to individual and personal experiences that may or may not correspond to what is indicated on an EEG tracing. For example, people who are aroused and then questioned during EEG stages Awake 1, Awake 2, Sleep 1, and even Sleep 2, may all report that they had been awake. It has been reported that a slow, rhythmic sound such as someone's breathing, if picked up by a sleeper during Stage 1 or 2, is heard as a more high-pitched and much more rapid noise than it really is. The sleeper's experience also appears to be related to the way that arousal takes place. If awakened while still feeling "present" to their own thought, persons are likely to be startled and to become suddenly alert, but if awakened after they have lost a sense of their own "presence" and are caught up in a dream situation, they will either awaken slowly or else incorporate the disturbance in the dream and continue sleeping.

5. REM (rapid eye movement) activity appears to define a special, "paradoxical" state of light sleeping.

A second discovery in Kleitman's laboratory[10] established definitely what had been suspected by many other investigators. It was that periods of dreaming are accompanied by rapid, synchronized movements of the eyes. This type of eye movement is quite different from what can be observed in most individuals as they are falling asleep—a slow, rhythmical, but nonsynchronized swinging of the eyeballs. The latter is a sensitive indicator of the onset of sleep.[11]

Kleitman called this phenomenon REM, for *rapid eye movement*. It turned out to be an indicator for a state so remarkable that it has been called "paradoxical sleep." This is because its EEG pattern is very similar to a waking record, yet its other characteristics are not. The muscles, for example, are almost in a state of paralysis during this state. The EEG record of the REM state is so similar to that of Stage 1 sleep that they are listed in the same column in Figure 9.4.[12]

Both REM and non-REM (NREM) sleep are stages of light sleep, very close to the awake state. A record of the various sleep stages that a normal adult goes through in the course of one night would therefore look like Figure 9.5. Here both REM and NREM appear in Stage 1, as the sleeper moves in and out of deep sleep toward awakening.

Periods of REM sleep in adults occur about every 90 minutes, for a total of 1½ to 2 hours in an 8-hour span, or between 10 and 30 percent of the night. It is much more frequent in infants, as much as 50 percent of the sleeping time being REM, but only a little less frequent in old age. Most of the REM period is taken up in

Fig. 9.5. Typical stages in one night's sleep for a normal adult. There is an initial period of deep sleep, then a brief period of REM sleep followed by a period of deep, dreamless sleep. For the rest of the night, there are alternating periods of moderate sleep, light NREM sleep, and light REM sleep.

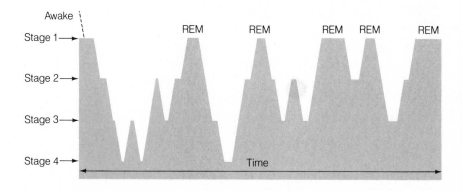

dreaming, and for some time this was considered by sleep researchers to be the mark of REM sleep. However, it now appears that there are many more differences between REM and NREM states, so many that although both may occur when a person is asleep, these really constitute two different kinds of sleep.

REM sleep. Although the EEG indicates that this is a stage of light sleep, it is marked by a blocking of both motor and sensory activity. The REM sleeper is unlikely to sleepwalk or sleeptalk, and is less susceptible to stimulation. What is extremely active, on the other hand, are autonomic functions. Males may have erections (unrelated to sexual arousal, because it occurs in newborn infants). In both females and males the variability of heart rate, breathing rate, and systolic blood pressure° may be 50 percent greater than in NREM sleep. REM dreams are the kind that we usually remember—very visual, filled with vivid images, and emotionally meaningful, like odd or remarkable fantasies. As Figure 9.5 indicates, REM sleep occurs later during a sleep period and is always preceded by at least one period of Stage 3 or 4 sleep without dreams.

NREM sleep. In contrast to REM sleep, and although the EEG indicates about the same level of wakefulness, in NREM sleep there is regular or minimal autonomic activity occurring during the earlier hours of sleep. There is also a greater potential for motor and sensory activity. NREM is a state of relative freedom from emotional activity, with cognitive activity resembling thinking more than fantasy[13] (unless a nightmare intrudes on the NREM state). Sleepwalking and sleeptalking occur during NREM. EEG activity during NREM sleep undergoes changes, the deeper stages of sleep being accompanied by brain waves that are generally higher in amplitude, lower in frequency, and more synchronized or regular.[14]

Both REM and NREM sleep are apparently required for normal functioning. Studies have been done on cats in which they were awakened just as REM periods began so that over the course of some time they became in effect REM-deprived. This produced severe effects: irritability, anxiety, fatigue, and finally disorganization and a psychoticlike state marked by hypersexuality. If deprived of their normally occurring amount of REM sleep, some humans will increase the proportion of REM in subsequent periods of sleeping, apparently to make up for the loss.[15] Some aspect of REM is therefore a biologically necessary experience, as much as the need for (NREM) sleep in general.

But the differences between the two states (REM and NREM) are more striking than their similarities, raising the question of why two kinds of sleep should be necessary. In the REM state, there is activity of those parts of the brain related to emotion and also of the nervous system related to arousal and emotional states. Accompanying this are usually dreams of vivid, emotional, fantastic quality. In the NREM state, there is a relaxation of these systems and accompanying cognitive activity of a quiet thoughtlike quality. In REM, the motor apparatus is inhibited, while in NREM it is quieted but seemingly mildly active and ready for action. Finally, REM sleep comprises much of the sleeping activity of infants—in premature babies as much as 80 percent. As one careful study has shown, REM bursts occur in the brain activity of normal adults all during the twenty four-hour cycle, whether they are awake or asleep, lying down or sitting up, or with eyes open![16]

It seems possible, then, that the individual has two related biological needs. One is for rest and recuperation in various degrees of depth, which appears as NREM sleep in Stages 1 to 4. The other need, appearing as REM sleep, involves the exercise of certain primitive functions that are associated with older parts of the brain and the organism (older in an evolutionary sense). REM sleep, then, might

systolic blood pressure. A reading made of circulating blood against the wall of the arteries. The systolic reading is made at the high point where the heart contracts to empty its blood into the circulatory system.

occur mostly at night or during periods of NREM sleep because at these times there is less interference by the demands of the environment and less need to be motorically active. If this is so, it would follow that the REM state is not necessarily a part of sleeping and that REM dreams are not a necessary aspect of the state. The suggestion makes some sense and accounts for the known facts, but it is quite speculative. Since we do not really know why any living creatures sleep, it is even more difficult to say with confidence why any of us do what we do during sleep.

Dreaming

Dreaming has always occupied a very special place in human affairs. Its content appears to be related, although in sometimes very odd ways, to significant aspects of our waking life. At the same time, the dream is the most personal of all phenomena. It is so personal, in fact, and so close to the very core of myself, that my own dream may be hidden from me, its creator. I may not recall any of it, many of its details may be lost when I awake, and, even if prodded or helped to recapture it, the dream may make no sense to me, much less to others.

Understandably, dreams have always been considered essentially mysterious, filled with portent and significance about the world, suggestive of hidden depths in the person. In a thorough review of the history of dream beliefs and dream theories, Van De Castle concludes that there are "apparently well-documented cases in which dreams have stimulated literary masterpieces, contributed to original theorizing about scientific phenomena, and led to vast political changes. Even our major religions. . . may owe their origins to inspirations revealed in dreams."[17]

---

6. To understand dreaming a distinction must be made between tonic and phasic states of the autonomic system.

For some years, it has appeared that objective studies, based on the use of the EEG and similar instruments and inspired by the discovery of REM phenomena, would finally enable psychologists to develop a sound theory of dreaming. All the evidence is not in, but at this point we can summarize what is known, to see how much the hope has been realized.

REM referred to rapid, synchronized, sometimes jerky movements of the eyes while the dreamer, eyes closed, appeared to be sleeping. The original discovery was that ten persons, awakened when they showed REM activity, reported in three quarters of the instances that they had just been dreaming, but, if awakened when no REM activity appeared, reported dreaming only 7 percent of the time.[18] On the basis of a very large number of studies since that time, it now appears that eye movements of the REM type are usually associated with dreaming, especially if the dreamer is experiencing active participation in the dream. Dreams of the same sort may, however, also occur in as many as 10 percent of the instances in which the dreamer is in a NREM state of sleep. When REM sleep occurs together with dreaming, the way that the eyes move may be related to what is being dreamed—for example, the eyes will sweep horizontally if the dreamer is scanning a scene.

There is thus some relation between REM and dreaming, but the parallel is by no means precise. More intensive studies of other aspects of the REM and NREM states have indicated that much more than dreaming is going on. In the

Fig. 9.6. Elias Howe, the inventor of the
sewing machine, had a (phasic) dream in
which savages were thrusting their spears
down at him, spears with holes in their
points. He awoke from the dream with the
key idea for a workable sewing machine —
to use a needle with the hole in the point
rather than in the head.

REM state, the dreamer's body is essentially paralyzed for voluntary motor and
muscular activity. The brain effectively blocks the activity of nerve cells in the
spine, so that the dreamer can dream of, say, moving a limb without the activity
taking place. This condition, which has been called *tonic*[○] because it shows its
effect on muscle tone, is interrupted from time to time by phases or bursts of
activity, mostly in the autonomic nervous system. The heart and the breathing
apparatus change their rhythms, the pupils change size, the middle ear contracts,
the muscles twitch, the temperature of the brain goes up, blood pressure rises,
penile and nipple erections occur, and gastric secretions increase. In addition, the
eyes begin a period of rapid, jerky, synchronous movements, the phenomenon
that was first discovered and that gave a name to this curious condition of the body.
The more this *phasic*[○] activity, as it is called, occurs, the more vivid and fantastic
are the REM dreams reported if the dreamer is awakened at this point.

Thus we seem to have still another distinction to add to the original distinctions between waking and sleeping, and the more recent distinction between REM
and NREM states. Our newest distinction is between tonic and phasic states. It
now turns out that although REM and NREM states are different in many ways,
they are not completely dissimilar. Dreams are not related precisely to either REM
or NREM states. Rather, the type of mental activity that dreamers report is most
closely related to whether the individual is in a tonic or a phasic condition of sleep.
If phasic activity should occur during a NREM period, there may be a dream
experience and a report of a vivid, emotional, and fantasylike dream. If tonic
activity should occur during a REM period, the report will be of no dreaming or
else of quiet, thoughtlike activity (Figure 9.6).

The quest for a dream theory by means of objective measures of sleep states
has reached just this far. To see what may be learned by approaching the problem
from another direction, we turn now to subjective evidence regarding dreaming.

7. Views of dreaming based on the person's inner experience usually distinguish between the person's awake, rational side and "dark," hidden side.

Nonindustrial societies, which anthropologists used to call "primitive,"
make use of dreams in quite a different way than we usually do in modern West-

tonic (activity). A condition of sleep in
which muscular activity is inhibited.

phasic (activity). A condition of sleep
in which phases of marked autonomic
activity occur.

ern society. Their members have two kinds of dreams. The first is like the one that we have—personal, sometimes remarkable, often requiring interpretation. The second kind is related to the life of the society or tribe—dreams of obvious significance, filled with known and familiar symbols of the group, of great emotional and social import, and closely related to an important event; for example, the dreamer's initiation rites. The latter may not even occur as a dream but as a vision, perhaps gained in a trance and perhaps aided by drugs, starvation, or fatigue. It seems to be the product of a special state that the individual may achieve under the influence of powerful social symbols and rituals. The first kind of dream, like ours, seems to reflect temporary or long-term issues in the passage of one's life.

That there can be two kinds of dreams, under two different sets of influences, suggests that this experience is not only a biological phenomenon but a condition by which the dreamer expresses a status and a role in relation to the rest of society. Just as we might expect, such a condition is understood differently in each society. Our own Western tradition, for at least the past few centuries, has emphasized two roles belonging to the adult. One is open and on the surface, the other hidden, primitive, and unsocialized. The first, the social side of a person, is the role of reason, order, control, and maturity. The second, the person's "dark side," is the role of animal instincts, unreason, antisocial phenomena, most feelings, and, of course, sexuality. The dream theory arising from this split is simple: Dreams are a way of expressing that dark side of the personality that cannot be expressed in the clear light of day, in the social arena.

Freud's contribution. At the end of the nineteenth century, Sigmund Freud brought together the set of beliefs that had been circulating in Western society for more than two centuries. These were beliefs concerning the split between the social and the antisocial, hidden parts of the person. In a book first published in 1900, called *The Interpretation of Dreams,* Freud spelled out his dream theory, in which he publicly discussed his own dreams and their significance (an absolutely unheard-of thing for a professional to do at that time). He used his interpretation of his own dreams to conduct a psychoanalysis of his own neurotic problems, and he advanced a comprehensive theory of the personality that included both dream states and awake states.[19]

The dream theory itself was almost mechanically simple. It said that we all have wishes, at the conscious level as well as at the unconscious. We spend our lives trying to gratify them, with more or less success. If they are conscious and thus acceptable to ourselves, either we work to gratify them or we give them up. But if they are unconscious and therefore not acceptable in conscious thought, they keep driving for satisfaction, and we cannot recognize them in order to give them up. They may find an outlet in our waking lives in a variety of ways: in slips of the tongue, in jokes, in uncontrolled outbursts, in neurotic symptoms, even in choice of occupation or artistic creation. But they find their chief outlet under those special conditions when our conscious, censoring minds are at rest, during sleep. These unconscious wishes, representatives of the dark side of the personality, make their appearance in just enough disguise to evade censorship. Hence the curious and fantastic quality of dreams and also their susceptibility to multiple interpretations.

Freud's great contribution was not just to propound this theory of dreams, which was not his alone, but to link the theory to a comprehensive psychology of the personality. He said that the process by which the dream was formed and then expressed was exactly the same as the process by which we do everything else in our waking lives. There were not two sets of processes, one belonging to the open side and one to the hidden side of the personality. Rather, there was only one process, most clearly spelled out in dreams. Our conscious, waking life was simply another and rather less important version of it. Freud had, in effect, turned upside down our Western view of the personality and how it worked, by saying that our unconscious life was more important than our conscious life.

The Senoi contribution. An anthropologist named Kilton Stewart began in 1934 to visit the Senoi, a nonindustrial society of about 12,000 persons who lived in the nearly inaccessible rainforest of the mountains on the Malay Peninsula. This seemingly primitive group had apparently been able to develop a peaceful and stable society without police or prisons or even corporal punishment and without any known instances of serious conflict or personal violence. All this was accomplished, too, with no tradition of inherited authority. Their only honorary title was "Healer," and their social organization was based entirely on free choice by the individual.

Central to the socializing process among the Senoi was the careful training of each child in using his or her own psychological resources. These inner resources appeared primarily in one's dreams. And so the children were educated through their dreams in ways of mastering the forces in themselves and in the world around them. In turn, the children played a similar role at daily "dream clinics" in educating other persons, including adults, for the dreams of children were accepted and understood as important messages concerning ways of acting.[20]

For example, during the day a child sees the black smoke of a fire that some adults have set to clear a piece of land. Dreaming about this at night, the child awakens in fright, telling of images of choking. The parents' response is first to offer comfort, in the manner of parents the world over, but then to advise the child how good the dream was. What you must now do, they say, is to go back to sleep, reenter the dream and then go deep into the smoke — for in it you will surely find a treasure. This is the sense of such a dream — it points to a treasure that can be brought back to the community. Most often this is a gift or a contribution that only this particular child can make, to help in his or her personal growth or to assist in developing appropriate feelings and images in other persons.[21]

To the Senoi, all dreams are potentially good. It is a good thing, for example, to die in dreams, for that exhausts the negative force of one's antagonist. To kill in dreams is also good, for the one who is killed must have been a representation of an evil force working against the dreamer. In this way, by each individual facing and overcoming the negative forces at night, the atmosphere for the group is kept clear and positive during the day.

Our own "advanced" view, in Western society, a view best expressed in the work of Freud, is, rather, that we must learn how to fight the real battles during the day, in order to keep our nights more peaceful. We would advise someone: Express your aggression appropriately during the day, and then you will be assured of not having disguised dreams of aggression at night. The Senoi would say that your aggression is your feeling, your personal force, so you must learn to handle it appropriately during your dreams, in order that all of us may live together more peacefully during the day.[22]

Induced states

In his recent book *The Natural Mind*, Andrew Weil[23] reviews all the known states of altered consciousness and concludes that they are similar in many ways, that they differ from one another only in degree, and that the less extreme of them shades off into our accustomed, normal state. He finds that all the states that differ from our normal, awake one have certain characteristics in common. There is a more or less obvious loss of awareness or of the "social ego," shown to a mild degree in simple absentmindedness and extending to an extreme degree in states of total ego loss (such as schizophrenia). There are changes in the experience of the body, especially in regard to physical lightness. There is a greater or less loss of time sense, in the extreme case becoming a feeling of timelessness. There is an increased access to buried memories and sometimes to unfamiliar feelings.

These characteristics are found in quite similar form whether the state is induced by meditation, drugs, hypnosis, fasting, or religious ecstasy. In a study of 150 experienced users of marijuana, Tart found a similar agreement as well as a communality with nondrug experiences. His subjects reported heightened sense perception, increased and more vivid imagery, alterations in space and time perception, and changes in memory, feelings, and sense of one's own ego.[24]

From this kind of evidence, we might infer that there are really no separate states that we can call *altered*. People in many different states appear to act in much the same way. They can even furnish objective evidence (such as filling out scales or questionnaires) that show striking similarities between persons and among the different states. Yet when subjective evidence is offered differences between the states are often as evident as their similarities. If asked, I would have no difficulty at all in distinguishing among my own states of consciousness — that I am awake, half awake, fully asleep, waking up from sleep, drunk, stoned, high, in transition toward or from one of these states, have achieved a peak of mystical ecstasy, and so on.

But if I make a claim on the basis of such subjective evidence, it may be objected that I am the only witness for my own case. Can such evidence be accepted as valid data in a scientific discipline? It is a question that has haunted the study of induced states of altered consciousness. To explore some answers to this question, we will look at two major varieties of induced states: the hypnotic and the meditative.

8. Hypnosis, which may consist of more than one kind of state, has been explained as a special state of consciousness or as a special social role.

Although different forms of hypnotic trances have been reported from very ancient times, the phenomenon as we know it today is recent. In 1784, there appeared the first recorded instance of what was initially called *somnambulism*[⊙] — meaning that while asleep the person was capable of complex motor acts (Figure 9.7). It was a "generally accessible second state of consciousness which could be put to a rational purpose (while) the semisleeping subject remains in verbal contact."[25] For a long time, it was believed that the state was induced by the flow of "animal magnetism"[⊙] from healer to patient, a belief based on the enormous successes of Franz Anton Mesmer, a charismatic Austrian physician whose name still lives in such words as *mesmerize*.

Eventually the notion of "suggestion" took the place of animal magnetism as the supposed force. Even today we speak of some persons as being more "suggestible" than others. But regardless of the forces that are presumed to bring about the state, it remains just what it was almost 200 years ago: a situation in which, under conditions of concentration and focusing of attention, coupled perhaps with heightened belief or motivation, many persons can be brought, or can even bring themselves, to experience and to act in altered ways.[26]

People differ very much in their susceptibility to hypnotic induction procedures, and a number of scales and tests have been developed to assess individuals on this dimension. But there appears to be no question that, given the right condi-

somnambulism. Sleepwalking.

animal magnetism. Mesmer's term for a "magnetic fluid" with which he claimed to effect miraculous cures. The cures were, in fact, effected by hypnotism or suggestion.

Fig. 9.7. The first recorded case of somnambulism, the precursor of modern hypnotism, may have occurred under this tree on May 4, 1784. (From Van den Berg, 1974, p. 69)

tions, some persons will do some or all of the things listed in the marginal material. The question now is, How can we explain this?

One school of thought on this topic argues that under hypnosis the person is in a special state of consciousness not quite like the normal, awake state. It is evidently not a sleeping state, either, for EEG traces are like those of the waking state rather than any of the recognized stages of sleep.[27] Further, it is possible to induce hypnosis without any suggestion concerning relaxation. If hypnotized people are stimulated with pain-producing instruments, they may report feeling no pain, yet their brain activity in response to the stimulation is just as great as if they were experiencing pain. Thus, if anything is changed in this state, it is most likely not the nerve pathways.[28] All this evidence says what hypnosis is not, but it does not answer the question of what it is. For this we turn again to hypnotized persons, who do report that their own experience is changed. They often know they are being influenced, and they may even be aware that they are able to oppose the influence, but they "choose" to allow the influence to take over.

In direct confrontation with this view of hypnosis are other views that claim that we have no need to talk about such a special state. Sarbin, for one, has argued that the hypnotic state, so- called, can be explained in simpler and more familiar terms.[29] It is a role that subjects adopt under certain social pressures, much like the roles that we play as obedient employees (when inwardly we may feel rebellious), or as swaggering toughs (when inwardly we may be quite afraid). A similar position has been argued for some years by Theodore X. Barber, who has been able to reproduce most of the known hypnotic phenomena simply by persuading or bribing people to do the same things.[30]

Hypnosis and pain. Because it would appear that we need more evidence to settle the issue, we now turn to the phenomenon of pain, for which it is possible to gather both objective and subjective evidence at the same time and in response to the same experimental conditions. In one study described by Hilgard,[31] pain was induced by having people squeeze a measuring instrument called a *dynamometer* while their upper arms were tightly bandaged with a tourniquet. The increased blood flow caused by squeezing the dynamometer is blocked by the tourniquet, resulting in increasing pain. The person's ability to withstand the pain is then read off directly on the dynamometer. Hypnotized people, instructed not to feel any

Persons in the hypnotic state have been observed to

- Behave and experience as though they were at an earlier time of their lives (age regression)
- Dream in accordance with the hypnotist's suggestions
- See, hear, smell, and even touch what was not physically present (hallucinations)
- Fail to sense what was physically present
- Be unable to remember, after the hypnotic session (amnesia)
- Carry out suggestions at a later time, with no sense of why they are doing so (posthypnotic suggestion)
- Experience dramatic changes in their awareness of the passage of time
- Show physiological changes, such as blisters or marks on the skin resembling religious stigmata

pain, were able to continue the exercise without giving evidence they were in pain.

However, there still remains a critical question: Were these people somehow blocking out the pain as a result of the hypnotic suggestion, or were they truly experiencing the pain but, being highly motivated, were controlling their expression, continuing the pressure, and sturdily insisting they felt nothing? To answer this question, Hilgard gathered one more kind of data from his participants by means of another measure that is claimed to be an accurate gauge of the presence of pain. It is a measure of the systolic blood pressure at the middle finger, which should increase sharply under conditions of pain. When this additional measure was taken, it did *not* show an increase for the hypnotized persons. This led Hilgard to conclude that they were not merely covering up the normal experience of pain but were in fact in some different, "dissociated" state.

Other studies have shown that hypnotized people are able to produce tissue changes in accordance with suggestions. If they were stimulated on both forearms to a degree that would normally produce inflammation and some mild tissue damage, these persons produced the expected results on one arm but less damage on the other arm when they were instructed that the latter was insensitive.[32] Blisters on the skin have been produced by hypnotized people although the only stimulus was the suggestion that they were being burned. In one study, when the hypnotist suggested to participants that they were experiencing pressure and pain from a metal headband being tightened around the scalp, they were able to show the appropriate respiratory and emotional changes, although other results, such as changes in blood pressure, skin temperature, and pulse rate, were not well reproduced.[33]

Pain is, of course, a very complex phenomenon. It includes the subjective and reported experience, physiological reactions such as increased pulse rate, changes in feeling, and an increase in anxiety that is quite distinct from the pain experience itself. The first of these, the experience, can apparently be eliminated by hypnosis. Associated feelings can also be controlled under hypnosis. Physiological reactions can be markedly altered, although very nearly the same results can also be brought about without the hypnotic induction procedure. Finally, the associated anxiety can also be controlled by nonhypnotic means. In short, evidence from pain studies provides a mixed picture as to the nature of the hypnotic state.[34]

Experiencing hypnosis. When the subjective evidence is examined, it appears that hypnosis may not be a single state that is experienced in the same way by everyone. Consider another study reported by Hilgard.[35] Some subjects score low on a hypnotizability scale, while others score high. When they are all hypnotized and given the suggestion not to feel pain (analgesia),[○] the lows show a moderate analgesic[○] effect and the highs a marked analgesic effect. However, when they are not hypnotized but merely told that a medication given them will reduce the pain (although it actually has no such effect), the lows again show a moderate analgesic effect, but the highs show no effect at all.

Our interpretation of these results is that the lows can be placed into a suggestible state, a kind of mild hypnotic trance, by any suggestion from someone who seems to be an expert; and that this will then produce moderate hypnosislike effects. The highs, on the other hand, may depend much more on their own interpretation of the situation. When this interpretation leads them to the experience of actually being hypnotized, they will show marked hypnosislike effects. The first response, showed by the lows, we might call the *placebo*[○] experience. The second response, by the highs, is much closer to a familiar "hypnosis" experience. It might then be conjectured that in the placebo experience I am in the state

analgesia. The inability to feel pain.

analgesic. Pain-killing or pain-lessening substance.

placebo. An inactive substance substituted for a drug and given to the subjects of a control group in an experiment.

of actively needing what is offered or said to me. In the hypnosis experience, I allow myself to passively incorporate whatever is offered.

9. Subjective evidence suggests the existence of still other states, which are familiar as meditation° or as yogic and Zen achievements.

As we have seen, subjective evidence indicates that there may be many different states of awareness, each marked by its own mode of personal experience. The objective evidence, on the other hand, indicates that there are a limited number of basic states that can be modified by the person's motivation or set or physiological condition. But both kinds of evidence suggest that normal adults are capable of many alterations of consciousness, even though the resulting changes in experience and feeling may not always coincide with changes in behavior.

Extraordinary states. The question of how extreme these alterations might become is one that has attracted, terrified, fascinated, and angered thinkers for many centuries. Many persons, for example, have had the experience of sudden bursts of great energy under emergency demands or conditions of extreme stress. Is this completely reducible to a biochemical phenomenon? To take another example, there is a mode of controlled perception that is reported by some devotees of Eastern mystical practices. They claim that, under proper conditions and given the right motivation, training, and setting, it is possible to "merge" completely with what one sees, to "take over" the visual target and incorporate it. (Note our embarrassing shortage of adequate English words to discuss these matters.) When this happens, it is claimed, the target appears in an absolute and astonishing purity, its colors radiant and perfect, its shape the very ideal of that object.

This is an extreme notion, granted, but for just that reason it provides a fitting introduction to more familiar and less extreme instances. There is now a great deal of scattered evidence concerning unusual states of awareness, many of them instances in which normally involuntary phenomena are brought about on a voluntary basis. When this happens, one's entire field of awareness can change.[36]

Yogic and Zen states. Many practitioners of yoga have demonstrated voluntary control over physiological processes such as heart rate.[37] Years of devoted training are said to be necessary for these achievements. As is now well known, however, untrained persons can, with brief practice and appropriate laboratory procedures such as operant conditioning, learn to control the production of alpha waves in the brain.[38] They can learn to regulate their blood pressure and even, under hypnosis, to control the distribution of blood to their two hands so that the temperature in one is increased while the temperature in the other is decreased.[39] One such person was extensively studied during research on the states associated with different brain waves. He learned to maintain production of alpha waves, to eliminate pain, and to minimize bleeding. His description of his own experience was that it was similar to "depersonalization." That is, he was in a state in which he believed that he was sticking a needle in *an* arm rather than in *his* arm; that he was in some way moving *outside* of the body that was his; and therefore that this body could become an object for him.[40]

In studies of meditators who use simple techniques of concentrating on a word or phrase (mantra), EEG records show that their sustained alpha rhythm is

meditation. A process of conscious concentration on something—object, idea, or feeling—for an extended period of time. The goal is often to achieve an altered state of consciousness.

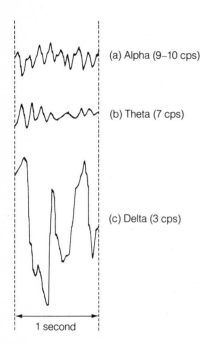

(a) Alpha (9–10 cps)

(b) Theta (7 cps)

(c) Delta (3 cps)

1 second

Fig. 9.8. Brain waves at three phases of
meditation. The *delta* waves shown at (c)
normally occur only in the very deepest
sleep or in conditions of coma. The waves
at (a) occurred at the start of meditation
when, with eyes closed, the meditator was
repeating a mantra phrase. Those at (b)
occurred during deep concentration. If the
EEG record is to be trusted as indicating
different states of awareness, these results
are of some significance; they were taken
from the scalp of an experienced yogic
meditator.

easily interferred with by presenting some outside stimulus. This, in effect, is
what happens to us when we are simply relaxed and resting. By contrast, EEG
studies of Zen Buddhist meditators show no alpha blocking in spite of repeated
presentation of external stimuli.[41] This may indicate a difference in how much the
meditative state is "insulated" from the world, or perhaps how "deep" the state is.
Yogic states of meditation also differ from relaxation in regard to the activity of the
sympathetic nervous system (increased in meditation) and breathing activity
(much less in meditation).[42] How the difference is accomplished by the meditator,
however, is not clear (see Figure 9.8). It has been suggested that stimulation of the
reticular activating system of the brain will block sensory messages and thus
insulate the person from external stimuli. Perhaps the concentrated attention of
the meditative states is achieved in this way.

Are there states of consciousness?

From an outside viewpoint, distinct and different states of consciousness can
be inferred on the basis of many kinds of evidence. The EEG record is one such
source of evidence. For example, it gives us indications of different states that may
vary from frenzy, through excitement, and down to sleep and finally coma. It is
possible to put the objective evidence together and to develop a theory that helps to
explain the various states. This is just what has recently been accomplished in
regard to the different states of sleep, although it has yet to be accomplished in
regard to, say, hypnosis or meditation.

From an inside viewpoint, however, the evidence is often so different that it
cannot always be reconciled with evidence gained from an outside viewpoint. As a
result, the inside viewpoint does not always define the same states nor even define
them with the same precision. Thus, from an inside viewpoint there may not be a
relatively large number of equivalent states of consciousness but rather one central
"home state" that each individual experiences as normal and to which the individual returns after experiences in other states. It may be, too, that only from this
home state can the person think about or communicate about other, possible
states. Finally, from an inside viewpoint it is not always easy to mark off the
boundaries between states. They tend to shade into each other in ways that are
often difficult to describe or report.

The question of whether there are different states of consciousness will thus
be answered in different ways, depending on whether one takes the inside or the
outside viewpoint. But, whatever answer we arrive at, at the present state of our
knowledge it appears that both approaches, the inside and the outside, may be
needed in order to pursue the study of consciousness.

Summary

1. Our normal, waking state is just one of the many possible states of consciousness.

2. Natural states of consciousness appear to occur spontaneously in the course of
our normal living, while induced states require special influences or intervention by others to be elicited.

3. Unlike other states of consciousness, the awake state is communal or consensual, not individual.

4. The study of altered states is a major concern of the psychophysiologist, whose approach is to invoke or alter an activity and then to assess the effect on specific physiological functions.

5. Two kinds of psychological set can be distinguished: Implicit set is potentially known only to the person; explicit set is known to both the person and to others, such as an experimenter.

6. Sleep can be defined through behavior, instrumentation, or experiential report.

7. EEG records of sleep indicate two "awake" stages and four successively deeper "sleep" stages.

8. In general, the REM (rapid eye movement) state is accompanied by high arousal, emotionality, and vivid dreams, while the NREM (non-rapid eye movement) state appears to be related to relatively lower arousal and affect, with dreams of a more thoughtlike quality.

9. The occurrence of dreaming is not linked precisely to either REM or NREM states.

10. Dreams are a biological phenomenon as well as a condition in which the dreamer expresses role and status relations to society.

11. One of Freud's major contributions was a theory of dreams that was tied to a comprehensive theory of the personality.

12. To the Senoi group, all dreams are potentially good because they provide both insight and information about one's feelings, as well as a way to master one's impulses.

13. Weil's thesis concerning altered states is that, in comparison with the awake state, they all show a more or less obvious loss of awareness of the "social ego."

14. Hypnosis has been shown to be capable of reducing pain reactions and modifying physiological responses, especially if both need and willingness to surrender are high.

15. Practitioners of yoga and Zen have demonstrated voluntary control over many physiological processes.

Excursion III

About time

This excursion will help you to think about our relationship to time. You will begin to understand how the topic can be discussed in terms of personal time, public time, and the regularity of biorhythms. Because we find ourselves embedded in time, all animal and human behavior is affected by time.

You will find that time perception depends largely on one's own experiencing. You make your own time. It will become clear that we can live our lives in the future, the present, or the past, with different consequences for each. Specific factors in our time experience will be suggested as affecting our ongoing behavior and even the rate of our aging.

Time is everywhere. In this excursion, you will be introduced to some of its many facets. Moreover, you will come to understand that time can be viewed from either an inside or an outside viewpoint. It presents us with a dimension that is invisible from the inside viewpoint, yet can be seen everywhere, as change, when approached from the outside viewpoint.

An American psychologist, Paul Bakan, has noted that "Books devoted to the psychology of time are rare, and most standard textbooks either omit or barely mention the problem of time."[1] Indeed, the average person, psychologist or not, rarely thinks about time. St. Augustine expressed our attitude very well, some 1,600 years ago, when, in answer to the question, "What is time?" he said "As long as no one asks me, I know the answer; the moment I want to explain it to an enquirer, I do not know." Time is simply taken for granted, for it is all around us and nothing can ever happen outside of it. Our relation to time is like the fish's relation to water, and it has often been remarked that the fish will be the last creature to discover the existence of water.

Varieties of time

Time is more varied than we think. It is the uninterrupted and endless flow that is marked off by our watches and clocks. But it is also the framework for our most diverse experiences.

Mohammed, music and marijuana. Muslim legend has it that Mohammed's donkey, on leaping up to heaven, tripped over a jar of water—but by the time the donkey and Mohammed had returned to earth, having visited each of the seven heavens and been touched by God, not a drop had yet been spilled from the jar. Mozart once described how he put his great musical compositions together in his head. When they were done, he said, "I do not hear it in my imagination at all as a succession—the way it must come later—but all at once, as it were. It is a rare feast! All the inventing and making goes on in me as in a beautiful strong dream. But the best of all is the hearing of it all at once."

We may reply that both of these examples are impossible, for there can be no instantaneous or even stretched-out time. But is this so? A common experience under the influence of marijuana is that time is distorted. For example, someone may report, "It was a good two-mile or longer walk, and at times it seemed that certain segments of it were stretched out or expanded." Or else, " When I left the curb, I could tell that any approaching cars were several blocks away. However, it seemed to be taking me forever to get across the street. I looked down at my feet and they seemed to be going fast enough, but when I would look to the other side of the street, it seemed to still be a far way off."

In these drug experiences, you will note, the person seemed to be aware of two varieties of time at once. The intrusion of one of these kinds of time on the other is similar to our common experience when we are bored or impatient. Trapped at a deadly boring lecture, I may look at my watch after what seems to be a very long time, only to discover that a mere four minutes have passed. The kind of time that I feel it ought to be is determined by the clock; it marks itself off independently of my ongoing experience. The other kind of time is more personal, and it directly reflects the experience that I am undergoing. These are the two varieties of time and their relations, that we will now consider.

Experiencing personal time. The first time that as a child you stayed alone in your house, waiting for older persons to return, may have seemed to you interminably long. By the fiftieth time you did the same thing, however, you were accustomed to the experience, and time seemed to pass "normally." Public, clock time is not what had changed, of course. What changed was your experience of time passing—or more precisely, your comparison of your own psychological time with what you knew about clock time. Our personal experience of time is always the result of our comparing our own ongoing situation with what we know, or think we know, about the passage of clock time. And we can, apparently, make this comparison even in sleep. In one study, three of ten persons showed that they were able to awaken within ten minutes of a preset time during the night.[2]

The variations in how we experience our own psychological time in relation to clock time are endless. On happy occasions, time may seem to fly, whereas when we are in mourning or waiting or passing a dull day time seems to drag. Our personalities have an important effect, too. If I am the kind of person who likes to have things over and done with, my experience will be much more affected by a situation in which time seems to drag; whereas if I tend to take things easy and wait them out my comparison of my experience with clock time will lead to a different sense of time passing.

---

1. Our time experience is related to whether we experience it as process or as duration, and also to the number of targets in our attention.

Process and duration. Piaget[3] has suggested that one of the most important determinants in time experience is the *position* from which we consider time passing. If we attend to the passing of time as it happens, or in the moment, or if we vividly relive its passing as though it were happening now, we would be attending to its *process*. If, however, we attend to the time that has already passed, judging it by looking back on it, we would be attending to its *duration*. When our attention is to the process of time, it is experienced as a flow or movement going on right now. When our attention is to the duration of time, it is experienced as a "space" of time spread out between our present moment and some moment in the past (see Figure E3.1).

As an example of the latter—when people were aroused from sleep in an experiment and asked to estimate the duration of their interrupted sleep, they calculated the distance between their present moment and a specifically remem-

Fig. E3.1. For many persons in this situation, time is empty and therefore seems to drag while it is passing. But it also seems empty in retrospect—and so the person also has the retrospective sense that it has slipped away too fast.

bered moment before falling asleep. If dreams had intervened during this time, the earlier moment was experienced as further back in time.[4]

Some interesting relations can be shown between process-duration and how fast time seems to pass, if we add one additional variable: the number of targets that one attends to. In Table E3.1, we show the four possibilities.

Access to public time

We know of time in one other way, the time of clocks. This is a public time, a consensual time, the time that most of us would say is "real" time or the time that "it is." If it is experienced individually, in what we have just discussed as personal time, it will seem quite variable from one situation to another and its units may not be the same from one person to another. But, if it is known publicly and socially, it will be referred to an instrument such as a clock, it will be judged the

Table E3.1. Experiencing time.[a]

	Process	Duration
Few targets	(Impatience) Time passes slowly.	(Foxhole) Time passed rapidly.
Many targets	(Childhood) Time passes rapidly.	(Vacation) Time passed slowly.

[a] When we are in the state that we call *impatience*, our attention is concentrated on the passing of time in the present moment (process), and it is narrowed down to very few targets; time then seems to be moving slowly. The typical experience of childhood, on the other hand, is of concentrating on many targets in the moment, of devoting brief attention to many different things; and time is experienced as moving fast. Soldiers trapped in a foxhole during combat, necessarily concentrating on few targets, typically reported when the air raid was over that they were surprised so much time had passed; that is, experienced as duration, time had passed rapidly. During vacationing, and because of the novelty of the situation, our attention is likely to be scattered over many targets. If we attempt to judge how much time has already passed we will be surprised to find that time has been passing so slowly.

same by anyone who can "tell time" by means of a clock, and its units will be the same from one day to the next, or from one century to the next, or from one person to another. As we have said, normally a person's time experience rests on their comparing the passing of their personal time with the knowledge of public time.

There are two ways that the person's time experience can be studied, the one from an outside approach and the other from an inside approach.

Reaction time: the outside approach. The field of experimental psychology began with this kind of study, carried out in laboratories in Germany in the 1880s. Accurate timepieces were used to determine, to the thousandth of a second, how long it took people to carry out simple movements. A stimulus, such as a flash of light, would be presented, and the person would be instructed to respond as rapidly as possible, by pressing a button. The time between the light flash, or stimulus, and the button pressing, or response — which in adults is normally about one third of a second — was called one's reaction time.[○]

Reaction time can be affected by very many factors; for example, one's age and physical condition and motivation and amount of practice and even whether one is responding to a visual or an auditory stimulus. The relation between age and reaction time is that for most persons the reaction time is longer for older persons. It is shortest, under ideal conditions, for people in their early twenties — which is one reason that champion sprinters are usually of this age, whereas marathon champions may be as much as ten years older. If a young person and an elderly person are both asked to respond as fast as possible but the older one takes twice as long to respond, we can infer that the same length of experienced time ("almost immediately") is measurably different. That is, the older person experiences a greater chunk of (public) time as immediate, or as passing rapidly. We would conclude that the older one gets the faster one experiences the same amount of (public) time as passing — and older people usually report that time seems to be passing uncomfortably fast.

Perception of time: the inside approach. In the inside approach, which has also been productive of a great number of experimental studies, people are asked to estimate how much clock time they think has passed under certain conditions.[5] For example, people would be put to work on two kinds of tasks, one interesting and one boring, and asked when they had finished how long they thought it had taken them. The results are usually clear-cut in showing that people's judgment of time duration, or of how much time they thought had already passed, is markedly affected by their situation and activity. Even such a brief event as the saying of a sentence may be affected. A sentence made up of nonsense syllables is judged as having taken longer to say than a meaningful sentence of the same number of syllables.[6] This would be consistent with our earlier suggestion that in duration judgments of time, a smaller number of targets (in this case, a unitary meaning of a sentence) leads to experiencing time as shorter.[7]

In a remarkable series of experiments, Aaronson[8] hypnotized people and suggested to them that one of the "tenses" — past, present, or future — was either nonexistent or expanded for them. Under conditions of no past or no future, they became immobilized, reporting an experience of a deathlike state in which time was "collapsed." They estimated time as being much shorter than would have been stated on the basis of clock time. People's comparison of their personal time with their public time can thus be markedly influenced. Under normal circumstances, however, and perhaps as a result of many years of experience, adults are able to estimate the duration of short blocks of time (up to about a minute) with accuracy.

reaction time. In an experimental situation, the term used for the time between the onset of a stimulus and the occurrence of a response.

2. Public time may be socially organized in different ways by different groups of people.

Every organized social group, large or small, has its own public, consensual time, the time that the members of the group agree that "it is." In modern societies, we are so accustomed to clocks that we easily come to believe that clock time is the only time that "it" can be. In actuality, the time we all agree on is in some ways quite arbitrary. We change it from season to season and from place to place, calling it "daylight saving time" as distinct from "standard time." We set our own watches by "it," perhaps seldom bothering as to how accurate "it" is. Recently the U.S. Naval Observatory changed its method of keeping time, and thus its standard of public time for all the rest of us, when it switched over from a mechanical device to an atomically powered device. Although few of us suspected it, when this was done the public time to which we all have access was changed by a small fraction.

And even the instruments on which we depend for marking off this passage of public time are more recent than most of us suppose. In one form or another, water clocks have been known for about 5,000 years, but they did not usually serve to determine the one public time of a society. That happened only with the introduction of accurate mechanical watches and clocks, which have been in common use for less than 400 years. Public time is something quite new in human history, at least in the sense of a single, impersonally fixed time for everyone.

Before the advent of such a single public time, different social groups organized their public times in individual ways. This was particularly true in earlier societies when life was lived much closer to the cycles and seasons of nature. As the British psychologist John Cohen has said, "For all the cultures of antiquity as well as in the mythologies of all peoples, time has a varying quality. It is divided up into holy and secular, lucky and unlucky periods. . . . Each day is animated by some personal spirit and one's good or evil fortune on a particular day is due to that day. In Homer's *Iliad*, the quality of time varies with the seasons and with the weather."[9]

Even in our highly mechanized culture, the days of the week are experienced by most of us as different; the week is not made up of seven equivalent days but of seven periods that vary in important ways, as shown in Figure E3.2.

Maurice Farber had eighty college students rank the days of the week in an order of preference, from most to least liked.[10] The results are shown in Figure E3.2 in terms of the average ranking that each day received. Monday, the period of the "Monday blues," is the least preferred day and Saturday the most. Surprisingly, Friday ranks slightly above Sunday, although on Friday the students have to go to classes while on Sunday they do not. Clearly, one's future time perspective is what determines one's preference, so that Friday is preferred over Sunday because a free weekend is better to look forward to than a week of school work. The Monday blues also occur on Sunday.

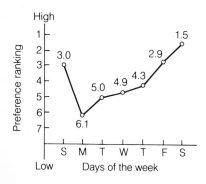

Fig. E3.2. Preference rankings for the days of the week. (From Farber, 1953, p. 254)

Aging in time. One of the most important determinants of our experience of time is our age. Yet, as we all know, we age at different rates during different periods of our lives. Our biological clocks do not always run at the same speed. Nor do the biological clocks of different persons necessarily keep the same time, for one person may age much faster than another.[11] It has been suggested that the rate of our individual aging may be a function of how we live our time; that is, the way that as individuals we "access" public time. If we manage to be fully concentrated on the time of our life, experiencing it as process, our biological clocks may run more slowly, and we will age more slowly—or live longer, which is another way

Table E3.2. Some relations among objectives, clock time, experienced time, and biological time.

| Public (clock) time | How time is experienced | | Biological clock of aging |
	As process	As duration	
1 year	If one is absorbed in few targets, time seems slower	If one is absorbed in few targets, time seems faster	9 months
1 year	If one is "present" to oneself, a compromise between absorption and scattering of attention is felt.		1 year
1 year	If one's attention is scattered, involved in many things, time seems faster.	If one's attention is scattered, time seems slower.	15 months

of saying the same thing. The relations can be summarized in a chart (Table E3.2).

These relations are meant to suggest that the body will age (biologically) at the rate that we feel time is passing (its process) rather than at the rate that in retrospect it will seem to have gone by (its duration). If our experience of time as process is one of absorbed attention to few things, as happens with especially withdrawn persons, time will seem to us to be passing slowly—and our biological "clocks" or our aging process will conform to this experience. We will age more slowly, or in other terms, we will seem to be younger than our stated age. This is what, in fact, we see in the extreme of the withdrawn person, the form of schizophrenia known as *catatonia:* Such persons often have remarkably babylike faces. On the other hand, if we involve ourselves in a scattered type of attention, flitting rapidly from one thing to another, we will have the constant experience that time passes very rapidly—and our biological clocks will conform to this. Like the jetsetter, we will age rapidly. Hyperactive children, whose attention is marked by this kind of "flitting" activity, often look older than their stated ages.

A third possibility, shown between the other two in Table E3.2, is a compromise between the first two. It consists in being "present" to oneself, neither fully absorbed in few things nor lightly attending to many things, but simply being where one is. Under these conditions, time is experienced as passing "normally," and our biological clock proceeds at a rate in accordance with public time.

Living our time

3. Because it "takes time" to do anything, all behavior, animal or human, is embedded in and affected by time.

All behaving necessarily takes place in time. It takes time to do anything. This is true of animals as well as humans: "Their behavior at any given moment takes into account what has already happened and what is about to follow; in other words, it allows for the succession of events."[12] It is, of course, very difficult to discover how it is with animals, who cannot tell us about their ongoing experience. However, one line of work may give us some clues. When rats are placed in a closed container known as a *Skinner box,* they can be trained to press a little bar, projecting from the wall, in order to obtain the reward of a food pellet. The timing of the rat's response as well as of other associated conditions can then easily be recorded for comparison. In one study, the rats were trained, in about a hundred trials, to recognize that a buzzer would sound for 3 seconds each time the animal pressed the bar, and that food would be delivered when the buzzer had finished sounding. Now the rats were presented with a new problem: A delay, varying from 1 to 81 seconds, was interposed between the time the buzzer sounded and the time the food was delivered. Will hungry rats wait around after the buzzer has finished, thus showing that they still connect the sound of the buzzer with the delivery of food even across such a gap in time? In other words, can a rat extend its own act so as to bridge across an interval of more than a minute? The results showed that rats make such a connection, or bridge, up to about 9 seconds, but after that interval they are less and less likely to continue pressing the bar for the delivery of food.[13]

From this experiment we might conclude that a rat cannot become bored, for what we experience in boredom is that the beginning and end of the same event have become separated beyond the point at which we are comfortable; we therefore keep wishing that it would end. If we were like rats, no event lasting more than 10 seconds would continue being for us the same event. We would do just what most animals do when they are caught in a situation that drags on: We would fall asleep. This is a sensible substitute for boredom that many students have discovered.

Feedback and delay. In the early 1950s, there appeared the first reports of an interesting phenomenon called *delayed auditory feedback,*© or DAF.[14] Although it had been known for a long time to public speakers and sound engineers, the development of tape recorders during World War II made it possible for the first time to reproduce the phenomenon experimentally. The procedure is this: Normally we hear our words at about the same time that we say them, with almost no delay; but if a tape recorder with multiple heads is so arranged as to delay our own hearing of what we speak—by about .15 to .3 seconds—we begin to stutter, to repeat or duplicate syllables, and to speak louder. With practice, one can overcome the effect to a great extent. That the phenomenon is not entirely a matter of the delay is shown by the facts that the effect is not as severe with female subjects as with males, and that it rarely occurs with children under four years of age.

The major significance of delayed auditory feedback, however, is that it reminds us dramatically that any ongoing behavior that we can monitor as we do it (which would seem to include just about all our meaningful acts) must take place in its own cycle of timing. The interference that occurs in DAF studies on speech can also be shown if people clap their hands, or whistle, or even play a musical instrument.[15] But most strking of all are the results if a delay is introduced into our visual monitoring cycle; that is, our seeing of our own acts. In one series of studies, subjects performed simple writing or copying tasks in front of a television camera. Their writing hand was screened from them by a cloth, and all they could see was their hand on a television screen in front of them, but the image had been passed through a device that delayed the visual feedback by about .52 seconds. Under these circumstances, as shown in Figure E3.3, their performances deteriorated markedly—and, unlike the DAF studies, they were not able to overcome the effect. No matter how hard they tried, they could not overcome the effect of the delay.[16]

Pacing. Regular or repetitive behavior, made up of the same action repeated over and over, usually paces itself with great regularity. Observe people walking and

delayed auditory feedback (DAF). Feedback in which a recording of a subject's voice is played back not simultaneously but a moment later. It may lead to interference with speech patterns.

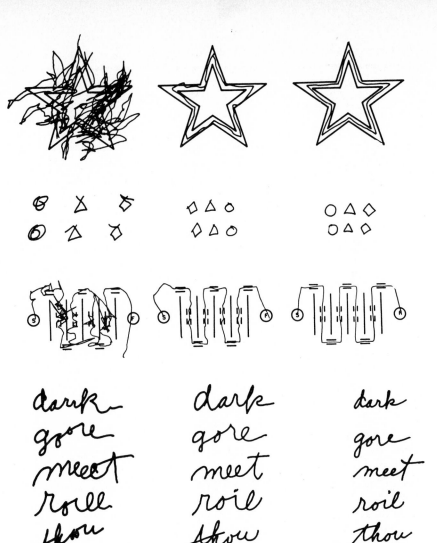

Fig. E3.3. Sample records of some tasks performed under delayed visual feedback. (From Smith, McCrary, and Smith, 1960, p. 1014)

you may be surprised to find how regular is their pace, under a wide variety of conditions. For adults in the United States, a pair of left-right steps usually takes up about 1 second, except in some large cities where the rate increases by about 20 percent. The rate is seldom affected by age, weight, or sex, but it may vary as a function of one's height. The time-boundedness of ordinary actions is shown very clearly in films that are slowed down or speeded up. Slowing down by as little as 20 percent produces an effect of dreamy unreality. Speeding up by the same degree results in jerky and equally unreal behavior. The world of action as we perceive it is paced at a familiar and constant rate to which we adjust ourselves.

Spoken language is perhaps the most obvious example of a time-bounded and conventionally paced form of ongoing behavior. Even one's sentence length is keyed to the rate of speaking: the longer the sentence, the faster one speaks.[17] Public speakers take advantage of this phenomenon by taking up more time than is expected in uttering a thought so that the trivial is made to sound profound.

4. Regular biorhythms° affect every process in nature, each in its own predetermined way, with possibly some influence from environmental forces.

biorhythms. Cyclic changes in physiological processes.

Table E3.3. Biorhythms and athletic performance.

In relation to that individual's physical biorhythm (thirty-three-day cycle), predictions of the following athletic achievements were	
Correct (at or near a peak day)	Incorrect (at or near a low or "critical" day)
March 8, 1971: Joe Frazier successfully defended his heavyweight crown against Muhammed Ali (Ali was very near his "critical" day).	March 2, 1962: Wilt Chamberlain set an NBA scoring record of 100 points in a single game.
November 2, 1974: Ali defeated George Foreman to regain the title (Foreman was very near his low point).	October 8, 1956: Don Larsen pitched the only perfect game ever achieved in the World Series.
May 6, 1954: Roger Bannister ran the first mile under four minutes.	May 25, 1935: Jesse Owens set five world records in track in one day.

All life is an expression of cycles and rhythms, from the wake-sleep cycle of all creatures to the menstrual cycles of humans. Recurrent diseases such as malaria have their flareups every few days, arthritis symptoms get worse on a weekly rhythm, and asthma attacks tend to occur in the evening. Just about every important bodily response is tied to a specific time in the day-night cycle of activity, from susceptibility to epileptic seizures to allergic attacks, from responses to medication to the probability of family quarrels, the production of amino acids, or the individual's heart rate. It is now well established that each process in the body has its own natural rhythm and that these dozens of internal clocks are not necessarily running at the same speed.

Experimental interest in what used to be called the body's "chemical clocks" goes back to work by a biologist, Hudson Hoagland,[18] in the 1930s and before that to the researches of Hermann Swoboda, a psychologist at the University of Vienna, and Wilhelm Fliess, a physician and friend of Freud in Berlin, about 1900. Extensive data appeared to indicate that two bodily rhythms, one of twenty-eight days referring to one's emotions and one of twenty-three days referring to one's physical state, were jointly influential in determining how the individual reacted to life stresses. A third major cycle of thirty-three days, referring to brain activity and the intellectual life, was later added by an Austrian engineer, Alfred Teltscher. Very recently there has been a revival of interest—aided by the marketing of simple calculators and charting methods—in the way that these biorhythms might affect our daily lives. Some governmental agencies in Japan and in Europe have been sufficiently impressed as to organize work schedules around the biorhythmic "clock" of their employees. Like most predictive methods, results that are somewhat better than chance can be obtained for large groups of people, but they are not precise enough to be of much use in predicting the day-to-day activities of individuals. Some examples of correct and incorrect predictions are given in Table E3.3, for outstanding athletic performances in relation to the physical cycle.

There is now a very large literature on human and animal biorhythms.[19] Interest in the phenomenon has undoubtedly been triggered by the large number of persons who suffer from "jet lag," a period of malaise and low energy immediately following a jet flight across a number of time zones. The exact cause of jet lag is not known, although it is usually explained away rather glibly as a consequence of upsetting one's normal routine of eating and sleeping. This alone could not produce such a unique effect, for many of us have had occasion to lose sleep or miss meals during a holiday or an emergency. More likely is the explanation in terms of a disturbance of one's total milieu. Normally, each of us "locks in" a large number of our internal clocks⊙ in an overall pattern to our day-night activities and to the

internal clock. The hypothetical mechanism that regulates cyclic variations in the body's physiological systems.

varied influences and activities in our environment. When this overall pattern is suddenly disrupted, because we are plunged into a setting that is on a different schedule, it may result in forcing all of our internal rhythms to readjust quickly. If they do not all respond at the same rate, the harmony of our "internal environment" becomes disturbed, and we experience the general, nonspecific upset known as *jet lag*.

A major question concerning biorhythms is whether they are primarily the expression of genetic programs built into the organism or are primarily the result of the influence of environmental forces. In humans, for example, infants begin life by napping as many as ten times in a twenty-four-hour period. Gradually, the ten naps become two daily naps plus an eight-hour sleep, then only one nap, and finally a rhythm of about fifteen hours awake and nine hours asleep. Is this developmental change due more to changes in the growing child's internal clocks or to increasing conformity to the fixed scheduling of one's environment? The answer has been sought in experiments on animals; for example, by transporting oysters from the Atlantic coast to Illinois to determine if their tide-related rhythm of opening their shells would change in a new time zone (it did);[20] and also in studies of humans, for example, by one man's staying alone in a cave for fifty-eight days to see whether his perception of time passing would remain accurate with no external cues (it did not; he guessed he had been underground only thirty-three days).[21]

Both results suggest that at least some internal clocks can be strongly influenced by environmental factors. Thus, some major cycles, such as the body temperature's high point in the daytime and low at night (for humans, of course; the reverse is true for nocturnal animals), are easily altered by social influences, whereas the rhythmic production of certain chemicals in the urine is not. Similarly, the human menstrual cycle is normally between twenty-four and twenty-nine days, but it can fairly easily be altered by cultural and social pressures. In some closely knit preliterate societies, most of the women menstruate at about the same time each month.

The major cycle—fixed by nature but in certain ways alterable by circumstance—is called the *circadian,*© a term meaning "almost daily" to refer to the fact that it nearly corresponds to the twenty-four-hour night-day cycle on this planet. Sleep cycles, activity rhythms, and even the changes in many plants are all manifested as circadian rhythms. Yet the female menstrual cycle and some biorhythms of blind persons show lunar cycles.[22]

It may be that external cycles do not cause internal cycles, but that when the two "lock in" together behavior is most effective. Salk has shown that babies in nurseries are quieter, cry less, and gain weight more rapidly when they experience in their environment some regular, beatlike stimulation. The commonest example of this is rocking. Equally common, although less evident, is the mother's heartbeat while they are being cradled or held. In Salk's experiments, the effective stimulus was the tape-recorded sound of a heartbeat that was played in the nursery.[23]

The tenses of living

Time enters our lives as the very basis of experiencing, not simply as a topic on which we can make judgments. James Thurber once described very well the tenses of everyday life: "Two persons living in holy matrimony... must avoid slipping into blasphemy, despond, apathy, and the subjunctive mood . . . (or) the gloomy sub-cellar of the pluperfect subjunctive, a place in which no marriage can thrive. The safest place for a happily wedded pair is the indicative mood, and of its tenses the present is the most secure. The future is a domain of threats and worries,

circadian rhythm. A recurring biological rhythm of events that is approximately twenty-four hours long.

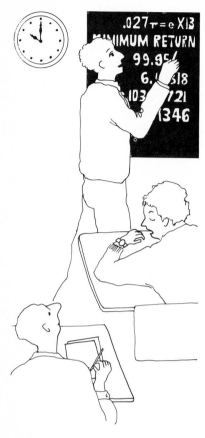

Fig. E3.4. There is not one clock in the room, but many. The "real" clock may say that thirty minutes have passed since the class began. A teacher who had been involved and animated, however, might now turn around and say, "A half hour gone already? I thought it was more like ten minutes." For the bored student at (a), however, the time might have seemed more like an hour. For the hard-working student at (b), experienced time and public time might well coincide.

and the past is a wasteland of sorrows and regrets."[24] It has been suggested that people who are predominantly of the "feeling" type live mostly in the past, "sensing" people in the present, and "thinking" people in the future.[25] This seems appropriate when we consider the practicality of sensing persons and the anxiety, indecisiveness, and planning that often occupy the thinking type.

The time of one's life may change markedly from one occasion to another, a fact that Shakespeare summarized in a famous passage in *As You Like It* (Act 3, Scene 2.) Time, he said, moves too slowly for the maiden "between the contract of her marriage and the day it is solemnized," yet it "ambles" properly for the rich man who "lives merrily, because he feels no pain." For the thief on his way to the gallows, however, time "gallops... for, though he go as softly as foot can fall, he thinks himself too soon there." Here the urgency of the situation overrides any personality characteristics.

Adults are often well aware that time has a quite different texture for children, who, not yet having gained the benefits of educational and social pressures, seem to experience time as less differentiated, less future-oriented, and less linked to the weight of the past. The tense of childhood life is surely the present plus a short-term future. It has been remarked, with understandable annoyance, that no child under the age of ten has ever been known to turn off a light when leaving a room. What is gone is gone, and for the child only the present and an immediately engaging future really exist.

The tenses, then, are not just temporal places that we know about impersonally but are deeply felt aspects of our experiencing. A clock, marked off in absolutely equivalent units and ticking off its endlessly similar seconds, is unrelated to past, present, or future. But humans, and perhaps some animals as well, experience themselves and their lives in terms of the present (the tense of doing), in terms of the past (the tense of "done-with," memory, sadness, and regret), and in terms of the future (the tense of "to-be-done" and therefore the home of hope as well as anxiety and challenge). See Figure E3.4.

An experiential study. In order to study the experience of time from the inside, we may consider the major elements in this experience.[26] They are

Experience is directed. All our conscious experiencing is directed toward something. If I look, I must look *at* something (or else *at* nothing in particular). If I am afraid, I am afraid *of* something. If I think or remember, I must think *about* something or have a memory *of* something. There must be a target for every experience, and the target is a part of the experience.

Targets of experiencing differ. One respect in which they differ for us is in how memorable they are; that is, in how well we remember them later. Their memorableness, in turn, may depend on some of their characteristics, such as their novelty. Additionally, targets may be inner, or "mental," or else outer, in the environment, such as visual targets.

We experience targets in different ways. For example, we may look at something, or we may hear something. We may attend to targets carefully, or casually. We may concern ourselves with what we attend to, or we may not.

In regard to time experiences in particular, as we discussed earlier, our experience may be in the form of process (what is going on now) or in the form of duration (what has already happened).

With these elements interacting in our experience of time, many combinations of results are possible. Some possibilities were listed in Table E3.3. As a concrete example, consider the situation of someone who is forced to spend some period of time in an atmosphere, such as a hospital or a nursing home, which can take many different forms. Suppose this person were reasonably content in regard

Table E3.4. The elements in our experience of time.

If our experience is of significant targets, then, under these conditions:	Process		Duration	
Number of targets	Few	Many	Many	Few
Target is inner or outer	Inner	Outer	Outer	Inner
then time will appear to pass	Slowly	Fast	Slowly	Fast

to the hour-by-hour passing of time (that is, time did not seem to be either dragging or going by too fast), but was upset by their duration judgment. That is, when looking back on the time that had already passed, it seemed terribly slow. The person might then say, "It doesn't seem possible that only three days have passed since my surgery." What might one do to change the experience of duration so that this unpleasant feeling might be avoided? Table E3.4 suggests an answer. One should spend as much time as possible in continuous attention to a small number of targets, preferably targets that are "mental." This can be done by deliberately losing oneself in thoughts of one or two very important matters.

On the other hand, suppose one wanted to have time pass in such a way that, on looking back on it, it would seem to have passed slowly. This is what one might want to do if what is going on is pleasant at the time. In this case, the best tactic would be to concentrate on as many different visual targets as possible, particularly any that are personally significant and positive. This can be done, for example, by having available an album of treasured photographs that are scanned rapidly.

Observations of existing situations support these inferences. Older persons in nursing or convalescent homes, who have available few significant visual targets, quickly become habituated to what is available to them. Their experience of time passing (process) is that time drags. It becomes, for them, enormously stretched out. In some instances, this slowing of time is so extreme that their experience can be termed *distorted*. When we talk to them, we find that they are, by our "public" standards, disoriented in time. This is an experience sufficiently distressing to anyone to lead to other symptoms of anxiety and even panic. The apparent loss of memory for recent events, found so frequently among such elderly patients and taken as a natural sign of encroaching senility, may in fact be no more than their response to continued experiences of this sort. If so, a changing and stimulating environment, especially when it is peopled by others who have some positive significance for them, will often produce seemingly miraculous recoveries.

Summary

1. Time experience can be modified in a number of ways, including drugs and feelings.

2. The flow of (personal) time can be experienced in the moment (as process) or in retrospect (as duration), or else as public time, which is the time of clocks.

3. The fewer the number of remembered targets (events), the shorter will be one's estimation of duration.

4. Research shows that even the familiar seven-day week is not experienced as seven equivalent days but as seven different periods that vary in both meaning and significance.

5. The more one's attention is absorbed in a few things, the more slowly will time pass in the moment (as process).

6. Any ongoing behavior that we can monitor as we do it takes place within its own cycle of time; it therefore "takes time" for us to do it.

7. Delay in the feedback of one's visually observed behavior will interrupt the normal cycle, with severe negative effects on performance that cannot be voluntarily corrected. A similar phenomenon in another modality, called *delayed auditory feedback* (of one's own voice, usually), is less severe in its effects and can be controlled to some degree.

8. Spoken language is deeply embedded in time, and all its characteristics are thereby affected. For exmaple, the longer a sentence, the faster one speaks, with the result that most sentences take about the same amount of time to utter.

9. Almost every important bodily function is tied to some specific cycle that is usually related to our day-night rhythm.

10. At least some of these "internal clocks," however, can be strongly influenced by environmental factors.

11. Most rhythms are circadian, or approximately daily (sleep cycles and activity rhythms, as well as some physiological and hormonal processes), but the female menstrual cycle in humans is unusual in being linked to the lunar cycle.

12. For children, the tense of living is the present plus a short-term future, whereas for adults the tense of living is the past and the future.

13. It appears that one can learn to modify time experience through controlling one's attention.

Part three

GROWTH

Becoming an individual

In this chapter, we will trace the normal development of individuals, beginning with conception. At each age level, we will look briefly at the continuing story of development and, in particular, at how the two sexes are both alike and different. In addition, for some of the age levels we will treat in detail selected problems that exemplify important issues in the study of human development. In order to emphasize the importance of differences between the sexes, we will chart the course of development in terms of a pair of children: a girl and a boy who are twins.

At the start, you will see how the infant demonstrates survival competencies from the very beginning of life. You will then learn the way that children develop on schedules that are partly species-specific and partly an individual matter. It will be shown how infants enter the world of childhood with the development of speech and the upright posture and how they develop into the socialized world of their peers in the preschool years. The importance of cognitive development during the school years will be shown, with its deemphasis on bodily experience. Finally, as a problem that typifies much of development, you will see the way that moral development proceeds in stages, from an emphasis on the concrete and personal situation to an emphasis on abstract principles.

10

Growing up: from birth to puberty

The story of growth and development brings with it questions that are different from those we raised in earlier chapters. Some of the questions we will be raising in this and subsequent chapters are "What is the normal course of development? How does it differ between the sexes? How is it displayed in such specific areas as language, motor abilities, intelligence, and personality? And (on a practical level) what can I as an adult do to help in the optimal development of children who may be in my care?"

Developmental psychology, as this area of study is called, differs from other areas of study in another important respect. In studying development, we do not ask, "What are people like?" Rather, we ask, "How do people change?" Thus, as we will see, theories of development must take into account not only principles of people's behavior and experience, but also how that behavior and experience may change from one time to another and what might bring about the changes.

A third difficulty in the study of growth and development is that much of it is concerned with individuals who are unable to provide data in the form of reports. Until they are at least old enough to answer questions intelligently, young children cannot tell anyone how things appear to them, what they are feeling or thinking, or why they act the way they do. In this respect, they are like animal participants in research studies—although, of course, they are also uniquely human. Developmental psychology thus imposes a special demand on experimenters to develop ingenious ways of testing out their hypotheses about very young children. In addition, it requires a great dependence on careful and even intuitive observation, especially if the investigator is interested in evidence from the inside view, as we have been in this book.

Before and after birth

1. Beginning at conception, the human child shows survival competencies as well as psychological abilities.

The human fetus© develops both psychologically and behaviorally during the entire prenatal period. At birth, it is not merely a complicated physical organism that then starts to develop as an individual in an environment. Rather, its development throughout the fetal period, even from the moment of conception, has been that of a living organism in interaction with its environment. Pregnant women can certainly testify that this growing organism profoundly affects their physical and emotional state, their appearance, their activities, and their very lives. Similarly, the fetus just as surely would report that the mother as an environment provides a continuing and changing effect on its condition, activities, growth, and prospects. Embryos do a lot of moving around before birth, some more than others. They can respond to pressure and temperature changes and to sound, and they can be conditioned, by Pavlovian procedures, to move at the sound of a bell. Thus, at birth they are well prepared to demonstrate a quite remarkable repertoire of skills, some of which are listed in Table 10.1.

The twins at birth. Our twins will not be identical, of course — that is, not the result of the splitting of a single fertilized egg. They will develop from two eggs fertilized at the same time, and so they can be either the same sex or of different sexes (the arrangement we will assume here). At the very beginning of prenatal growth, the fertilized egg is undifferentiated as to sex, although it does have a specific arrangement of chromosomes that will determine whether it will become female or male.

This basic, undifferentiated human structure is female oriented, and (con-

Table 10.1. What the newborn human infant can do.

Reflexes

Turn its head and mouth toward a touch (rooting)
Suck whatever is placed on its lips or in its mouth
Blink to avoid something approaching its eyes
Curl its hand in a grasp when stimulated on its palm
Fan out its toes when stimulated on the sole of its foot (Babinski reflex)
Turn away from an unpleasant stimulus

Psychological abilities

Respond selectively to the human voice
Discriminate between two sounds only one note apart
Visually attend to patterns and to colors (with a preference for looking at the human face)

Localized abilities of the head and face

Breathing, sucking, chewing, turning, seeing, hearing, crying, vomiting, coughing, gurgling, vocalizing, rooting

fetus. An unborn human from approximately the end of the second month of pregnancy to birth.

trary to the story of Adam and Eve) it must be specifically influenced by whatever is in the Y chromosome to become a male (see Figure 10.1). This is apparently accomplished, in the embryo, by the Y chromosome inhibiting the development of the uterus and Fallopian tubes of the female while enhancing the development of the Wolffian ducts of the male.[1] In any case, not only the sexual anatomy but the entire structure of the embryo is affected by whether it becomes female or male: "All the cells in the entire body of a female are different from those of any chromosomal male."[2]

Perhaps because the female starts out with a greater amount of genetic material—there being more in an XX than in an XY combination—she will be significantly less prone to disorders that are genetically carried, such as color blindness and hemophilia. She will also live longer than her brother and be more resistant to infection and disease at every age level. This will happen in spite of the fact that at birth she will be 5 percent smaller, a weight difference that will increase as the years go on until it reaches 20 percent or more. She will always be weaker and less muscular. Her vital capacity, or lung capacity, a factor in physical activity, will always be less. On the other hand, her rate of growth, beginning at conception, will be greater than his: She will have a fetal period that is one or two days shorter, will grow teeth faster, and will mature sexually at least a year or two ahead of him.

2. Prematurity of birth is related to the child's later status but only in a complex interaction with other factors, physical and social.

What long-term effects do prenatal and birth conditions have on children's development? It has always seemed that one of the most straightforward ways to test this out was to compare children who, because of premature birth, weighed less and were less developed than full-term infants. In Table 10.2, we summarize the results of two studies on the same group of children, the first when they were

Fig. 10.1. If Michelangelo had been aware of modern research on embryonic development, he might have painted this picture instead.

forty weeks old and the second between three and five years later. Prematurity is usually defined in terms of birth weight rather than fetal age, because it is never possible to know with precision how early a baby is born. In these studies, babies of 2,500 g (about 5½ lbs) were compared with babies under 1,500 g (about 3⅓ lbs) and with those falling between. Each baby above 2,500 g was paired off with a baby below 2,500 g so as to be matched on the following characteristics: ethnic group, season of birth, hospital where born, number of previous children had by the mother, and socioeconomic status of parents. The two groups of approximately 500 babies each, then, can be assumed to have been nearly identical on every characteristic except birth weight.

The babies were all assessed by a pediatrician when they were between eight and seventeen months of age, the average testing age of the group being forty weeks. The pediatrician was never told if a baby was full term or premature. He administered a neurological examination and a developmental scale devised by Arnold Gesell and his coworkers at Yale.[3] Between three and four years later, the children were contacted again and retested with the Gesell Scale as well as with some items from a standard intelligence test.[4]

Two conclusions may be drawn from these data. The first is that for both neurological and intellectual functioning, both earlier and later in development, birth weight is related to status. The higher the initial birth weight, the greater the percentage of children who test at the normal level or better. A second conclusion is that 1,500 g seems to be a kind of dividing line. Above this point, we find a few effects of prematurity, but below this point the effects are striking. One in every eight children below 1,500 g will be seriously defective or developmentally abnormal. This sharp distinction between groups persists into early childhood. Studies of children who are later referred to clinics for "behavior disorders" such as incorrigible behavior in school show that as many as 6 percent of the white children and 17 percent of the black children are prematures.[5]

May we conclude from these results that the length of prenatal development directly affects later neurological and intellectual growth? Not quite. For we should notice, first, that the results are far from invariant. According to Table 10.2, approximately seven out of eight babies who weigh less than 1,500 g at birth do *not* develop as defective or abnormal. In addition, studies of premature babies in hospitals suggest that a major factor in their impeded development may be their treatment immediately after birth. Because they appear in need of special care, they are often kept in incubators and therefore receive less handling and loving than babies of normal birth weight. When they are treated more like normal babies, they often catch up in their development.

Table 10.2. A study and a follow-up of the relation between birth weight and later neurological and IQ status. The lower the birth weight, the more premature the infant.

If birth weight was	Number of babies	The percentage of children who tested in various categories was								
		At forty weeks of age						At three to five years of age		
		Neurological			Intellectual			Neurological		
		Normal	Uncertain	Abnormal	Average or Above	Borderline	Defective	Normal	Questionable	Abnormal
Below 1,500 g	57	50.9	36.8	12.3	77.1	10.6	12.3	51.9	31.5	13.0
1,500–2,500 g	443	76.7	21.6	1.6	95.5	3.2	1.3	77.1	36.7	1.2
Above 2,500 g	492	88.4	11.0	0.6	97.4	1.4	1.2	87.3	9.1	0.7

Source: Data from Knobloch and others, 1956, table 2, and from Harper, Paul A., Fischer, Liselotte K., and Rider, Rowland V., "Neurological and intellectual status of prematures at three to five years of age," *Journal of Pediatrics,* 1959, 55, pp. 679–690, table 1B.

Other factors, too, appear to be influential, aside from the simple fact of birth weight. The chief of these is socioeconomic level. It is now well established that prematurity occurs far more frequently among mothers at the lowest socioeconomic levels, although we do not know whether this is caused by diet, prenatal care, maternal habits, unknown psychological factors, or even smoking (which has a marked effect on the fetus and which is more frequent among lower-class pregnant women).[6] A recent and very careful study in North Carolina concluded that social class is as significant a factor as prematurity or birth weight in determining the rate and level of a child's development.[7]

3. Children normally develop on a schedule that is partly species related and partly individual.

We have raised the question of how the two major influences, biological and individual, interact in the course of early development. Two sorts of evidence are relevant here:

- There is a great deal of evidence, from both human and animal studies, of what is called *maturation*,© or the natural process of biological development. In a classic study done in the 1920s, Leonard Carmichael anesthetized tadpoles so that they had no opportunity to practice swimming movements during their first stages of development. When released into the water, after the anesthetic had been allowed to wear off, they then swam at the same time and in exactly the same way as tadpoles that had been allowed to develop normally. Carmichael concluded that there is a maturational "program" that can develop even in the absence of external influences or practice in movement.[8]

   In one of the first major studies using motion picture equipment, Arnold Gesell and his associates at Yale studied infants in a wide variety of experimental conditions during the first five years of their lives. They concluded that most of the major developmental advances occur on a regular schedule that is very nearly the same for the majority of children of both sexes. The head is raised from the crib at about the end of the first month, babies are able to sit up unassisted by about the fifth month, they crawl during the next few months, and they start to walk at about the end of the first year. Not only do these major steps in development occur at the same time for most babies but they also occur without assistance, often in spite of assistance, and usually in spite of resistance. Most importantly, all infants show the same series of stages. Gesell concluded that there was a biological, species-related program that developed in the individual unless conditions were so extreme as to seriously prevent it.[9]

- In addition, there are individual differences, the individual's own plan for development, that shows up sometimes in spite of opposition from the environment. In another early study that used motion pictures, Lois Ames compared two children at three ages—at the end of their first year, then when they were five, and again when they were twelve years old.[10] She found a persistent, individual difference in their visual perception, ways of grasping and contacting objects, and even the timing of their motor behavior. In a quite different area of study, Anna Freud, the daughter of the founder of psychoanalysis, described the often astonishing resilience displayed by British children during the severe personal disruptions they suffered in World War II. Of the children she studied, those who had the benefit of a strong

maturation. The completion, through heredity and environment, of developmental growth processes in the body. Also, the actual growing process.

character formed early in family life were able to put up with quite serious hardships and tragedy. Their ways of reacting preserved individual characteristics in the face of great environmental pressures.[11]

Individuals are often capable of making their own way successfully in spite of such adverse influences as extreme isolation or deprivation.[12] Apparently most individuals are equipped to be resilient in the face of adversity, even at a very young age. Thus, the course of growth is not simply a response to given biological and social conditions but one that makes room for each person to exercise their own choices. In one series of studies, for example, Kagan tested children in many different societies, comparing them at various ages on tests of cognitive ability. He found that even under circumstances of what appear to be minimal environmental stimulation and support, as in certain very poor villages in Guatemala, children may appear quite retarded in infancy, but the differences between them and middle-class American families disappeared by the preadolescent years.[13]

The first month

4. Infants show individual response preferences almost at birth, particularly in their visual discriminations.

Within the first few days after birth, our twin infants will have begun to stabilize their eating and sleeping patterns—not randomly but in some sensible relation to what is going on in their environment. Their major activities will be digestion and sleeping, they will take in nourishment and excrete it, and they will spend about three quarters of their time in a series of long naps. Both these kinds of activities, although they serve different biological needs, will depend very much on the kind of atmosphere, or emotional climate, in which the infants find themselves. Tension, distraction, rejection, or inconsistency will be reflected immediately in the infants' bodily functions.

Even the activity of sucking, so basic to nourishment and growth, appears to serve two distinct purposes, as close observation has shown. Healthy, full-term infants appear to suck in two different ways. One is a "nutritive" and continuous sucking that is fitted to the flow of milk, at the rate of about one suck per second. The other is a "nonnutritive" sucking in which alternating periods of sucking and resting occur, with a frequency rate of about two sucks per second, and that can be elicited at any time except during sleep or intense excitement. The nonnutritive sucking appears to be an expressive reaction to stimulation or anxiety.[14]

In the first month of life, human infants focus best on visual targets about 10 inches away, and this just happens to be the average distance from nipple to eye in the adult female. The infants are thus nicely equipped to begin what will soon become the single most engaging activity for them: looking, particularly looking at other people's faces. Eye-to-eye contact begins very early. In a pioneering series of studies, Fantz presented various patterns to infants of various ages, from less than forty-eight hours to six months, and determined how much time they spent looking at each (Figure 10.2). The determination was made by noting what was reflected in the infant's pupils. Clear-cut preferences were evident before the infants were two days old, and they did not change appreciably: About 15 to 20 percent of the time was spent looking at patterned targets, as opposed to about 5 percent spent looking at a plain gray target. The most preferred target of all was one resembling the human face.[15]

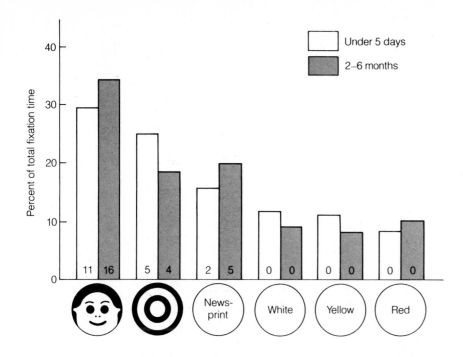

Fig. 10.2. Infants show preferences for patterned visual stimuli almost from the day of birth. (From Fantz, 1965, p. 804)

It had long been known that human infants are able, almost from birth, to discriminate differences in color and to follow a moving target. To these findings, Fantz now added two more that are of major importance. First, infants are also able to make rather fine discriminations and to show preferences in regard to patterns. Second, they seem to begin life with a built-in preference for one kind of pattern, the human face. Monkeys, on the other hand, appear to start out with a preference for monkey faces. As yet it is not possible to decide between two explanations: the first, that infants of each species come equipped with a built-in detector for adult faces belonging to their own species, and the second, that recognition of adult faces is based on the fact that these are the first stimuli presented to them under biologically important conditions in infancy.

When the human infant's pattern of fixating is carefully studied, however, it turns out to be more complex than the simple activity of directing the gaze at one object rather than another. The human face is extremely mobile, as we all know, continually moving and changing expression. At some moments of repose it can be very still. The infant responds to these distinctions by fixating the entire face of the mother when she is moving or changing expression, but fixating a single detail when her face is still.[16] Even at this early stage of development, then, the infant does not simply direct its gaze, nor even simply select one target out of those available, but seems to actively try to put information together. As we will see, this active organization of its perceptual world, constantly in tune with environmental changes, will be the mark of much of the activity of the growing child.

At the ripe age of two weeks, then, the twins will be stabilized and evident members of their immediate community. They will discriminate and respond visually to a range of stimuli, will have begun to make crawling "movements," and will start to respond appropriately to the human voice. Their change to a more advanced mode of life will first be evident at about three weeks of age when they try to hold their heads erect. They will now be ready to advance to a stage in which they are not restricted to a prone position.

The twins in the first month. The very first thing that the parents noticed, when the twins were born, was their sex — probably even before noticing whether they had the requisite number of fingers and toes. What the parents saw at this moment will now begin to determine almost everything important about the twins for years to come. What will matter is not so much the fixed differences between the twins of different sexes (which will turn out to be very few) as it is what the parents, the family, and society in general will do about the differences in their gender. As far as is known, every society that has ever existed enforces certain significant distinctions between the sexes. It is these *created* differences that will matter as much as, perhaps far more than, any built-in differences between the twins.

In the first months of life, the mother is visually the most important person in the twins' world. Perhaps as a consequence of the boy's higher levels of testosterone (the male sexual hormone), he may show more activity than his sister, and his mother will begin by paying more attention to him. But this kind of attention will begin to decrease by the end of the first month, just as it does in the case of monkey mothers. The mother's choice of attention, to either the girl or the boy, will now begin to depend on her individual preferences and also on how the twins act. In general (although this will vary, depending on the mother), parents both expect and prefer a boy to be more active, and so they will permit more activity and movement on his part, perhaps even encourage it. If it is shown by the girl, they may have more difficulty accepting it and are less likely to encourage it.

The subtle exchange of messages during these early weeks is a two-way communication. If the girl is larger than average, does more kicking, or has a louder voice, she will affect the parents differently, for better or worse, than if she is a small, sweet child who seems very "feminine." If the boy is normal or above in size and weight and moves in an active and physical manner, he will seem to the parents to be "all boy" and will begin to determine how they in turn respond to him. These distinctions may outweigh the mere fact that the twins differ in gender.

5. Studies on infant monkeys show that basic infant needs are for bodily contact and socialization.[⊙]

Ordinary observation of infants, of their obvious need to cling and to be held and rocked, and of their obvious satisfaction when these contact needs are satisfied, should suggest to us that this is as fundamental a "drive" as hunger or sleep. What we would like to know, however, is just what it is in the total infant-mother relation that is so crucial in the infant's life. Some years ago a psychiatrist, Margaret Ribble,[17] shook up her profession with a report of her observations in some maternity wards. She noted that there were striking differences among mothers in the way they mothered their babies and that failure in this respect was immediately evident in the state of the infant's health and the rate of its development.

What could not normally be done to human infants was then done experimentally to other animals, when Harlow and his coworkers at the University of Wisconsin began to raise monkeys under specific conditions of deprivation. You may recall that this was discussed in Chapter 3.

One of Harlow's major findings had to do with the long-term effect of isolation. Monkeys raised in isolation from others of their kind invariably develop severe and even irreversible disturbances. They withdraw from the world and spend their time in self-directed behavior that is either meaninglessly repetitive, such as head banging and rocking, or else destructive, such as pulling or tearing at their fur and skin. The males are unable to engage in appropriate sexual behavior, and so they do not father offspring. The females are equally inept as sexual part-

socialization. The process in which an individual, from childhood on, internalizes the values of society.

ners, although they can be impregnated by an active, normal male. In such cases, they turn out to be cruel, destructive, or insensitive monkey mothers, seemingly completely lacking in the feelings normal to female animals under these conditions.

Mitchell has summarized the results of many studies comparing isolates with normally reared monkeys.[18] They may be divided into two sets of results, the one referring to effects that disappear or diminish as the animals grow up, and the other referring to effects that seem to be ineradicable:

- Effects on infant isolates that lessen with time: awkwardness in their movements; submission to others by crouching, cowering, and fewer facial signs of threat; stereotyped rocking movements and a wide range of bizarre movements and postures; more "screech" calls (a sign of withdrawal or fear), and more grimaces of fear.
- Effects on infant isolates that persist into adulthood: The isolates, whether male or female, show many abnormalities of sexual posturing, which is the behavior necessary for completing the sexual act. They display stereotyped movements in the cage, such as jumping and somersaulting. They retain a few idiosyncratic movements that are bizarre. They emit fewer "coo" sounds (a vocalization associated with distress at strange conditions). And they direct much more of their behavior toward themselves rather than toward their peers.

Similar findings have been reported when puppies rather than monkeys are used as subjects.[19] Significantly, in laboratory rats equivalent pathological changes can be produced in behavior, in physiological functioning, and in brain tissue either by feeding the animals a markedly inadequate diet or by raising them in the absence of environmental and peer stimulation. Starvation of any sort, whether in food or in environmental support, appears to produce about the same result in any species: retardation in intellectual, emotional, and social development and often permanent impairment in adaptive ability.[20] Even the "critical period" of such deprivation seems to follow the same rule across species: The earlier the deprivation, and the more long-lasting, the more severe will be the subsequent results. The British psychiatrist John Bowlby, who was one of the first to study deprivation and separation in children, has summarized his conclusions in the same vein: "It is now demonstrated that maternal care in infancy and early childhood is essential for mental health. This is a discovery comparable in magnitude to that of the role of vitamins in physical health."[21]

The second to the sixth months

6. An important development in this period, evidenced in both motor and perceptual ways, is a "stabilization" of the infant's world.

During the second month, a new "stage" of development begins to appear in the infant. It can be described in two ways, as a physical maturation or as a gain in perceptual skills—but, as we will see, these are two ways of saying the same thing. (See Figure 10.3.)

Consider first the observable changes in physical appearance and motor ability. By the second month, the twins have lost their "birth" appearance and now appear firm and individualized to the sight as well as to the touch. Their skin takes

Jean Piaget is the most influential contemporary psychologist of childhood development. His theory of stages in the growth of thinking, as worked out over the past fifty years, rivals that of Freud in completeness and importance. (See the pages on Piaget in the Epilogue.)

Piaget distinguishes three major stages that apply to all children, although each individual may progress through them at a somewhat different rate. They are (1) The sensorimotor° stage of "practical intelligence," in the first two years of life; (2) The stage of concrete operations,° in the preschool and elementary school years; and (3) the stage of formal operations,° beginning at about age eleven.

We will present descriptions and examples of these stages and their substages at appropriate pages in this chapter.

Fig. 10.3. Jean Piaget.

sensorimotor. Piaget's first stage of cognitive development (until two years old), in which the child learns to distinguish self from environment and to develop a feeling of worth.

concrete operations. Piaget's third stage of cognitive development (from seven to eleven years), in which the child develops a cognitive system that organizes the events of the external world into a logical structure.

formal operations. Piaget's final stage of cognitive development (from age twelve to adulthood), which is characterized by abstract thinking and concept formation.

on a glow of vitality and serves as an expressive organ, changing color with their changing moods and states of comfort. At this point, they also start to take up their own space, by deliberately moving from one position to another rather than remaining where circumstances have brought them. During this month, they become able to hold their heads erect at will and then their chests as well. Within a few weeks more, they will be able to maintain a sitting position with a little help.

The distinction we are emphasizing here is between moving and being moved. An object that must be moved may react, if the appropriate patterns are built into it; but in order to have an *experience* of acting or reacting, it must be capable of doing its own moving. Initially its own movements will be disorganized, perhaps random, but very soon, as in the case of our infants, certain movements will become organized enough to be experienced by them as what they want to do; that is, as efforts, as goals to be reached. If we, as observers, watch what is happening, we will get the inescapable impression of the infants *trying* to lift their heads, of struggling to turn over, of reaching intentionally for a bright object, and so on. These are impressions that we could never possibly get from watching a billiard ball heading toward a pocket or a leaf flipping over in the wind—although mechanically these too are motions. What we are observing here in the case of the infants is the beginning of organized experiencing.

The results of this development are apparent in many ways. Piaget noted that at about the age of four weeks his child repeated an accidental movement, sucking a finger, that had apparently given pleasure. And, as Bruner has shown in laboratory studies, infants four to six weeks of age can learn to actively work on their environment to get what they want. In no more than one or two learning trials, they learn to vary their rate of sucking on a nipple in order to turn on lights that attract them. As their space of perception and action begins to become organized for them, their visual skills seem to improve in leaps. Fantz, in his studies of infant visual perception, reports that, when allowed to choose between a flat, painted model of a head and a solid form, a clear-cut preference for the solid head appeared "suddenly" at two months of age.

As the world starts to get organized for the infants "in their heads," they give evidence that for them certain transient stimuli, even those from their own bodies, have stability. By two months of age, they visually recognize the mother, and within another few weeks they respond to their own internal changes to the extent of stabilizing their schedules of feeding and sleeping. Regularity and organization of experience go hand in hand during this period. In Fantz' data, infants below the age of two months are just as likely to look at a picture shown repeatedly as at a new one. But at the two-month turning point they start to become "bored" with the familiar and prefer the one that is novel. Familiarity is not possible unless experience is organized so as to lead to a statement like, "Wait, haven't I seen that one before?"

As Figure 10.4 shows, the smiling response makes its appearance in the second month, in response to any nodding, smiling, humanlike facial stimulus, and remains in the infants' repertoire for the next few months.[22] It has disappeared by the age of eight months, not because the infants no longer welcome faces, but because they will smile only at familiar faces.[23] Along with this specifying of perception and response goes an improved ability to focus their eyes on a target and the ability to organize their experience of time in terms of a future. They select particular sounds, such as the mother's voice or footsteps, and anticipate her arrival. And, finally, it is during this period, as they approach the sixth month, that the infants improve sufficiently in coordination of hand and eye so as to prepare to take the step that defines their next "stage" of development: getting to know that the world is permanent and stable even when it is beyond their reach or out of their sight.

The twins from two to six months. The most surprising aspect of the twins' development is that they show so little difference at this age. Surely the adults around them know that one is a girl and one a boy. Given the strong attitudes that adults have about the sexes and the quite different ways they act toward the two twins, we would expect the infants to begin very soon to respond in observably different ways. Such observations are easy enough to make. For example, one long-term study compared two groups of infants who were black and two who were white in a middle-class "private practice" setting and in a lower-class clinic setting. It was evident as early as the age of eight weeks that the development of organized motor behavior was fastest in the black clinic babies, a little slower in the black private practice babies, and slowest in the two groups of white babies. But no sex differences were apparent[24] — nor, in another study of 1,400 infants from one to fifteen months were any sex differences found on any scale of mental or motor development.[25] In a survey of every study that could be located in which sex differences were assessed in infancy, Maccoby and Jacklin could find no firm evidence of differences in the use of the senses, learning ability, or social development.[26]

It is almost certain that the twins are treated differently, but it seems equally certain that, in most important aspects of their development, they proceed at the same pace and in about the same way. The girl may have a slight edge in postural development, perhaps because she is somewhat less active in a gross sense. The boy's physical activity may emphasize more use of large muscles. Such slight differences in kind of movement should be mentioned at this point, because they may be the seed of what will become the outstanding observable difference between them in the next twelve months. This is the behavior known as *aggression*, to which we now turn.

The problem of aggression. Although it does not really show itself until the children are another year older, aggression needs to be discussed at this point

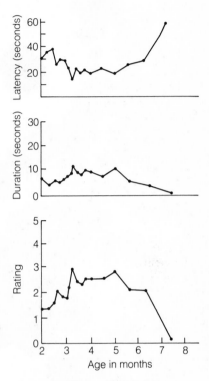

Fig. 10.4. The "natural history" of the smiling response in infants. Three kinds of measures were used: the latency, or the delay before the infant responded; the duration of the smiling response; and a rating of the degree of smiling. The response typically peaks in the period of three to six months and drops out (at least in regard to strangers) by the eighth month. (From Polak, Emde, and Spitz, 1964, p. 107)

Piaget: Early sensorimotor thought

Beginning at birth, the twins are at work on their environment, using their innate behavior patterns. What they do modifies their environment, which in turn modifies their behavior. Their behavior, largely exploratory, gradually forms into observable activity involving both senses and muscles (hence the word *sensorimotor*), and together with this, internal "models" or representations in the mind. This is the origin of intelligence and thinking. It is hardly thinking as we know it, however, since it is tied closely to action and is unique to the individual's action pattern.

Example: As a result of exploratory activity, the twins "discover" that waving an arm will make a rattle suspended above them move and make noise. They then begin to repeat the action deliberately — Piaget, 1966b.

because it originates here, in the ways that the twins begin to organize their space and themselves in it. Hartup,[27] in reviewing what is known about the development of aggression in children, points out that we do not know exactly, for any species, how later aggressive behavior is built up out of earlier motor patterns. It does seem reasonable that growing children, like the young of other species, "learn" to be aggressive in the course of rough-and-tumble play with their peers. More generally, the possibility of later aggression is initiated in the way that infants "carve out" their individual space of movement. As much research has shown, one of the most enduring characteristics of being an individual is the personal space that one has around oneself, that area within which another person's entry (except at times of intimacy) is felt as an intrusion.[28]

Maccoby and Jacklin report that the only significant difference in the preschool years between girls and boys is in their physical and verbal aggression. However, this does not mean that boys are more aggressive than girls; the matter is a little more complex than that. Aggression is a form of social behavior, and so it is not apparent until children are old enough to begin playing with each other. When they do so, boys usually play more actively with other boys than they do with girls or than girls do with each other. As a result, boys both give and get more aggression than do girls — but primarily from other boys. This holds true no matter what the circumstances or provocation and no matter how the aggression is expressed or measured.

Thus, it is true that aggression is more frequent in boys than in girls, but largely because males are aggressive against each other. Boys are no more aggressive with girls than girls are with girls. It has been suggested that boys may "excite" each other through mutual threats to each others' personal space and that this element begins a snowballing sequence leading to aggression as a generalized form of social behavior.[29]

Six months to one year

7. Crawling and walking begins in the period between six months to one year, allowing the child to perceive a fully stable world in which things are experienced as permanent.

At six months, the twins have established reasonably stable and identifiable places for themselves as persons. They can now sit up, occupying a position, so to speak. From this base, they now begin to reach out, and an increasingly coordinated eye-and-hand control soon develops over what is within their reach. By the end of the sixth month, they do not just pick up objects but grasp them, using their fingers differently in accordance with the shape and size of the object. The richly varied world is very soon felt, seen, held, brought close and pushed away, all in meaningful actions.

Imitating. It is just about at this stage that infants also begin to show a capacity for imitating. This is a poorly understood and often misunderstood phenomenon, far more complex than it may seem. Suppose the mother does a little rhythmic action in front of the twins: She holds her left hand in front of her, palm upward, and brings her right hand down on it, slapping it and making a sound. The twins soon begin to imitate it, everyone laughs delightedly, and the little incident, so full of mystery, passes off without a thought. But just what is it that the twins have done? The mother brought her right hand down on her left, and so did they. The question to be asked is, how did they know which hand to use? The mother was facing them, and so her right hand was on their left side. But then how did they make the shift to their *own* right hands, which are on the other side? We adults might easily figure it out. We might say to ourselves, "Let's see, she's 180 degrees turned around from me, so if her moving hand is on my left, I have to make a 180-degree switch of hands to make up for that."

But of course this is not what happens. How do the babies do it? We can get some clue by considering first what they do *not* do. Their action does not simply resemble that of their mother; they do not simply use their left hands to do what her right hand does. Imitation is apparently not the same as resembling. However, they do not go through a process of which we adults are capable—to say to oneself that a 180-degree turn is required, and so on. They do not mechanically follow the mother's action, and they do not logically figure out the mother's action, but apparently accomplish something that falls between these two.

But monkeys also imitate, as their keepers well know. This suggests that imitation does not require a spoken language, or even thinking, only those characteristics that the higher apes share with humans. These include an upright posture, a great reliance on visual channels for information, and a special kind of contactful stance in relation to significant figures such as the mother. We suggest that this latter is what the twins were able to accomplish. They literally put themselves in the mother's place—and then the rest was easy. If we as adults feel that this trick of taking another's position is difficult, perhaps it is because we have so rarely used it in recent years. But in all probability it is one of the fundamental forms of relationship through which human and ape infants coexist with significant figures in their environments.

Now notice what happens as the twins begin to move around and as they develop a more and more highly individualized place for themselves in their world. They will find it increasingly difficult to assume the position of another person. To have developed a formed and individualized world in which I am the center means that I can no longer easily shift over to someone else's place in *their* world. This may be why most adults do so poorly at imitation. It is a skill that they once needed and had, but lost—and as we will now see, they lost it at the point in development where they became able to move around freely.

The developmental formula we are suggesting here is that immobility makes possible full participation in another's stance; and mobility then eliminates participation. However, this in turn makes possible the perception of others as stable.

Object permanence.[°] Between six and nine months, the twins begin to move around on their own. Usually they start by crawling, although there are many individual variants of the development of this motor pattern. For the first time, they are in charge of the changing array of perspectives that present themselves for each thing that we adults call a *fixed object*. Notice the psychologists' unusual emphasis here: We are saying that an object is only fixed, stable, and permanent— that is, what adults call a *thing*—if the perceiver can perceive it as fixed, stable, and permanent. Otherwise, as far as the perceiver is concerned, it is not an object but a mirage, not one thing but possibly many. (See Figure 10.5.)

Piaget pointed out a significant change that takes place around the age of nine months. If we show the twins an object that attracts their attention and then, while they watch, hide it under a cloth, they will, at seven months, turn away. For them the object is no longer present to their vision or touch, and so it has ceased to exist. But if we try this when they are nine months old they will not turn away but try to look under the cloth for the hidden object. They have now reached a new developmental level in which objects are not only seen but *known*. What is

Fig. 10.5. The reality wall. Once the baby has achieved the stage of object permanence (see text), the toys in the other room are real for that baby *because they are now absent*. This is how we, as adults, know that something is real— because it can disappear behind a wall. If it could never disappear, we would then know it is only a mirage or a figment of our imagination.

object permanence. A term coined by Piaget, referring to a child's awareness that a hidden object still exists and does not cease to be because it cannot be seen.

perceived is not just changing sensation but a thing in its own right, which exists even though it is not evidently present. To grasp the overwhelming import of this distinction, imagine what it would be like if we were in a world in which we were never sure whether all the images that appear to us were phantoms or solid reality. How relieved we would feel to discover something of whose existence we could be sure, even if it came and went. This is what we as adults might feel if we lost our touch with a world of things, the world that the twins have just entered.

Separation anxiety.[○] At just about the same time that they develop a sense of the permanence of things, the twins reach a similar achievement in regard to people. During the preceding few months, they have shown an increasing attachment to their mother and have begun to lose one of the great charms of infancy — the ready and smiling welcome to any and all persons who will be pleasant to them. They are now starting to be wary of strangers and may burst into tears even when one approaches with the best of intentions.

In addition, during the period around nine months of age, they display for the first time a sense of their mother as a permanent aspect of the environment. She becomes real for them in a new sense, exactly as things are becoming real: she too can disappear and then reappear, as the same permanent object of their attention and love. But only with object permanence can you miss something. And so, because their feelings for her are much stronger than their feelings for this or that object, her disappearance upsets them. For the first time, they begin to show anxiety and distress when she is gone. Then, as they become more familiar with her pattern of activities, they will show anxiety even in anticipation of her departure. It is not entirely a matter of attachment to the mother, of course, for if the twins are familiar with other adults, separation anxiety is displayed concerning them as well.

8. Stability of one's world soon leads to the first stages of the independence of oneself—the basis of one's "social image."

Another development appears at about nine months. It consists of attaining a relatively stable and permanent sense of oneself as an individual distinct from the environment.[30] This is a much more complex kind of development than the others, and it does not come about as quickly. Rather, it begins during the second half of the first year of life as a stance of deliberate stubbornness and independence. It constitutes the twins' first use of themselves to make a statement of power and influence to another person. The situation in which it occurs is when they are toilet trained.

To understand the psychological meaning of this situation, we may look very briefly at a very well-known theory of child development. Based on Freud's ideas and worked out in detail by one of his earliest followers, Karl Abraham, the theory states that every child goes through a fixed sequence of stages of development and that difficulty at one stage will show up in later years as specific defects or exaggerations in one's character. The first of the stages is the *oral*, because at this point, in the first six months or so of life, the infant's life was centered largely in and around the region of the mouth. It is at the oral stage that the growing child learns how to take in what the world has to offer. So the successful mastering of this stage will show up all through life in personality traits related to taking in and giving out, receiving and rejecting.

Piaget: Later sensorimotor thought

By the end of the twins' first year, their exploration of their environment has turned into active "experimenting." Their internal models, or representations in their mind, are being put to work in new and different situations, and are no longer tied directly to the action patterns that produced them. Once this happens, they are directed, not by links between action and object, but by new links between mental representation and environment. A major result is that they can now "think about" an object as external and permanent.
Example: A ball rolls beneath the couch, and they actively seek beneath and behind the couch for it. Here their action is directed, not by an action link to a ball they can see, but by their own mental representation of a ball that they know about and remember.
During their second year, they are increasingly active, in many different situations. By the end of this year, their mental representations are largely independent of external objects. They have become, in Piaget's term, *images*. The twins are almost ready to "think about" the world in addition to acting in it — Piaget, 1954.

---

separation anxiety. Feelings of apprehension experienced usually by children when they are separated from their mother or mother substitute. It is most common in the second half of the first year of life.

Then, toward the end of the first year, according to this theory, the child's life energy shifts, to become centered around the anal region of the body. It is at this point that a great deal of attention begins to be paid by adults to what children are doing to, and with, their excretory functions. To hold oneself in and refrain from soiling so as to go to the potty at appropriate times and places, often becomes the single overriding criterion of whether the child is growing up and is becoming a socialized being. In Freud's theory, pleasure becomes centered on the anal region. The theory would then predict that childhood difficulties at this stage will show up in later life as some form of inadequacy of control over impulses, as problems related to holding back, keeping clean and orderly, and maintaining independence without stubbornness.

Now, to get back to the twins. We can see that the Freudian theory of development describes a key change occurring at this stage. It concerns the twins gaining a clear-cut sense of themselves, at least as much as they can achieve through independence. They discover, for example, that they can influence their mother's attitude and behavior and mood, and perhaps even the atmosphere of the household, by what they choose to do or not do with their excrement. This is power on an unbelievable scale, at least for these children. How it is worked out, in the undercover struggle that often ensues, will determine many later characteristics of the twins' self-perception. In any case, the self, as a sensed core of permanence within one's individual experience, finds its origin at this stage of development, along with the newly gained sense of the permanence of objects and of persons.

At this stage, the self is still thoroughly grounded in the body. During this period of development, the twins learn to present themselves in specific ways to other persons, ways that will become characteristic for them, expressed in a language of body postures and movements. The child who becomes independent through fear will begin to live in, and express through, a different body from the child who learns to become independent in a climate of love and respect.

Twin differences. The boy and the girl will still be quite similar in their rate of development and in their abilities. Because the boy is a little bigger, he may often seem to be stronger or more active, perhaps even more destructive. But it is just as likely that this will be counterbalanced by the girl's greater "forwardness." Their steady progress in socialization is composed of two aspects: what they are as individuals and what influences are brought to bear on them by adults. Although they may not display too many important differences as individuals, there will now be a steadily growing distinction in the kinds of influences *on* them. For this reason, as they become more and more socialized they will begin to show more and more sex-related differences. We might state this in another way—that increasingly the difference between the twins will be the consequence of the way they are shaped by the adults around them.

The evidence concerning observed differences between the sexes at this age may be summarized briefly. Brought into a clinic or a laboratory to be tested, boys will show a little more of the behavior called *dependent*. They will cling more to their mothers and be more upset when the mother leaves. However, these conclusions are based on fairly crude observations. It is just as likely that more refined observation would indicate subtle messages from mothers to their sons. Because mothers expect male children to be more independent and self-sufficient, they indicate in subtle ways less patience with dependent behavior, and the boys' reactions thus often appear relatively more clinging.

As they approach the age of one year, become mobile, and start to assert their independence, the twins are on the threshold of the socialization process. More and more of their activities will come to be related to other children. More and more of the judgments made about them and the pressures put on them will be related to how they seem to compare with other children. We should therefore expect that they will now begin to be socially molded into a girl and a boy, still similar but increasingly different.

The second year

9. With the development of an upright posture and the beginning of grammatical speech, infants enter the world of childhood.

Two major accomplishments bridge the second year of life—at its start, the attainment of walking upright, and at its end, the attainment of grammatical speech. By the twenty-fourth month, the twins will have mastered the fundamental social requirement of toilet training. They will be able to move around independently and in the same way that older persons do. And they will have mastered the fundamentals of communicating with others and expressing themselves by language. The course of their development from this point on will be largely a matter of refining and extending the basic skills already grasped.

The upright posture. We will discuss language development in a later chapter. Here we want to indicate related developments that occur along with the twins' acquisition of a spoken language, and we want to try to relate this development in turn to the acquiring of upright posture. Between twelve and fifteen months, the twins pull themselves up to that permanently upright position that they will retain as "correct" for the rest of their lives. Humans are the only species in which this occurs. It is true that many other species can assume a position of uprightness, but it is not their "correct" posture. Penguins customarily walk, or waddle, in an upright position, but their "natural" place is in the water, where they swim as well as fishes. Laboratory rats, and other rodents in the wild, will rear on their haunches, but it is clear that this is a special pose that is adopted under unusual search conditions. The higher apes walk on their legs. But they do this only when being led by a larger or older animal or by a human, or when this is the only way to get from one place to another. The customary posture of the higher apes consists in using all four limbs as needed for locomotion. This is a pose that is almost never seen in human adults.

Yet this posture, unique to humans among all the species on earth, is not one that might have been selected out in evolution for its efficiency. It puts excessive strain at three points in the skeletal-muscular system: at the base of the neck, at the base of the spine, and in the feet. We pay a price for uprightness, in our sore feet that give out years before the rest of our bodies, in our chronic lower back pains, and in the pains that we suffer in the neck and across the shoulders. What do we get in return? Simply stated, we gain the feeling of being at home in a very special position vis-à-vis the world. We can make our sensory contacts at whatever degree of distance that we choose. We are not drawn to whatever attracts us, as all animals are who are built to follow their noses. We are close when we wish to step close yet removed when we wish to keep our distance. It is this postural ability to make and keep our chosen distance that furnishes the uniquely human perceptual command of our environment (Figure 10.6).

Symbolizing. If I point my finger toward something to which I am attending and then try to get my dog to notice what I am pointing at, the animal will look at

Fig. 10.6. It is the upright posture that makes possible keeping one's distance while surveying it. Language accomplishes in words what is here shown in vision: to avhieve both distancing and participation at once.

my finger, not at my target. But a two-year-old child will look at the target. The dog notices what it notices; it can never take in the whole situation of which it is a part, although it can perhaps "tune in" to the emotional climate of a situation. More important, the dog can never detach itself in thought from what it is noticing in order to grasp what that target refers to. It has no way of handling the phenomenon of *referring to.* Therefore it cannot understand pointing.

The two-year-old, however, is fully capable of mastering a symbol, or that which has meaning in its own right and also refers to other meanings. Children at this age can look at a picture — which in its own right is only a smudge of colored ink on some paper — and grasp that it refers to some kind of target in the real world. And, because what they grasp is not just the picture but the picture as a representation, or the picture in its referential aspect, they are able to identify the picture, even though it may not be concretely anything like the real-world target. Children at this age have no difficulty at all in looking at a 1-inch-high picture of a horse, colored green, and viewed from above — all characteristics different from any real-world horse that is perceptually available — and saying, "Horsey!" They have no difficulty in grasping that the area within a picture's frame is not a space in the real world but a represented space (although there is, of course, a real-world space behind the picture). It is only a picture; a distinction that is forever beyond the capabilities of all animals below the level of the higher apes. Two-year-olds delight in movies, in television, in storybooks with pictures — most of these delights being beyond the capacities of other species except some of the primates. The evidence is not at all clear as to how close the monkeys and the apes come to humans in these respects, although it increasingly appears that individual apes can handle most of the pictorial symbols that humans use.

As we will see later in this chapter, Piaget puts the ending of the earlier stages of intelligence at about this point in development. Somewhere toward the close of the second year, as the child learns speech and the grasp of representational thought, there comes to an end that kind of practical intelligence that he calls *sensorimotor.* Unlimited new worlds now begin to open up, bounded only by the child's imagination and experiences. New forms of intelligence now make their appearance.

The twins' second year. They will reach and then pass the various stages of motor development at about the same time and in the same way — crawling, standing up while holding on, taking steps between two supports, and, finally, walking on their own. They will differ as persons, rather than only because of their gender, in regard to personalities, likes and dislikes, and individual habits of eating, sleeping, or interacting with their family. The boy will still be a little larger, but not yet significantly so. And, if the father is typical, he may treat the boy differently, using a little more roughness or even corporal punishment, while usually treating the girl as though she were more fragile.[31]

Since the pioneering studies of Dorothea McCarthy[32] in 1930, it has been more or less accepted that the most evident difference between boys and girls in the early childhood years is their language skills. McCarthy's analysis of the recorded speech of seventy-three girls and sixty-seven boys, aged from about one-and-a-half to four-and-a-half years, indicated that on most measures the results favored the girls. They developed speech at earlier ages, and at every age level their speech was more developed than that of boys. Similar results were found a few years later, by Jersild and Ritzman,[33] in their analysis of the recorded speech of forty-five girls and forty-three boys, aged one-and-a-half to six years. The differences, while consistently in favor of the girls, were usually small and not statistically significant. More recent studies, on the other hand, have either failed to find any differences or have found them to be quite small.

It is difficult to draw any firm conclusions on the basis of these data. Perhaps

Piaget: Early concrete operations

Beginning in the second year, the twins are using language. But during their preschool years language is an accompaniment of their thinking rather than a tool in its own right.
Example: At age two, one of the twins, if left alone, may say, "Mommy gone." Here the verbal statement serves as an alternative to the child's internal representation. The mental activity or operation in this case, and for the next year or more, is what Piaget calls *concrete:* It is tied to the immediate and specific situation rather than being abstract and general.

Thinking and language develop together during this period. It is not until the close of the preschool period that the twins will have developed, on the one hand, logical tools in their thinking and, on the other hand, conceptions that they express in language. Thus, their explanation and understanding of events will result from simply juxtaposing images or from dependence on their egocentric point of view.
Examples: In juxtaposition, the child says, "I lost my ball because I'm not playing with it." In egocentrism,$^{\odot}$ the child is asked, "How many sisters do you have?" "I have two—Mary and Joan." "And how many sisters does Mary have?" "She just has one sister, Joan"—Piaget, 1967.

egocentrism. Piaget's term for the inability of young children to be able to imagine the world from any point of view not their own.

nuclear family. A family structure consisting of parents and their offspring.

the most appropriate inference is that during nursery school years, perhaps beginning as soon as they start to talk, girls expend more of their energy in finer and more personal movements, such as speech. In contrast, boys expend their energy in more large-muscle activity. This may then appear as a slight but not significant advantage in favor of girls in regard to the rate of maturing of their speech patterns. In some settings, especially those concerned with schooling, this advantage pays off in better performance and a more rapid development of close ties with female teachers and school aides. But the differences, although they may often be found, are small enough to be applicable only in general, not always to individuals.

The preschool years

10. During the preschool years, the major thrust of development is toward peer socialization, resting on an identification with one or more adults.

By the age of two, the growing child has completed the biological development and preparation that is ordained for its species. In this respect, it is like its close biological kin, the chimpanzee: In the first eighteen to twenty-four months, it acquires all the equipment that it will need for its adulthood. This equipment is motor, perceptual, sensory, and linguistic. It is all present and now needs only to be developed in degree, either by maturing from the inside, as it were, or by getting socialized from the outside.

The most important kind of development that will take place over the three or four years, before the child enters school, will be what is called *socialization*. The requirements for being accepted into nursery school, which are usually satisfied by the age of three, express very well the level that the child has now achieved: Nursery school children must be capable of separating themselves from their mothers for a few hours at a time, they must be toilet trained, they must be able to communicate their wants and needs, and they must be ready to occupy themselves socially in the company of their peers.

This last requirement is the most difficult to describe but will be central in the nursery school child's adjustment. Our phrase describing the requirement was rather cumbersome. We mean by it that the child can stick with an activity for more than a few moments at a time, so that activities can be carried out with a group. In addition, we mean that the individual child is more interested in engaging in these activities with peers than alone. Finally, we mean that the play with peers is not yet a joint effort, not cooperative, not a true interaction, but rather being agreeably in the presence of one another. Achieving this level carries the children into a world in which socialization becomes possible. This will be their principal occupation during the years prior to formal schooling.

It is in these years, too, that the separate influences of father and mother begin to be felt. Children below the age of two are usually primarily concerned with the mother and only marginally concerned with the father. This changes as soon as they are old enough to talk, to think, to express themselves in terms of an absent member of the family, and to associate with peers from other families. Then the child can be influenced by any number of adults.

Most of the data that we have concerning such influences is in fact derived from studies of traditionally organized, or nuclear families,$^{\odot}$ which consist of two parents, each with a fixed role and schedule, plus children of different ages. To an increasing degree, however, families are assuming forms that are different than this traditional pattern, with results that are as yet not known. In a number of societies—for example, in the kibbutzim,° or collective settlements, of Israel— children are not reared in families at all but in groups that are run by the community. Many communes follow this pattern. Single-parent families are becoming increasingly common, especially in urban centers. As divorce rates increase, with patterns of marriage, divorce, and remarriage taking the place of unbroken marriages, many children experience a succession of adults who play the role of a parent. Still other children move back and forth between two or more families, with changing parents as well as changing siblings. And, particularly among minority families at or below the poverty level, the sheer struggle for survival gives rise to forms of nontraditional caring. As Carol Stack[34] has described in a recent study, extensive networks, based on loose kinship or even friendship, provide a way of sharing whatever goods or facilities are available in rearing children. Mothers, fathers, exparents, older siblings and stepsiblings, grandmothers, aunts, current or former boyfriends or girlfriends—all may function as necessary within a broad "network of mutual obligation."

Identification. It is during the preschool years that there emerges a new and complex phenomenon, identification. As we have discussed, children can imitate at a much earlier level. It may even happen that they are observed to resemble one or another adult. Identification, however, is more than either of these. It consists first of all in having a sense of who you are, even if only dimly and even if it is more wanting than knowing (Figure 10.7). Second, it consists in patterning yourself on your perception of another person. Very young children can imitate, as can most of the apes and monkeys—but identification seems to become possible only on the basis of the abstractions that human language allows.

Identification,° or the self-conscious modeling of one's social self on that of someone else, becomes the most important basis for the developing personality during the preschool years. It is the time when little boys begin to act like little men, when little girls become girlish, feminine, or womanly, play with dolls, and act like their mothers and teachers. They may never again be this close to the parents' image. For some children, it is almost a caricature, but it does at least serve a constructive purpose: Identification and its consequent adopting of defined sex roles fits the child into social roles, which are overwhelmingly sex defined in most cultures.

A male child who strongly identifies with his very masculine, overbearing father might, if asked whether he ever cries, say with great emphasis, "No I don't—I'm a *boy!*" In this reply, he tells us, not just the fact of his gender, which we could easily have discovered in other ways, but also some details of his social identity: He claims proud membership in a group of humans who view with great, masculine scorn any creature who is weak enough to cry. Since this characteristic is, if at all, only minimally biological in origin, we conclude that this detail of his identity has been socially conditioned—quite probably through the process of identification with a male parent who holds unquestioningly to this attitude concerning crying. We might even predict that this is a father who says of his son's troubles, "Good for him. Toughen him up a little."

The twins in the preschool years. The concept of identification enables us to trace the most important way that the twins now come to differ from each other in their behavior and in their personalities. Training in their sex roles will begin, accomplished primarily through the development of a sexual identity. This term does not mean simply that they think they belong to one gender or the other, for both would have been able to tell you, since they began to talk, whether they were girl or boy. Rather, their sexual identity will be the end result of a series of stages that can be understood in terms of the following distinctions:

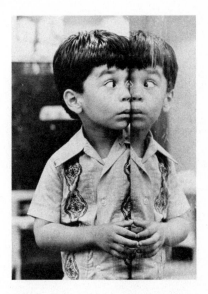

Fig. 10.7. The age of a developing social identity, leading to the question posed to a mirror: "Who are you?"

kibbutz. A collective farm community in Israel.

identification (in development). The process of learning social roles in childhood by copying or imitating the behavior of others, particularly adults.

- There is a child's gender, or biological identity. Except for cases that are largely of medical concern, this characteristic does not raise a problem for investigation.
- There is the degree of the child's masculinity or femininity. This refers to those characteristics that a particular society or cultural group associates with one or the other gender. For example, the habit of swaggering in some societies is considered to be a necessary characteristic of one's being masculine. A positive attitude toward being a mother in many societies is considered a basic characteristic of the feminine personality.
- Finally, there is one's sexual identity—a term used to describe the complex of attitudes that people have toward their individual gender or masculinity and femininity.

In our pair of twins, the girl will be of the female gender. She will display relatively few qualities of femininity before the age of two, will show more and more of such qualities as she is socialized in her preschool years, will also show some masculine qualities in this and later years, and will in this way develop a sexual identity that sums up her attitudes toward this aspect of herself as a person. The boy twin's development will follow analogous lines. For both of them, the developing of a mature, ideal sexual identity will involve "the earning of a sense of self in which there is a recognition of gender secure enough to permit the individual to manifest human qualities our society, until now, has labeled as *unmanly* or *unwomanly*"[35]—unmanly for the male and unwomanly for the female. That is, ideally each twin will know his or her own gender, will be acquainted with characteristics called *manly* or *womanly* by their culture, and will adopt for him- or herself some appropriate mix of the two. This achievement may be somewhat more difficult for the boy twin than for the girl, because he is likely to show, earlier and more strongly, a preference and identity closely related to his own gender. This is because in our society females are permitted a greater latitude.

The usual behaviors observed in the preschool years concern giving and taking, being active and passive, being aggressive and compliant, dependency and independence, affiliation and distance. In these respects, the results of studies on sex differences are very mixed. In the earliest preschool years, the boy may show greater dependence on his mother, the girl greater dependence on her like-sex peers. But again, the major differences on these important dimensions are not so much in the actual behavior of the twins as in what is expected of them and in what is seen by expectant adults. The remarkable extent to which cultures agree in the way girls and boys *ought* to differ is revealed in a survey of 110 different cultures, most of them nonindustrialized: In 85 of these societies, girls are expected to be more nurturant° than boys, and in 89 of them boys are expected to be more reliant.[36]

While these social pressures are operating, a persisting and "natural" difference is making itself evident. We have noted that, from the earliest months, the boy will occupy space in a more "encompassing" way than will the girl—a distinction that we said may be related to persistent findings in relation to aggression, especially aggression between boys. In a pioneering investigation of the first five years of life, Arnold Gesell and his associates at Yale found that in one test of an activity involving large-muscle movement in space (throwing a ball), boys were clearly superior as early as three-and-one-half years of age (Figure 10.8). Girls, on the other hand, were superior in such activities as dressing themselves.[37] If we observe adult males and females who have no particular professional skills as they throw a ball, the difference that makes itself evident in the preschool years is still evident. The female normally keeps her elbow close to her body in throwing and in effect pushes the ball, using her shoulder and torso. The male sweeps his arm

nurturant. Developmental characteristic of a person that emphasizes helping, taking care of, or sympathizing with others.

Girls   Boys

Fig. 10.8. Even at preschool ages, girls and boys take up space in different ways, as shown in these examples of throwing a ball. (From Gesell, 1940, Plate 17)

around, up, and then down, releasing the ball at the appropriate point of a long descending arc, for much greater velocity and accuracy. The difference is not in strength, not in agility, not in anatomy, and not even in practice, but in the way that the two sexes differentially occupy space by the use of their muscles. It is, as we suggested in an earlier chapter on the human body, just one more instance of the skeletal-muscular system as our primary "social system."

The early school years

11. The early school years are the years of training in "cognitive" pursuits that deemphasize the body and in which both sex and class differences are evident.

The influential theory of development advanced by Freud divides the years of childhood into four stages:

1. In the first year of life, approximately, the *oral* stage is defined by the young child's intake. It is a period of rapid growth, learning, and absorption of what the world has to offer.
2. In the second year of life, the *anal* stage is defined by the child's beginning to take an independent stand as a little person, a social being with individual ideas and preferences and character.
3. In the third year of life, the *phallic* level (which refers to boys rather than girls, because psychoanalysis was always limited in its understanding of the female) is defined by identification with the father, the personality and activity of a "little man," and immature sexuality with the mother as object.
4. Following the resolution of the sexual conflict implied in the previous stage—a conflict called the *oedipal crisis*©—the child enters the *latency* period, in which sexual drives are put aside and energy is used in substitute fashion for learning in school.

In the Freudian view, it is no accident that schooling always starts about the age of five or six, for this is just the time that children turn their (sexual) energies in new directions. Non-Freudian theorists would say that society has usually decided to begin formal training of the young at this age. Under this social pressure the children begin to occupy themselves with their new career as students. Whether the Freudian view, emphasizing biological forces as the causes, or a non-Freudian view, emphasizing social influences, is more correct, the fact is that in practically all organized societies children begin at this point to become full-time students. It is a career that will occupy them for at least the next ten years, and, for some, the next ten to sixteen years. In modern society, human beings spend more

oedipal crisis. In psychoanalytic theory, a child's attachment to the opposite-sex parent and hostility to the same-sex parent.

Piaget: Later concrete operations

As a result of the years of using language and experiencing social interactions in the elementary school years, the twins have learned to communicate (which usually requires listening to and taking account of the other person's view) and to think in increasingly more abstract and less ego-centered ways.

Example: At the start of this period, the child may ask, "Does the clock stop while I'm asleep?" By the end of this period, the child is well aware of, and can think about, a world of events that can go on independently.

The twins' operations, or mental activities, now begin to refer to classes of objects and events, and finally even to qualities of objects and events. They can do thought problems, which are posed entirely in language and thought about by means of operations, and express the answers in language, all without concrete links to objects or actions. Their observations become increasingly accurate and organized. A major accomplishment is the beginning of what Piaget calls *conservation,*⊙ or the ability to deal with something mentally by holding it constant — that is, to conserve it in the mind while manipulating it. The twins gradually come to be able to conserve quantity, space, length, area, volume, and so on.

Example (of conservation of quantity): The ability to recognize that the same quantity is present in containers A and B, although their shapes are different, or in B and C, although they differ in width — Piaget, 1966a. See diagrams at right.

conservation. Piaget's term for the ability of the child to distinguish that the amount of a substance is not changed — that it is conserved — even when it is placed in a different container or setting that makes it appear different.

time in school than they do in any other single kind of setting. They spend more time sitting in groups listening to a teacher talk than they do in any other single kind of activity, except (in some cultures) in watching television.

The single most important characteristic of schooling, however, is not that it is essentially passive and receptive but that it emphasizes cognitive activities and the control of body-based impulses. Children have already learned, in the immediate preschool years, to control their excretory functions, their emotional outbursts, their eating habits, and their impatience. To this is added, beginning in the first grade of formal schooling, hours spent as though these controlled aspects did not exist. The child has gone from knowing that one has to urinate but controlling it, to no longer knowing that one has to urinate because one is fully occupied with the joys of reading. This step is a major shift in the relations between mind and body, and those children who make the step easily will be the best students. The chief influence toward making this step is the authority of the teacher.

Middle-class children do better at this than do lower-class children, quite probably because their background and family culture predisposes them to an emphasis on cognitive rather than bodily activities and to accepting institutional authority. Lower-class children, whose experiences with authority and social influence are more likely to have been either negative or rigid, have more difficulty adopting the attitudes conducive to being good students. Their dispositions are much more toward learning by doing-in-movement than toward learning through controlling their movement and "getting into their heads." American children from non-English-speaking cultures — Chicanos, Chinese, Japanese, other Asians, some eastern Europeans — as well as black children — are often from settings where the language is not standard white English. They often have difficulties following what is said and do well in school only if their own culture's attitudes toward cognitive activities and toward authority conform to those of American school settings. In general, girls do better than boys in the early grades; it takes boys some years to learn how to learn in ways that are most useful in school (Figure 10.9).

During their first few years of schooling, children may appear to be more or less overwhelmed — by the system, by the new phenomenon of an authority figure who knows everything, and by the incredible kinds of new things to be learned. Then, somewhere about the age of nine or ten, at about the fourth-grade level, a change usually occurs. Teachers report that the children fairly suddenly become less accepting. They begin to organize themselves in cliques and groups and, for the first time, in sex-determined pairings and groupings. They are able to learn new kinds of material, because they are beginning to move from practical and person-centered modes of thinking to more abstract levels. At the same time, many of them become harder to teach. To some degree as well, their relative success in different school subjects will depend on their sex and their individual personalities. Skill at spelling for example, seems to bear some relation to an individual's conflicts with authority.[38]

The twins in the early school years. The two are now clearly different — in their size and appearance, in much of their behavior, in their preferences and activities, and, most of all, in their friends. For the first few years of school, the boy and the girl will live in two different minicultures, gaining a great deal of their

Fig. 10.9. At this age, boys' activities take up more space than do those of girls.

pleasure from the fact that the minicultures are separate. The most obvious distinction and the most obvious basis for competition in the first few grades of school will be between the sexes.

Social pressures to keep the differences alive between the boy and the girl will also be very strong at this time. The girl will be taught to be "grown up" and socialized, but to accomplish this while controlling expressions of aggression. The boy, on the other hand, will be educated, with some greater difficulty, in being "grown up" and controlled, but to accomplish this while hiding any expression of tender emotion. These differences will show up, as we noted earlier, in regard to their general educability. The most important single subject in the first two years of school is reading, an entirely cognitive activity that demands concentration on small printed signs and an adeptness at following a kind of language that does not sound like spontaneous talk. The girl can fit herself to this rather arbitrary activity much easier than can the boy. This in turn will underlie her generally better performance in school subjects (for, in school as elsewhere, success breeds success.) One of the most striking pieces of evidence in regard to this general personality difference in the elementary grades is that the newly discovered "illness" known as *hyperkinesis*, or *hyperactivity*,$^{\circ}$ is found three or four times as frequently among boys as girls. It seems very probable that, whether or not some kind of slight brain damage is associated with this condition, a major element in its appearance is the child's reaction to the situation of discipline and authority in the classroom — and in this respect, as we would expect, boys react quite differently than girls.[39]

Being fitted to one or another sex role is an advantage to the girl in the early grades and will gradually become an advantage to the boy in the upper grades. However, sex-role typing that is extreme will usually be a disadvantage. The girl

hyperactivity (also hyperkinesis).
Intense, restless activity in children, accompanied often by an inability to concentrate or complete a task.

will do best if she is feminine but not too feminine. The reason is that school subjects that require abstract thinking, concept formation, and the manipulating of symbols (for example, arithmetic) are interfered with by too "passive" and receptive an attitude. Similarly, the boy will benefit from being masculine but not too masculine, because his tendency toward being active could interfere with the concentration and attentiveness that is needed in school tasks. Their popularity, too, which is both an important measure of their adjustment and an important factor in their development, will depend on sex-role adjustment that is not too extreme; that is, neither overly feminine nor overly masculine. As many studies of adults have shown,[40] those who are unsuccessful in adult roles, particularly as parents, are very often caricatures of the extremes of masculinity or femininity.

12. Moral development proceeds in stages, from self-centered to a concern for others, and from an emphasis on the concrete situation to an emphasis on abstract principles.

One of the most significant ways in which children develop into adults is in regard to their moral standards and behavior. We all seem to recognize that there are attitudes, and social behavior related to them, that reveal distinctive levels of morality. We are usually agreed that some such levels are "higher" or more "mature" than others. Consider for example, the following letter from a mother regarding her teenage son, which appeared in the syndicated column of Ann Landers:

Our sixteen-year-old son and his friend are in serious trouble because some stupid person put temptation in front of him. Being human, they couldn't resist it.

Juddy and a fifteen-year-old pal were walking along the street last evening, and they saw a 1970 Chevrolet with the key in the ignition. On a moment's impulse, they decided to go for a little ride. These boys didn't mean to steal the car—they just wanted to have some fun. They were picked up two hours later in a nearby town. The police treated them as if they were murderers.

Please say something about irresponsible adults who tempt kids and expect them to be superhuman. Everyone in town is talking about our son, and it has made his father and me sick. We would like you to print this letter and comment.

Proud Of Our Boy.

What this parent fails to condemn, perhaps may even covertly encourage, is a kind of morality in which one's own impulses, as long as they are well meaning, are sufficient excuse for any behavior, even though it may involve breaking the law or causing another person some loss. In support of this dubious moral standard, the parent puts the blame for her son's act on the owner of the car, who is accused of putting temptation in front of him. It is strikingly similar to the attitudes and excuses we might find in very young children.

Morality, then, appears to have its developmental aspect. It has therefore occurred to a number of theorists that in the normal course of development children can pass through increasingly more mature stages of morality. The example just given certainly belongs at one of the immature stages—and it suggests that adults who may have reached mature levels in other aspects of their personality, such as intelligence or sexuality, might still be at a "childish" level in regard to their moral attitudes.

The initial steps toward developing a "stage" theory of development were taken by Freud. During the 1920s and the 1930s, Jean Piaget extended the notion of stages of development. In one of his studies,[41] he observed children of different ages as he engaged them in the game of marbles. On the basis of his observations, he formulated a sequence of stages in children's consciousness of rules and application of rules. He found that only at the conclusion of the preschool years do children appear to become aware that their collective play can be governed by rules. In turn, only toward the end of their elementary school years do they recognize and accept the notion that rules have an abstract and independent status. This is, rules are what everyone knows. Still later comes the notion that rules are what everyone obeys. In this development, rules are first unknown, then slowly recognized and codified over the course of time, and finally are known and accepted as independent, guiding principles.

The development is not easily achieved. In a recent series of studies, Loevinger and her associates[42] assessed moral development by means of a personality test in which children were asked to fill in incomplete sentences. Their results suggest five levels of increasing maturity:

1. An *impulsive* level, in which personal responsibility is not even recognized.
2. A *self-protective* level, in which the concern is with avoiding blame rather than taking responsibility.
3. A *conformist* level, in which one gets by through a technique of letting the responsibility reside in rules and authorities.
4. A *self-conscious* level, in which one's own responsibility is determined by what other persons think.
5. A *conscientious* level, in which one is responsible because one is accountable to one's own inner standards. They found that at the fifth- and sixth-grade levels most of the children were at or below the conformist level.

The most elaborate studies of moral development have been done by Kohlberg,[43] who assesses the children's level by asking them what should be done in instances of moral conflict. For example, they are given a situation, in the form of a story, in which a desperate husband, trying to save his wife's life, steals a drug because he cannot afford the inflated price being charged for it. Based on results that appear to hold up in many different societies, Kohlberg distinguishes three levels of moral development, each with two sublevels or stages. They are listed in Table 10.3.

The growth in one's "moral philosophy" can be seen if we compare typical answers given at various stages to the story of the husband who steals a drug to save his wife's life. At Level 1, the child's morality is a matter of circumstance. Thus, a Stage 1 answer might be simply, "No, he shouldn't steal it because if he does he'll go to jail." At Stage 2, the answer might be, "Yes, he can do it, because if he ever gets sick then she'll do the same thing for him." Notice that the level of moral development in the child's answer is not determined by whether the child says, "Yes, he should" or "No, he shouldn't" but by the reasoning involved.

At Level 2, there emerges a realization of the importance of rules in a more abstract sense. Typically, a Stage 3 answer would be, "No, because if he's found out his friends will know he's a crook." At Stage 4, the child might say, "No, it's illegal to steal anything." At this level of moral reasoning, the important element is what is right or proper, either in the view of others or in the view of society in general. Kohlberg's researches indicate that the majority of adults act in accordance with a personal moral philosophy that is at this level. The more "advanced" Level 3, in which morality rests on principles by which one tries to live, is found in the minority of persons past the age of sixteen. At Stage 5, for example, the person might say, "He would have to take it. The right to life is more important than the right to make a profit." At Stage 6, a typical answer would be, "Yes, of course. How could he live with himself if he let another human being die when he could help?"

It is uncertain whether there are simply few adults who are as morally "ma-

GROWTH
Becoming an individual

Table 10.3. Stages in the development of one's own "moral philosophy," as determined by Kohlberg.

Level 1. Morality is determined by circumstances such as what one does or what one has to do or wants to do.

    Stage 1. One should do right in order to avoid punishment (at ages eight to ten and below).

    Stage 2. One's responsibility goes only as far as satisfying needs or making an exchange with other persons (between ages eleven and thirteen).

Level 2. Morality is determined by conforming to established rules, conventions, or authorities.

    Stage 3. One should be "good"; one should help others because that is what is (stereotypically) considered proper (at about age thirteen).

    Stage 4. One should obey authority and do one's duty (between ages fourteen and sixteen).

Level 3. Morality is a matter of prinicple, of standards that are shared by everyone and internalized by each person.

    Stage 5. One should avoid violating the rights of others and should abide by what is generally agreed on (at about age sixteen).

    Stage 6. One should act in terms of individual principles in the form of a conscience, principles that have some larger meaning.

Piaget: Formal operations

The stage of formal operations, which is usually achived at about the fourteenth year, is the culmination of the development of intelligence. Not all children achieve it, nor do all adults think in this way all the time. But its characteristics are at the basis of adult reasoning as we know it.

The twins have now mastered a set of operations that consists of a formal system of thought. They can now operate in the abstract—that is, independently of any specific content—to solve problems and to manipulate the environment by thought alone. Piaget has described the achievement in this way: Earlier (concrete) operations used observations to build theories about events, whereas later (formal) operations use theories so as to organize operations. Thus, science, formal logic, and independent creative thought are now possible.

---

ture" as Level 3 requires or whether "mature" levels of moral development follow a different course than Kohlberg outlines. It may be, for example, that from the viewpoint of the person concerned, the highest level of morality does not consist in conforming to an abstract principle, as Kohlberg maintains. Rather, adult morality at the highest level of development might consist in putting oneself in the place of another person. Self-sacrifice, then, which is not mentioned in Kohlberg's listing, would rate "higher" than acting for a principle.

If this were so, we would expect that the level of people's morality would differ from one situation to another and from one interpersonal relation to another. And this is in fact what is most often found. Beginning with studies as far back as the 1920s,[44] the evidence indicates that children are not usually consistently honest or dishonest. They appear to act, not in accordance with abstract principles of virtue, but in terms of how they see the situation, including the other people in it. Most persons are honest in many situations. Quite probably most persons would be dishonest in at least a few situations. What people actually do seems to result from weighting the costs and benefits as they see them in order to arrive at the most workable solution. If any moral principles are involved, especially at the highest level, they may have to do less with abstract or ideal propositions than with the good or harm that might be done to others.

Summary

1. Developmental psychology is concerned with how people change, but some ingenuity may be required to obtain data on this in regard to infants and young children.

2. The human embryo can respond to pressure and temperature changes and to sound and can be conditioned by Pavlovian procedures.

3. At the outset of prenatal growth, the fertilized egg is undifferentiated as to sex—although its chromosomal makeup will determine its eventual gender.

4. Although the female is smaller and weaker than the male, she will grow faster, live longer, and be more resistant to disease.

5. The higher the birth weight, the greater the percentage of children who test, both neurologically and psychologically, at or above the normal level.

6. Prematurity is influenced by many factors, but the best predictor of it is the mother's socioeconomic status.

7. The course of normal growth is not simply a response to given biological and social conditions but also includes the exercise by each person of his or her own choices.

8. Within the first month of life, infants can make visual discriminations, respond appropriately to the human voice, and demonstrate their needs to cling and to be held and rocked.

9. In the period from the second to the sixth month, the infant begins to attempt intentional movements; shows a typical smiling response, especially to the human face; and expresses anticipation as well as familiarity.

10. In the preschool years, aggression is found more frequently with boys than with girls, but largely because males are aggressive against each other. Boys are no more aggressive with girls than girls are with girls.

11. In the period from six months to a year, the child begins to crawl and walk, as well as to show a capacity for imitation, object permanence, separation anxiety, and a relatively stable sense of self.

12. Freudian theory suggests that childhood difficulties at any stage of development will appear later in life as some form of inadequacy.

13. At the beginning of the second year, the child attains an upright posture and, at the end of this year, gains grammatical speech.

14. The two-year-old child has a command of meaning and symbol that enables understanding things in their own right as well as references to other things.

15. During the nursery school years, girls expend more of their energy than do boys in such activities as speech, whereas boys expend their energy proportionately more in large-muscle activity.

16. The self-conscious modeling of one's social self (indentification) becomes the most important basis for the developing personality during preschool years. Sex roles also begin to be defined at this time.

17. Sexual identity is the result of one's gender, the degree of masculinity or femininity, and the complex set of attitudes that others have toward one's gender and masculinity and femininity.

18. Preschool boys appear to take up more lateral space than do girls, as a reflection of the different way they use their bodies.

19. Beginning with the early school years, there is a progressive emphasis on cognitive concerns, at the emphasis of a concern with the body. Differences in regard to sex and to social class also play a part here. Psychoanalytic theory described this stage of development with the appropriate term *latency period*.

20. Middle-class children do better than lower-class children in regard to the authority structure of the classroom.

21. Studies of moral development indicate that, like other cognitive functions, it can be traced through a series of progressively more abstract and less concrete stages.

This chapter will help you learn about the measurement of individual differences in ability. Some important problems inherent in measuring people's abilities will be clarified, and the history of intelligence testing will be traced. You will see how the interest in intelligence testing began and flourished. A detailed discussion will be offered of the construction of the intelligence test (or IQ test) and the assumptions it is based on.

Major flaws in the IQ test will be discussed. The IQ may be a meaningless score, the effect of the testing situation is not accounted for, and the statistical basis of scoring contains built-in deficiencies. You will learn something of the weaknesses in such fixed categories of IQ as genius and mentally retarded. Intelligence, as defined by these tests, will be shown to be essentially the ability to profit from traditional schooling. You will see how the results of the tests, reflecting rather restricted abilities, are then used to make group comparisons.

Toward the end of the chapter, we turn to the central question of hereditary and environmental influences on intelligence. The current state of the controversy will be reviewed. Performances on intelligence tests will be shown to be complex and multiply determined; they cannot be linked to specific gene patterns. Finally, you will see why this question should probably not be raised in the present state of our knowledge and with presently available measuring instruments.

11

Individual differences in ability

Differences are very easy to spot; children can tell you how two things are different long before they can tell you how they are alike. One reason for this is that differences exist everywhere. No two things, anywhere, are exactly alike. In this chapter, we will consider some of the problems in measuring differences between individuals. Our theme will be that the history of such measurement in psychology has been less than satisfying and that the most familiar application, the measurement of differences in intelligence, has largely turned out to be a lost cause.

Measuring individual differences

1. The results of measurements depend as much on the instruments used as on what is being measured.

Measuring by categories. When we use the term *measurement*, we usually think of applying something like a ruler and marking off the appropriate number of units. But the term actually has a much broader meaning. Measurement consists of ordering or arranging your data according to some known system. The simplest kind of measurement, then, involves sorting data into categories—for example, all the people you like, and all the people you don't like.

One defect in such a system of categories is that it is not *exhaustive*. If you applied it to the people you know, you would probably have a fair number of persons left over who do not fall into either category. Other groupings, such as male *vs.* female, would be exhaustive in all but the very few cases in which you

Fig. 11.1. These persons are all "alike," at least until we choose to make finer distinctions among them.

could not arrive at a decision. This problem arises every four years when physicians for the various Olympic teams have to decide whether specific individuals whose chromosomal and hormonal balance is unusual ought properly be placed with the women's or the men's team of a country.

Fingerprinting, a widely used method for identifying persons, also measures them by placing them into various categories. Our modern system of classification by fingerprints, now used by law enforcement agencies all over the world, was not devised until 1891. It consists of six different levels of categorizing, each successively more refined, with a grand total of approximately 1.5×10^{14} different arrangements possible. Since there are about 4.5×10^9 different people in the world, there will be only 1 chance in 300,000 that two different persons will be similarly classified. If they were, we would say they have the "same" fingerprints.

But it is clear that the notion of identical fingerprints depends not only on the people we are classifying but also on the measuring system that is used. Given the figure of 1 in 300,000, it is not impossible, but only unlikely, that two persons will be found to measure out the same. They would not then be classified as "identical" persons, of course, because there is a very great likelihood that they would also differ in age, name, and place of residence. However, in the very remote case that a law-abiding citizen would be found to have the same fingerprint classification as a known criminal, an obvious solution to the confusion is open to law enforcement officials: They would simply add another subcategory to their system of classification, thereby making their measurement still finer.

Thus, measurement depends in important ways on methods or systems or instruments for measuring. Any differences that we find will depend in important ways on the means that we have for detecting them. But this is mostly a matter of practical decision (Figure 11.1). If two people differ by 1 millimeter in height, we say they are the same height—not because we cannot measure a difference this small, but because the observed difference in height does not make much of a difference in practice. However, if two beams of pure light differ by only 1/100 of a millimeter in wavelength, we say they are certainly two different colors. Similarly, we can say that for all practical purposes all the pages in this book are of the same size, but if for some reason we had to distinguish them, there would be no problem in making fine measurements to do so. The point is that the terms *same* and *different* have no absolute meaning but depend on how the two items are compared, what methods of measurement are used, and even what purpose the measurement serves. As we shall see, this conclusion is of critical importance when we come to consider differences between people.

Measuring by observation. Many kinds of measurement, especially those concerned with people and their characteristics, are made by the use of controlled *observation*. Here, one person makes judgments about another. For example, each year a new winner in the Miss America contest is chosen by a panel of judges, the final choice being entirely dependent on the judges' views of which candidate is the most deserving. There is no ruler marked off in units of "deservingness," nor even a ruler marked off in units of charm, or beauty, or talent. The judges are entirely dependent on their individual observations and the personal judgments they then arrive at.

Of all the observable characteristics of persons, one of the most evident is the size and shape of the body. We have no difficulty "measuring" someone as tall, short, fat, thin, lean, muscular, or whatever. For centuries, scholars have been intrigued by the possibility of classifying all human physiques in terms of a simple and orderly system. One could then try to find relations between such body types and other categories, such as personality, ability, or even kinds of abnormality. Unfortunately, significant relations of this sort have not been found, except in extreme cases, such as severe neurosis associated with being extremely fat or extremely thin.

However, much energy has been expended anyway in somatotyping,⊙ as it is called, beginning in modern times with the work of Ernst Kretschmer.[1] Working with mental patients, he classified all human bodies, except for a small number of very deviant physiques, into three major types: the round, whom he called *pyknic*;⊙ the slender, or *leptosome*;⊙ and the intermediate or muscular, whom he called *athletic*.⊙ Further, he claimed that one of the two major types of severe mental illness, the manic depressive,⊙ was found predominantly among those of a pyknic physique, and the other major mental illness, the schizophrenic,⊙ was found mostly among the leptosomes. More recently, Sheldon[2] has extended Kretschmer's work to nonhospitalized persons (male college students) and observed the same three general categories—the fat, the lean, and the muscular (Figure 11.2). Sheldon carried his observations a number of steps farther, first, by rating people on a scale of 1 to 7 on each of the three characteristics and, second, by relating the characteristics to components of the body. The "fat" component, which he called *endomorphy*,⊙ corresponded to the soft visceral tissues; the muscular component, or *mesomorphy*,⊙ to bone and muscle; and the "slender" component, or *ectomorphy*,⊙ to the nervous system and skin. An extreme endomorph, or very obese person, would then be scored 7-1-1, whereas a very thin person would score 1-1-7 and a person with a balanced physique perhaps 4-3-4. In later studies, Sheldon and his collaborators attempted, although without great success, to relate these varieties in somatotype to differences in personality.[3]

Measuring people. Ever since the problem of measuring people's characteristics was first seriously considered, about the middle of the seventeenth century, it was known that measurement along dimensions, or quantitative measurement,⊙ had many advantages over qualitative measurements.⊙ During the seventeenth century, modern, mathematically based science, especially the science of physics, began to be developed on the basis of Galileo's work. It very soon occurred to the "natural philosophers" of the day that perhaps people could be subjected to the same kinds of measurements as were being used with natural phenomena.[4]

But it was immediately evident that measuring the characteristics of people presented new kinds of problems. Psychology, it seemed, was not about to become

somatotyping. A method of classifying people into groups by measuring their physiques.

pyknic. Kretschmer's term, used to describe a body type that is plump and round. The people with this body type are usually friendly and contented, according to Kretschmer.

leptosome. Kretschmer's term for a slim body build. In his view, people with this build are often intraverted, tend to daydream, and lack rapport with their environment.

athletic. Kretschmer's term for the body type he associated with the normal personality.

manic depressive. A psychotic reaction described by mood swings, from excessive elation and euphoria in the manic state, to severe depression and despondency in the depressive state.

schizophrenic. A psychotic condition characterized by general withdrawal from reality; it can include hallucinations, delusions, and inappropriate emotional response.

endomorphy. Sheldon's term for a physique characterized by heaviness, particularly with a prominent abdomen.

mesomorphy. Sheldon's classification of an athletic body type, marked by a prominent bone and muscle structure.

ectomorphy. Sheldon's term for a physique characterized by thinness, fine hair, and a sensitive nervous system.

quantitative measurement. The statistical measurement of variables involving numbers and quantities.

qualitative measurement. The statistical measurement of attributes (such as good or beautiful) that are not stated numerically.

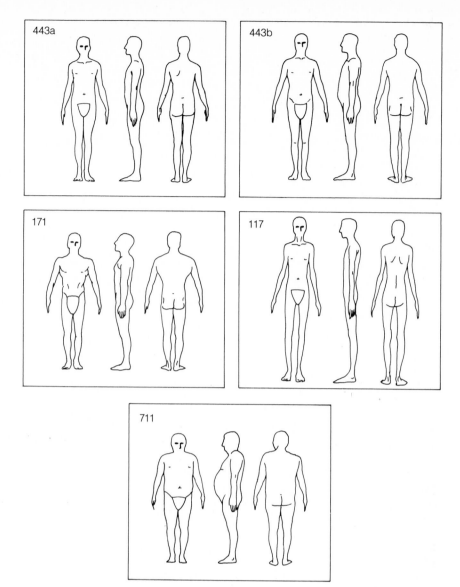

Fig. 11.2. Examples of Sheldon's typology of male somatotypes. Nos. 443 a and b are common American adults; No. 171 is the "Li'l Abner" type; No. 117 is the "Phi Beta Kappa" type, according to Sheldon; and No. 711 is an extreme. (From Sheldon, 1954, pp. 37, 66, 220–221, 325)

achievement. A psychogenic motive that enables a person to master difficulties and be successful.

assessment. The general term for measuring by means of a test.

a science as easily as physics or chemistry had. Two problems in particular made the task so difficult that it was not to be solved for another 200 years.

The problem of hidden data. The first of these problems is that much of the information that we would like to obtain in regard to people's characteristics is not on the surface or directly accessible for measurement. It is always in some way hidden, so it always has to be inferred. The length of a table, for example, can be measured directly: We simply measure its length. But how do we measure someone's musical ability? It would be evident, if at all, only when the person performed musically.

Yet this is not what we are after. We do not want to know what the person *has* done—which we call *achievement*©—but what the person *can* do, or their ability. This cannot be measured directly, but must be got at indirectly, perhaps in terms of something that we take to represent musical ability. A similar problem arises in regard to any other human characteristic, whether it is beauty, or intelligence, or level of moral development, or degree of anxiety. In every instance, we are forced to a somewhat roundabout and indirect method of assessment, which we then call a *test*.

The problem of units. An even more serious problem concerns the units of measurement that we might use. Surely we cannot hope to have a quantitative science, on the model of physics, if we do not make our measurements in terms of some standard units such as inches or millimeters. But it turns out that the (psychological) units we might use to measure people's characteristics, although seemingly numerical, do not behave like numbers. Suppose we place a yardstick against one table and measure the table's length at exactly 36 inches; then place another yardstick against a second table and measure that, too, at 36 inches; and, finally, place the two yardsticks end to end and obtain a total of 72 inches. In this way, we would demonstrate that our units of measurement are *additive;* Whether on yardsticks or on paper, 36 of our units plus 36 of our units adds up to 72 units, and we could then confidently predict that if we placed our two tables end to end alongside a 72-inch measuring stick, they would correspond, within slight errors of measurement.

But now suppose we do the same thing with a pair of psychological measurements. We measure the IQs of two relatively stupid people and then add up the separate IQ's on paper. Will the sum be a useful prediction about their joint intelligence—for example, how they might perform if set to work on a task together? The very notion strikes us as peculiar—just as peculiar as the notion that my perception of one dim light, followed by my perception of another dim light, somehow could add up to my perception of a bright light. Units of psychological measurement, unlike those used in the natural sciences, may be expressed in numbers but are not numerical. They are not additive; they do not even have a zero point. The idea of zero IQ simply makes no sense.

Not all of these ideas were clear to psychologists of a century or two ago. As we shall now see, the development of psychological tests, particularly those of intelligence, ran into many such problems.

The history of intelligence

2. With the help of techniques for handling masses of data, called *statistics*, and a firm faith in science, the testing movement began a hundred years ago.

Two important developments came together in the nineteenth century to make possible the mental testing movement. The first of these consisted of new techniques for handling numbers. It came about in this way: If you make the same measurement on many different people, how can you best organize and summarize the long list of numbers that you obtain? This problem may arise when many different measurements are made of the position of a star or when one counts up the number of shoes of various sizes that are issued to soldiers. There is one simple way of summing up such a collection of measurements. You find the smallest measurement and the largest measurement in your collection, and then either subtract the smallest from the largest to get the range,⊙ or else divide the larger by the smaller to obtain a proportion⊙ (as in Table 11.1). These two simple measures of variability⊙ provide a kind of handle by which one large collection of measurements can be compared with another collection.

During the first half of the nineteenth century, two mathematicians of genius, a Belgian astronomer named Adolphe Quetelet and a German physicist named Karl Friedrich Gauss, laid the foundations for the field that we now call

range. The difference between the highest and the lowest scores in a frequency distribution.

proportion. In general, the ratio of one value to another. Specifically, balance that is particularly pleasing or esthetic.

variability. A measure of the degree to which scores in a distribution cluster around some central measure.

Table 11.1. Some extremes of variability. Accurate observation and recording of variability, or degree of difference, is difficult under even the best of conditions. When the data consist of extreme instances, observation is likely to be influenced as well by problems of instrumentation — and, in the case of records of historic importance, by such factors as vanity, local pride, the chance of commercial gain, and, of course, carelessness. This table presents some instances of extreme variability that are as trustworthy as we can get.

Phenomenon	Range (Low to High)	Proportion
Height, adult human male	26.5 in to 8 ft 11 in	1 to 4.0377
Weight, surviving human infant at birth	10 oz to 24 lbs	1 to 38.4
Weight, adult human male	5 lbs to 1069 lbs	1 to 213.8
Size, living mammal	1.5 in to 108 ft	1 to 864
Weight, adult bird	.07 oz to 63 lbs	1 to 14,400
Diameter, one-celled living organism	.000004 in to .6 in	1 to 150,000
Weight, insect	1/5,670,000 oz to 3.4 oz	1 to 19,278,000
Size, mammal at birth	1/140th oz to 7 tons	1 to 31,360,000
Weight, living mammal	.078 oz to 152 tons	1 to 62,358,974
Weight, plant seed	1/35,000,000 oz to 40 lbs	1 to 22,400,000,000

Source: Data from McWhirter and McWhirter, 1963.

statistics.[○] Some simple statistics are known to all of us, for example, the average of a group of numbers or, as statisticians call it, the *arithmetic mean.*[○]

Quetelet and Gauss also pioneered in developing ways to represent geometrically the characteristics of any large grouping of data. As we all know, the simplest way to do this is by means of a graph,[○] which gives us at a glance some basic characteristics of our data. For example, the graph in Figure 11.3a shows that, of all the professional basketball players now active in the United States, none is 5 ft tall, some small percentage is 7 ft or over, and the majority are between 6 ft 2 in and 6 ft 8 in tall. On the other hand, we can graph a collection of measurements on any natural phenomenon that is widely distributed in nature, such as the height or chest measurements of all the seventeen-year-old males in North America, or the width of all the leaves on the oak trees in Oregon. In such a case, we obtain a bell-shaped figure that is popularly known as a *normal curve*[○] (Figure 11.3b). It is not "normal," of course, merely very common when large amounts of naturally occurring data are shown.

The second major nineteenth-century development that led to mental tests was a belief, still widely held today, that science was an effective tool for making a better world. As this belief came to be widespread, particularly among progressive educators and reformers, it provided the motive force for their efforts to assess and train all persons on an individual basis. It is not hard to understand why the most rapid growth of a new rational science of individual differences took place in America, the youngest and most active of political democracies.

Two names are most closely associated with this new movement, although their backgrounds and characters were very different and their interests quite far apart. One of these was Francis Galton, the most remarkable of British gentlemen scientists. A cousin of Charles Darwin, he was influential in making the new field of testing a scientific discipline. Through his own extensive studies, he invented the questionnaire and the "Galton whistle" for calling dogs. He founded the field of eugenics[○] and contributed importantly to the early history of statistics. And he

statistics. The branch of mathematics that deals with the analysis of sets of scores for groups or individuals.

mean. The arithmetic average, found by dividing the sum of a group of scores by the number of items.

graph. A diagram representing successive changes in the value of a variable quantity.

normal curve. The symmetrical, bell-shaped frequency distribution in which the mean, the median, and the mode are identical.

eugenics. The science that deals with improving races or breeds of animals. It is usually used in regard to controlling human characteristics through heredity.

carried out the first large-scale testing program, at a walk-in laboratory which he set up at the Crystal Palace in London, at the Great Exhibition of 1851.

Yet his tests of mental imagery and hearing and speed of movement were a loose collection of separate investigations rather than instruments for assessing any important psychological characteristics. It remained for a young American, J. McKeen Cattell, to take the next step.

Cattell studied in Europe and came home to establish a university clinic for

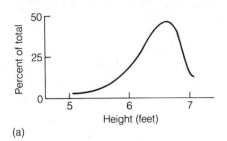
(a)

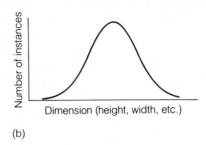
(b)

Fig. 11.3. (a) Basketball players are certainly selected for height. (b) The height of all seventeen-year-old American males is "normally" distributed.

the sole purpose of making psychological measurements on human beings. He introduced the term *mental test* in 1890—and the fact that he had to coin the term indicates that at this time the idea was far from self-evident that people could be objectively tested for their mental characteristics.

What intelligence is. It may seem odd that educators and scientists had to be taught, by a few pioneers, that abilities could be tested. But the fact is that you cannot measure the amount of something unless you have some idea of what it is and where to look for it. Now, intelligence, or a person's general ability, is obvious enough to an observer. We can all perform the simplest of measuring acts: the intuitive judgment of how "smart" someone is. But is this the same as testing them? For obvious reasons, it is not. My judgment of someone may differ from yours, and we would have no common scale or units by which to compare them. Nor would we be sure that you and I are judging the same thing or mean the same thing by the word *smart.*

Until a phenomenon is defined, then, it cannot be properly measured. Cattell, for his part, was convinced that intelligence was a kind of elaborate complex of sensorimotor skills, and so he thought his collection of simple measures was quite adequate as a measure of general intelligence. British psychologists, on the other hand, during the early years of this century were very much influenced by the work of C. E. Spearman.[5] His statistical analyses of people's test scores led him to propose that every individual had a store of what he called **g**, or "mental energy."[☉] The more **g** one had, the more intelligent one would test on different measures.

Some American statisticians have tended toward the view of a more democratic organization of the structure of intelligence—that it is composed of a number of independent general abilities. L. L. Thurstone[6] called these *primary mental abilities,*[☉] referring to one's facility in regard to verbal meanings, numbers, space, induction (a form of reasoning), rote (or literal) memory, word fluency, and perceptual speed.

In all of these views, the abilities being measured are closely related to what students display in schoolroom classes. In fact, it would not be inaccurate to say that the abilities that are discovered by testers are precisely those that are required in order to get good grades in school (as, indeed, they were intended to be). No mention is made of any other possible skills, aptitudes, or gifts. Athletic ability, for example, is never mentioned. Nor is the ability to work skilfully with the hands, as is shown by persons who do not seem to need training in order to handle tools or work with wood or cloth or know how machines work. One psychologist, J. P.

g (mental energy). Spearman's term for a "pool" of general intelligence.

primary mental abilities. The abilities identified as making up general intelligence. These relatively independent abilities include verbal, numerical, perceptual, and spatial reasoning.

Guilford,[7] makes some place in his scheme for what he calls "divergent production," a kind of ability that he feels is basic to all creative work, but in general creative abilities and the arts are neglected in these theories.

In addition, it seems evident that these views are not really theories of intelligence. None of them help to answer the question of what intelligence is. It may seem curious that testers can proceed to develop tests and produce elaborate schemes concerning the structure of something that they have not quite defined. Yet this is, in effect, what was done for many years. When asked directly, the response of the testers was often something like, "Well, intelligence is what the intelligence tests test."

The problem of definition and the issue of theory were hardly matters of central importance. The field of intelligence testing became one of the most active in all of psychology and probably the one in which psychologists gained their greatest reputations and made their most significant contributions to education, yet it was all done with surprisingly little interest in theory.

3. Binet and Simon solved most of the problems of constructing an intelligence test; their work was rapidly Americanized for a mass market in testing.

How to construct a test. In order to see how it is possible to develop elaborate tests of intelligence without stating in detail what it is that is being measured, we need to look briefly at the work of some pioneers. The most important of these, by far, was Alfred Binet, a French educator and experimental psychologist. With his colleague, Henri Simon, he had as early as 1895 raised serious objections to the simple sensorimotor tests of intelligence that were then in vogue.[8] The French government asked him to devise some means for identifying schoolchildren who were slow learners, so as to be able to give them special help. He and Simon therefore set about developing a test that, as they hoped, would tap complex mental abilities. The Binet-Simon tests that resulted were the first "scale" of intelligence, for the test items were grouped according to age level and the children were given so many months of mental age⊙ credit for each test they passed[9] (Table 11.2).

Binet and Simon solved most of the problems of test construction so well that their scale became the standard for all others for the next four decades. Brought to the United States, it was issued in a translated and Americanized version by Lewis M. Terman of Stanford University in 1916. He modestly used the name of his institution rather than his own name, and so the test has been known, in its revisions of 1937 and 1960, as the Stanford-Binet test.⊙

The contributions made by Binet and Simon may be summarized in the form of answers to the major questions that confronted testers. First, if you have no theory of intelligence, how can you measure someone's performance on your test? What yardstick do you use? The answer was to make two assumptions: First, if general intelligence was a characteristic of the human species, it was probably distributed throughout the population according to the same principles as were other biological characteristics such as height or chest size; that is, in the form of the familiar bell-shaped curve (see Figure 11.3b). Thus, if questions are devised so that at each age level a large sample of normal children obtain scores that fall into this distribution, the questions are probably representative. A second assumption was that, if general intelligence was such a characteristic of the species, it ought to increase regularly with age. Thus, test questions would be picked that are neither

mental age (MA). A score developed by Binet and Simon for intelligence testing. If the test is representative of, and standardized to, a certain age group, children of a certain age should have the same mental age.

Stanford-Binet Test. An individual intelligence test designed by Terman and based on the earlier Binet tests.

Table 11.2. The items of the 1908 Binet-Simon Intelligence Scale.

Three-Year Level. Points to nose, eyes, mouth. Repeats sentences of six syllables. Repeats two digits. Enumerates objects in a picture. Gives family name.

Four-Year Level. Knows sex. Names familiar objects when shown: *key, pocket knife, penny.* Repeats three digits. Indicates which of two straight lines is longer.

Five-Year Level. Indicates the heavier of two cubes. Copies a square with a pen. Makes a rectangle from two pieces of cardboard, copying a model. Counts four pennies.

Six-Year Level. Indicates which is right hand and left ear. Repeats sentences of sixteen syllables. Chooses the prettier in pairs of faces. Defines familiar objects in terms of use. Executes an order with three parts. Knows age. Knows morning and afternoon.

Seven-Year Level. Tells what is missing in unfinished pictures. Knows numbers of fingers on one hand and both hands, without counting them. Copies a picture with pen. Copies a diamond with pen. Repeats five digits. Describes pictures as scenes. Counts thirteen pennies. Knows names of four common coins.

Eight-Year Level. Reads a passage and remembers two items in it. Adds up the combined value of different stamps. Names four colors—red, yellow, blue, green. Counts backward from 20 to 0. Writes short sentence from dictation. Gives differences between two objects from memory.

Nine-Year Level. Knows dates: day of week and of month, month, and year. Recites days of week. Makes change in a play transaction. Gives definitions of familiar objects, above the level of use. Reads a passage and remembers six items in it. Arranges five blocks in order of weight.

Ten-Year Level. Names months of year, in correct order. Recognizes all varieties of coins. Constructs a sentence including three given words. Answers easy comprehension questions. Answers hard comprehension questions (may not get majority correct).

Eleven-Year Level. Points out absurdities in contradictory statements. Constructs a sentence including three given words (higher standards than at ten-year level). Names sixty words in three minutes. Defines abstract terms—*charity, justice, kindness.* Puts words, arranged in a random order, into a sentence.

Twelve-Year Level. Repeats seven digits. In one minute, finds three rhymes for a given word. Repeats a sentence of twenty-six syllables. Answers problem questions—a test of common sense. Gives interpretation of pictures.

Thirteen-Year Level. Draws the design that would be made by cutting a triangular piece from a folded paper. Rearranges in imagination two triangles and draws the result if rearranged. Gives differences between pairs of abstract terms.

Source: Peterson, 1925, pp. 193–195.

too easy nor too hard for students of each age level. Specifically, 50 percent of all the children at a given age level should answer a question correctly in order to assign it to that level. In this way, one would accumulate a set of questions for each age level, and the score obtained by a particular child would then be a way of comparing that child with his or her age group—for example, just at the average, or above average, or perhaps somewhat below average (which was the aim of the tests in the first place).

Second, even if you get some tests, how do you ever know that what you are testing is really a child's intelligence, and not some other characteristic? One answer was to compare the results with a familiar standard, teachers' judgments.

Binet and Simon were well aware that such judgments are not perfect. In fact, they carried out a number of ingenious experiments to test this standard, but it was, at the beginning, the best kind of standard available. The issue here is referred to as the *validity*© of a test. Aware that how a test is administered can affect its validity, Binet and Simon insisted that intelligence tests be given individually by a trained and sensitive examiner, who would observe all the important aspects of the child's performance.

Binet's American fate. Unfortunately, the individual and clinical approach advocated by Binet and Simon was largely ignored in the United States, in the rush to turn their testing instrument into an efficient, mass-produced educational tool. Henry Goddard, of the Vineland School in New Jersey, learned of the test in France and brought it to the United States in 1911. He soon embarked on a hard-sell campaign. The Binet test, he proclaimed, was always accurate to within one or two points, and it was valid and reliable even in the hands of untrained teachers. Further, because the test was a means for tapping "native" ability, it could be used to support Goddard's extreme views concerning the inheritance of intelligence — that some families had "good blood" and some did not, and that "bad blood" was the cause of alcoholism, poverty, prostitution, and criminal behavior.

Although test specialists such as Goddard and Terman maintained a firm belief in the importance of heredity — or, as they usually called it, "breeding" — they thought of themselves as very democratic in their views. It was their conviction that intelligence tests were ideal tools for picking out talented persons of all classes, who could then be trained to take their proper places in society. As the tests came to be more widely used in the United States, first on a mass scale with millions of recruits during World War I and then in school systems during the 1920's, the leaders of American psychology were thus united in two beliefs: first, that intelligence, being hereditary, was the major cause of some people's miserable position in life and, second, that the intelligence test, being able to spot this hereditary characteristic in anyone, was a democratic tool for the betterment of society. As we shall see, the problems raised by these two somewhat contradictory beliefs are still with us.

The flawed IQ test

Two kinds of inspiration had joined to produce the modern IQ test — the clinical and scholarly inspiration of Binet and Simon and the organizational and technical inspiration of psychologists during a period of optimism and growth in America. Here we take a look, in summary fashion, at some of the test's more serious flaws.

---

4. Major flaws in the IQ test are the facts that MA (mental age) is a meaningless measure, that the effect of the testing situation is not accounted for, and that the statistical basis of the test contains built-in deficiencies.

Measuring the Eye-Q. During the nineteenth century, an ingenious Dutch ophthalmologist, Hermann Snellen, devised what might be called an "Eye-Q" test, which is still in use. He made up a wall chart consisting of letters of different sizes, and asked his patients to read the letters from a distance of 20 ft. Anyone who

validity. The extent to which a test measures what it is supposed to measure.

could do as well as the average person, by reading the line labeled 20 at the 20 ft distance, was given an "Eye-Q" score of 20/20. Those persons who could do no better than read a larger set of letters at 20 ft received a different score. For example, if the best they could do at 20 ft was to read the letters read by the average person at 100 ft, their Eye-Q would be 20/100. Each eye was tested separately and received a fractional score that could range from 20/10 to 20/200, or from very farsighted to very nearsighted. These scores were a shorthand method for stating how an individual compared to a person with average or "normal" visual acuity.

Binet and Simon had labeled their test scores "mental age" or (MA) and had suggested that each child's MA should be compared with that of other children of the same chronological age (CA). The obvious next step was that, instead of a fraction, the comparison of MA and CA be expressed as a decimal, or even more efficiently, as a decimal multiplied by 100 to eliminate the decimal point. Thus, any eight-year-old child who obtained the same mental age score as the average for eight-year-old children would be scored at MA = 8; and, because the CA in this case was 8, the intelligence quotient,° or IQ, would be MA/CA, or 8/8, or 1.00 × 100, or 100. Another eight-year-old whose MA was only six years would receive an IQ of 6/8 or 75; whereas an eight-year-old with an MA score of 10 years would have an IQ of 10/8 or 125. In the Terman revision of the Binet-Simon tests, each of six tests at every age level gave the child credit for two months of mental age, so that it was possible to obtain MAs at any two-month interval from the low end (two years) to the high end (superior adult).

But now consider some difficulties with these scores. Suppose we have three children who score as follows:

	Child No. 1	Child No. 2	Child No. 3
Chronological Age (CA)	6	10	14
Mental Age (MA)	10	10	10
Intelligence Quotient (IQ)	166	100	71

All three receive the same score on an IQ test; therefore all three are said to have the same mental age. But would anyone claim that, by any criterion, the "intelligence" of these three children is the same? The first would be a very precocious child of six; the second would be an average child of ten; and the third would be a subnormal child of fourteen. Do these children in any meaningful way have the same "mental age"? It is clear that the use of MA and IQ serves here to distort rather than to reveal the level of these children's ability.

Nor does an equivalent MA score always mean the same thing even in comparing two persons of the same IQ, for the simple reason that in any test composed of a large number of items, it is possible to obtain the same final score in many different ways. One person may pass all the items involving words, another may fail all the verbal items but pass all those involving numbers or spatial concepts. To say that both have the same "intelligence" is, again, a distortion of the facts. In one study, in which mentally retarded and normal children of the same mental age were compared for performance on the Stanford-Binet, the patterning of ability was very different; of thirty-one items on which the two groups usually differed, the mentally retarded did better on twelve and the normals on nineteen.[10]

David Wechsler,[11] who developed another widely used test of general intelligence, the Wechsler Scales for both children and adults (Figure 11.4), simply substituted a score, or point scale, for the MA. Separate scores are available for the verbal items on the test and for the nonverbal, or performance items, as well as a total score combining the two subscores. In addition, Wechsler provided two other

intelligence quotient (IQ). A measure of intelligence obtained by dividing the person's mental age (determined by a standardized test) by the chronological age and multiplying by 100. An IQ of 100 is, by definition, average.

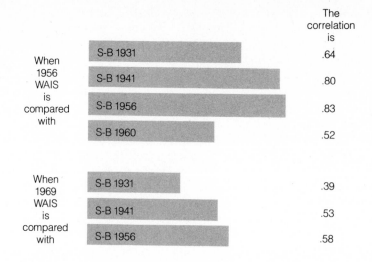

When 1956 WAIS is compared with		
S-B 1931		.64
S-B 1941		.80
S-B 1956		.83
S-B 1960		.52

When 1969 WAIS is compared with		
S-B 1931		.39
S-B 1941		.53
S-B 1956		.58

Fig. 11.4. Illustrative correlations between different versions of the Wechsler Adult Intelligence Scale (WAIS) and different versions of the Stanford-Binet (S-B). A correlation of .50 would be at the lower level of acceptability when validating one test against another. Note that there is a direct relation between the size of the correlation and the number of years intervening between two tests. (Matarazzo, 1972, p. 246)

kinds of scores. For the first, Wechsler established a standard based on the results from 500 people aged twenty to thirty-four, which is presumably the age when adults are in their intellectual prime. Any individual's scores can be compared with this standard to obtain something like the familiar IQ. For the second type of score, Wechsler used as a standard ten different age groups. An individual can then be given a "deviation IQ" that denotes how far they deviate from the norm from their own age group. Such data are often very useful for research purposes, in studying changes in ability with age.

Giving the test. As Binet and Simon were well aware, the results of a testing are only as valid as the situation itself. If the person is treated like an object to be studied in an experiment, the situation will then be an experiment but not a test. Any object can be studied experimentally, if it will stay still long enough to be measured. But testing a person is something else, for it requires that people know they are being tested; that they recognize the difference between test instructions and test tasks; that they try to do their best, in accordance with the examiner's demands; and that they be aware of their own errors and make a continuing effort to correct them. Animals cannot be tested, nor can infants, although both animals and infants can be observed, or experimentally studied, and their performances assessed. It is even doubtful whether severely retarded persons can be tested, which suggests that test results obtained from such persons should be viewed with great caution.

A certain kind of situation is, so to speak, built in to standard tests of general intelligence. Since the days of the first large-scale group tests of intelligence given to recruits in World War I (the Army Alpha and Army Beta tests), the situation has been the same: Specific problem questions are given by means of verbal directions, and people are required to complete them, using pencil and paper, within specified time limits. The content usually consists of vocabulary tests, verbal problems such as analogies or anagrams, school skills such as arithmetic, general information, and ability to follow directions, and tests of logical reasoning. Speed is a critical factor on many items, thus penalizing certain groups and individuals.

The situation that is mimicked here is, of course, the classroom examination so familiar to products of our school system. Schoolroom-type tasks, presented in a classroom setting and by typical academic means, are assumed to be an appropriate means for measuring one's innate intellectual ability. We should therefore not be surprised that when people of all ages are tested by even the best of tests, such as the Stanford-Binet, mental age appears to increase regularly up to about the age of fifteen or sixteen, when it levels off, and then declines from about age thirty until old age. This is precisely the result that would be expected if the test were essentially a glorified academic examination — for the schooling of most persons stops in the mid-teens and is then retained for another ten or fifteen years, after which it is gradually forgotten or displaced with other skills and content. The suspicion appears to be well-founded that results on even the best of intelligence tests may be tied more closely to educational than to biological factors.

The structure of the test. Some of the major flaws in the IQ test arise directly from the way it is put together. It was accepted from the very beginning of the testing movement that, because general intelligence was largely a biologically determined characteristic, males and females would not differ in how much of it they had. As a result, when items were selected for inclusion in these tests, any item that unfairly penalized or rewarded one of the two sexes was carefully screened out for if it had been included, one sex would have automatically scored higher, and that would have been contrary to the "theory" underlying the test. In short, tests have always been constructed so as to *minimize* differences between the sexes. Therefore, any use of the tests to distinguish females from males would be unrevealing.

However, tests have always been constructed so as to maximize differences between those who could profit from conventional schooling and those who could not. It so happened that in the course of recent history, groups that differed by ethnic background or by socioeconomic level also came to profit to different degrees from their schooling. This difference showed up on the tests, which were carefully devised to detect just such differences. We should hardly be surprised, then, that ethnic groups differ on tested intelligence, for this is just what the tests were permitted to show. But it might well be argued that what the tests detect here is simply what has been built into them, not some innate intellectual characteristics of the people. Many tests cannot detect differences between males and females; equally, most detect differences between ethnic groups in our society. Neither fact has anything to do with whether males and females, or blacks and whites, differ innately in general intelligence.

Similarly, the items on standard tests of ability have been selected so as to show differences between persons; they would contradict the very assumptions of intelligence test "theory" if they could not distinguish individuals from one another. It can be shown mathematically that the best way to achieve this sensitivity is to select items that are passed by 50 percent of subjects at each age level. For example, items that are passed by everyone or failed by everyone in an age group are discarded as useless. But the better the items are for this purpose, as it turns out, the less sensitive they are to differences or gains because of growth. The best item for distinguishing between individuals in the seven-year-old group is one that is answered correctly by half the seven-year-olds. But the best item for distinguishing, say, between seven-year-olds and eight-year-olds may be one that is passed by 0 percent of the seven-year-olds and by 100 percent of the eight-year-olds. No test can do both jobs well.[12]

High and low IQs

Just as we seem to have no trouble intuitively categorizing other persons in terms of how bright they seem to be, so we find it easy to identify those special individuals who appear to be either extremely high or extremely low on this characteristic. When intelligence tests were first developed, it was optimistically felt that at long last it would now be possible to make precise identification of persons who were either gifted or retarded in comparison with the norm.

5. Mental retardation, originally stated simply in terms of low IQ, is now recognized and treated as a complex mode of cognitive and social adjustment.

Originally for humanitarian reasons, and later for reasons of social control (as we shall see), interest in selecting and treating those with low IQs has always been intense. Before the advent of the intelligence test, it was not possible to separate out the intellectually retarded from those who were brain damaged, or afflicted with some congenital condition, or emotionally disturbed, or perhaps simply grossly neglected. Then, when the first standards were established to categorize low-IQ persons by means of intelligence tests, such terms as *moron, imbecile,* and *idiot* came into popular usage. For many years, intelligence tests with all their weaknesses were used to classify people according to fixed rules that involved these derogatory labels: Those below IQ 20 were idiots, those with IQs from 20 to 50 were imbeciles, and so on, regardless of any other characteristics.

In 1913, the more forward-looking British passed a comprehensive Mental Deficiency Act. It was finally realized that mental retardation, if it was recognizable at all as a condition, had to be defined primarily as a lack of social competence and that the IQ was only one of the measures that might be used to arrive at such an assessment. It is now generally agreed that four general groups of retardates should be identified, based on assessment of IQ as well as on their level of social behavior.[13] They are (1) the profoundly retarded, with IQs below 20, whose deficiencies are personal and who often cannot even care for their own needs, therefore requiring institutional care; (2) the severely retarded, with IQs of 20 to 35, who can care for themselves but need special training; (3) the moderately retarded, with IQs of 36 to 52, who can function vocationally, especially in semiprotected settings, but who may need help and support to maintain themselves as independent citizens; and (4) the mildly retarded, with IQs to about 70, comprising three fourths of all retardates, many of whom can master a trade and conduct their own lives.

In spite of a vast research literature on the subject (a 1963 bibliography listed 16,000 books and articles), it cannot be said that we know why people differ so markedly in intelligence or what causes most of the cases that are subsequently labeled as mental retardation. Some conditions are understood. For example, there is the condition known as *hydrocephalus,*⊙ in which an excess of fluid within the skull produces pressure on the brain and consequent severe malfunctioning. Down's syndrome⊙ includes a typical face shape, conformation of the features, small size, and changes in skin texture and size of fingers, and is known to result from an abnormality (an extra chromosome) in the person's genetic endowment. In the vast majority of instances, however, children are labeled as mentally retarded simply because they seem unable to fit into the normal social and educational patterns pursued by most children. Mental retardation, then, is not so much an identifiable condition as a label that is affixed for a variety of often unrelated reasons.

In a recent study by Janet R. Mercer,[14] a sociologist, 6,900 persons labeled as mentally retarded were studied to determine whether the label that had been given them was in any way related to nonintellectual factors. She found that to a disproportionate degree her sample was male, physically disabled, and made up of poor persons and members of minority groups (blacks and Mexican-Americans). Her analysis of how these persons came to be so labeled revealed an interesting pattern. Certain children are perceived by their teachers as failing to keep up with the majority of their schoolmates. Usually these "troublemakers" are boys, of minority status, and from homes below the poverty level. It is these children who

hydrocephalus. An excess of fluid in the brain, causing enlargement of the head and wasting away of the brain.

Down's syndrome. A mental deficiency of genetic origin, physically distinguished by a slanting forehead and extra eyelid folds. Also called *mongolism.*

are then tested at their teacher's request, with the legitimate excuse that the teacher would like to know whether they are unable to do schoolwork or have some other reason for their failure. As a result, a disproportionately large percentage of the children seen by the tester are boys of minority status from poor homes. As a consequence, such children are overrepresented in the final group. Thus the stereotype gets reinforced, although the labeling cycle may have begun with the best of intentions.

The consequences of such labeling for the individual are surprisingly little known to the public. Until very recently and in most of the United States, the mentally retarded were treated far worse than the mentally ill. Perhaps more serious than the treatment itself was a fixed set of ideas, which held in its grip both the keepers and the kept, the staff of the institutions as well as the patients housed there. Both groups believed that the condition of the patients, firmly labeled as retarded, was hopeless and unchangeable. Yet the evidence now abounds that, except for a suprisingly small number of persons (estimated at no more than 3 percent of all retardates) who are physically or neurologically incapacitated, the vast majority of persons now labeled as mentally retarded are capable of lives very much like the rest of the population.

This view has found official formulation in a principle that is known in the Scandinavian countries as *normalization*.[15] A similar approach in the United States, known as *mainstreaming*, is described as "placing children in the least restrictive environment" (Figure 11.5). One particularly dramatic example of this practice occurred in relation to a recent national conference in Sweden that dealt with problems of housing the mentally retarded. The conference was planned by the mentally retarded.

None of the questions concerning the condition we call *mental retardation* are, of course, solved simply because a country adopts a more humanitarian approach. The importance of such an approach is not that it provides answers to problems of theory, nor even that it offers new approaches to practice, but rather that it helps to break us free of a pattern. Whether or not it was done deliberately, approaches to the mentally retarded had become locked into a set of practices that were guided by certain beliefs: that people differed very much in their native intelligence, that these differences could be validly detected by intelligence tests, and that those far enough below the population average were incapable of independent functioning and had to be put away in institutions and stripped of all their rights. It is at least probable that the first of these beliefs is not true, that the second is unfounded, and that therefore the third does not follow.

Fig. 11.5 Mental retardates, (a) traditionally and (b) under modern conditions of "normalization."

6. High-IQ persons, the so-called geniuses, are not usually distinctive; their test scores do not appear to be related to their life patterns.

Geniuses. We owe our contemporary usage of the term *genius* to Lewis M. Terman. When he began his monumental *Genetic Studies of Genius* in the early 1920s[16] by selecting the 1,000 most gifted children in California, with the hope of following them throughout their lives, he rather arbitrarily picked an IQ of 140 as the lower limit of what he called "genius." There was no significant basis for this; the number 140 in the IQ scale has no particular meaning. But the notion has entered the popular literature and is still found in newspaper articles.

As we know, some persons test very high on instruments to measure general intelligence. But just what it is that is being measured in these persons is as much

normalization. The Scandinavian practice of training the mentally retarded by arranging their lives to be as close to normal as is possible. In the United States, a similar approach is called *mainstreaming.*

of a mystery as in the case of the mentally retarded, where we do not usually know what causes them to score so low. High-IQ persons are rarely distinctive in any way. In one study of eight boys and 4 girls, all of them scoring above IQ 180, Hollingworth[17] found that their family backgrounds were at the moderate socioeconomic level, that they had not walked nor talked at particularly early ages, that they did not show adult achievement that was in any way commensurate with their presumed intellectual abilities, and that they were all considered "problem children" when young.

Other evidence supports this conclusion. Most of our great adult achievers showed no more than ordinary promise when young. Bright youngsters, on the other hand, do not necessarily make outstanding adults. Terman's group of gifted children, who are still being studied on a regular basis, have not shown adult achievement beyond what would be manifested by any select group of white, healthy, college-educated, middle-class adults. Those rare children of "genius" whose adult achievements live up to their early promise are invariably those who have been chosen and pushed—sometimes overwhelmed—by a proud and ambitious parent. Typical of these are the late mathematician and founder of cybernetics, Norbert Wiener, and the nineteenth-century philosopher Karl Witte, who at the age of nine was translating books in English, French, Greek, Latin, and Italian and became a full professor at the age of twenty-three.

It may be said of both groups of IQ-extremes, the mentally retarded and the geniuses, that their unique performances on the IQ test appear to have little connection with the pattern of their lives. What they become is more a matter of how they are labeled, and perhaps how they label themselves, than it is of any single recognizable characteristic in them—certainly not of any characteristic that can be spotted by means of a test of intelligence. This should certainly alert us to consider such test results with great caution.

The IQ in society

No other area in psychology has, through the years, led to as much strong feeling, high hope, and controversy as the testing of human abilities. When tests were first introduced, they were welcomed with great enthusiasm as instruments that would revolutionize the educational system. It was expected that they were going to be the foundation of new and far-reaching methods for selecting and training society's leaders and for weeding out the unfit. By World War I, they were considered the ultimate in a rational process of fitting the person to the job. During the 1920s, they were looked on as the foundation for a new psychology. Even today, although tests of all sorts are in some disrepute, their strengths and weaknesses provide material for the most intense quarrel that the academic scene has witnessed since the debates over evolutionary theory a century ago. In this final section of the present chapter, we will summarize the background and implications of the current dispute over heredity and environmental influences on ability and performance.

---

7. Intelligence, as defined by the tests used to measure it, is essentially the ability to profit from traditional schooling.

The first question that has to be asked, if we are to discuss the social uses of testing, concerns the nature of the ability that we test for. Not every human characteristic is subjected to testing; not even those characteristics that, like intelligence, are intuitively grasped by everyone. There are no psychological tests for how pretty someone is, or how charming, and there are very few tests for such general traits as creativeness, or artistic ability, or passivity, or even how loving someone is. Yet all of these are evident to a casual observer, and they seem to differ among persons, and they are probably important in human life. Why did psychologists pick out just certain characteristics and abilities around which to build a testing movement? And are the kinds of tests that are used in any way related to the characteristics chosen to be measured?

To emphasize how precisely psychologists have chosen their target for testing, consider the two modes of intelligence that Cattell[18] has suggested can be distinguished by appropriate tests. The first of these he calls *crystallized intelligence*,© defined as abilities that are evident, in the classroom, in the form of good vocabularies, retentive memories, reasoning abilities, ordered thinking, and high grades. The other kind of intelligence he calls *fluid*;© it has to do with being able to see into situations, or to grasp things in a useful and often personal way. It is likely to show up in the classroom as alertness, perceptiveness, or individualized insight. Although Cattell found that the two types of intelligence tend to be found together in a person, they are rarely given the same importance in school examinations, in standard intelligence tests, even in teachers' judgments. Tests zero in on crystallized rather than fluid intelligence, just as teachers do.

To define standard tests in this way is not to condemn them. It may be argued, as Vernon has done,[19] that tests that enable us to predict school success are useful and should be encouraged rather than eliminated—at least, as long as you believe that schooling is a good thing and that Western societies provide a desirable way of life for their citizens. Given the existence of highly developed societies and the special skills and abilities that improve one's chances of success, it would seem desirable for teachers and other educators to have available refined instruments for selecting out talent, for classifying students, for allocating resources, and for predicting outcomes. Intelligence and aptitude tests do this job very well.

However, it is often pointed out that schooltype tests are really not very useful for predicting what a person will do outside of school—except that they do enable one to predict other schoolroom-type behavior, such as grades on various examinations. But the grades one gets are not useful for predicting anything at all about performance in later life. The evidence from repeated studies shows very clearly that there is little relation between the grades one gets in school and the degree of one's success in life (Figure 11.6). It is true that college-educated persons make out better than others with only high school educations, but it seems to make little difference what college one went to or what grades one received while there.[20] In the testers' terms, most tests of ability have very poor predictive validity.

To a surprising degree, testers appear to be locked into the pursuit of schoolroom-type skills, the assessment of which demands specific kinds of measuring instruments. As a result, most tests are remote from real life and from the situations to which they are supposed to be related. Thus, applicants for positions as policemen in many cities are required to take an intelligence test, although there is no evidence that the items on such tests bear any meaningful relation to performance on the job. What is needed, as McClelland has put it, is a program of testing for competence, that is, tests that involve actual sampling of the performances in question. "If you want to know how well a person can drive a car . . . sample his ability to do so by giving him a driver's test. Do not give him a paper-and-pencil test for following directions."[21] For example, because there is almost no situation in life in which one is required to do word analogies, such a test cannot ever be a good predictor of any performance except one involving a limited range of academic skills.

Fig. 11.6 The relations between one's work experience and one's income, given the same amount of education, for males whose fathers rated either low (L), or medium (M), or high (H) on an occupational scale. The status of one's father, apparently, helps to determine how much money a man makes all his life. (From Hauser, 1973, p. 139)

crystallized intelligence. According to Cattell, the composite of all of a person's culturally conditioned acquisitions, such as social information, skills learned in school, and factual data.

fluid intelligence. Cattell's term for neurologically determined capacity for insight that is independent of culture or sensory experience.

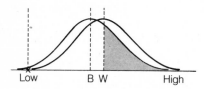

Fig. 11.7. Two "normal" distributions of intelligence test scores in children. The curve on the right is that usually obtained when large numbers of black children are tested; the one on the right is obtained from white children. B = the average score of the black children; W = the average score of the white children; X = the lowest score in the white group. The shaded portion shows the 25 percent of black children who exceed the average of white scores. (See discussion in text.)

8. Group comparisons unwittingly influenced by social class factors are used unfairly to stigmatize individual members of the groups.

In addition to all these reservations, we may raise further questions about the way that tests are used to compare, not individuals, but groups of individuals.

The distinction between comparison of individuals and comparisons of groups is exemplified in Figure 11.7. It represents a common finding when intelligence tests are used to compare a large number of black schoolchildren and an equally large number of white schoolchildren, with each group falling into a bell-shaped distribution. The difference in average IQ that is often found is, as here, about twelve IQ points. Only 25 percent of the black children equal or exceed the average score of the white children.

Notice that both these statements refer to group comparisons. But if we want to make a statement that applies to an individual, we have only to look at Point X on the figure. As can be seen, more than 95 percent of all the black scores fall above this point, in spite of the difference in averages of the groups. In regard to any individual, then, it would not be possible to predict whether that person would score higher or lower than a member of the other group. Thus, the groups differ measurably, but individuals may or may not differ.

Group comparisons are easier to make than statements about individuals, especially if any differences do exist. It is therefore not surprising that the history of the testing movement has been dominated by them. The actual groups compared, however, have changed with the times. In the days when the term *social class* had some meaning, testers were busy making comparisons along this dimension, invariably discovering that the better class of people scored higher. Extreme instances of these studies became famous; for example, Henry Goddard's[22] elaborate genealogical study of what he called the Kallikak Family.

On searching through the family records of a female inmate of the Vineland School, Goddard discovered that during the Revolutionary War, one Martin Kallikak, "in an unguarded moment steps aside from the paths of rectitude and with the help of a feebleminded girl (a barmaid), starts a line of mental defectives that is truly appalling." Kallikak, himself of good family, then returned home and fathered another line of descendants through marriage with a respectable woman. Practically all the descendants on the "good" side were respectable, often prominent members of the upper class. Of the other line, less than 10 percent turned out to be normal, 143 were feebleminded, and a large number were criminals, prostitutes, and alcoholics over a span of four generations. To Goddard, this was conclusive proof that mental defect was inherited, supporting a view that he expressed very succinctly: "If all the slum districts of our cities were removed tomorrow and model tenements built in their places, we would still have slums in a week's time, because we have these mentally defective people who can never be taught to live otherwise than as they have been living."

Now, today, of course, we would dismiss this as nonsense — but its historical importance cannot be denied. Goddard represented the position of those who believed firmly in a single and perfectly measurable psychological trait called *intelligence*, inherited, like the color of one's eyes, and so powerful in one's makeup that it influenced the entire pattern of one's life. His conclusion, that the only way to keep the planet from being overrun with mental defectives was to sterilize them wherever they could be found, was seriously discussed during the 1920s, and major elements of his view are considered respectable even today.

Class, race, and intelligence. But social class is no longer considered a legitimate basis on which to make comparisons between groups. In its place, there has been revived the notion of "race," a term that is supposed to distinguish various subgroups of the human population. The human gene pool contains determinants of a very wide range of characteristics, including skin color and shape of hair follicles—as well as height, eye color, and susceptibility to many different diseases, among hundreds of others. Thus, it is not at all difficult to denote a group that differs from most whites in terms of skin color and appearance of the hair. But even if such a group could be discovered whose ancestry were guaranteed to be "nonwhite" for many generations, there would still be no justification in calling them a separate "race," because under conditions of free interbreeding the two groups would absorb each other in a few generations.

If such groups, called "races," cannot be legitimately distinguished on genetic grounds, we may well wonder what their distinction consists of.[23] The answer would appear to be that, given the present structure of American society, individuals chosen largely on the basis of their skin color, such as blacks, Mexican-Americans, Asians, and native Americans, do in fact constitute unique and definable groups. They share a common culture, they usually speak their unique dialect of American English, and they are more often found at the lower end of the socioeconomic scale. Racial comparisons, so-called, are in fact comparisons of groups that differ in these ways. That is, "racial" comparisons are in fact comparisons of social classes. The findings concerning group differences, then, have to be understood in terms of these group characteristics.

The comparison group, or those to whom other "races" are compared, is made up, at least in Western countries, of the dominant white majority. They are typically represented in Terman's sample of gifted children—who were overwhelmingly white and middle class. Terman was convinced that members of this group had individually inherited their gifts, and that having these gifts was what made them do well on intelligence tests, get good grades in school, go through college, live decent middle-class lives, attain some success in life, and produce children who repeated their parents' life pattern.

Unless one believes that such a constellation of characteristics, represented in such a diverse variety of life activities, can be inherited in predictable fashion, an alternative explanation must be entertained. This is that Terman's group were perfect examples of a social class that, being dominant in American society, is able to express itself and to perpetuate itself. Their scores on the intelligence test merely reflected their membership in a group to which the educational system is geared (Figure 11.8).

Fig. 11.8. What if conventional tests of intelligence were based on what each cultural group is able to accomplish in its own setting?

9. Performance on an intelligence test is a complex, multiply determined performance that cannot be linked to specific genes.

Many investigators, who ignore these serious issues of kinds of ability, kinds of tests, and comparisons between groups, plunge into large-scale questions of social policy, using data from IQ testing to support their position. The major question that they raise is whether, or to what degree, one's innate intelligence is caused by heredity or by environment. It must be emphasized again that such a question is answerable only if all the other issues we have considered in the present chapter are firmly settled—when in fact they are probably unanswerable in the present state of our knowledge. But, because the question has been raised repeatedly and because it gives rise to endless serious debate, we must report on the controversy at this point.

If the issue in question concerns heredity as a factor influencing one's tested IQ, we have to be very clear just what we mean. It is now generally accepted by geneticists and ethologists that one cannot speak of genetic *causes* of behavior. As we discussed in Chapter 1, specific genetic determinants, when they affect succeeding generations in observable ways, work only through changes in structure. The best we can say is that in regard to the characteristic we are interested in, our population will differ between individuals; it will show variability. We can then try to make some statement about how much of this variability or how much of the differences between individuals, can be attributed to genetic influences. Note that we do not ever say that genetic factors *cause* individuals to do one thing or another. The most we can say is that genetic factors have some influences on *differences* between individuals in what they are or do.

Any statement about genetic factors, then, will have to include certain important reservations. The first of these is that we can only speak of contributing genetic influences, never of sole causes. In even the simplest case, we cannot usually make a definite statement about how genetically carried factors mix with other influences. If this is true in regard to very simple genetic instances, such as determinants of wing shape in the fruit fly, it is even more significantly true in regard to complex human characteristics such as tested intelligence. It is probable that in every living individual, no matter what its species, genetic factors at the molecular level continuously interact with a variety of other factors—prenatal conditions, birth conditions, and subsequent environmental life conditions. The sex of some flies can be changed by altering the temperature they experience just before birth. What factors, then, might affect major human psychological capacities, from the moment of conception to the day the individual enters school?

Additionally, in considering the genetics of ability, we should bear in mind that separate abilities can be inborn but not necessarily inherited. There are many distinct abilities, such as those involved in playing chess or succeeding in athletics or interpersonal relations, that differ between individuals. Yet it is hardly possible

Fig. 11.9. A family tree, showing the apparent inheritance of distinction.

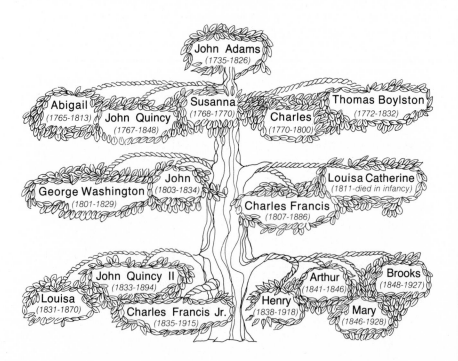

to make a case for their inheritance; they do not seem to run in families. Emily Dickinson's sister made no name as a poet. We look in vain for the works of William Shakespeare, Jr., or for philosophy written by Aristotle's mother or father. There are exceptional instances of musical families, such as the Bachs, but they are no more common than families who were all executioners, such as the Sansons of France. And if we cannot make a case for the inheritance of clearly measurable abilities, it is unlikely that a case can be made for that much more loosely defined general ability we call *intelligence* (Figure 11.9).

A final reservation concerns the possible relations between genetic factors, built into the species through millions of years of evolutionary change, and behavioral characteristics, which are unique to a small portion of the population of some societies that have existed for only a few centuries. It may well be that human beings carry with them, as part of their genetic program, elements relating to the most general kinds of "ability"—perhaps an ability in the form of stores of "vital energy," which might then get expressed as leadership, courage, inventiveness, ingenuity, or mastery of the environment. But it is extremely unlikely that such a broad and adaptive characteristic is equivalent to excellence on IQ tests in modern Western society in the twentieth century. The gap between these two kinds of abilities is so wide that it becomes perilously close to nonsensical to talk of "genes" that affect performance on the Stanford-Binet.

The state of the controversy. Yet it is just such statements that are repeatedly made, by researchers and scholars who become involved, once again, in an old but enduring quarrel: Do hereditary or environmental influences contribute the major effect on variability in human intelligence? The argument we have presented over the past pages has, we hope, made it clear that this question, as it is phrased, should perhaps not be asked in the present state of our knowledge. Every single term in the question is enmeshed in so many reservations and cautions that the question cannot be phrased in a scientifically useful way.

But the issue comes up again and again. Most recently it was revived by Jensen in an article in *Harvard Educational Review*.[24] He reviewed a very sizable literature on the heredity-environment issue and concluded that the evidence strongly supported a hereditarian position. He argued (once again) that whites as a group were genetically superior to blacks in what he terms intelligence of Level I (the ability to learn concepts and to manipulate them cognitively) but not in terms of intelligence of Level II (ability to learn by rote or in terms of associations of ideas). He assured his readers that he was raising these questions primarily to set the stage for discussion and a "no-holds-barred" inquiry. And then he concluded with a plea that society's resources be directed toward teaching blacks basic skills at a low level rather than attempting to educate them beyond their capacities.

As might have been expected, reaction to this publication was swift and strong, and it has continued for the past number of years. In 1974, Jensen estimated that 117 articles had been published directly discussing his original paper.[25] With the issue thus reopened after it had seemed to be laid to rest, some of the major data on the subject has been reexamined, with surprising results.

Through the years, the argument over heredity *versus* environment in influencing the IQ has been based very largely on a few types of studies. Recognizing that it is not possible to do a controlled laboratory experiment with humans, investigators have resorted to what might be called *experiments in nature*—that is, circumstances in which the two influences might be assessed separately and so compared. The ideal situation in which this occurs, although admittedly rare, is one in which two identical twins (whose heredity is, presumably, precisely the same) are separated at birth and then reared in environmentally different surroundings, and finally tested. If they test the same, this would be clear proof that heredity was the major, if not the sole, influence. This is, for example, how we know that skin color is entirely under the influence of one's genetic endowment. No matter what the different environments, skin color remains determined by one's family heritage. But if the twins tested differently, in ways that could be predicted from knowing their separate environments, we would have to conclude that it was environment that had the greatest influence.

A vast amount of energy has been spent, through the years, in tracking down such cases, as well as other kinds of cases which, while not as clear-cut, would furnish additional data. These latter include:

- Comparisons of the intelligence of nonidentical (fraternal) twins, either of the same or of different sex.
- Comparison of children's IQs with that of their parents, and of children with their siblings, particularly of children who are reared in homes other than their natural ones.
- Studies of adopted children, comparing the IQs or educational level of their natural parents with that of their adopted parents.

Although these studies differ widely and the results are very difficult to summarize, it seemed until recently that two very general conclusions might be drawn (very cautiously) from the data. The first was that the closer any two persons were in their biological makeup the more they resembled one another in their performance on an IQ test (Figure 11.10). But that, second, the IQ was flexible enough so that quite large changes might reasonably be expected, in the individual case, under strong environmental pressures. Jensen's article, with its attempt at reinterpretation of the data to suggest a much stronger genetic effect, reopened the issue—an event that was generally welcomed by investigators even though they may have deplored his hasty use of his conclusions to make serious inferences concerning political and social policy.

At this point, another element was introduced. In a wide-ranging and severe attack on the "hereditarian" view, Leon Kamin[26] argued that most of the data on which this case rested were quite inadequate. Major studies of identical twins, he maintained, could not be trusted. In particular, he attacked the work of Sir Cyril

Fig. 11.10. The range of correlations in IQ between parents and their children, for different circumstances. A total of fifty-two studies are summarized. Notice that the closer the relationship between children and parents, the higher the correlations. (From Erlenmeyer-Kimling and Jarvik, 1963, fig. 1)

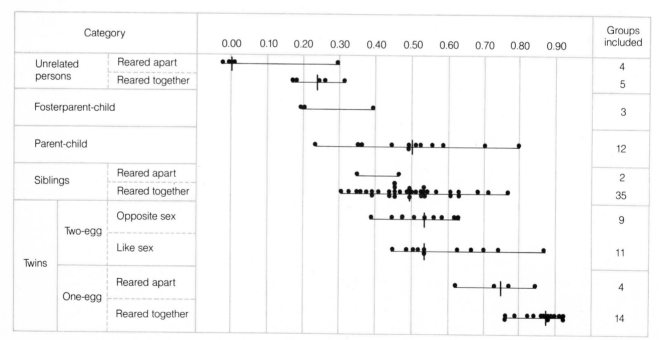

Table 11.3. A comparison of the average IQs of different groups of children.

The figures in Rows 1, 2, and 3 are from studies that have been made in the past on these groups of children. The figures in Rows 4, 5, and 6 are from data in the Scarr and Weinberg study, which is discussed in the text. The natural children of the families that adopted black and interracial children in this study have an average IQ of 116 (Row 6). This is what would be expected in such families. If they had adopted white children, we would expect the IQ of the children to be 112 (Row 3). Some of these families adopted black and interracial children in early infancy, so that the children had very nearly a lifetime of exposure to the above-average environment. In this case (Row 4), their IQ's averaged 110. Other families adopted black and interracial children who were already in their childhood years. The average IQ of all the adopted children in this study, both those adopted in infancy and those adopted later, was 106 (Row 5). From these figures, it is possible to make a judgment about the different effects of racial background and environmental influences.

Group	Average IQ
1. Black children in the United States	90
2. White children in the United States	100
3. White children adopted by above-average white families	112
4. Black and interracial children adopted in early infancy by above-average white families	110
5. Black and interracial children adopted in infancy and childhood by above-average white families	106
6. Natural (white) children of above-average white families	116

Burt, a British educational psychologist, now dead, on whose original work most of the hereditarian argument has rested.[27] The resulting scandal for a while filled the correspondence pages of the London *Times*. It appears that Burt, long revered in psychological circles, may have misrepresented his findings, fudged his data, and perhaps even invented one or two collaborators in his research.[28]

At this point, what should be a serious question for science and for the social uses of science had degenerated into melodrama. Some useful lessons may be learned from this sequence of events: that no one is immune to weaknesses of logic, especially when strong feelings or biases are involved, and that a meaningless argument has no possibility of being resolved by hard facts. But more important, we are left with the question of what to make of more than half a century of technically brilliant and useful work. We may well ask whether the testing movement can ever be rescued from the position to which its excesses have brought it.

A recent careful study by Scarr and Weinberg[29] pinpoints the major problems involved. One hundred and thirty black and interracial children who had been adopted by above-average white families in Minnesota were tested for intelligence and school achievement, and their results compared with those of the families' natural children. The results are presented in Table 11.3, Rows 3 to 6. They show clearly that adoption and rearing by advantaged white families provided a 10- to 20-point "boost" in IQ. Further, the earlier the children were adopted, the greater the "boost." However, even in this study it was not possible to separate the effects of genetic inheritance from the effects of environment, for in American society these two usually go together. Black mothers have more premature and defective babies than do white mothers, because their living conditions and physical status are worse. In addition, black mothers provide their children with less advantageous living conditions, diet, and environmental stimulation, because they are lower on the socioeconomic scale.

In regard to educational applications the kindest recommendation at this point may be that tests of such characteristics should be abandoned, at least until educational opportunities are completely equalized in all classrooms and at all levels. In regard to cross-cultural implications, we must conclude with Philip Vernon that "when we contrast very different groups . . . the modes of thinking, the conceptual structures, and classificatory categories are so different that it is simply impossible to measure genetic differences."[30] As Michael Cole and his colleagues have recently shown in studies of African societies, the highest types of cognitive abilities are demonstrated in all cultures, but in each culture quite differently, thus making comparisons impossible.[31] It may well be that human ability, like any other expression of human experience, can only be understood in the light of its background and the situations in which it naturally occurs.

Summary

1. Measurement is in major part a function of the methods or instruments used for measuring.

2. A number of different systems of classification have categorized human bodies into three general types: the round, the slender, and the muscular.

3. Measurement of the characteristics of persons is made more difficult by the fact that the quantities that can be stated do not seem to behave like numbers.

4. The modern movement in mental testing became possible because of two developments: new techniques for handling collections of numbers and a growing belief that science was an effective tool for improving people's lot in the world.

5. Definitions of intelligence have not been very satisfactory, because they tend to say nothing ("intelligence is what intelligence tests test") or to rest on weak theory.

6. Binet and Simon solved most of the problems in constructing a test of general intelligence, including problems relating to the distribution of intelligence in the population, the development of intelligence in childhood, and the techniques by which examiners could administer the test.

7. Major weaknesses of the IQ test appear in relation to its scoring, its statistical basis, and the effects of administration.

8. Mental retardation has been at various times: an IQ label; a method of stigmatizing social deviants of all sorts; and, more recently, a mode of adjustment that is multiply caused but amenable to training. The vast majority of those labeled *mentally retarded* are capable of living lives similar to the rest of the population.

9. Neither mental retardates, scoring low on IQ tests, nor so-called geniuses, scoring high, appear to pattern their lives in ways that are related to their categorization on the test.

10. Intelligence, at least as defined and tested by IQ tests, appears to be best understood as the ability to profit from traditional schooling.

11. Cattell has suggested two kinds of intelligence, the crystallized and the fluid; testing programs tend to focus on the former.

12. Evidence from many studies indicates little relation between one's school grades and one's level of success in life.

13. The history of the testing movement has been dominated by statements about groups, although such statements may hide equally significant data about individuals in the groups.

14. Racial comparisons, such as are often made using intelligence tests, are in reality tests of social class differences, because race and social class are highly correlated in all modern societies.

15. Social class differences in intelligence test results reflect the makeup of the social and educationally dominant social class.

16. Although genetic influences on the sources of behavior may well exist, it appears inappropriate to link genes to specific behaviors, as is sometimes done with intelligence tests as the measure.

17. In the present state of our knowledge and with the present instruments we have available, we are not equipped to make an adequate assessment of the relative roles of heredity and environment in regard to any ability.

18. Tentative conclusions from twin studies are that the closer two persons are in their biological makeup the more similar their test scores are. However, within this comparison, test scores are sufficiently adaptable under environmental influences to make prediction for any individual or pair quite risky.

In this chapter, you will learn about the factors that make human communication possible. An understanding of signs and symbols will help you distinguish more primitive forms of communication from human language. You will then follow the controversy surrounding the question of innate *versus* learned factors in language development.

Human language will be discussed in terms of three major characteristics: its distancing, its openness, and its "aboutness." You will come to understand how it is that natural human languages consist of orderly collections of rules. In these terms, you will follow a discussion of the special variety of language shown by the higher apes, a variety that seems to lie between animal gesture and human grammatical speech.

The three chief forms of communication will then be presented: address, influence, and expression. The first of these forms the bulk of the present chapter. In closing, some aspects of expressive communication will be discussed, including the way that emotional meaning occurs by way of the body as well as through speech.

12

Communication and language

No living creature seems to be able to get along without any contact with others of its kind. If nothing else, it must make such a contact at least once, in a mating act that will help to carry on its species. Living creatures at all levels are involved in far more than single or isolated contacts, both with their own species and with others. One of the most important categories of such "interbehavior" is communication. As a form of social behavior, communication is such a broad category that it is not easy to arrive at a sufficiently comprehensive definition of it. Our thesis in this chapter will be that communication, whether at the animal level in the form of communicative behaviors or at the human level in the form of language, is a transaction between sender and receiver in a situation that is meaningful to both.

1. Communication requires a sender and one or more receivers.

Communication means more than language, for language is only one of its specialized forms (Figure 12.1). As a start, we may say that communication always involves some relation, or transaction, between two creatures, one of whom serves as sender and the other as receiver. It may not seem necessary to emphasize these points, but the fact is that they have often been ignored. For example, the field of linguistics, the study of languages, was for many years solely concerned with the structure of words as they were spoken. Consider what was left out or ignored under such an emphasis. No consideration was given to the fact that if language is spoken, it must be spoken *by* someone. Such speaking-to must take place in a situation, must be directed, and must be meant to serve some purpose. Yet linguistics presumed to study language as though all of these aspects of the communication were irrelevant; as though it were not, in fact, communication at all.[1]

Communication and behavior

Much of the early study of animal communication was carried on while ignoring these necessary aspects of communication. A wealth of information, often painstakingly gathered, has been accumulated through the years on one of the fundamental communicative patterns among birds, their species-typical© songs; yet surprisingly little attention has been paid, until recently, to the behavior of the receivers of these elaborate communications. The behavior of the sender was studied as though it took place in a vacuum, directed nowhere and for no known purpose.

A half-century ago an Austrian entomologist, Karl von Frisch,[2] discovered that when a foraging bee finds a source of food for the hive and returns, she quickly communicates to the other bees the location of the food source. It is done by means of an elaborate "dance" or wiggling of the abdomen. The distance is indicated by how long the dance takes, and the general direction in relation to the sun is indicated by the way the bee orients herself inside the hive. But, because the inside of a hive is dark, the dancer provides a "backup" system of communication: She emits a steady hum, whose duration indicates the distance to the food source.

A great deal of ingenious effort was spent, through the years, in studying the pattern of behavior of the sender of these communications. It was clear that, in their specific way, these bees were "talking"—but not until very recently have investigators bothered to ask whether any bees were "listening." The communication was studied as though it took place in a vacuum. When the emphasis shifted, however, there was quickly discovered what is now recognized as a major characteristic of all communication—that it is not symmetrical. That is, in any communication, what goes on in the sender may not be equivalent to what happens in the receiver. There is very often a loss of information between sender and receiver, there is frequently a change of information, and there may even be an increase of information. There is some evidence that the "dance" of one bee serves only to trigger extended search flights by other bees in a general direction and that much of their actual success in locating the food is due to their sense of smell. They track down the food on the basis of odors picked up from the sender bee, odors caused by food particles originally picked up when the food was discovered.

Communications that serve as triggers are among the commonest signals found among animals. They are particularly important in mating patterns, in which a single brief posture or movement triggers off an entire preset sequence of behavior in an animal of the opposite sex. It is a highly efficient system of communication, for a trigger that uses a very small amount of energy in the transmitter serves to release a great deal of energy in the receiver. If the family dog is outside at about its feeding time, only a brief whistle may be needed to bring it bounding to its feeding dish. In a professional football game, the referee who measures the position of the ball on a fourth-down play need only point briefly in one direction to evoke an enormous roar from the crowd. These, like many communications, are asymmetrical.

Levels of communication. Communication among insects does not seem to be directed from one sender to one particular receiver. Rather, it takes a form that might be summarized in the announcement: "To whom it may concern—this is the nature of my present state; and I expect that this will lead you to doing something about it." Among higher animals such as primates, however, communications may be either of a similar type—for example, "To whom it may concern, this is how I feel right now"—or else of a one-to-one type, as though the animal were saying: "Hey, you! Do this."

One consequence of this distinction is that different modes of communica-

Fig. 12.1. The international traffic signs, now in almost universal use, communicate meaning without words.

tion are used by these different creatures. When communication is of the "To whom it may concern" form, it is first necessary for the sender to get the receivers' attention. As advertisers are well aware when trying to get the attention of humans, the way to do it is to offer a stimulus that intrudes on one's attention, that literally breaks through or forces itself into one's selective perception (Figure 12.2). In advertising, color and movement, novelty and contrast, as well as specific appeal to sexual motives, are all used for this purpose. Among insects, such communication takes the form of smells or sounds rather than what can be seen; for the nature of a smell or sound is that it falls on the receiver whether the latter is ready and attentive or not. Smells and sounds are intrusive.

Another consequence is that at the level of "To whom it may concern" communication, what is sent out must linger, for it may not be received or attended to immediately. Smells and touches serve this purpose best, vision and hearing the least. For this reason, ants leave behind a trail of odor molecules for their fellows, not a trail of footprints nor a train of sounds. At the level of primate behavior, on the other hand, apes use different modes of communication for different purposes. Sounds are used when the purpose of the communication is to break in on the attention of others, such as to sound an alarm at the approach of a predator or to scare off another ape with a threat. Visual displays, however, are used in one-to-one communications to convey more personal information.

Fig. 12.2. One purpose of advertising is to grab the reader's attention.

2. Sounds, as used in human language, serve as the most effective kind of symbols in communication.

Among humans, all the preceding communications are possible, and others as well. We can send communications back and forth to people in general (as the words of this book are being "sent" to a multiplicity of unknown readers); to a group in a face-to-face situation (as when an actor or speaker faces an audience); or from one person to another, as in every instance of direct talk. We use our bodies to send visual signals, just as many animals do (although we are less willing, as a species, to do it openly or in full awareness). Most of all, we depend on the use of organized sounds, in what we call *language*, surely the most remarkable of achievements in communication.

On the face of it, using sounds for communication would seem to be the least efficient of all means, for the sound is gone as soon as it is produced. It leaves no trace behind it, and therefore it requires the sender to "capture" and somehow preserve it in order to make use of it. How much more certain and effortless it would be if instead of sounds we each produced a little picture or structure when we wanted to communicate something. Then our receivers could take their time studying the communication, refer back to it, and always be certain they had it right. What advantage can there be in using a scheme that requires more effort on the listener's part and raises so many more possibilities of error or loss? Why would any species have developed a system of communication such as we use in speaking? The answers to these questions will introduce our discussion of language.

Signs and symbols: From communication to language. For any living creature, the environment is filled with messages that come and go, increase and decrease, change or remain constant all the time. Indeed, an environment might be defined as one's collection of available messages. Some of the signals conveyed by these messages are intrinsically or "naturally" connected with their meaning. For example, the smell of smoke is, for most creatures, connected with heat, fire, danger. Hence the behavior of a forest full of varied species of animals when

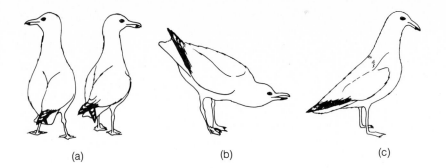

(a)   (b)   (c)

Fig. 12.3. The "turning away" position of the two herring gulls in (a) is a *sign* of appeasement, and the preparatory, upright stance of (c) is a *sign* of threat and readiness to attack. The peculiar "forward" stance of the bird in (b), however, serves rather as a *signal* that the bird probably will not attack but will fight if attacked. (From Tinbergen, 1960, pp. 119, 120)

smoke begins to signal an approaching forest fire. Such "naturally" connected signals are called *signs*.⊙

Signs also occur in the course of the behavior of living creatures with one another. Many female animals in heat emit specific odors and even display specific body markings or positions, which function as signs to convey messages that begin a mating process. The advantage of having such signs available is that their presence guarantees sexual behaviors that ensure the survival of the species. Yet such sign mechanisms have certain disadvantages. They are very specific, and so cannot be used in other types of situations, such as in signaling that food has been discovered. They occur, not on demand, but only on a limited number of occasions. And they usually involve the animal totally, so that a great deal of attention and energy is expended to carry through the behaviors intended by the message.

A more efficient system has been developed by most species. Its main features are as follows:

- The signal that is sent from sender to receiver has no "natural" connection with the content of the message. The dancing bee wiggles its abdomen, and this "means" food; the foraging ant leaves drops of a scent behind, and this "means" that an approaching animal is a threat. Such signals, which are arbitrary and traditional rather than "natural," are called *symbols*.⊙

- Symbols utilize only a part of the sender's anatomy and do not involve the creature totally. The creature is thus free to do other things while sending the message. Indeed, as we go up the scale of creatures, from the most fixed to the most flexible arrangements of behavior among members of a species, we find that symbols become more and more subtle, using less and less energy, and involving fewer and fewer parts of the anatomy (Figure 12.3).

The ultimate symbol, then, involving very little energy and requiring the sender to act very briefly and minimally, would maintain all the advantages of symbols over signs. It would be an event that occurs, does its job, and disappears, just as words do when we speak them. This may be the essential difference between living things and machines. A machine or nonliving structure can only convey a message if it leaves itself or a changed part of itself behind—as do the pyramids or the mountains or the beds of rivers. A living creature, on the other hand, can create an event that in turn affects its situation and its environment of other creatures; that event can do its job and then disappear. Nonliving things leave only other things behind, for as long as they will last, but living things leave behind their memories, the odor of their histories on the winds of time.

sign. In linguistics, a message that is "naturally" connected to its meaning. For example, heat is a *sign* of fire.

symbol. In linguistics, a specialized message that is uniquely or even arbitrarily connected with its meaning. For example, a pointing arrow is a *symbol* of a direction.

3. The major characteristics of a human language are its distancing, its "openness," and its "aboutness."

Surely the most highly developed, the most complex of all systems of communication by symbols is the language of humans. Its characteristics have been summarized by C. F. Hockett, whose list is given in Table 12.1. A number of these characteristics have been discussed in the preceding sections—for example, that its signals are arbitrary and that they disappear quickly. Others need some additional emphasis. One characteristic is that the channel for the communication is primarily the voice, which is then heard by the receiver. The consequences here are that each sender has the same access to their own signals as do the receivers. Thus, I can hear my own words as soon as you hear them. The sender is then in a position to correct the message, and more than that, to ensure its accuracy, to remember it, and most important of all, to think about it.

Distancing in language. This characteristic leads in turn to some significant although perhaps unexpected aspects. Consider, first, the fact that as a speaker I can hear my own speech. This leads to the continuing experience, beginning in my early childhood and lasting all my life, of splitting my behavior into two parts whenever I speak. In every communication that I make, I can say what I mean to say, and I can also hear what I mean to say. Being able to maintain this dual role enables me to develop a skill that is probably unique to humans—to maintain an attitude toward my own speech at the same time that I am speaking. One obvious result is that I then can (if I choose) engineer a split between my speech and my intent—that is, I can use my language to tell a lie. As soon as children learn to talk, they begin to learn to lie; and, as we all know, the smoothest talkers are often the most accomplished liars.

A second result is that I can mean one thing but say something that is altered from my meaning, perhaps because my feelings get in the way, or because I am not motivated to communicate properly, or because I am confused or tired or under the influence of drugs. An administrator in the Federal Aviation Administration was motivated to gloss over the fact that bureaucratic mismanagement is related to the large number of preventable air crashes. He issued an order that for the unpleasant, if accurate, word *crash* there was to be substituted the phrase "inadvertent contact with the ground." An impressive clinical literature testifies to the frequency of "slips of the tongue," instances in which an intent to say one thing is blocked and changed by a feeling, resulting in saying something quite different. A spokesman for a municipal transit system, trying to defend the system's poor scheduling record, was recorded in the following verbatim pronouncement: "And by and large we are achieving this, despite the fact that sometimes because of difficulties our own calculation for what is happening shows that the offset which

Table 12.1. Characteristics of human language.

1. It is made up of signals rather than signs, and therefore
   a. It is extremely variable.
   b. Its contents are arbitrary.
2. Its messages disappear soon after they are produced.
3. Any person can learn the language, and can be either a sender or a receiver.
4. It is primarily spoken, and therefore
   a. It can be directed from one person to another.
   b. It can be heard by the sender as well.
5. There can be a split between one's intent and one's production, and therefore
   a. The sender can lie.
   b. Senders can know about, or think about, their own messages.
6. It is infinitely open.

Source: Based in part on Hockett, 1961.

is the offset from the ideal schedule in the computer and what is actually happening in the real world in the system does appear at variance."[3]

The openness of language. Human language shares one characteristic with many other systems of communication—it is made up of quite small units that can then be combined in a very large number of ways. This means that there can be a larger number of different messages than there are different units, an obvious advantage for any message system. Exactly how many different messages are possible, however, depends on factors other than the number of units. The most important single factor here is that the communication consists of more than the combining of so many units into a message. It consists also of a *message in context*. It is delivered by a specific individual with a background, experience, and skill. It occurs within that individual's total current frame of reference and in a situation that is understood by the two participants.

The possible variations, given all these interacting factors, are clearly almost infinite. If to these we add what was mentioned earlier, that every human communication can represent, in diverse ways and to varying degrees, the intent of the speaker, we have the possibility of an infinite number of different communications based on a rather small number of word units.

The aboutness of language: Another time, another place. By far the most important of the characteristics of human language, perhaps the one characteristic that can never be shared by other species, is its displacement,° as linguists call it. By means of language, we are enabled to talk about things that are not present. The messages of all other species are never addressed to any other situation than the one in which the sender is presently engaged. A troop of baboons is well equipped to stand around, having just finished a meal of tasty shoots, and make sounds to each other that signify, "Wonderful food" or "I feel stuffed"—or whatever else they may be moved to communicate in regard to their present situation. But baboons can never stand around a spot where they once ate a meal and discuss the situation that is no longer at hand: "Say, wasn't that a great meal we had here last week?" or "I really believe the shoots are better across the stream."

Animal communication, complex though it may sometimes be, is limited to expressing the present state and situation of the sender, whereas human communication—for reasons that are not completely clear—enables the speaker to break free of the immediately present situation (Figure 12.4). We can talk about a time or a place that is not here; about the past or about the future; about the possible, the probable, and therefore the impossible and the improbable; about what is not real and could never be real. We can talk endlessly about matters that we ourselves have invented and that would not exist if we did not bring them into existence by our talk and our thought—about unicorns, and Love, and the dirty Reds and the filthy imperialists, and next summer's crops, and nothingness, and whether pigs have wings.

The development of language

How did this remarkable achievement ever come about? Unfortunately, there is little that we can do to recapture any evidence for the origins of language within the human species. Recent intensive studies of the skeletons of prehistoric humans indicate that their jaw bones were shaped so as to have rather complex muscle groups. From this, it has been concluded that they were equipped for the delicate and elaborate muscular movements required for human speech.[4] Other than this, however, we do not know (and probably will never know) specifically how or when language developed in humans.

displacement (in language). A basic characteristic of human languages—their symbolic character, by means of which we are able to talk about phenomena that are not physically present.

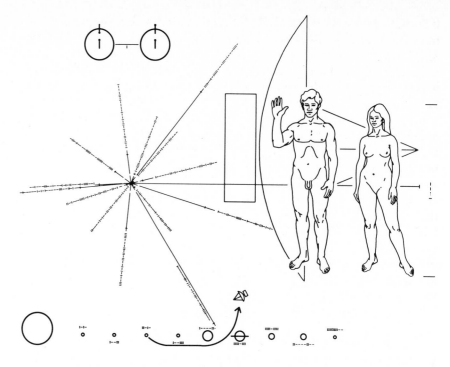

Fig. 12.4. Recently NASA sent this engraved metal plate off on a voyage beyond our solar system, in the hope that it might be found by some far-off civilization. If it is ever found, at some unimaginably distant space and time, it will surely serve as an example of a basic characteristic of human communication—its distancing.

It is possible, however, to study the way that present-day children almost universally learn to speak their own native languages. This would certainly not be direct evidence of the origins of language, but it might well help us to understand the role played by different influences. Current interest in this topic, which is very high, is largely prompted by the innovative contributions of the linguist Noam Chomsky. Following his work, an hypothesis has been expressed most forcefully by Slobin,[5] that the sequence by which language development occurs in children is universal.

4. Children do not learn to use words but to speak a language.

Chomsky is not a psychologist but a linguist. Within his own field, his contribution has been to show that traditional linguistics, based on the intensive study of units of language and their combinations, is simply unable to explain the kinds of meaningful speech produced by humans. In addition, he has attacked the theoretical position of the leading figure in modern behaviorist psychology, B. F. Skinner. The controversy thus sparked has been extremely fruitful for the progress of the field of psycholinguistics.[○]

The great controversy: Chomsky versus Skinner. The problem that both Skinner and Chomsky start with is the same. Because no child is born able to speak and no child begins to speak before its second year of life, we must conclude that speaking, like walking, is part of one's developmental progress. If so, it must come about by way of some combination of two major influences. One influence is maturation. By this, we mean that the child is so organized biologically that at a certain point in development it displays its speaking behavior—in the same way that humans usually display their walking ability at about a year of age or their dying behavior during their seventh or eighth decade of life. The other influence

psycholinguistics. The psychological study of languages.

is learning, by which we mean that influences from the environment normally train the child in the behavior called *speaking*. It is most probable that both influences are at work in every case—but what made the controversy in this instance was that the views were stated in extreme form. Skinner claims an almost total influence in the form of learning, Chomsky an equally great influence in the form of innate neurological structures.

Skinner's position,[6] as expressed in his book on what he called "verbal behavior," is related to his own lifetime interest in the uses of language—he is himself a skilled, successful writer—and is based on the successes achieved by the functional analysis© of behavior in rats as well as humans (see Chapter 7). Functional analysis consists of finding links between a unit of behavior and the consequences of that behavior; for example, between the rat pressing a bar in a Skinner box and the probability that reward will follow the bar pressing. For Skinner, understanding how some kind of behavior develops reduces to finding an appropriate unit of behavior to chart, determining the kinds of positive and negative reinforcements associated with it as consequences, and then charting the links between the behavior and its consequences. In verbal behavior, or speech, the unit is, for Skinner, the word. The reinforcements are the behaviors of significant other persons of one's "verbal community," especially parents, and the consequences are the child's verbal behaviors.

Chomsky's own studies in linguistics,[7] however, led him to conclude that what was learned in the course of language development was not that certain words or sequences of words, were reinforced "right" or "wrong," as Skinner claimed. Children did not seem to learn words when they learned to speak. Rather, the only way that one could describe what happened was that they seemed to learn the *rules* of speech. But since no such rules were ever taught (and in fact, are only taught, if at all, much later in school, as rules of grammar) Chomsky concluded that human beings are born with some innate equipment that enables any child to learn whatever language in all the world is spoken by its family. Chomsky therefore claimed that all normal human beings are born with a "perfect knowledge" of a universal grammar. The contrast with Skinner's position could hardly have been more striking.

Stated in this extreme fashion, the controversy is useful as a statement of positions as well as of a set of problems to be solved. For example, it can hardly be denied that some sorts of learning must take place in the course of language development. This is evident in the fact that all children learn, not some universal tongue, but their own native speech. There is also evidence concerning the speech sounds that children make. Languages differ very much in the phonemes© they contain. Swahili, for example, a widely used African language, contains a wide variety of "click" sounds that are not used in English and are very difficult for English-speaking persons to imitate. Adult Japanese cannot usually say the English *l*, and adult Americans cannot easily articulate the Parisian *r*. Yet any child born in a Swahili-speaking culture grows up making appropriate click sounds, just as American-born Japanese children say the English *l* perfectly. However, it is also known that young children imitate only those sounds that they already uttered in infancy. Because any normal child *can* utter any human phoneme, it must follow that the collection of phonemes that children hear and then imitate is learned in infancy—and quite probably by the process of instrumental conditioning that Skinner describes.

A maturational view. However, an increasing body of evidence supports the view that human language simply could not be acquired only by a process of conditioning. Children do not only acquire a vocabulary of words. At the same time they start to speak, they also come to command a wide range of related

functional analysis (of behavior). Skinner's term for the systematic observation of the contingencies that affect behavior.

phoneme. The smallest and most basic unit of sound in a given language.

behaviors—pointing, understanding symbolic representation in the form of signs and pictures, knowing sequences of musical notes in the form of tunes, and even understanding more than they can say! This suggests that they develop, not a list of words or word sequences, but a capacity to express themselves and to make use of the expression of others in those symbolic forms of which language is the best-known example.

Further, children learn many words that are quite necessary for speech but that are never defined and indeed seem undefinable. These are what have been called the "little words" of a language—for example, the English words *of, but, and, or* (or the French words *et, en, pas*). The word *and*, to take only one of these, is used correctly as soon as children begin to put words together. Yet they are never told what it means, they are never instructed in its usage, and they are never given the one example or instance that tells what it means or when to use it (because, of course, there *is* no such example). It is hardly conceivable that the word is correctly learned through some process of correction by reinforcement.

Equally telling is the evidence concerning children's gradually corrected errors in talking. Children's speech is, by adult standards, very bad. A two-year-old may say "All gone doggie" and a three-year-old may ask, "Why the dolly won't eat?" yet as careful observation shows, parents rarely correct the structure of such sentences. Indeed, most of the child's early utterances, although lacking proper word order or even many necessary terms, are greeted with great approval. If learning takes place, as Skinner would claim, by a process of positive and negative reinforcement of one's behavior, we would have to predict that young children will never learn to eliminate their errors and gradually conform to adult speech. But, because this is what happens, we must conclude that language development proceeds in some ways that are not describable as operant conditioning. Modeling is probably one of these ways.

5. All natural languages are orderly collections of rules—and this is what children really learn in language development.

We do not usually think of the rules of a language. When we speak our native tongue, our experience is simply that we are saying it right, not that we are following any rules. And, indeed, if we are not familiar with grammar we might well be at a loss to tell anyone what the rule is that we use so easily and correctly.

And this is just where the psychological problem lies. If we do use rules, but if we do not consciously know the rules, and especially if we have never been taught the rules, how did we learn them so well? In order to appreciate the significance of this problem, you as the reader are now asked to furnish some evidence to compare with that already gathered on a number of young children. As you know, in English we put the adjective before the noun it modifies. We say "the red house" but not "the house red." However, we sometimes use two adjectives to modify the same noun—for example, "the big red house"—so we need to have a rule that governs which adjective should come first. Take a moment to write down a rule that will cover every possible case in which two adjectives are used to modify a noun, a rule stating which adjective comes first. Your rule should be so exact yet so simple that someone who is just learning to speak English can memorize and use it.

In all probability, you found this to be a difficult task. Perhaps we should simplify the problem. Suppose we consider only two kinds of adjectives: adjectives of intensity (such as *big*) and adjectives of classification (such as *blue*).

Quite probably you still were not able to develop a single rule. Yet of course each of us is well able to use any adjective or noun, in any combination, without error—just as though we did in fact know the rule. In English, the rule is this: the adjective that can be variable always precedes the adjective that is fixed. "Big" can be varied (bigger, biggest), whereas an adjective describing an architectural style (colonial) cannot; therefore we would say "the big colonial house" but not "the colonial big house."

Patrick Suppes[8] has collected a great deal of linguistic data in an investigation comparing the language development of three children—Lingling, who speaks Mandarin Chinese; Philippe, who speaks French; and Nina, who speaks American English. The data were gathered between the children's twenty-third and thirty-ninth months. In both Mandarin Chinese and English, the word order for adjectives is the same, but in French it is somewhat different. In spoken French, adjectives of intensity precede the noun, but adjectives of classification follow the noun. (Some differences between Philippe's speech and that of Nina are shown in Table 12.2.) Suppes' evidence is clear that by the age of two, children know the rules for their native language that govern the placement of adjectives—rules that you, even as an adult, may not be able to articulate.

An even more complex example is given in the child's use of the word *all*. Suppes quotes the American child, Nina, who says, quite properly, *all gone* as well as *all these clothes* and *all of they gonna go in here*. In the first usage, *all* is what is called a *universal*, such as is used when we say "All quadrupeds have four legs." But in the other two usages *all* means something more like "in this context or situation," its flavor having been altered by association with *these* or *of they*. These distinctions are so subtle that they cannot really be discussed short of a digression into general logic—yet at the age of two, a normal child manipulates the variations with precision.

None of this is explicitly taught—although it may be done by adults and copied by the child. But what is modeled in this way is a sequence of individual examples, never the general rule. What leads the child to know that this is the right way to say something? For example, how does the child master the "rule" that goes something like this: "If I say *I*, it refers to me, but if my mother says *I*, it refers to her"? Chomsky's answer, which has come to be at the basis of much current work in psycholinguistics, is that the normal human infant comes equipped with a neurological "program" that enables dealing with the deep structure⊙ (as he calls it) at the heart of all human languages.

Some of the strongest evidence in support of the fact that children learn to speak through mastery of unspoken rules is in the kinds of mistakes that they make. As soon as children learn to use the past tense of a verb, they begin to make grammatical errors—for the simple reason that every language contains what we call *irregular verbs*. An irregular verb is one that does *not* conform to the rule. If children get the irregular verb wrong, it suggests they are going by the rule when

A "rule" problem in English

There are many words in English that begin with the prefix *un*. Examples are *uncover, uncoil, undress, unfasten, unfold, unlock, unroll, untangle, unwind*. But there are also many other words for which we would reject the prefix *un*. Examples are *unbreak, unheat, unopen, undry, unpress, unsleep, unwalk, unlook*. What is the general rule that distinguishes these two groups of words?

Table 12.2. Some differences between French and English speech.

	English	French
Noun	*thread*	*filet*
Adjective 1	*little*	*petit*
Adjective 2	*yellow*	*jaune*
Noun + Adjective 1	*the little thread*	*le petit filet*
Noun + Adjective 2	*the yellow thread*	*le filet jaune*
Noun + Adjective 1 plus Adjective 2	*the little yellow thread*	*le petit filet jaune*

deep structure. Chomsky's term for the underlying or semantic meaning of a sentence.

Fig. 12.5. Bilingual children learn more than one "channel" from self to object and so their cognitive processes are often enriched by learning more than one language. However, the fact that they have more than one channel available does not mean that they can shortcut the process by translating from one language to another. It is quite common for seven-year-old children to be fluent in two languages but be unable to deliberately translate from one language to another.

articulation. Speech; making sounds.

they should not. Thus, the child will very soon learn that a past tense is made by adding *-ed* to the form of the present tense; "I walk" becomes "I walked." Applying this rule in all innocence, the child will then offer the familiar mistake, "I taked it." If children learned only by imitation or a simple form of conditioning, they would never make such mistakes. The fact that these are among the most common errors of childhood suggests that they are going by general rules rather than particular examples.

Stages of language development. The question of how this remarkable development comes about is now being intensively investigated, although the problem is so complex that studies are still at the beginning stage. Newborn infants spend the critical first few weeks of their lives making random sounds that are mostly variations of breathing, such as coughs, burps, and gurgles. In addition, they have a repertoire of distinctive cries to express important differences in their bodily states—a cry of hunger, a cry of distress, perhaps a cry of anger or frustration as well. These cries gradually get more precise during the next few months, with variations in pitch, in intensity, in articulation,[☉] and even in patterning, often individually distinct.[9] At the end of this period, when they are sitting up and in a position to interact with the world and with others on a face-to-face basis, the development of speech as such can begin. Interestingly, and perhaps not accidentally, it is just at this point that children who are born deaf end their babbling and turn silent.

During the last half of the first year, the child imitates the specific sounds of the surrounding verbal community. Its babbling appears to be a method for learning and practicing the speech sounds, the elements, and the intonations and rhythms that identify the language around it. Some time after the first birthday (the age varying somewhat by sex, cultural influence, and individual differences) the child begins to say recognizable words, to put words together, and most important, to show that it intends to use language in context (Figure 12.5). This latter "purpose" of language was, curiously enough, the last to be noted by linguists and psychologists and was first emphasized by Bloom in her analyses of children's grammar, where she distinguished the form from the function of their speech.[10]

Roger Brown has summarized Bloom's finding thus: "She found evidence that the child intends to express certain meanings with even his earliest sentences, meanings that go beyond the simple naming in succession of various aspects of a complex situation, and that actually assert the existence of, or request the creation of, particular relations."[11] The "rules" that the child appears to learn, then, may be based on an understanding of the ways that one gets along with other people. This helps us to understand how it is that even at an early stage of language development, when children are still talking in a kind of "telegraphic speech" (for example, "Mommy gone"), they are able to respond appropriately to a situation stated in the complex command "Where's the baby's shoe?" and distinguish it from, say, "Where's the shoe's baby?"

Language, culture, and politics. One of the most important gains from the new emphasis on context that one finds in modern psycholinguistics is that for the first time languages and dialects can be studied in their own right. Older approaches in linguistics were restricted to classifying formal rules of grammar and therefore set up one way of speaking as a standard. Resulting was a tendency to treat dialects as inferior versions of one "good" or proper way of speaking a language. But, with the recognition that learning to speak a language is essentially a learning to get along in one's own ongoing contexts, the emphasis shifts to studying how well the child—or the adult—is able to use language to do what has to be done in one's individual situations. In this latter view, there are no "best" languages, and indeed no ideal forms of language. Every mode of speech serves the same function and probably does as good a job. In this respect, languages do not differ, only cultures and environments do.

Because all people are engaged in the same kinds of endeavors, often by very similar means and in psychologically similar ways, their separate languages are just different, not better or inferior. The practical import of this view has already been widely felt in linguistics, in sociology, and in education. One important result has been in regard to that specific form of English that is spoken by some blacks in the United States. Traditional linguistics would have considered this inferior, because it was an "ungrammatical" variant of standard or "good" English. As a consequence, urban black children were often either dismissed as unteachable or forced to conform to the standards of proper English.

Extensive studies of black English, however, have indicated that it is not a substandard variant of correct language but a legitimately different dialect in its own right. It is, in the words of one group of linguists, "a well-ordered, highly structured, highly developed language system which in many ways is different from standard English."[12] The remarkable fact is that this distinctively different language with its own rules was spontaneously developed by a widespread group and learned by successive generations. It does its job as well as any other language we know. And all this happened, not as something taught in schools, but simply as one important by-product of an ongoing culture.[12]

Language and survival. Everything that we know about communication in general, and its development into human speech in particular, suggests that we have here an activity that must be closely related to survival functions. Like other patterns that are necessary for survival, communication is either preprogrammed or is learned very early in life; it is developed by every normal member of the group or species; there seems to be no way to keep the individual member from developing it; and without it the individual never becomes a fully functioning member of the group.

The forms of communication that an individual shows, then, do not seem to be the results of learning in the ordinary sense and certainly not, in humans, like the learning that takes place in school. It is, as we have said, closer to maturation or development than to learning in the ordinary sense. A great part of it may be built in, as it clearly is in the case of communication patterns among many species of animals and as it may be in the case of deep structures of syntax in humans. But the remaining part, especially in humans, must be a special form of learning. This is why we give it the unfamiliar label of *survival learning.* It is meant to refer to instances of change, growth, maturation, and development that share certain features. Among these are the following:

- It takes place with often astonishing rapidity — as we see, for example, in the number of new words of speaking vocabulary that very young children can acquire or in the fact that they seem to be able to pick up a speaking knowledge of a new language in a few weeks.
- It seems to be related to critical periods in development — indicated by the well-known imprinting phenomenon in fowl, as well as in the fact that young children can easily learn accents of speech that adults can usually never learn.
- It seems to be related to critical periods in development — indicated by the well-known imprinting° phenomenon in fowl, as well as in the fact that young children can easily learn accents of speech that adults can usually never learn.
- Once learned, it appears to be so deeply built-in that one no longer has the

syntax. The grammatical arrangement of words in a sentence showing their relationship.

ability to "know what one knows"; for example, as in our way of knowing the words of our native tongue. As one who speaks English as a native tongue, if I look at a chair in front of me, I "know" it is a chair. It is not that I see this object, know it in some way, and also know that the word for it is *chair*—not at all. That would describe, rather, my use of a language not native to me; for example, I look at this object, know it is a chair, and also know that the French word for it is *chaise*. The difference for me is that it *is* a chair (the English word) whereas for me the French word *for* it is *chaise*. There is absolutely no way that I can go back behind my own knowing in English and apprehend this object as nameless. My learning of the English word is now buried beyond recall.

Language in apes

Although the different primates (such as chimpanzees, monkeys, or gorillas) use elaborate systems of communication, including many different kinds of vocal expressions, it can hardly be said that they possess a human kind of language with spoken words and a grammar. In fact, anatomical and acoustic studies have indicated that no living creature but the developed human has the anatomical capacity to make the three basic vowel sounds that underlie all languages—*i* as in *heed*, *a* as in *dot*, and *u* as in *toot*.[14] Yet higher apes do appear to be capable of the muscular, gestural, and probably cognitive activities required to communicate with humans. For this reason, many attempts have been made to teach language to primates.

6. The higher apes appear to be able to learn a language that is somewhere between natural animal gesture and human speech.

In the 1930s, a husband and wife team of psychologists named Kellogg attempted to rear a chimpanzee named Gua in their home;[15] and in the 1950s two other psychologists named Hayes tried the same thing with a chimpanzee named Vicki.[16] These and more recent studies with the higher apes have produced clearcut results in regard to development and socialization. The animals quickly become accustomed to living like human children. In addition, they are both intelligent and lovable, and they develop more rapidly than do human children in motor abilities, so that it is often easier to train them in the elementary social graces. However, dedicated efforts to train some of these animals to articulate words have never succeeded, even though they can learn to understand many words.

Ameslan: The new approach. It occurred to two ingenious psychologists, Beatrice and Allen Gardner of the University of Nevada at Reno, that, even if a chimpanzee could not be taught to speak words, it might well be possible for the animal to learn to "sign" as deaf people do—to learn Ameslan,⊙ or American Sign Language. This is a true language that is used by large numbers of hearing-impaired persons in North America. For this purpose, in 1966 the Gardners bought a female chimpanzee who was about eleven months old (her exact birthday was not known, since she had been born in the wild and brought to this country by an animal dealer). They named her Washoe and installed her in a furnished trailer in the back yard of their home. She was treated as a human child being reared by deaf

Ameslan. American Sign Language, a system of hand signals used by the hearing-impaired; the language taught to Washoe and other chimps.

parents. That is, her companions spoke only Ameslan in her presence, plus some occasional calls and cries (Figure 12.6). Using a mixture of three methods—shaping, molding, and modeling (see Chapter 7)—they taught her a vocabulary. Washoe was very soon able to express a variety of wants, to answer questions and be tested on her signing abilities, to conduct conversations, and even to reveal what seemed to be her thoughts.[17] After about four years of training and testing, Washoe was moved to the University of Oklahoma Primate Center, where her training has continued under the direction of Roger Fouts.[18]

Understandably, a great deal of excitement has been generated among psychologists and linguists over these studies. For the first time since humans and apes came to know each other, the communication barrier between them seems to have been bridged. Experimentalists can now ask questions never before raised concerning the origins of language in the individual and concerning the possibilities of language in animals other than humans.

As we will see, the data gathered and lessons learned in the Washoe project were impressive, but its limitations were also evident. Washoe was, by most criteria, linguistically disadvantaged. She had spent the first year of her life with no training in Ameslan, and her teachers for the next four years were not perfectly skilled in signing. She had no age mates to play with or to share her new language with. And her opportunities for natural learning of a language were seriously limited by interference from the formal demands of the experimental testing procedures. For comparison, imagine a human child who hears no speech until the age of a year, who is then kept exclusively in the company of adults with a poor command of speech, who never plays with another child, and whose time is very much taken up with what must seem like pointless testing.

Washoe's achievements. In the first fifty-one months of her training, Washoe learned a total of 132 different signs. This does not mean that these were all that she knew, however. For the Gardners to accept a sign as reliably "known," they used extremely strict and conservative criteria, far more strict than we might use when we say that a human child has learned a word. No sign was even entered in their report as a new sign in Washoe's vocabulary until it had been reported on three independent occasions by three different observers. Following this, it was not considered a stable, or reliable, item in her vocabulary until it was reported to occur spontaneously and appropriately on each of fifteen consecutive days. The count of 132, then, is quite probably far lower than the number that Washoe either used or understood.

In Table 12.3, we present a breakdown of Washoe's first 132 signs, categorized by the order in which they were learned and by their usage. A number of comments are in order. The bulk of the signs, understandably enough, were nouns, referring to the objects in her environment, and their rate of acquisition increased

Fig. 12.6

| Quick | Brown | Fox | Jumped | Over | Lazy | Dog |

Table 12.3. The first 132 signs learned by Washoe, by category.

Category of sign	Example	Within first 16 signs learned	Between 17 and 36 signs	Between 37 and 86 signs	Between 87 and 132 signs	Total
Noun	*flower*	1	9	17	25	52
Action noun: referring both to a noun and to its related action	*food/eat*	2	5	9	3	19
Appeal, request word	*come/gimme, more, tickle*	8		5	3	16
Pronoun	*you*, names of humans		4	7	5	16
Locative: adverbs of place or direction	*in, out*		1	1	1	3
Adjective	*red, same*		8			8
Verb	*bite, open*				4	4
Emotion words	—	*listen hurt sorry funny please*	*good*	*quiet enough no*	*can't goodbye who different same*	14

Source: Data from Gardner and Gardner, 1975, table A1, pp. 259–267.

steadily. In addition, some of her earliest signs, as well as a percentage of the signs that she continued to learn, were appeals. Of the first nine signs that she learned, eight were of this type; *come/gimme, more, up, open, tickle/touch, go, out, hurry*. This kind of sign was always made in a situation in which she was in effect asking that her companions do something to her ("tickle") or for her ("come/ gimme"), in much the same way that a human infant might lift its arms to a parent and say "Up." It is significant that two other chimps in a more recent project followed almost exactly the same sequence of learning: Moja's first four signs were *come/gimme, go, more,* and *drink;* and Pili's first four were *drink, come/gimme, more,* and *tickle.*

Finally, Washoe learned a series of signs that we have termed "Emotion words," because they appear to serve a quite unique function. Signs such as *listen, funny,* or *can't* seem to serve the purpose of expressing a feeling about or an attitude toward an ongoing situation. They are emotional or expressive additions to an ongoing situation, meant to articulate her affective participation rather than just to identify something or to appeal for something. Similar expressions are found in the vocabularies of human children, especially in their spontaneous vocalizations during play.

It is apparent that Washoe's linguistic achievements are remarkable and that in many ways they correspond structurally to what might be seen among human children. The Gardners have taken this to be their major experimental task, to order their data in such a way that legitimate comparisons might be made with the stages of language development in human children. Referring to standard measures of developmental language competence, they conclude, "If Washoe had been a preschool child, then by these standards her replies would place her at a relatively advanced level of linguistic competence."[19] Not only in terms of single words but in terms of word combinations as well, Washoe's development approximated that of children. Her first two-sign combination, "gimme sweet," was made when she was approximately twenty-one months of age, very close to the average for human children. An analysis of her first 294 recorded combinations of two signs agrees very well with the results obtained by Roger Brown in his studies of five young children.[20]

Prospects for research. On the basis of what was learned from the Washoe project, the Gardners have embarked on one that is considerably more ambitious. Four new chimpanzees have been obtained, each within a few days of its birth. They are being signed to from the first day, just as a deaf human mother might begin immediately signing to her newborn baby. In addition, the adult companions for these new chimpanzees are all fluent in Ameslan, and most are in fact deaf themselves. Because the four new chimps were brought in at different times, the animals will have a community of peers of various ages. This situation approximates quite closely what they have in their natural state. In this project, the animals will be followed all the way to maturity, in order to explore the limits of linguistic development in chimpanzees. These animals can apparently learn a language; the appropriate questions, the Gardners would now say, are only "how much human language, how soon, and how far they can go."[21]

Preliminary answers are already at hand to the first question that is usually asked: If chimpanzees who can sign are reared in each other's company, do they "talk" to one another? The answer is that, as far as can be determined thus far, they do, but only minimally. One reason for this is that their necessarily restricted life does not permit them the same opportunities for risk or challenge that are naturally available to them in the wild. Life as a pet is predictable, even a little dull. A second reason is that these animals already have a very adequate gestural language that they use extensively and naturally. Ameslan is for them an artificial language and perhaps biologically not needed. But the indications of a growing "language culture" are there, and as the animals begin to rear families the opportunities for signing will increase. (Washoe gave birth to a baby, but it died soon after birth, so that she had no chance to sign to it.) And other possibilities have opened up as well. Moja enjoys using crayons for drawing pictures and will already make a specific drawing on demand and then answer correctly when asked later what it is (Figure 12.7). All the animals give indications that the language they are learning is not simply a set of arbitrary gestures memorized by rote but as much a part of their lives and development as is the speech of human children. Their signs during

Fig. 12.7. Moja's drawing for *berry*.

infancy are "infantile" in form, as is found among humans and as seen analogously in the "baby talk" of humans. And, just like a human child, Washoe would talk to herself. As the Gardners describe it, "We have often seen Washoe moving stealthily to a forbidden part of the yard, signing *quiet* to herself, or running pell-mell for the potty chair while signing *hurry*."[22]

Other laboratories and other investigators are currently engaged in pursuing the general topic of language in apes, sparked by the Gardners' pioneering projects. At Oklahoma, Maurice and Jane Temerlin have reared one chimpanzee, Lucy, as a human child and have just introduced a younger chimpanzee into the household. Their Ameslan training was conducted by Roger Fouts. (Among the findings: Lucy was taken to see the movie *Planet of the Apes*, but she wasn't interested.) At Santa Barbara, David Premack is studying the linguistic and cognitive capacities of a chimpanzee, Sarah, by training her to "speak" through the use of plastic symbols for words.[23] At the Yerkes Primate Center in Georgia, Duane Rumbaugh and colleagues are engaged in a similar project, training a chimpanzee named Lana to "speak" by pressing the appropriate panels on a computerized display.[24] Thus Washoe's scientific heritage grows.

7. Three major forms of communication can be distinguished: *address*, or conveying information; *influence*, to persuade another person, and *expression*, to convey an emotional state.

The work on language in apes suggests that there may be many possible forms of communication and language. Within humans, too, more than one form of communication may be going on at any one time; and, at different stages of development, these forms may play different roles. To conclude this chapter, we will discuss one of these forms, *expression*. The form that we call *address* has been discussed in this chapter, and the form we call *influence* will be reserved for a later chapter in the social psychology of propaganda.

The most universal of all varieties of communication, but one about which the least is known, is *expression*. In a general sense, expression refers to the outward manifestation of an inner state. It communicates the condition of the individual. Because one important aspect of the current state of an individual is the emotional, we would expect to find a significant emotional component in expressive behavior and communication. Because the manifestation of a condition or inner state can occur by whatever channels are available, we would also expect to find that expression takes place in complex ways that cut across ordinary channels.

Table 12.4. The semantic differential. How would you rate the word *democracy* on the various scales?

	Democracy					
Good	x	x	x	x	x	x	Bad
Strong	x	x	x	x	x	x	Weak
Rough	x	x	x	x	x	x	Smooth
Heavy	x	x	x	x	x	x	Light
Fast	x	x	x	x	x	x	Slow
Cold	x	x	x	x	x	x	Hot

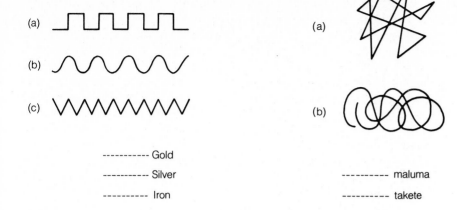

----------- Gold

----------- Silver

---------- Iron

---------- maluma

---------- takete

Fig. 12.8. Match each word with the "best" drawing. Our ability to do this is a consequence of the connotative meanings in even "meaningless" words. Most persons will match *maluma* with the "round" drawing and *takete* with the "angular" one. (Scheerer and Lyons, 1957) In the other group, most persons will match the first drawing with iron, the second with gold, and the third with silver (Irwin and Newland, 1940)

Finally, because expression refers to the total current state of the individual, we would expect that its communication involves nonverbal as well as verbal means. We will consider some important kinds of expressive communication in terms of these three aspects.

Connotative meaning. The words we use for communicating carry a heavy baggage of associations, emotional implications, and partial meanings, based in part on their sounds and in part on their meanings. It is surprising how many words referring to small things have a tight, pinched sound — *thin, bit, chip, slit, wink, pygmy;* how many referring to a loud or startling event have the sound of *blare, glare, flare;* or how many referring to wet smoothness have the sound of *sliding, slipping, slick.* Asked to rate nonsense words for their positive or negative connotations on a scale of –3 to + 3, people not surprisingly gave a mean rating of –1.61 to *ickatt,* –.15 to *fleab,* and + 2.2 to *gliss.*

Findings such as these are usually explained by saying that words have both denotative° and connotative° meanings, the former referring to what a word specifically denotes, in the dictionary sense. A major difficulty faced by adults who learn a foreign language is that they usually know the denotative but not the connotative meanings of the foreign words. They can compose telegrams but not poetry.

An ingenious technique for assessing the range and richness of connotative meanings has been developed by Charles Osgood and his associates at the University of Illinois.[25] Called the *semantic differential,°* it requires people to rate test words on a number of different scales, each scale being defined by a pair of adjectives of opposite meaning (Table 12.4). Individuals as well as groups can then be compared on their responses to different test words.

It might seem strange to rate a word such as *democracy* in terms of such adjectives as *heavy* and *light.* In a denotative sense (in terms of its dictionary meaning), the word *democracy* communicates information only about a certain kind of political system. But connotatively, as we all know, *democracy* (and most other words as well, as shown in Figure 12.8) communicates layers and shadings of meaning that ramify into quite unlikely areas. For this reason, few people have any great difficulty making such ratings, and a high measure of agreement is found among persons of similar backgrounds and attitudes. As we might expect, *democracy* is usually rated more "good" than "bad"; but perhaps we might be surprised to find that *success* is rated more "hot" than "cold."

Osgood's semantic differential technique is based on extensive studies of the

denotative meaning. The primary or socially accepted definition of a symbol or concept.

connotative meaning. The meaning beyond the denotative meaning; the emotional meaning of a symbol or concept.

semantic differential. A method developed by Osgood that measures the connotative meaning of words by using rating scales and factor analysis.

connotative meanings assigned to a large number of words. These led the investigators to conclude that three major dimensions of meaning accounted for most of the ratings assigned to words. The most important of these dimensions is *value*— that is, we assess the meaning of a word in terms of how "good" or "bad" it seems to us. (If you try this out for yourself, you will see how easy it is to rate almost any word on a value dimension, simply by asking: Is this closer to good or to bad?) A second major dimension is *power*; that is, how "strong" or "weak" the word's meaning seems. A third dimension is *activity*, or the degree to which the word has a connotation of being active rather than passive. The three dimensions suffice to "locate" any word in our shared world of meaning. In practice, the semantic differential uses not only the basic adjective pairs that describe the dimensions, but similar or related pairs. For example, on the value dimension, a pair of adjectives might be *clean* and *dirty*, on the power dimension *large* and *small*, and on the activity dimension *tense* and *relaxed*.

Emotional expression. By word and by gesture, by posture and stance, by body as well as language, we express our emotional states continuously. Even if we happen to be emotionally controlled, it is the control that we express; if we try to hide the expression, what is revealed is our individual mode of hiding expressions. There is no escape from emotionality; hence there are no choices except to express, mask, or alter it. Emotional expression is transient, and it is often not accessible to the individual in whom it occurs. So, in spite of its fundamental and pervasive importance, it is nearly impossible to pin it down for assessment and study.

It is most curious that, in spite of the difficulty that serious investigators may have in trying to get a handle on emotional expression for purpose of scientific or scholarly study, these same investigators in their daily lives, like people in general, do not seem to have such problems. Normally we get along with one another quite sensibly. We usually know, or are pretty sure we know, the emotional state of ourselves and of other persons. We can even accomplish this across the boundaries that normally separate the species. Owners of dogs are usually well aware of the animal's emotional state, and there is strong evidence that the reverse is just as true. In his long-term, day-to-day observations of the mountain gorilla in its natural habitat in the mountains of the African Congo, George Schaller expresses himself in confident terms in his description of some of the animals: "There was recklessness in his face and a natural mischievousness, which even his inherent reserve could not hide." Or this: "I could see hesitation and uneasiness, curiosity and boldness and annoyance."[26]

Yet all this is done on the basis of the most fleeting impressions, and with no training—for there are no schools in expressiveness nor in reading it. (We might well suspect that schooling would so organize the art as to make it unworkable.) As Charles Darwin said a century ago in his own work on the subject, "It has often struck me as a curious fact that so many shades of expression are instantly recognized without any conscious process of analysis on our part. No one, I believe, can clearly describe a sullen or sly expression; yet many observers are unanimous that these expressions can be recognized in the various races of man."[27] It was Darwin's view that this similarity of expression and of its recognition across diverse cultural groups was the strongest argument for a "single parent-form" for the various human groups.

This gap between practice and knowledge has been summarized by one investigator in terms of five possible reasons. First, we are so familiar with expressions, our own and others, that we have difficulty even seeing the phenomenon as a problem. Second, expression is very personal, and impersonal study tends to destroy such objects even as it aims to observe and explain them. Third, expressive phenomena are so fleeting that we are often at a loss to capture or repeat

Fig. 12.9. Duchenne at work with a willing subject.

them for careful study. Fourth, expressions are so many and so unique that they pose great problems in reducing them to the generality required for systematic knowledge. And, finally, expression as well as our perception of it is always global, and so it cannot easily be reduced to units or parts for analysis and explanation.[28] For all these reasons, and in spite of many years of interest and study, there is still lacking a complete theory. Only recently have some advances been made.

The study of expression, extending back at least to the period of the Renaissance in western Europe, has usually depended on techniques for capturing or producing these fleeting phenomena. Thus, the problem began to interest scholars as the art of portraiture began to be developed in the early Renaissance. One of the earliest results of such study was the "theory" of Della Porta that characteristic human expressions could be classified according to their similarity to animal types. Some centuries later, Johann Lavater explained expression in terms of the spirit's influence on the muscles of the face and body, which in turn is sensed by others intuitively rather than rationally. Then, with the discovery of ways to use the new magical tool of electricity and the related discovery that muscles can be triggered electrically, Charles Bell offered a theory of the "machinery" of expression. This theory seemed to be supported when Duchenne was able to produce facial expressions by stimulating muscles with electrical current (Figure 12.9). The motto became: "One expression is related to one muscle action, and this correspondence is built into the musculature." This laid the foundation for Darwin's thesis that such built-in "programs" for emotional expression are part of our species' inheritance. With the development of photography as a usable tool at the end of the nineteenth century, the problem was again revived, and extensive studies were made to classify facial expression. A typical example is the elaborate series made by Rudolph in 1903, using a talented actor whose posed expressions were photographed and then touched up by drawing (Figure 12.10).

In the era of modern psychology, experimental studies have taken over. A very active area of study has been what is called *nonverbal communication.*[⊙] We make our way with other persons by means of an endless series of such communications, expressed without words and known without training. Expressions, whether of face or body, are true actions, for we can stare down someone as surely

Fig. 12.10. Some examples of the complex and expressive pictures produced by Rudolph.

nonverbal communication.
Communicating or giving clues to meanings of behavior through use of body language, body tensions, or gestures.

as we can knock that person down, and we can express our status as certainly by our relaxed and confident posture as by the title on our office door.[29]

The most significant and extensive of recent work has been that of Paul Ekman,[30] who has studied a number of cultural groups around the world, from those in advanced societies such as our own to tribes in New Guinea whose members have had only minimal contact with the products of industrial civilization. Using very elaborate film and videotape procedures, he has shown that most facial and bodily expressions are universally similar among humans, both in the way they are done by the expressor and the way they are perceived by the partner. Facial expressions in particular can be almost unimaginably complex and subtle — as is evident from the samples of Rudolph pictures — but the "message" appears to come through. Ekman has suggested that this is because in every case the expression is "built up" on the basis of common, elementary units. To this we may add that, however the message is grasped or known, it is in its expression a form of behavior. Therefore it occurs in an existing situation that is already meaningful to both participants; it serves a purpose that can be known to both; it is evidently directed toward an existing state of affairs and is related to the individual's goal. As it appears in the behavior of living creatures, communication in any of its forms makes sense because it is a series of communicative acts.

Summary

1. Communication, a transaction between sender and receiver(s), is not symmetrical. What occurs on one side may not be duplicated on the other.

2. In advertising, the "to whom it may concern" form of communication tries to capture attention through color, movement, novelty, and content, especially sexual content.

3. A sign is a form of communication that usually occurs as a spontaneous display involving the animal to a major degree.

4. A symbol is a different form of communication that appears on a more deliberate basis and involves the animal less totally.

5. Humans are able to separate themselves cognitively from the fact and even the meaning of their own speech.

6. Human language, like all great rule-ordered symbol systems, is made up of a relatively small number of small, independent units that can be combined in a large number of ways.

7. One of the great advantages conferred by a true language is that it enables the speaker to talk about what is not present or even could not be present.

8. Chomsky's view of the basis of language is that it rests on an innate neurological program that permits any normal child to learn any language that is part of its speech community.

9. Skinner's view, by contrast, is that no other equipment is needed for language learning than for learning in general, because it is acquired in the same way as other performances.

10. Children begin their speaking careers by imitating all the sounds in their environment, but they end up speaking only the language spoken by their associates.

11. Children develop a capacity to utilize abstract symbols in many guises, of which language is the prime example.

12. The development of speech proceeds from differentiated breathing sounds and cries, to babbling the local sounds, to forming words, and finally to forming words into grammatically appropriate combinations. Children seem to learn rules rather than words.

13. Because all languages serve the same function and do it in the same way, it is probable that languages do not differ in their complexity or level of abstraction. Only cultures and environments do.

14. Language learning often seems to take place with astonishing rapidity and may be tied to certain critical periods in development.

15. Although efforts to teach chimpanzees to articulate words have never succeeded, recent efforts to teach the higher apes to communicate by way of Ameslan (sign language) have sparked new lines of research. It is not yet clear whether signing serves the same purpose in domesticated apes as speech does among humans.

16. Analysis of connotative meanings, by Osgood and his associates, has extracted three major dimensions of meaning in words: value, power, and activity. This finding has served as the basis for constructing the *semantic differential* as a measure of connotative meaning.

17. A large variety of emotional expressions (facial as well as gestural) are recognized, even across species, without any seeming conscious attempt at figuring out what they mean.

18. According to Ekman's researches in different cultures, most facial and bodily expressions are similar across cultures, both in the way they are expressed and in the way they are perceived.

The focus in this chapter will be on the search for consistency in people. Is there some thread in each of us that runs through time and that can become part of our identification? Are there personality types? If so, how can we discover them? These are some of the questions raised in this chapter.

Tests for consistency will be shown to refer to factors related to persons, traits, and situations. You will be introduced to some of the problems in the testing situation, such as reliability and validity. Then you will see how consistency either within or among persons can be reflected in bodily organization of the individual as well as in the national character of societies.

The comprehensive theories of Freud and Jung will be reviewed and their relation to the problems of consistency discussed. Biological factors will be touched on as a possible source of consistency in persons. You will learn about a number of major kinds of tests for personality characteristics. Finally, a view of the problem from the inside will allow you to consider some relations between consistency and familiarity.

13

Personality: the consistency of personal history

"He began to wonder whether we could ever make psychology so absolute a science that each little spring of life would be revealed to us. As it was, we always misunderstood ourselves and rarely understood others. Experience was of no ethical value. It was merely the name men gave to their mistakes."—Oscar Wilde.[1]

If we think about the people we know, but think of them as *persons* rather than as other people, we will find that we can say a number of things about them.

- They are different, yet they are also alike.
- Each one can be described in terms of their characteristics.
- Each one seems to remain what they are, year after year.

The describable uniqueness of persons is what we usually call their *personality* and is the topic of this chapter; their stability, or consistency, is the main theoretical problem in explaining personality, and so most of the chapter will be devoted to it.

The problem of consistency

It is fair to say that psychologists do not agree on how to describe personalities in general, nor even on whether they can be described; nor on how to explain people's uniqueness and stability of personality.

Puzzles of personality. On the one hand, each person seems to remain the same individual over long periods of time (Figure 13.1). Yet it is not at all difficult to find two different situations in which a person will act quite differently, just as though there were no consistency of personality. And it is true that each person can be described as a whole, just as though the individual personality were a single

Fig. 13.1. If you meet someone after a lapse of many years, you expect that they have changed in some uniquely individual way, but you also expect to meet someone who is still the same person. That is, you expect both change and consistency.

unit, yet each individual also seems to be "made up of" a lot of separate elements that can be identified and described one at a time.

In short, although we go about our daily interactions with a commonsense faith in people's uniqueness, consistency, and wholeness, much of our own experience with them casts some doubt on our naive "theories" of personality. In a famous experiment that was originally meant to show how gullible students were in judging their own personalities, Forer[2] had students fill out a supposed personality test called a "Diagnostic Interest Blank." He then handed them his interpretations of their results—but what they did not know was that they had all received the same general interpretation. It contained the kinds of statements that are usually found in commercialized astrological readings, statements that probably apply to everyone and that each of us would agree apply to us. For example, they were told, "You have a tendency to worry more than you should" or "Your mood changes sometimes from day to day." The students did not suspect anything was wrong with the descriptions but agreed with them. Hence Forer concluded that he had demonstrated gullibility on their part.

What he may also have demonstrated, however, is that many general statements about people's personalities are applicable to most of us. After all, we are like each other in a lot of ways, and we see ourselves as similar to other persons. We like to think of ourselves as unique, and quite probably we are—but we also see ourselves as like others, which may also be true. We may even think of ourselves as indescribable—yet we would probably also agree that meaningful statements can be made about us, and we are usually eager to know what they might be. Thus do contradictions abound in the study of personality.

Two approaches to consistency. One of the most widespread beliefs about personality is simply that there is such a thing. That is, most of us would probably agree that individuals do in fact have characteristics that add up to personalities. Now, when we make such a claim, we are also implying that individuals "have" something that remains consistent over time. That is, we are implying that there is a consistency about the individual personality. This may seem so obvious as to leave no room for argument, but the fact is that as an issue in psychology it is far from settled.

One well-known characteristic of personality is a person's honesty. We might therefore ask: Can it be said that in general one person is more honest than another? Again, notice what this question implies. When we ask it, we are implying that each of the two persons who are being compared "has" this characteristic in greater or less degree, and also "has" it in some consistent way. We imply that to be honest is to be that way in most, if not all, situations, or else that to be dishonest is to act dishonestly most of the time. Can such statements be legitimately made about people? In concluding Chapter 10, we referred to a study by Hartshorne and May[3] in the 1920s, in which schoolchildren were given various opportunities to cheat. For example, after they had taken examinations and found out the correct answers, they were given access to their own papers with the opportunity to change their answers. What they did not know, however, was that their papers had already been photographed.

The results were clear in showing that no individual child was consistent, regardless of situation. There did not seem to be a general characteristic of honesty that could be applied, in greater or less degree, to each child. Rather, each one displayed an individual pattern of response to the different situations, sometimes showing honesty and sometimes not. Thus, our widely shared belief that people will display the same characteristic across situations was not supported in this study—nor in most such studies conducted since then.

However, some personality theorists have not been too impressed with this kind of result. They have argued, in accordance with widespread, commonsense views, that there is a great deal of consistency to be found if we know how to look for it. In addition, personality theorists have claimed that such consistencies have their origins quite early in life, when personality differences begin to arise. Personalities are thus said to be learned in the course of development and then persist throughout the life span.

Thus, we have two major views of personality. The first is that there are no consistencies to be found within the person; if any apparent consistencies are found, they are caused by people being in similar situations. The second view is that each person has a unique personality that remains consistent. The two views have in turn led to two major approaches in studying personality. They are as follows:

- Situation-centered approaches, in which explanations are sought in the situations that individuals encounter.
- Person-centered approaches, in which explanations are sought in individual's characteristics or disposition. These are therefore also called *dispositional*© approaches.

The situational approach

---

1. According to the situational approach, prior experience, observation of other persons, and expectancies are the three bases of consistency in individuals and in people in general.

To understand the situational approach, one must first put aside the ordinary notion of the "person." It is true that there are individuals, but they are to be thought of as biological organisms that display certain behavior. The only information that is available to us about them is the behavior that can be observed. All

dispositional. In personality, a method of attributing causes of events or actions to fairly stable characteristics within a person (for example, traits or attitudes).

that can be said in regard to consistency is that a specific individual repeats the same behavior in many different situations. We are now going to try to explain this consistency without invoking the idea of a "person" who contains some element giving rise to the consistency.

The first and simplest explanation we might offer is that an individual displays the same behavior many times because the situation repeats itself many times. This is in fact true for much of our lives. An undertaker is likely to refrain from smiling during the daylight hours, not because his "person" carries around a characteristic of solemnity, but because he spends his working hours in a mortuary where levity would be out of place. Roger Barker,[4] a leading social psychologist, has pointed out that we need know only the situations that persons are in to be able to predict a great deal about their (consistent) behavior. "In church," he remarks, "we behave church. In a post office, we behave post office" (Figure 13.2). Thus, we are often able to identify mentally disturbed people simply by the inappropriateness of their behavior, and we are also willing to excuse the behavior of young children on the same grounds. Because we recognize that certain situations call for appropriate behavior, we are immediately aware if the rule is transgressed.

One of the leading proponents of a situational approach, Walter Mischel, points out that one cannot rely only on a knowledge of individual differences to build a theory of personality.[5] The reason is that a science of personality aims at predicting how people will behave, for prediction is the final test of whether a theory works. If you could not predict how people will behave, your theory as to their consistency would be incorrect. But, if their behavior is individual, no general prediction is possible. Therefore a theory that starts with individual differences cannot provide the basis for a general theory of personality.

If, as Mischel says, a pure "person" theory leads only to predicting individuals and rules out general statements about personality, no theory seems possible. But it can also be argued that if a pure situation theory fails to make room for the individual, no personality theory is possible either. The only workable resolution of this dilemma is a theory that combines some elements of both views. Mischel's position, for example, makes room for factors that belong to the situation as well as factors that belong to the person. It is closely related to the *social learning theory* that was discussed at the end of Chapter 8.

Cognitive-situation theory. In this approach, an attempt is made to explain the two kinds of consistency that can be found. The first refers to the fact that each person appears to maintain a unique but recognizable consistency across many situations. The second kind of consistency has to do with people in general: Broadly definable characteristics can be found in human beings that seem to apply across situations. Cognitive-situation theory therefore offers a number of ways to understand personality, as follows.

The individual's earlier experiences, in the form of social learning, have led to certain cognitive "conditions" that are unique to each person. Most of these

Fig. 13.2. If we knew nothing about this young man except that he was in these three situations with his girlfriend, we would still be able to predict a great deal — about his behavior, his feelings, even the details of his autonomic functioning.

conditions take the form of expectancies; that is, what the person expects will happen in a situation. If as a teacher I usually expect my class to be unruly, I am likely to act stern. This is not because I "have" such a characteristic in my personality, but because it fits my expectancies in this situation. In addition to such expectancies, individuals tend to cognitively "transform" situations or find individual meanings in them. Each person may be consistent in doing this, but individual cognitions are likely to be so unique that no general rule can be stated as to how people in general will do this. Thus, in two different ways one can explain people's consistency of behavior without resorting to the notion of individual personalities.

Still another way that cognitive-situation theory offers for understanding personality is based on the fact that as people observe each other, they usually come up with characterizations that cut across situations.[6] Each of us tends to find consistencies in other persons, although in fact the consistency may lie in our own judgments rather than in any characteristic of others' personalities. This would help to explain how people can appear to be consistent even though they do not "have" any consistent personality characteristics.

Social learning theorists will admit to some characteristics that belong to individuals. However, they are cognitive, or related to perception and the intellect, rather than associated with personality in the usual sense of the term. These characteristics are

1. Social *competencies,* or ways to get along in a social world, simply by virtue of having lived so many years. Girls "know how" to act like girls and boys like boys. Adults can be citizens, sports lovers are knowledgeable followers of sports, and so on.
2. Personal *strategies* or means for organizing cognitive input, particularly in what concerns other people.
3. Stable *hypotheses* concerning how other persons will act.
4. Individual *meanings* and *values* that each of us places on certain events or classes of events.
5. And, finally, more or less fixed ways to control and regulate one's own behavior in the face of various influences.[7]

All these differ from person to person, and they are an important basis for why we seem different and unique to others.

To summarize, we may say that situational theorists have not succeeded in eliminating the person or in explaining consistency entirely in situational terms. Rather, theirs is a shift in emphasis, from the purely personal and individual to the behavioral and general.

Testing for consistency

The test of a theory is whether it leads to any consequences: A theory must be to some degree practical. In regard to personality theory, the obvious practical consequences of a theory are its successes in enabling one to assess people's personalities, to relate the assessment to their behavior, and to predict how they will act under given conditions. It is the first of these that has been of greatest concern in this area, and it has led to the thriving field of personality assessment. Here we discuss the kinds of assessment that are feasible on the basis of a situational approach.

Persons, traits, and situations. Consider the difficulties facing a tester who wants to get some information bearing on the problem of consistency. Let us suppose that he or she has devised a test to assess some aspect of one's personality and gives the test to Person A. The results of one testing will hardly tell anything useful about consistency; some repeat data are needed. If the same test is given to Person A every morning for a week, the seven testings might be of some use, but only if the tester manages to rule out two possible sources of inconsistency. The first is in the test itself; for surely the same test given seven times in a row will generate its own special practice effect. The second source of difficulty will be in the testing situation: The seven testings can only be trusted if the tester has made sure that the situation remains unchanged all week.

One might rule out the practice effect by devising seven separate but similar tests and using one each morning—but in that case there would have to be some additional, external guarantee that the seven tests are in fact equivalent. And if one could not make sure that all seven situations are equal, one would have to take that into account in assessing the results regarding consistency.

Now, if this complex arrangement is multiplied by the number of persons that one wants to test and if that result in turn is multiplied by the number of different elements of the personality that we want to assess, it will be clear that the problem of consistency presents serious technical difficulties. Cattell has suggested that there are three sources of difficulty here, which he calls *persons, traits,* and *occasions.*[8] That is, inconsistency may arise because people change, or because their traits change, or because the occasion (the situation or the test, or both) changes.

His work has consisted in determining just what traits can be discovered to exist in all persons and make up the totality of their personalities. Before reviewing his findings, we will look at two characteristics of the tests themselves.

Reliability and validity. We have been discussing consistency of the personality, which in practical terms refers to whether the same phenomenon can be guaranteed to reappear under different circumstances. A related feature of personality tests is their reliability⊙—that is, the degree to which they can be relied on to give the same results under repeated use. Test-retest reliability,⊙ as it is called, is surely a basic feature of a useful test. If the test were lacking in this feature, it would be like a ruler that changed its length under every variation in temperature or humidity: We could not trust its results because we could not rely on the instrument.

Equally important is the test characteristic known as *validity*—that is, the extent to which it does, in fact, test what it is supposed to test. A ruler on which someone had changed the lettering (but not the units) from "inches" to "centimeters" (assuming that the user could not detect the error by inspection) might be completely reliable—always giving precisely the same measurement. But it would be quite invalid in that it would not be measuring what its labeling says it measures (Figure 13.3).

Validity is trickier to achieve than reliability in constructing a test, largely because there are a number of independent ways that it can be done. When students do a class project that involves making up a questionnaire, they usually depend on what is called *face validity.*⊙ They choose the items in their questionnaire because, on the face of it, the items look like they will produce the information that is wanted. This is a perfectly legitimate approach for many types of questionnaires, especially if the material is uncomplicated and there is no reason to suspect that people cannot or will not answer truthfully. In a typical project, for example, some students wanted to test the hypothesis that skiers who preferred downhill skiing were more gregarious and extraverted than those who preferred cross-country skiing. Their questions, which had face validity, were therefore of

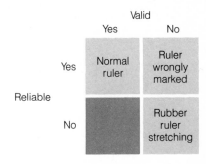

Fig. 13.3. The relations between reliability and validity. Notice that if the measuring instrument is not reliable it makes no sense to ask whether it is valid.

reliability. How dependably a test measures what it is supposed to measure.

test-retest reliability. A method of checking the reliability of a test by readministering it a second time, or by the use of a formula that approximates a second administering.

face validity. A form of validity based on appearance or on association with the job to be performed.

the following type: "Do you prefer to have one close friend or a lot of casual friends? Do you consider yourself more extraverted or more intraverted?"

This may be a satisfactory approach in making up a questionnaire, but it turns out to be flawed as a basis for a personality test. First, the personality characteristics we may want to test for are not usually so simple or elementary as the facts we want to obtain in a questionnaire. For example, anxiety is a more complex phenomenon, requiring more elaborate questioning, than is someone's preference for one activity over another. A second reason is even more difficult to deal with. It is that people do not usually answer completely or truthfully when they take a personality test. They may not be able to tell the whole truth. They may prefer to put themselves in a good light. They may not want to reveal their private worries or feelings or attitudes to a stranger. They may not understand themselves fully, even though their intentions are to be accurate and honest. And the most significant aspects of their personalities may in fact not even be at the level of conscious awareness.

To get around these difficulties while still making sure that their test will measure what it is supposed to measure, test constructors resort to some form of what is called *empirical validity*.$^{\odot}$ It is a method that is somewhat foreign to everyday thinking, and so it requires some explaining. The method consists of selecting test items, not because they seem valid (face validity) nor even because their validity is supported by a theory of personality, but simply because they do the job. They may therefore be *seemingly* irrelevant; that makes no difference. For example, if we discover that anxious males, and only anxious males, prefer brown shoes, we might include in our test for anxiety the item "What color shoes do you prefer to wear?" Although this example may appear to be extreme, it typifies the approach: Items are chosen for a test simply because they do in fact distinguish between categories of people, regardless of whether this fits with theory or even with common sense.

2. Raymond Cattell's approach, based on mathematical analysis, yields clusters or *surface traits*,$^{\odot}$ and factors or *source* traits.

Cattell begins with the observation that individuals are usually consistent, and therefore predictable, in how they appear to others. In fact, this is his straightforward definition, that your personality is simply what makes you predictable. But then, rather than intensively examine or analyze persons, he turns to the problem of personality in general. His question now becomes "What is the smallest number of general 'traits' that will adequately describe the personalities of most people?" Cattell's work has yielded two different categories of general traits.[9]

First, he has determined what characteristics of people are usually found together. This was done by listing every term in the English language by which someone's personality might be described and then by reducing this large number to a manageable amount by combining those with similar meanings. Between fifty and sixty such clusters resulted, which Cattell has called *surface traits*.$^{\odot}$ They are what people observe in each other, and they are the basis that people generally use to predict how others will act. Thus, what Cattell has done by means of this "cluster analysis" is to organize the perceptions that people have of each other's personalities.

empirical validity. Validity based on observation and/or measurement.

personality trait. A fairly constant and measurable characteristic of a personality that gives the person's acts his or her own "color."

surface trait. Cattell's term for a trait that can be observed directly at overt levels of behavior.

Table 13.1. The major underlying source traits of the personality, as isolated by Cattell's analysis. The four source traits labeled with *Q* numbers were obtained from people's self-ratings, using a method called the *Q-sort*.☉ It has been argued by some personality researchers that perhaps no more than six of these factors really have a sound basis in the data (Peterson, 1965). Cattell cautions that the names given in this list are meant to be no more than useful labels. In the present state of our knowledge, he says, we might better use numbers.

A: Outgoing *versus* reserved	K: Polished, cultured
B: Intelligent	L: Skeptical
C: Emotionally stable	M: Unconventional (in a self-absorbed way)
D: Actively impulsive	N: Calculating, socially adept
E: Dominant	O: Moody, guilt-ridden
F: Alert	Q_1: Radical *versus* conservative
G: Conscientious, responsible	Q_2: Self-sufficient
H: Self-confident, carefree	Q_3: Careful, controlled
I: Sensitive, introspective	Q_4: Physiologically irritable
J: Independent, nonconformist	

Second, Cattell has used sophisticated mathematical techniques to analyze the results of tests given to large groups of people. By means of these techniques he has isolated nineteen "unitary influences" that appear to underly the personalities that we observe in each other. These underlying influences he calls *source traits*.☉ They are listed in Table 13.1. Cattell has constructed a number of tests of personality, based on these source traits, and has used them in an extensive testing program on individuals as well as on groups in many different countries. He has also raised the possibility of using these tests to distinguish between hereditary and environmental influences in personality formation, because he claims that a source trait can be either hereditary or environmental in origin, but not both.[10]

3. National character is a social reality based on shared situations; it is a consistency that others perceive.

No one who has traveled to another country has failed to comment, at one time or another, on how different those "foreigners" are from one's own people. Some of us are even certain that we can identify citizens of specific other countries simply on the basis of how they walk, or eat, or wear clothes, or make love. Psychologists too have been attracted by the notion that different groups are identifiable simply because of where they live. The literature on what may be called *national character*☉ is quite large, and it has recently been spiced by the addition of studies based on situation theories of personality—because, if your bias as a personality theorist is toward the significance of the situation, you will be likely to emphasize large-scale situational influences, such as nation or culture or society, as well.[11]

Yet, in spite of this widespread interest in national character and the even more widespread conviction that it can be observed and described, the very concept remains fuzzy. Do large groups or societies really share a distinctive character?

source trait. Cattell's term for an underlying trait that determines visible bahavior.

Q-sort. Stephenson's term for the procedure he developed to measure self-concept. The test is unique in that the subject sorts cards into piles that range from "most" to "least" characteristic of the self.

national character. The general behavior characteristics, attitudes, and patterns found in a nation.

If they do, have we any way to describe it precisely and usefully? And would such descriptions be similar to the personality portraits we might make of single individuals (Figure 13.4)? In a review of the many descriptions of the national character of the Hindu people, Sinha[12] notes their similarity: The people as a group are repeatedly described with such terms as *passive, mild, dependent, conforming, subordinate to family and social sanctions, inner directed, indecisive,* and *emotionally insecure.* These are just the words that might be used to describe individuals in a society. Is the concept of national character, then, nothing but the concept of individual personality multiplied?

In an extensive review of theory and research on national character, appropriately commissioned by the International Social Science Council and UNESCO, Duijker and Frijda[13] list the major ways in which national character has been defined:

■ In its broadest sense, a national character consists of the personality structure, or the major personality characteristics, which are shared by the members of a

Fig. 13.4. National character is often displayed in style of clothes. What might be said about each of these "national characters" on the basis of their attire?

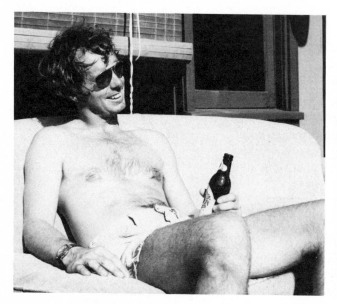

group.[14] For example, it appears that Freud's cultural group, in late nineteenth-century Vienna, shared a personality characterized by control over one's emotions, conscientiousness, hard work, and a denial of the body. The stereotypes© that many of us have about other groups constitute this kind of definition.

■ The attitudes, values, and personal beliefs that are held in common by most of the members of a group. For example, some groups or cultures, even some nations, may be extremely religious and others much less so.

■ In terms of a situational approach, national character may be defined in terms of the norms of behavior that are found in a group—such as the siesta found in tropical countries or the drinking patterns that differ from one country to another.

The concept of national character has an uncertain status in personality theory. There is not much consensus on what the concept means or even how it might be studied. Yet most observers seem to be certain that there is "something there" to be studied, a conclusion with which travelers would probably agree. National character is admittedly a social reality, but as yet it has not been tied to the reality that we call the *individual personality*.

We suggest that this problem can be resolved in part if we consider the phenomenon from an inside viewpoint—that is, from the stance of the individual. We have noted before that people are always in some situation. In any one country or culture, there is a strong likelihood that people will share many situations—such as a greater or less familiarity with automobiles, or a rigidly ordained and enforced distance between classes, or a great respect for anyone in uniform, or even a casualness of attire in public. The commonality of these situations, customs, and behaviors is what the observer sees. This in turn is what the observer "pins" on the individual person and then labels as an indication of national character. This helps us to understand, too, why we have difficulty perceiving the reality of our own national character—because such commonalities are not observable targets, to be seen in others, but the basis and background to everything that we ourselves do.

A national character may be made up of many elements. Do typical driving habits differ enough from one country to another so that the nation can be identified in this manner? One journalist has argued that a country's style of architecture may fit its language. The public buildings of Soviet society, he says, in some instances perfectly match the language: St. Basil's Cathedral, ornate and logical yet baffling, could well be "a monument to the Russian verb"—Tucker, 1976.

The person-centered approach

A person-centered approach to understanding personality is close to our own commonsense, "naive" notions about others. It says simply that each person carries inside some characteristics that remain more or less constant and ready to be expressed, so to speak, on the appropriate occasion. Some explanation for the constancy has to be offered in order for this view to become a theory of personality.[15] For example, in Sheldon's theory, which we discussed in Chapter 11, constancy of the personality is explained on the basis of consistency of one's body type. With S. S. Stevens, Sheldon undertook to compare body type and personality in a large sample of college students.[16] Because their statistical procedures have been criticized by other writers, their conclusions must be considered suggestive rather than well established. The endomorphic or "fat" type of body, they stated, is associated with a personality that is inclined to immediate, sensory pleasures and appetitive satisfactions. The mesomorphic or "muscular" body type is associated with an active, outgoing, achieving personality type. And the ectomorphic or "lean" type of body is associated with a personality devoted to less social and more cerebral interests. A great deal of everyday wisdom supports this formulation, that people are organized in bodily ways that reveal their personalities. This may be because the two aspects, the bodily and the characterological, are different expressions of a single psychobiological unity.

stereotype. A preconceived belief, usually biased, concerning a certain individual, group, or nationality.

Fig. 13.5. Freud in his aspiring youth, at the peak of his career, and in his old age. Is any consistency of character apparent?

free association. A technique used in psychoanalysis, in which a patient says whatever comes to mind.

4. Freud's great life work led to our only comprehensive theory of personality, centered on two conceptions: psychosexual development and the unconscious.

Freud's career. Sigmund Freud's life span is the best single indicator of his influence on our modern world. He was born in 1856, three years before Darwin published *On the Origin of Species* (which introduced the theory of evolution to the Western world), and lived until 1939, two years after Hitler invaded Austria. His life thus spanned the entire Victorian era and the beginning of our modern world (Figure 13.5). His work was very largely responsible for the vast changes in attitude and behavior that mark our current period. It was said of him, when he died, that he was no longer simply a man but an entire climate of opinion.

Freud began his work as a physician and experimenter who specialized in neurology. He shifted to using hypnosis with neurotic patients, with whom he developed a method of free association$^\circ$ and then a theory of mental functioning to explain his findings. He was our first "shrink": In a real sense, he invented the profession of psychotherapy and devised most of its original techniques (see Chapter 17). In the course of his forty years of active practice and writing, he revived the dream as an object of scientific interest. He built a worldwide organization and profession of psychoanalysis that is still flourishing. He made the topic of sexuality, particularly sexuality in childhood, both respectable and theoretically significant. And he constructed, over the years and with many changes, our only comprehensive theory of the human personality. In the course of this work, he wrote a total of twenty-three brilliantly composed volumes of case studies, psychological theory, art criticism, anthropology, personality and child development, and social philosophy.[17]

In every sense, Freud was a great man—in his originality and genius, in his dedication, in the breadth of his vision, in his influence on modern life, and certainly in his great moral courage. It is not possible to present a brief summary of his work or his ideas that does them justice, but it may be possible here to at least mention his major contributions: the key concepts in his theory and the personality "types" that derive from Freudian theory. In general, his contributions consisted of (1) a set of interrelated concepts that add up to a picture of the psychological functioning of both normal and abnormal persons; (2) a collection of practices that constitute a method of psychotherapy; and (3) a philosophy that aims to help us understand all human history and all its cultural manifestations, from religion to drama, from social organizations to the causes of war.

Freud's personality theory. It may not be accurate to say that Freud had a theory of the human personality, if by the term *theory* we mean what is meant in the physical sciences: a logically interlinked set of terms and propositions derived by a formal system from a limited number of basic axioms. Perhaps a better description would be, as one psychoanalyst has written, that his work is "a collection of miscellaneous ideas, insights, and intuitions"[18] gained from his clinical experience, his thinking, his exploration of himself, and the scientific and cultural atmosphere of his times. Together, these ideas and insights have entered our language and even our everyday thinking. As a result, most of us today would find it difficult to talk about personalities without using such terms as *ego, unconscious, defense mechanisms,* or *Freudian slip.*

Unconscious. This term is the chief pillar of Freud's theory. However, it is often misunderstood in two different ways. First, many people think of the term as referring to a "place" like a compartment in the head or in the brain. Freud did not mean this. For him, the term *unconscious* was an adjective, not a noun. It meant a quality that most of our personal experiences have; they are unconscious ideas or images or memories rather than conscious ones. A second common misunderstanding concerns how such experiences get this quality of being unconscious rather than conscious. It occurs by a process that Freud called *repression*.○ This is not the same as suppression; it does not refer to a process of "pushing" something out of consciousness. Rather, the mechanism of repression itself operates unconsciously. Given the kind of personality that each of us has, the mechanism operates automatically and unthinkingly on selected kinds of material. We do not know it is happening, and so we do not usually have any conscious control over its occurrence.

Some of what is unconscious may at times take on conscious qualities. This occurs in four ways. First, our conscious mental activities may be tricked, so to speak, by the use of various *defense mechanisms*,○ as they are called. This enables some material to take on conscious qualities without arousing anxiety in us as a conscious warning signal. The major defense mechanisms are listed in Table 13.2. Second, our conscious state of consciousness may be altered, as in sleep or under the influence of hypnosis or drugs, thus allowing unconscious material to be expressed. Third, unconscious material may appear in disguised form; for example, as a joke that we make, as a neurotic symptom, as an artistic production, or as a slip of the tongue. Fourth, under extreme circumstances we may suffer a temporary or extended alteration of our personality during which unconscious forces erupt, as in an outburst of uncontrolled emotion or in a schizophrenic episode.

Agencies. There are three major agencies, or functioning elements, of the personality in Freud's theory. The first is the id,○ a reservoir of instinctual (biological) energy, sexual and aggressive in character, providing the source of power for the personality to function. The second is the superego,○ an unconscious element that is incorporated into the personality in childhood on the basis of orders and restrictions from our parents. Because it is unconscious, each of us experiences it in the form of a controlling inner voice, perhaps even a harsh one, that says no. Because it was received from our parents, it serves as a major carrier of tradition between generations. The third agency is the ego,○ an "executive" agency that is largely unconscious but partly conscious. Its major purpose is to mediate among "three masters," as Freud called them: the id, the superego, and the demands of the world. These three agencies work together along the lines of a steam engine—that grand model of nineteenth-century science and progress (Figure 13.6). A boiler, the id, produces energy that seeks outlets. They are controlled by the ego as well as the valves, which represent one's defense mechanisms. Meanwhile, high above and beyond reach sits the ancient engineer, one's superego.

Development. As we discussed in Chapter 10, Freud saw childhood development as proceeding through a sequence of psychosexual stages.○ This name comes from the fact that stages of *psychol*ogical development are determined by one's *sexual* energy and where in the body it is centered. One's particular adult personality is determined by which stage had captured the greatest amount of energy during the course of one's development. The stages, and the consequences of each for personality organization, are as follows.

To start, in the first year of life, the *oral* stage centers around the mouth. Prolonged emphasis or difficulty here would result in a predominantly oral character, which is marked by grasping or sucking tendencies, swings from optimism to pessimism rather than by mature realism of outlook, childish wishfulness of thinking, and identification with rather than relationships with other persons.

repression. The basic defense mechanism, in which one excludes material from conscious awareness.

defense mechanism. Freud's term for unconscious processes that defend an individual against anxiety. The pattern of one's typical defense mechanisms determines the makeup of one's personality.

id. In Freud's theory of personality, the reservoir of impulses that seek immediate gratification of primitive needs.

superego. In Freud's theory of personality, the unconscious part that acts as a "super" conscience, expressing the ideals the person learned as a child.

ego. In Freud's theory of personality, the part that is rational, "executive," and interacts with the external world. It is also the individual's conscious concept of self.

psychosexual stage. Freud's term for a stage of growth and development that is characterized by investment in a zone of pleasurable stimulation.

Table 13.2. The Freudian defense mechanisms.

The two basic mechanisms, in the sense that the functioning of the personality depends on them, are

> *Repression.* Normally the personality operates so as to assign whatever is experienced an unconscious quality; this operation is called *repression.* Some experiences may then take on conscious qualities, either immediately or at a later time. Some experiences may remain repressed, often for one's entire life.
>
> *Projection.*☉ This is the basic mechanism in interacting with other persons. Different impulses and thoughts are constantly arising in each of us that we do not want to accept as belonging to ourselves. We then "assign" them to another person, projecting them and thus finding in others what we are afraid we will find in ourselves. The very young child who says of a playmate whom he or she has just hit, "He hit *me,*" is demonstrating projection at its earliest level. A more advanced form is shown in this example: On days when you feel particularly grouchy, you may well find that other people look mean.

Two primitive defense mechanisms, in the sense that they point to a lack of development in the personality, are

> *Regression.*☉ Under stress, one will behave at an earlier psychosexual level than one does normally — for example, becoming helplessly ill at a time of personal crisis.
>
> *Denial.*☉ Either perceptually or cognitively, refusing to experience what is there to be experienced: to hear no evil, see no evil, and hence speak no evil.

The other major defense mechanisms are

> *Identification.*☉ In its special meaning within Freud's theory, this refers to acting in terms of the characteristics of another person, usually as mediated through the superego.
>
> *Intellectualization-Isolation.*☉ Every thought normally has an emotional component, derived from the impulses of one's instinctual life. In isolation, the rational and emotional components are kept apart. In intellectualization, the rational part is expressed in a detached way, with the emotional part cut off.
>
> *Rationalization.*☉ In place of what one really wants to say or do (with its freely expressed wish), one provides a seemingly rational explanation or excuse. The most familiar form is "sour grapes," which is a way of saying "I never did want them" as an acceptable substitute for saying "I'm very disappointed that I didn't get them."
>
> *Reaction Formation.*☉ Changing an unacceptable impulse (and its expression) to its more acceptable opposite is called *reaction formation.* Often this is accompanied by an exaggeration. Thus, when Lady Macbeth used this defense, a perceptive observer could say, "Methinks the lady doth protest too much" — meaning that she exaggerated her protest and also that the protest was probably masking its opposite.
>
> *Sublimation.*☉ This term refers to displacing instinctual energy from one object to another that is more acceptable. Freudian analysts might say that if someone's impulse is to peer at sexually desired but forbidden objects, sublimation would lead to a career in photography in which peering is accomplished but with more acceptable objects seen in the lens.

projection. A defense mechanism in which one keeps material from awareness by ascribing one's own undesirable qualities to others.

regression. A return to infantile or primitive behavior when confronted by insecurity or frustration. With insecurity, there is usually a return to behavior experienced when younger. When a person is frustrated, the regression may be expressed in acting childish.

denial. The basic defense mechanism in which an individual refuses to accept or think about a threatening external situation. One simply denies reality.

identification (in Freudian theory). A defense mechanism that involves taking on the characteristics of an admired person.

intellectualization (also isolation). A defense mechanism in which one detaches oneself from an emotionally threatening situation by handling it in abstract or intellectual terms.

rationalization. A defense mechanism in which one tries to justify oneself by giving socially acceptable reasons for otherwise unacceptable behavior.

reaction formation. The mechanism of concealing a motive from oneself so well that one expresses its opposite.

sublimation. A defense mechanism in which a socially accepted activity is substituted for an unacceptable motive or behavior.

Next, in the second year of life, the *anal* stage develops, when toilet training and the learning of organized obedience, order and cleanliness occur. Difficulties at this stage might result in an adult character with problems concerning self-control of socialized impulses, tendencies to excessive orderliness, stinginess, or obstinacy, and rigidity and compulsiveness in the face of opposition rather than reasoned or

Fig. 13.6. The Freudian model of the personality.

socialized independence. Three, the *phallic* stage in the third year (for males) is marked by a preoccupation and immature identification with the father's prowess and potency. This may lead in adulthood to a childish preoccupation with an image of machismo, bravado, and hollow potency, like an eternally swaggering little boy. Four, the *latency* period that allows the male child's resolution of the *oedipal conflict* with his father over his mother. This is a period of suppressed impulses and of socialization through the agency of school, culminating in, five, the start of the period of adult *genitality* in early adolescence.

Adult character "types" have their origins in oral, anal, and phallic conflict resolution, for the male. The case is much less clearly spelled out for the female and the evidence much less clear, particularly in regard to a possible "oedipal" conflict with the mother over the father. In any case, in this theory one's adult personality is the result of specific ways that were found to handle sexual energy through the biologically fixed stages of early childhood development.

If we were to ask, "In Freud's theory, what makes for consistency of personality?" the answer would have to be that these key features are never clearly spelled out. The best that we can say, perhaps, is that each individual develops a personal reservoir of memories, thoughts, and images with unconscious qualities. This store of psychic content, unique to each person, can be expressed only through the "channels" that were selected in the course of one's psychosexual development. By comparison, we may briefly consider another psychoanalytic theory of the personality, that of Carl Gustav Jung.

5. Jung's picture of the organization of the personality is more elaborate than Freud's and more closely tied to myth and symbolism.

Originally Freud's major disciple, Jung broke away for theoretical and personal reasons and went on to a productive lifetime of clinical and scholarly work. He lived until 1961 and during the last two decades of his life became increasingly more influential with younger persons whose interest was in mysticism, symbolism, and the spiritual. Jung's writings were as voluminous as those of Freud, but of

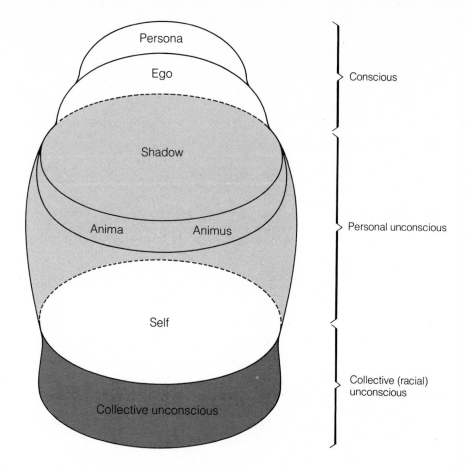

Fig. 13.7. Jung's conception of archetypes of the personality.

collective unconscious. Jung's concept of the universal unconscious that is the "pool" from which all people draw.

archetype. According to Jung, an inborn predisposition to function in a certain way toward the environment. The predispositions are drawn from a universal unconscious and are represented by such ideas as God, Earth Mother, and so on.

animus. Jung's term for the masculine attributes of a woman's personality.

an entirely different temper. Rather than elaborate a social philosophy or the details of a psychological account of the personality, as Freud did, Jung turned toward those common elements, to be sought through history and through culture, of myth and symbol and what he called *archetypal modes of thought*. In support of this, he tracked down material in thousands of dreams, in legends, in art of all cultures, in religious symbols—in short, in all the universal wellsprings of human thought and feeling. His view of the individual personality can only be understood against this background of interest in the universal.[19]

Personality structure. The structure of the personality, for Jung, is made up of aspects that belong to the human race collectively, plus other aspects that belong to the individual (Figure 13.7). They are, first, the collective unconscious,⊙ that inherited source of energy and images and symbols, given to all of us at birth, as part of our biological inheritance. Second, within the collective unconscious are tendencies to form certain universal images or symbols or themes of thought. We experience these consciously as archetypes,⊙ images or symbols that recur repeatedly in legends and myths, such as the Hero, or the Great Mother.

In addition to these structures that we share with all other humans, there are individual structures of the personality, some within the (personal) unconscious and some conscious. The third, the major unconscious structure, is the self, which is that personal totality by which each of us organizes conscious and unconscious into a working whole. Fourth, there develops through childhood in each of us a pair of unconscious structures: in the female, the animus,⊙ constituting her nonconscious self-image that is "male" and does not correspond to her conscious self as female; in the male, the anima,⊙ the disowned "female" aspects that do not fit his self-portrait as a male. Fifth is the structure closely corresponding to the Freudian personal unconscious, called here the *shadow*.⊙ Sixth, and finally, there are two structures that belong to the conscious part of the personality, the ego, or the organizer, and the persona,⊙ the conscious social mask that we present to others.

It is clear that this is a complex and impressively broad-ranging view of how the personality is constituted. It goes far beyond the work of Freud in its inclusion of influences from biology, psychology, culture, and history, although it puts much less emphasis on developmental aspects, except in regard to the growth of the animus or anima and the two conscious structures, ego and persona. Jung's scheme is much more future oriented than Freud's, much more emphatic in its statement that one is always growing and changing, and much less tied to the tragedies and traumas of one's past.

Personality functioning. Quite separate from the structures of the personality are Jung's conceptions of certain personality functions, or the way that the individual acts. Because each person tends to emphasize some of these functions in a consistent way and to deemphasize others, Jung's theory of personality functioning may properly be called a *typology*.⊙ A basic functional distinction is between intraversion⊙ and extraversion,⊙ terms that are familiar to most of us because they have become part of our everyday language. They refer to general tendencies to turn our energy either inward or outward. For Jung, people differ in how they grasp things or gather information about the world, either by way of *sensation* (concrete, practical experiencing) or by way of *intuition* (grasping possibilities in a global way). People also differ in how they judge or decide, either by *thinking* (the use of cognitive processes) or by *feeling* (the use of emotion-laden value judgments).

The four possible combinations of grasping and judging—sensing and feeling, sensing and thinking, intuition and thinking, and intuition and feeling—constitute four major types of personality. But in every individual there is some balance of emphasis on the various kinds of functioning, so that many more than four types are possible. In all, it is a remarkably rich and fruitful conceptualization of personality functioning, so rich indeed that it provides no simple answers to our question concerning consistency and organization.

6. Biological factors in personality provide a basis for continuity. Cognitive factors leading to free choice suggest, rather, a discontinuity.

Person-centered theories such as those of Freud and Jung stress development, but we should note that the mere fact of development does not guarantee either the organization or the consistency of a personality. There is some evidence for both continuity and discontinuity.

In an elaborate longitudinal study of middle-class children in Kansas, Escalona and Heider[20] found that the children differed measurably in activity level from birth and that this distinction became the basis for consistent differences in later years. Some children "engage" the world, others "withdraw" from the world, not necessarily to an extreme degree, but sufficiently so that individual differences in personality are apparent. More recently, Thomas, Chess, and Birch[21] reported on a fourteen-year study of children in New York City, with similar findings.

anima. Jung's term for the feminine characteristics of a man's personality.

shadow. Jung's term for the "animal" behavior in humans, corresponding to an "individual" unconscious.

persona. Jung's term for the mask of social conformity each person wears.

typology. A viewpoint that individuals tend to fit into biosocial categories. Kraepelin was the first to classify according to physiological types.

intraversion. The psychological type Jung classified as inward and withdrawn.

extraversion. The psychological type Jung typified as being outgoing and socially oriented.

Not everyone agrees that assessing the personality is to be encouraged. Here is a portion of a letter written, during World War II, by Winston Churchill concerning supervision of psychologists and psychiatrists:

"I am sure it would be sensible to restrict as much as possible the work of these gentlemen, who are capable of doing an immense amount of harm with what may very easily degenerate into charlatanry. The tightest hand should be kept over them, and they should not be allowed to quarter themselves in large numbers upon the Fighting Services at the public expense. There are no doubt easily recognizable cases which may benefit from treatment of this kind, but it is very wrong to disturb large numbers of healthy, normal men and women by asking the kind of odd questions in which the psychiatrists specialize. There are quite enough hangers-on and camp followers already."—Churchill, 1950

existentialism. A philosophy that holds that individuals have the freedom to make important decisions and are responsible for their own lives.

functional autonomy. The theory that motives sometimes become independent of their origins and that the original intent is forgotten or put aside.

projective test. A technique used in the measurement of personality characteristics in which the subject is presented with a neutral or ambiguous stimulus and then asked to describe it or tell a story about it.

Beginning at birth, children seem to differ on a dimension of inward-outward, similar to what Jung emphasized as extraversion-intraversion.

The Freudian view of development puts a heavy emphasis on biological determinants and places much less stress on the critical events of one's later years. Therefore it assigns the greatest importance to the very earliest period of life. One Freudian analyst, Bruno Bettelheim,[22] who has done remarkable work with disturbed children as director of the Orthogenic School in Chicago, has gone so far as to say that programs such as Head Start are really a waste of time. His argument is that, according to Freudian theory, the major (and presumably irreversible) aspects of one's character are already established by the age of three, which is the point at which Head Start programs attempt to intervene.

Allport's view. A contrasting view may be found in the work of an American personality theorist, Gordon Allport.[23] He was greatly influenced by modern European thinkers associated with the philosophy known as *existentialism*⊙ and was concerned with working out a theory that allowed the individual a maximum of freedom and change in the development of a personal life and character. Allport was fond of pointing out that what may have been a perfectly sound and understandable motive in early life might disappear and its place taken by quite a different motive in later years. He referred to the emergence of such new determiners as functional autonomy.⊙ He gave as a typical example the case of the boy who in early years became a sailor as a means of escape from his parents' home and influence but who remained a sailor because, as the years went by, the escape motive disappeared and he grew to love the sea for its own sake. Thus, a rebellious personality of early years might be replaced by an accepting personality of later years, a developmental sequence that could not be explained in terms of continuity.

Allport viewed the life span as influenced primarily by biological factors in the early years and by factors associated with cognitive and rational elements in the later years. Similarly, Carl Jung saw the life span as divided about in the middle, approximately at age forty, when one's extraverted emphasis as a youth changes over to one's more intraverted personality as a mature person. One becomes reflective rather than active, and spiritual interests begin to take over from social and intellectual ones. In this kind of view, discontinuity plays as important a role in development as continuity.

Assessing the personality

Assuming at least some organization and consistency of the personality, how might one test for it? In a person-centered approach, the sources of consistency will be sought in each individual, usually by means of some test (hopefully, one that overcomes people's normal inclinations to cover up or dissemble when they feel they are being probed). Two major approaches have been used for such assessment.

Projective tests. The ideal test of an individual's personality, it would seem, is one in which people display the full range of their (often hidden or even unconscious) personality characteristics without knowing that they are doing so. The perfect instrument might then be one that has subjects leave the testing session unaware that they had furnished what amounted to an X ray of their personalities. They would have, so to speak, projected their "psychological insides" out into the outer world for a skilled examiner to see.

It is this metaphor that provides the basis for the group of personality tests that are called *projective*.⊙ They consist of procedures that on the surface seem to bear no relation to characteristics of personality, that are not given or taken as tests

Doctor RORSCHACH,
I'm ready for
my TEST.

Fig. 13.8

in the usual sense but that are more like activities that the tester may observe and then interpret. The key element here is that these procedures are not tests that are scored but activities that are interpreted. Thus, they do not usually have formal scoring systems but, rather, elaborate interpretive systems. As a consequence, they can only be used effectively by a trained and skilled professional, in contrast to the typical objective test, which may be administered and scored by a technician or clerk, or even by machine.

The grandfather of all projective tests (Figure 13.8) is the well-known inkblot test called, after its inventor, the *Rorschach*.[24] It was developed by a brilliant Swiss psychiatrist, Hermann Rorschach, who was one of the bright lights of early psychoanalytic thought in Europe before he died in 1922 at the age of thirty-eight. In this test, the person is simply asked to look at each of ten inkblots in turn and to tell what they "look like" or "seem like." The request is so unstructured, the task so wide open, the procedure so little connected with testing of personality, that people respond in ways that can be interpreted, by a skilled examiner, as a wide-ranging and deeply probing personality picture.

Some aspects of the interpretation are scorable, in the sense that subjects can be compared on one or another aspect; for example, the percentage of one's responses that include a reference to the color of the blot. But usually skilled interpretation is emphasized in using the Rorschach. The test is found most often in clinical settings, such as clinics and mental hospitals, where it may be used to help in arriving at diagnoses, or psychotherapists' offices, where it may be used to help pinpoint problems that need to be worked on. Like many other clinical procedures, such as interviews or even psychotherapy, the argument as to whether the results achieved are accurate or useful is still unsettled.

Here we present a number of examples to indicate the way an examiner may make use of projective test material.

Rorschach test. A projective test, commonly known as the "inkblot" test, in which symmetrical inkblots are shown and the subject is asked to interpret them.

- To a card that resembles a batlike creature, the person (P) responds by saying, after an unusually long pause, "Well, might be a butterfly." The examiner (E) waits for the person to continue and finally says, "And anything else that you see?" P: "Well, that's about all I could see." (This is much less than people normally respond to this card.) E waits for more material and is about to take the card away when the person adds, "Could be—oh, a flying fish, or some . . . [Pause] Could be a kite, I guess." E waits again and then asks, "And anything else?" P: "That's it."

- To another card, which resembles a looming human figure with large feet, a different person says, "Ah—He's got huge feet, and he's standing facing anteriorly—facing, or rather—well, bending over backward so his head is at a level lower than his feet. His pants are ragged, his shoes are worn. He has the head of a monster—sort of a caterpillarlike head or dragonlike head. . . . And there's some interesting effects of shade and light here, that form a picture within themselves—just the light and dark shades. Light and dark shades—the face of a man. Probably a god, or the features of a god—a long Hebrew nose, hollowed cheeks, a masklike face, and the long hair of the ancient Hebrews. His eyes are absent. They're much more powerful than they would be otherwise."

We hardly need much more material to tell us that here are two quite different approaches to the task. One is minimal, the other almost maximal. The first person's responses might suggest hypotheses concerning low intelligence, lack of energy, depression, even an inability to perceive things in an orderly and organized way. The responses of the second person, on the other hand, suggest someone who may be more intelligent, more verbally skilled, perhaps artistically gifted, energetic and active, attentive to details, but perhaps also fearful or the prey to his or her own imaginings. In giving and interpreting a test such as the Rorschach, the examiner develops these statements as hypotheses and then continually checks them throughout the examination, discarding, replacing, and improving them until some coherent portrait of the test subject's personality emerges. As with all clinical skills, such interpretation is more art than science. It can be learned, usually by practice in the presence of a guide and model, but it cannot be taught in the ordinary sense.

Objective tests. For large-scale testing, for purposes of research, and for relatively inexpensive and rapid screening of people, tests are needed that offer neither the advantages nor the disadvantages of projective tests. The latter may, in the hands of skilled examiners, provide in-depth interpretation of an individual personality. By the same token, however, they are time consuming and require the services of trained professionals. Objective tests supply much more limited or even more superficial information, but they are inexpensive and efficient. An entire field of test construction, embracing statistical techniques as well as personality theory, and closely tied to its sister field of intelligence testing, has been developed as a basis for such objective testing of personality.

The most widely used of all objective tests of personality, the Minnesota Multiphasic Personality Inventory (MMPI),⊙ gets its name from its place of origin, its aim of tapping many different aspects of the personality, and its overall purpose.[25] The complete test consists of about 550 questions that people answer about themselves—as to whether the item is true of them, or not true of them, or if they cannot say. The test is then scored so as to produce fourteen different subscores, or scales.

Minnesota Multiphasic Personality Inventory (MMPI). The most widely used, objective, paper-and-pencil personality questionnaire.

- Three of the scales are designed to provide information about the person's test performance itself—for example, whether this person can be trusted to be telling the truth in responding.

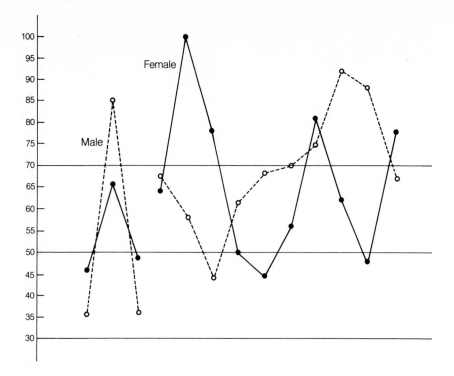

Fig. 13.9. Two MMPI profiles, one of a young man who may be psychotic and the other of a middle-aged woman who is suffering from depression.

- One scale assesses a person's degree of involvement with other persons, in terms of the familiar intravert-extravert dimension.
- One scale assesses a person's standing in regard to masculinity and femininity.
- Four scales refer to mild to moderately severe personality problems, often called *neurotic* difficulties (see Chapter 15). These scales are meant to detect such problems as an overconcern with one's own bodily state, various bodily complaints, and certain kinds of nonconformity or antisocial attitudes.
- The last four scales refer to serious personality problems, usually called *psychotic* difficulties (see Chapter 16).

The separate scores are usually displayed for convenience in the form of a profile, as in Figure 13.9, from which a trained examiner can read off whatever information is desired. Although it may seem that the separate scales are weighted toward a concern with mental illness, the MMPI is widely and successfully used in schools and in industry to provide personality profiles of the "normal" population.

One of the most useful features of a test such as the MMPI, and one of the major reasons for its wide applicability as a research instrument, is that subsets of the total pool of items may be pulled out to form separate scales and then used as tests in their own right. Some 200 such scales have already been reported in the literature—each of which has, of course, had to be separately validated.

A concluding word on consistency

The problem of consistency of personality, which we have said is central to this topic, may not have been completely resolved in our discussions of either person-centered or situational approaches. We now want to conclude this chapter by briefly considering consistency from the inside viewpoint.

Consistency appears in two major ways: either as a consistency of my own ongoing experience; or as a consistency that I may observe in other persons. The first, we suggest, is basic to the second.

Fig. 13.10. We usually ask for consistency of both persons and the "frames" within which they act. In our dreams, we are willing to give up the consistency or stability of the frame. Perception of instability in both persons and their frames may occur only in states of confusion, psychosis, or delirium.

My own ongoing experience is made up of both novelty and familiarity. To be more precise, in my experiencing I seek both novelty and familiarity. A personal world that was forever novel and changing, with no anchors at all in what was familiar, could not persist for me more than a brief time. It would very soon lead to unbearable excitement, confusion, and finally exhaustion. This is probably one of the ways that some persons experience a state of loss of control. Yet a personal world with no novelty at all, and no expectation of novelty, a world of unending sameness, would very soon cease to be experienced as familiar. It would soon be felt as monotonous, then deadening, and finally hopeless. It might not be experienced as loss of control but rather as a state in which control has been given up to some overwhelming influence (Figure 13.10).

It is to avoid these two untenable extremes that we all keep working to achieve some balance between the new and the familiar. In order to keep things consistent, so as to have the continuing experience of familiarity, I usually select what is known, or perceive things in accordance with what I have learned and dealt with before, or treat what is relatively new as though it were relatively old. This is part of my continuing, individual process of organizing my unique world of meanings.

As a consequence, the ongoing processes that I know as my own experience are, for me, more or less equated with consistency. To experience is, in major part, to experience the familiar; I could not easily have it otherwise. And, similarly, I tend to experience other persons in a consistent and familiar way. I could not easily handle their continuing novelty, and so I tend to understand them in ways that are familiar to me. In sum, experiencing means consistency, just as it also means novelty. The most "natural" thing in the world for me is to be familiar to myself and for other persons to grow to be familiar to me. This may be why one of the common early signs of that radical disorganization of experience that we call "going crazy" consists of seeing one's own familiar face in the mirror, or the face of a friend or relative, as somehow changed and unfamiliar.

This consistency of experience is basic to all our observations of other people.

When I look at other persons, I "naturally" perceive them in ways based on my own consistency. In addition, I experience some of this same process as it operates in them, which tends to support my own sense of the familiar in our interactions. And, finally, whenever social situations do in fact repeat for myself and for others, the experience of consistency is thereby deepened. If you were to ask me, then, I would say with great confidence that the world of people is indeed a stable place — but unless I were a theorist of the human personality I might not be able to tell you why this is so.

Summary

1. Many general statements about people's personalities are applicable to most persons and would be accepted by them as applicable to themselves.

2. The differences in people's response patterns may be a result of different situations; their similarities may be a result of the situation repeating itself.

3. Situational theorists would attribute the consistencies we find in others more to characteristics of our own judgments than to characteristics in those we judge.

4. Situational theorists of personality do not appear to have succeeded completely in eliminating the notion of the person or in explaining consistency of personality entirely in situational terms.

5. Cattell's approach to personality theory rests on mathematical techniques that yield surface traits and source traits. His methods enable him to make comparisons between groups, across cultures, and between generations.

6. People appear to be organized in bodily terms, in structure as well as function, so that aspects of their personalities are expressed.

7. National character appears to be a social reality perceptible by most persons; it may be defined in terms of personality characteristics, values and beliefs, or norms of behavior.

8. Freud's theory of the personality stressed internal mechanisms related to the alternatives of conscious and unconscious; defense mechanisms; and results of development through the oral, anal, phallic, and latency periods of psychosexual development. Personality consistency is explained in this theory in terms of one's personal reservoir of (unconscious) memories and images.

9. Freud's major disciple, Jung, proposed a theory of personality that also included the structures and forces related to the collective unconscious of the human species.

10. Biologically oriented personality theories such as Freud's tend to stress the consistency and continuity of personality. Theories that are more "cognitive," such as that of Allport, stress the element of free choice and therefore imply discontinuity and personality change.

11. Projective and objective tests, two methods for assessing the personality, differ in that projective procedures result in clinical documents that need not be scored and must be interpreted, whereas objective procedures result in test scores and profiles that provide information that is more limited but easier to obtain.

12. The major projective test is the Rorschach, or inkblot, test; the most widely used objective test (aside from the instruments devised by Cattell) is the Minnesota Multiphasic Personality Inventory (MMPI).

13. A major advantage of the MMPI is that subsets of the pool of items may be pulled out to form separate scales that can be used as tests in their own right.

14. Persons seek both novelty and familiarity in their lives; and the latter can be an important source of personality consistency.

Can age-related changes be predicted solely on the basis of knowing a person's chronological age? We will discover in the course of this chapter that not very much can be predicted with confidence. You will learn in this chapter that prediction is most accurate in regard to factors removed from personal experience but decreases in accuracy as one focuses more on areas close to personal experience.

In this chapter, you will also learn about what are called *stages of life* and about some theories that attempt to define them. Some of the problems and methods involved in studying the life span will be elaborated. A number of extensive life span studies will be presented to demonstrate the problems.

In discussing theories of the aging process, it will be shown that specific bodily decrements, particularly in the senses, can be charted but that cognitive changes are less easily measurable, because they depend as much on attentional and motivational factors as on decline associated with aging. Personality changes with age will be reviewed, particularly in reference to changes occurring in late maturity. Finally, cultural and social influences on the facts of aging will be documented, in particular the impact of new standards for retirement and for leisure. You will see that much of what has been called *aging* is a sociocultural phenomenon that differs widely among societies.

A couple who are in their thirties live in a town where there are two night clubs, one catering to people in their twenties and one to people who are over forty. Because they are between the two groups in age, our couple have gone to both night clubs. Here are some differences they have observed.

	In the "twenties" club	In the "forties" club
Conversation	Nonverbal, between sexes	Verbal, between people of the same sex
Atmosphere	Competitive, vigilant, serious	At ease, joking, laughing
Mood of patrons	Hungry, searching, sexually unsatisfied	Stimulated, sexually satisfied but bored with it
Auditory foreground	Music	Conversation
Movement, communication	Table to table, communication between groups	Communication within groups

Thinking about these differences on the way home one night, one of our couples says suddenly, "Listen, let's not go back to that 'forties' night club again. It makes me feel uncomfortable." To the question of why, this person says, "I don't want to be like that—and the place reminds me that I *will* be like that."

This is the kind of question that we will be discussing in this chapter: Is it inevitable that someone who is now about thirty years old will in ten years be like most forty-year-old persons? And, if so, does this mean that we can predict what

14

The life span: changes in personal history

By the time you are Real, most of your hair has been loved off, and your eyes drop out, and you get loose in the joints and very shabby. But these things don't matter at all, because once you are Real you can't be ugly, except to people who don't understand. — Williams, n.d., p. 4

people will be like if we know only their age (Figure 14.1)? Our thesis in this chapter will be that prediction is possible, but not for all people. In addition, we will indicate that experience is predictable, but only from the inside.

The stages of life

Although the psychological study of children has a long and rich history, the psychology of adulthood and aging is quite recent. Developmental theories—those of Freud and of Piaget are the best known—stop at early adolescence. As a result, "theories" based on folklore or on literary imagination have had as much influence as psychological theories in establishing popular notions about the later stages of life.

How much of the change from one stage to another is fixed in advance for the individual, and how much is open to chance, to the individual's uniqueness, or to free will? Freud's theory was explicit in its emphasis on determinism based on biological principles. Erikson's theory, which derives from Freud's, postulates equally fixed stages. A distinctively different view is expressed by Joseph Campbell in discussing mythological tales of the course of life: "Maturity, like all coming to oneself, requires a break with what has been inherited."[1]

1. In Erikson's psychoanalytic view, development through life consists in mastering eight sequential "crises."

Fig. 14.1. Which is the reality of old age, which is our stereotype, and which is our fantasy?

Erik H. Erikson began his career as an educator in art and then came under the influence of Sigmund Freud's daughter Anna. After personal training in psychoanalysis and in the Montessori method of children's education, he came to the United States in the early 1930s. Here he began a fruitful career as a child analyst, social theorist, biographer, and student of native American culture. Although his theory of life span development is clearly indebted to the thinking of Freud, it differs in two important respects. First, it is a theory of the entire life span, not just that portion up to adolescence. Second, it is less biologically based and places more emphasis on social influences on development.[2]

Erikson sees the development of a healthy personality as the consequence of meeting and weathering certain predictable "crises"—although this term does not refer to extraordinary emergencies but only to life's important way stations, marked by "normal stresses and strains." At each stage, life dictates that a crisis is experienced. It can be resolved, with the result that a new and positive component is added to the growing personality, or it is not resolved and a less healthy component is added. However, there is no guarantee that a crisis once surmounted will be put behind one forever. One may achieve a resolution and then lose it, or else the same crisis may appear again and again. Crises do not appear out of nowhere and disappear forever, but are always present in some form in the personality itself. Their overt appearance is experienced by the person as a "critical alternative" between a more or less positive resolution. The successive stages, expressed in terms of the identifying crisis at each point, are as follows:

Crisis 1: Basic trust vs. basic mistrust. In the first year of life, when the constant flow of goodies from the mother begins to slow down, the infant must "choose" between an enduring conviction that the world is a safe, just, nourishing place (basic trust)° and a suspicion that the world is not to be completely depended on (basic mistrust). This is the most fundamental of developmental crises, the one that can provide, if it is surmounted, a lifetime "bodily conviction" that in the end things will be all right.

Crisis 2: Autonomy vs. shame and doubt. During the period of toilet training in the second year, in the course of the battle between holding on and letting go, between self-control and overcontrol of self and others, the child may achieve a sense of dignity and personal independence. Erikson calls this *autonomy*. If not achieved, the alternative is a burden of shame and self-doubt relating to personal independence.

Crisis 3: Initiative vs. guilt. In the preschool years, as capacities for moving around, for talking, and for thinking develop, the growing child faces a new crisis: between an "unbroken initiative," based on self-activation and energy, and a powerful sense of guilt, often sexual in content, about competitive, ambitious, independent strivings.

Crisis 4: Industry vs. inferiority. In that new "world all by itself" called *schooling,* the child may achieve a "sense of industry"—the ability to make and do things, to be effective in the social world of adults. This is preliminary to assuming "a constructive role in a healthy society." If not, this period of development will result only in feelings of inadequacy or inferiority.

Crisis 5: Identity vs. identity diffusion and role confusion. We now come to the end of childhood and to the adolescent years, in which everything comes to be questioned. The issue now is whether the individual will integrate previous identifications with adults into a personal identity. By this term *identity,* which has come to be associated with his thought, Erikson means a sense of oneself that constitutes an integrated adjustment to appropriate social roles. If it is not achieved, there is a danger of identity diffusion or perhaps the start of a lifelong search for instant identities. If the crisis is surmounted successfully, a path is cleared toward adult concerns with marriage and an occupation.

basic trust. Erikson's first stage of psychosocial development in which the child, during the first year of life, learns to trust or mistrust the environment.

Crisis 6: Intimacy vs. isolation and self-absorption. Erikson sees sexuality in young adulthood as an appropriate fusion of two forms of intimacy, sharing and distancing. One's developed identity is now used in order to establish a basis for intimacy with others, with failure laying the basis for two forms of interpersonal difficulty—formal and stereotyped relations, or a continuing search for intimacy.

Crisis 7: Generativity vs. stagnation. The concern now is with parenthood or, in a larger sense, with that social or civic concern that expresses a guiding interest in coming generations. Achievement leads to productive ties in the present, coupled with ties to both past and future; failure leads to stagnation in an impoverished personality.

Crisis 8: Integrity vs. despair. In the middle to late years of adulthood, a sense of human integrity can arise out of accepting fully what one has become: "If we will only learn to let live, the plan for growth is all there."[3] A sense of personal fulfillment is one alternative, a despairing sense of failure and an unconscious fear of death is the other.

These are Erikson's life stages (see Figure 14.2) and crises, based not on laboratory research, but on a kind of anthropological field research among different groups—native Americans, his clients in psychotherapy, and historical figures.[4]

Objections to Erikson's scheme. Attractive as it may seem, Erikson's developmental scheme has come under fire from a number of critics.

- Psychoanalysts have complained that Erikson strays too far from an orthodox position. Nonpsychoanalysts, in turn, complain that his views are nothing but disguised psychoanalytic theory.
- The central notion of crisis may have some value in pointing to the tensions of living, but it still overemphasizes the pathological and the negative aspects of growth.
- The stages are too few and too broad, and the nicely organized sequence may not apply to all persons. Some evidence indicates that women are as likely to meet and resolve Crisis 6, on intimacy, before Crisis 5, on identity, as the reverse,[5] and that creative persons can resolve the crisis of generativity without ever resolving the crisis of intimacy.
- Like most thinkers influenced by psychoanalysis, Erikson has some difficulty in seeing the lives of women in terms of forces belonging to women and not simply derivative of forces belonging to men.
- Little is known about the effect of cultural pressures on the length or importance of these stages—but it is probable that the effect is considerable.
- Erikson speaks of change, but he has no theory of how change occurs.
- Erikson assumes that a crisis once resolved usually fades into insignificance.

Fig. 14.2

However, the course of life may well offer and reoffer very similar life crises.

- Children may not be as influenced or determined as the scheme calls for. They may, for example, bounce back from earlier failure or find delayed success at a later time.
- In general, it may be that "crisis" theory is most applicable to extreme cases — for example, to those unique historical figures whom Erikson has studied, such as Luther or Gandhi, or to deviant individuals who are likely to be met in clinical practice.

Studying the life span: Methods and problems

2. The three major methods for study of life span changes are longitudinal, cross-sectional, and cross-sequential.

There are problems to be faced in every branch of study, derived partly from the topic and partly from the methods and people available for study. The study of changes related to the life span presents some special problems of its own. There is, for example, the general problem of variability — that is, the fact that groups of people at any age level may be so individually unique that no general conclusions can be drawn about them as a group. In addition, studies in which older persons are studied may face the general problem that researchers and the people who work for them tend to be young, middle class, verbally and academically skilled, and science oriented. When they meet older, less educated, nonverbal people who have often not had contact for many years with testing situations, the encounter may consist of two groups of strangers trying to find a common language for communication. And there is also the problem that tests that are used in life span research were often developed and standardized on younger persons who may have very little in common with those who are being tested.

The longitudinal approach. When life span research began in the 1920s, the method that seemed most appropriate was simply to choose a convenient group of people and then to arrange to follow them, through repeated testing, for the rest of their lives. The approach was called *longitudinal,*° for obvious reasons. All of the major early studies in this field were of this type, including the project conceived by Terman for the study of intelligence (Chapter 11) and the Berkeley-Oakland study, which we will review below.

The longitudinal approach has many advantages:

- A longitudinal study enables one to study crises and turning points in their naturally occurring sequences, as they happen, and in detail.
- People are not compared to some average, which may not exist, but to themselves as they change.
- The experimenter can choose whether or when to study long and short periods of time or to study trends that are transient as compared with those that persist.
- All the data that one obtains are collected on the spot, so that there will be few errors caused by faulty memory.
- One can develop hypotheses at any stage of the study and then test them out at later stages.
- Because of their long-term connection, researcher and participant can get to know each other well, which does not usually happen in short-term studies.

longitudinal study. A research method in the study of development in which a person's behavior is observed over a long period of time.

- Most important, the sum of the data on an individual provides a rich, almost biographical account of a life unfolding and developing through time.

However, as experience has been gained with the longitudinal approach, its disadvantages are evident.[6]

- As the same people are seen, and tested repeatedly, they may become familiar enough with the tests to improve with practice. According to one estimate in regard to the Berkeley-Oakland study, this may have added as much as ten points to the tested IQ of some persons over the years.
- Information is inevitably lost, as offices are moved, fires occur, or files are misplaced.
- The staff changes, and new staff may bring with them new ideas or theories, perhaps new methods or even different ways of using older methods.
- If subjects are lost, there is no way of knowing — and accounting for — how they would have changed the results if they had remained.
- Procedures are always changing, in any field of study — new tests, new and usually better ways of handling data, and often new concepts and theories.
- Social changes, usually unpredictable (for example, wars or depressions), may change the lives of the people in ways unrelated to the aims of the project.

In short, everything connected with a large-scale study will change with time, and there may be no way to separate out these effects from those caused by the "normal" process of aging. Nor will the researchers who embark on such a project have any guarantee that they will themselves live to see its culmination.

The cross-sectional approach. A much simpler, easier, and less expensive way of studying age-related changes in people was also developed during the earliest years of this field. Called *cross-sectional*,[○] it consists of selecting a number of different groups, each group being of a different age, and then testing them all at the same time. The comparisons that can then be drawn will, presumably, be a measure of how age is related to the variable being tested. For example, if one is interested in whether tested intelligence declines with age, one simply tests a group of ten-year-olds, a group of twenty-year-olds, and so on, and then compares the group results (Table 14.1).

Because the method is so easy, particularly by comparison with a longitudinal approach, many early studies were cross-sectional. The conclusions that these studies offered were in agreement in one important respect — that marked and even dramatic declines occurred in most human capacities as a consequence of getting older. The curve of the growth of intelligence showed this capacity increasing steadily until the age of fifteen or so, then leveling off, and at about the age of thirty beginning a slow but steady decline into the senility of old age.

Then the first returns began to come in from longitudinal studies, which had been proceeding while the cross-sectional results were being accumulated. What the longitudinal results now revealed was just the opposite — that most important capacities did not decline with age; in fact, many showed an increase. It was a dramatic discrepancy, which had a sobering effect on research in aging. Researchers were now forced to look very critically at their approaches and methods — with what turned out to be beneficial effects. Out of this examination came a clear understanding of an unsuspected factor. We now turn to a discussion of this element.

The cohort[○] problem. Let us suppose that we want to do a study to answer the question, "Does age affect a tennis player's ability?" If we tried to answer this question by means of a cross-sectional approach, we would select, say, 50 tennis players at each of a number of age levels — 50 players aged twenty, 50 aged thirty,

cross-sectional study. A research method in the study of continuity of behavior in which behavior characteristics are sampled at different ages.

cohort. In developmental studies, a group whose members are similar in some measurable way.

Table 14.1. An arrangement for either longitudinal, cross-sectional, or cross-sequential study of age-related changes. There are five groups of testees, as shown in the column at the left. They are tested on the dates shown. The groups tested on a testing date are indicated by small circles (○). The connecting lines and arrows are identified as the different kinds of studies. For example, if the group born in 1955 is tested every five years from 1960 (when they are five years old) to 1980 (when they are twenty-five years old), the result would be a longitudinal study.

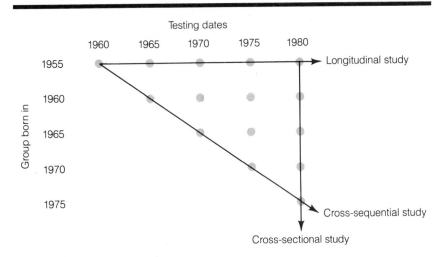

and so on—and have them all engage in a big tournament. If our players in each age group were representative of their age levels, the final standings in our tournament would tell us whether age is related to tennis-playing ability. Probably most of us would predict that age would in fact be related, and that the final results would indicate that tennis-playing ability declines markedly with age.

However, there is a characteristic of our cross-sectional groups that has not been mentioned. Take the group of sixty-year-old players as an example. If they learned to play tennis when they were twenty years old, in 1936, the game that they learned was very much different than the game that is played and taught today. A good player of 1936, like a good college football player of that time, was rather small (by contemporary standards) and fast and depended on a repertoire of tricky shots rather than on power. First-rank players of today are appreciably bigger and stronger, and theirs is much more a game of power. (The difference is also evident in other sports, such as football and basketball.)

If someone became a first-rank player shortly after 1936, the level of ability that was attained might well be preserved for some time—so that a longitudinal assessment would indicate very little decline in ability. But if that 1936 player continued playing the same way and was now compared with a 1976 player, the difference would not simply be in age but in strength and style as well. There would be no way to separate out the effects of age from the effects of change in style and strength. The term that is used to describe the group to which someone belongs is *cohort*. Our cross-sectional groups of people are, by definition, age cohorts—but they are also tennis-style cohorts.

Most things change with time, not only styles of tennis playing (Figure 14.3). For example, attitudes toward such matters as sex surely change with time. Thus, the average thirty-year-old of today has different sexual attitudes than did the average thirty-year-old of a generation ago. If they are both tested today, when one is aged thirty and the other is aged sixty, and if we find a marked difference in attitudes toward sex, are we entitled to conclude that age alone has brought about the difference? We are not, because, while they belong to two different age cohorts,

Fig. 14.3. The persons who put ads like this in a newspaper differ from their parents not only in age. They also belong to different attitude cohorts.

they also belong to two different sex-attitude cohorts. People of different ages differ in many other respects than age; they differ in all the ways that change with time, which includes just about everything that we might be interested in studying. The cohort effect, then, is unavoidable and will always produce a difference between results from longitudinal and from cross-sectional approaches.

One proposed approach, the cross-sequential,⊙ would take advantage of the best in the other methods while avoiding the cohort effect. Developed by Schaie,[7] it involves an elaborate (and often expensive) arrangement such as is shown in Table 14.1. With this arrangement, we might, for example, run a conventional longitudinal study, as shown, following the group that was born in 1955. Or we might do a conventional cross-sectional study, with all the testing done in 1980. Finally, we might do a cross-sequential study. Here the people would always be fifteen years old at the time of testing, but, because they have been born at different times, the cohort effects caused by this drop out.

Whatever method is used in such studies, it appears that the issues we have raised really refer to two different kinds of developmentally based psychologies. They have, in fact, been identified as a *developmental* psychology and a *differential* psychology. A differential psychology is aimed at finding out the ways that people show stable personality characteristics, so it uses cross-sectional methods to compare individuals and groups. This has been the history of the testing movement, particularly intelligence tests—which are built on the premise that intelligence is a stable characteristic of the person.[8]

In the method of developmental psychology, on the other hand, the emphasis is on the ways that people change, so the longitudinal approach is preferred. This has been the method of choice in the field of personality, where it is assumed that important characteristics change and grow with time.

The Berkeley-Oakland study

3. Results on the Berkeley-Oakland sample of white persons studied for almost fifty years indicate a stability and resilience not predicted by any theory.

The earliest longitudinal studies were based on repeated measures of IQ, because this was the only instrument available that was standardized and could be used on people of any age. Soon thereafter, other measures were introduced, making possible full-scale studies of growth. One of the first of these, covering a very wide range of developmental factors, was begun in 1928 in Berkeley, California, under the direction of Nancy Bayley, to study growth and changes in intelligence. One year later, a second study was undertaken at Berkeley, this one under the direction of Jean MacFarlane, to follow the personality and social development of 248 normal infants. And in 1932 a parallel growth study was begun in Oakland, a neighboring city, under Harold Jones. The results for the three were gradually merged into one comprehensive study that is still continuing, with its participants now into middle age.

Predictions. One value of such longitudinal studies is that they give us a chance to test out our predictive measures, so as to answer the question: "Knowing what people are like at one age, can we predict what they will be like in that respect at a later age?" Answers to this question vary according to what is being measured. Physical measurements can be predicted quite well. Scores on intelligence and

cross-sequential study. A method in developmental research that combines features of both longitudinal and cross-sectional methods.

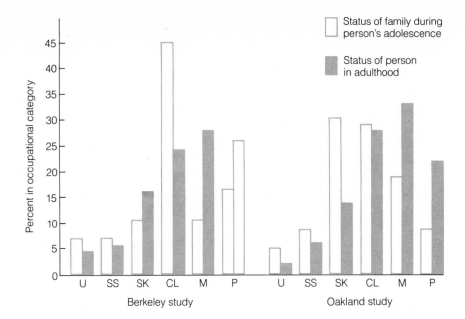

Fig. 14.4. How occupational status changes between adolescence and adulthood. U = unskilled worker; M = managerial; P = professional. (Data from J. Block, 1971)

ability are a little less predictable. Scores on personality measures are still worse; and predictions based on measures of social adjustment are just about useless. To state the conclusions in a different way, we may say that in the average individual the course of growth is stable, and therefore, predictable, for some characteristics but not for others.

The data in the Berkeley-Oakland study show that most persons are capable of great variation in the course of growing up and of weathering difficulties and developmental crises that might seem to an outsider to be extreme. Mary Cover Jones, who was associated with the Berkeley studies almost from their beginning, notes that at least half of the people turned out to be more stable in personality than had been predicted.[9] The error in predicting had come about because investigators had mistaken transitory crises for serious problems.

The most predictable aspect of these people's lives, aside from some physical characteristics, was simply that they maintained their status as a cross section of the American white middle class as they grew up. They settled into jobs and professions, married, sometimes divorced, and had an average number of children. Perhaps because American society as a whole was stable during these years, their lives were also. However, one continuing and therefore finally predictable change was found to occur, as we can see in Figure 14.4. A person's socioeconomic status, as indicated by a comparison of the kind of job held by father and then by child, improved in the years between adolescence and adulthood. Thus, in the Oakland sample, only 10 percent of the people as adolescents lived in families in which the father belonged to the professional class, but 22 percent of them became professionals themselves in adulthood.

In regard to characteristics of personality, and contrary to what Erikson would have predicted, these people did not seem to pass through well-defined stages of growth. Rather, those who in childhood fell into one personality grouping, such as being closely tied to their families' values, did not change much nor go through marked crises. Those who came from less harmonious or less stable families or who showed some opposition to their families' values at an early age might themselves change in the course of evident crises. Studies of older persons[10] have usually indicated the same: Persons who achieve some stability of personality in the early years (as do many persons from conservative, stable homes) are not likely to alter as they get older.

Theories of aging

4. Theories, required for predicting age-related changes, have been either of the general "wear-and-tear" type or releated to specific systems.

There is very little good information on decline during the middle years, from about thirty-five to about sixty—on whether it occurs at all, or in what way. Earlier evidence based on cross-sectional studies must now be viewed with caution. Some theories have been proposed, but they are based largely on observations made of persons who are already in the later stages of serious decline. The only generalizations that seem appropriate are (1) that all living creatures seem to have a more or less fixed life span that is species specific and (2) that, within this span, the individuals within a species age and decline at about the same rate.[11]

"Wear-and-tear" theories. The most general statement that can be made about aging is that it is a process of "slowing down." Birren refers to "a basic change in the speed with which the central nervous system processes information."[12] With increasing age, there thus appears a "generalized brown-out in behavior." Some recent evidence in support of this view comes from studies of heart disease in what is called the "Type A" personality—that is, the kind of person who is constantly pressing and straining in the race of life.[13] Such persons often show a significant slowing of reaction time—just as though they needed more time to process perceptual information,[14] suggesting that as they build toward a heart attack they are engaged in a kind of premature aging.

A related theory has been offered by Hans Selye[15] as part of his continuing investigation of the way that living organisms handle stress. He suggests that the mechanism that normally regulates response to stress becomes less efficient with age, perhaps because it can respond effectively just so many times. As the individual becomes less able to cope with stress, the breakdown process begins to snowball, ending in death. Related to this view is another, which states that every organism accumulates certain internal "waste products" of metabolism and that these pile up to a point at which they interfere with effective self-regulation of bodily functions.

"Body system" theories. Other theories of aging select one phenomenon or system of the body and attribute the aging process to its failure. For example, it has been noted that the body's individual cells have a limit on the number of times (approximately fifty) that they can multiply. As the years pass, an increasing number of cells will stop multiplying. The organs in which they are located will then slow down or cease functioning, and the person will die. A related theory has it that each cell of the body is "programmed" to function only so many times in whatever it does, and as this program runs out the various parts of the body will slow down. Still another version points out that the body normally accumulates "errors" within its cells, caused by random mutations in reproduction or perhaps to cosmic radiation or even to the effects of atmospheric pollution. As the effects of these errors build up, normal bodily processes will slow down or even reverse, thus leading to death.

Specific systems in the body are also implicated in the aging process. For example, some chemical substances in the hypothalamus are known to increase with age, leading perhaps to progressive interference with the transmission of nerve impulses. The body's elaborate system by which it maintains an immunity against foreign substances (which is why a patient's body may reject a heart transplant from another body) is known to alter with age. The aging process, then, might consist of an increasing difficulty in rejecting foreign substances, coupled with an increasing tendency to "reject" the body's own tissue—the latter being what seems to occur in such age-related diseases as arthritis.

The body in aging

5. After the normal growth spurt of adolescence, the body reaches a physical peak and then declines in regard to sensory, respiratory, circulatory, and muscular functioning.

Individuals show great differences in the level of their capacities as they age. In addition, many individuals vary within themselves, so to speak. One person may have the complexion of a fifty-year-old and the kidney functioning of someone who is eighty. Toscanini, the great orchestral conductor who was musically active until his death in his nineties, had the physical appearance of a very elderly man but the motor skills, the stamina, and even the auditory acuity of a man of forty.

Varieties of deficit. Changes related to the use of the senses have been the most widely studied of all age-related changes in the body. They may begin even before adolescence: The lens of the eye shows some signs of hardening in many persons even at the age of ten. However, for most persons, the years of adolescence and young adulthood represent a peak of sensory efficiency. Beginning at about the age of thirty in some persons, but in others not before advanced middle age, the sensory apparatus shows specific deficits. Peripheral vision becomes less efficient, and the individual also becomes increasingly less able to change focus from near to far, and vice versa, with ease. Hence the common need for bifocals. There is a drop in the ability to hear higher frequencies. Because such frequencies form a major component of human speech, the older person may complain that people are "mumbling." It is significant that this loss is far more common among the elderly than a lessened ability to hear sounds as such. Older persons do not suffer from a "lowered volume" but from a selective deficit. Therefore it is usually more helpful to them if the speaker enunciates clearly than if the speaker talks loudly.

Other changes related to sensory functioning are less common. There is a lessened ability to maintain balance as one ages, especially when looking down, hence the person's tendency to fall. This is coupled with a decreased ability to recover from injuries to the bones, often referred to as "fragility" of the bones. The evidence in regard to taste, touch, smell, and sensitivity to pain is not very clear and is probably greatly subject to individual differences of experience and motivation as well.

These findings are so familiar that they are often taken for granted. However, in a study that was specifically directed at the performance of older persons who were both highly trained and extremely motivated, quite different results were obtained. Among airline pilots aged forty to forty-nine,[16] a slight decline in sensory acuity was noted, but there was no particular decline in performance. The author of the study suggests that the skills involved were very much overlearned. The pilots may also have had unsuspected reserve capacity, and their performances may have depended not only on sensory functioning but also on the factors of motivation, experience, and the cognitive processing of information.

A warrior bard in ninth-century Wales expressed these universal feelings as he felt himself facing his inevitable decline:

> Before I was decrepit, I was splendid;
> My spear was foremost, was first in attack.
> Now I am hunched over, I am weary, I am wretched . . .
> The four things I have always hated most
> Have converged on me at the same time:
> A cough and old age, disease and grief . . .
> Maidens do not love me, no one visits me, I can't get about.
> O death! that it does not come to me.
> — Ford, 1974, pp. 77, 81

The effects of disease. In the early 1960s, an intensive study of the aging process in forty-seven healthy, elderly men was begun by the U.S. Department of Health, Education, and Welfare. In a follow-up study some eleven years later, it was found that about half of the men, originally aged sixty-five to ninety-one, had died in the interim — and it is this finding that is of interest to us here.[17]

Among the original forty-seven men, twenty had been discovered to have a chronic medical condition, although still in mild enough form that they would be classified as healthy. However, of these twenty men, fourteen (or 70 percent) had died, whereas only ten (or 37 percent) of the nondiseased persons had died. In addition, those with chronic disease had performed worse on every test used except reaction time, where age alone seemed to be a factor. The results suggest that disease may be a major if unrecognized factor in aging. There are four important diseases that affect a significant number of older persons — hardening of the arteries, high blood pressure, and the various forms of arthritis and cancer. All are similar in their slow and often hidden onset, their probable multiple causation, and in their long-term effects in the form of chronic disability. It has therefore been suggested that they are not so much distinct diseases as conditions associated with the process of aging. In any case, these diseases and a number of others are so common among elderly persons that in a large sample it may be difficult to find more than a few cases of "true" aging independent of any disease.

Changes other than those in sensory functioning are also critical in the aging process. The most important of these concern related functions of the respiratory, circulatory, and muscular systems, which together furnish and use oxygen as a fuel for muscular activity. These interrelated systems show a very rapid spurt in capacity and efficiency during the years of adolescence. For example, blood pressure as well as lung capacity and muscle mass all increase at this time. The systems usually maintain their peak efficiency during the twenties and in many persons through the thirties. At this time, however, the bodily processes by which oxygen is supplied to the muscles begins to become less efficient, particularly in regard to its "bounce-back" capacity, or its ability to recover from stress (Figure 14.5).

The decrease in functioning, once begun, begins to accelerate as the individual reaches the sixties. It is often associated with what is called *high blood pressure*, a condition that is actually associated with thickening of arterial walls rather than with a marked change in the blood pressure itself. The consequence of these changes in functioning is lessened ability to do sustained physical work, changes in physical appearance, and in many persons the appearance of diseases such as chronic respiratory ailments, high blood pressure, and arthritis. Problems specifically related to brain and nervous system functioning, such as loss of memory or signs of senility, do not usually appear for another decade, when the individual is at or beyond the age of seventy.

The Duke study. In the first major and continuing interdisciplinary study of aging that was based on a thorough medical assessment, Duke University Medical School in 1955 embarked on a longitudinal survey of 256 volunteers who were originally between sixty and ninety-four years of age. A first report[18] was issued in 1970, based on medical, neurological, and psychological assessments, social history, and retirement data. It comprises an enormous mass of data that will require some years of careful study and from which it is not possible to draw any simply stated conclusions. However, even a cursory review of the findings shows that the major change that takes place with advancing age is in physical capacity but that this varies very much between individuals. A minority of the volunteers "actually showed improvements in physical functioning, in skin conditions, in blood vessels, and in increases in sexual activity."[19] An average decline was seen only in medical and neurological function but not in social and psychological aspects.

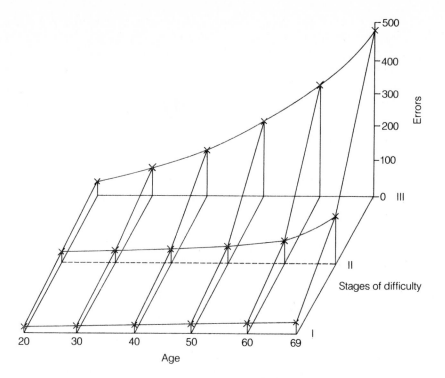

Fig. 14.5. A related kind of functional loss with age can be shown if people are set a task involving transposing from sight to touch and vice versa. This graph indicates that when the task is relatively simple (Stage I), older persons make no more errors than younger persons; but as the task is made progressively more difficult (Stages II and III), the age differential increases markedly. (From Welford, 1959, p. 600)

Contrary to expectation, there seemed little overall decrease in level of intellectual functioning, in willingness to take risks, or in memory (all of which are traditionally thought to be associated with the aging process), and little increase in feelings of loss or neglect.

These results were obtained on a local sample that consisted entirely of volunteers. Therefore the researchers are justifiably cautious in drawing general conclusions, preferring instead to consider their findings as hypotheses, summarized as follows:

■ Evident decrease in physical capacity can be found in half the people, but the other half show either no decrease or even some improvement.

■ Persons of lower socioeconomic status show a greater impairment in medical and neurological functioning. No sex differences are apparent.

■ Typical physical impairments that are found include difficulties with gait, tremors, skin disorders, circulatory problems, and some EEG abnormalities.

■ Normally, reaction time slows with age, but this seems to be related in part to practice and to people's lack of exercise.

■ Sexual activity continues in about half the men between seventy-two and seventy-seven, and among one quarter of the men over seventy-eight. Sexual activity and interest remain high among a surprisingly large percentage of the aged, although more so for men than for women.

Psychological changes in aging

6. Cognitive skills are so intermingled with factors of practice, motivation, test anxiety, and background that clear-cut conclusions cannot be drawn.

Dear Abby:

I need help. My husband is ninety-one, and for the last two years Arnold has had no desire for sex, and I am only seventy-three and I still need a man.

Arnold is a jealous person and he follows me everywhere so there is no chance of even meeting anyone else. Is there something the doctor can give him to pep him up a little? If that is hopeless, maybe the doctor can give me something to quiet me down. It is no good this way.

Young at Heart

Dear Young:

It might be easier to quiet your desire than to rekindle Arnold's. Ask your doctor.

Intelligence. Remarkably little sound data are available on intelligence test performance among the elderly. A comparison of people in the Duke study with those in another study in Kansas City revealed a curious difference: Persons in North Carolina did better on tests of verbal ability, and persons from Missouri did better on tests of numerical and spatial ability.[20] No national norms exist, even for a single country, that can be used as a standard for persons past sixty.

Only recently have careful longitudinal studies begun to dispel the myth of a universal decline in general intelligence. It is now recognized that motivational factors of all sorts play a major role in intelligence test results, especially so when the people in the study are elderly, out of practice, perhaps institutionalized, and certainly unfamiliar with contemporary testing procedures and results. (These factors all serve as cohort effects.) Only a few kinds of performance that are directly dependent on speed seem to show a clear-cut relation to the aging process, and this does not usually happen to a marked degree until about the age of sixty.

Cognitive and motor skills. Most tests of cognitive skills involve factors that are related to motivation or else to sensory functions, thereby making it difficult to assess cognitive functioning directly. As an example, many studies indicate that older people take longer to be conditioned by Pavlovian procedures; it is not known whether this is also true for operant conditioning. Why this should be so is not clear. There may be a change in learning ability with age, or perhaps in memory, or in attentional or motivational elements. In regard to memory, the picture is almost as mixed. Many tests appear to show a deficit in short-term memory in older persons, coupled with an excellent ability to retain events that are long past. However, when the process of remembering and recall is more carefully examined, it appears that the apparent deficit may really be a defect in attention or in initially grasping the material to be remembered. When older subjects are permitted to take in the material in their own way, short-term memory appears not to be affected by increasing age.

The various processes entering into the performance of a cognitive skill seem to overlap — memory, learning, attention, ability, motivation, anxiety, and fatigue, among others. Individuals may age differently in regard to each of these factors, so that it may finally be almost impossible to separate out their different effects. The example of automobile accidents is a case in point.

As the level of their insurance rates indicates, young drivers have the most accidents — although they are certainly the best equipped group in regard to skill, alertness, and speed of reaction. Older drivers, often poorly equipped as regards neuromuscular skills, have fewer accidents than one might expect. Some of the reasons are obvious: Younger drivers drive faster, take more chances, and get into situations that are intrinsically more dangerous. However, some older drivers who do not themselves get involved in accidents may play a role in causing them to happen to other people — as, for example, by driving so slowly as to make other drivers impatient.

Given this mixed situation, the complexity of the data is understandable. If one counts only the number of accidents per thousand persons in any age group, the rate decreases with age. This is in part caused by the fact that fewer persons in the older age groups do any driving. Yet, if one counts the number of accidents per thousand *drivers* in the various age groups, the rate remains about the same with increasing age. Finally, if one counts the number of accidents per thousand *miles* driven in each age group, then the rate increases with age. It is a matter, not of a general factor such as accident proneness, but of different driving circumstances.

Some generalizations. Some general conclusions emerging from many years of study are

- Even familiar tasks become difficult for older persons if they are rearranged in novel ways—as shown in the increasing difficulty that such persons have in driving tasks such as looking backward to back up or park.
- It appears to become increasingly difficult to "tune out" irrelevant information—which may help to explain why older persons wander off the subject.
- Older persons have much more trouble than younger with tasks that are externally paced. They do better when they can proceed at their own pace.
- With age, there seems to be increased caution, although the reason is not clear. It has been suggested that industry might take advantage of this characteristic by assigning such persons to inspection jobs on assembly lines.

In general, cognitive functioning seems to require increased attention, especially after one reaches the age of fifty. However, if performance levels do drop appreciably with age, the drop is most likely to be associated with a neurological, sensory, or physiological process that may be related to disease rather than to the aging process itself.[21]

---

7. Two established findings regarding the relation of age and personality are that people show consistency of personality and that people are more inwardly directed as they age.

Personality and time. For many persons, the period of being away from home at college is one of the most important influences on their personality. The effect may not be to alter basic personality patterns, but significant changes do occur that may set the stage for the adult personality. They include a greater openness to mutual relations at a mature level; an increased social competence, based in part on a more firmly established self-esteem; and a broadening of intellectual and cultural interests. Other changes are the tempering and stabilizing of moods, greater goal-directedness, a flexibility in self-control, more independence in thinking, increased trust in one's own impulses, and, often, more liberal modes of thought.[22]

In the years following college, a general turning inward is often observed. In some persons, this may appear in the form of increased rigidity and dogmatism, greater intolerance and conformity, and a heightened preoccupation with one's health.[23] In other persons, the inward turning is manifested as a lessened concern with one's uniqueness, coupled with a greater emphasis on links with one's family, with friends, even with society and humankind.[24] In either case, with increasing age most persons show less and less tendency to change their personalities, in the absence of extreme life crises, and so they appear to others as "set in their ways" (Figure 14.6).

These general changes over time, however, are usually the joint result of persons interacting with their situations. For example, as opportunities open up for women whose personalities make them "unfit" for traditional female roles, they find it easier to adopt styles of living that emphasize their independence. They will now be adapted to their circumstances, whereas in other times they might have been judged as neurotically incapable of mastering the crisis of aging. At any age, personality adjustment is a continuing and delicate balance between person and situation, as both keep changing. Thus, in the Duke study it was found that even the presence of certifiable neurotic symptoms did not enable the investigators to predict whether a person would be incapacitated or hospitalized. That depended on the presence and support of family and friends and, most important of all, on the person's relation to a work situation.

Figure 14.6 Many persons are able to "settle in" contentedly to the pleasures and limitations of old age.

The Kansas City study. During the 1950s, a major study was carried out in Kansas City on about 700 noninstitutionalized men and women who ranged in age from forty to ninety. On the basis of repeated interviews over a seven-year period, a number of basic personality "styles" were identified. These related to how well the individuals appeared to be adaptive, competent, mature, armored, or turned inward—all of these styles being joint products of person and situation.[25]

The most important single finding to emerge from this study was, in the words of the author of the report, that "the self becomes institutionalized with the passage of time." In some persons, this is seen as becoming more fixed, in others as behavior that is more predictable. Still others are observed to turn in on themselves, to come closer to discovering themselves, to accept themselves more for what they are, to become more consistent or more rigid. In every case, however, it is a matter of circumstances that come more and more to fit the person, as well as vice versa. Adaptive aging, at least as revealed in this study, appears to consist of an appropriate balance between turning inward and breaking out, between settling into old ways and acquiring new freedoms.

Age and social status

8. Age is defined in any society in terms of social standards and custom, socioeconomic status, and personal milestones.

There are no absolute definitions of different ages nor of what it means to be young or old. Older persons do not themselves offer such definitions, for until they are about seventy most persons consider themselves as adults or as middle-aged but not as old. It may be that this is why the elderly function so poorly as a power bloc, even though in numbers and purchasing power they are becoming increasingly important in both economic and political spheres. The age limit that was officially set for retirement, sixty-five, is somewhat arbitrary. It was originally selected, in the nineteenth century, by the German chancellor Bismarck as the point at which people were first eligible for social security.

Age grading. When Pierre Trudeau was elected prime minister of Canada at the age of forty-eight, many persons remarked, "How young to be a prime minister." Many of these were the same persons who, when he was married two years later at fifty, said, "Awfully old for a bridegroom, isn't he?"[26] We express this same attitude, of what is sometimes called *age grading,*⊙ when we admonish someone to "act their age"—insisting that the important phenomena of life are appropriate only to certain ages.

In modern industrialized societies, age grading usually involves a negative evaluation of the status of older persons, an attitude that is all too often shared by oldsters themselves. Specifically, students from the third-grade level to the college years share a negative view of their elders. When asked about themselves and their lives, persons up to the age of forty show a positive attitude, at which point their feelings about their later years become increasingly negative. In one study, people were asked to pick out the three age levels that they considered most important in life. At least two thirds of the persons in each age group up to thirty-nine picked a future year as one of the most important; but at age forty the percentage selecting a future year dropped to about one third—and no one older than forty-nine picked a future year.[27]

The economics of age status. It may well be that a defining characteristic of aging, at least in the United States, is a deteriorating economic status. The National Institute of Mental Health has estimated that of the 10 percent of the American population who are over sixty-five, a disproportionate number fare badly and receive minimal assistance. This 10 percent of the population comprises 24 percent of first admissions to mental hospitals and occupies 30 percent of the beds in mental hospitals, yet in outpatient clinics they receive only about 3 percent of the care.

This is not a temporary problem that is likely to go away. Rather, since our population is getting older, the problem is likely to get worse. By the year 2000, there will be more than 60 million persons in the United States who are over sixty-five, but only the first steps are being taken toward even a recognition of their status as an ignored minority. One of the more active and militant of national organizations working to improve conditions for the elderly, the Gray Panthers, has been occupied primarily with such everyday matters as banking facilities (because banks are hesitant to make loans to persons who may not live to repay them and because older persons are therefore often forced to carry cash and so become victims of mugging), the use of transportation (because very few city busses are equipped with facilities to aid persons who use canes or walkers), and health care (because house calls by physicians are almost nonexistent, yet older persons need continuing contact with professionals involved in preventive medicine).

For those older persons who are economically disadvantaged, life can become increasingly difficult as the general standard of living in society improves. If laws are changed to help them, the help often lags behind the fact of their poverty. More than 5 million elderly persons have incomes below the poverty level, and more than 16 million do not have sufficient income to qualify for paying income tax—a situation that is made worse as living costs go up with inflation and improved standards. From specialty foods to better automobiles, improvements in general living standards have an increasingly negative effect on older persons, because they are likely to be either retired or on Social Security or at a maximum salary for their work.

On working. Next to their physical well-being, the most important concern of men—and to an increasing degree, women—who have passed the age of thirty is their work and career. It is a concern that used to be called the *work ethic,*

age grading. The practice of defining persons or their acts entirely in reference to chronological age.

Figure 14.7 The "leisure ethic" may now be replacing the work ethic.

meaning the set of attitudes in which working is highly valued for its own sake. There is no verb in the English language exactly meaning "to leisure," quite probably because there has never been a need for it. According to the work ethic, it is good to work. Everyone ought to work rather than do nothing or, worse yet, be a drain on those who do work. People should strive to use their work to make something of themselves, for leisure, although it may be pleasant, is really wasteful and in any case is deserved only by those who have earned it.

It is a refrain that is familiar to all of us, either because we have grown up having to work or because we have grown up hearing our elders say it to us. But it may be changing—and, if so, there will be profound, even revolutionary repercussions in society. The work week is getting shorter in every industrialized country, and leisure-time activities are becoming increasingly the focus of most people's year-round concerns (Figure 14.7). In some European countries, whose social practices may be more advanced than those of the United States, the attitudes that once supported the work ethic may be disappearing. In Denmark, thousands of the unemployed collect about $470 a month each in unemployment compensation and, quite free of guilt, use the money to live inexpensively in vacation resorts in Spain.

Whatever one's attitudes about working, however, work remains a significant factor in the way that one adjusts to age-related changes. The kind of work that one does plays a major part in determining the socioeconomic status that directs one's activities and preferences and style of life. No other factor in life, apparently, is so important in determining health, illness, and personal satisfaction. It has been verified repeatedly that one's socioeconomic status is more significant than the factors of age, ethnic group, or even sex in determining whether one gets ill, how severe the illness will be, and how great the disability resulting from it—and the major determinant of socioeconomic status is the kind of work that one does. A systematic understanding of the life span will have to make as large a place for the factor of work as for the factor of age itself.

The retirement milestone. A comprehensive view of age-related changes in life will also have to take into account those event markers that have appropriately been called *milestones*.[28] Some milestones in life are enforced by the culture and are age specific; for example, the year that one starts school. Other milestones are as strongly influenced by the culture but are less age specific, such as getting married. And still others are unique to each person as regards their time of occurrence but certain to happen, such as the death of one's parents, or less certain to happen, such as getting divorced.

The most significant milestone in one's work life—and therefore in the lives of many persons—is retirement, at least in that majority of cases in which one has been at one place or job for most of a working career. Among men in the United States (but not among women), the retirement age has been steadily dropping. In 1900, at least two thirds of all working males were still working at age sixty-five. By 1960, the percentage had dropped to about one third, and by 1975 it was closer to one fifth. And as the number of early retirees has increased, so has the proportion of persons who have retired because they wanted to. There is an opposing trend, consisting of those who want to keep on working for as long as they can. But data show that in general people do want to retire, that they will do so as soon as they can, and that as a rule their health improves after they retire. The event is a major milestone, but, contrary to what is usually thought, it is not necessarily a crisis.[29]

9. Societies differ very much in the way they treat their aged members, the best treatment being found in societies that are neither too rich nor too poor.

Societies are known to deal differently with the fact that their members get older and die. When conditions are marginal in terms of survival, as in some Eskimo families, individuals will reach an age when they can no longer contribute and must be completely dependent on the others. Because living conditions do not allow for the luxury of a noncontributor, the Eskimo culture has ritualized the acceptance of a stark necessity: The old person says goodbye to the others and goes off alone to freeze to death on the ice. Among these people, death is called the Snow Walker.

Although not all societies have found the same solution to the problem of surplus members, the same basic principle seems to apply everywhere—that the way older persons are treated is a succinct expression of their value to society. Simmons[30] studied the operation of this principle by comparing seventy-one societies according to two criteria: their level of industrial development and available resources and the way they treated their aged members. He found that in the very poorest social groups, those in which there were no resources to spare, older people became surplus and so were either killed off or left to die. In the very wealthiest societies, where perhaps the interest in resources comes to outweigh the interest in people, old people who could no longer contribute to the accumulating of resources or who were not self-supporting were shunted off to institutions or ignored.

The net value of an older person in advanced societies often depends on the ties that they can maintain with families, friends, institutions, and organizations. In an extensive study of some 2,500 older persons in the United States, Denmark, and Great Britain,[31] it was found that their living arrangements were less restricted than might be thought. About 5 percent lived in institutions, about 10 percent were bedridden or otherwise unable to leave their homes, another 10 to 20 percent were somewhat restricted, but the remaining two thirds were unrestricted in their mobility. This largest group, still maintaining their chosen ties, were active, well adjusted, and quite different from the picture of lonely and neglected older persons.

These data seem to indicate that aging need not be synonymous with decline unless a society elects to make it so. Older persons, regardless of their age, prefer first to live alone and with some independence if they can, second to live with relatives, and third to live with strangers in an institution.[32] It is this last choice that becomes the greatest threat to the life of an older person, for it means that the last chance of keeping a tie with the rest of the world has been lost. Only persons who are already hopelessly out of touch with active life will give in to institutionalization without a struggle. For those who are not, the move itself is highly traumatic.

This helps to explain what seems a contradictory set of findings concerning the effects of institutionalization on the aged. It is usually found that institutions do not have a bad effect on those who live in them. The reason, as we can now see, is that institutions house either those who are already in bad shape or those whose entry was traumatic to them. Once these negative factors have been accounted for, the factor of residing in the institution has no additional negative effect. And, of course, as the inmate stays longer in an institution reentry to the community becomes progressively more difficult and risky. What communities need, then, is not more institutions where the death of its inmates can be hastened, but as one writer has put it, to "rebuild our communities in ways that permit greater contact between the generations."[33]

Changes in the life span

Two interwoven sets of possibilities exist in an individual's life. On the one hand, as we discussed in Chapter 13 on personality, consistent pressures from biological and social sources bend the individual back toward stability, resisting any influences for change. On the other hand, people do not remain the same. Not much is known about the sources of change, or how it comes about.

The late bloomers. If people were consistent in their growth patterns, we would find that those who show great talent in adult years would have given advance warning long before that. But this does not always happen; many people are late bloomers. A surprising number of individuals who achieved great fame or success as adults showed very little promise either as children or as adolescents. Leonard Bernstein, the composer and conductor, was uninterested in music and displayed little talent, but in early adolescence, for reasons that remain a mystery even to himself, he suddenly bloomed as a bright, articulate, and musically gifted person. Andre Gide, the novelist and critic, recalled in later years that he was quite an ordinary schoolchild, perhaps even well below the average. Darwin was, as a youth, a poor student who showed little promise. Gandhi was, until his early manhood, an undistinguished and unimpressive lawyer. Einstein showed very little intellectual brilliance until well into his twenties, and the same can be said of both Freud and Albert Schweitzer.

The list could be made much longer—but not to prove that no one ever shows promise nor that anyone who is dull in childhood is bound to change in the course of time. A list showing consistency from the earliest years could just as easily be composed. Rather, this list suggests simply that radical and unpredictable changes can and do occur at almost any point in life. If this happens, a new person is created, with a kind of second inheritance. We do not yet know, because we have not really been interested in studying, the way that these changes come about.

One possibility that may underlie such spurts in personal growth is diagrammed in Figure 14.8. Normally, or at least in terms of our conventional understanding, the growth curve is according to the solid line. But if the normally expected growth is delayed, as shown in the dotted line, and if the cause of the delay is then removed, we might see an unexpected spurt in growth.[34] An illness or even a tumor might be the cause of the delay. Equally, a suddenly favorable influence might cause the spurt: a favorable environmental situation, the effect of a special person, a change in diet, the removal of some stress, or a decision on the part of the individual.

A major difference between Freud's view of development and the views of Piaget or Erikson is that the latter do make some place for changes such as we have just discussed. In Piaget's scheme, in particular, growth from one stage to the next is not determined entirely by automatically occurring biological impulses. Rather, change occurs if an appropriately prepared and developed organism comes in contact with a setting or with information that the organism can use and learn from. Thus, changes that occur may or may not be consistent with patterns of previous growth and so may not always be predictable.

Aging and personal history

10. Major events of life now occur much earlier than in former years, with consequences for most aspects of living.

Since about 1900, major life events have been taking place at earlier and earlier ages. Marriage, the birth of children, the period that children spend at home, even retirement from work, have all been occurring at younger ages, with significant results in terms of the familiar stages of life. Being adolescent, being a young unmarried, being married and a parent, and finally being a grandparent, now occur earlier. As a result, more "free time" is left in the closing years of the life span.

This shift is not an isolated social change. Rather, it is part of a much broader movement toward an increase in one's years of personal freedom. As a consequence of important changes in attitudes and behavior, especially since World War II, this free period both begins earlier and ends later in life. For both sexes, self-responsible life begins earlier. The voting and drinking age drops, and credit cards and checkbooks are commonplace among teenagers. Sexual activity is countenanced at a younger age. Young people travel around the world on their own. They are self-consciously a major commercial market, and they may live alone, without parental restrictions. In addition, they also make increasingly more significant contributions at younger ages. The group of advisors immediately surrounding President Carter average less than thirty-five years, which is an age at which a century ago a young man would just have been seriously considering marriage. Adults at the age of sixteen, contemporary young people in many countries now begin their free periods at the earliest age in history.

The same change is occurring at the other end of the life span. People do not settle in to one job in which they grow old but preserve their options to retire, or to have tandem careers, or even to hold multiple jobs. Their good health lasts longer, and so they are free to travel, to indulge in sports, to a more advanced age. Older persons act younger—just as many younger persons act older. Reentry programs for older persons seeking new training or brushing up on old skills are a flourishing new sector of our educational systems. The free period of the life span is thus being extended at both ends, in many cases from sixteen to sixty-six or even seventy-six

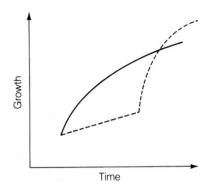

Figure 14.8 One possible mode of growth in the late bloomer.

Figure 14.9 The ultimate stage of personal "freedom."

(Figure 14.9). One of the major lessons gained from the initial Kinsey reports on sexuality is probably applicable in any area of living: The earlier one begins, the longer one is likely to last. The free period is now in many cases as long as sixty years.

We began this chapter with the general question of whether age-related changes can be predicted, in any sphere, solely on the basis of knowing the person's chronological age. The material that we have reviewed in these pages has suggested that not much can be predicted at all, particularly in regard to how the person will change. Prediction works best in regard to those aspects of growth that are the most removed from personal experience—for example, one's physical characteristics such as height or weight. The closer one gets to the realm of personal experience, the less is prediction possible (Figure 14.9). We suggest that this is because, as we said, experience itself is unpredictable—and as the free period of the life span increases both in extent and in quality, it may be difficult to construct a comprehensive theory of life span development. One step, however, has been taken: We now know what many of the important variables are.

Summary

1. Erikson's theory of life span changes is that a series of stages must be lived through, each in the form of a "crisis."

2. Three methods have been developed for studying life span changes: the longitudinal, the cross-sectional, and the cross-sequential, each with its specific advantages and disadvantages.

3. The term *cohort*, referring to a group with a common characteristic, is widely used in the study of age-related changes, because age groups are also cohort groups in many different ways.

4. Results from longitudinal studies indicate that predictions of changes in individuals are good for physical characteristics, less so for intellectual and other ability-related characteristics, and poor for measures of personality and social adjustment.

5. Results from cross-sectional studies will usually show larger age-related declines in capacity than will results from longitudinal studies on equivalent populations. The differences are caused by the effect of cohort characteristics.

6. There is relatively little trustworthy information on decline for the age period between thirty-five and sixty years.

7. Some results suggest that disease may be so important a factor in aging that we should not refer to aging itself but only to disease-linked changes.

8. Individual differences are not only important at any age level, but they tend to increase with advancing years, thus making prediction of an individual course still more difficult.

9. Major established findings on decrements with age indicate a decline in most areas of sensory functioning and a decreasing ability to bounce back from physical stress.

10. The major change in cognitive functioning with age is that it seems to demand greater attention, especially after the age of fifty.

11. As people age, their personalities appear to become more fixed as well as more inwardly directed.

12. Because of the wide variation between persons and because in each person the parts of the body may age at different rates, it is not possible to arrive at a precise definition of a specific age and its characteristics.

13. Socioeconomic status is more significant than chronological age, ethnic group, or gender in predicting the existence and severity of physical illness.

14. In general, and in spite of much anecdotal evidence to the contrary, most people want to retire, and their health improves after retirement.

15. Cultures that are neither wealthy nor marginal appear to be able to give the best treatment to their aged population.

16. Although the status of many older persons is marginal, in terms of health as well as financial resources and social amenities, this is not true for more than a small percentage. Most older persons, in fact, prefer to live alone, with the maximum independence they can sustain.

17. There is an increasing tendency in modern times for the major milestones of one's life (marriage, birth of children, retirement, death of spouse) to occur at earlier ages, with the result that many persons have a lengthy "free period" at the end of their lives.

Death and dying

Death is a personal as well as a social, cultural, and biological matter. In this excursion, you will learn about the independent meanings of aging, dying, and death. You will find that people typically die as they have lived, within the limits established by their culture. In modern cultures, as will be seen, the significance of dying is diminished, while death itself is sensationalized.

It will be suggested that people tend to pass through typical phases in approaching their deaths. Moreover, they differ in the ways they cope with death as well as in the ways they choose to die. These differences in meaning will help us to understand some of the questions surrounding suicide. It will be shown that suicides want as much to escape as to die. Finally, we will see how the significance of one's mortality can influence one's meaning of death, and thus a continuing awareness of one's own death can add meaning to one's life.

On the morning of December 2, 1915, following a stroke and expecting death at any moment, the novelist Henry James said: "So this is it at last, the distinguished thing!" He died on February 28, 1916.

Nothing is so obvious as death, nothing so little known. We ought to live in the knowledge of it, yet it is and has been our most taboo subject. Still, the terrible secret that each of us must die is now more open, to be talked about by everyone, to be studied and written about, even to become the subject matter of a new discipline, thanatology.

Our thesis here is that death is a biological, personal, cultural, existential phenomenon and that it can only be fully understood in the light of these four aspects.

The Biology of Death

1. It is useful to distinguish among the process of aging, the aspect of living we call *dying*, the decision to decline, and the ending called *death*.

In spite of years of intensive research, not much is yet known about how it is that at some point in the life of every living creature it appears to enter a declining stage and finally dies. There are some minor differences between individuals, but most of the members of the same species have about the same life span. Yet there is still no hint of what the mechanism might be that triggers all members of the same species to die at about one certain age, an age that differs from that of another species. In the thinking of biologists today, the triggering mechanism is most probably in the brain, functioning as a central point, rather than scattered among the billions of cells of the body.

Aging and dying. We are so accustomed to seeing people first age and then die that we take it for granted that these are two sequential parts of the same process.

Fig. E4.1. People age in different ways. Mae West, although admitting that in many ways she looks and feels her age of eighty, will also insist that in other ways she is "the equal of four women of twenty."

However, they need have no connection. One can die without aging, as people do who die at any age from a sudden heart attack or as a few rare persons do who work busily and productively to an advanced age and then suddenly die within a few days or weeks. On the other hand, one can age without dying, as in the case of many elderly persons, particularly in nursing homes, who seem to be sitting around, sometimes for years, while they wait to die. Such instances provide an argument for the thesis that each of us has a more or less preset time to die and that we will meet this appointment unless accident intervenes.

Even when the immediate cause of death is known and can be interfered with, we are usually at a loss to trace out the connection between aging and dying. In the case of spawning salmon, it is known that at a fixed point in the developmental cycle the adrenal glands of the fish very quickly produce large amounts of hydrocortisone, and that this serves to drive the fish back upstream toward its spawning grounds. However, by the end of the spawning period the excess of cortisone has become toxic, and the fish is killed off by the very chemical that caused it to reproduce. If we surgically control the cortisone production in advance, the salmon will not spawn and thus will not die in that year, but will die of other causes the next year.

The aging process should properly be called *aging processes,* for it appears to consist of many different events, all interlinked. No two major parts of the body age at the same rate—and in fact, this may be the greatest source of individual differences in aging (Figure E4.1). One person's hair becomes gray quite early, another's remains dark until old age. One becomes rigid and forgetful; another remains alert and youthful in attitude. If skin cells from a young member of the species are transplanted to an older individual, they appear to age at their own rate, independently of the age of the rest of the body. Even within an intact organism, certain organs such as the liver have their independent rate of age and may sometimes grow in a healthy fashion at the same time that the rest of the organism is in decline. As a result, there are a very large number of theories current to explain why we age and an almost equally large number to explain why we eventually die, but no comprehensive theory to link the two kinds of events.

Decline and dying. As we discussed at some length in Chapter 13, the two major kinds of aging studies, longitudinal and cross-sectional, do not give the same results. In an attempt to trace out the differences, Riegel and Riegel[1] conducted an elaborate study on older Germans, consisting of intelligence tests administered on three separate occasions, in 1956, in 1961, and in 1966. The results unexpectedly revealed a phenomenon which they call "terminal drop." Their essential data on this phenomenon are as follows:

In 1956, they tested a total of 380 people (190 men and 190 women) with a standard test of intelligence. Their ages were fifty-five to seventy-five.

In 1961, five years later, they attempted to retest all the people and found that 62 had died in the interim. This left 318 subjects, but 116 of these refused to be retested. Their second sample thus consisted of 202 persons.

In 1966, after another five years, they attempted to conduct a third testing on the 202 who had been tested in 1961, and found that 50 of them (24.7 percent) had died in the interim.

Now for the unexpected finding: Of the 116 who had refused a second testing in 1961, 50 had also died, but this constituted 43.1 percent—almost double the percentage of the group who had agreed to be retested in 1961.

The authors conclude from these figures, and taking into account some other data as well, that within about five years of death many persons go into a phase of *decline*, in some cases marked dramatically as a terminal drop, in which they give up and prepare to die. These findings are in agreement with what is found in many older persons who react to the loss of a spouse by seeming to give up interest in life and soon dying. The Riegels' data indicate, interestingly enough, that the phenomenon of decline may occur at any point between the ages of fifty-five and seventy-five. They suggest further that if the individual has lived past the age of seventy-five, death then occurs more or less randomly, as a consequence of individual factors such as genetic background, state of health, life circumstances, available medical care, and the accidents of life and infection.

Personal Death

Because death has been for so long a topic quite removed from the thinking of the average adult, we have forgotten how closely one's death is linked to the style and substance of one's life. But with the rediscovery of death as a legitimate topic of thought, we can now take seriously the most fundamental fact of all concerning our individual death: that it is inseparably an important part of our individual lives.

2. People typically will die as they have lived—at least, if their culture will permit it.

Asked how they would prefer to die, people usually answer in ways that are predictable from their personalities. Normally extraverted persons would usually choose to die in some "active" way—by fighting off death with the help of modern medicine or, if this is not feasible, by dying more or less suddenly while engaged in what they want to do. Many such persons would also prefer the consequences of their dying to be meaningful in an active way, and so they would wish to have parts of their bodies used for scientific purposes. The extreme extravert might opt for a final thrill in death, such as dying by jumping out of an airplane. Intraverted persons, on the other hand, prefer a quiet death, perhaps by peacefully fading away, or even more commonly, by dying in their sleep.

That these are not just idle preferences but deep-rooted feelings about a central part of one's life is indicated by the fact that many persons do in fact die in unique and personal ways (Figure E4.2). Freud's last years were a constant, courageous struggle against cancer, for which he refused medication on the grounds that it would dull his thinking. He seems to have chosen the time of his own death. He requested some sleeping medicine, knowing that in his weakened state it would kill him. Similarly, Fritz Perls' last words were to a nurse who scolded him for resuming his chain smoking very soon after major surgery. Quite in consonance with his lifetime insistence on being his own person, he said in return, "Young lady, don't you tell me what to do"—and then fell back dead. And the distinction between Presidents Lyndon Johnson and Harry Truman, one an outer-directed man and the other an inner-directed man, were summed up clearly in the difference between Johnson's sudden death of a massive heart attack as compared with Truman's lingering decline into death.

It has been suggested by Keleman[2] that there are "styles" of dying that may not be overtly expressed but that function, like myths, to direct the way that many people live and die in culturally specific terms. They are

- Death is heroic; for example, the death of a Japanese kamikaze pilot is part of a heroic tradition.
- Death is a joke: Specifically, death is, in the Hindu view, a kind of bitter cosmic joke.
- Death is noble: Therefore, like Socrates or like modern martyrs for a political cause, one dies willingly.
- Death is pain: Therefore, in the tradition of contemporary technology, one ought to pass away while thoroughly drugged.
- Death is a problem to be solved: Given sufficient research funds, we will find the answer.
- Death is an illusion: It is not death but only one more step along the endless wheel of one's fate, through successive reincarnations.

Five reactions. Yet when the actual time comes, and the individual faces death alone, the psychological reactions appear to be remarkably similar. Kübler-Ross[3] has found that in the majority of persons, almost regardless of age, the personal reactions to imminent death pass through five phases (although not every individual achieves the final phase):

1. *Denial.* In effect, the person says, "No, there has been some mistake. It is not true. It is not happening to me." For most persons, abundant evidence soon becomes available, from self or from physician or from family, and so this phase is often brief. A relatively few persons persist in denial and die without admitting that it is happening to them.

Fig. E4.2. People die in their own individual ways. Shown here are various reactions of victims of a firing squad.

It is a beneficial exercise to contemplate one's death with the seriousness that it deserves. Because it is not easy to know where to begin on such a task, here are some questions to consider:

1. If you faced death in the near future, what would matter most?
2. What can anyone do to prepare for their own death or for that of someone very close?
3. What might make you feel you were better off dead?
4. If you had to make an irrevocable decision right now, between immortality (but staying at the age you are now) and dying in twenty-four hours, which would you choose? Why?

(Questions 1, 2, and 3 modified from Weisman, 1972, p. 157)

2. *Anger*. The person now fights back as though to beat down impending death. In the course of this, persons may become extremely difficult, even irrational, but this passes over if they are allowed to express their anger fully. One of the most frequent, and poignant, cries that is heard through the anger, a cry for which no answer is possible, is, "Yes, but why me?"

3. *Bargaining*. Half accepting death, the person now attempts to strike a bargain, as a last means of fighting it off. One may bargain with family or, more specifically, with the physician and medical staff. (Wealthy patients may give large grants at this time.) The bargaining may seen irrational to an observer, but it is very meaningful to the dying person, especially if it takes the form of the plea, "Just let me live a while longer."

4. *Depression*. At this point, the fight seems to be gone, and it may even appear that the dying person is about to slip away into death. This can happen, but not if the dying person is allowed a period of self-mourning. In that case, there is a good chance that he will achieve the final stage.

5. *Acceptance*. Having fully accepted one's death, it is now possible to die with dignity and in peace. This is not at all the same as resigning oneself more or less apathetically to an unavoidable fate. Rather, one enters into one's own death as the final, necessary stage in having lived one's own life. Kübler-Ross has quoted one such person, who summed it up in these words: "It is all right. I am not happy, but it is all right."

3. The act of suicide may, paradoxically, be an expression of a last, despairing wish *not* to die.

For many years, it was argued that suicide, like sexual activity, should not be openly discussed because the very mention of it would exercise an irresistible fascination. If college newspapers printed the story of a student's suicide, it was argued, a rash of imitative suicides would immediately follow. The argument has some basis in psychological fact, but not any more than did the similar argument about sex. Indeed, now that suicide can be viewed as a legitimate topic of psychological and sociological inquiry, the first result has been that suicide prevention is now a real possibility in many cases, precisely because the topic is confronted, discussed, and studied.

The field of sociology can boast of the first major study of suicide as a social phenomenon, Émile Durkheim's classic survey in 1897. But it was two psychologists, Farberow and Shneidman,[4] who revived modern interest in the subject in the 1950s. Their studies, and their activities in setting up suicide prevention centers, have given us much of the information we now have as well as methods for helping persons who have reached the point of seriously contemplating suicide.

Most persons have, at one time or another in their lives, given more than passing thought to killing themselves. It is therefore not a rare or extreme possibility for the average person, nor is it a sign of being mentally ill. Rather, it seems to be an expression of a quite specific experience.

All of the evidence, inside as well as outside, suggests that suicide attempts do not occur primarily because the person feels depressed or beaten down by the conditions of life. Nor does suicide appear to be related primarily to one's feelings of aggression turned inward, as a popular theory based on psychoanalytic thought suggests. Interviews with persons who have attempted suicide, as well as talks with people who are actively thinking about it, indicate very few feelings of aggression, either against self or others (Figure E4.3).

Fig. E4.3. A suicide, at the instant between life and death when the decision was made to slip from restraining hands and jump.

Suicide attempts do occur, however, under conditions that seem almost the opposite of the preceding views. The lowest point of the day, for most of us, may be what are called the "wee hours" of the morning, and certainly among the higher points of the day are the hours of late afternoon. Yet far more suicides occur during the latter than during the former period. Similarly, suicides occur more often in the spring than in the winter, and they occur remarkably often during holiday seasons. Suicide attempts were more exceptional than we might suppose in the terrible conditions of the Nazi concentration camps. They dropped dramatically during the period of the blitz in London, during World War II. They are more frequent among adolescents who stay at home after high school rather than go away to the strange, unsettling, lonely life of a strange campus.

The description that seems to best fit the experience of an individual about to commit suicide is this: At this point, the individual feels almost a total mismatch between self and world. Here are some examples. If I find myself in a difficult or almost impossible set of conditions (for example, as a prisoner in a concentration camp), I experience no mismatch between my own state and the state of the world. My experience is, rather, that I am the victim of present circumstances. Similarly, if I awaken at 2 A.M. and see how dreary everything is, my own sadness will not be experienced by me as a mismatch — for my feelings now match my circumstances. But it is precisely when my feelings run counter to what I see around me that I will be in trouble. If the circumstances call for general joy, but I feel depressed; if the situation requires achievement, but I feel myself completely unable to achieve — these are the times when I am most likely to feel suicidal. Thus, suicides occur during holiday celebrations, or in the pleasant part of the day, or more frequently in cities such as San Francisco than in presumably less desirable living places, or more frequently among whites than among blacks (in spite of the admittedly less desirable living conditions experienced by most blacks). But they occur less frequently during situations of general social unrest or chaos, and they occur less commonly among oppressed groups.

This also helps us to understand a little more about the critical moment when, so to speak, some decision is made. The person who makes the actual attempt does not appear to be aimed so much at dying as at getting out of an impossible, "mismatch" situation. Suicides want just as much to get out as to die. As a consequence, the overwhelming majority of persons who are thinking seriously about suicide weigh the pros and cons over some period of time, give all sorts of indications to others as to what they might do, and even carry their uncertainty into the act itself—for example, by making an attempt that might not succeed.

Finally, it is for the reasons that we have been reviewing that the majority of suicides leave notes behind them. If someone were really engaged fully in ending their life, rather than in making a final attempt at resolving the crisis of their life, they would hardly leave a note behind, for it would be of little consequence to them (unless they believed, as not too many persons do, that they would be able to sit up in heaven and observe other persons reading the note and doing something about it). It is the suicide note that is the last clue, and the most important clue, telling us that the suicide attempt is not so much an attempt at dying as a gamble with living—a despairing wish not to die, in short, a final cry for help (Figure E4.4).

The most effective means of suicide prevention rests on this way of understanding the person who is thinking of suicide. If, at the moment of final decision, someone could step in and make the person pause, many suicides might be prevented. The problem is that someone who is at this point of despair is not likely to be seeking out the company of other people. The suicidally inclined person will make the attempt precisely because they have isolated themselves from the help of others. What is needed is a means for them to communicate anonymously, so to speak, with someone who is a stranger yet helpful and knowledgeable. The suicide prevention centers that work by telephone furnish an ideal way of satisfying these conditions. As the conditions of modern society bring an increasing number of persons to thoughts of suicide (an increase of more than fivefold in less than ten

Fig. E4.4. The comparative percentages of those who either attempted or committed suicide, by sex and age, in Los Angeles County during one year. (From Shneidman, Farberow, and Litman, 1970, table 3)

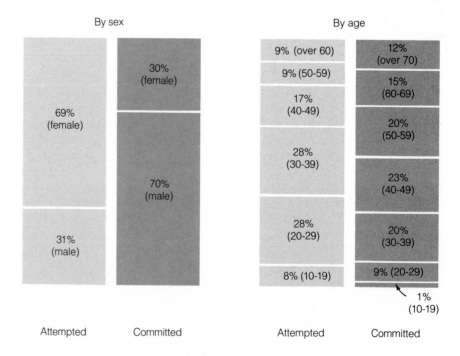

years), its technological achievement, in the form of telephone communication, has also brought about the most helpful means of prevention.

Culture and Death

Dying and death, like other major aspects of human life, are also very important cultural and social phenomena. Quite probably the earliest ritual practices developed by prehistoric humans concerned death. Carefully arranged gravesites, complete with bodies laid out in crouched positions, rows of stones, and various sorts of beads and other adornments, have been found in caves in the Swiss Alps that date back more than 100,000 years. Much of religious practice, in all cultures, pertains directly to death and the possibility of an afterlife.

No more than a century ago, particularly in European countries, death was a common and familiar event in everyday life. There was as yet no widespread technology to control infection, indoor plumbing was rare, and medicine could not do much for most diseases. Among the poorer classes, the young died at an appalling rate, and the old died in their time, and they all died at home. The average person had been in the immediate presence of dead bodies at least half a dozen times before reaching adulthood.

Against this background, death was in former years much more a part of life than it is today. It was not a matter to be shunned or a taboo to be mentioned by means of euphemisms such as "passed on" but was dealt with directly and was even celebrated at the wake. It was not unusual, in small European towns of a few centuries ago, for someone who was dying to pass their deathbed hours in the public square, greeting friends, saying goodbye, and glorying, for at least a brief time, in a position of respect. Under such circumstances, death was an occasion for sadness but not for shame. No one would have dreamed of hiding away the dying as we do, in tomblike terminal wards of hospitals or in old-age homes.

4. Public attitudes toward executioners, the official dealers in death, reveal a mixture of fear and fascination.

The attitude of many persons toward death is interestingly suggested by people's behavior toward a very special class of public servants: the executioners who carry out official killings demanded by the state. Without exception, executioners have occupied unique places in society, at least since the Middle Ages, when they first became necessary adjuncts of the operations of cities.

The story of the Sanson family, executioners in France from 1635 to 1889, through war and revolution and changes in government, exemplifies the horror that ordinary persons felt for what the family did.[5] The daughters in this family were not allowed to marry men who were not themselves executioners—and so the executioners of seventeen French cities were interrelated in a unique kind of clan. A document attached to the front door of an executioner's house warned the public not to enter, not to touch a member of the family, or if a message had to be delivered, to drop it on the ground. Their houses might be painted red; merchants might not sell to them; and on one occasion, when a young woman agreed to dine with a man who later turned out to be an executioner, she sued him for having violated her honor. And more than a century later, when Robert Elliott[6] was appointed executioner at Sing Sing Prison, he at first could not bring himself to let his teenage daughter know, although the rumor soon spread in his neighborhood

Fig E4.5. The curious fascination of death.

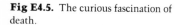

and he had to protect his family against the attacks of children who taunted him as a killer.

However, the public attitude has never been pure revulsion (Figure E4.5). There are always many more job applications for such a post than can be accommodated, some of them as sober as that of the girl who wrote Elliott: "I'm graduating from high school, and I haven't yet made up my mind concerning what I want to do. Would you recommend getting a job like yours?" Hangmen get as many requests for their autographs as do movie stars, and the public will plead and even bribe to be permitted to witness executions. When they do, the air is that of a frantic carnival. In seventeenth-century Nuremberg, in Germany, the hangman Franz Schmidt made quite a profit selling pieces of the corpse to superstitious folk, and the body itself had to be quickly removed or else it would have been stripped clean of clothing by the revelers who came to watch the proceedings.[7]

The two attitudes, of fear and of fascination, must sometimes be brought together and reconciled as well as possible. Harry Allen, for twenty-seven years the official hangman for Britain, finally retired when capital punishment was abolished (except for killing a policeman or a prison guard). Hoping to supplement his pension, he opened a pub. He had to close it soon after, however, for each day it would fill up with viewers who came in simply to stare at him, silently, in fascination and in fear, perhaps in love and in hate. This is how everyone, both executioners and their public, resolves an almost unbearable tension between our twin attitudes toward dying and death. The revulsion and horror and fear, on the one hand, and the fascination and attraction and even wonder, on the other, hold all of us as captives of our feelings. The lessons of history, expressed in every Western culture, thus have a great deal to teach us concerning how we confront death and even how we deal with such related feelings as aggression.

The Meaning of Death

5. Death can be fully understood only if it is viewed as one of the central meanings of human existence.

We may get some idea of the centrality of one's own death if, by the right kind of question, we can get individuals to contemplate seriously the possibility of their own deaths. Here is one such question:

Let us suppose that a number of atomic scientists, responsible for stockpiling hydrogen bombs, have made a series of terrible blunders. As a result, their entire supply of radioactive material is going to explode. Nothing at all can prevent it. When the explosion occurs, the whole world will be blown up with it, including everyone, without exception. This is going to happen in just twenty-four hours. Therefore you, like everyone else in the world, know that you have just twenty-four hours to live. The question you now have to answer is this: In this situation, how would you choose to spend the twenty-four hours?

A question very much like this has been given by researchers to wide samples of respondents. In general, people of all ages have no difficulty taking the question seriously. The major choices are as follows:

- To spend their final hours with those to whom they feel closest — for example, with family or other loved ones. In addition, many persons would prefer that the final scene be passed in a particular place that has meaningful associations for them, such as their family home, or a special place outdoors.
- To live it up, either by doing something they had always wanted to do and put off doing or by doing again something that was most meaningful or enjoyable to them. Sexual fantasies are particularly common in this kind of response.
- To do something never before attempted, such as calling up the President or jumping a motorcycle over a line of cars or even reading a special book that they had never gotten around to.
- To spend the time in meditation, contemplation and waiting, or prayer, either alone or with a select group of others.

Prospects for immortality. Another approach to confronting persons with the prospect of their own dying and death is to pose for them death's alternative — immortality. The question may be asked, "what would it be like to be immortal?" To make matters simple, it can be further assumed that immortality as any of us might achieve it would guarantee our remaining at precisely our present age forever.

The consequences of immortality are most curious. If I were to have forever to live, I would soon realize that I also have forever in which to pass each moment of my life, and therefore forever for every single act, large or small. Would I then still experience a tension regarding the present moment or an urge to get it over with? Or, would I remain endlessly suspended in the experience of a moment that had neither beginning nor ending, the trough of a wave in a timeless existence? And without a tension pulling me toward a future, what would happen to hope, to anticipation, to fear or anxiety, even to restlessness, impatience, and boredom? Could I ever be surprised? Challenged? Finally, would I be able to experience these feelings in regard to anyone else? If hope and fear were lost to me, I could hardly have them in regard to another person, either as threat or as promise, and I would hardly understand their appearance in others when they were directed toward me. I would become, in the end — or perhaps immediately on assuming immortality — a mere presence, unmoving and unmoved, utterly alone in the absolutely equivalent presence of everyone else.

Some arguments can surely be made for the positive side of immortality, but the considerations just mentioned suggest that it is the very fact of our own mortality, known to us as the ground for all our experience, that may make possible all the richness that makes life worth living. Children perhaps find a way around this, as is suggested by some of the evidence concerning children's attitudes toward dying and death. At least in young childhood, life is present oriented, in an innocence that rules out the concerns that bind us to our social worlds. Perhaps they gain some of the rewards of immortality without suffering its consequences. But for the rest of us, who have grown older and into a guiding sense of our own mortality, the lesson that life may have taught us is simply that personal time has to have a stop; this central fact of our lives is learned by facing our own mortality.

In the face of death, What can our attitude to our own dying be if we accept this requirement fully? One answer is given by a respondent to the atom bomb question that was discussed earlier. This young woman wrote simply: "But I would keep on doing exactly what I'm doing now—because, if not, what am I doing it for?"

In a long-term series of experimental studies with terminal cancer patients, Joan Halifax, a cultural anthropologist, and Stanislav Grof, a physician and psychotherapist, have found that with the careful use of psychedelic drugs such as LSD-25 the dying person can go through his own dying with a full acceptance of it.[8] In the course of guided drug experiences, these patients have come to accept their own dying as a necessary passage in their lives—not only an intellectual acceptance but in some complete sense, as indicated by their spontaneous reports of wellbeing and of feelings of harmony with themselves and with some order that transcends their lives.

The wisdom and personal peace that sometimes come with a personal aging process that is fully lived and accepted indicate that, late in life, some persons in our culture learn more about how to live by coming to accept and face their own death. In one of his many instructions to Carlos Castaneda,[9] the Indian *brujo* (wizard or sorcerer) Don Juan says that the whole trick in life is simply to live with death always at one's left hand. For it was here all the time—the distinguished thing. This may have been what Plato meant when, asked on his deathbed for some advice about living, he said, "Practice dying."

Summary

1. Because aging, dying, and death are distinguishable as phenomena, one can age without dying or die without aging.

2. No two major parts of the body age at the same rate.

3. In many persons, there can be seen a phase of decline preceding their death, in which it appears that the person gives up and prepares to die. Some evidence indicates that this phase can be predicted as much as a year in advance.

4. Personality differences may lead to distinctively individual preferences in regard to choice of the type of death.

5. In individuals actually facing death, similar psychological reactions occur, which Kübler-Ross has organized into five stages: denial, anger, bargaining, depression, and acceptance.

6. Study of suicide attempts and with failed suicides, as well as extensive communication by way of suicide hotlines, all combine to suggest that suicides want just as much to escape an impossible situation as to die.

7. Awareness of one's personal death can help one live more fully in the moment.

8. The meaning of immortality will vary from person to person; its significance is that it points to the central importance of mortality in our lives and therefore to the central importance of death for the living.

Part Four

SITUATIONS

The social psychology of individuals

I n this chapter, you will be able to review the different views of
abnormality. It will be shown that each group or society defines
abnormality in terms of its own standards. Much of what is called
maladjustment and *deviance* may be understood better with reference to its social and historical context.

We will discuss the different types of neurotic conditions, all
with their central factor of anxiety. To these distinctions we will add
others, relating to influences stemming from one's character, one's
mood, and one's setting. You will be able to trace some of the links
between personal and social factors in such disorders as depression and
multiple personality, and you will then see how an understanding of
these relationships has brought about some new approaches to the
problem of treating these conditions.

A major change has occurred in recent years in the field of abnormal psychology:
Abnormality was originally defined in a narrow way, but the development of the
field has been marked by a steady broadening of approaches. Abnormality was first
conceived as a condition belonging to an individual and to elements within the
individual. Later it came to refer to broad characteristics of the whole person, then,
to the individual in a social setting, and, most recently, to total social situations. As
the understanding of abnormality has broadened, so have approaches to treating
it—from an original emphasis on the individual, to broader approaches involving
whole families and even communities. We will be tracing this development in the
present chapter.

1. Basic ways of defining *normal* rest on some method of counting or on some approximation to an ideal.

The simplest way of approaching an understanding of the abnormal is to start
with a definition of what is normal. The abnormal, then, would consist of any
serious defection from the norm. We can distinguish four commonly offered ways
of defining normalcy:

- In the *statistical* definition, the normal is considered to be whatever is average
  or occurs most frequently (the modal). We use this kind of definition when
  we excuse a child's misdemeanor with the statement, "Oh, it's just normal
  behavior for a four-year-old."
- The *social* definition says that normalcy consists of what the society or the
  culture or the group generally accept. When the U.S. Supreme Court defines
  pornography as that which is offensive by contemporary community standards, the justices are resting on a social definition of normality. Note that
  what the society says is normal may not be the same as what is statistically
  most common or average, for here the term *normal* is given some special
  value.
- The *theoretical* definition relies on a theory of the personality, so the definition
  can now be as varied as one's theory. Developmental theories, such as the

Getting along: adjustment and deviance

Fig. 15.1. The same behavior may be described quite differently if it occurs in Western culture (shown on the left) rather than in Eastern culture (shown on the right). What Westerners might describe as the aimless behavior of someone who has nothing to do and nowhere to go, Easterners might describe as the fulfilled behavior of someone who has attained a high level of no-attachment.

psychoanalytic, imply that to be normal is to be at the appropriate level or state for one's age.

■ The *ideal* definition is related to the theoretical definition and is one in which normality is defined as an ideal. By the ideal definition, in contrast with the statistical definition, normality is very rare.

Identifying the abnormal

2. A first problem in identifying what is abnormal is that each group or society defines it according to its own standards.

What is considered as abnormal in any group usually depends heavily on the current standards of the group and on what they collectively consider as outside the limits of acceptability. In 1850, a man was jailed for exhibitionism—because he insisted on displaying his bare torso at a second-floor window. To torture another human being is, we would all agree, an abnormal act—but not if it was done by the official executioner in Elizabethan England. And what of the 20,000 persons who on August 14, 1936, gathered in a carnival spirit, complete with booths, popcorn, and souvenirs, to witness the lynching of a black man at Owensboro, Kentucky?

At one time or another, human societies have encouraged and even sanctified the most barbaric kinds of behavior. We are quick to condemn them today. But, when we do so, we might well bear in mind that societies, including our own, have also accepted beliefs and practices so strange as to be delusional by any rational standards. (Figure 15.1.) During the Nazi era in Germany, the majority of the normal, adult population apparently believed that an identifiable group of "Aryans" existed and that they were biologically different from Jews. Less than a century ago, most respectable adults firmly believed that children who masturbated would become insane, a belief they clung to in the face of the fact that they themselves had probably masturbated as children or young adults. A case reported by an Italian physician in 1882 concerned "the disgusting story of two sisters affected with premature and perverse sexual disease" (they had both masturbated since early childhood). We are told that "even a white-hot iron applied to the clitoris had no effect in overcoming the practice."[1] Whose behavior would we today describe as abnormal, that of the girl or that of her physician?

3. A second problem is that abnormality, like other psychological characteristics, tends to be identified by the methods used to detect it.

The problem here is very much like the one that we came across in Chapter 11, where we discussed the early attempts at measuring intelligence: How do you detect or measure something if you have no good definition of it, if you lack a theory about it, and if it seems to vary from one group to another? Now, a century or more ago, no one stated the question quite this way. In fact, an important part of the problem of understanding abnormality, for them, was precisely that they could not state clearly what their problem was. Here is an example.[2] In 1665, when a group of sober citizens grappled with the question of whether a widow named Amy Duny had practiced witchcraft on a number of children, a series of careful "tests" was applied in court. For example, it was felt that the children who had accused the woman might be malingering or "counterfeiting their distemper." As an experiment, the accused was brought over to one girl "whilst she was in her fits," but the child's view of the witch was blocked and someone else actually touched the girl's hand. This produced the same effect as the touch of the woman herself, which suggested very strongly that the child was engaging in a "mere imposture."

In the face of this and similar evidence, the jury took only half an hour to convict poor Amy Duny, and she was later hanged. As for the children, they all recovered from their "ailments" within a half hour of the verdict being announced. We may therefore ask: How did it happen that this woman was convicted even in the face of evidence to the contrary in court? The answer seems to be that no one in the courtroom, apparently, doubted that witchcraft truly existed and that some persons were capable of practicing it. Given this firm and common belief, they differed among themselves only in the ways that they preferred to detect it. That there was an "it" to detect, they had no doubt (Figure 15.2). Under

"What in layman's language is called a *vice* and in the law is called a *crime*, is often in medicine diagnosed as a *disease.*" — Krafft-Ebing, 1886

Fig. 15.2. Women who had special skills and who competed with male physicians were once singled out and attacked as witches.

such circumstances, the odds were always heavily against an accused person. Almost anything she said could be turned against her.

If the investigators share a collective certainty that witches exist in their community, it is almost certain that some of the people they accuse will be found guilty—that is, they will be identified as witches. The methods used to reach this conclusion will not be unbiased but will be specifically designed to prove the case; for example, tying an accused woman to one end of a log and forcing her under water. If she did not drown after being kept under for three or four minutes, that proved that God had aided her, and so she was not a witch. But if she did drown under these conditions (as most women will), it was proof that she was a witch. The method here was not a neutral test, but a means of proving an already established case.

A modern diagnostic experiment.[3] A professional actor was tape-recorded in a conversation with a therapist. He presented himself as a mathematical scientist, well adjusted and happy, who had read a book on psychotherapy and wanted to talk about the topic with a professional. In the course of the interview, of course, he talked about himself as well.

The tape recording was then played to a number of groups of listeners, who are listed in Table 15.1. The four experimental groups were all told, by someone of obvious status and prestige, that the tape they were about to hear was that of a man who was actually quite psychotic. Of the four control groups,[⊙] the first three were professionals who were (1) given no suggestion about the man's state; (2) given the suggestion that he was mentally healthy; or (3) told that the interview was part of a new personnel policy in a large business concern. A fourth control group (4) consisted of the jury in a mock sanity hearing.

In the absence of any suggestion concerning the possibility of psychosis, none

Table 15.1. The percentage of judges who diagnosed a tape-recorded interviewee as mentally ill.

	Number of judges	Percentage who judged speaker as		
		Psychotic	Neurotic	Mentally healthy
Experimental Groups				
Psychiatrists	25	60	40	0
Clinical psychologists	25	28	60	12
Graduate students in clinical psychology	45	11	78	11
Law students	40	18	73	9
Undergraduates	156	30	54	16
Control Groups				
1. No prestige suggestion	21	0	43	57
2. Suggestion: mental health	20	0	0	100
3. Personnel interview	24	0	29	71
4. Mock sanity trial	12	0	0	100

Source: Data from Temerlin, 1970.

control group. The group, in an experiment, which is similar in all respects to the experimental group, except that it is not exposed to the independent variable that is being studied.

of the judges in the control groups made this diagnosis, although such a choice was available to them on their answer sheet. By contrast, 60 percent of the psychiatrist judges made this diagnosis. In general, the more closely a group of judges was identified with the mental health profession, the more likely they were to see psychosis.

The conclusion that is strongly implied by this evidence is somewhat disturbing: Advanced training and more strongly felt identity as a professional does not necessarily lead to judging clients more accurately. Rather, it may lead to being locked ever more tightly into one's expectations, just as the learned experts were in the trial of Amy Duny. One inference that may be drawn is that no really fair-minded assessment can be made unless another alternative is given equal weight: that the condition being judged does not even exist.

Neurosis and anxiety

In modern psychological theory — that is, for about the past hundred years — two major forms of abnormality have been identified, neurosis[☉] and psychosis.[☉] We will deal with neurosis in the remainder of this chapter and with psychosis in Chapter 16.

---

4. In every theoretical approach to understanding neurosis, a central factor is *anxiety*.

Fig. 15.3. Anxiety for some persons is a normal mode of existence.

The only characteristic of neurosis that seems to be common to all viewpoints is *anxiety*. Behaviorally oriented clinicians have defined neurotic behavior in terms of anxiety, for example: "Conditioned anxiety is usually the central component of neurotic habits."[4] Freud considered the problem of anxiety to be the central issue in neurotic difficulties, so he worked and reworked his views on the subject over a twenty-year period.[5] Anxiety is probably the most widespread and familiar of all distress feelings, so much so that we all know what it means. Psychologists, however, have had difficulty defining it.[6]

Anxiety may range from the mild form of temporary nervousness and upset to extreme and severe forms in which the person is overcome by what seems an explosion of the autonomic nervous system: The heart beats fast; one perspires, especially at the extremities; dizziness or nausea may occur; trembling is felt; breathing becomes irregular or too rapid or out of control; vision may blur; the face is flushed or pale; and a feeling of panic comes over one. The condition may come and go very rapidly, or it may persist long enough to be recognized and labelled an "anxiety attack." It may happen only once, a few times, or quite frequently, and it may even persist as a chronic state. It may be related to one kind of situation only, or it may happen under so many circumstances that it cannot be linked to one kind of trigger (Figure 15.3).

In short, anxiety is a variable condition that resists any simple explanation. To make matters even more complicated, anxiety to a mild degree is generally agreed to be a positive rather than a negative characteristic of one's adjustment. A total lack of anxiety, as is found in some kinds of criminals or in certain personality disturbances, seems to be itself a mark of neurosis. Normal adjustment appears to require a low level of anxiety so as to keep the person alerted, engaged, and properly concerned with productive achievement and constructive relations with other persons. Too much anxiety, however, or too little, are either neurotic conditions in themselves or perhaps (as Freud thought) signals of some other, possibly more dysfunctional condition.

neurosis. A mental disorder characterized by anxieties and conflicts that interfere with behavior but are not so severe that the affected person breaks contact with reality.

psychosis. A major psychological disturbance in which the individual breaks contact with reality, a break that often includes hallucinations or delusions as part of its framework.

The experience of anxiety. Normally we find ourselves in situations that we have either chosen or accepted. And so normally we do not mobilize ourselves to a state of alertness against the strangeness or danger of our current situation. But it may happen that circumstances bring us to situations in which we do not feel "at home" in this way. If this happens, one possible response might be the state of diffuse arousal that we call *anxiety*, in which we are charged up but not necessarily able to pinpoint a specific target.

There are groups of persons for whom such a situation is the customary order of things, and so we would expect to find that their general anxiety level is high. Typical of such groups are the mentally retarded, who understandably usually find themselves in circumstances where they feel they do not belong, that they do not fully grasp, that make demands on them that seem important and necessary but cannot possibly be fulfilled. Yet in the face of this, they cannot pinpoint anything specific that is identifiable as threatening. Tests of mentally retarded persons, using any of the standard measures that have been developed to assess *general anxiety,*[7] indicate that they have an appreciably higher level of anxiety, at all ages, than persons of higher intelligence. Similarly, when cultural groups are compared within a society, as when blacks are compared with whites, anxiety levels are found to be chronically higher among those who belong to the nondominant segment and who therefore are likely to feel less "at home."

Specific anxieties. If one can construct a test as a measure of general anxiety, it should be possible to construct a test to measure anxiety states that occur only in specific situations. The most common such situation is the taking of an examination, as most students are well aware. A number of ways of measuring such test anxiety[°] have been devised.[8] Almost equally common is stage fright, the state of anxiety that overcomes one just at the beginning of a situation involving speaking or presenting oneself in public.[9] Actors and actresses describe this sort of "public" anxiety as their own clue to themselves that they are sufficiently primed to give a good performance.

Persons who are prone to anxiety in regard to a specific situation often show specific patterns of muscular tension as part of the expression of their anxiety. Evidence for this is that the anxiety state is incompatible with muscular relaxation. When the tension pattern is eliminated by means of some technique of relaxation of the muscles, the anxiety also disappears. This general finding, first clinically demonstrated by Jacobsen in the 1930s,[10] now forms the basis for effective therapeutic treatment of many anxiety-related states such as fears and uncontrollable impulses. We discuss this extension in greater detail in Chapter 17 under the heading of behavioral therapies.

Symptom neuroses

---

5. Based on psychoanalytic theory, the first workable theory of neuroses classified them according to symptoms arising in specific areas of the personality.

The classification of neuroses began with the work of Freud, who established psychotherapy as a legitimate specialty within medicine and supplied it with its first theory and technique. Prior to this, professional treatment of abnormalities of personality and behavior had been in the hands of physicians, as part of their regular practice; if the disturbance was serious enough, it was diagnosed and

test anxiety. Worries, fears, and other symptoms that occur specifically in examination situations.

treated by physicians known as "alienists" in mental hospitals. Understandably, then, the specific neuroses that were first "recognized" and treated resulted from Freud's theory—and, as the theory changed, so did the neuroses.

The neuroses diagnosed and treated by the first generation of psychoanalysts, in the decade just before World War I in Europe, were what we would now call *symptom neuroses*. They consisted of identifiable symptoms, in the form of certain behaviors and experiences, and they fell into three broad classes: defects or abnormalities of cognitive functions such as thinking and decision making, defects of the emotional life, and defects of impulses and drives.

Abnormalities of cognition: Obsessive and compulsive neuroses.[⊙]
The complaint that these persons bring to a psychotherapist is that much of what they think or do does not come about in the normal way (because this is what they want, or because this is what they are used to, or because this is what the situation demands) but because they seemed to be forced to it. Without their asking for it, obsessive ideas or thoughts enter their mind, or they find themselves impelled to go through certain compulsive actions. To some degree, of course, these symptoms are part of the ordinary workings of the personality. All of us can think of occasions when we could not get a phrase or a tune out of our minds, or we felt literally compelled to get up out of bed to see if we had really set the alarm. But the obsessive is truly occupied with these kinds of ideas, often to the degree that they crowd out ongoing thinking and planning. They are, in addition, often painful or disturbing ideas that run counter to the person's own moral standards. Thoughts of killing a close friend or relative are examples, ideas that have been aptly described as "ego alien." The compulsive, too, may become so preoccupied with the repetitive doing of certain things in a ritual fashion, such as washing the hands dozens of times a day, that the normal conduct of affairs is interfered with. This is also carried out with the clear sense that it is wrong, silly, or senseless.

Ordinary processes of thought and action, by which we usually keep our lives decently in order, may also be interfered with by other obsessive and compulsive symptoms. Orderliness may become so exaggerated that the person gets completely lost in detail and becomes quite anxious if one tiny detail is overlooked or changed. Keeping one's things together and in order may become exaggerated to the degree that we call *miserliness*. Persons who show such symptoms are well aware of what they are doing and are also acutely conscious that their symptoms may be irrational and disruptive, but their experience is that they cannot help it. Thus, to the disruption caused by their symptoms, they add a constant anxiety about themselves. Their condition is doubly distressful, and often is accompanied by feelings of depression as well.

Abnormalities of emotion: Hysterical neuroses.[⊙]
Most of the early cases of psychoanalysis fell into the hysterical category, perhaps because these conditions were better understood. They consisted mainly of disturbances of normal states of feeling and sensation, in contrast with the usual control that people exercise over their emotional lives and their expression of feelings. Hysterical patients would show unusual extremes of feelings and unusually rapid swings of mood. They gave the impression of being giddy, or excitable in a shallow way.

The theoretical notion that was at the heart of early psychoanalytic theory was repression, which referred to maintaining one's impulses at the unconscious level. In this view, hysterical neuroses, and their symptoms, were the result of failure of repression, usually in the kind of personality that relied too heavily and too exclusively on repressive mechanisms for control of impulses. Thus, the condition known as *amnesia*,[⊙] in which the person simply blocks out periods of time, was the result of massive repression, used in a kind of wholesale fashion.

As a typical example, the person might suddenly develop a curious paralysis

369

Getting along: adjustment and deviance

**Case study 15.1:
Worry, doubt, contamination: the obsessive**

A. G., thirty-seven, married, father of three children, Scotch Presbyterian minister, worried since his fourteenth year about "three branches of thinking": (1) that he might cheat someone, (2) that he might get things dishonestly, and (3) that he might poison someone. In any money deal—paying of a bill or street car fares, drawing of checks—he always felt that he cheated some other man. He felt so disgusted that he never told anybody, not even his wife. His wife, however, wrote in a letter about his peculiar habit of staring at a piece of money: "If he gives me any amount, he will ask over and over again how much he has given me." When buying things, the patient always felt that he gave too little money and that the clerk gave him too much change. . . .
When he reads a newspaper or a magazine he always has the feeling that he will receive some illegitimate aid on the examinations that he passed years ago. The most recent was twelve years before his admission (to the clinic). "I argue to myself like this. This building [Phipps Clinic] was not built when that happened, or this paper, or this book not printed when that happened. Then I look to see when it was published, or I overcome it with a great deal of pressure. Sometimes it makes me feel very depressed. They are rational arguments, but they ought not to be necessary."
The feeling of poisoning someone was not
(continued)

obsessive-compulsive neurosis. A neurotic reaction in which the person is plagued with the repetition of persistent disturbing thoughts or the compulsion to repeat ritualistic acts.

hysterical neurosis. A psychological disorder characterized by physical symptoms (such as paralysis) or loss of sensory functions (such as amnesia).

amnesia. Loss of memory, particularly of past or personal experiences.

so strong. "I feel that there might be some poison in the cup; through some inscrutable way I have left poison in the cup after having taken it from the table dish. I never feel this way about the dishes or cups of other people, or the general dishes. I never have anything on my person to put in the cups, but I cannot get rid of the feeling that I have left something in the cup which someone else will drink. Like a servant might chance to drink what is left in the cup. . . . I have tried by the dint of willpower to prove the absurdity of these things. I succeed for a while, but the case comes right back, and I am unable intellectually to convince myself."—Straus, 1948, pp. 60–62

**Case Study 15.2:
Living in hot water: the
hysterical neurosis**

A twenty-six-year-old married white woman was admitted to the hospital for psychiatric consultation complaining of painful hands and feet. She stated her hands and feet tingled then "burned" until she was frantic, and she claimed that her only relief was in putting her hands and feet in cold water. Physical
(continued)

conversion hysteria. A neurotic reaction in which psychological conflict is converted to bodily symptoms. The person then shows illnesses that have no physical basis.

belle indifference. Janet's term for the air of indifference hysterics have toward their physical symptoms. For example, paralysis, instead of arousing anxiety, is accepted calmly.

voyeurism. Peeping-Tomism; sexual pleasure obtained by peeping or observing.

exhibitionism. Generally, a tendency to show off; specifically, deviant sexual behavior in which a person obtains pleasure by exposing the genitals.

of one whole side of the body, which is a condition that is not possible on a neurological basis; there are no nerve centers in the body that control it in this symmetrical fashion. Such a condition is often called *conversion hysteria,*[⊙] because, according to the theory, the denied impulse or wish had been converted into a physical expression. It is often explicitly and obviously symbolic in its expression, yet the patient, on being confronted with this rational explanation, will show a naive or even indifferent lack of awareness. Hysterical neurotics are renowned for this ability to remain blandly innocent of the significance of what is often quite clear to others, a state that is termed *belle indifference.*[⊙] However, with the increasing sophistication of adults in general, and of patients in psychotherapy in particular, the classic hysterical neurosis is now being seen less and less frequently.

Abnormalities of impulse: sexual "neuroses." In an era when only the most daring pioneers talked openly about sexual matters and when standards of conduct were rigidly enforced, it is hardly surprising that most of the problems brought to early psychoanalysts were disturbances of the sexual drive. Nor is it to be wondered at that so many kinds of sexual behavior were considered deviant. We have moved some way from this position of nearly a century ago, but powerful reminders of earlier views are still with us. Thus, the official position of the American Psychiatric Association, repeated in practically all textbooks in psychiatry and psychology, is still that individual preferences in sexual practice, even when they harm no one, can be considered as evidence of personality disturbance. It has been argued, however, that, on a purely rational basis, individual preferences for satisfying the fundamental biological drive of sexuality should no more be considered indicators of neurosis than, say, highly individual preferences in satisfying the hunger drive. If a middle-aged man gains his "eating" pleasures solely from cottage cheese, it may be that this is no more and no less neurotic than his gaining his sexual pleasures from wearing women's clothes.

Yet many kinds of neuroses are still defined in this way. There are those persons whose preference is to stand at a distance and satisfy themselves by looking without touching: the voyeur.[⊙] Parallel to this curious choice is that of the exhibitionist,[⊙] who wants to be looked at—again without making physical contact. In another version of the preference for remaining at a distance, there is the fetishist, whose sexual pleasure is found in possessing, fondling, and perhaps even wearing an article (usually of clothing) belonging to the desired person. It seems to be characteristic of these "distancers," just as it is of their more recent counterpart, the voice of the obscene phone call, that they gain an illusion of control by never risking the intimacy in which control has to be shared. The voyeur, secretly watching yet without being seen; the flasher, suddenly appearing to stun an abashed spectator; the fetishist, owning a very personal part of the target person; or, as we find today, the obscene phone caller, safely terrifying the listener late at night—all these persons have chosen patterns of sexual expression in which open and intimate contact is eliminated.

In one respect, too, these variants on sexual preference share a characteristic. They are often remarkably specific in their actions, almost to the point of turning the scenario into a ritual, repeated down to the last detail. A surprising number of individuals gain sexual excitement or even satisfaction by means of unique practices that might seem most odd to their neighbors. Some people get their greatest sexual pleasure having intercourse in unlikely places—in a self-service elevator, under the dining room table, anywhere but in bed with the lights out. Some persons have reported that they prefer to be stimulated by having the partner pelt them with tennis balls. Some wear costumes, or ask that the partner make certain sounds or say specific words, or require that a phone call be made during the act.

The history of prostitution, regardless of country or era, is replete with amazing tales of the requests made by regular customers.

This should not be at all surprising to personality theorists. Since Freud, it has been accepted that the sexual impulse in all its varieties and modes of expressions is at or near the very center of the human personality. If this is so, we should not be surprised to learn that all the imagination and ingenuity of which humans are capable may be engaged to channel the precise expression of one's sexuality. Any dimension of human relations might then become a significant channel for sexual expression, as in the sexual neuroses called *sadism*[☉] and *masochism*.[☉] Sadism ranges from the symbolic and harmless to the brutal and violent. Here the person expresses the controlling, aggressive element of power that runs through all relations between persons. Masochism, as the acceptance of this element, is its logical counterpart.

If we may judge from recent evidence in countries all over the world, it appears that many different sexual activities once suspect as abnormal are becoming acceptable as individualized expressions. These include homosexual preferences and life-styles; sexual activity that begins early in life or continues into old age; very frequent sexual indulgence, or none at all; specific practices, such as oral sex; sexually oriented language in what used to be called "mixed company"; masturbation as a preferred practice; and the enjoyment of explicit sexual material in print or picture. A recent bestseller, *The Joy of Sex*,[11] sums up this historic change in attitude: When sex becomes a joy rather than a burden or a moral stance or a sickness, sexual neuroses will disappear.

Abnormalities of drive: psychophysiological disorders. A final category of symptomatic neurotic disturbances also harks back to psychoanalytic theory. This is the group of conditions that are commonly known as *psychosomatic disorders*.[☉] They are medically discernible conditions that, according to theory, represent the expression of psychological problems and specifically the expression of certain feelings in disguised form. Such deviant expressions were known in early psychoanalytic work, and in fact were often studied in the form of conversion hysterias. But it was only in the 1930s and 1940s that they began to be systematically described. The list is surprisingly long, and includes asthma, supposed to be related to problems of dependency and specifically to the inability to articulate cries of longing; arthritis, supposed to be based on repressed feelings of rage; colitis, similarly supposed to be based on repressed and overly controlled anger; thyroid problems, supposed to be related to problems in experiencing and expressing fear; and some forms of ulcers, supposed to be derived from lifetime conflicts in the expression of needs to be taken care of. More recently, and in the same line of thought, proneness to heart attacks has been claimed to be related to personality conflicts.[12] Even a disease as diffuse and as little understood as cancer has been described as related to a disturbed life of impulse and feeling.

The weaknesses in these claims, however, should also be pointed out. It is extremely difficult to establish definitely that certain kinds of conflicts in the personality are the direct cause of certain observable physical conditions. Indeed, probably the links are never so simple nor so clear-cut as to prove this proposition. Some remarkable coincidences are often found on extensive examination of individuals. For example, repeated clinical evidence suggests that asthmatics are simply different people from arthritics. In addition, careful studies of subjects who are put under stress conditions suggest that most persons have individualized and quite stable patterns of autonomic response.[13] (See Figure 15.4.) One might then guess that, under proper conditions of continued stress during the early years of life, some persons would be prone to develop stresses that would finally lead to physical breakdown in a specific way.

examination showed . . . severe blistering of the hands and feet, with no other objective findings in the skin, nervous system, or elsewhere. Six weeks prior to admission, attacks of burning pain had started in the extremities. These attacks had lengthened in duration and increased in frequency and severity despite treatment. . . .

Since the beginning of her present condition the patient had been "neglecting her children and only did work that was absolutely necessary. . . ." [Her husband] said that she had spent all day every day recently soaking her hands and feet in cold water, acting depressed and unhappy, and that she did not improve with medication. Her husband was a hard-working farmer and the patient had assisted him with his work as well as attending to her housework prior to the onset of this illness. . . .

During the course of . . . discussions the patient acknowledged that with all the work and the difficulty . . . of making ends meet on the farm, she had been worried about a second pregnancy. And she said that she was afraid that "another child would land me in hot water"—meaning she felt as extended as her resources allowed with her one child and efforts to please her husband. It later also became apparent that she had worried about "getting into hot water" before marriage, when she had occasionally participated in sexual intercourse. Moreover, soon after marriage and then after each delivery the patient had been treated for urinary infection, during the course of which, briefly, she had suffered from burning pains on urination.—Abse, 1966, pp. 217–218

masochism. The sexual gratification a person receives from pain, whether self-inflicted or inflicted by another person.

sadism. A deviant behavior in which sexual gratification is received from inflicting pain on another person.

psychosomatic disorder. A physical illness that has psychological origins.

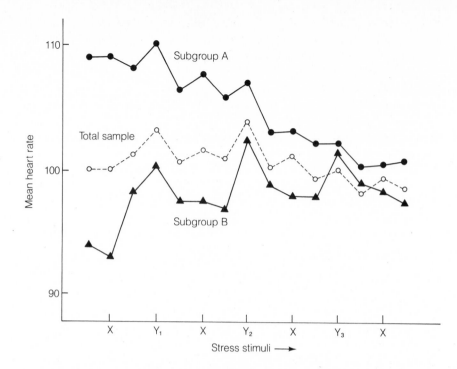

Fig. 15.4. Different degrees of stress were administered to a group of hospitalized patients: X = minimal stress (an interview), Y_1 and Y_3 = medium stress (taking a blood sample), Y_2 = maximal stress (a planned stress interview). Although the group as a whole maintained nearly the same average heart rate during all conditions, one subgroup began the sessions with high anxiety (subgroup A) and was not particularly affected by the stresses. Another subgroup (B) remained relatively calm *except* at times of situational stress. (From Glickstein et al., 1957, Fig. 1, p. 104)

Case study 15.3:
The curious "sexual" impulse

A case of fetishism. P., laborer, aged twenty-nine. Family heavily tainted. Emotional, irritable, masturbated since childhood. When ten years old, he saw a boy masturbate into a woman's handkerchief. This gave the direction to P.'s sexual life. He stole handkerchiefs from pretty girls and masturbated into them. His mother tried every means to break him of this habit; she admonished him, took the stolen handkerchiefs away and bought him new ones, all in vain. He was caught by the police and punished for theft. He then went to Africa and served in the army with an excellent record. On his return to France, he resumed his old practices. He was only potent if the prostitute held a white handkerchief in her hand during the act. He married in 1894 and sustained his virility by grasping a handkerchief during coitus.
A case of symbolic defilement. A man had an inamorata who would allow him to blacken her hands with coal or soot. She
(continued)

fetishism. A deviant sexual behavior in which a person focuses sexual interest on an article of clothing or a special part of the body.

But this can hardly constitute a sufficient explanation for the very large number of instances of common diseases. The explanation along strictly psychosomatic lines also leaves out the effects of many other kinds of influence, from diet to air pollution to infection to congenital predisposition to the stresses of modern life. It can certainly be argued that all so-called physical diseases are in some way linked to personality changes or crises, because the human organism works as a psychosomatic unity — but this biologically sound view is quite different from a claim that specific disease conditions are the consequence of neurotic difficulties.

Behavior disorders

6. Defining neurotic conditions in terms of their behavioral traits has the advantage of indicating directly an appropriate therapy.

A theory of neurosis that is similar to the Freudian but somewhat broader as well as somewhat more practical is offered by behavioral therapists. In this view, all of our behavior is nothing but the collection of habits that we have learned. Therefore, what are called *neuroses* are only our individual sets of maladaptive habits. Most important, because they were once learned by the person, they can be unlearned; the habit can be broken, or new habits can be substituted. Out of this viewpoint, there has emerged a very lively current practice of therapeutic treatment usually referred to as *behavioral therapy* (see Chapter 17). As might be expected, the conditions that are treated by this approach are usually those that can be isolated and defined as a specific set of behaviors; for example, a child's habit of refusing certain kinds of food or of acting in a demanding fashion toward the mother; or a woman's panic whenever she has to go shopping alone; or a man's desperate fear of flying in airplanes. A sampling of such neurotic conditions would be:[14]

- A person acts inappropriately in regard to the situation, because for this person the stimulus has been conditioned to "control" the behavior in a functionally inappropriate way. For example, a young man becomes uncontrollably angry at a small slight, or displays extreme anxiety.
- A person appears to behave appropriately but experiences his or her own actions as negative, leading to feelings of distress or discomfort — for example, cases of depression, self-hatred, or apathy.
- A person lacks essential social and behavioral skills, because of poor learning in the past — for example, being unable to be normally assertive.
- A person typically responds to the "wrong" reinforcers — for example, the alcoholic.
- A person's environment lacks appropriate reinforcers, leading to such reactions as, for example, loneliness.

Many of these behavior disorders, it will be noted, might also be described in terms of another point of view, such as the psychoanalytic. The advantage gained from the behavioral formulation, however, is not simply a matter of rewording. Rather, the source of the maladaptive learning is identified in each case, whether it is in the stimulus or reinforcement conditions of the environment or in the learned reactions of the person. Once this identification has been accomplished, certain therapeutic procedures are directly indicated — for example, to alter the reinforcing conditions of the person's current environment.

As a result of this kind of precision, behavioral therapy procedures have become known for their success in treating conditions that can be identified and described as isolated reactions or habits. The most successfully treated of such conditions have been the phobias.© A phobia can be precisely identified and labeled. It consists of a specific item of behavior whose presence as well as absence can be exactly verified, so that one knows when it exists and when it has been eliminated. It can be handled as a learned reaction even though neither client nor therapist may know its exact origin. A compulsion, such as the irresistible urge to wash one's hands, is also a specific item of behavior that can be treated even though one may not know how it originally arose or what it "means." A behavioral approach to neuroses bases its diagnoses on conditions or problems that can be defined in behavioral-environmental terms. What would not be dealt with, however, would be problems of character, which by definition have no single, precise behavioral expression, or severe disorders that are expressed in a general disorganization of the person's life.

Character problems

7. Developments in psychoanalytic theory have led to identifying neuroses in terms of character and style.

One of the most important developments in psychoanalytic theory and practice began in the 1920s. As we described a few pages back, Freud's followers had identified various kinds of neurotic conditions in terms of the specific symptoms displayed by their patients. A major assumption behind this approach was that the persons who displayed the symptoms were not themselves defined. They were considered to be simply neutral carriers of their symptoms, in much the same way that, according to behavioral therapists, people are neutral carriers or displayers of certain behavioral traits. It was this assumption that was challenged by the psycho-

then had to sit before a mirror in such a way that he could see her hands in it. While conversing with her, which was often for a long time, he looked constantly at her mirrored hands, and finally, after a time, he would take his leave, fully satisfied.

A case of masochism. X, a model husband, very moral, the father of several children, had times . . . in which he visited brothels, chose two or three of the largest girls, and shut himself up with them. He bared the upper portion of his body, lay down on the floor, crossed his hands on his abdomen, closed his eyes, and then had the girls walk over his naked breast, neck, and face, urging them at every step to press hard on his flesh with the heels of their shoes. . . . After two or three hours, he had enough. He paid the girls with wine and money, rubbed his blue bruises, dressed himself, paid his bill, and went back to his business, only to give himself the same strange pleasure again after a few weeks.
— Krafft-Ebing, 1965, pp. 143, 182, 561–562

**Case study 15.4:
Wanting to be fed: the
psychosomatic ulcer**

If the wish to receive, to be loved, to depend on others is rejected by the adult ego . . . [and] cannot find gratification in personal contacts, then often a regressive pathway is used: the wish to be loved becomes converted into the wish to be fed. . . .

A twenty-three-year-old university student had his first hemorrhage from a duodenal ulcer when he was was eighteen years old. This was preceded by only a short period of stomach distress. . . . The patient's most conspicuous personality trait was his extreme casualness, which reflected his marked control over the display of emotion. . . . As a child the
(continued)

phobia. An exaggerated and unrealistic fear of something.

patient had been quiet and obedient, whereas his brother, three years older, had been aggressive and independent. . . . When the patient was thirteen, the brother died and two years later the father died. These events were of crucial importance in the emotional development. After the death of both older male members of the family, the mother turned to the patient with all her own dependent needs. She consulted him concerning important decisions, forcing him to become a substitute for both the older brother and the father—a task for which he was emotionally unprepared. His casualness and show of imperturbable security were but a defense against insecurity and dependence, which became overwhelming under his mother's exaggerated expectations. . . . In overt behavior, many peptic ulcer patients show an exaggerated aggressive, ambitious attitude. They do not like to accept help and burden themselves with all kinds of responsibilities—the type that is so often seen among business executives. This is a reaction to their extreme but unconscious dependence.—Alexander, 1950, pp. 102, 104, 113

analyst Wilhelm Reich, in an influential book called *Character Analysis*, first published in 1927.

The meaning of character. In order to understand the importance of the term *character*, consider the following example. A few years ago, a high school football coach published an article in an athletic magazine in which he expressed quite bluntly his views on current trends among young athletes.[15] They were, he said, in danger of becoming effeminate as a result of certain abhorrent practices, such as wearing their hair long. In support of his view, the coach offered a number of his other attitudes. He noted, for example, that God made man to dominate women and therefore God meant for men to wear their hair short; that long hair is effeminate and therefore people who wear it this way will not be able to conquer the Chinese and Russian communists; and that wearing one's hair long represents a lack of self-discipline and an absence of respect for authority, and therefore will lead men into lives of crime, drug abuse, and sexual perversion.

Notice that the attitudes expressed by the writer of this article encompassed politics, religion, sexual behavior, dress, grooming, and social institutions. Yet quite probably you, reading this example, are not too surprised. The separate attitudes somehow seem to make a coherent mix. Perhaps you might even have formed an image of the man who expressed them—an image of his appearance, his bearing, his voice, and even his method of enforcing discipline on the playing field. Taken together, they are all expressions of his character—a term that refers to the whole person.

The quite new conception that Reich introduced was simply that one's entire character might be one's neurosis. Freud as well as a number of his closest colleagues had suspected since 1908 that specific difficulties in infancy and childhood might lead to certain kinds of adult character—for example, that difficulties in getting through the stage of toilet training might be the foundation for character traits centering around orderliness, parsimoniousness, and punctuality.[16] Reich's view was that these traits of one's character permeated everything that one did—ways of moving, of talking, of thinking, of perceiving. If one was neurotic, then it was because one was a neurotic character. People sustain their individual characters, neurotic or not, by means of the physical conformation of their musculature. Their habitual ways of moving and acting and expressing themselves are nothing but their individual patterns of muscular tension, patterns that they have built up all their lives in the form of what Reich called "body armor"[17] (see Figure 15.5).

Fig. 15.5. One's armor may be both inside and outside.

Reich's theory of the bodily basis of character has not been accepted by the majority of psychoanalysts. (As we will see in Chapter 17, he had to found his own school of psychotherapy.) His view of the importance of character has been enormously influential, however. It has made possible a broadened conception of neurosis. It is now more customary to think of neuroses, not as collections of isolated deviant symptoms or traits, but as disorders of the entire personality, usually expressed in the form of characteristic ways of living neurotically.

Neurotic styles. In a recent formulation based on current views of character, Shapiro[18] has described a number of what he calls *neurotic styles,*⊙ which are "identifiable, in an individual, through a range of his specific acts . . . that seem characteristic, respectively, of the various neurotic conditions." This is an interesting development in the theory of abnormal personalities, for it combines the best features of the concept of character and the concept of neurotic difficulties. Shapiro offers a number of major neurotic types, which should be compared with the symptom neuroses we described earlier.

- The *obsessive-compulsive* character is marked by rigidity of thinking and by the lack of an emotional life. There is a great quantity of activity, especially of a routine or technical nature, which is often accompanied by experiences of effort, deliberateness, will, duty, and the sense of "should." There is a lack of a natural, realistic, or easy conviction about the way things are. Appearing in its place is a constant sense of doubt or skepticism.
- The *paranoid* character is marked by a suspicious, prejudiced, often rigid style of thinking, by keen perception and observation, and by an acute and narrow attention. Reality contact is not so much with what is obvious and natural as with its hidden "indicators" of significance. Behaviorally and even muscularly, the style is marked by an alertness, as though the person is at the ready to counterattack. The inner experience seems to be as though the person were sustaining an "internal police state."
- The *hysterical* character is marked by thoughts that are global, diffuse, and impressionistic rather than factual; naively accepting rather than judgmental or doubting; and transient rather than stable or organized. Perception seems always to be at the mercy of emotion, which in turn may be explosive, unorganized, not pinpointed, and quite changeable.

Disorders of mood and setting

8. Some disorders cannot be reduced to the individual but appear to reflect and express the individual's place in a social setting.

The neurotic conditions we have considered thus far have been those in which persons (or those immediately concerned with the persons, such as parents) have recognized that they have a problem. The identification and labeling of other conditions, however, is not a matter of someone's recognition about him or herself, nor does it arise from someone's theory about personality. Rather, in these conditions the total interaction between person and social context is disturbed. Therefore, as this interaction changes, for example from one period of time to another, the labeling also changes.

Depression. This condition, an exaggeration of the feelings of sadness that are so much a part of normal living, is judged as neurotic only when it is either extreme

neurotic style. Adler's term for the characteristics that are organized as a defense against feelings of inferiority; also, a term referring to a kind of neurotic character.

**Case study 15.5:
When life is hopeless: the
depressive**

She is in her late forties, and her dark red hair is lined with a dull grey. All the lines on her face turn downward and her light brown eyes move constantly. . . . She has been ill before, but for her every time is like the first time. . . .

For her, being ill means waking before it is light, a clutching gnawing vague pain inside, the beginnings of a dull headache, and a feeling of terror. Before she is properly awake, she worries that she has overslept, will miss the train, be late for work, has she adequate clothes for the weather, will it snow; then, awake, she feels alone, utterly alone, utterly useless, utterly without value, facing a meaningless day that will be a constant battle with which to cope. The ache seems so bad she thinks she cannot get out of bed; it seems that no one cares whether she lives or dies; she cannot read, she cannot write letters, her bedroom is in a state of shocking disorder but it does not seem worthwhile to tidy it. She stays in bed too long and then, heart pounding, breathing fast, races ineffectually through her morning chores, terrified that she will be late for work. . . .

Her behavior takes a heavy toll on everyone around her. Her children have seen it all before, of course, but to them also, every time is like the first time, or worse, because in the back of their minds they remember how she whispered, once, 'I can't go on' or raged in a darkened room 'You'd be better off without me,' and they are nagged by the fear of suicide. They understand that she is ill, but even their understanding and their kindness are *(continued)*

postpartum depression. Symptoms of depression often brought on after giving birth and lasting from about two to six weeks. Physical exhaustion, hormone changes, and personality conflicts seem to be probable causes.

in degree or so persistent as to interfere with everyday functioning. All of us have felt depressed at one time or another, and perhaps for some persons it is a central aspect of their character.

Depression is not a symptom, nor is it a kind of character or temperament. Rather, it is a definable mood that colors the person's entire life. Like anxiety, it may be brief or prolonged, mild or severe. Some types of depression appear to occur in response to a specific life situation, such as the *postpartum depression*© shown by some women in the period after giving birth to a child; the *menopausal depression* that is one of a complex of characteristics sometimes shown by women during this transitional period of life; or the "between contracts" depression, so-called because it appears with some frequency in insecure entertainers who are between contracts and fearful that they will never get another. Depression may be of two general feeling types. A sad, apathetic, resigned set of feelings is marked by a slowing of behavior, loss of appetite, and seeming acceptance of defeat or loss. A bitter or resentful set of feelings is marked by self-accusation and guilt, on occasion leading to suicide.

Although depression is so much a matter of almost intangible mood that it seems difficult to explain, there have been two major theories offered. The earliest of these was Freud's, who noted the marked similarity of depressive reactions to the behavior of people in mourning.[19] He theorized that depression was a fundamental possibility in early childhood development. It was related to experiences of oral deprivation, and it came about because normal aggressive responses were blocked and then turned inward against the self. More recent psychoanalytic thought has emphasized the complexity of depressive feelings. For example, in one current view, depression may occur as a result of difficulty in handling one's aggressive feelings, or on the basis of loss of a love object, or even as a recurrence of infantile depressive feelings, which in turn were based on guilt and anger.[20]

Another, quite different view of depression, this one along the lines of recent behavioral theory, is that of Seligman.[21] On the basis of extensive experimental work with animals, he has proposed that depression is a state of learned helplessness. For reasons connected with the circumstances of the individual's life, a pattern of reaction is set up that progressively convinces the individual that fighting back is useless, that there is no way out. At some point, the spiral of stimulus and response begins to turn downward, further convincing the individual that nothing can possibly be done. This in turn results in a habitual mode of response to all situations, which we then call *depression*. It can occur in animals as well as in humans and consists of a helpless and resigned pattern of putting up with negative circumstances.

In accordance with behavioral theory, because the causative sequence is known, the appropriate therapy is then evident. One involves the depressed individual in new behavior, which then results in developing more constructive habits of response.

It is on this basis that Seligman explains the success of antidepressant drugs, which undercut the psychological basis of old behavior patterns and thus make new ones possible. Supportive evidence is found in experimental work with animals (Figure 15.6). For example, a dog made severely "depressed" by the repeated application of unavoidable punishment is made to act in new ways by being pulled repeatedly, on a leash, through the "danger zone" into a safe area. This results in new behavior, which produces results counter to the dog's pattern of expectations. A different attitude then takes over in place of a former stance of cringing or resigned helplessness.

Multiple personalities. Around the end of the nineteenth century, when educated persons were just becoming aware of all the fascinating discoveries being made in the new psychology of the mind, when Freud's startling new theories were being talked about in Europe and America, the most dramatic of all cases was that known as *multiple personality*. Such persons, when they were found, were not considered "sick," but rather unusual or even gifted persons from whom much might be learned. Hypnotism was still a mystery and far from common; automatic writing and similar performances were beginning to be accepted as manifestations of powerful psychic influences. Professional circles were buzzing with curious ideas mixed of spiritualism, the new psychology, religion, superstition, and abnormal psychology. In this atmosphere, the discovery of a person in whom there seemed to coexist, side by side, more than one complete personality, upset all previous notions of "the mind" and seemed to provide startling evidence in support of such notions as the Freudian unconscious. The cases of Eve and Sybil, discussed in our opening Message, are modern versions of this phenomenon.

On historical grounds alone, we might claim that the multiple personality is a new phenomenon. Therefore it may well be related to some new elements in the history of Western society, as is argued by Van den Berg[22] (see Chapter 9). It is Van den Berg's position that, over the past two centuries, in European and American societies, the undivided self of the normal adult became split. Thus, the normal adult can now be hypnotized (a very new phenomenon in human history), can give evidence of unconscious motives (an equally new phenomenon) and shows evidence of such split-self possibilities as ESP and multiple personality.

Whether this is so or not, it is evident that multiple personality has remained a rare phenomenon, restricted mostly to young women, and somehow old-fashioned. The expression of multiplicity in one's personality strikes many observers as contrived. When it is made clear that the individual in question is not simply acting or faking, then we begin to feel that such a person, capable of blocking out total areas of her life, is similar to the old-fashioned hysteric of Victorian days, who maintained with conscious innocence a repression of all things sexual. Whenever her repressive defenses were threatened, she would close off her consciousness and faint. The same mechanism enabled her to close off one part of her personality from another.

The phenomenon of multiple personality is certainly related to historical changes, particularly to changes in the status of women (Figure 15.7). It may have served as an indicator, as the new century began, of what women could express if they dared; but it soon gave way to more effective techniques of expression.

Hyperactivity in schoolchildren. During the 1960s, when discipline in many institutions, including schools, began to be called into question, there appeared on the American scene a remarkable upsurge of a disturbing behavioral pattern. It resembled a condition that since the 1930s had been diagnosed as MBD, or "minimal brain dysfunction." Presumably this is brain damage that is minimal enough to be undetectable by conventional neurological techniques yet sufficiently serious to influence the child's behavior. The "new" pattern was soon labeled *hyperkinesis* and, on the basis of previous successes in treatment, began to be treated with drugs.

Inexplicably, the first successful drugs turned out to be strong stimulants such as dexedrine, benzedrine, and ritalin (some of them known to the street addict as "speed"). Many different drugs have since been used in the treatment of hyperkinesis, including both depressants and stimulants, all seeming to have about the same general effect. Apparently any chemical that suddenly and markedly alters the child's state of consciousness results in a temporary alleviation of the behavioral symptoms. As more and more cases of hyperkinesis appeared in schoolroom classes, parents turned in desperation to school authorities, who in turn appealed to the medical and psychological professions. It was some years

drained by the emotional demands that never stop. . . . The most difficult demand for everyone around her is that she simply does not hear what is said to her. She does not want to know what anyone else thinks. It is impossible for her family to have relationships with her. Their posture is that of punching bags. After a few weeks, they are punched limp, drained, exhausted. — Mendels, 1970, pp. 2–5

(a)

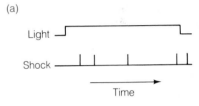

(b)

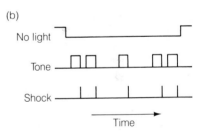

Fig. 15.6. In an experiment by Badia and Culbertson (1972), laboratory rats were given unpredictable and unavoidable shock while a light was on (condition a). Another condition (b) consisted of the same number of unavoidable shocks, but always signaled by a tone. Like other experimental animals as well as humans, rats prefer the latter situation, in which information provides them with a sense of control. Under condition (a), they become "depressed" and refuse to escape even when escape is available. (From *Hopelessness: On Depression, Development and Death* by Martin E.P. Seligman. W.H. Freeman and Company. Copyright © 1975)

Fig. 15.7. When women are restricted to a single role in life, developing a "multiple personality" is sometimes a way to break free. If a man plays many different roles, he is more likely to be described as well-rounded or as having a multidimensional personality.

before research studies could establish that the stimulants being used did not serve to slow down the hyperkinetic children but rather organized their attention.[23] The term *hyperkinesis* was therefore probably not appropriate for their condition.

Hyperkinesis is apparently a collection of different behaviors. They include: (1) deficits in learning and in perceptual-motor skills such as reading and coordination; (2) extreme hyperactivity, distractibility, and unpredictable fidgetness; (3) impulsiveness of both behavior and emotion; and (4) a short attention span.[24] Most professionals, however, seem to agree that it is a true disease, even though its causes are not known. In the words of one review, "It is clear that a significant portion of the childhood population suffers from behavior disorders which express themselves in hyperactivity and accompanying learning problems."[25]

Estimates vary as to how many children are currently receiving regular dosages of drugs in order to keep their behavior manageable in the schoolroom. It may be as high as 30 percent in some school systems. What is clear is that the same tendency of theory to lead to diagnosis by mental health professionals is in operation here, as in the case of the XYY condition we discussed in Chapter 1. Hyperactive behavior is found overwhelmingly among males, very largely in city school systems, to a significant degree among minority children, and almost exclusively in countries that are highly industrialized and undergoing rapid social changes. Why should such a definable disorder, which is presumably based on malfunction of the brain, suddenly appear in this select group of human beings at a specific point in history? As we have noted in preceding chapters, all behavior takes place in some situation. Hyperkinesis takes place in contemporary school classrooms (Figure 15.8). It may be less than appropriate to "explain" hyperkinesis, then, without taking into account the state of contemporary educational practice.[26]

Some research data. In studying disorders that may be related to the social context in which they occur, it is necessary to observe changes in the context itself and then to see whether they are associated with changes in the disorder. To do this, one can choose between two kinds of research strategies. The first would be to compare the disorder as it appears in different social contexts—for example, by comparing one culture with another. The second, more elaborate strategy would be to follow a large number of cases over a period of many years, as the context changes with time. (The two strategies are analogous to the longitudinal and cross-sectional approaches that we discussed in Chapter 14.)

We do not have too many careful research studies of the long-term progress of personality and behavioral disorders in childhood. Do disorders come and go, or do they persist and perhaps get worse? Does it make any difference how or when they are treated? How are they related to the children's home environments and specifically to what kinds of parents they have? These and similar questions need to be raised and answered before conclusions can be drawn concerning the causes and cures of supposed disorders in children. One study was carried out in England on the records of 6,000 children, aged five to fifteen, who had been in difficulty as maladjusted in the classroom.[27] There were the following results:

■ It appeared to make no difference, as judged by the rate of subsequent improvement, whether the children had or had not been seen at a child guidance clinic. Approximately two thirds improved in either case.

■ When children who were brought to the clinic were matched for severity of disturbance with children not brought to the clinic, it appeared that mothers who brought their children were significantly less accepting and more anxious than those who did not. In other words, whether a child was seen at the clinic for treatment was more a matter of the mother's condition than of the child's.

■ Maladjustment that consisted of patterns of behavior unacceptable in school

Fig. 15.8. How a classroom might appear
to a certain kind of overactive male. Its
combination of authoritarianism and
absence of firm limits might seem to him
like an uncontrolled explosion of
activity—and his resultant behavior might
then be called *hyperactive.*

(for example, aggression or withdrawal) appeared to be transient. Disturbances of this sort might come and go regardless of form of treatment.

■ On the other hand, gross characteristics of the personality, such as how active
the child was, tended to be permanent from an early age—a finding that
agrees with that reported independently by American investigators in long-
term studies of children from birth.[28]

■ Generally, specific habits or symptoms such as bedwetting also had a tendency
to persist, regardless of treatment.

■ Observation of both children and parents suggested that when obvious maladjustment was present and persisted in the face of either treatment or the
passage of time, it was usually associated with a disturbed family situation.

These findings do not support the view that deviant and antisocial behavior
in children is the result of some sort of pathology in the child alone. They suggest,
rather, that most maladjustment is either part of the child's pattern of growth; or it
is related to the child's long-term character as it expresses itself in a given situation;
or it is nourished within a deviant family setting. A more broadened conception of
neurosis may therefore be needed.

The psychopath and the modern age

**9. A change in terminology, from psychopath to
sociopath, suggests two views of the origin of this
condition: (1) in the person or (2) in society.**

One type of antisocial neurosis poses some distinctive problems. There is a
kind of person who used to be diagnosed as a *psychopathic personality.*⊙ The
diagnostic term has recently been changed to *sociopath.* It is a significant change

psychopathic personality. A
character disorder typified by behavior
without regard for society's laws, lacking
anxiety or guilt.

in terminology, for it indicates two different ways of describing this category of persons: either as victims of a mental illness within the personality or as those whose style of behavior and mode of relating to others reflects certain features of the modern world.[29]

Originally the adjective *psychopathic* referred to anyone who acted in a deviant way. We now use the adjective neurotic for the same purpose. Partly under the influence of early psychoanalytic theory, but more importantly because of the growing recognition of a distinct class of troublemakers, the term psychopath was applied to those who for more than a century had been called "moral imbeciles." That is, it referred to persons who did not show any recognizable symptoms of common neuroses, who were clearly not emotionally disturbed and whose only clear-cut psychological symptom was a lack of anxiety and perhaps some impulsiveness.

Certain kinds of criminals, particularly confidence men, clearly belonged in the category of psychopath. However, it soon became increasingly evident that the behavior itself was not restricted to the criminal class. The psychopath can be the "hero" of an age in which we all play games and where the best gamesman usually wins. "Free from responsibility, free from guilt, free from anxiety, he pursues his interests without compunction, manipulating others to reach his goals. Corporation president, statesman, educator, physician; his calling is irrelevant; his features are everywhere the same."[30]

Yet there is also a significant personal element in what makes the psychopath tick. Such persons are detached, without real concern for others, and hollow where the heart should be. They do not appear to be maladjusted or neurotic in the usual sense, yet they seem to lack a sense of humanity, of the feeling and empathy that binds people together in a working community of interest. They often possess an intuitive skill at perceiving and manipulating others. They can be cruel in a senseless and almost infantile way and can apparently go through life without strong attachments. In the extreme, the charm that they use against anyone may be so great as to seem magical to those they victimize — as it apparently was in the case of Hitler and of Charles Manson. (The latter may have also been deviant in other ways, but in addition they showed many prominent psychopathic traits.)

The background of such persons often shows a history of neglect, rejection, and lack of love. This makes understandable their lifelong project of taking revenge on the world. They are often impulsive to an extreme degree, self-centered, and incapable of delay in gratification, with no sense of what constrains the rest of us in our interpersonal contacts. In all, theirs is a complete character neurosis in the traditional sense, as well as a socially conditioned neurosis.

These are the two views that clash over the psychopath. Quite possibly both views are more or less valid. In the most extensive recent discussion of psychopaths, Harrington concludes that they may be seen in four different but related lights: as victims of an illness or neurosis, as those who have adopted a specific means of survival, as possessors of a specific and deliberately adopted life-style, and as revolutionaries in an age of crumbling social values.[31]

Neurosis and the current scene. The problem of the psychopath is particularly relevant to our understanding of neurosis in its relation to the current social scene. Increasingly, young persons who get into difficulty because of their antisocial behavior pose the problem of how their behavior is to be understood. That is, the question is whether their neurosis is personal, in the sense that they are maladjusted as individuals, or social, in the sense that their situation is unlivable.

Recent trends in understanding neurosis seem to lean toward the latter view. We do not mean by this that current theory in abnormal psychology explains neurosis only in social rather than personal terms. Rather, we mean that there has been an increasing tendency to include in our explanations the social context in which the neurosis occurs. The earliest attempts to understand neurotic conditions attributed them to elements of the individual personality, which were the person's unique symptoms. A somewhat broader view then explained neurotic conditions as collections of behavioral traits. A still broader conception took in the whole of the person's character. The emphasis then shifted to disorders that were expressions of the person's total relationship of mood or style to a living context. Finally, in most recent formulations, many neurotic conditions are seen as representing failures of adaptation within a total family, social, or even societal setting.

Parallel to this successively broadened emphasis has been a change in treatment approaches. The earliest forms of systematic treatment were those carried out by the single professional such as the psychoanalyst. This form of practice slowly evolved into groups of clinicians working together in professional clinics. Out of this, during the 1950s and the 1960s there arose the first community health clinics, which aimed to service large segments of the population. Finally, full-scale programs of mental health care are now being developed, which incorporate still larger population groups.

The more recent position in regard to treatment has been described in this way: "We increasingly are willing to acknowledge that the problems of the designated client often are as much rooted in his community's tumultuous social structure and fragmented care-giving system as in his personal psyche."[32] To overcome the fragmentation of the social setting and its facilities, services are now being located within larger institutions such as general hospitals, or else "human service networks" are being organized to link together such separate facilities as are available (Figure 15.9). In this way, a wide array of services and facilities can be brought to bear on problems defined by the needs of an individual client, whether that client is an elderly person or a brain-damaged child or a hyperactive teenager. This emphasizes that there is only one society and that together we make it work or suffer its failures.

Fig. 15.9. Treatment places that were formerly housed in medical and judicial settings are now found in neighborhoods, thus bringing the professional to the client.

Summary

1. Standards of the group usually determine the boundaries of normal and abnormal behavior.

2. Advanced training and strongly felt identity as a professional does not necessarily result in judging clients more accurately, according to studies of the process of diagnosis.

3. Anxiety is a central characteristic of neurotic conditions.

4. The mentally retarded, like other persons of marginal and uncertain status, have higher levels of anxiety than do persons of higher intelligence.

5. Persons prone to anxiety in specific situations tend to show specific patterns of muscular tension as part of their expression of anxiety.

6. A characteristic of the obsessive-compulsive neurosis is that the individual complains of the disruptive effect of thoughts and ideas, or actions, which seem both impelling and "ego alien."

7. Hysterical neurosis is marked by emotional swings, often accompanied by a bland unconcern or innocence.

8. The variety of psychophysiological disorders (asthma, arthritis, ulcers, and so on) have been linked to particular personalities or to life crises.

9. Reich's contribution to the understanding of neurosis was his conception of character as being carried in the body, in the form of one's defensive "muscular armor."

10. Neurotic styles, similar to the categories defined in terms of symptoms, have been identified: they include the obsessive, the paranoid, and the hysteric.

11. When antidepressant drugs are effective, they undercut the psychological basis of old behavior patterns and make new ones possible.

12. The phenomenon of multiple personality appears to be related to historical changes, in particular the changes experienced by women during this century.

13. Long-term studies of disturbed children suggest that their difficulties fall into three groups: a pattern of growth; the child's character as it is expressed in a given situation; or the consequences of a deviant family setting.

14. A continuing diagnostic and theoretical puzzle in the field of neurosis is the psychopath, whose gift for manipulation and inability to effect enduring relations with others points to either personal characteristics or historically conditioned roles.

15. A recently offered view of adjustment and deviance is that the problems of clients may be as much rooted in the social structure of the community and its care-giving systems as in their personal psyches.

F ollowing our discussion of deviance and adjustment, we turn to the radical break with the social context that is termed *psychosis*. In this chapter, you will be introduced to the topic of psychosis as an apparently universal human condition and as the most personal of all experiences.

We will survey some of the major ways that have been offered to understand the psychotic condition, as well as the often inadequate ways that society chooses to deal with it. Major categories of psychosis will be presented, with their background in the history of hospital psychiatry. Then there will be presented a scheme for following the natural course of psychosis through its three major stages—an initial buildup period, a stage of acute excitement, and a final period of stabilization and readjustment.

You will then learn of the effects of social custom on admission to hospitals and in particular the effects of one's social class standing. Some difficulties in understanding and dealing with the hospitalized psychotic will be offered—for example, whether the psychotic person exercises control through interpersonal manipulation or is simply a victim. Treatments such as drugs and electroshock are discussed, along with more recently discovered measures. In conclusion, two major ways of understanding psychosis will be contrasted by way of a well-known research study. These are (1) the view that psychosis is a condition carried around inside the person and (2) the view that it is a response to the social context.

16

Getting along: psychosis

In the preceding chapter, we distinguished between the personality disturbances called *neuroses* and the breakdown of personality that is called *psychosis*. In the present chapter, we will first discuss the psychotic state, what it looks like as well as what it seems like to the person involved. We will then discuss various theories concerning the origin and cause of psychosis and the two major approaches to understanding it.

The state that we call "being normal" is characterized by a reasonably stable organization. What is it like, then, if this organization is felt to be falling apart in its very foundations? There may be no way for the individual involved to describe what is happening. Our everyday language does not provide terms with which to describe a radical transformation of our ordinary, sensible, meaningful world. Nor is an observer likely to find it easier to describe what is seen as happening. The observer is likely to report that the affected individual seems to be doing all sorts of things that make no sense and perhaps also that attempts at communication do not succeed. And, to make matters still more difficult, it is probable that no two persons ever have exactly the same experience when they become psychotic. The person who is in the throes of this experience may complain to others of "being eaten alive by evil forces" or that "the world is coming to an end, and I have been appointed to save it." The affected individual may report, in panic, a conditon of being completely victimized by overwhelming forces, or may boast of being totally in control of the universe. The individual's behavior may explode out of control or freeze into immobility. Descriptions give us at best only a hint of what this condition is like.[1]

The psychotic state

1. Psychosis is an apparently universal human condition, with its own characteristics and stable rates of occurrence.

Some statements about what psychosis is like

A psychotic patient in a mental hospital scribbles in his notebook:

Nothingness. Is just plain blank. It's void. It has no affiliations with anything. It has nothing to do with anything.

A man who thinks he is going crazy writes in his diary:

The earth is disintegrating, and it is cooling down. It is still warm, but not for long, and God therefore wants love. . . . The earth is the head of God. God is the fire in the head. I am alive as long as there is fire in my head—Nijinsky, 1968, pp. 50–51

A writer describes the moment when it happened to him:

What used to happen so often in thought, now had happened for keeps: I could not turn. To make that movement would mean rolling the world around on its axis. . . . Instead, I performed, or imagined performing, a wild wrenching movement—and the globe did not budge—Nabokov, 1974, pp. 199, 200.

The condition that we call *psychosis* has many names (Figure 16.1). It is known in the practice of the law as *insanity*, in medical circles as *schizophrenia*, in literary terms as *madness*, and in common language as being *crazy* or *cracking up*. It is probably as old as human culture itself. In the Old Testament, we can read a case description of Nebuchadnezzar that is familiar in our own day: "He was driven from men, and did eat grass as oxen, and his body was wet with the dew of heaven, till his hairs were grown like eagles' feathers, and his nails like birds' claws" (Daniel 4:33). We can also read a description of how someone might pretend to be crazy, and do very much what you and I would do: "And he [David] changed his behavior before them, and feigned himself mad in their hands, and scrabbled on the doors of the gate, and let his spittle fall down upon his beard." (1 Samuel 21:13)

It is a condition that spares no group, no culture, no class. Although many cultures appear to have their specific symptoms of severe disturbance, there is a great deal of evidence that the core of the psychotic experience is similar in all cultural groups. It is reported in documents all through history, and every language that has ever existed has apparently had some words that meant "crazy." As Table 16.1 indicates, even a partial listing of well-known persons in Western history who may have been psychotic indicates that it is one of the most pervasive of human experiences.

It may be that this condition is not a specific state but rather one of the major possibilities that are open to some human beings. Being a Mozart or a Shakespeare is another such possibility whose causes we cannot grasp, whose occurrence we can neither predict nor foster nor prevent, and whose existence we cannot particularly change. Apparently a limited number of people are, for some reason, able to be Mozart-like or Shakespeare-like. A slightly larger number, for equally unknown reasons, are able to become psychotic. Their condition might best be described as living just outside the boundaries of what it means to be human—and therefore in any particular society they are described in terms of the human

Table 16.1. Some well-known persons who were probably psychotic.

Caligula, Roman emperor	August Strindberg, writer and mystic
Sylvia Plath, American poet	Ezra Pound, critic and poet
George III, king of England	Friedrich Nietzsche, philosopher
Friedrich Hölderlin, German poet	Robert Schumann, composer
Lucia Joyce, daughter of James Joyce	Vladimir Nabokov, writer
Adolph Wölfli, Swiss painter	Zelda Fitzgerald, writer,
Edvard Munch, artist	wife of F. Scott Fitzgerald
Arthur Rimbaud, poet	Waslaw Nijinsky, dancer
Mary Lamb, essayist, sister of Charles Lamb	James Forrestal, first U.S. Secretary
Vincent Van Gogh, artist	of Defense

Source: Friedrich, 1975.

boundaries that seem most salient. Societies explain the psychotic as the one who breaches just the one set of boundaries that, in that society, must not be breached. Madness may be the only unforgivable sin.

The psychotic population. The figure most commonly quoted in regard to the frequency of psychosis is 5–10 percent of the adult population. It appears in so many textbooks, in precisely the same phrasing, that perhaps students and their teachers may be excused for accepting it as established truth. Thus: "estimates suggest that one out of every ten people born will be hospitalized for mental illness in the course of a lifetime."[2] In fact, this estimate is based on a misunderstanding of some data published in 1953. Admissions to mental hospitals are not absolutely constant; a study based on 127 years of available data indicates that hospital admissions rise as the economy falls, and vice versa.[3] In addition, the average number of hospitalized patients with mental illnesses has dropped steadily since tranquilizing drugs were introduced in the 1950s. However, the number of admissions in recent years has stayed about the same: "The number of persons admitted and readmitted each year has remained quite close to one half of 1 percent of the total population ever since 1930 — as far back as census data are available."[4]

Detailed studies help to answer the further question of who makes up this population of hospital admissions. It appears that these victims of psychosis are not produced by processes of industrialization, nor by the stresses of war or of economic depressions, but rather by relatively sudden social upheavals for which they have no resources to cope.[5] Thus, in one decade, or in one country, the majority of new admissions may be made up of young men who have recently been through combat in a war. In another time or place, it may consist of migrant or immigrant groups who have been unexpectedly displaced. Although psychosis is the most deeply and personally felt of all human experiences, its onset is at the same time the expression of a specific relation between individual and environment.

Although admissions to mental hospitals tend to remain fairly constant, the number of persons who are actually in treatment at any one time varies in accordance with a number of factors. The most important of these is the kind of treatment available. This was seen very clearly during a major change in the 1950s, when hospitals began to use tranquilizing drugs in large quantities. They were therefore able to discharge many of their patients.

In 1950, when the population of the United States was about 151 million, some 550,000 patients were hospitalized as mentally ill and the figure was steadily rising; but in 1970, when the total population had climbed to more than 200 million, the hospitalized total had dropped to 338,000. However, individual states, which have the primary responsibility for care of psychotic persons, vary markedly in the number of persons they hospitalize and also in how much they spend. California, which discourages such hospitalization, had only 9,246 occupying hospital beds in 1973, representing 1 in 2,500 of its population, whereas South Carolina was hospitalizing 1 in 500 of its population and Vermont and Pennsylvania about 1 in 600. As a consequence, California spent some $83 million on its hospitalized mentally ill in 1973, while Pennsylvania spent $170 million and New York $420 million. In most states, hospital and other forms of care for such patients represents a substantial portion of the annual budget, as much as 20 percent.

Yet, in the face of this enormous investment of buildings, equipment, and funds, not very much is spent on the individual patient. On the average, states spend about $25 per day per patient who is hospitalized, a figure that includes the salary of professional and custodial personnel. When this is compared with hospital costs for other medical specialties, it is clear that psychotic patients in mental

MUNCH, Edvard. *The Shriek.* 1896. Lithograph, printed in black, 20 5/8 X 15 13/16", sheet. Collection, The Museum of Modern Art, New York. Mathew T. Mellon Fund.

Fig. 16.1. Edvard Munch's drawing entitled *"The Shriek"* may have been derived from his own experiences.

hospitals are not receiving much in the way of treatment. Most hospitals average about one full-time staff member for each patient, including professional, administrative, custodial, and caretaking employes.

The patients who are in mental hospitals consist of those recently admitted, and generally being processed for rapid discharge and return to their families (the 1.5 percent figure already mentioned), and those who are chronically disturbed to the point that hospital personnel have given up hope for their recovery. It is the latter group that receives—or, more accurately, fails to receive—the treatment available for the figure of $25 per day. Yet interestingly enough, it is just this chronic group on which most theories of psychosis and its treatment are based.

The natural history of psychosis. Three fairly distinct phases seem to characterize the usual history of the psychotic condition. There is an introductory or buildup period, which finally erupts into an acute phase, followed by a period of adjustment and stabilization.

The buildup period may begin in childhood, perhaps as a consequence of disturbed family conditions. People who later become psychotic are often described as withdrawn in childhood and adolescence, although this characteristic is by no means a clear indication of a later breakdown. There is a specific condition of childhood, known as *autism,*° which resembles psychotic conditions in some ways, but aside from this disorder psychosis is rarely found in childhood. Serious personality and behavior disturbances before early adolescence are thought to be directly caused by brain damage. The preadolescent period, however, may serve as a building ground for later psychosis.

The acute phase is the period during which the person is demonstrably "crazy." This period is sometimes referred to as a "psychotic break," in the sense that the individual makes a break with social reality and acts in ways that necessitate intervention by others. The conventional picture of crazy persons that is held by the public really refers only to this period. It may be brief, sometimes lasting no more than a few hours, or it may extend for years. The use of tranquilizing drugs in recent times has the specific effect of cutting short this phase of the psychotic condition. In most societies, at least in modern times, the result of this period is that the individual undergoes involuntary treatment, usually in a mental hospital.

The adjustment period is the time during which the psychotic person makes some more or less stable adjustment to having passed through the very rapid period of transformation of the acute phase. The adjustment is usually in the form of a radically altered way of life. This may be in a hospital, where the person settles into the existence of a "chronic" mental patient, or it may be a changed pattern of living out of the hospital, or in some instances a life that is creative and enriched. Some nonindustrial societies, such as native American tribes, have ritualized a sequence in which specially gifted persons, having passed through an acute phase, settle into an adjustment phase in the role of healer or *shaman.*[6] Industrialized and urban societies, on the other hand, tend to concentrate their forceful methods of treatment (such as electric shock or drugs) in the acute phase and to deal with the adjustment period by various custodial methods. These include: continued hospitalization, returning the patient to the situation that precipitated the acute phase, or more helpfully, creating special settings.

Typical of the latter are the Halfway Houses, whose origins in the United States go back to 1913 but which became widespread only after World War II. Of the more than 200 now permanently in operation, most house the younger and

autism. A form of childhood psychosis in which the child does not communicate with other humans and shuns contact with others.

more promising patients, who usually stay for four to eight months during which time they become adjusted to the transition between hospital residence and independent living in the community.[7] According to some surveys, residence in such homes reduces by about one half the patient's chances of returning to the hospital after discharge. A more longstanding version of these protective environments is the unique town of Gille, in Belgium, where for the past two or three centuries most of the townspeople have put up expatients in their homes as a substitute for continued hospitalization.

How one describes the general characteristics of psychotic people depends on which of the three phases of the condition is in evidence. When they begin to show specific symptoms that we commonly associate with psychosis (such as acting "strange," becoming violent or out of control, talking incoherently or with odd ideas, or complaining of hearing voices), they are entering what we have termed the *acute* phase. Here their behavior often resembles a caricature of the personality they have always shown. Isolated and withdrawn persons may become even more so, hiding when others approach or refusing to take care of themselves or their surroundings. Those who have been prone to variations of mood may now begin to swing even more wildly between extremes, from suicidally depressed states to states of uncontrollable and excessive grandiosity. Two major forms of psychosis are generally identified:

Manic-depressive psychosis, now less common than it was half a century ago, is usually marked by alternating periods of depression and mania. In some cases, however, the person remains for most of the time in one of the two, either in a state of deep depression or a state of exalted mania. The depressive state is marked by uncontrollable expressions of guilt or despair and usually by delusions of being responsible for unforgivable sins. The manic state is characterized by excessive energy, endless activity and talk, disorganized behavior, and irresponsible plans and schemes.

Schizophrenia is a term now used to refer to most cases in which the person is psychotic. It includes a wide variety of disturbances in all spheres of activity. The person's emotional state may be "flat" and withdrawn or excessively silly and uncontrolled, and it is usually unrelated to the ongoing situation. Patterns of thought may be scattered and disorganized, or peculiarly overorganized in the form of delusions.⊙ Sensation and perception may be affected, the person reporting hallucinations,⊙ in the form of distortions of vision or hearing, hearing voices, or imagining nonexistent visions or smells (Figure 16.2). Interpersonal relations are often seriously affected, the person seeming to others to be odd or strange and showing behavior that is often excessive or antisocial, such as running nude in the streets or setting fire to a bedroom. The recent social history of the individual may be marked by patterns of disturbance, such as quitting many jobs, becoming homeless, breaking ties with family and friends, or neglecting personal appearance.

These varieties of psychosis are referred to as *functional,*⊙as distinct from the *organic* psychoses.⊙ The latter may show many of the same symptoms, but their course during what we have termed the *buildup* phase will usually be different. Organic psychoses show a more sudden onset, with few or no ties to the person's earlier personality type. The course of treatment will also be different, because in the case of organic psychoses the physical cause will often be discovered, and the effects of treatment will be evident very soon. Organic psychoses that are caused by damage or deterioration to the brain and central nervous system produce irreversible effects that can neither be alleviated nor treated and in fact often show a

delusion. A false belief or thought that is often a symptom of paranoia.

hallucination. A false perception; misinterpreting of imaginary experiences as being real perceptions.

functional psychosis. A severe mental disorder that has no physiological or medical basis.

organic psychosis. A severe mental disorder caused by some physiological problem, such as disease, drugs, or injury.

Fig. 16.2. "Suddenly the room became enormous, illuminated by a dreadful electric light that cast false shadows. Everything was exact, smooth, artificial, extremely tense; the chairs and tables seemed models placed here and there. Pupils and teachers were puppets revolving without cause, without objective." (From Sechehaye, 1951, p. 77)

downhill course. This is in contrast with the functional psychoses, in which the period after the acute phase is one of responding to treatment and restoring some stability and adjustment.

2. Admission to a mental hospital for psychosis is often based on archaic legal custom rather than on the requirements of treatment.

The diagnosis and treatment of psychosis is not just a field for mental health professionals. An equally important part is played by members of the legal profession such as lawyers and judges, as well as by the complex of laws and regulations that define the way society is to deal with those who are deviant.

State laws, the means by which the will of the people in regard to psychotic persons is supposed to be expressed, have been described as "a mélange of statutory ineptitude."[8] Every state in the United States has a law covering the involuntary hospitalization of those who are judged to be, somehow, incapable of caring for themselves. The decision is officially made by a team of psychiatrists, but in fact in the vast majority of states such commitment proceedings are a formality. Most persons who interfere with others in an odd way, or who frighten or upset the people around them, may be judged as commitable and hospitalized without their consent. It is most revealing that the police are often unlikely to arrest a husband for beating his wife, even when they witness the act in the couple's home, on the grounds that this would constitute interference in a "domestic quarrel," but that they will quickly arrest and take away a husband who is accused by his wife of hearing voices. In other words, people in our society are more likely to be locked up for being "odd" than for certain forms of physical violence.

Once hospitalized on an involuntary basis, the patient may be deprived of many of the ordinary rights of citizens, the specific punishment depending on the state. In many states, a person once committed automatically loses all rights to vote, to serve on a jury, to practice most of the major professions, to drive a car, to make a contract, or even to sue someone.

These restrictions do not apply, of course, to persons who have voluntarily committed themselves to a hospital, nor are they equally severe in all states. But some stigma is universally attached to being hospitalized, whether voluntarily or not. It is for this reason that the process by which hospitalization is brought about is a matter of central concern. It ought to be a process based entirely on professional considerations. Unfortunately, it almost never is. The proceedings are conducted as though they were legal rather than psychological. The evidence, such as it is, is introduced by hospital staff members who are usually disposed to assume that the patient is sick until proven well. The patient rarely has the opportunity or the necessary skills to undertake a defense, and the decision is made by a judge or a jury of laypersons rather than by an independent panel of professionals. What enters into the statistics, then, is the result of this kind of proceedings. And the hospital, in turn, organizes itself to deal with persons whose entry into the institution is accomplished by these means.

All this can be brought about because a husband is convinced his wife is depressed, when she may be only dissatisfied and seeking a change in her status; or because an elderly person is somewhat eccentric and gets upset over a fancied injustice in a store; or because a young adult panics as a consequence of some drug usage. An example that is not at all unusual: "In the name of psychiatric treatment, a man who has disturbed the peace by falling asleep in a California laundromat can be incarcerated for the remainder of his natural life, provided prison psychiatrists first label him a 'mentally disordered sex offender.' "[9]

Treatment as punishment. Given the mode of entry that we have just described as commonplace, it is not surprising that treatment following admission often leaves much to be desired. It is not at all difficult for a sensitive observer to find examples of inhumanity, in varying degrees, that serve to defeat the very purpose for which the patient has been brought to the hospital.

In February 1967, Niels Erik Bank-Mikkelsen, director of the National Service for the Mentally Retarded in Denmark, visited a 3,400-bed hospital for the severely mentally retarded in one of our wealthier states. In a news conference that followed, he described what he had seen: One staff member for each twenty-five children at a meal, trying vainly to supervise patients who were incapable of even the simple act of chewing and swallowing food. Fifty women, ten of whom were naked, crouched on the bare cement floor of a "recreation" room. The practice of cleaning off the patients, who were mostly incontinent, by periodically washing them down with a hose. As many as ninety men and women wandering in and out of toilets in an area immediately adjacent to the dining room. "In our country," he said, "we would not be allowed to treat cattle like that."

From the point of view of many patients and expatients, as well as of those who are advocates for them, enforced hospital treatment cannot be anything other than punishment, and the mental hospital is indistinguishable from a jail. From the point of view of an often overworked staff, however, this is the only institutional setting in which it is possible for a psychotic patient to withdraw from the world and try to reconstitute a shattered life. It should be clear that there is very little deliberate villainy involved here, only a terrible discrepancy of power between patients and staff.

Whatever the degree of its goodwill, the hospital staff has the power of life and death over its inmates, for mental hospitals are one example of what have aptly been called *total institutions.* Prisons are classic examples of total institu-

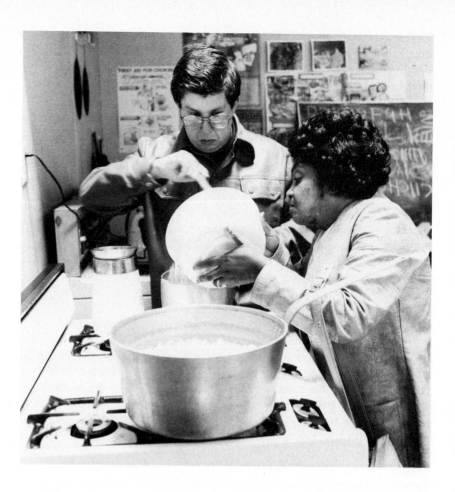

Fig. 16.3. Here a patient is being trained in a simple household task. Is it a good thing or a bad thing to control people for their own good?

tions. Other examples would be monasteries and convents, the military, old folks' homes, and mental hospitals. Each of these institutions has its own methods, rituals, and traditions, its own particular approaches and techniques, as well as its own rationale and purpose, but they all do the same thing. They attempt to bring about some significant change in each inmate by totally controlling every aspect of the person's life — appearance, behavior, habits, scheduling of time and arranging of place, mode of speech, and ways of doing ordinary things like walking, eating, or communicating with others (Figure 16.3). As the sociologist Erving Goffman has shown in a series of brilliant analyses, mental hospitals or asylums accomplish these aims more successfully than any other type of total institutions, for they enlist the aid of professional groups that can then convince the inmates that it is all being done in their own best interests.[10]

Theories of psychosis

Although literally hundreds of theoretical explanations have been offered as to the origin and cause of psychosis, the major theories fall into three main groups. Each of the groups, in turn, leads to its own form of treatment.

3. Psychosis has been explained as a physical condition, as a developmental disorder, or as a response to conditions of life or society.

Psychosis as a physical condition. The most widespread theory concerning psychosis is that it is an illness whose cause is not yet known. The brain is usually held to be the affected organ, and a large number of hypotheses have been offered concerning possible biochemical "errors" in the brain that produce the psychotic state. Although initial results in some research have been promising, none of these hypotheses has yet proven out. The difficulties here have to do with the almost insuperable obstacles in the way of carrying out definitive research. An adequate test of whether a particular chemical in the blood or the brain is the major cause of a psychotic condition would require the following:

1. Two groups of people, one group clearly psychotic and the other not, the two groups being matched, person for person, for age, mental and physical condition, and way of life
2. Sufficiently long-term study of the two groups, to determine the differences between them in regard to the presence or absence of the chemical, but with no significant changes occurring in either group during this time
3. If at all possible, an experimental arrangement in which volunteer subjects are given the chemical to determine if a psychotic condition is produced, ideally under "double-blind" conditions in which neither volunteer nor tester is aware of whether or not each person is actually receiving the chemical or a placebo

In addition, all relevant conditions of diet, activity, social pressures, and environmental influences would have to be equated for all groups during the period of study. Such elaborate studies have not been carried out.

A closely related hypothesis, which states that the physical cause of psychosis is inherited genetically, seems to have had more success. When identical twins (who share the same heredity) are compared with nonidentical twins (who share the same parents but not precisely the same heredity), the results indicate that there is a measurable genetic component in psychosis. If one identical twin, for example, is schizophrenic, the likelihood is about 40 percent that the other one will be. But if one nonidentical twin is schizophrenic, the likelihood is no more than 15 percent that the other will be. This sort of finding does not yet constitute firm proof, for it can be argued that identical twins also usually share a more similar environment than do nonidentical twins. In addition, the mechanism by which psychosis might be transmitted genetically is not known. Finally, a genetic explanation leaves open such questions as this: If psychotics marry less frequently and therefore produce fewer offspring, how can we explain the apparently stable rates for the condition over long periods of time?

As one example of the problems raised by such studies, we may consider the very thoroughly studied four girls, quadruplets, who all became schizophrenic and who were the subject of exhaustive investigation by the National Institute of Mental Health (NIMH). The results have been reported by David Rosenthal.[11] The girls' pseudonyms in the report were based on the initials NIMH: Nora, Iris, Myra, and Hester.

By an elaborate series of tests it was concluded that the four were (with a 99 percent probability) identical quadruplets from one egg, and therefore shared the same genetic makeup. However, they differed markedly from birth and maintained their relative positions all through life (Table 16.2). Hester, the smallest, weakest, and "sickest" of the four, with the lowest birth weight, was always the most disturbed, became psychotic at the earliest age, and had the least positive response to treatment. Iris, the next smallest at birth, occupied the second position in regard to psychosis and recovery as well. Nora was the variable one, at times being the strongest and most well adjusted but at times resembling Iris. Myra was always the strongest of the four, and her subsequent career bears this out. On the

Table 16.2. A comparison of some major events in the lives of the Genain quadruplets.

Event	Nora	Iris	Myra	Hester
Birth weight	4 lb 8 oz	3 lb 5 oz	4 lb 4 oz	3 lb 0 oz
First psychotic episode	Age 20–22	Age 22	Age 23	Age 18
Condition on admission to NIMH hospital	Unhappy about it but agrees to hospital	Doesn't care	Does it to help her sisters	Unaware of what is going on
Course of treatment	After 1 year, discharge to state hospital; marginal adjustment living with mother	Discharge to state hospital, then readmitted	After 1½ years, much improved; discharge in 3 years, now married	Still in hospital, on "back" ward, poor prognosis

Source: Data from Rosenthal, 1963.

basis of these data, gathered over many years in one of the most exhaustive case studies ever done, it is clear that being genetically equivalent is compatible with marked differences in life adjustment.

An explanation of psychosis as a physical condition logically leads to the use of physical treatments. Of these, by far the most widely used is drugs.

Drugs that are used in treatment fall into a number of classes of chemical compounds, but in general they produce the same effects on psychotic patients. They eliminate or markedly decrease symptoms of confusion, delusion, or violence toward self or others. In this way, they make the patients considerably more manageable. As a result, most traditional measures of restraint, such as padded cells, straitjackets, and physical abuse, have disappeared in modern mental hospitals (Figure 16.4). Yet although the patients are rendered more manageable as well as more accessible to other forms of treatment (such as group psychotherapy), they are not as sedated or dulled, as they might be, for example, if they had been given opiates⊙ or barbiturates.⊙

Following on the remarkable success of tranquilizers, a wide spectrum of other drugs has been introduced for use in mental hospitals—and increasingly, for use in outpatient treatment as well. The hospital psychiatrist has today an array of drugs to use singly or in combination for the individual patient. They include tranquilizers of different potency and speed of action, depressants to calm patients who are too active or aggressive, and stimulants to energize patients who are depressed or withdrawn. Their practical value in alleviating the symptoms of psychotic behavior, if not the condition itself, has encouraged some investigators to believe that psychosis is therefore a condition caused by a chemical imbalance, one that can be cured by the appropriate combination of drugs and diet. One of the most intriguing such theories is that of Humphrey Osmond and his associates, who have developed a form of treatment they call *megavitamin therapy*, and have founded an association, the American Schizophrenia Association, to promote its cause.[12] The treatment consists of massive doses of a number of different vitamins, coupled with a diet that is high in proteins and low in carbohydrates. For reasons unknown, it does in fact succeed with some patients in restoring them to what seems to be their prepsychotic state.[13]

opiate. Opium and its derivatives, morphine, heroin, and codeine. More generally, a sedative drug.

barbiturate. A class of drugs, used as sedatives, that depress the central nervous system.

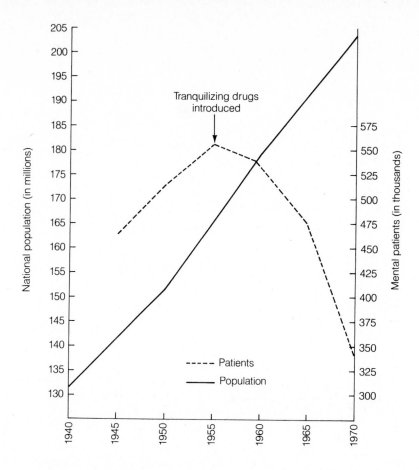

Fig. 16.4. Although the population of the United States has increased steadily since 1940, the number of patients in state and local mental hospitals has decreased since about 1955, when tranquilizing drugs first came into use in hospitals. (Data from U.S. Census Bureau and U.S. Public Health Service)

The problem of diagnosis. One of the main results of the drug "revolution" in psychiatry is that it has all but eliminated a former reliance on medical-type diagnoses. If drugs will change the patient and eliminate most of the symptoms on which diagnoses are usually based, there hardly remains any need to trouble oneself about a diagnosis, because the chief purpose of a diagnosis in medicine is to help one to choose among various kinds of treatment.

Diagnostic labels had been under fire in the treatment of psychosis for a long time before the widespread use of tranquilizing and energizing drugs. The arguments against diagnoses were very compelling. Diagnostic categories have almost no relation to possible causes. They do not lead to particular treatments. Most patients get about the same kinds of treatment in any case, and variations in treatment occur mostly because of specific acts the patient performs (such as becoming violent or refusing to eat), or because of the particular treatment center or professional staff and their traditions and preferences. There was, then, almost no rational basis for the continued use of diagnostic categories in regard to psychosis.

Yet hospitals, clinics, and the journal and textbook literature that described their work all persisted in retaining the traditional categories. The most widely used of these were the classical subdivisions of schizophrenia: the paranoid, the hebephrenic, the catatonic, and the "simple" types. Some hospitalized psychotic patients were, it is true, describable on a particular day as mostly shallow and silly (the hebephrenic characteristics) rather than mute and immobile (the catatonic symptoms). Therefore it might seem that one label rather than another was indicated. But, as a large number of studies showed, it was not possible to get even trained professionals to agree with each other on what label to apply. In addition, most patients changed from week to week and certainly from year to year, and at any one time the typical patient might show a mixture of characteristics from different subtypes.

To complicate matters still more, even such fundamental diagnoses as whether a patient is or is not psychotic were found to be so variable as to be almost useless. In one study on the admitting ward of a large urban psychiatric hospital, it was shown that the patient's presenting symptoms were not the main determinant of a diagnosis of severe disturbance. More influential were two other factors: (1) the availability of community resources for this patient at this time and (2) the particular circumstances under which the diagnosis was made—that is, whether it was made during daylight hours by a skilled, relaxed, experienced staff member or during the small hours of the early morning by a tired, somewhat anxious junior staff person.[14]

Treatment by shock. The physical approach, involving the application of an external treatment to a "diseased organ" of the body, found its perfect expression in the introduction of a form of treatment still used, electroshock therapy.☉ Ugo Cerletti, an Italian psychiatrist, introduced the method on April 15, 1938, when he applied an electric current to the head of a thirty-year-old patient. The patient, an engineer who had been picked up by the police for wandering in the railroad station of Rome, apparently dazed and delusional, was strapped down and given an 80-volt shock for .2 seconds. When this did not even produce a loss of consciousness in the patient, Cerletti and his assistants discussed whether to increase the voltage. At this, the patient—who had apparently been "out of contact"—said clearly and solemnly, without his usual gibberish: "Not another one! It's deadly!" Although this statement, made under such circumstances, shook Cerletti's determination to proceed, he conquered his "fear of yielding to a superstitious notion," and applied another shock, of 110 volts, to the patient's head. He does not state whether the patient was "cured."[15]

Like most physically based treatments now in use, electroshock therapy does appear to benefit some patients. It is particularly useful in cases of severe depression. Its supporters argue that, although the method may seem somewhat barbaric, when properly administered in combination with a muscle relaxant it is not felt by the patient and inflicts no permanent harm. It is therefore used in most institutions that treat psychotic patients and will probably continue to be used until less severe methods are found or until greater understanding of psychosis is achieved.

Psychosis as a developmental disorder. A major alternative to the physical explanation of psychosis is that it is a result of the person's individual developmental history. This puts the burden of blame, so to speak, on the individual's family, for they usually are by far the most powerful influence in one's development.

In a specific version of this view, a group of family therapists and communication theorists some years ago proposed what they called the *double-bind hypothesis*☉ of the origin of psychosis.[16] According to this hypothesis, the behavior that we call crazy in the psychotic person is only the natural consequence of a lifetime of trying to make sense out of paradoxical and contradictory demands by other family members. Persons condemned to grow up in such a twisted web of demands and influences have found that no matter how they responded, it was wrong. If they ask, they are too demanding; if they do not ask, they are too independent.[17] Suppose a boy wants to go outside after a rainstorm, and his mother insists he put on his boots. He protests that none of the other boys will be wearing boots, and that it is babyish, and that it has stopped raining. She answers, with all the power that

electroshock therapy (ECT). A form of therapy that consists of passing an electric current through the head and producing temporary unconsciousness. It is most frequently used to treat severe depression.

double-bind hypothesis. Bateson's hypothesis that a cause of schizophrenia is the inconsistent demands parents convey to preschizophrenic children. The verbal level and the action level conflict and produce stress, which finally becomes unbearable.

only a mother can muster: "Only babies imitate whatever anyone else does—if you want to be a big boy, you'll wear your boots even though the others make fun of you as a baby for wearing them."

What can a child do with such messages? If he agrees, he is a baby, and a big boy too; and if he disagrees, he is a big boy, and a baby as well. All he can learn, in this unlivable situation, is somehow to live in its terms. Perhaps this helps us to understand the adult schizophrenic who sends home a Mother's Day card with the scrawled message: "Happy Mother's Day, Mom. You've always been like a mother to me."

Many families in which one or more of the members is clearly psychotic have now been studied at length, with major emphasis on the way that they communicate, the roles that they maintain, and their patterns of expression of feeling. Such studies are weak in one important way: They are undertaken because one or more of the members has already come to the attention of professionals or the law. Thus, there is no way to tell whether one or more members started out as deviant and then affected the family; or whether the family structure and patterning was itself pathological and led to psychosis on the part of some member; or perhaps that some interplay between individual susceptibility and family structure is the cause. But given this weakness in the studies, there is clear agreement that in any family in which one or more members are psychotic, the chances are very high that the atmosphere and relationships within the family will be disturbed. It may be a matter of how feelings are expressed or hidden, or a matter of the network of interpersonal relations, or a matter of the strength of the ties that bind them as members of the same unit, or, finally, a matter of authority and power.[18] (See Figure 16.5.)

In such a setting, it has been suggested that one member is "selected"—or perhaps simply falls into place—as the scapegoat, the one on whom all the blame can fall. This person is the one who eventually comes to the attention of the outside world as psychotic.[19] Viewed from this perspective, psychosis might well be considered our most pervasive social disease. It might also help us understand the phenomenon of the "evil genius," that influence by someone close that is often the pressure leading to psychosis—such as the influence of James Joyce on his daughter, of Diaghilev on Nijinsky, of Elisabeth Nietzsche on her brother.

Psychosis as a social response. A third view of the cause of psychosis is consistent with social learning theory (see Chapter 7). It suggests that psychotic individuals, even in their most extreme and deviant states, are engaged in attempts to satisfy sensible needs. Their behavior can therefore be understood as responses to their own lives or their own societies. Two lines of evidence are relevant in regard to this view. The first concerns the behavior of psychotic patients in mental hospitals, and the second concerns relations between psychotic behavior and the particular culture in which it occurs.

Social-psychological evidence. If an individual in the midst of a fundamental personal crisis has finally been admitted to a hospital with a diagnosis of schizophrenia, and experiences the hospital as a haven, the patient may then begin to behave in ways that ensure continued, safe hospitalization. This behavior would then be diagnosed by the staff, who see it as evidence that the patient has a chronic mental illness. The patient, in fact, having found the most acceptable of places to live, is now behaving in ways best suited to maintain the new situation.[20]

Contrary to what has been maintained concerning hospitalized psychotic patients, their behavior when not under pressure from the staff is not necessarily either confused or wild or mysterious. The overwhelming majority of psychotic persons spend their time quietly and sensibly. They quickly fit themselves into

Fig. 16.5. A child may be mortally afraid of his or her parents and at the same time control them through anger. Such confusions of power relations often occur in "psychotic" families.

Most of how you're treated in Hollywood Hospital, and, I suspect, most others, is determined by how you are dressed. If you have on a suit and tie, there's no such thing as a locked door. With nothing but a sheet, there's no such thing as an open one. I started at ground zero. I didn't even have a sheet. Moving up the ladder was painfully slow. Slippers are the first goodie after the sheet. If you continue to be good, you get the most ridiculous, ill-fitting pajamas you can imagine. If all goes well after that, you get better-looking pajamas and more mobility. Then come ridiculous pants, and so on and so on till you start getting some of your own clothing back, and then the big day when you get shoes. Shoes are the biggest day in the career of a patient.

All this saves the staff a lot of time. They can just look at a patient and know they're dealing with a "pajama, stage 3" and act accordingly. — Vonnegut, 1975, p. 173

impression management. A social skill (often studied in hospitalized mental patients) enabling one to influence how one is perceived by others.

the rather boring routine of the mental hospital. They may persist in some of their symptoms in the same way that the rest of us bring some of our habitual behaviors with us when we travel to foreign countries. But mostly they stay to themselves and prefer not to socialize with other patients, with the staff, with well-meaning volunteers, or above all with their families. And they resort to more "acute" symptoms when they feel that their newly won status is threatened by change or interference.

It may be argued, of course, that anyone who chooses to live out their life in a drab mental hospital, in the company of an unprepossessing lot of mental patients, doing nothing more than waiting for the next meal, must really be sick. The argument makes some sense — but it clearly changes the meaning of the term *sick*. The meaning here is no longer a medical one, but a value judgment concerning what other persons ought to do with the problems that they see in their own lives. Some persons apparently reach the point at which they turn toward this way of life as the only one that is reasonable or liveable.

Research carried out on hospitalized mental patients and supported by observation that is not prejudiced toward an exclusively physical view tends to support such a social-psychological theory of chronic psychosis. It has been shown that hospitalized mental patients adopt general roles or styles of life, some of them becoming loners and others more gregarious, some serving as hard workers and others remaining close to their wards. The tactic used is called *impression management*⊙ — in this case, to impress the hospital staff.[21]

In one study,[22] thirty hospitalized patients were divided into three groups of ten each. The first group was taken, one at a time, to an interview, and on the way each patient was told that they were to be judged to see whether they were ready for discharge. Members of the second group were told that the interview was to judge them to see whether they should be sent back to a "worse" locked ward. Members of the third group were told only that this was an ordinary interview to obtain data for their record. If one hypothesizes that such patients have settled into the level of adjustment that they prefer, it would be predicted that they would object to both the first and second possibilities but be unconcerned about the third. Therefore, it would be predicted that in order to avoid the first possibility, being discharged, they would act "sick"; in order to avoid the second possibility, they would act "well"; and they would act their usual selves in regard to the third possibility. When portions of each interview were later judged by professionals who had no knowledge of what each patient had been told, this was in fact just what was found. The patients successfully created the impressions in other persons that they needed to in order to maintain their own status quo.

Cross-cultural evidence. The possibility that membership in a particular society was related to one's chances of becoming psychotic, or to the type of psychosis that was developed, was a barely explored issue in the late nineteenth century and is by no means resolved even today. It was probably the influence of medical views that for so long kept scholars from seriously studying cross-cultural relationships. Curiously enough, some of the evidence for such studies was right at hand, in the wards of great psychiatric hospitals. It had long been noted that patients of lower class and education did not usually develop "refined" psychoses — that is, conditions marked by elaborate delusional systems or marked depressive features. Such symptoms were the property of the higher-class patient, the one of greater education and refinement. Now, this distinction is just what is often found in a comparison of psychotic persons in nonindustrialized and industrialized societies.

According to many studies reviewed by Opler,[23] most psychotic conditions in

Fig. 16.6. Craziness may be evidenced in ways that are similar from one culture to another, or in ways that differ very much.

nonindustrialized cultures tend to be disorganized, confused, and eruptive, with a great deal of unsystematized rage and anxiety. Typical of the sudden and explosive "attacks" that afflict some members of these cultures is the condition of going berserk[☉] or running amok[☉] (Figure 16.6). Systematized delusions are quite rare. In more developed cultures, including our own, people who become psychotic tend to withdraw, to build their own delusional worlds, to refer their problems to themselves, and therefore to show symptoms of shame and depression. These are similar to the differences that are diagnosed as manic-depressive psychosis versus schizophrenia. As one writer has put it, in contrast with the delusional system-atization and self-referential depression that one sees in persons under stress in "literate cultures," members of preliterate cultures "do not commonly withdraw into themselves to create a little dream world where everything can be ideally ordered. . . . The individual is psychologically faced outward, he is a 'tribal' man, and, under duress, he directs his anxieties and hostilities outward toward the material world."[24]

This is not to say that cross-cultural evidence has established a specific kind of psychosis for different societies or cultures. There is a great deal of evidence, but it is mixed. According to one review, a fair conclusion would be: "Psychopathology emerges as a caricature of its culture, or as a continuation of socially learned behavior patterns. Psychopathological ideas and acts represent culturally shared experience applied in the wrong way, at the wrong time, and in the wrong place."[25] This conclusion, they add, is based on suggestive rather than on compel-ling evidence. All that can be said with some certainty is that changes in forms of psychosis often appear to reflect major changes in culture.[26]

amok (or berserk). Frenzied behavior; running wild. A form of psychotic behavior seen in some Asian cultures.

Understanding psychosis

Behind the various theories of psychosis we have just discussed can be found two major approaches to understanding this condition: the dispositional approach and the situational approach (see Chapter 13).

■ The *dispositional* approach to understanding psychosis assumes that it is a condition or state that one carries around within oneself. It may be a transient condition, like anger, or it may be a long-lasting state like a protracted illness. In either case, since it resembles having a disease, it is best treated by medical-type approaches.

■ The situational approach to understanding psychosis assumes that it is a way of life that represents the individual's total response to the perceived situation. The best analogy might be the developmental stage that is called *adolescence*. Because it does not resemble a disease, psychosis should be dealt with by procedures of rehabilitation or education in nonmedical settings.

In the remainder of this chapter, we will compare these two approaches, and conclude with an experiment in which they are contrasted.

4. The dispositional approach to psychosis, expressed as medical treatment, diagnoses and treats it as an illness in a hospital.

By far the most familiar view of psychosis is that it is an illness. Most journalistic accounts concerning crazy people use the term *mental illness* and include such statements as "a victim of schizophrenia, the commonest of the severe mental illnesses." All of the familiar words used in talking about psychosis are medical: *illness, diagnosis, cure, symptom, hospital, prognosis,* and *treatment.* The professionals are all either doctors or people who act like doctors. And the modern tradition of humane care and treatment of psychosis has been almost exclusively medical.

This view has by now entered so deeply into our everyday thinking that many persons find it difficult to think of psychosis in terms other than the medical. But a little thought will indicate that the medical view may not be applicable to this condition. Strictly speaking, medical models are applicable only to conditions in which some foreign physiological influence takes over the functioning of a person's body and causes it to work in a maladaptive way. The influence may be accidental, such as a bullet from someone's gun or a blow on the head. It may be in the form of a virus, as in pneumonia, or of a poisonous substance, such as is found in contaminated food. But, whatever its form or its source, the foreign influence was originally independent of the person's body and then entered and changed the body. In this view, treatment consists of eliminating either the foreign influence or its effects, a cure is accomplished when this happens, and the body is restored to something like its original state. The term *body* is used here in a physical sense. Even when it is the "mind" that is being treated in this approach, it is assumed that a physical organ (such as the brain) is being treated or cured.

One of the chief antagonists of this approach, the psychiatrist Thomas Szasz, has argued that mental illnesses are not, in this sense, illnesses. One cannot "catch" a mental illness, nor can one transmit it to others.[27] Rather, one undergoes some significant change as a person, much like falling in love or becoming an adolescent. The fact that these conditions can be changed by the use of drugs does not prove that they are illnesses. One may, for example, speed up or slow down an adolescent's passage through this stage of life by the use of appropriate drugs.

The mental hospital. Although Western society has always maintained one or another kind of asylum in which disturbed persons might be temporarily housed,[28] they have not always been large institutions. In the London of Shakespeares's time, a small hospital holding no more than twenty-five patients at a time sufficed for the needs of a good-sized city (Figure 16.7). This was not because there were not a lot of disturbed persons wandering around, but because until the eighteenth century the government did not maintain large-scale establishments to provide such services for its population. One of the major products of the French Revolution and the change in thinking that accompanied it was the establishment of hospitals, together with the conviction that society itself bore a responsibility for the humane care of its deviants and unfortunates.

Within a century after this, every major country in the Western world had begun to set up institutions for the care and treatment of all sorts of unfortunates, including those whom we now call *mentally ill*. There was no generally accepted way of understanding such persons, of course; that came only in the nineteenth century. They were simply housed, protected from themselves, from each other, and from society, and permitted to stay if they could not leave and leave if they preferred not to stay. Then, as modern societies became industrialized, there arose a lower class of less educated workers whose lives were harsh and without much hope for change. Certain countries such as the United States began to receive large waves of working-class immigrants. As a result, hospitals became dumping grounds for those who showed, in often strange ways, an inability to cope with their situations.[29] Under such circumstances, patients rarely received individual attention or study. This in turn made it still more difficult for even the best physicians to develop a theoretical understanding of the phenomenon they confronted. The myth, still persistent, that this is a mysterious malady with no con-

Fig. 16.7. The eighteenth-century patients of Bethlehem Hospital in London, according to an engraving by Hogarth. On certain days, the patients made extra money (which was used to improve their food budget) by permitting visitors to view their antics for a penny (hence our modern word *bedlam*). Accounts of Bethlehem indicate that on nonvisiting days the patients mostly sat around quietly—just as they do in mental hospitals today.

nection with reality, had its origins during this period of the nineteenth century.

In the United States, the major figure in the development of mental hospitals, the founding mother of our state hospital system, was Dorothea Dix, a woman of almost pathologically high energy, herself the product of a life marked by serious neurotic disturbances and depression. She was quite incapable of maintaining what we would term normal relations with other persons, but she singlehandedly browbeat twenty different states as well as the federal government into constructing huge hospitals to house an increasing population of the mentally ill. Her concern was not with what happened in the hospitals but with their existence as institutions to carry out the government's most humane goals, the treatment of the mentally ill as a separate group.

The systematizers. In Europe, hospital building had also proceeded apace. By the 1880s, huge institutions housed a largely chronic population of psychotic patients who lived under minimal standards and whose care consisted of occasional sedative medication and the opportunity to be removed from the pressures of family and society. Then a German psychiatrist, Emil Kraepelin, undertook to bring order to this mass of disparate clinical material. His model was internal medicine, then just beginning to flourish with the help of the developing chemical industry. Good medicine demanded, first of all, careful and precise description of observable symptoms and then the grouping of the symptoms into a rational classification based on the assumption of specific and independent disease processes.

Kraepelin's monumental achievement, which earned him the name of the father of descriptive psychiatry, was to organize all the acutely disturbed patients into two major groups: (1) Patients of higher intelligence, higher social standing, or more education, whose illness took the form of regular cycles, from a low point of severe depression to a high point of extreme mania (hence, the manic-depressive) and (2) a much larger group, often of lower social class, intelligence, and education, whose illness, he thought, usually began in puberty and thereafter pursued an inevitable downhill course toward complete dementia (a condition he called *dementia praecox*).[⊙]

It was a system that had worked well with medical patients, including the fairly large number of psychotic patients whom Kraepelin treated for purely physical conditions. These included the organic psychoses, such as might be induced by chemicals, by the consequences of advanced syphilis, by chronic alcoholism, or by little-understood diseases that affected the central nervous system such as Huntington's chorea or certain inherited conditions. Then, as now, it was recognized that many such strictly physical causes, as well as accidents and other traumas, could lead to conditions that were similar to the so-called mental illnesses. Kraepelin simply assumed that all were the result of physical causes, probably biological and genetic in nature, that had not yet been discovered. He then proceeded to describe and classify all his cases according to one set of principles.

But there was as yet no theory. It remained for Eugen Bleuler, another brilliant hospital psychiatrist in Germany, to take this step. Bleuler was a genuinely original thinker who rivaled Freud as a true systematizer of ideas. His contribution was to take Kraepelin's classification and "explain" it by means of a universal theory of psychological functioning. In this view, thought processes and emotional processes together make up the web of one's psychological functioning. Some persons, for reasons that were often as much developmental as physical, become victim to a progressive splitting apart of these two major kinds of processes; their thinking and their emotions, instead of collaborating, begin to separate, and the desperate efforts at adustment that the person now makes to pull the processes together is observable to others as the acute symptoms of psychosis. Bleuler did not believe that the condition began in puberty nor that it took an irreversibly down-

dementia praecox. An earlier name for schizophrenia.

hill course, but that it could occur at any age and that it was both understandable and curable. Because the major characteristic of the condition was a splitting apart of central psychological processes, he termed the condition *schizophrenia*, or "splitting illness" (now often, and quite incorrectly, referred to in the popular press as "split personality").

Because both Kraepelin and Bleuler had accomplished the great feats of theory, the idea that schizophrenia was a single disease remained unquestioned for almost a century. Because their model was the medical illness (although, to his credit, Bleuler viewed the condition as a true psychological disorder), the psychotic patient was hospitalized, diagnosed, and treated, and above all was viewed as a victim of a disease, just as are victims of pneumonia and strokes.

5. The situational approach to psychosis suggests that this condition is to be understood as behavior in a social context, frequently the behavior of a victim.

The situational view is that psychosis is not an illness but a state in which the person's fundamental problems in living become too much, and the person then collapses in the face of the problems, turns away or gives up, and undertakes a radical reorganization of personality, of life stance, perhaps of the totality of experience. Such a person is not ill, is not properly to be called a *victim*, and does not need hospital treatment but rather some safe and secure place to pass through and to recover from the crisis.

Social class and treatment. During the 1950s, there occurred the first studies in which a major situational factor, one's socioeconomic class, was studied in its relation to personality disturbances. A sociologist, August Hollingshead, and a psychiatrist, Frederick C. Redlich, published a pioneering study[30] in which they directly attacked the question of whether one's socioeconomic class was related to one's chances of becoming psychotic, to the diagnosis one might receive, and to the treatment that one then gets. They located 1,891 persons, comprising just about the total number of adults who were receiving treatment for neurosis or psychosis in the urban area of New Haven, Connecticut. With the cooperation of private practitioners and the staffs of hospitals and clinics, they assigned each of the patients to one of five socioeconomic classes. Their analysis of the resulting relationships showed a disturbingly clear pattern: (1) The lower the patient's socioeconomic class, the more likely the person was to be receiving some form of treatment; (2) The lower the patient's socioeconomic class, the more likely the person was to be diagnosed as psychotic and the less likely to be diagnosed as neurotic; and (3) The lower the patient's socioeconomic class, the more likely the person was to be treated in a hospital and not to be receiving private psychotherapy.

These results were not peculiar to one period of time, for they were replicated in a follow-up study done about ten years later.[31] They indicate clearly that Kraepelin's intuition was correct: Differences in social class are related to differences in one's type of "mental illness." His own intuition, therefore, casts doubt on his conviction that he was dealing with a purely medical condition with physical causes.

Blaming the victim. To the degree that they ignore social and cultural factors in evaluating and treating disturbed persons, psychologists and psychiatrists may be accused of serving as agents of an unjust society. Unwitting agents, perhaps, but agents nonetheless, and with even greater power over their clients because of their obvious sincerity in pursuing only the aims of treatment and cure.

This legitimate accusation has recently been taken up by social critics within the helping professions and made the starting point for a severe attack on clinical psychology and psychiatry. The basis for the attack is a Marxist critique of psychological theory. These critics would maintain that, just as human behavior is influenced by social forces, so is human consciousness. Therefore the situation in which many "sick" persons find themselves is a direct consequence of the "sick" society in which they must live. The solution, they would then argue, is not to give the patients psychotherapy, for this would simply serve to adjust them to an unjust order.[32] The solution would be to change the social order.

In an extension of this argument, Beit-Hallahmi[33] has recently argued that psychologists in particular have been guilty of social control in the guise of treatment. "The importance of interpersonal and social conflicts tends to be obscured by our preoccupation with internal conflicts . . . [for] a major function of psychologists today is to rationalize inequality." He notes that there is a persistent tendency on the part of psychologists, especially those in clinical specialties, to look for, and find, the sources of human problems in what goes on inside people's heads. The way they act in the world, especially the way they act with persons who are closest to them, is given less emphasis. If, then, people are seen to be in disadvantaged positions, psychologists have a strong tendency to find the causes for their troubles in the persons' personalities or attitudes or abilities (Figure 16.8).

In short, the tendency of many professionals to "blame the victim" may make it difficult for them to perform services that are genuinely useful to their clients. Explanations involving "person blame" so diffuse the responsibility for people's difficulties that the professionals may do more harm than good. As one survey of this problem concludes, "person-blame interpretations are in everyone's interests except those subjected to analysis" — that is, the patients themselves.[34]

The Rosenhan study.

The two approaches that we have been comparing are not easy to put to experimental test. In one study by Rosenhan, however, current medically oriented practice in hospital psychiatry was examined by a simple yet ingenious method.[35] Over a three-year period, eight adults (five men and three women) obtained admission to a total of twelve different mental hospitals and then reported on their experiences. The eight persons consisted of Rosenhan himself and seven volunteers, none of whom had a history of any psychological abnormality. In each instance, they called a hospital and requested an appointment. They then showed up at the admissions office with the single complaint that they

Fig. 16.8. From the point of view of the jockey, the horse has taken over (a situational explanation); but from the point of view of the crowd watching from the stands, the jockey is probably at fault (a dispositional explanation).

had been hearing "voices." The voices seemed to be saying "empty" or "hollow" or "thud." No other symptom was reported.

Aside from falsifying their names, vocation, and employment, the pseudo-patients answered all other questions truthfully. One of them was admitted once with a diagnosis of manic-depressive psychosis, and the other times the admitting diagnosis was of schizophrenia. On admission, all the pseudo-patients immediately dropped their "symptoms" and behaved normally and cooperatively; their only ward activity, aside from going with the group to whatever was organized for them, was to make notes on their experiences. This they did quite openly, because no one seemed to be concerned about their doing so.

None of the pseudo-patients were detected. All were eventually discharged with the diagnosis of "schizophrenia in remission"—a vague phrase that is meant to refer to the fact that the "disease" has receded to a state of latency but is still present. Rosenhan notes that this discharge diagnosis is of some importance, because the sanity of the eight participants had never been detected. The discharge diagnosis thus implied that they were in fact schizophrenic and remained so, not that either some mistake had been made or that they had been cured. As Neisser[36] later commented concerning this study, its most important finding was simply that the diagnoses arrived at for the eight pseudo-patients were not hypotheses, as a diagnosis should be, but irremovable labels. By this study, the scientific pretensions of psychiatry had been dealt a serious blow.

Rosenhan puts the essential question in this form: "Do the salient characteristics that lead to diagnoses reside in the patients themselves or in the environments and contexts in which observers find them?"[37] In medicine, the salient characteristics, the evidence, reside in the patient. This is why physicians take your pulse, listen to your heart, or take a sample of your blood. For example, a patient is never diagnosed as pregnant only because she is examined in a maternity clinic. The only acceptable evidence for such a diagnosis would be evidence from the patient herself, quite independent of the context. Alternatively, when we say of some persons who try to enter a restaurant and are refused admission, that they are not well dressed, we do not refer to their personal, "inner" characteristics. We mean that, in this context, by the standards currently in force at this restaurant, they are not dressed the way they should be. But, as we all know, the restaurant may change ownership, or dress habits may change, and these same people may be welcomed at another time and be described as acceptably dressed.

If a gynecologist mistakenly diagnoses a woman as pregnant, and she then has her regular menstrual period a few weeks later, the physician would hardly "interpret" this incident as further proof of her pregnancy. Yet this is just what happened in the case of the eight pseudo-patients: The way they were perceived was shaped entirely by the diagnosis that they carried. Their note taking was viewed by the nursing staff as a form of compulsive, therefore pathological, behavior. One patient who paced out of boredom was immediately judged as nervous. Another's statement that he had been closer to his mother than to his father during early childhood, but had reversed this relationship as he got older, was written up as "having a long history of considerable ambivalence in close relationships."

From beginning to end these eight persons were perceived as though everything they said and did was caused by something inside them, in this case a disease called *schizophrenia*. If they paced up and down as a normally bored person might, they were viewed as sick people who were nervous—which was then seen as part of their sickness. And if they are sick, with a sickness that probably will stay with them all the rest of their lives, their subsequent behavior has to be understood in terms of their sickness.

There is an alternative view, not yet fully spelled out in theory or practice but one that might form the basis for psychology. In this view, it is emphasized that

There must be something the matter with him
  because he would not be acting as he does unless there was
  therefore he is acting as he is
  because there is something the matter with him

He does not think there is anything the matter with him because
  one of the things that is
  the matter with him
  is that he does not think that there is anything
  the matter with him
therefore
  we have to help him realize that
  the fact that he does not think there is anything
  the matter with him
  is one of the things that is
  the matter with him
—Laing, 1970, p. 5

whatever people do, no matter how odd or different, they are acting in terms of the situation as it appears to them. No behavior at all ever takes place in a vacuum—not even the supposedly free behavior of the laboratory, for the laboratory is itself a significant social context that is perceived by participant and experimenter in ways that profoundly affect them both. When the context is ignored, as it is in the medical view of psychosis, the staff will find themselves dealing with psychotics in ways that sensible observers can spot as ludicrous or harmful. In Rosenhan's study, a nurse casually opened her blouse to adjust her bra in the presence of a group of male patients—not because she thought they were blind, but because she was convinced they were out of touch with reality (as all schizophrenics are "known" to be) and therefore could not be affected by her act. When the rest of us spot this act as somehow wrong, as faintly cruel, we are saying that we are able to appreciate the human situation of female nurse and male patients—an appreciation that both nurse and patients, for different reasons, may lack.

Summary

1. Psychosis appears to be a universal human condition and is surely the most deeply felt and radically influencing of all conditions.

2. An overview of the course of hospital admissions for psychosis suggests that the rates are constant except for specific changes, which are usually the result of sudden social upheavals for which one segment of the population lacks resources with which to cope.

3. The natural history of psychosis may be divided into three phases: an introductory or buildup phase that may extend into childhood; an acute phase, which is the phase identified in the lay mind as "crazy"; and a period of readjustment and stabilization, spent in a mental hospital in most contemporary societies.

4. The two major categories of psychosis are manic-depressive and schizophrenia.

5. Organic (physically related) psychoses differ from functional (not related to physical causes) psychoses in having a more sudden onset, an identifiable physical agent as cause, and little or no relation to the personality structure of the patient.

6. The most widespread theoretical explanation of psychosis is that it is a true illness but that we do not yet know its cause.

7. There is some evidence for a measurable genetic component in psychosis.

8. The fact that two or more persons are genetically equivalent (as in the case of the Genain quadruplets) does not seem to conflict with marked differences in their life adjustments.

9. Drug therapy in mental hospitals, consisting of tranquilizing and energizing drugs, has all but abolished former reliance on forms of restraint and physical treatments.

10. Diagnosis of psychotic conditions is unreliable even in the hands of trained professionals.

11. Electroshock therapy is still used and appears to be specifically indicated in cases of severe depression.

12. If one or more family members are psychotic, it is highly likely that the family atmosphere will be disturbed and its relationships deviant.

13. Well-adjusted mental patients, even those considered severely disturbed, are capable of adopting and sustaining identifiable roles and life-styles. These serve to produce specific impressions on the hospital staff and to assure some stability in the patients' lives.

14. The two major figures in the history of hospital psychiatry, whose influence and work established the medical approach to the treatment of psychosis, were Kraepelin (who organized the symptoms into manageable clusters of diagnoses) and Bleuler (who organized the material into a systematic theory and gave us the term *schizophrenia*).

15. Studies pioneered by Hollingshead and Redlich have established links between one's socioeconomic status and one's diagnosis and mode of treatment. The lower the status, the more likely one will be diagnosed as psychotic, be treated in a hospital, and receive organic rather than verbal treatment.

16. Rosenhan's study in which persons posed as psychotics in a hospital indicates that in the majority of cases the patient is judged not on the basis of personal characteristics or behavior but on the basis of the context in which the patient is seen: A covert situational approach is expressed in a dispositional formulation.

In this chapter, you will be shown the way that psychotherapy as a discipline developed at a specific point in modern history. From the later nineteenth century until the present, as you will see, psychotherapy offered a series of continually changing models of interpersonal interaction.

The psychoanalytic movement will be traced, from Freud's beginnings to contemporary neo-Freudian thought. Rogers' quiet revolution will be discussed, followed by the major innovations of the behavioral therapies, and more recently, the new developments that build on the insights and innovations of Reich. You will be able to see a developing orientation in which emphasis is placed on self-education and self-growth rather than on the diagnosis and treatment of forms of illness.

17

Psychotherapy

In the eyes of the public, psychology is almost equivalent to psychotherapy. The latter is by far our most well-known activity. No other figure is as familiar as the white-coated "doctor" who treats people for their emotional problems, usually with the help of the psychoanalytic couch. Some of this is only popular myth, some of it based on historical fact and some on contemporary practice. In this chapter, we will survey the major approaches to the flourishing field of psychotherapy, organizing our discussion in terms of its historical development.

The invention of psychotherapy

Psychotherapy arose to fill a number of needs at the end of the nineteenth century. Among these were

- The need for a comprehensive and rational account of why people acted the way they did. Darwin had laid the foundation for such a natural science of biology. Now it was needed specifically for people.
- The need felt by many people to understand themselves and their place in a rapidly changing world.
- The need specifically felt by women to understand themselves, with a view to changing their status in a male-dominated society.
- The need felt by both men and women to break free of social restrictions in regard to their sexual impulses.

Psychotherapy was invented, and then offered to a willing public, in answer to these needs. It soon became a profession and even an institution in its own right.

---

1. Bertha Pappenheim and Sigmund Freud jointly devised the techniques and underlying theory of psychotherapy.

In the early 1890s, Freud was shifting his practice from clinical neurology to the treatment of what were then called *nervous disorders*. He was not yet using the methods that we associate with his name. One of his great interests was hypnosis, which he shared with an older friend and colleague, Josef Breuer. They both used it in treating the disorder that was then called *hysteria*©—a collection of symptoms and experiences of dissociation and disorganization of the personality. The two clinicians decided to collaborate on a volume, to be called *Studies on Hysteria*, in which they would present five of their cases as well as a brief theoretical communication by Freud and some additional discussion by the two co-authors.[1]

By far the most interesting of the cases they presented was that of Anna O., as they called her. In those days, a medical case written up for publication had to include great precautions against revealing a patient's identity, especially if the authors had been bold enough to discuss some details of her sexual life. She had been a patient of Breuer about twelve years before, a bright and independent-minded young woman from a wealthy Jewish family in Vienna. Her real name was Bertha Pappenheim, as was revealed many years later by Ernest Jones, the official biographer of Freud. In later years, she moved to Germany where she became a famous figure in philanthropy and social work, a field that she helped to found. She wrote, traveled widely, directed institutions and organizations, edited scholarly works on history, and after her death had a postage stamp issued in her honor.[2]

She was clearly a gifted person, and it is hard to believe that this is the same person as the severely neurotic patient that Breuer describes. In the early phases of her treatment, she was acutely disturbed, with neuromuscular and sensory disorders, garbled speech, and visual hallucinations. After one suicide attempt, she had to be hospitalized, and at this time she would speak to no one but Breuer—and to him only in English. Then she became a "multiple personality," with one of the personalities exactly ten years behind the other. Apparently Breuer could often bring about a shift between the two by showing her an orange.

But in all these varied disturbances, Bertha kept to her own course. While hallucinating, she often used to mutter to herself. One day, when someone repeated back what she was muttering, she began to turn her expression into a more or less coherent story. As she kept at this, it evolved into a continuing, dramatic dialogue about herself with her ill father, for whom she was caring. In this way, she was able to be relieved of each day's accumulation of distress, anxiety, and negative feeling. She called the method her "talking cure" or, in a very apt phrase, "chimney sweeping." Breuer was able to facilitate the process by putting her in a light hypnotic state, and in this way through the winter of 1881–1882 the two of them each day "relieved her of the whole stock of imaginative products."

We might ask, in some surprise, "But if she simply wanted to complain about what was bothering her, especially in regard to the care she was giving her father, then why in the world didn't she do it directly? Why did she develop symptoms and then have to clear them away by this roundabout method?" The answer is simple enough. Some people, perhaps many people at some times in their lives, are not capable of being this directly in touch with their own feelings. This is just what psychotherapy may help them to do. Bertha seems to have been one of the first persons to do this on a regular basis.

Elaborating the method. Bertha now took an additional step, again entirely on her own. Following her father's death, she herself took a turn for the worse. Her sad, dramatic tales turned into sequences of hallucinations, which could only be relieved by Breuer putting her into a state of deep hypnosis. She called these states "clouds," and in them she would describe all her fears and visions. (Again, we see, she needed some external mechanism to help her express what she was deeply feeling.) Then, after another year of this, she began to show two distinct states of consciousness, one of them her normal one and the other, usually occurring dur-

On his psychoanalysis Woody Allen has said, "When I first started going, I was worried my personality would be changed to conform to a norm representing a typical middle-class Viennese of 1920. Now I would be willing to settle for that."—*San Francisco Examiner* & *Chronicle*, December 7, 1975, p. 5 of Sunday Punch section

hysteria. A form of neurosis in which mental conflicts have been converted into physical symptoms such as paralysis or tics.

ing the evening, located precisely one year earlier in time — that is, in the winter of 1880–1881. In effect, she relived the previous winter, day by day, with an exactitude that could be verified by the entries in her mother's diary as well as by Breuer's own case notes.

She now began to concentrate on the six-month period from July to December, 1880, just prior to the "year-earlier" time that she had been working on. Many of her symptoms had originated during this period. She worked on each symptom separately, going back over each occasion on which it had appeared until, by tracing backward in time, she came to its initial occurrence. Then she would deal with it, usually by talking about it and expressing the strong feeling associated with it. With this, the symptom as it currently existed would be removed. It was almost as though she had found a means to reach back into the recesses of her mind and turn off a switch that had been left on for many years — but of course this is the analogy that occurs to a twentieth-century reader of the case. In her earlier "talking cure," she had been working on problems that were current for her. In this elaboration of her method, which psychoanalysts later came to call *abreaction,*° she revealed and then worked through problems that were long buried.

As an example of what she was able to accomplish by this method, Bertha traced her phobia of drinking water back to an incident years before. She had seen her lady companion's little dog lapping from a water glass, but she was too polite to express her disgust. She then developed an inability to drink water, but she did not know why. Now, years later, having abreacted the incident, the symptom was gone for good.

Again, we may note that Bertha supplied the clinical material, then devised a method for dealing with it and applied the method to herself. She was patient and doctor, all in one. Her final contribution to the history of psychotherapy may, however, be the most dramatic of all. First she announced the termination date of her own treatment. On June 7, 1882, she declared, she would be completely cured — and this in fact did appear to occur after she relived the origin of one more experience. But that was not the complete story. Breuer had discreetly left out of his account some other details that he told privately to Freud, and which Freud later revealed to the translators of his work. These details had to do with Breuer's final visit to Bertha.

He had expected not to see her again, since she had said she was cured. Then she called him back, and he came to her house to discover her in a condition of false childbirth, loudly proclaiming that she was giving birth to his child. The poor man, some thirty years her senior, was frightened off. He immediately took his wife away on a "second honeymoon" and did not speak about the case for many years. This was why it was only published when he and Freud began to talk about it ten years later. Breuer wanted nothing to do with the sexual implications of his therapist-client relationship with Bertha, implications that she had quite clearly spelled out for him in their final meeting.[3]

Transference and free association. Thus did Bertha leave her legacy of theory and practice all through the early years of psychoanalysis. Breuer did not really ever grasp what was going on. Although he was an astute clinician, he was no theorist, and one suspects that Bertha used him, so to speak, for her own purposes. It was Freud's gift, however, to be able to realize what she had done and, once he had studied her successes, to weave them into a theory and a method. She had bewildered the gentle Breuer with her final scene of a hysterically imitated childbirth. But Freud saw that she was trying to say that in the course of her treatment she had developed a strong and positive attachment that had strong sexual overtones, and that her cure was possible only when this too was expressed and its consequences squarely faced.

abreaction. A cathartic process used in psychoanalysis that reduces the anxiety or tension by having the patient psychologically relive the event that caused the problem.

In that Victorian setting, such sentiments were completely inadmissible, yet, as Freud reasoned, they must have colored much of the relationship and perhaps even been the basis for her trust in Breuer. Building on this basis, Freud was later to come to one of his most useful therapeutic concepts, which he called *transference*.[☉] He suggested that, in the course of treatment, the patient "goes back" in time and reproduces much of the individual infantile situation, complete with its powerful sexual attachments, that lie at the core of every adult neurosis. The analyst becomes a screen on to which the patient now transfers the strongest of these feelings. In a real sense, the analyst becomes for the patient a desired parental figure, and the childhood neurosis is now replayed in the therapy session with the analyst as substitute parent (Figure 17.1).

Fig. 17.1. In the course of psychoanalytic treatment, the patient develops a "transference neurosis." Its cure marks the end of the analysis.

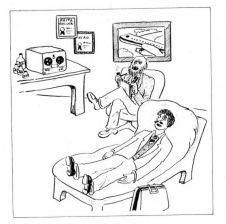 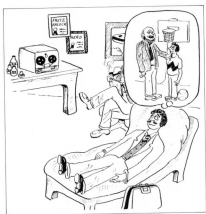 

Freud referred to this process of regression and replaying as *transference*, and the neurotic attachment that was thus induced he termed a *transference neurosis*.[☉] To cure the adult neurosis, which was what had brought the patient into treatment in the first place, one develops a transference neurosis and then cures it—and this was precisely what Bertha Pappenheim had done all on her own. She had worked up her own positive transference to Breuer and then brought it out into the open by openly expressing its sexual basis. Once this was done, she could be freed of the neurotic attachment to him and hence to the parental figure that he represented. Breuer was perhaps too close to the situation to see it clearly—or to see that, if there is transference from patient to analyst, there may also be some element of countertransference[☉] too, going in the opposing direction.

Bertha had introduced another element also, in her "chimney sweeping" technique. But Freud had only partially glimpsed its effectiveness. Then, a decade later he unveiled it as free association. In this procedure, the patient is encouraged to lie down (hence the analytic couch), relax, and, without looking at the analyst, begin to say whatever comes to mind, regardless of its content, totally without hesitation or self-censoring. But in the beginning it was his inventive women patients, not Freud, who insisted that this method be given a fair trial. When Freud tried to question one patient about her stomach pains, she told him that she did not know what caused them. He made the mistake of asking her to remember by the next day. "She then said in a definitely grumbling tone that I was not to keep on asking her where this or that came from but to let her tell me what she had to say."4

Here in embryo was the psychoanalytic method of psychotherapy—free association by the patient, which led to a transference neurosis and its cure. The combined efforts of two innovative geniuses, Pappenheimer and Freud, gave us a profession that is still growing today and still producing new forms.

transference. A psychoanalytic term for the phenomenon in which the patient transfers to the analyst feelings formerly held toward other people who have been important in earlier life.

transference neurosis. In psychoanalysis, an intense attachment directed to the therapist, originating from childhood attitudes toward the parents.

countertransference. A reversal of transference; a process whereby the therapist develops personal feelings about the client derived from the analyst's own earlier life experience.

2. Psychotherapy is an interpersonal situation in which the focus is entirely on the experience of one of the participants.

Psychotherapy is so much a part of our lives today that we tend to take it for granted. We often equate it with interpersonal activities that resemble it—for example, counseling of a younger person by someone older, or friendly advice and support given by a sympathetic friend, or even the dormitory bull session in which secrets and personal feelings are shared. Psychotherapy is all of these, but we suggest that it is distinguished by a characteristic that is unique among all the variants of a planned interpersonal relationship. The conducting of a psychotherapy session is based on an attempt at totally concentrating on the world of experience of one of its participants, the client. The other participant, the psychotherapist, is also involved in an individual world of ongoing experience, but it is deliberately mobilized in the service of the client exclusively. And this is the nature of the psychotherapist's technique, the mark of the psychotherapist's skill, to be able to mobilize one's own experience totally in the service of a client's experience.

The therapist's ability to accomplish this has been called by many names; perhaps the most appropriate is the term that forms a key element in Carl Rogers' view of the therapeutic process. His term is *empathy*. This is his description of what happens: "I let myself go into the immediacy of the relationship where it is my total organism which takes over and is sensitive to the relationship, not simply my consciousness. I am not consciously responding in a planful or analytic way but simply in an unreflective way to the other individual, my reaction being based (but not consciously) on my total organismic sensitivity to this other person. I live the relationship on this basis."[5]

Fig. 17.2. A flowchart of the major influences, beginning with Freud, in the history of clinical thought and practice. (a) Neo-Freudians—socially oriented psychoanalysts of the 1920s and 1930s, including such figures as Erikson, Fromm, Sullivan, and Horney; (b) body approaches—practices such as structural integration (Rolfing), massage, sensory awareness, and other therapeutic and nontherapeutic work involving direct body contact; (c) Eastern thought—movements and practices such as yoga, meditation, Zen, and the martial arts; (d) T.A.—transactional analysis, a system of individual and group therapy devised by the late Eric Berne; and (e) the behavioral therapy movement—here linked to Freud by dashes, to indicate that much of its original impetus derived from an opposition to Freud's views.

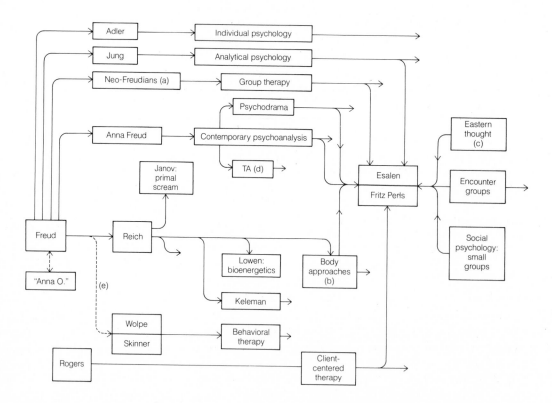

Clients cannot usually talk about their own participation in the same way; if they could, they would not be in the role of client. Rather, their activity, at least at the beginning of the process, is an individualized mix. Their own experience is accepted and denied, expressed and distorted, known and unknown. As they gradually find their way through the often terrifying world of their own experience, they usually learn how to lessen the distance that most persons keep between themselves and their selves. When this is achieved, they can then accept themselves for what they are and be whatever they are — not necessarily to be like their therapists, but simply to be like themselves.

Approaches to psychotherapy differ in how they bring about this kind of result — in how the therapist functions and in what is expected of the client. Our summary review of the major varieties of psychotherapy will be facilitated by reference to the lines of influence shown in Figure 17.2.

The psychoanalytic tradition

Freud's influence lives on in the direct line of orthodox psychoanalytic thought and practice. Today, this dominates the teaching of psychiatry in most medical schools and also in the work of a number of psychoanalytic schools that broke away from classical psychoanalysis. In addition, Freud left an enduring impact on all of contemporary Western culture. He was a very great man — a fact that we are likely to forget today, now that we are aware of some of his weaknesses and have become accustomed to the innovations in thought that he brought about. Our world would be vastly different if he had not lived, for he completely altered the moral climate. He provided our only theory of psychological functioning, established our only means for changing people without harming them, and had an incalculable influence on all the arts and on much of our social science.

One of Freud's weaknesses was that he tended to be dictatorial, with the ability to attract a wide and disparate group of followers who then disagreed with one another and often with Freud himself. One of those who joined him early and left before World War I, engendering feelings of bitterness that were never healed, was Alfred Adler.[6] An ardent socialist — as contrasted with Freud's devoutly middle-of-the-road position — with interests in education and child development, Adler refused to accept Freud's emphasis on sexuality as a primary motivating force. He founded his own psychoanalytic school, which he called *Individual Psychology*;○ it has come into prominence recently as a movement closely related in thought and approach to humanistic psychology.

Carl Jung, the other major figure who broke with Freud before World War I, was almost the opposite of Adler — a conservative, religious, scholarly Swiss physician with an interest in cultural anthropology, symbolism, and spiritual and cosmic themes. His work, too, has steadily increased in importance, largely because it is in tune with contemporary concerns with myth, legend, and the occult.

Among those who remain in the direct line of Freud's work, much of the original format of psychotherapy has been retained. The couch is still used, and the patient appears at regular hours, often once a day, for analyses sometimes lasting for years. Within Adler's group, psychotherapy has become more informal, often resembling counseling. For the Jungians, psychotherapy relies more heavily on dreams and on person growth that is guided by cosmic and universal symbols.

An important group known as the neo-Freudians○ are identified by their common emphasis on social rather than biological factors in personality theory.[7] Arguing that human beings are basically social rather than biological creatures, they view interpersonal difficulties as being caused primarily by interpersonal situations. Karen Horney,[8] for example, one of the early woman analysts, was the first to treat female clients as different from males. Personality problems, she

Individual Psychology. Adler's school of psychoanalytic thought and therapy.

neo-Freudian. The group of modern psychological theories and theorists based on a modification of Freud's thought.

Case study 17.1:
Classical psychoanalysis

The material that follows is taken from the first, second, and last sessions of the psychoanalysis of a ten-year-old boy named Richard. The analyst is Melanie Klein, an Austrian physician who during the 1920s and 1930s in Britain pioneered in child psychoanalysis. We have chosen this material as an example of psychoanalytic procedure because it demonstrates very clearly the activity of the analyst in interpreting a patient's productions.

The analysis in this case consisted of ninety-three sessions over a four-month period during World War II. Richard had come with his parents to spend the war years in a village in Wales where Klein was staying. A precocious and musically gifted child, he had become increasingly withdrawn, frightened, and dependent on his mother. He was afraid to go out by himself and in particular to associate with other children. In addition, he had periods of severe depression and showed many hypochondriacal⊙ symptoms.

At the opening of the first session, K. (Mrs. Klein, the analyst) sat down at a table where she had laid out some toys and writing material. R. (Richard, the patient) sat down and ignored the toys, "looking at her in an expectant and eager way, obviously waiting for her to say something. She suggested that he knew why he was coming to her: He had some difficulties with which he wanted to be helped." He immediately began to talk about his worries and fears—not only of the other children but about the war. He was very concerned about what Hitler might do to the Poles and Austrians, and he mentioned that K. was Austrian. Then he remembered some other worries, for example, that he wondered about people's insides and about how blood flowed inside of people.

K. now asked him if he was worried about his mother as well. R. then told about his fears, at times amounting to terror, concerning his mother's health. He recalled an accident she had once had. "In the evenings he often feared that a nasty man—a kind of tramp—would come and kidnap Mummy during the night"—although he, Richard, would come to her rescue. K. asked if he thought the tramp might hurt her, and R. said that he might.

K. now suggested that the tramp was very much like the Hitler who attacked people such as Austrians—for example, K. herself. K. then added, "At night he might have been afraid that when his parents went to bed something could happen between them with their genitals that would injure Mummy."

R. was surprised and frightened at this interpretation,⊙ and apparently did not know the meaning of the word *genitals*. They then discussed the word and its relation to sexual intercourse and childbirth. R. remarked that Daddy was a very kind man and would not hurt his mother. To this, K. said that perhaps R. had contradictory thoughts about his father. "Although Richard knew that Daddy was a kind man, at night, when he was frightened, he might fear that Daddy was doing some harm to Mummy. When he thought of the tramp, he did not remember that Daddy, who was in the bedroom with Mummy, would protect her; and that was, Mrs. K. suggested, because he felt that it was Daddy himself who might hurt Mummy."

R. showed both anxiety and surprise at

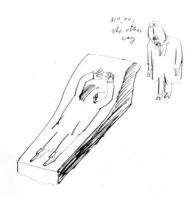

No, no, the other way

Fig. 17.3

hypochondriasis. A neurosis in which an individual is excessively concerned with physical wellbeing.

interpretation. In psychoanalysis, the analyst making the patient aware of resistances, as well as explaining symbolism.

group psychotherapy. A type of therapy in which individuals work within a group and, with the aid of a leader, help each other solve problems.

maintained, are different for a female in a male culture, and this difference is not significantly a matter of the biological distinctions between the sexes.

Unable to accommodate themselves entirely to Freud's thought, the neo-Freudians either joined or organized other schools of psychotherapy, and in the course of this they radically altered the practice of the profession. We owe to them our contemporary, informal format in which therapist and client face each other across a desk or simply in separate chairs. In addition, we owe to them and to those they taught the special format known as *group psychotherapy,*⊙ in which from four to ten patients meet with one or sometimes two psychotherapists to share their treatment with the therapist as well as with their fellow group members.

The practice of psychoanalysis. As our psychoanalytic Case Study 17.1 indicates, the patient is given no instruction in dealing with individual experience (Figure 17.3). This aspect of the method is handled by free association. In effect, the patient simply lets experience "happen" as it will, without trying to make it happen but equally, without trying to interfere with it in any way. The justification in psychoanalysis for such a free-form approach to one's own experience is that the bulk of one's experiencing is assumed to be unconscious. Therefore, there is no way one can "get in touch with it" consciously. However, if one lies back and gives up the use of conscious mechanisms of control, the unconscious significance of the experience will appear—perhaps not to the patient, but to the analyst, who then interprets it.

This method, therefore, rests on two pillars—(1) the patient's unconscious, which produces certain products in the course of free association and (2) the psychoanalysts's skill in interpreting and organizing these products. The patient's this interpretation, but he appeared to accept it. He did not accept every interpretation, and in fact actively rejected some, but seemed eager to use certain ones (such as this one) to talk about himself. This ended the first session.

At the second session, R. arrived early, apparently eager to begin. He immediately started to tell about some other worries and fears to add to those mentioned the day before. "He feared there might be a collision between the sun and the earth and the sun might burn up the earth; Jupiter and the other planets would be pulverized; and the earth, the one planet with living people on it, was so important and precious." In addition, there were all the small countries in Europe that Hitler might take over.

K.'s interpretation was that the "precious earth" was his mother, and the people on it her children; the small countries were also the children, R. and his friends. "The sun and the earth in collision stood for something happening between his parents." The other planets that might be pulverized stood for children who might get hurt if they came between the parents.

The analysis continued in this way, with R. offering this kind of material and K. interpreting it. She also dealt with his other productions: his gestures, his expression, his behavior in the treatment room, his drawings, his use of the objects and the furniture in the room, and his dreams and fantasies. By the final session, he had obviously formed a deep attachment to her, and was very silent and sad at the prospect that the relationship was about to end. "This whole session was characterized by long pauses and obvious efforts to speak, still to do some work, and not to give in to his depression." When he caught a fly and put it out of the window, K. made the interpretation that "flies had played various roles in former sessions. Sometimes he had killed them (and then they had often stood for bad babies or even for the bad Daddy). At other times, he had set them free . . ." He then began to talk lovingly of his father, and she explained this as his wish to have someone to replace K., someone who was nearly as good as his own mother.

R. now went into the kitchen and drank some water. K. "interpreted that if he could not have the good breast, he wanted now to take in the good penis of the father." R. responded by extended fiddling with the clock on the table, then by talking about how good K. was and how nice he himself was. He went about the room catching and killing flies, and then settled down to empty K.'s purse and count the money in it. She interpreted this as his wish to take as much milk as possible from her before they parted. "His killing 'all the flies' was to protect Mrs. K.—and Mummy—against the bad babies whom he felt she contained and who would endanger her."

As the session ended, R. "used every opportunity to touch Mrs. K." He was clearly fighting against his feelings of depression, hoping against hope that "he would see her again and would continue his analysis." When they went into the village where he was to take the bus, "he quickly took leave of her and said he would rather she did not see him get on the bus."—Klein, 1975, pp. 19–24, 462–464

experience is, so to speak, "handed over" to the skilled ministrations of a knowledgeable guide, who does not need to resort to empathy but in fact should maintain a neutral half-distance, or what Freud called "free-floating attention."

Rogers: The quiet revolution

Most innovators in psychotherapy have been medically trained. Carl Rogers, one of the few who came out of academic psychology, worked originally in a child guidance clinic and then with young adults in a college setting. Out of this practice, he developed the view that psychotherapy ought not to rest on the notion of curing an illness but on the idea of assisting people in unblocking their own potential for growth. Left to their own experience, in an atmosphere of acceptance and trust, he thought that it might be possible for most persons to see their way through what was currently troubling them. All that they might need was the support to find their own way in an atmosphere that he first called *nondirective*© and then *client-centered*.©[9]

3. Rogers turned psychotherapy inside out by allowing the client to find and direct its course.

Rogers' quiet revolution in psychotherapy was to return it to its original concept. He took seriously the idea that this was a unique interpersonal situation

nondirective therapy. Rogers' earlier term for his approach in psychotherapy. See *client-centered therapy.*

client-centered therapy. A form of humanistic, nondirective therapy developed by Rogers and based on the theory that people can work out their problems in a supportive atmosphere.

**Case study 17.2:
Client-centered psychotherapy**

During the late 1950s and early 1960s, Carl Rogers and his associates undertook a research project involving the use of client-centered procedures with hospitalized schizophrenic patients. The excerpt that follows is from a session with one of these patients, a young man in his twenties, whom Rogers had been seeing for about eleven months. The sometimes lengthy silences that appear in the tape of the interview are noted in the transcript. The letter *T* stands for *therapist*, and the letter *C* for *client*.

T: I don't know why, but I realize that somehow it makes me feel good that today you don't have your hand up to your face so that I can somehow kind of see you more. I was wondering why I felt as though you were a little more here than you are sometimes and then I realized well, it's because . . . . I don't feel as

though your're hiding behind your hand, or something.
[fifty-second silence]
And I think I sense, though it could be mistaken, I think I do sense that today, just like some other days when you come in here, it's just as though you let yourself sink down into feelings that run very deep in you. Sometimes they're very bad feelings like last time and sometimes probably they're not so bad, though they're sort of. . . . I think I understand that somehow when you come in here it's as though you do let yourself down into those feelings. And now. . . .

C: I'm gonna take off.

T: Huh?

C: I'm gonna take off.

T: You're going to take off? Really run away from here? Is that what you mean? Must be some, what's, what's the . . . what's the background of that? Can you tell me? Or I guess what I mean more accurately is I know you don't like the place but it must be that something special came up or something?

C: I just want to run away and die.

T: Uh, hum. Uh, hum. Uh, hum. It isn't even that you want to get away from here *to* something. You just want to leave here and go away and die in a corner, huh?

[thirty-second silence]
I guess as I let that soak in I really do sense how, how deep that feeling sounds, that you, I guess the image that comes to my mind is sort of a, a wounded animal that wants to crawl away and die. It sounds as though that's kind of the way you feel that you just want to get away from here and, and vanish. Perish. Not exist.
[one-minute silence]

C: All day yesterday and all morning I wished I were dead. I even prayed last night that I could die.

T: I think I caught all of that, that . . . for a couple of days now you've just *wished* you could be dead and you've even prayed for that . . . I guess that. The one way this strikes me is to live is such an awful thing to you, just wish you could die, and not live.
[one-minute, twelve-second silence]
So that you've been just wishing and wishing that you were not living. You wish that life would pass away from you.
[thirty-second silence]

C: I wish it more'n anything else I ever wished around here.

T: Uh, hum. Uh, hum, Uh, hum. I guess you've wished for lots of things, but Boy! It seems as though this wish to not live is deeper and stronger than anything you ever wished before.

---

in which the focus was to be entirely on the client's experience. He differed from Freud and other psychoanalysts on this issue more than any other. To Rogers, the troubles that clients brought to a therapist were not caused by uncontrollable biological impulses but more simply, by ineffective ways of using themselves. Therefore what they needed was not a skilled interpreter who would remain at a neutral distance from them and translate as a visiting anthropologist might the primitive thoughts of a savage, but a fellow experiencer who would share with them the process of feeling oneself as a unique and promising human being. The two would then be, in the words of the psychiatrist-philosopher Karl Jaspers, "partners in destiny."

The practice of client-centered therapy. In the Rogerian setting, the traditional roles of doctor and patient are very much deemphasized. Rogers' term was not *patient* but *client*, and the two were always on a first-name basis. (By contrast, imagine one of Freud's patients calling him Sigmund.) To this informality of structure, Rogers added an insistence that most of the familiar medical concepts no longer applied—concepts such as illness, cure, psychodynamics, symptom, or interpretation. The status gap between client and therapist was nearly eliminated, and the direction of psychotherapy now became a function of the client's discovery of a hidden potential for independence and self-direction.

In a famous statement, Rogers summarized what he considered the "neces-

[one-minute, thirty-six-second silence]
Can't help but wonder whether it's still true that some things this friend said to you—are those still part of the thing that makes you feel so awful?

C: In general, yes.

T: Uh, hum
[forty-seven-second silence]
[After an additional interchange concerning their next appointment, since the hour is nearly up, the therapist says:]

T: And another thing I would say is that . . . if things continue to stay so rough for you, don't hesitate to have them call me. And, if you should decide to take off, I would very much appreciate it if you would have them call me and . . . so I could see you first. I wouldn't try to dissuade you. I'd just want to see you.

C: I might go today. Where, I don't know, but I don't care.

T: Just feel that your mind is made up and that you're going to . . . leave. You're not going to anywhere. You're just . . . going to leave, huh? [fifty-three-second silence]

C: That's why I want to go, 'cause I don't care what happens.

T: Huh?

C: That's why I want to go, 'Cause I don't care what happens.

T: Uh, hum, Uh, hum. That's why you

want to go is because you really don't care about yourself. You just don't care what happens. And I guess I'd just like to say . . . *I* care about you. And *I* care what happens.
[thirty-seond silence]
[Client bursts into tears and unintelligible sobs]

T: Somehow that just . . . makes all the feelings pour out.
[thirty-five-second silence]
And you just weep and weep and weep. And feel so badly.
[Client continues to sob, blow nose, breathes in great gasps]
[thirty-four-second silence]
I do get some sense of how awful you feel inside. . . . You just sob and sob.
[Client puts his head on desk close to microphone, which magnifies his gulping, gasping sobs]
[thirty-one-second silence]
I guess all the pent-up feelings you've been feeling the last few days just . . . just come rolling out. [Blows nose]
[thirty-two-second silence]
There's some Kleenex there, if you'd like it . . . Hum. [sympathetically] You just feel kind of torn to pieces inside.
[one-minute, fifty-six-second silence]

C: I wish I could die. [sobbing]

T: You just wish you could die, don't you? Uh, hum. You just feel so

awful, you wish you could perish.
[Therapist laid his hand gently on the client's arm during this period. The client showed no definite response. However, the storm subsides somewhat.]—Excerpted from a tape by Carl R. Rogers, "Two Interviews with Mr. Vac," by permission of Carl R. Rogers and the American Academy of Psychotherapists

---

sary and sufficient" conditions for bringing about positive change in the personality:

- The therapist is able to accept the client in a positive way, with no preconditions attached, an acceptance that Rogers called *unconditional positive regard.*[○]
- The therapist achieves a full and accurate sense of the client's personal world of experience, a form of understanding that Rogers called *empathy.*
- The therapist's acceptance and understanding are both expressed in such a way that they are communicated to the client.[10]

As Case Study 17.2 shows, the technique requires simply that the therapist accept and reflect back the feeling tone of what the client says, no more. There is no interpretation, nothing added by the therapist to express a theory, nothing in the way of judgment, no mention of illness or cure. The emphasis is restricted entirely to whatever constitutes the client's present world of experience, no matter how blocked or contradictory or self-defeating that may now be.

The rationale behind Rogers' deceptively simple approach is that in most clients there has developed a condition in which what the person thinks or imagines or wants is somehow separated from the self-image. Thus, one might want to have sex with a partner but experience guilt because such an act is inconsistent with one's self-image. If this split continues, the gap may become more than the

unconditional positive regard.
Rogers' term for complete acceptance of a person in therapy.

person alone can resolve—but in a client-centered setting, in which wishes are freely expressed through the avenue of feelings, the self-image may become softened and the gap bridged. The specific problem may not be solved—for there is not always a simple solution to a difficult problem. But the anxiety and self-torment that accompanied the problem may be lessened as the person "grows through" the condition of being caught in this kind of problem.[11]

The behavioral therapies

This major movement in modern psychotherapy had its origin during the 1950s in the work of Joseph Wolpe, a South African psychiatrist who was influenced by modern learning theory. Brought to the United States by Wolpe and by Arnold Lazarus, the movement was further influenced by followers of B. F. Skinner. Academic and experimental psychologists, who had kept themselves separate from psychoanalytic and other clinical work, were now ready to use their skills and background from service in World War II to develop a psychotherapeutic approach that would be solidly grounded in psychological theory and research.

Behavior therapy is currently the fastest growing of all approaches to psychotherapy. Behavioral therapists have been particularly active in opposing what they term the "medical model" that is implied in psychoanalysis and its offshoots. They argue (1) that psychotherapy is a form of education, training, and habit formation, not a means of inducing personality change; (2) that the doctor-patient relation is not the only possible model for such a procedure; (3) that change can be effected by methods other than "talking out" one's problems; and (4) that there is no need for such concepts as unconscious nor for such practices as searching out and reconstructing the client's childhood history.

---

4. Two major forms of behavioral therapy are systematic desensitization,° or deconditioning of anxiety-related states, and operant therapy,° or retraining in more appropriate behaviors.

Systematic desensitization. As developed by Wolpe and Lazarus, the systematic desensitization approach to psychotherapy rests on the idea that so-called neuroses are simply maladaptive forms of behavior that are kept alive through the mechanism of anxiety. The technique does not look like conventional psychotherapy, but it has been very effective as a therapeutic technique. It is based on the principle, taken from the learning laboratory, that one behavior can eliminate another by being practiced as a substitute for it. Thus, to conteract and eliminate the client's anxiety, the client is first trained in a technique of muscular relaxation, because anxiety is assumed to be a form of muscular and autonomic tension. Thus, the client counters an anxiety state by practicing a learned relaxation technique. Second, the patient and therapist together make up a list of possible situations, known as a *hierarchy*, that are associated with the phobia and are arranged in order of increasing severity.

If, for example, the problem is a phobia related to flying in airplanes, an item low on the hierarchy might be seeing a newspaper photograph of an airplane. An item a little higher might be seeing a real airplane at the airport. Still higher on the list would be the behavior of walking up to an airplane and looking at it. Given such a list, the client pratices each of them, either in real life or in imagination, beginning with the least anxiety producing. If an item results in anxiety, the relaxation procedure is used to counteract it—and in this way the client even-

systematic desensitization. A behavior therapy technique in which exposure to anxiety-arousing situations takes place systematically until the subject is desensitized to them.

operant therapy. A form of behavioral therapy, based on operant conditioning, in which the therapist tries to eliminate the elements in the client's background and environment that are causing the problem and also to provide positive reward for learning appropriate behavior.

tually reaches the point of being able to handle the actual phobia-producing situation without anxiety.[12]

Operant therapy. Working with mentally retarded and brain-damaged children, Lindsley in the 1950s showed that even the most difficult and helpless cases might be retrained by the use of operant techniques. Here was one of the first practical applications of the conditioning procedures (see Chapter 7) that had been developed in the laboratory. The approach is based on a presumably universal principle of learning: that the probability of occurrence of any behavior is determined by its consequences. There is no need for the subject or client to understand what is going on or to cooperate. Thus the most unreachable persons might now become candidates for therapeutic retraining in acceptable modes of behavior.

One example is an adult male, so severely brain damaged that he has been bedridden since birth and is unable to take care of any of his physical needs. He is conditioned to assist in his own feeding. The procedure consists in shaping his feeding behavior through the use of a sugar solution on his tongue as a reward. He learns to turn toward the food, to open his mouth, to take in food and not spit it out, and to swallow it.[13] In another example, autistic children who are unteachable because they are mute and refuse contact with adults, are successfully taught to speak through a patiently worked-out process of individual shaping of mouth movements and sounds.[14] Bandura argues that the learning process called *modeling* is an important aspect of all psychotherapy.[15]

The range of applications of contemporary behavioral therapy is now quite large, and in a typical conference one might find presentations on education and teaching, organizational management, alcoholism and drug abuse, sexual problems and stress-related illnesses, population control, stuttering, hyperactivity, and getting along with one's boss. Workshops in assertiveness training° might typify the procedures that are used. Participants are first taught something of the behavioral principles involved. They are then engaged in role-playing situations that provide elementary training in recognizing their individual cues for anxiety. They are given instruction in techniques of relaxation or imagery to reduce the anxiety. Additional training provides them with specifically useful behaviors such as "body language," the use of eye contact, techniques of listening, complimenting, revealing and nonrevealing, and how to judge situations. Finally, it allows for intensive rehearsing in low-threat situations where the participants can support one another.

The practice of behavioral therapy. The behavioral therapies came out of a tradition of theoretical opposition to psychoanalysis. For its first few decades, as "behavior modification," behavior therapy offered itself as a new set of discoveries in applied learning theory (Figure 17.4). But in fact, as London once pointed out, its principles and methods were already in use.[16] Did it, then, have a unique set of practices? Case Study 17.3 indicates that it now does, for it combines various forms of behavioral engineering with a number of nonbehavioral operations—imagery, fantasy, role playing, rehearsal, and self-exploration. Indeed, it seems to resemble good therapy in general. If anything, it is a philosophy, a point of view toward human experience that is unique about this approach to psychotherapy. It has been well described as "a general orientation to clinical work that aligns itself philosophically with an experimental approach to the study of human behavior.[17] As in any good experiment, the person's experience is admissible, but only in the form of behavioral data—that is, in ways that are always under the experimenter's control. Just as in psychoanalysis—although for very different reasons—a gap is maintained between therapist and client, and the latter's ongoing experience is kept under strict control.

As a result, behavioral therapy is both unique and valuable, but only to the

assertiveness training. A form of behavioral training in which individuals are positively reinforced for being assertive or aggressive in situations where they are normally passive or vacillating.

degree and in the way that a sound technology is. It can rationally organize a disordered array of elements, in this case the elements of someone's behavior. In the face of the anxiety and distress felt by someone whose life is out of control, or who cannot cope with the environment, behavioral techniques bring about a sensible order of things that the client can live with.

In one of its most effective examples, the behavior of a whole ward of patients is changed for the better through a controlled system of exchange that is called a *token economy*.[18] Specified items of behavior (for example, buttoning one's clothes) earn or lose the patient's credit, in the form of tokens, toward desired privileges such as trips to the store for candy. The procedure is particularly effective with hospitalized mental retardates, for whom it appears to organize and simplify what must be a very confusing world. Every requirement that is significant for them is broken down into small and manageable units. They are told specifically what they have to do, and what will be the consequences of not doing it. Usually a large, highly visible indicator such as a blackboard is installed so as to mark the step-by-step achievement of each individual. Even severely retarded or withdrawn patients thus learn very soon how to accommodate themselves to this simple and just arrangement. In effect, they learn to do what the rest of us can do without thinking — to conduct themselves in such a manner as to maximize their chances of being rewarded.

The net effect of most neurotic or maladaptive conditions being to make things seem confused, frightening, upsetting or difficult to control, these techniques of behavioral engineering are bound to lessen the anxiety, to bring the world into order, and thus to "cure" the neurosis. But, because the techniques consist essentially of ways of managing the patient's experience and behavior — rather than allowing the experience to happen or to encourage its full potential — the behavior therapies are bound to work best when the patient goes along with them without questions. The best patients for this approach are therefore those who are relatively unsophisticated and nonreflective. Behavior therapists themselves, when they go into therapy for their own personal growth, almost never choose to go to behavior therapists.

The techniques, in fact, will work even better when the patient is in a condi-

Fig. 17.4. Four different groups (a control group receiving no treatment, a group receiving only attention, a group receiving insight-type psychotherapy, and a group receiving desensitization behavioral therapy) were assessed before and after treatment in a stress situation (speaking before a group). These are the results on two different measures of anxiety. (Compiled from Paul, 1966)

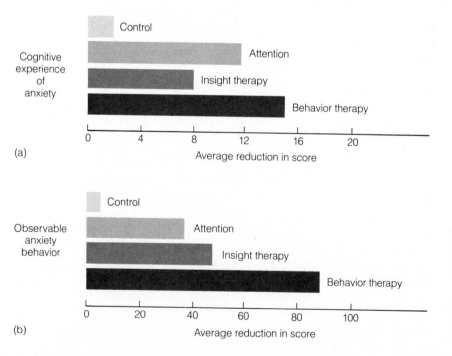

token economy. A training method based on positive reinforcement, such as tokens, used at mental hospitals. See *token learning.*

**Case study 17.3:
Behavioral therapy**

This case presents, in summary form, the behavioral treatment of a thirty-five-year-old woman, married and the mother of two children, who comes to the therapist with complaints of anxiety, depression, and feelings of helplessness and dependency. These feelings keep her from acting as an independent and responsible adult.

At the outset of the therapy, she is in a state of distraught, even childish anxiety—nervous, unkempt, and openly afraid that she is "going crazy." The first thing that the therapist has her do is fill out a form on which she lists all her complaints and problems. He discusses this list with her and then gives her a "homework assignment"—to list all the situations that make her anxious. In addition, he immediately assigns her a specific task: to try to smile at people and note their reactions, in this way teaching herself that she does indeed have a predictable effect on other persons.

The major training begins with instruction in how to relax voluntarily, on the assumption that muscular relaxation is incompatible with anxiety and therefore relaxing oneself will lessen one's anxiety. Over the next few sessions, the client's use of this technique helps her a great deal

with her anxiety outside the clinical setting. The therapist now begins to work on her depression by advising her to try doing things on her own, and by giving her some sound advice concerning how to cope with such feelings. In a later session, he engages her in imaginary rehearsal of effective ways of managing her daily schedule so that the vicious cycle of lassitude, depression, and greater lassitude can be broken.

All of this results in obvious improvement in both her outside behavior and her feelings about her behavior, and these results are reinforced by further suggestions for relaxation and by the therapist's encouragement. She now continues to practice her relaxation techniques, obtains further encouragement from her husband, and is able to follow through on what is rehearsed in imagination in the office. As a consequence, she is able to enlarge her social life and carry it off without anxiety, as well as to do many new things on her own. When this improvement brings home to her the fact that she lacks assertiveness, the therapist starts to work on this by having her keep a daily record of her successes and failures in asserting herself. She reports back on what she does, and the two of them discuss the ways she might improve. When she reports anxiety about being home alone, the therapist

suggests she work out a schedule involving progressively longer periods of time by herself. When she complains of being depressed, he works out with her a program of new activities that might bring her pleasure. And when she shows some of her newfound assertiveness by canceling too many appointments, he firmly reminds her that she will be billed for future cancellations.

Future problems, concerning feelings of low self-esteem and guilt or difficulties in being assertive with her friends, are handled by these methods of counseling, scheduling, rehearsal training, and reporting back on her successes and failures. Finally, when circumstances unexpectedly force her to spend an entire day alone in the house, and she finds that she is able to take it in stride, it is clear to the client as well as to her therapist that they have turned a corner. The remainder of the therapy consists essentially of cleaning up some loose ends.—Goldfried and Davison, 1976, pp. 3–4

---

tion of ignorance or helplessness—and the worse off they are in these respects, the more likely it is that behavior therapy will be the most successful approach. It gives its best and most dramatic results with conditions that are not amenable to other approaches—such as the severely retarded or brain damaged, the backward schizophrenic, or the mute, autistic child. Arnold Lazarus, one of its leading figures, sums ups its strengths and weaknesses thus: "The application of behavioral procedures is singularly appropriate whenever specific deficits emerge. People who cannot stand up for their rights, individuals who cannot enter crowded places . . . and people who cannot control their bladders or their tempers may all benefit from conditioning and other special retraining techniques."[19]

Reich and the rediscovery of the body

It is customary to think of psychotherapy as a form of talking. This is entirely true of psychoanalysis and its derivatives, and largely true of behavioral therapy as well. At this point, however, we come to a radically different procedure in psychotherapy. We may summarize it as an attempt to change people, not by altering their ideas, attitudes, thoughts, and memories, but by altering the way they experience their own bodies and conduct themselves bodily. In psychotherapy, this approach, one of the major innovations since Freud, is owed to Wilhelm Reich, one of Freud's most brilliant and controversial followers.[20]

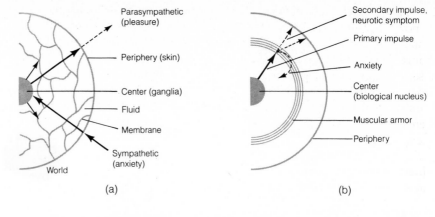

Fig. 17.5. Reich's conception of the basic functions of the vegetative nervous system: (a) naturally, in an unarmored organism, and (b) in an armored organism, showing an inhibition of primary impulses resulting in anxiety and neurotic symptoms. (From Reich, 1971, pp. 261, 262)

Reich's contributions are inextricably entangled with his career and his own personality. He began as a close and respected follower of Freud but broke away in the early 1930s, partly on theoretical grounds (Figure 17.5) and partly because he had developed a technique involving direct work on his patient's bodies. In the same year, he was expelled from the international organization of psychoanalysts as being too political and from the Communist Party for being too clinical. He left Germany and only a few years later had to leave Norway after a violent controversy over his claim to have discovered the secret of biological life forms. In the United States, he pursued a number of careers. He developed his approach to psychotherapy, but he also claimed to have discovered "orgone energy,"⊙ the basis for all matter and energy in the universe. He ran afoul of the medical establishment, and the U.S. Food and Drug Administration seized and burned his books and journals. Brought to trial for some of his work with orgone accumulators, he refused to defend himself before a nonscientific jury,[21] and was sent to prison where he died a year later, in 1957.

---

5. Reich's therapeutic innovation, vegetotherapy, opened a new dimension in understanding the basis of character and neurosis.

Reich began the modern psychotherapeutic movement that rests on the rediscovery of the body. In his early, ground-breaking work, *Character Analysis*,[22] he had enlarged the scope of psychotherapy by showing that each person presents a total, individual character that is expressed in voice, posture, gesture, mannerism, stance, and movement. He then went on to show that character in this sense is carried in one's body armor. This is the specific organization and structure of the body that each person develops to maintain his or her character as a lifetime stance. The therapeutic procedure that he developed, which he called *vegetotherapy*,⊙ aimed at releasing and dissolving the body armor by a direct attack on the musculature of the body.

Reich's approach should not to be confused with a current fad of interpreting various elements of what is called *body language*⊙—a process that assumes that one's body is a kind of neutral communicator that flashes various signals. The approach inspired by Reich, rather, attends to how people live in and experience their own bodies as manifestations of their character. This includes the structure and conformation of their figures; how they sit and stand and walk; how they express themselves in face and stance and gestures; how they breathe; and how they are "put together" physically.

orgone energy. Reich's term for the cosmic force that underlies all matter and energy in the universe.

vegetotherapy. Reich's therapy based on the dissipation of sexual tension through dissolving bodily armor and reaching full orgasm.

body language. A nonverbal communication in which body tensions and movements give clues to what a person is feeling or thinking.

The rediscovered body may help us to explain many of the conditions that are now called *altered states of consciousness*. Our waking state is defined by our denial of our bodies; we identify the state by what goes on in our heads. But every change in our "normal" state, without exception, is brought about only by means of some important alteration in our bodies. This is how we go from our normal waking state to sleep, to dreaming, to drugged conditions, to delirium, or to meditative states. They are all states in which the body is inserted into consciousness and therefore plays a different role—and so perhaps they should properly be called *altered states of the body*.

Bioenergetic therapy.$^{\ominus}$ Bioenergetic therapy is the system of psychotherapy that was pioneered by Alexander Lowen, a psychiatrist who was originally trained

---

**Case study 17.4:
Bioenergetic therapy**

This is a description of a treatment session by Alexander Lowen, the founder of the method of bioenergetic therapy. The patient, Bill, was a mathematician, an intelligent person who suffered from chronic depression and an inability to work.

Physically, Bill was a young man with a thin, tight body that could be described as *asthenic.*$^{\ominus}$ He had broad shoulders, a narrow pelvis, and extremely tight, tense legs. His chest, which was rather large, was depressed in the region of the sternum, and his abdominal musculature was severely contracted. Owing to this, his breathing was limited to his thorax. While his arms and legs were strong, they were not integrated with the rest of his body. Despite an apparent strength, there was a weakness in his body. The split in his personality was also manifested in his facial expression. In repose, his face looked sad, tired, and old, but when he smiled he brightened like a young boy. The conflict between optimism and dejection led him into dangerous activities, in which, fortunately, nothing happened.

Bill was a rock climber; one of the best, he said. He had made many ascents of steep cliffs without any fear or hesitation. He had no conscious fear of heights or falling. He was not afraid because in one part of his personality he didn't care if he fell. . . .

It became obvious that Bill was terrified of falling. His defense against this fear was to subject himself to situations in which this could happen, to prove that he had nothing to fear. Such a tactic required an exaggerated control of his body, especially his legs. His legs were tight and tense, he could hardly bend them; his ankles were

frozen, and his arches so contracted that contact of the feet with the ground was greatly reduced. In view of his physical handicaps, he was the last person one would expect to climb rock walls, but he compensated for his handicaps by a strong will. Thus, he lived on an emergency basis, fighting each challenge with all his strength to prove that nothing would happen.

As long as this charade continued, nothing would happen to bring Bill out of his depression. He had to learn to let go; his will had to weaken its grip on his body. At this point in his therapy, I asked Bill to assume a position of stress that is used by skiers and other athletes to strengthen their leg muscles. Such body exercises have the effect of concretizing emotional attitudes and making the patient aware of his problems through the perception of his physical rigidities. In Bill's case, the exercise was designed to make him conscious of his fear of falling.

Standing at the edge of the couch, Bill bent his knees and leaned forward so that all the weight of his body was on the balls of his feet. He could maintain his balance by arching slightly backward and touching the couch with his fingers. Athletes generally hold this position for a minute or so. When I asked Bill how long he could remain in it, he said, "Forever." Since this meant indefinitely, I asked him to try. He held the position for more than five minutes while his legs trembled and the pain increased. When the pain finally became too great, Bill didn't fall. He threw himself down on his knees, as if indifferent of consequences. He repeated this exercise several times, until it became apparent that he was afraid to let the sensation of falling develop. Bill sensed that his legs would not let go. I interpreted this physical attitude as Bill's unconscious resolve to stand on his feet at all costs.

Psychologically, this meant that he would "stand alone." He unconsciously rejected any dependence on others and denied his need for contact and intimacy.

At our next meeting, Bill reported the breakthrough of a strong feeling: "That night, after our last session, I had my first nightmare. I awoke thinking there was someone in the room. I must have screamed. Awake, I thought I saw a figure at the door. I was scared to get out of bed. Finally, I heard my cat, and when I called to it I felt better. This experience reminded me of my childhood fears. I realize now that my going to bed late is due to my fear of falling asleep. . . ."

Bill's nightmare was the first breakthrough of his repressed feelings. He recognized that the strange figure in his dream represented his father and that he must have been in awe of him as a child. As he grew up, this awe was covered by an attitude of arrogance since "nothing did happen"; he was neither punished nor cast out. However, the underlying feeling of doom persisted in Bill's unconscious mind and was transferred to his work situation. His psychology of desperation demanded that he challenge the authorities to see if they would retaliate, while at the same time he was terribly afraid of losing his job. Bill had devoted his life to mastering the technique of surviving on a precipice.—Lowen, 1967, pp. 106–110.

bioenergetic therapy. Alexander Lowen's method of psychotherapy, combining elements of both Freud and Reich.

asthenic. An individual who is generally tall and lean with slight muscular development.

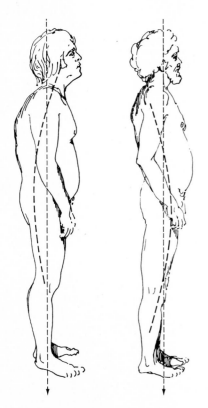

Fig. 17.6. Two modes of misalignment. The light dashed line represents the line of gravitational influence; the heavier dashed lines show how the person may "oppose" gravity in individual ways. (From Kurtz and Prestera, 1976, p. 30)

Here is one client's description of a result of rolfing: "At one point in this session, the work focused on a location lower and somewhat more lateralized in my abdomen. When Bob first began at this point, I almost immediately felt grief-stricken. My efforts to maximize these feelings led to my eventually sobbing. This crying was the deepest and most complete that I have ever experienced. While this crying grew, I felt very much like a small, lonely, and quite sad little boy."

structural integration. Rolf's treatment (also called *rolfing*) by body manipulation that is designed to realign the body correctly in relation to gravity.

by Reich. His method has been to combine a Reichian emphasis on the body and on character types with a "talking therapy" on a psychoanalytic model. An excellent and prolific writer, Lowen has had a wide influence through his teaching and through a series of popular books that clearly describe his clinical approach. They provide the best introduction to current body-oriented psychotherapy.[23]

Reich had described his vegetotherapy as a means of restoring "biophysical equilibrium" through the release of vegetative energies. His method, he said, aimed to "develop those attitudes, movements, excitations, and natural breathing rhythms that are specifically characteristic of the patient's personality."[24] Lowen adopted this approach, and added to it. In every respect, he said, the individual is a unity of body and mind, with psychic and somatic processes always working together. The unity that we call the *person* is essentially an elaborate system of energy flow, and what we call *clinical* or *neurotic problems* are essentially blocks or disturbances in the normal flow of energy through the body.

This energy is experienced by the patient and observed by the therapist as a flow of excitation that is marked by warmth, grace, freedom, and the look and feel of "aliveness." In Lowen's view, the upper half of the body normally "charges" the organism with energy, through the breathing mechanism, and the lower half of the body discharges energy, largely through the mechanisms of motility. One's character and one's typical way of getting along in the world are therefore related to how these two halves of the body are formed, how they are experienced, and how together they carry out one's intentions through expression and movement. The person who is typically "stiff necked" is thereby expressing a rigid stance of power and pride. The person who "can't stomach things" is making a significant life statement concerning sources of, and blocks to, pleasure.

Rolfing. No other area in the clinical field is currently as actively cultivated as that concerned with direct work on patients' bodies. Much of it was sparked by Reich's innovations in psychotherapy, but it comes as well from a number of long-standing educational and training traditions in Europe. Perhaps the most striking of these is the practice known as *structural integration*, or *rolfing*,© after its inventor, a biochemist named Ida Rolf.[25] She began her researches on muscular functioning while at the Rockefeller Institute and eventually developed a method of realigning the body through forceful manipulation of the muscular fasciae (the membranous sheaths that cover the bundles of muscles beneath our skin). Her basic concept is gravity: that our muscles are used to provide our stance within a gravitational field, and therefore that the way we align ourselves in standing and movement is a continuing interplay between gravity and our built-in muscular patterns of holding (Figure 17.6). By manipulating the fasciae, in a form of very deep massage, these rigid structures can be broken up, thus making possible a new and more adaptive alignment of the parts of the body.

Although Rolf had originally developed the method as a form of physiotherapy, it has gradually changed into a psychotherapeutic technique. Its practitioners have discovered—just as Reich could have predicted—that each person's body alignment is at the same time an emotional attitude, for the person always acts as a psychophysical unit. Any intervention that changes the person in one way can therefore bring about a change in another way as well. As the history of psychotherapy has shown, psychoanalytic methods, although exclusively verbal, have often served to bring about striking bodily changes—alleviating tensions, even helping cure the so-called psychosomatic illnesses. It is to be expected, then, that the reverse can happen. Systematic work on one's bodily alignment, as with the rolfing procedure, would allow breakthroughs in the expression of long-denied feelings, changes in interpersonal relations, even the retrieval of long-buried memories.

Fritz: The Gestalt approach

During the 1960s, perhaps as a major expression of that turbulent decade, many separate currents in the field of psychotherapy came together in the work and person of an elderly expsychoanalyst named Frederick S. Perls. The place was the Esalen Institute in California, the prototype of what are now called *growth centers.* Perls had been influenced by Jakob Moreno, the inventor of psycho-drama;⊙ by Carl Rogers; by his own lifetime interest in the theater; by psycho-analysis, in which Perls received his training; by Zen Buddhism; by the work of Reich, who had been one of his analysts; and by the small-group work of social psychologists in America and England. Born in Germany in 1893 and trained as a psychoanalyst, Perls had fled to South Africa to avoid Hitler's regime and then came to New York at the age of fifty-three to begin developing his own approach to psychotherapy, which he called Gestalt Therapy,⊙ a unique blend of psycho-analysis, existentialism, and theater.

After a decade in New York, another in Miami, and a search around the world for a place where he might feel at home, he came at the age of sixty-nine to Esalen, where he spent five years glorying in his role as Fritz, the first American guru. He found his first major audience among the post-Freudian generation of middle-class professionals, as well as among the younger generation who were just finding their own voice. Preaching a revolution of the senses and a reliance on being present and fully aware, he expressed perfectly the attitudes and ideals of that period, its alienation and its desperate break with the past. A restless, tortured man who described himself as "a lonely bum who loves to joke," he finally set up his own community on an island near Vancouver, British Columbia, where he found some peace during the last six months of his life.[26]

Here is Fritz' philosophy: independence, awareness, excitement, and living in the now, and the Golden Rule of "do unto others what you do unto yourself." His endless search for a nod of approval from the Freudian system that he nearly demolished (Figure 17.7); his fierce honesty and his genius for tearing apart pre-tense; his matchless clinical skills and his inability to systematize his thought; his dramatic innovations in technique and his high theatricality—all these add up to a historic figure.

The theory of Gestalt. Perls was not as interested in explaining people as in helping them to gain "self-knowledge, satisfaction, and self-support." Nor was he a systematic thinker, let alone a writer. The bulk of his work is recorded on film and in various verbatim transcripts of his workshops.[27] However, some of his separate insights are memorable:

- There are five "layers" of the neurotic personality. First there is the game-playing, phony layer, the level of behavior within which we play games and act "as if." At this level can be seen the eternal conflict between one's *top dog* (which is similar to the Freudian superego) and one's *under dog.* The second layer is the *phobic* layer, or the level of "shoulds" and of avoidance, of the mechanisms that we use to avoid discovering life. The third layer is the *impasse,*⊙ or "stuck point," which is reached when our feelings are caught between full expression and distortion. At this point, we feel that there is simply no way to resolve our problem. Fourth, there is the *implosive* layer, the set of inner forces that keeps one's feelings down and that produces the deadness or lack of feeling of which so many neurotics complain. Fifth is the deepest, *explosive* layer, the wellspring of energy that contains a potential for our explosions into joy, grief, anger, or orgasm. (In these concepts, Perls' debt to Freudian theory, expressed so feelingly in his own autobiography, is most evident.)

The Gestalt prayer

I do my thing, and you do your thing.
I am not in this world to live up to your expectations
And you are not in this world to live up to mine.
You are you and I am I,
And if we find each other, it's beautiful.
If not, it can't be helped.

—Perls, 1969b, p. 4

---

psychodrama. A form of play acting devised by Moreno. It is used therapeutically to act out roles or situations that are pertinent to people and their problems.

Gestalt therapy. Perls' eclectic combination of psychoanalysis' resolution of internal conflicts, humanism's concerns for self-actualization, and behaviorism's emphasis on awareness and feeling.

impasse. Difficulty without a solution, or a situation from which there is no escape. Perls' term for the "stuck point" in therapy.

Case study 17.5:
Gestalt therapy

This is a portion of a recorded and videotaped session with a thirty-eight-year-old woman, Barbara. The setting is a circle of about twenty persons, with Barbara (B) seated in the "hot seat" next to Fritz Perls (P). She has done some work with him before.

B: I wanted to be a good girl and have a magnificent dream for you with lots of goodies in it. I didn't manage that, but something else happened, which is maybe just as well. Last night I was in bed, and it's happened to me for a long time — though not very frequently — and what happens is I become totally paralyzed and I can't move at all. I can't move my toes and I can't open my eyes — I can't do anything. I'm just totally paralyzed. And I get very frightened and then it goes away. It seems like a very long time, but I think it's just a few minutes — maybe not even that long. But it's like I can't do anything, and what it made me think of was, uh, my inability to handle myself when I get frightened or angry. [Takes a long drag on her cigarette] I just get immobilized — so that I'm the same when I'm awake as when asleep, I'm still paralyzed.

F: All right. Could you tell the whole story again and imagine that you are responsible for all that happens. For instance, "I paralyze myself."

B: Um, all right. Um, I paralyze, I paralyze myself. . . . I immobilize myself. I won't allow myself to feel anything or behave any way if it isn't civilized and good. I won't let myself run away when I'm afraid; I won't tell people I'm afraid. I won't, uh, fight back when I'm angry or hurt. I won't ever let people know that I have bad feelings. [Starts to cry] I won't let them know that I hate them sometimes, or that I'm scared to death, and um . . . I put myself sometimes, to punish myself, in a state of panic where I'm scared to do anything. I'm scared to breathe, and then I torture myself with all the bad things I'll let happen to me. That's all I can think of right now. [Sniffs] Fritz, I don't want to cry because I think that crying is very bad for me. I think I hide behind my tears. But I don't know what I . . . hide.
[B is slapping her thigh with her hand as she talks]

F: Can you do this again? With your right hand. Talk to Barbara.

B: [Slapping her thigh and laughing] Barbara, you need a spanking!

F: Spank her.

B: [Still slapping] You're a bad girl because you're phony and dishonest! You lie to yourself and to everybody else, and I'm tired of it because it doesn't work!

F: What does Barbara answer?

B: [Voice rising] She answers that she never learned how to do anything else.

F: Say this in quotes.

B: I never learned how to do anything

- There are four basic "neurotic mechanisms." First is introjection, or taking in without true assimilation. Typically, the introjector does as others would like him or her to do. Second, there is projection, the reverse of introjection, or placing aspects of one's self out in the world as disowned. Projectors do to others what they accuse others of doing to them. Third, there is confluence, or the loss of boundaries between self and world or between parts of the self. The fourth mechanism is retroflection, in which one turns one's own behavior against the self. Retroflectors do to themselves what they would like to do to others.

- For Perls, maturation toward independence and self-sufficiency is the central theme of psychotherapy. It occurs only to the degree that the person can transmute environmental support into self-support. It comes about when

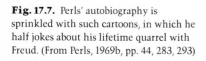

Fig. 17.7. Perls' autobiography is sprinkled with such cartoons, in which he half jokes about his lifetime quarrel with Freud. (From Perls, 1969b, pp. 44, 283, 293)

else. I know about doing other things. I know that there are other things to do but I don't know how to do them.

F: Say this again.

B: I don't know how to do them! I can only do them when I'm in a protected, supporting kind of situation; then I can do it a little bit. But if I'm out in a cold situation by myself I'm too scared. And then I get into trouble. I get myself into trouble.

F: Ya.

B: And then I get mad at myself after I've gotten myself into trouble, and then I punish and punish and punish. [Spanks thigh again] And it's like there's no end to it, and I'll never be satisfied. [Starts to cry]

F: Say this to Barbara: "I'll never be satisfied with you, whatever you do I'm never satisfied."

B: Barbara, I'm never satisfied with you. No matter what you do, it's never good enough! . . .

F: Now go into more detail. Stick to your imperatives, and each time give Barbara some prescription—what she should do to follow up.

B: Um. . . . Don't be a mime, a chameleon!

F: Tell her how she should achieve this—not to be a chameleon.

B: Figure out who you are, and what you want to be and what to do, and do it! Don't try to go around looking for other people to imitate all the time. You've imitated thousands of people, and where has it ever gotten you? You still feel like an empty shell. You've got to decide who you are, and what you want to do!

F: Tell her how she can decide.

B: [In a scolding tone] You know what your own tastes and interests and values are. You've known for a long time. They're never. . . .

F: Come on, start figuring out.

B: Well you have to develop . . . you have to do two things: You have to make a real effort to learn from other people who are much more experienced and skilled than you are and at the same time you've got to be yourself. You can't go around imitating Fritz or Virginia Satir or Dr. Delchamps or whoever the consultant of the moment is, or wherever the last seminar you went to was or the last workshop. Don't do that, that's bad! Because you're not them and you can't just go through the motions that they go through, and say things they say, and do any good for anybody. They'll know that you're a phony.

F: You mentioned my name. So, tell me, what am I? What are you copying of me?

B: Fritz, you're a man who works with people and lets them use him—you let people use you to grow.

F: Ya.

B: And I want to do that too, and I think that what you do really works . . . but I can't play Fritz. That won't work because I'm not you and my tendency would be to imitate you.—Perls, 1969a, pp. 199–203

---

one's environment furnishes just the right balance of support and frustration. The neurotic person's symptoms serve the purpose of enabling continued dependence on others rather than independence and self-direction, and these neurotic mechanisms are as varied as human ingenuity and desperation can devise.

The practice of Gestalt therapy. To exemplify and teach this philosophy, Perls developed a method that he called *individual therapy in a group*. The participants sat in a circle and took turns in the empty chair, or "hot seat," next to Perls, who worked with each person in the presence of the others. The techniques came from every source in the history of psychotherapy. However, Perls gave major credit to Carl Rogers for his "feedback" technique—in which the client confronted his or her own images, fantasies, and thoughts and set up a dialogue with them. The major difference, Perls noted, was that Rogers fed back statements, while he himself helped the client obtain feedback of complete feeling experiences.

Perls was also inspired by Reich, not toward direct work on the body but to lead his clients toward concentrating on their immediate, sensory experience. He called this arena of experience the *now*. The goal was to reintegrate those parts of themselves that they had disowned or would not acknowledge. As Case Study 17.5 suggests, Perls' aim was always to establish a "continuum of awareness," an ongoing experience of one's own possibilities and excitements, honestly faced, risked and lived out. To those who were afraid to take such emotional risks, he would say, "After all, a mistake is only another way of doing something."

Psychotherapy now

Psychotherapy began as a discipline similar to other practice in medicine, but through the contributions of Reich and then Rogers, it has been revolutionized from the inside. In former years, clients had, to an embarrassing degree, been selected and treated largely because they resembled their therapists' self-images: They tended to be youthful, attractive, verbal, intelligent, and successful (hence the term "the YAVIS syndrome"). More recently, however, psychotherapy has been moving toward a relationship in which client and therapist are equals and in which therapy is a part of one's real life rather than an isolated exercise in a clinician's office. A great number of clients now come to mutually supportive settings that do not require therapists—to encounter groups, leaderless seminars, sensitivity training, peer counseling, or consciousness-raising groups.[28]

In other respects, too, contemporary psychotherapy appears to be moving toward the aim of growth and education rather than cure, in an approach more situational than dispositional. We have noted in this chapter that the psychotherapeutic relation is unique in that it involves a deliberate focus exclusively on the client's ongoing experience. Different approaches to psychotherapy may be distinguished by how they arrange for this to happen. Psychoanalysis permits experiencing to happen in the patient, although its understanding is reserved for the analyst. Behavior therapy allows experience, but only to the degree that, as behavior, it can be managed by the therapist. Rogers restored to psychotherapy the primacy of experience, perhaps backing away too far from the therapist's role as experiential guide. Lowen superimposed the psychoanalytic approach on Reich's substantive contribution, the lived body. Perls took as his task the defeat of sophisticated patients at their own game. They were able to use psychoanalysis, not as a means of exploring their own experience, but as a means to support their neurosis, and Perls offered an array of techniques that made this game too costly to play.

Summary

1. Psychotherapy had its beginnings at the end of the nineteenth century, when it was devised by Bertha Pappenheim as a patient of Freud's colleague Josef Breuer.

2. Psychoanalysis provides a method in which problems that were long buried can be revealed and worked through. Its method is to recreate in the analytic hour the patient's infantile neurosis in relation to the parent(s), and then to cure it.

3. The psychoanalytic method depends on production of and then interpretation of unconscious material supplied by the patient through free association.

4. The neo-Freudian method, an outgrowth of classical psychoanalysis, was responsible for making the psychoanalytic approach more informal, more widely used, and more attuned to the life situation of the patient.

5. Rogers' client-centered psychotherapy, a derivative of his self theory, allows its clients to unblock their own potential for growth. This is accomplished by the technique of reflecting back the feeling tone of the clients' statements, without judgment and without interpretation.

6. Behavior therapies, currently the fastest growing of psychotherapeutic approaches, utilize a range of experimentally oriented procedures. Among them are (1) systematic desensitization, in which an incompatible response (relaxation) is practiced together with the unwanted response until the former substitutes for the latter; and (2) forms of operant therapy, in which the patient is retrained in more acceptable behaviors.

7. Reich's vegetotherapy, the first of the body-based approaches to psychotherapy, began a trend in which clients undergo change as a consequence of direct work on their bodies.

8. Reich's notion of body armor refers to the specific organization, attitude, and even structure of the body that the person develops as an expression of character.

9. The procedure known as *rolfing* aims to realign the body in the gravitational field through direct manipulation of muscular fasciae. Although entirely a body manipulation, it appears to function psychotherapeutically for many of its clients.

10. Fritz Perls was interested in helping people gain "self-knowledge," satisfaction, and the ability to be self-supporting. His mix of methods, borrowed from Moreno, Rogers, Freud, and Reich, aimed at guiding people toward the independence that he identified as emotionally mature.

11. Contemporary psychotherapy appears to have a major thrust toward growth and self-education, as distinct from its historic thrust toward forms of cure.

We now turn to the field of social psychology, concerned with relations between people. Two major approaches are available: an inside approach, concerned with the individual's awareness of others, and an outside approach, concerned with the observed effects of others on an individual. The basic social psychological arrangement, we will see, is a dyad, a two-person relationship involving their mutual behavior.

You will review the problem of social facilitation, concerned with how the presence of others affects one's behavior. Both animal and human evidence will be offered to show some of the relations between social facilitation and the nature of one's performance. A related topic, the process of social comparison, follows, in which it is shown how people evaluate themselves, under conditions of uncertainty, by comparison with similar others. Evidence from studies of anxiety will be discussed, especially in relation to the factor of one's birth order.

You will then take up the distinction between actors and observers in social relations, and the way in which this distinction affects how one explains the causes of behavior, one's own and that of others. You will be able to see how, in each individual, enduring characteristics known as *attitudes* furnish guidelines for such ongoing processes. Some of the important elements of attitudes, such as their degree of positive and negative feelings, will be discussed, as well as the ways that attitudes seem to be organized within each person. The curious relations between one's attitudes and one's behavior will be discussed and, finally, the socially important topic of how attitudes can be changed.

18

Social psychology: awareness and effect of others

In this and the following chapter, we take up the topic of social psychology. This specialty in psychology deals with people's awareness of other persons and the effect that other persons have on them. In the present chapter, we will discuss the awareness and effect of other persons as persons, either individually or in small numbers. In Chapter 19, we will discuss the awareness and effect of other persons as organized groups.

The dyad

"You can't cheat an honest man," W. C. Fields once said. What he meant by this wise remark was that it always takes two to cheat: a dishonest cheater, who is looking to put something over on another person, and a dishonest victim, who wants to get something for nothing but is outsmarted by someone cleverer. As we all know, if there is no cheater the game cannot begin. But, as we need to remind ourselves, if there is no eager victim the game falls apart. Cheating is no different from any other sensible social situation: It takes place with at least one other person, and it requires that they both do their part. It is therefore a fine example of the simplest situation in social psychology, called a *dyad*.© It consists of two persons joined in an interaction that requires both of them.

dyad. A two-person group.

Fig. 18.1. There are many kinds of dyads, each with its own "natural" distance between the participants.

1. The essential characteristics of the dyad are that behavior in it is reciprocal or mutual and that the two persons share a situation.

Many dyads are reciprocal and even symmetrical. For example, to meet someone is also to be met by that person (Figure 18.1). Other familiar examples are spouses, and lovers, and friends. Other dyads are reciprocal but asymmetrical; for example, pairings such as teacher-pupil, attorney-client, and parent-child. But in all of these one member of the dyad needs the other if the situation is to continue. If there were no parents, there could be no children, and, equally, if there were no children, then an adult could not properly be called a parent. If you and I are friends, then each of us is a friend to the other, and if I stop being a friend of yours you will not usually keep calling yourself a friend of mine. Similar arrangements are found in animal behavior. For example, the wolf that preys on a herd of elk needs the herd for food; and, equally, the herd needs its accompanying family of wolves in order to assure that the older and sickly elk are weeded out.

In the dyad, the behavior of one member affects the other, whose reaction in turn affects the behavior of the first, in what is called a "behavioral loop." Elaborate behavioral rituals in animals can sometimes be built up in this way, especially in sequences related to mating and sexual behavior. Any deviation or failure on the part of one member of the dyad will disrupt the sequence. For example, if one member of a sexual pair of monkeys is inept because it has been reared in isolation, it will be rejected by a potential mate. Appropriate behavior, then, involves seeking out a partner with whom the proper situation of mutuality can be established. This is why a Peeping Tom does not buy a ticket to a striptease show, where he might gaze to his heart's content but runs some risks in order to look at someone who would not choose to be looked at. The two members of an established dyad may even recognize their need for each other. Thus, Jean Genet, in his play *The Balcony*, has the judge say to a penitent thief, "You won't refuse to be a thief? That would be wicked, it would be criminal. You'd deprive me of being!"[1] These two participants are not simply separate entities communicating back and forth to each other, but two parts of an ongoing social situation that is meaningful to both. The situation is, in fact, so meaningful that if one refuses to take part or refuses to play the appropriate role, the other becomes unable to act. (We will discuss the social psychology of roles in Chapter 19.)

The presence of other people

Neither dyads nor other groupings of people need necessarily involve themselves in an organized relation. It often happens simply that people are in each others' presences for some length of time. I might find myself sitting next to someone on a bus ride between cities, and for an hour or more we are in each others' presence. Or, you may leave one place, where you have been alone, and walk across campus in the presence (but not the company) of a large number of other persons. The effect of others' presence was first studied in the 1890s, when it was noted that cyclists usually rode faster when competing with others than when competing only against themselves. Similar findings were reported, in dozens of studies, for both humans and animals. It appeared that many creatures will do an activity faster or better or more often when in the presence of others of their kind than when alone. For this reason the phenomenon came to be known as *social facilitation.*[⊙]

However, as we will see in the rest of this chapter, social facilitation is only one consequence of people's awareness of others and of the effect that people have on each other. We will begin with what seems to be the simplest case, in which people are simply present to each other.

2. The presence of others affects one's behavior. The effect depends on the situation and on what is being measured.

In a large office where many typists are at work, should they be separated from each other so as not to interfere with one another's work, or should they be seated in groups so as to share each others' company? And will the two kinds of seating arrangements have different results in terms of work output? Will hens eat more when they are penned in groups than when they are kept in isolation? These and similar questions are often of practical importance, and different kinds of evidence need to be considered in arriving at an answer.

The evidence from animal life. Many insects will die quickly if isolated from others of their species. In bees, this effect has been traced to the fact that they actually feed each other nutritional necessities such as vitamins and sugar. The presence of peers may also affect physical structure, such as the length of wings in some insects. And a sow will often fail to develop a normal sexual structure if she is never given the chance to be in the presence of a boar.[2]

The presence of peers during certain periods of development may also have a profound effect on later behavior. This has been shown with monkeys who were reared in isolation from birth and who then show pathological behavior in play and in sexual activities. But whether the presence of peers has a positive effect depends on the situation. With laboratory rats, as well as with birds and some insects, overcrowding results in a decrease in such positive behavior as reproduction and an increase in such negative behavior as aggression.

When the topic of social facilitation was first studied, the animal evidence seemed clear-cut. It appeared to point to the simple conclusion that the presence of peers has a facilitating effect. If hens are allowed to eat until they are completely satiated and are then placed in a room with more food and other hens present, they will resume eating. If ants are allowed to move dirt in order to build their nests, they begin work quicker and move more dirt when working in groups of three than when working alone.[3] And the other animals do not have to be engaged in the same task; sometimes their mere presence can have a facilitating influence.

One explanation offered for these findings is that competition is involved. Thus, among most animals, survival often depends on finding enough food. We would then expect that competitive behavior in the presence of food is biologically

social facilitation. A term for the increase in motivation or performance that is brought about by the presence or effect of other people.

adaptive. The animal that is more competitive for food increases its chances for survival, especially in times of food scarcity. The same might hold for other "survival" behaviors such as nest building among ants. However, social facilitation effects are found in other animal activities, such as learning a maze, that are clearly unrelated to survival, suggesting that this explanation may not be widely applicable.

A more useful explanation, applicable to both human and animal behavior, has been offered by Zajonc.[4] He suggested that the presence of others usually has the same effect, to increase the level or strength of some activity. However, the results will differ depending on the individual's state in regard to the activity. If it consists of one or more responses, or behavior, that are already known, the individual will then perform that behavior more effectively, and the presence of peers will seem to be facilitating. But if the individual has not yet learned the behavior, or is in the process of learning it, an increase in activity is just as likely to disrupt the behavior or to reinforce an incorrect response, with the result that the presence of others will seem to have an inhibiting effect. As we will see, Zajonc's theory helps to clear up many of the puzzles in the study of social facilitation.

The evidence from human performance. One important difference between human and animal evidence is that humans can be asked how the situation appears to them. That is, they can be used to provide evidence from what we have called the *inside approach,* whereas with animals such evidence can only be inferred. It has long been known that people will perform academically at a higher rate — for example, by finishing a test faster — when others are present. However, their increased quantity of activity may or may not be accompanied by an increase in the quality of their work.

How might this discrepancy be explained? One way is to ask the performers. When this is done, people report that the significant element is how they view the situation. The presence of others will affect the quality of their performance if the situation seems to them to be one of competition or if they feel that they are being tested or judged. Cottrell's interpretation in terms of evaluation apprehension,[5] is based on this sort of evidence. In this view, the performer's perception of others who are present — whether they are neutral, for example, or likely to be critical, evaluative, or in competition — will have a significant influence on whether their presence is facilitating or inhibiting (Figure 18.2).

The apparently simple question of the effect of the presence of others can

Fig. 18.2. An attentive audience will facilitate the performance of the pro but not that of the amateur.

now be answered, but in a rather complicated way. When a task is either simple in itself, such as crossing out all the capital letters on a printed page, or when it is so well learned that it seems simple to the person, the presence of others is likely to have a facilitating effect on performance. But when the task is inherently complex, such as a creative problem or a complex lesson to be learned, or when it is still being learned and so appears complex to the person, then the presence of others is likely to be inhibiting. To this basic effect, we add another — that dominant or learned responses are even more facilitated when others present are seen as evaluators. If the response is not dominant or the behavior not well learned, however, evaluation lowers the quality of performance.

One practical application to academic work may be drawn from these findings. It is usually better to study alone, because this is a situation in which the desired behavior is still being learned. Once the material has been learned, however, it is better to be tested on it in a group. In addition, the better learned the material is, the bigger the group to be tested on it. Thus, if you have studied for a test but do not know the material too well, you should sit alone in a corner, but if you know it well, choose a seat for the test that is near other persons — especially your friends rather than competitors.

The knowledge of other people

The phenomenon called *pluralistic ignorance*⊙ refers to a situation in which a number of persons each know or think the same thing, yet each is unaware that any of the others may think the same way. The phenomenon may occur, for example, in communities where custom forbids the open discussion of sexual matters. A number of members of the community may have similar sexual attitudes or urges, and all of them may feel guilty, yet each may be convinced that no one else could possibly be as wicked as they. Thus, the knowledge that each individual has about other persons (even though it is mistaken, as in this case) may powerfully affect how members of the community feel about themselves.

A most important inference to be drawn from phenomena of this sort is that people are influenced in important ways by the presence of other persons even when those other persons are not physically present. We cannot be sure whether this also occurs with other animals, but in the case of humans it adds one more dimension of complexity to the general topic of social facilitation.

---

3. Processes of social comparison enable us to evaluate our current state, especially in situations of stress or uncertainty.

Much of our everyday behavior is aimed simply at checking things out, usually for purposes of evaluation. We pass silent judgments on other persons, as well as on the state of the weather, the way our automobiles perform, or how well other persons drive. In addition, we may seek out additional information to assist us in making our judgments, as when we take a more careful look or a second look at something noticed only casually. In most such judgments, some more or less objective standards are available. However, judgments and evaluations that we might try to make about ourselves often lack objective standards. If, for example, I want to know how good my poetry is or how charming my smile is, I can hardly resort to some known standard. What I can do is compare myself with others. Such processes of social comparison,⊙ according to Festinger, form the basis for many of our perceptions and cognitions in the social realm.[6]

pluralistic ignorance. A situation in which individuals are each unaware that the others feel or behave in the same way as themselves.

social comparison. Festinger's term for processes by which people measure their own behavior, ideas, and so on by the standards of others.

Such comparisons usually are not made with reference to people who are physically present. Rather, they are made with reference to all the people we have known whose characteristics are relevant to our present situation. I will evaluate myself as a poet by comparison with other poets. Usually, however, my comparison will be with other persons who are similar to me. Thus, I will not compare my poetry with that of Shakespeare but with the work of others who are at roughly my level of ability or development or fame. And their level, at least as I view it, will then be an important factor in furnishing me with accurate knowledge about myself.

The stress situation. The notion of social comparison processes helps us in understanding certain social situations—in particular those in which explanations of social facilitation do not suffice. For example, if a number of people are asked to participate in a psychological experiment that involves receiving electric shock, they are likely to become both uncertain and anxious. They may ask themselves, "How severe will the shock be? Will it hurt? How will I react?" (Perhaps, also, "How can I get out of here?") Suppose we now ask what effect the presence of the others in the group might have on each participant. It is not likely that the explanations we arrived at in the preceding section, concerning social facilitation effects, will be of much help here.

Yet it is clear that being in a group under such stress conditions is likely to have different results than being alone. In a series of studies on variations in this situation, Schacter[7] used as his measure the tendency of his participants to affiliate. That is, they were made anxious and then asked whether they wanted to wait alone or with others until their turn was called. As might be expected (and as expressed in the familiar saying, "Misery loves company"), people who are uncertain and anxious prefer to wait with others. However, this choice was not made under every condition; misery does not love just any kind of company. People generally choose to wait with others who are in about the same situation as they are—not, for example, with persons who are not anxious or with persons who are much more anxious.

Why should people who are made anxious or uncertain tend to see other persons as supportive or as desirable company? Schacter has used the theory of social comparison to explain his findings, and a great deal of subsequent research seems to support it. In this interpretation, it is suggested that people in a state of anxiety are looking for some basis for evaluating their situation. As noted earlier, in the absence of objective standards we usually resort to comparing ourselves with others, and we tend to choose for this purpose people who are like us. This is just what the anxious participants in Schacter's studies did. When they were given some information about the others in their group, so that they did not have to spend time with the others in order to have a basis for comparison, the tendency to affiliate was reduced (Figure 18.3).[8]

An explanation of these persons' affiliation in terms of social comparison processes does not rule out other needs that they may also have had. For example, anxious people may prefer being with other anxious people in order that they can all support each other. But the social comparison interpretation provides the clearest and best-supported explanation thus far offered. In addition, it provides a link to a related series of experimental results. One of Schacter's most intriguing findings was that the tendency to affiliate under conditions of anxiety was related to the person's birth order. Specifically, firstborn children are more likely to choose to be with other persons in situations of stress, uncertainty, or anxiety. (They also tend to be more "people oriented" and to be more easily influenced by others.) Apparently, firstborns are less confident in rating or evaluating themselves, especially in regard to their emotional states. This leads to their greater need to check out their self-evaluations in the company of others who are in the same or similar states. It

Fig. 18.3. In this setting, would you prefer to wait alone or with others? If with others, would you prefer them to be braver than you, less brave, or the same? How does this relate to your own birth-order position? (See text.)

may also explain why, with a less firm basis than later-borns in knowing about their own emotional states, they are more easily influenced in becoming anxious.[9]

The actor and the observer

So far in this chapter we have shifted back and forth between an inside and an outside approach to our topic. We have discussed, on the one hand, the effect that other persons might have on an individual—that is, the social facilitation phenomenon as viewed from the outside, as by an observer. On the other hand, we have discussed the individual's awareness of other persons, which is the social facilitation process as viewed from the inside, as by an actor. This distinction between actor and observer, or between the inside and outside views of situations involving people, was also discussed in the introductory Message that precedes Chapter 1. There we referred to the complexities that might be involved in comparing the two approaches. At this point, in our discussion of some of the central topics of social psychology, we take up some of these complexities.

The situation that we are concerned with here is the dyad. Here, let us say, are two persons who share a situation. Each is influenced by the other, in a continuing interaction. Each is also engaged in a continuing and necessary effort to make sense out of the ongoing situation. That is, from the inside view (of either of the participants) there is a continuing effort at understanding and explaining what is going on, especially with the other person.

Now we come to some of the complexities. In the first place, each of the two persons in a dyad is both an actor and an observer. Each is engaged in seeing the situation from the inside, but at the same time is engaged in seeing the other person from the outside. How the participants might explain themselves, then, might very well be different than how each participant explains the other. And, in the second place, it may be possible for some persons to assume two different views regarding themselves. They may privately "know" about themselves, which would be an inside view of themselves as targets. And they may also see themselves as an observer might, which would be an outside view of themselves as targets.

As we shall now see, one of the most actively studied areas in social psychology concerns the interaction of inside and outside approaches to the study of the dyad.

Attribution

4. Attribution° takes two general forms: dispositional and situational.

The pioneer in theory and research on this topic in social perception was Fritz Heider, a social psychologist at the University of Kansas whose background was in the very productive psychology of Germany in the 1920s.

As we discussed in Chapter 5, under the heading of consistency as a social motive, Heider's interest was in the way that we organize events in causal terms. We see two events happen in sequence, such as a batter's swinging bat coming in contact with a baseball and then the ball changing direction and heading toward the left field fence, and we spontaneously perceive the event in causal terms. The ball's flight was caused by being hit by the bat. As he generalized his analysis of

attribution. Process of inferring from an individual or from his or her behavior specific underlying causes or conditions.

such perceptions, Heider constructed a rather complete psychology of interpersonal relations, in which he described what he called the naive "psychology of common sense," by which we all make sense out of our ongoing experience of people and events.[10] You will notice that Heider does not construct this theory. Rather, his interest here is in describing the informal "theory" that ordinary persons construct and use.

In our everyday, commonsense psychologies, we usually place a great deal more weight on persons than on nonpersonal influences when we are trying to figure out why something happened. In the terms introduced by Heider, terms that we found useful in an earlier chapter on psychosis, we assign more causal influence to dispositional attributes (those belonging to people) than to situational attributes (those belonging to the environment). The degree to which we all tend to do this was shown in a recent study in which subjects worked in pairs, one of them as questioner and one as answerer in a quiz game, while observers watched.[11] The questioner's task was to ask ten questions whose answers were known to the questioner. After the quiz, both contestants as well as the observers rated the questioner and answerer on their general knowledgeability. Questioners were always rated as more knowledgeable, by themselves as well as by the other persons. This held true even when the roles of questioner and answerer were chosen by lot and did not depend at all on actual knowledge. In other words, when asked to make a judgment about the two contestants, observers conformed to the tendency to credit the person rather than the situation. In answering the implied question, "How explain the fact that the questioner has more information than the answerer?" they did not say, "Because that person was lucky enough to be chosen to be questioner rather than answerer" but rather "Because that person is more knowledgeable."

The finding in this experiment has been repeated in dozens of others. When I try to explain a person's behavior, if the person is someone else I will depend on a dispositional explanation; but if the person is myself, I will depend on a situational explanation.[12] The student who receives an unexpectedly low grade on a paper is more likely to explain it in terms of the instructor's personal characteristics (tough grader; mean; or temporarily angry because of fight with spouse) than in terms of environmental influences (standards set by the department or level of performance by the rest of the class). In this case, the student is acting as an observer and taking an outside view of the instructor's behavior. But if the instructor were asked to give a self-report of the causes of this same behavior, it would be much more likely to stress the situational causes. In this case, the instructor, as the actor in the situation, takes an inside view of it. In other words, the major conclusion that is to be drawn from work on causal attribution is that the outside approach leads to stressing dispositional causes and the inside approach leads to stressing situational causes. One of the great gains from work on this problem is that it has made possible many different kinds of comparison of inside and outside approaches.

One other finding in this experiment needs to be mentioned. You will notice that questioners were rated as more knowledgeable even when they were rating themselves. That is, when questioners were asked to explain their behavior, they often responded as though they were observers of themselves, not actors reporting their own behavior. This is one of the complexities that we mentioned earlier. People can behave as actors or as observers when they are trying to understand their own behavior. If they behave as actors, they will explain their own behavior in situational terms — as when I strike out in the office softball game and look at the bat in disgust. If they behave as observers, they will explain their own behavior in dispositional terms — as when I am able to achieve some "distance" from my own weaknesses and explain my batting performance as another example of my athletic ineptitude (Figure 18.4).

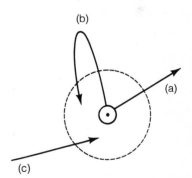

Fig. 18.4. Three forms of attribution: (a) when someone takes the role of an actor and attributes the cause to the situation; (b) when someone takes the role of an observer of his or her *own* behavior and so attributes the cause to some characteristic of him- or herself; and (c) when someone takes the role of an observer of another person and attributes the cause of behavior to some characteristic of that person.

Influences on attributions. Attributing causes to someone's behavior need not, of course, result in "accurate" or valid explanations. The general tendencies we have just discussed may lead people astray just as often as they lead them to understanding social situations. Here are some typical factors that may lead to invalid attributions or to attributions that do not conform to the general principle that we stated.

- The higher the status that we perceive for the person we are observing, the more likely we are to explain the person's behavior in dispositional terms. We tend to see high-status people as being in charge of their own lives and knowing what they are doing and low-status people as more likely to be the victims of circumstances.
- The less admirable or desirable the behavior, the more likely are we to attribute its cause to the person rather than the situation. It may be that we reason like this: that person must really have wanted to do such an act.[13]
- We are more likely to attribute the cause of some behavior to the person if it is done under various circumstances or if it is unique in some way.[14] Thus, an act of heroism is explained by some characteristic of the person rather than by the necessary equipment having been available, or the conclusion is drawn that someone must really like you if they are as nice to you away from the job as on the job.
- Actions that are highly personalized, or directed at one person, are more likely to be explained in dispositional terms. If a flowerpot falls from a window ledge and does not appear to be aimed at anyone in particular, I will conclude that environmental forces caused it to fall; but if it flies through the air quite directly at some person I will attribute the incident to some person's intent.

Attitudes: Pro and con

We have now discussed the general effects of persons on one another, under the heading of social facilitation; some of the processes by which persons know about themselves in comparison with others; and some of the ways that people explain to themselves the causes of their own and others' behavior. One other major topic remains to be discussed in connection with people's awareness of and effects on each other. It is the long-term, enduring cognitions that people seem to carry around with them and that seem to be a basis for their perceptions as well as their behavior. These enduring cognitions are called *attitudes*.

---

5. An attitude is a complex of feeling and knowledge, or belief and intention, that a person uses in an evaluative way.

Our usual state of mind seems to have three major components: some information or *knowledge* about the target of our perception or thought; some *feeling tone*, or emotional coloring, or value judgment; and some tendency to *decision* or acting in regard to the object. The components are knowing, feeling, and intending; together, they sum up to an attitude.

The study of attitudes has been central to the field of social psychology since the 1920s, when the phenomenal growth of communications media — advertising, radio, and then motion pictures — made it evident that large-scale manipulation of people's attitudes was politically feasible. Franklin D. Roosevelt, the first "radio" president, made very effective use of this medium to persuade and influence the electorate. Hitler, a few years later, made frightening use of the same channel of propaganda, even to the extent of mounting loudspeakers on street corners to blare out government announcements and speeches.

The measurement of attitudes was one of the earliest triumphs of psychology as a quantitative natural science, and helped to establish the field as a social science, in addition to providing the technological basis for modern methods of polling and opinion surveys. A number of different characteristics of attitudes seem to vary and are therefore open to measurement. For example, one can measure the amount of information that one has about the target, the nature and strength of the feelings associated with the attitude, the way that one attitude is related to others that an individual may hold, and even the relations among the various components of a single attitude. In addition, attitudes may be held in full awareness and be carefully thought out and reasonable, or they may be expressions of an individual's personal conflicts, and so may be unreasonable or irrational, or perhaps not even held consciously by the person.[15]

6. Positive feelings for others are related to familiarity and acceptance; negative feelings are a different phenomenon entirely.

The feeling aspect of attitudes has been widely studied, in part because the phenomenon of interpersonal attraction or liking appears to be so open to study among college students. By contrast, the phenomenon of dislike is less available for study and more difficult to examine in the usual research population.

The findings on interpersonal attraction are to be interpreted with a certain amount of caution, for they may often refer to superficial or contrived conditions and they may be divorced from data on related feelings such as disinterest, dislike, contempt, hatred, hostility, and loathing. Within these limits, however, the findings concerning liking—a one-to-one positive feeling—are clear-cut and definite. In general, people will be liked who possess, or at least appear to possess, certain basic characteristics: They are physically attractive (probably the most important feature of all, for both sexes),[16] friendly, and able to be interested in or flatter their partners. As some persons have always suspected, flattery will indeed get you somewhere, especially if it is not obvious as flattery.[17]

In addition to these basic characteristics of personality, there are others that help to determine degree of liking. Again in general, we will prefer or like someone who seems to be similar to us—although this basis for initial attractiveness may not of itself keep a relationship going.[18] In addition, the more familiar someone is to us, and the more exposure we have had to that person, the more they will be liked. If circumstances keep us close to or in the company of another person, we are apt to get to like them.[19]

Much of the data for these conclusions comes from laboratory studies in which, of course, variables must be strictly controlled. The weakness here is that the situation is usually artificial and the feeling that may be generated is shallow and of recent origin. To get around these difficulties, some social psychologists have tried to study the development and natural history of liking as it plays a role in acquaintance processes. This can be done by asking residents of a student housing project or a residential area which of their neighbors they know best or like best.[20] What is revealed in these studies appears to be not simply the phenomenon of liking, but rather a mixture of liking and familiarity. That is, more positive feelings are expressed toward neighbors who are more familiar, are seen or contacted more often, have no distinctively negative characteristics, and seem to show a reciprocal interest and liking (Figure 18.5). What is less often tested, of course, largely because of the intrinsic difficulty in carrying out such studies, is the nature and development of negative feelings.

The difference between positive and negative feelings is not simply one of degree. They are not two different ends of the same scale. Liking is not just the absence of dislike, and disliking is not just the absence of liking. In fact, they appear to be distinctively different areas of feeling, each with its own mode of development and its own consequences for one's experience and behavior. Negative feelings are both more complex and more specific. They may vary greatly in terms of intensity, and they are likely to be directed at a specific behavior or characteristic in the other person.

Liking, on the other hand, is much more a mode of acceptance. As long as someone is reasonably acceptable, even if we cannot pin down specific characteristics in them, we may accept and like them. Thus, if I get to know a couple who are my neighbors, I will probably like both of them about equally, especially if I have a fair degree of contact with them and if they are similar to me. But if my liking should change to dislike my feelings will be qualitatively different. My negative feelings will be directed at one rather than both, they will refer to specific items of behavior or attitude, and I will experience them as active and as impelling me to do something about them. Or, if my neighbors should move a block away so that I no longer see them as frequently, my liking would not then change to dislike but to lack of interest or perhaps a feeling of distance and strangeness. What we call liking, then, is a general, accepting feeling, but there may be a wide range of alternative possibilities of dislike, with quite different consequences for one's interpersonal relations.

Degrees of liking, even of love, can be measured, however, as Zick Rubin has done by means of a pair of scales (Table 18.1). Notice the difference between the items of the scales. Those on the Liking Scale are mostly judgments concerning the other person's positive characteristics, the assumption here being that if I can find enough of such positive characteristics in a person, my feeling will be one of liking. The Loving Scale, on the other hand, appears to tap the lover's deeper feelings. Indeed, it was specifically constructed around three feeling dimensions:

Fig. 18.5. If you were to rank these different people in terms of how much you might like them, the results should be comparable with those discussed in the text.

Table 18.1. Some 'Loving' and 'Liking' items from Rubin's scales.

From the Loving Scale:

I would do almost anything for _____.
If I were lonely, my first thought would be to seek _____ out.
It would be hard for me to get along without _____.

From the Liking Scale:

In my opinion, _____ is an exceptionally mature person.
_____ is one of the most likeable people I know.
_____ is the sort of person who I myself would like to be.

Source: Rubin, 1970.

intimacy, attachment, and caring or concern. Rubin has done a number of studies with these scales, mostly on young couples. The two scales appear to be tapping quite different feelings, for he has found that one member of a pair may score the other high on the Loving Scale and low on the Liking Scale. Love may indeed be blind, at least to some of the characteristics that lead to being liked.[21]

7. The way that attitudes are organized within each person suggests that they function in a coherent way.

In a previous chapter, we noted that a person's attitudes are often organized to form a coherent whole that we call the person's *character*. Here we consider the same phenomenon from a different angle, using as our example the following expressed attitude.

About seventy-five years ago, the Monaco correspondent of the London *Times* sent in the following dispatch about an accident with a cable car. "The funicular railways between La Turbie and Monte Carlo broke down yesterday. There were no casualties. Twelve Monacans were killed." At first reading, this seems contradictory—that is, until we realize that in the thinking of this correspondent, Monacan peasants were not people and therefore not to be included in a list of casualties. The attitude of the correspondent here is quite evident. Now, if we knew nothing else about him except that he had written this dispatch, we would in all probability be able to predict his attitude toward the then pressing question of voting rights for women.

There is common, even if sometimes implicit, agreement that everyone has a lot of different attitudes but that they are connected in some meaningful way. On a continuum ranging from the political right to the political left, one person's attitudes toward all sorts of social institutions will usually be found to cluster within a fairly narrow range. Indeed, we are all so accustomed to finding that people's attitudes cohere in meaningful clusters that we may be astonished to come across what seems to be an exception—for example, a pro football player who undertakes training as a Zen monk, or a county sheriff who leads a protest march of sharecroppers.

All of this may seem commonplace—yet it is worth examining. There is usually nothing in the content of one attitude to indicate why it should always be found in the company of certain other attitudes. Attitudes about the right of a citizen to own a private handgun would seem to have nothing in their content that relates to attitudes about sexual behavior or the use of cocaine or American foreign policy—yet, as we all know, specific attitudes on all these dissimilar issues are often found to go together. How can we explain the coherence of separate attitudes that seem to have so little in common on the surface?

A major socioclinical study,[22] carried out in the years immediately after World War II, gave some basic answers. A multistage research procedure was used on a large sample of white, adult, Protestant males. By means of a questionnaire, two groups were identified in this sample, one scoring high and one scoring low on a dimension that was called *authoritarianism*.⊙ Individual interviews were then conducted with members of both groups, who were found to differ importantly in regard to their personalities as well as to their family backgrounds. The high authoritarians, who are the target of our interest here, were those generally called *prejudiced* or *bigoted*. On the questionnaire, their answers fell into a pattern: accepting unquestioningly the statements of an authority, the more definite the better; categorizing persons into fixed groups; and willing to express hostility against persons entirely on the basis of their group membership.

The family backgrounds of the high authoritarians were found to have some interesting features in common. They had been reared in families in which power was openly exercised yet not allowed to be mentioned. Problems of status and rule making dominated every avenue of communication. Beliefs were treated as dogma, not to be questioned nor thought about. And domination by one adult figure was both arbitrary and rigidly accepted. Persons reared in this kind of atmosphere, it appeared, grew into adults with shaky and fearful control over their own motives. They were moralistic in a blindly, angrily conforming way, unable to know why they so fiercely condemned those who did not fit their preconceived patterns of defensive intolerance.

Although the theoretical bias of this study, which followed a psychoanalytic approach, has been questioned by other psychologists, it did establish the finding that attitudes, particularly those that are held strongly, will often cluster in a coherent pattern. The cement that holds the attitudes together, it seems, is a set of personality characteristics that help to determine what the person selectively perceives. What is perceived then helps to keep the pattern unchanged. Attitudes, it appears, are not accidental, not random beliefs, but vital expressions of our individual personalities. They have a life of their own.

The structure of attitudes. We have now discussed some aspects of the *feeling* components of attitudes and the fact that they appear to be organized within each person as coherent wholes related to the personality. We are now ready to ask how attitudes are held together. Do they, for example, all have the same "structure"? Of the four components related to an attitude—a belief, a feeling, an intention, and some behavior—is there one that is basic?

Fishbein and Ajzen[23] have recently suggested that the four major components involved in attitudes are interrelated, as shown in Figure 18.6. They offer the argument that of the four components, the fundamental one is the person's belief, based on the amount and kind of information one has about the target. In their view, humans are best described as "rational processors of information." People's attitudes and behavior are based on the information that is available to them, perhaps colored by some feeling and perhaps affected by some intentions that are related to their past experience. Other attitude theorists, however, have placed greater emphasis on the feeling component in attitudes or have pointed to the fact that it does not seem easy to demonstrate any close tie between one's attitudes and one's behavior.

authoritarianism. A social structure that subjects individual freedom to the control of an authority or society in which everyone has a specific place; also, a personality characteristic of such settings.

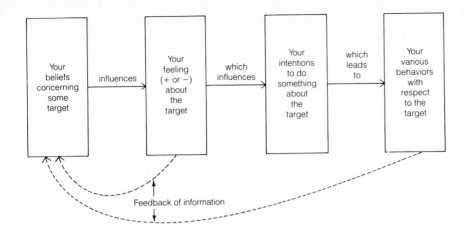

Fig. 18.6. How the different components of an attitude might be interrelated. (Based on Fishbein and Ajzen, 1975, fig. 1.1, p. 15)

8. Although a great deal of evidence appears to show that attitudes do not "cause" behavior, the issue may be more complex.

No issue in the field of attitude study has generated as much heat as the question of the causal relations between the attitudes held by a person and the behavior the person displays. If my attitude toward religion and churchgoing is both strong and positive, does this mean that I will attend church regularly? If I am prejudiced concerning certain minority groups, as measured on a reliable scale of attitudes, would you be willing to bet as to how I will act toward a member of such a group? To put the question another way: If I can be shown to hold certain attitudes, do these attitudes cause me to behave in any particular and predictable way? If my attitudes are changed, will this lead predictably to a change in my behavior?

Research on attitudes and behavior. In 1930, a sociologist, Richard La Piere, traveled across the United States in the company of a Chinese couple. They made a total of 251 requests for rooms or service and were refused only once. On returning home, La Piere wrote to seventy-nine hotels, some of them already visited and some not, asking whether service would be provided if he and his Oriental friends arrived. He received only one clear-cut yes answer and five "maybe" answers out of the seventy-three. He then wrote to 167 restaurants, half of them already visited and half not, making the same inquiry. Again, only one yes answer was received, and thirteen "maybe" answers, out of 167 inquiries.[24] The conclusion seemed clear, that attitudes as assessed by means of an impersonal request do not accord with behavior in regard to the same situation. A very similar study, done in New Jersey in 1952, obtained the same result when one black customer accompanied a group of whites. They were served in restaurants when they appeared in person but were refused when they applied by mail or by phone.[25]

These studies suggest that what people do is one thing, and what they say about what they do is something else. Attitudes and behavior do not always coincide. The evidence is even more telling if we look at instances in real life in which people's attitudes are changed: Does their behavior then change to fit their new attitudes? When the U.S. Public Health Service mounted a propaganda campaign to change people's attitudes toward smoking, repeated tests showed that it was successful. Attitudes changed measurably. However, smoking behavior did not change, either in the public at large or among those whose attitudes had seemed to change. Similarly, when the Nazi government undertook its first propaganda campaign against Jews, they were able to show that many Germans did change their attitudes in a negative direction, but there was little indication that this led to a change in people's behavior toward Jews. The conclusion seemed undeniable. Attitudes are not directly related to behavior, and specifically, attitudes may not "cause" or determine behavior.

However, a great deal of additional evidence seems to show that if anything, the reverse is true — that a change in one's behavior can lead to a change in one's attitudes. Racially integrated housing projects were first built in the United States in the years following World War II. Studies of the tenants' attitudes repeatedly showed that there was distrust and prejudice when they first moved in, but that this lessened in direct relation to the length of residence in an integrated situation. Further, there was usually a direct and positive relation between the degree of proximity (whether neighbors lived next door to one another, or two doors away, and so on) and the amount of attitudinal change. In this case, enforced behavior change led to changes in attitude.[26]

Thus, however the issue is studied, the answer seems to come out the same, that what people think and feel about other persons is not always reflected in their behavior. But such a conclusion runs directly counter to what many of us intuitively feel is true about ourselves: We do not hold our attitudes because of the way we act, but rather that we act the way we do because of the attitudes we hold. Further, if it were true that our attitudes do not cause us to act the way we do, we would be left with the question, What then does cause us to act as we do? Finally, if our thoughts and feelings are only a result and not a cause, what role do they play and of what social use are they?

Attitude change

9. Attitudes change in ways that relate sensibly to one's situation.

If attitudes are not reflected in behavior and do not significantly determine one's behavior, it should follow that changing people's attitudes is a process unrelated to their real-life situations. That is, if attitudes are in truth nothing but a kind of mental fiction, a set of beliefs floating around in people's heads, quite disconnected with what they do in real life, then their attitudes might be changed in the same way their thoughts are changed.

Attitude change has been, for this reason, a topic of central concern to social psychologists. In addition, the question of how attitudes are changed is clearly related to activities that are familiar in real life, such as persuasion, salesmanship, and propaganda. For this reason, it was the hope of social psychologists that they would be able to make some important contributions to these socially significant areas. It is a relatively simple problem to study in the laboratory. One simply measures some people's attitudes, presents some experimental conditions, and then measures what attitudinal change, if any, took place. In addition, there is available a different method, large-scale surveys or public opinion polls, by which mass changes in attitude can be assessed and related to social events. As a result, there is now a very sizable literature on the topic, and it is possible to put together a

Fig. 18.7. Research on attitude change suggests the following advice on how to be a good persuader:

Your manner:
- Try to be perceived as one who can be trusted and one who has authority and power.
- Be subtle rather than obvious.
- Come across as sincere; forget the sarcasm.

Your approach:
- Get the audience on your side — for example, have a good introduction; use humor; come out in favor of something the audience favors; try to convey the impression that you are similar to the audience; stay on the audience's level.
- Don't resort too much to strings of facts.
- Try to present both sides, with an impression of fairness, particularly if you sense that the audience may be disagreeing with you or if they may hear the other side from someone else.
- However, if the audience is friendly and warmed up or if you are only after a fast and temporary agreement by the audience, present only one side.

Some tricks:
- Try to involve the audience with you, even if only to the extent of getting them to nod when you say, "Isn't that right?"
- If you can get away with it, take a rather extreme position on something and then temper it.

set of instructions guaranteed to make one a more effective persuader in front of an audience (Figure 18.7). Such advice is less likely to be useful in one-to-one situations, but most situations calling for tactics of persuasion require that a single persuader face a group of persons rather than a single person. Persuasion is not quite the same as convincing; it is carried out at a distance, and it is less dependent on the immediate feelings of the listeners and their felt relation to the persuader.

The results of many years of study of persuasion, propaganda, and attitude change provide us with a basis for an answer to the question of how attitudes and behavior are related. A careful study of just what happens when a single individual is influenced to act in one way rather than another indicates that it is by no means a simple or unitary process. An experimenter may record the change by a single measure, but in fact the change may have come about in a number of ways. Kelman has identified three such processes: There is mere *compliance*, or going along with the group without much investment in the decision. In *identification*, a choice is made to go with a group or a leader rather than because of commitment to an idea. In *internalization*, agreement occurs because it fits in with one's personal values.[27] Few laboratory experiments have tapped the complex, value-laden process that Kelman calls *internalization*. For example, only if the rewards and punishments in an experiment are sensibly related to the experimental conditions will they produce behavioral change. If they are so extreme as to be unreal, they may produce compliance but rarely identification and never internalization — and they will then change expressed attitudes but not behavior.

A very extensive program of research on communication and persuasion was carried out from the 1940s to the 1960s by Carl Hovland and his group at Yale.[28] Out of this material, Hovland drew some answers to explain one of the most persistent of all findings: Laboratory studies always seemed to produce greater changes in attitudes than could be detected when people were repeatedly surveyed in polls. The answers rested on these differences between laboratory and survey approaches:

The audience. In the laboratory, the audience is completely exposed to each communication, and it is probably randomly divided as to being pro and con. In the survey, it is often self-selected as to opinion and often biased one way or the other.

The communication unit. In the laboratory, the communication unit is small and controlled as to size; in the survey, there may be a large and mixed bag of communications.

The communicator. In the laboratory, the communicator is the experimenter or teacher, someone with known authority or influence and immediately present. In the survey, it is someone more remote or strange, often with less influence.

The time interval. In the laboratory, there is a short interval between the time of the communication and the time its effect is tested. In the survey, this time is variable and may be much longer.

The issue. In the laboratory, the issue is chosen so as to be susceptible of modification by persuasion and dependent on expert opinion. In the survey, the issue is more socially significant, broader, and often personally held; it is influenced in many ways other than by experts.

To conduct a good experiment, participants are given both sides of an issue, but in the survey situation people are asked about only one side, and their past influences have been primarily one-sided as well.[29]

The result of these differences is that outside the laboratory people exercise much more initiative. When experimenters attempt to change people's attitudes in a laboratory, they usually involve the people in an artificial situation that is restricted and manipulated. What appears to happen, then, is that people's beliefs come and go with little relation to their behavior. But, if we recognize that this result is a consequence of the laboratory situation as much as it is of the way people really conduct themselves, then we are open to asking how people develop and maintain attitudes in real life. In this connection, Bauer suggests that all persuasion, and indeed all communication between persons, contrary to how it appears in the laboratory, is a two-way process. It is a "bargain" struck between speaker and listener that is based on "an exchange of values between two or more parties; each gives in order to get."[30] The results of persuasive efforts, like the end results of any other communication, are always a compromise between what one wants to achieve and the other wants to accept.

The trouble with basing theories of attitudes and behavior, and of their relations, only on studies of persuasion is that such studies rest on an unspoken assumption: that one side, the persuader, has all the initiative, while the other side, the audience, is merely a passive receiver of effects. In fact, people are actively at work when they form their attitudes and then when they behave in relation to them. Their behavior, in turn, may change their attitudes. This is what the material on attitude change has to tell us. With this notion in mind, we may now be able to offer a summary statement about behavior and attitudes.

Perception, attitude, and behavior. Our diagram of the various components of an attitude (Figure 18.6) some pages back, indicated that one's beliefs influence one's feelings, which in turn influence one's intentions, which finally lead to one's behavior. We then presented a great deal of evidence that seemed to suggest that this relationship does not always hold up. Measured attitudes do not seem to predict behavior or even to be sensibly related to one's behavior. Then we presented a series of counterarguments, to the effect that attitudes and feelings, the major components of attitudes, are real phenomena; they are sensibly organized, they show evidence of development and persistence, and they change in understandable ways.

If the components of attitudes, and the attitudes themselves, are real — in the sense that they form part of our ongoing life of experience — what is their relation to our behavior? We now suggest that Figure 18.6 will have to be modified, as in Figure 18.8.

Beliefs as well as feelings are important influencing aspects in that ongoing mix we call an *attitude*. To these familiar components, however, our diagram adds another — the individual's unique perception of the situation. It was this compo-

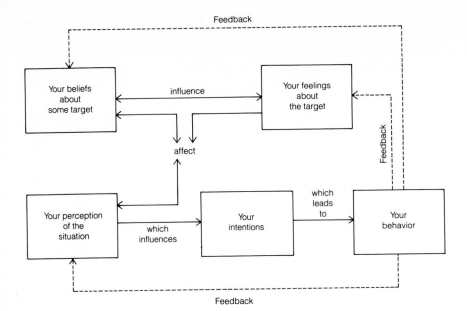

Fig. 18.8. The probable state of affairs in regard to the components of an attitude and their relation to behavior.

nent that was left out of our earlier diagram and that is left out of many theoretical accounts of attitudes in their relation to behavior.

The component we have called *perception* in our diagram helps us to account for many of the findings that were so puzzling in our discussion during this chapter. The results of laboratory and survey experiments on attitude change differ precisely because subjects perceive their situations differently under the two different settings in which to act. In short, people do what they do, in relation to other persons, because it usually seems to them the most reasonable thing to do under the circumstances of their own situation. What that situation may be, for any individual at a specific time and place, may not always be evident from knowing only the objective facts of the matter. The work of social psychologists, as we have reviewed it in this chapter — work on social facilitation, on causal attribution, on social comparison processes, and on attitudes and attitude change — has been to determine how the situation appears from an inside viewpoint and then to relate such findings to the outside view of social situations.

Summary

1. A dyad consists of two persons who share a situation and show behavior in it that is reciprocal, the behavior of each person in turn affecting the behavior of the other.

2. The presence of others, an influence first called *social facilitation* because it seemed to be positive, has complex effects: generally, an increase in quality of performance but a decrease if the presence is felt as competitive or judgmental, and positive if the task is simple or well learned, negative if it is complex or not well learned.

3. Effects on the level of social facilitation need not require the physical presence of other persons; social reality is equally effective.

4. Studies of affiliative behavior under stress show that misery does love company but prefers company perceived to be similar, and that the effect is more pronounced in the case of firstborns—a consequence of their greater tendency to be affiliative and easily influenced.

5. People tend to explain the causes of others' behavior in dispositional terms and the causes of their own behavior in situational terms.

6. The currently active field of attribution theory had its beginnings in the work of Heider, especially in his description of the "naive" theories by which persons explain each others' behavior.

7. An attitude is a complex of feeling, knowledge, belief, and intention to act which the person maintains in conjunction with other, similar attitudes.

8. In general, people will be liked who are physically attractive, friendly, and who are able to be interested in and flatter others.

9. Liking seems to follow our perception of another person as similar to us and is often the consequence of exposure and familiarity.

10. Liking and disliking are distinctively different dimensions of feeling rather than two opposite ends of the same dimension. Rubin's research indicates as well that liking and loving are distinctively different modes of attraction.

11. A great deal of evidence suggests that attitudes are somehow associated with behavior, but the causal association appears to be that behavior causes attitudes, rather than the reverse.

12. However, causal associations in the other directions also seem probable: Attitudes are related to behavior by way of people's perception of their situation.

In this, the second of our chapters on social psychology, we introduce again the inside and outside approaches to the study of interpersonal relations, but here our focus is on the ties between individuals and the groups they are in. We organize our discussion around the problem of the "good German," a problem that refers to attempts to understand the behavior of ordinary German citizens under the Nazi regime.

Two major lines of research stemming from interest in this problem will be presented: (1) research on climate and leadership styles in small groups, and their effects on individual behavior, and (2) research on the effects of a group consensus on conformity in individuals. Another set of issues related to these problems refers to the effects of group situations on individuals' helping and hurting behavior. It will be shown that one's knowledge of the situation plays an important part, as does one's felt degree of responsibility, especially as both are reflected in the way one sees one's own role in the situation.

In conclusion, it will be shown that groups are social realities that have their own dynamics, natures, and characteristics, all of which have been extensively studied. The structure of groups will be seen to affect their members, particularly as the structure and needs of the group are reflected in the chosen leader. Finally, the nature of psychological roles will be discussed, in terms of the expectancies that they prescribe between individual and group.

19

Social psychology: awareness and effect of groups

During the 1930s, the Nazi regime in Germany carried out an official program of imprisonment and killing aimed at specific minority groups. Homosexuals were the first to be systematically tracked down and thrown into concentration camps, where many died. Gypsies were next, and then Jews. Political dissidents considered dangerous completed the roster of those who were maintained in unlivable conditions in the camps, where they died in large numbers of malnutrition, exposure, disease, and brutal treatment. Finally, under the code name of the Final Solution, millions of Jews, in and out of the camps, were rounded up, gassed in large groups in specially constructed gas chambers, and their bodies usually buried in mass graves or burnt in open ditches.

The problem of the good German

For more than three decades, scholars have asked how a social horror on this scale could have occurred in any modern country, particularly in a nation as supposedly civilized as Germany. Yet the evidence is clear that a very large number of respectable German citizens, in all walks of life, participated knowingly in carrying out these atrocities. Physicians and chemists and engineers gave their services toward arranging the most efficient means of conducting mass killings. Ordinary people from the areas surrounding the camps earned extra money by doing part-time work at the reception depots, gas chambers, and burial sites. All of these persons were "good Germans," to use a stereotyped expression that is supposed to refer to the conforming personality of the average German citizen. How is their behavior to be explained? Is the "good German" a product of a sick society, and would any of us do the same if we were in similar circumstances? How much influence does the group and the society exert on an individual?

A number of major lines of research in social psychology are relevant to the problem of the good German. We have already discussed one of them, the study of the authoritarian personality in Chapter 18. One conclusion suggested by this research was that some kinds of extreme attitudes and behavior may be a result of people's personalities. These personalities can in turn be traced back to specific sorts of family atmospheres experienced during childhood.

Some persons, it appears, are so bigoted, rigid, and authoritarian that they will join in the oppression of others who are different from them. Other persons, apparently ordinary and decent in their everyday lives, can be influenced to perform an admittedly shameful act in the proper circumstances. Such conclusions do not suggest grounds for optimism regarding most people's behavior toward their fellows. In order to examine these issues in greater detail, we will consider two other lines of research. The first concentrates on the effect of group climates and leadership, and the second explores the meaning and effect of a group consensus.

The individual and the group

1. The climate of a group, especially as influenced by its leadership, is reflected in its morale, its productivity, and its interpersonal relations.

Social psychologists in the United States became interested in questions concerning group influence in part because the questions were brought to this country by scientists who were refugees from persecution in Nazi Germany. Among these scientists was Kurt Lewin, an original thinker and inventive researcher who sparked a dozen lines of investigation. His approach to the problem of the good German was to design a simple yet effective study in which the effects of various social atmospheres could be compared (Figure 19.1).

With the help of two younger colleagues, Ralph White and Ronald Lippitt,

Fig. 19.1. Two kinds of behavioral similarity, one derived from an external directive and the other from an internal state.

Lewin took over the supervision of a large after-school club for 11-year-old boys. The researchers acted as leaders of small groups of these boys, the original scheme being that they would each take a turn leading a group for a few months with either an autocratic, dictatorial style or a cooperative, democratic style. The schedule was arranged so that each leader would have a chance to play both leadership roles with each group. However, it very soon became apparent that one of the leaders preferred a style that came to be called *laissez-faire* — best described as "hang loose" or "do your own thing." The project as finally carried out, then, compared three rather than two leadership styles and the social climates they induced.

The project turned out to be more elaborate and time consuming than originally planned (as often happens in exploratory research on significant questions) and was in fact continued for more than ten years under the guidance of various leaders. The investigators were interested in the climate that they could produce, the behavior of the group members and their relations to each other, the feelings that group members had toward each other and toward their groups, and how well the groups accomplished tasks that they set themselves such as making masks for an entertainment. Under the autocratic style, decisions were made and enforced by the leader, and the activity of the group was task oriented° and centered on the leader's opinions and criticism. In the democratic style, decisions were largely initiated and effected by a group consensus, with the leader acting as a friendly guide who was on the same level as the group members. In the laissez-faire condition, the leader did not function as such but as one other group member, with his own preferences but with no power to initiate or enforce any direction the group might take. The laissez-faire group obviously had no parallel in organized human societies, but the other two climates were clearly meant as a comparison of social life in the United States *versus* Nazi Germany.

A wide range of methods were used to gather data — behavioral checklists, movies, self-rating questionnaires, and assessment of productivity, among others. The results were not unexpected, but they have some interesting implications for group behavior and perhaps for education as well. The autocratic leaders, and the climates they generated, were quite efficient in getting things done — although they usually had to be present to make sure of this. In their presence, the behavior of the group members was polarized toward them, resulting in effective behavior that was carried out without any particular pleasure and under conditions of submission. The degree of negative feeling aroused but unexpressed under these conditions was well revealed when the autocratic leader was absent. The groups then fell apart, engaged in a great deal of in-group aggression, and even found scapegoats on whom to vent their hostility.

The democratic and laissez-faire group members, on the other hand, uniformly displayed more positive feelings toward one another. The democratically led groups became highly self-motivated; performed efficiently, but never as well as the best efforts of the autocratic groups; and were usually pleased with themselves and with each other. The laissez-faire climate produced as much good feeling, which was expressed in a less controlled fashion, but did not couple this with productivity. They spent a great deal of their time fooling around, sometimes to extremes, and usually required the emergence of leadership from within the members' ranks to bring about any order or accomplish any work.[1]

Generalizations from the behavior of 11-year-old boys in voluntary semiplay groups need to be made with caution to the larger society of adults in nonvoluntary work situations. In addition, critics of this study have pointed out that it may have confused two significant factors: degree of control and degree of warmth.[2] In a recent study in which many of the conditions were duplicated for groups of boys in India,[3] an autocratically led group performed best and in addition led to greater

task oriented. One kind of activity by a person or group, in which the focus is primarily on getting a job done.

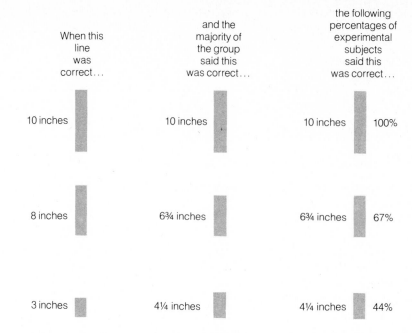

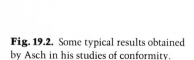

Fig. 19.2. Some typical results obtained
by Asch in his studies of conformity.

feelings of satisfaction among the members. This indicates that Lewin's findings may be applicable only to countries such as Germany and the United States, which share a common heritage of group climate and of an individualistic ego orientation. Finally, these results are restricted to males, who at the age of 11 are likely to show particular needs for external controls, because they have not yet become self-directed or self-controlling. Girls of the same age may well respond differently to the same adult models.

With these qualifications in mind and recognizing the great difficulties in studying the complexities of social influence on the individual, we may recognize that group and social conditions may have important effects on individuals' behavior. What is unclear, however, is how these effects work. In the next section, we review another line of research addressing this question.

2. Depending on their own personality and on the size and effectiveness of the group, most persons will eventually go along with the group consensus.

In a surprisingly simple study, Solomon Asch[4] began a line of research on what has come to be called *conformity*.[⊙] Asch trained seven or eight students to take part in an experiment on comparing the lengths of lines: They were to be unanimous in their errors on twelve critical trials in a series of eighteen (Figure 19.2). For each series of trials, a naive student was also in the group, always at or near the end position so as to make a judgment after those of the others had been given. The naive person's position on the twelve critical trials thus consisted of hearing seven or eight peers state, one after the other, that Line A was the same length as Line B, when in fact it was very clear to the naive subject that this was not so. (The judgment tasks were quite simple and in a free test were done correctly almost 100 percent of the time.)

The naive student was therefore in the familiar position of someone who finds that their view of social reality is in opposition to a unanimous social norm.

conformity. Behaving according to social norms; being influenced by group pressure.

What now happens? Asch found that his students split into three groups. About 25 percent of them steadfastly maintained their independence of thought, even when this meant going against a unanimous consensus of their peers. About 31 percent of them conformed to the group consensus on all twelve critical trials. The remaining 44 percent varied in their performance, depending on the difficulty of the judgment. In short, on any one trial, approximately 40 percent of a group of college students could be induced to make a perceptual judgment that was grossly in error, with no other pressure than the vote of seven or eight other students whom they did not even know.

In order to study this phenomenon under more varied conditions, Crutchfield[5] set up a situation in which people sat in individual booths and made their judgments in a variety of tasks by pressing buttons. Each person's booth was equipped with a panel, and they were told that the votes of the others would be flashed on their panel so as to indicate what other persons thought. In fact, Crutchfield manipulated the panel presentations to everyone, leading them to think there was a consensus one way or another. By this technique, he was able to test a number of persons at one time on a range of issues and problems. His results agreed with those of Asch as regards conformity to a group consensus: There is no difficulty getting college students or even professionals in various fields to agree to statements that conflict with their privately held views. For example, when army officers were tested on an independent basis, they all expressed a conviction that they would make good leaders, but when faced with an apparent unanimous disagreement with this statement, more than one third went along with the group.

The dissenter's experience. A very large number of studies, using these and similar techniques, have specified some of the processes that lead individuals to conform to group pressure. First of all, even the most gullible and conforming people make clear distinctions between being influenced by some persons and being pressured by a group. For example, in an Asch-type situation, at least three confederates are required in order to influence a naive person. Apparently a majority of two is seen, not as establishing a group norm, but simply as expressing some individual opinions. Conformity tends to increase as the size of the group increases, to the point where it levels off. People's personalities play some role in the conformity process, as seen in the fact that some persons always conform and some persons never do. However, a significantly larger effect comes from the nature of the task or judgment. Crutchfield found that conformity increased as the judgmental tasks became more ambiguous or more like guesswork. Most of us, for example, are not too sure about the number of hours of sleep that the average adult gets each night—and so, as we might expect, most persons will go along with a group consensus that the correct number is four to five hours, although this answer is in fact wrong.

The situation of the dissenter is not easy. Such a person, at odds with a community of peers, may find it impossible to share doubts and uncertainties with others in the group, because the very situation that leads to a consensus may keep individuals from talking to each other about their dissent from a consensus. In Hitler's Germany, for example, enormous social pressures were used to persuade the citizens that what the government was doing was both right and necessary. Under these conditions, individuals were inhibited from sharing their doubts with others. They tended to keep their doubts or disagreements to themselves, and this increased their conviction that they were each alone in their dissent.

The first step in producing conformity, it would appear, is simply to convince each individual that they are in such a situation. They will then find themselves in the Asch situation—a single vote against a unanimous opposition.[6] From their point of view, they have lost that identification with a group that builds the self-image and leads one to feel more important. They are therefore now more susceptible to pressure from the other subjects.

The power of unanimity was dramatically shown in Asch's work when one of the confederates was instructed to disagree with the majority. With the support of just this one other person, naive students now conformed only 5 percent of the time. The minimum required for conformity, then, is three persons; the maximum possible is 100 percent of the group. Between these extremes of very little conformity and very high conformity, such factors as personality, the nature of the judgment, and the characteristics of the setting interact to determine who will conform and under what conditions.

Helping and hurting others

The real-life problem with which we began this chapter, the problem of the good German, has to do with people's helping or hurting behavior under conditions of group pressure. In order to explore this question, social psychologists have designed experiments in which individuals found themselves in situations where helping behavior was called for or hurting behavior was expected. We will consider these two possibilities as they have been examined in two other major lines of research.

3. People will be helpful to others under some circumstances, depending on the situation and on their degree of knowledge and felt responsibility.

On March 26, 1975, a young man was beaten to death by some other young men in the presence of hundreds of horrified onlookers (including many of his friends) at a church fair in New York City. In 1964, a young woman named Kitty Genovese was killed by an attacker outside her apartment, who took half an hour to accomplish the job while thirty-eight of her neighbors watched from their windows. In neither case did any of the bystanders offer to intervene or to help, or even to call the police (Figure 19.3).

At first sight it might appear that our worst fears concerning the phenomenon of the good German are confirmed: Not only will people harm others, but they will not even lift a finger to help others. In an ingenious series of experi-

Collection, The Museum of Modern Art, New York

Fig. 19.3. This sculpture by Alberto Giacometti, entitled "The Piazza," expresses some of the effects of urban living that are studied in experiments on bystander apathy.

ments that were inspired by such events, Latané and Darley[7] have attempted to pin down the psychological and social factors operating in this kind of situation. Their procedure usually consists of putting persons in the role of unwitting bystanders to an emergency in which they might help if they wanted to. For example, with the cooperation of a store owner, they stage an obvious shoplifting scene in the presence of the store's customers. Observations are then made as to the circumstances under which customers will report the shoplifting to the store manager. Or they bring people into their laboratory for a supposed learning experiment. There the people are allowed to overhear what seems like an emergency in the next room, such as someone falling and calling out in pain. Again, observations are made as to the conditions that aid or impede the bystanders offering assistance. What they studied has been often labeled *bystander apathy*,° because that was the phenomenon supposedly evidenced in the incident involving Kitty Genovese. However, the name is not appropriate for all their results, because apathy is neither universal nor certain.

The situation of the bystander. Viewed from the outside, the bystander's situation seems simple. Bystanders are made aware of some emergency happening near them, there are other persons nearby, and they need only decide whether to intervene in a helpful manner. From the outside viewpoint, then, the relevant factors in the situation are the number of other persons present or available, and the type of others present.

However, when experiments are carried out to determine the effect of the number and type of others who are present, the results are mixed and not easy to understand. In one study, naive onlookers in a liquor store saw the staged robbery of a case of beer.[8] If only one customer was present when the event occurred, that person reported it to the store manager 65 percent of the time. But if two customers were present, they would report it only 58 percent of the time. However, in another study that simulated real-life conditions in the New York City subway, a man pretended to have fainted. Within five seconds of his fall, as many as 95 percent of the onlookers came to his aid; the percentage of those helping increased if he was also carrying a cane.[9]

Apparently the number of other onlookers present does not by itself determine whether help will be offered. The picture becomes a little clearer if we now consider a related factor, the type of other persons present and their behavior. In an experiment[10] in which this was studied, Latané and Rodin brought people into the laboratory to work on some puzzles and then had them overhear what seemed like an accident (but was really only a tape recording) in the next room. The sounds were those of the experimenter's assistant being injured in a fall from a ladder. How the bystanders now responded depended on the role and behavior of the person with them. The results are shown in Table 19.1. In this case, just as in the liquor store robbery, people are less helpful when someone else is present, but only if the other person is a stranger or an "apathetic bystander."

Two major explanations have been offered to cover these and similar results. Both explanations take into account the inside view, or the situation as it is seen from the point of view of its participants.

The "knowledge" explanation. This explanation is based on the plausible idea that we usually act only if we feel sufficiently knowledgeable to act with some confidence. Otherwise, and in view of the normal inhibitions that people feel about doing things publicly, we will refrain from acting, at least until we have more information. We usually look to others for such information, or to compare our own view of the matter—just as would be predicted in the social comparison theory we discussed in Chapter 18.

bystander apathy. The phenomenon in which people are willing to stand by and watch a crisis situation without feeling the need to respond.

Table 19.1. The percentage of bystanders who helped an apparently injured stranger under different conditions.

Alone[a]	Confederate[b]	Stranger[c]	Friend[d]
70	7	40	70

Note: Since 70 percent of the people gave help when they were alone, it can be figured out mathematically that 91 percent of the people should have given help when they were in pairs. Therefore the results for the other three categories are less "helping" than they appear.
[a]The individual was alone when the tape was played.
[b]A confederate of the experimenter was present, who ignored what was happening or dismissed it with a shrug.
[c]One other person was present who was a stranger.
[d]The person was with a friend.

Source: Latané and Rodin, 1969.

Additional experiments to test out this idea lend support to it. For example, the more aware someone is of the consequences of their action toward another, the more altruistically they are likely to act.[11] Or, the more clear-cut and less ambiguous a situation is, in terms of whether it is a serious emergency or not, the more likely subjects are to offer help.[12] These results support the notion that the apparent coldheartedness or indifference of bystanders and experimental participants is due, at least in part, to their lack of knowledge or certainty in the situation that is suddenly presented.

The responsibility explanation is based on the premise that we act in situations according to the degree of responsibility that we feel we can assume. Thus, the good German citizens who worked in the Nazi death camps were able to convince themselves that they were not personally responsible for what was going on or even for what they themselves were doing. It was something ordered by the state; it was a necessary wartime measure; they were simply obeying a strict schedule of commands issued by the camp director; and so on.

If subjects are less likely to do harm to others when they feel greater personal responsibility, it should follow that the amount of shock that is administered can be raised or lowered by giving different instructions to the "shockers." This was just what was shown in a clever experiment by Bandura, Underwood, and Fromson.[13] Using a situation in which people thought they were administering shock to others as part of an experiment in how people can best learn, the "shockers" were either assigned individually to a victim (in which case they would, of course, have to take sole responsibility for how much shock they administered) or were told that the level of shock they delivered would be averaged in with that of others. Under conditions in which the responsibility was "diffused" (the second condition), they administered significantly higher levels of shock.

To sum up this line of research on the question of helping others, when one takes into account the inside view of the situation, it appears that people will in fact be helpful. However, their helpfulness will be tempered by the factors we have just mentioned, social inhibition, the degree of their knowledge and certainty, and the "diffusion" of their feelings of responsibility. The presence of other persons does have an effect, but only as it raises or lowers the influence of these three factors.

4. People may be harmful to others if they see their own situation as requiring or admitting such behavior.

In one of the best-known psychology experiments ever conducted, Stanley Milgram[14] arranged to have people in a laboratory deliver electric shocks to another person as part of what they thought was an experiment in learning. They were faced with a panel containing thirty switches labeled on a scale from "slight shock" to "danger: severe shock" and then "X X X." When instructed to increase the severity of the shock at each mistake on a learning task made by someone in the next room (actually a confederate who received no shock at all), 65 percent of the people in Milgram's first experiment continued to the highest point on the panel, marked 450 volts. All of them were willing to administer shocks up to a level marked 300 volts, "intense shock," at which point the presumed victim in the next room was screaming in pain and pounding on the wall. Those who continued to administer progressively higher shock levels in the face of this kind of reaction did so when the experimenter pressured and exhorted them, although many of the "shockers" were clearly in great distress over what they were doing. Indeed, if subjects were paired with another "shocker" (in reality, a confederate) who continued administering shocks with no signs of distress, the number who continued all the way to 450 volts rose to 92.5 percent.

Summarizing a long series of follow-up studies of this situation, Milgram writes that people act the same, in terms of administering shock, whether the victim is female or male or even whether or not the victim is supposed to have a heart condition. However, they are less likely to proceed to the high end of the shock panel if pressure from the experimenter is lessened; for example, if there are two experimenters who disagree or if other confederates are paired with them as "shockers" and refuse to continue.[15] And, as shown in Table 19.2, this behavior is appreciably more "hurtful" than most persons think is typical of people.

Milgram's results are disturbing, and to some extent they seem to fit our stereotype of the good German. However, they need not be taken to imply that people are naturally cruel, any more than the results of the work by Latané and

Table 19.2. A comparison of what various judges and observers thought might happen in the Milgram study, as compared to what actually did happen.

Volts	25	75	135	195	255	315	375	435	450
Shock level	Slight	Moderate	Strong	Very strong	Intense	Extreme intensty	Danger: severe shock	X X X	

How far psychiatrists thought average people would go

How far average people really went, in the experiment

How far college students thought average people would go

Source: Data from Milgram, 1974; Bierbrauer, 1973.

Darley imply that people are naturally goodhearted. It would be more appropriate, in view of all these experimental results, to say that people cannot be properly described as either altruistic or hurtful in regard to others. They are capable of a range of behavior that extends from fairly negative to fairly positive; most persons are probably incapable of being either excessively cruel or remarkably self-sacrificing. Within that range, their behavior will be a result of how they see their situation, the pressures at work in it, and their own role in it.[16] In the Milgram studies, people found themselves in the role of agents in a scientific experiment, the conditions for which were spelled out with confidence and authority by the actual experimenter. They therefore acted more negatively than they might under most other circumstances—in some instances even overcoming their own natural reluctance in order to do so.

Dynamics in small groups

In the late 1940s, Lewin, ever the practical theorist,[17] suggested that the most direct way to explore the dynamics of behavior in groups was to arrange about half a dozen persons in a group situation and set them to work on a task—such as drawing up an agenda for a large meeting. If the groups were composed of social scientists who were themselves interested in group dynamics, two sorts of data would then be available: (1) outside data concerning what happened in the group and with the group, as an observer might report it, and (2) inside data offered by the members themselves, who would be able to report on their experiences and of how and why they did what they did. Finally, it was suggested that one way to examine the functions of group leaders would be to run groups in which there were no leaders, so that comparisons might be made. There were at this time a number of interesting results that had recently been obtained with leaderless groups at the Tavistock Institute in London.[18]

Organized and supported by the National Education Association, the first summer workshops in group development were set up in 1947 at a boys' school in Bethel, Maine. Because the aims were to use the groups for training leaders as well as group members in effective functioning, the name *T-group*© was coined. Very soon, however, an interesting discovery was made. In a leaderless group situation, group members were called on to carry on the group process themselves, and of course each person did so in terms of their own individual and personal approach to group pressure. As a consequence, an exercise that had originally been planned as a way of examining what happened to groups quickly turned into a most effective way of examining what was happening to individuals. Further, the members' own self-explorations, as they attempted to look at and talk about their own experiences, turned out to be very effective in bringing about changes in themselves.[19]

What began as a study of groups and group change, then, turned into an in-depth study of individuals and individual change. The T-group thus became one of the important contributions to the development of group therapy—and indeed, when trained group leaders such as William Schutz came to the West Coast in the 1960s, they brought with them the years of experience in T-groups, which they then applied in a closely related form as the encounter group.©

Varieties of small groups. What constitutes a group? Surely not just any collection of individuals. Not, for example, five persons standing close to each other in an elevator, and not the larger number of individuals pouring out of the exit gate of a stadium. We might agree, however, that the members of a Little League baseball team form a group, as do half a dozen Girl Scouts on a hike, or the

T-group. Sensitivity training group originated as a situation to aid awareness and problem solving. It usually has a facilitator who primarily sets the stage for expression and discussion.

encounter group. A small group designed for people to relate intensely and honestly to the other members of the group.

average family, or even a dozen political figures plotting strategy in a smoke-filled room.

A collection of individuals is a group partly because the persons spend some time together. More important, however, may be the fact that the members are linked together by bonds of more than passing acquaintance. They share common goals, and often common traditions, history, rituals or even a private, inner-group language. Within the group, each member plays a part that is reasonably stable over time — such as mother, father, oldest, baby, and so on. Perhaps most important of all, the group is a "something" that its own members are aware of, separately from their awareness of themselves or of each other.

What this means is that the concept of a group is not completely an artificial abstraction dreamed up by social scientists. It is a genuine social reality that is apparent to any reasonably perceptive person. Everyday observation suggests that groups do exist, that they can be distinguished from gatherings or other nongroup assemblies of persons, and that we can usually make some statements to describe how one group differs from another. Like other real phenomena in the world, groups form, develop, grow, change, mature, and decline. They engage in their own kinds of activities and produce results more or less efficiently. And they affect their members in unique ways, resulting in identifiable levels of group morale and satisfaction.

The concept of group is central to social psychology and rich in its implications. A number of major kinds of groups can be identified:

The membership group refers simply to any group to which an individual belongs, for short or long periods of time and with greater or less significance (Figure 19.4). It may be no more than the volleyball team chosen almost by accident during an afternoon on the beach, but it may also be the discussion group lasting for months as an adjunct to an undergraduate class.

The reference group© is a group with whom an individual identifies or feels some kinship because of shared ideals and goals. Membership is not a requirement, and in some cases the reference group may not even exist in any formal sense. A common example is the group of persons who constitute the class of a specific year of graduates. The class may not have a formal structure and may rarely gather in one place or carry out particular functions. On the other hand, it may have a permanent secretary who keeps track of addresses and sends out an annual mailing to remind its "members" of the get-together once a year.

What identifies this kind of group and often makes it important is the attitude of those who feel a tie to the group and the others in it. They usually have a special feeling for the others, as shown by how they will greet one another at reunions. They may contribute time and money solely because of their membership in the group, and they usually feel that their lives have been significantly influenced by "belonging" to the group. Their behavior, attitudes, feelings, and memories may all be linked to a group whose very existence depends on their feelings of belonging to it.

The significance of reference groups was shown in a study by Newcomb that was carried out in the 1930s. He examined changes in the attitudes of students who spent four years at Bennington College.[20] As often happens, the major change was in the direction of liberalizing their attitudes. This change appeared to have occurred through the influence of reference groups, in this case the type of classmate with whom each individual felt some ties. Newcomb found that only if reference groups changed did behavior change, and that this in turn led to changed attitudes.

Fig. 19.4. One may be present to a group without feeling oneself to be a member of it.

reference group. The social group with which one identifies and compares oneself; for example, work, church, and clubs.

The *primary group*⊙ is a specific kind of reference group that is usually more organized in a formal way. It is defined by the fact that it plays a key role in an individual's development. The classic example of a primary group is one's family, where as a growing child, in an intimate, face-to-face setting, one learns most of the basics about people and how to get along with them. Families serve a dual role in regard to group membership: In the early years of life they determine most of our developmental patterns, and in later years they may serve as the prototype of every face-to-face contact, whether at work, in small social groups, in therapy groups, or in marriage. In this latter function, the family serves as the most enduring of an individual's reference groups—even though its members may have grown up, scattered, or died.

A *"change" group* is a group that is formed for the specific purpose of bringing about some change in its members. One of the best known kind of change groups, the encounter group, has already been mentioned. Another familiar example is the therapy group that is brought together with a skilled person as therapist or leader. Two kinds of small change groups have been widely used. One of them is the T-group or encounter group,[21] in which members learn about themselves through the process of learning about their interpersonal relations. The other is the self-study group, which was pioneered by the Tavistock Institute in London,[22] in which the emphasis is on studying the group processes. As a by-product of such study, members may also learn about their own ways of relating to groups and particularly to authority in groups.

The study of groups in all their varieties is known as the study of *group dynamics*.⊙ It covers the types of groups, their structures, how they develop and change, their effects on individuals, and how individuals in turn affect the working of the group.

5. Small groups affect their members by way of the group structure and patterns of communication, the group leadership, and the roles they make available to individuals.

In a classroom demonstration devised by Bavelas, five persons line up side by side, facing away from the class. The instructor thinks of a number between 5 and 25, and they are each to raise their hand and show one to five fingers. The instructor will add up the number of fingers shown and tell them whether the sum is too high or too low—but this is all they will be told. They cannot communicate with each other nor see what the others are showing. Given this task, how many turns will it take for the group of five persons to arrive at the number the instructor is thinking of?

Surprisingly, many groups are able to arrive at the correct number in less than ten tries, and an experienced group may do it in even less. They do it by spontaneously adopting individual roles. One person will hold up three fingers each time. Another will be an "increaser," increasing the number of fingers held up by one on each trial, and another will take on the role of a "decreaser." If they take on roles, and quite probably only if they do so, they will succeed in arriving at the correct number, difficult though the task may seem.

It is a dramatic demonstration of the effectiveness of functional roles in the activity of a group. Roles are probably the basic element in the structure of a group,

primary group. A small group, such as family or friends, with which a person has had frequent, informal, and significant contact.

group dynamics. The study of how groups and people composing the groups interact and function.

the parts that make the whole work—indeed, so important that we will return to a discussion of them in one of the following sections.

Related to roles are patterns of communication. A group, like any other ongoing system, can be considered as primarily a processor of information. Its purpose is to produce and process information and to keep it flowing. A number of ingenious methods have been devised by social psychologists to compare the effectiveness of different communication networks—for example, by controlling the seating arrangement in a group and establishing rules for passing messages back and forth, or by restricting communication to telephones and controlling the possible interchanges through a telephone switchboard. The results of these studies indicate that communication patterns, like the group climates in Lewin's research, fall into three major classes: *centralized* patterns, in which information is channeled through one member, usually the leader; *equalized* patterns, in which information is more or less freely shared according to some arrangement; and *free-form* patterns, in which there are no structural restrictions and anything can happen. The three types are clearly analogous to, respectively, the autocratic, democratic, and laissez-faire group climates.[23]

Describing a group in terms of its communication patterns is one way of describing its structure. Further studies of how communication affects what goes on in the group indicate that the most important factor is how much is said rather than what is said. In small groups, most members talk about the same amount, but as the group gets larger, fewer and fewer members make contributions. This is understandable in terms of members' experiences in groups of different size. In a small group, my speaking does not expose me very much; but as the group size increases, I may feel an increased risk in exposing myself. Thus, as group size increases, the difference between the most and the least talkative member also increases, with the usual end result being that the leader is the most talkative of all. Indeed, in one study it was shown that all that may be needed to assure someone a position as leader is to ensure that the individual talks more than anyone else.[24]

A third significant factor in the structure of groups is their physical characteristics. Groups consist of people, who take up space and occupy places that are near or far in relation to each other. These physical characteristics, easily observable and understandable, are usually adopted spontaneously by the group members to serve the purposes they choose. In a college classroom, for example, note how students usually choose seats: some sitting in pairs or small, closely knit subgroups; those who want to declare their separate position sitting out on the fringes; and the rows closest to the instructor usually filling up last, especially if the room is small. The relations between members and the leader of a group are often directly depicted in the seating arrangement, as are the existing status distinctions. These seating arrangements help in turn to determine how the members act toward each other, toward the leader, and as part of the group process.

Just as we saw in regard to patterns of communication, physical arrangements are both the cause and the effect of group behavior. Cocktail parties crowd people together, and then the people at cocktail parties develop a spurious intimacy that makes for the special climate of a cocktail party. As Robert Sommer has shown in a series of studies on what he calls "personal space,"[○25] people make their habitats and habitats in turn influence what people do. In libraries, we select a personal distance from others that precisely expresses the privacy we prefer for library work, so libraries usually furnish settings in which such distances are possible. However, as Sommer documents, there are other settings that can be called "tight spaces": They constrain people through "hard architecture," and they do so in a rigid way than cannot be changed (Figure 19.5). Prisons are an obvious example, but to a surprising degree other "people-moving" settings such as airport waiting

personal space. The term for the physical proximity people will allow others without feeling uncomfortable or stressed. It varies from place to place and from situation to situation.

Fig. 19.5. Does physical closeness always bring discomfort? Perhaps not, if you are not too personally involved in getting the trip over with or if you are interested in what is going on around you.

rooms attempt the same thing; the designers' interests are more in whipping customers through a place than in providing a comfortable or meaningful experience in a setting. Unfortunately, school classrooms far too often fall into this category.[26]

Leaders and leadership. The central role in any group, and for this reason the one that has been most widely studied, is that of the leader. It may well be that the functioning of a group inevitably gives rise to the leadership role, and that a group cannot proceed in its absence. We sometimes observe what appear to be leaderless groups in real life, but closer observation will usually reveal that one or more persons are acting as "ghost leader"⊙—someone who does not occupy a formal leadership position but covertly and often quite effectively exercises key power and influence.

In many traditional families, the father occupies the formal role of leader, but ghost leadership is just as likely to be exercised by the mother or even by one of the children. In royal politics, a similar phenomenon used to be known as "the power behind the throne." The absence of an effectively functioning leader in a group seems to create a vacuum, which will soon be filled either by a ghost leader or by a candidate from the ranks—as was shown not too long ago in the success of an FBI agent in taking over the leadership of an underground faction of the Weathermen. And in some cases of rapid organizational change, there may even be more than one leader at a time.[27]

---

6. There is no universally best leader, although there are optimal leadership characteristics. Effective leadership depends on a fit between these characteristics and the needs of the group.

The leader and the group produce each other, help to develop each other, and may finally even destroy each other. Even in the most autocratic of settings, the relation between leadership and followership is never completely one-sided.

Under ordinary circumstances, as a group develops the leadership role will be

ghost leader. A member of a group who functions as a leader without formally or overtly occupying the role.

identified and occupied very early. Small groups can often proceed well along in their development without a formal leader, but in general the larger the group or the more immediate or complex its tasks, the sooner will a need be expressed for explicit leadership. Whoever does emerge, in some fashion, to take on the role of leader will therefore represent and reflect just the structure and level of development of the group at this stage. The leadership role is in effect a creation of the group—and this in turn determines the characteristics that a leader must have.

- A good leader will have to be an exemplar but not an idol, similar to the best characteristics of the group members but not exactly like any of them.
- However, the precise characteristics of a good leader will depend on the needs of the group at any one time. If the group is currently organized so that it is to begin and complete a clear-cut task, the best leader will be one who enables the group to function clearly and actively—even if the leader has to be somewhat bossy to do so.[28] At other times, the preferred leader may be an "emotional mentor" who can best create and maintain a desired psychological climate. The distinction is indicated very clearly in recent American political history. In the depths of the depression, in 1932, the American people turned to a charismatic politico, Franklin D. Roosevelt, who truly seemed able to get things done. In the decade after World War II, however, the national need was for a period of rest and recuperation, of coasting on goals achieved, and the obvious choice was a politically untried leader, Dwight D. Eisenhower, whose great strength was in bringing people together amicably and maintaining a pleasant interpersonal climate.
- Accomplishment on the part of the leader comes about as an expression of influence; so the leader is, in practice, the one who exercises the most direct and significant influence. Some helpful personal traits for good leadership will therefore be intelligence, gregariousness and outgoingness, high level of participation and communication, perceived status that is higher than that of the group average but not too high, and the absence of clearly negative characteristics.

Fig. 19.6. Two quite different Roosevelts, each a leader who fitted the needs of his own era.

In an extensive series of studies on the relations between leader characteristics and group characteristics, Fiedler[29] has shown that the process by which each influences the other can be broken down into two major aspects. On the one hand, there is the group's perception of the leader; on the other hand, there is the leader's attitude toward the group and its individual members. Leaders will function best when their efforts are properly focused in terms of the group structure. Thus, when the group requires a centralized, leader-dominant structure (as it might if it is *task oriented*, or if there is an emergency), the most effective leader will be one whose efforts are highly focused and channeled toward the members who will serve best in each capacity. But when the group's needs are for a less directive kind of leadership and a more democratic way of functioning, the leader will be most effective whose efforts are more widespread and equalized among the group members (Figure 19.6).

There is abundant evidence from work that adults have done with children—for example, in children's clubs or in residential schools—that in unclear situations, where decisions seem to be needed, the children prefer authoritarian to democratic leadership, if only to clarify the situation for everyone. However, when the situation is clear or no emergency is threatening, the group preference is for democratic leadership. When we translate this into national political terms, we can easily see why some would-be leader will try to convince the populace that a crisis is at hand that requires strong, firm leadership; and also why some followers, on their part, who constantly see the world in crisis terms, will eagerly welcome a leader who seems dictatorial.

The role of the individual

Psychology is about individuals; this book is about people. For this reason, it is fitting that we close this chapter by discussing the most significant psychological characteristic of individuals who behave in groups. This characteristic is one's role.© We have used the term in previous discussions, but without defining it or examining it in any detail.

An initial distinction should be made between a role and a position. Being the youngest child in a family is a position; that is, it is a social fact. However, associated with this position there usually is a set of behaviors that are expected of the person who occupies the position, such as going to bed earlier than the other children or (at least in some families) being the center of attention. Because of the expectancies associated with each role, it is a psychological and not simply a social phenomenon.

7. A psychological role, as distinct from a theatrical role or from the person or their position, is marked by specific expectancies of behavior.

Defining the role. In summing up a comprehensive review of the psychological literature on roles, Biddle and Thomas[30] define the role as "the set of prescriptions defining what the behavior of a position member should be." Basic to this definition is what they call a "person-behavior matrix"—that is, both inside and outside determinants must be accounted for in considering what a role is. According to this definition, a role (such as being President) remains relatively constant, while the persons who occupy it will change.

The central element here is that the behavior involved is more or less specified for the role. Both the person in the role and other persons who know the role hold certain *expectancies;* and, equally, their expectancies refer to certain *fixed* kinds of behavior. Psychologists have a name for such role expectancies; they call them *role prescriptions.*© Sociologists have their own name for the expectancies and the fixed behaviors; they call them *mores* or *customs.* It may not seem that our ordinary social behavior is much prescribed, but consider the commonplace example of the interacting roles of customer and clerk in a store. Only certain fixed behavior is expected of each. The clerk is expected to say, "May I help you?" or some similar expression—an expression, note, that would be ludicrous if used in many other settings. The interchange between customer role and clerk role is quite closely ordained by modern society, from its formal beginnings, including the restrictions on their topics of conversation, their manner of expression, and the feelings they may express. Young children do not ordinarily enact either role—but when they do so in playing, their behavior may become quite exaggerated, as though they sensed that the role behavior is formalized and "unreal."

The role and the person. Persons differ more than their roles. That is, there is an almost infinite variety of persons, but the number of roles in any society is fairly limited. Individuals vary in how well they can enact one or another role. For example, someone who is thrust into a managerial role but who is not fitted for it as a person may develop symptoms (such as ulcers) that reflect the disparity between person and role. On the other hand, continued experience in a role may lead to the disappearance of such distress symptoms. Bettelheim[31] describes the behavior of inmates of concentration camps who enacted the role of "good prisoner" until the

role. The way people function and behave as a result of their place in society, based on individual and group expectancies.

role prescription. The aims of the group that describe and prescribe how a person in the group has to behave in particular circumstances.

original stress associated with it disappeared. They were then often capable of participating without guilt in aggressive behavior against fellow inmates. Similarly, the bureaucrat may experience stress on first taking up a position but slowly become more bureaucratic as the years go by. Judges become more magisterial as they settle into and finally even "become their roles."

People enact roles, in the sense we have just described. They also play-act roles in a theatrical sense. The two are not the same, however. Psychological roles consist of sets of behavioral expectancies, as we can see, for example, in the cases of the customer, the judge, and the actor. Theatrical roles consist of behaviors within psychological roles. Thus, most people can enact the psychological role of actor, in which the individual behaves in constrained and often elaborate ways while ignoring the audience toward whom the behavior is, in fact, directed. Within this psychological role, the individual may play-act a specific theatrical role as the dramatic vehicle demands.[32]

Goffman has developed an elaborate account of role relations and social interactions based on the concept of role.[33] In his account, however, the role is much closer to a theatrical performance. In Goffman's view, social behavior consists of acting out one's "line," or behaviors that express the way one wants to present oneself in the situation. A major aim, according to this view, is to manage the impression that one makes on the other person, particularly in face-to-face encounters.

Role variations. From an outside point of view, roles differ in how well they are enacted by different individuals or in different situations. No two persons enact the same role in the same way, although there are sufficient similarities between different enactments to enable us to appreciate the clever mimic who can zero in on their essential features. From the point of view of the role taker, roles also vary in how central they may be to the person enacting them. It seems to be generally true that the more central the role is to the person, the more fixed will be the behavior associated with it. This can be seen in the difference in behavior between the instructor whose life is centered on teaching, as compared with the student who maintains a large number of equivalent roles and interests.

Role behavior is prescribed, as we said, but not all such prescriptions exert the same pressure on an individual (Figure 19.7). At a funeral, the role of a close relative to the deceased is very much prescribed, and therefore the close relative will be much more proper in behavior than will a friend of the family who just happens to be in attendance. Other roles, however, such as the "life of the party" (which some persons cannot resist enacting in a social group), prescribe very little and permit a great deal of imaginative or even creative leeway. The mourner role and the party role are so distinct that no one is immune to the difference in their prescriptions. This is why it is that someone at a party might entertain some friends by mimicking the role of a mourner at a funeral, but the reverse is unthinkable.

Roles differ as well in how they relate to other roles that the person may be enacting. We often find ourselves in two roles at once, in an arrangement that calls for one role to nest within another, as it were. The student who volunteers to be a subject in an experiment run by the same professor who will grade the student's term paper is enacting this role-within-a-role. So, even more curiously, was Anna Freud when she underwent a psychoanalysis by her father. The role that is nested within another role may be appropriate and helpful to the larger role, as often happens when the person whose lifetime role is "spunky little devil" finds a satisfying career as a critical writer on social reform. Equally, the smaller and larger roles may not fit each other.

The larger the context in which a role functions, the more likelihood that

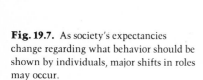

Fig. 19.7. As society's expectancies
change regarding what behavior should be
shown by individuals, major shifts in roles
may occur.

role conflict. Conflict that occurs when
a person is faced with role expectations
that conflict with one another.

there will be different sets of expectations and different kinds of norms exerting
pressure on the individual. When this happens, the person comes to hold mixed
expectations concerning role behavior that is appropriate in any situation, a condition that has been called *role conflict* or *role dissonance*.[©] One way to resolve the
issue is for the person to split one role into many. This, for example, is what many
women do when they discover that one set of pressures and expectations comes
from their families, a distinctly different set from some friends, and still another
set from other friends. In place of the unitary role of *woman*, the individual might
then behave in terms of an old-fashioned role when she visits her old-fashioned
parents, behave efficiently but in a ladylike manner in an office where the boss is
reasonable but conservative, and behave with a great deal more freedom when
backpacking with friends who share her views.

The classic example of role conflict is described in the rather weak joke about
the man who is watching his mother-in-law drive his new Cadillac over a cliff.
More precisely, role conflict occurs whenever expectancies are aroused that refer
to differing prescriptions for behavior. The authoritarian boss who discovers that
he is expected to unbend at an office party finds himself in such a situation, as
might the district attorney who is assigned to prosecute a close friend of the family.

With this discussion of the individual role, we complete our discussion of the
relation of individual to group. In the two chapters devoted to social psychology,
we have seen the usefulness of combining the inside and the outside viewpoint to
help us understand the complexity of that relation. As we have seen, individuals
are usually aware of the groups and society in which they claim membership; they
perceive them in the form of social reality. At the same time, groups and society

maintain a continuing pressure on individuals, some of it evident and some of it covert. From their own (inside) point of view, people act within social reality in whatever terms make sense to them and in whatever ways they feel are expected of them. From the (outside) point of view of an observer, people are influenced by and react to the effects of social forces. How the two sets of influences are resolved in each instance of behavior is the continuing problem of psychology.

Summary

1. A major research aimed at understanding how groups affect individual behavior compared leadership styles and climates in autocratic, democratic, and laissez-faire groups. Differences were observed in productivity, interpersonal relations, and level of ingroup and outgroup aggression.

2. A second major research on the same topic studied the effect of a spurious group consensus on individual perceptual judgment. Depending on personality and group characteristics, most persons will go along with a group consensus, at least on issues in which clear-cut answers or decisions are not available.

3. Conformity to a group consensus increases with the size of a group, with the ambiguity of the task, and with the individual's feeling of being alone in dissenting.

4. Research on bystander apathy, so called because it was sparked by such an incident in real life, has identified at least three important influences: the general social inhibition on acting in public, the degree of one's knowledge and certainty about a situation, and the degree to which one feels individually responsible or part of a collection of persons who share responsibility.

5. Milgram's important studies of obedience to authority indicate that people will behave in ways hurtful to others if they experience themselves as agents in a situation that requires such behavior.

6. Like other social phenomena, groups form, develop and grow, change, mature, decline, and set up relations with other groups.

7. Small groups affect the behavior of their members by way of the group structure, the patterns of communication, the group leadership, and the roles they make available to their members.

8. The leader and the group produce each other and affect each other. Firm leadership appears to be preferred by the group when the situation is unclear or there is an emergency. In addition, focused leadership is called for when the group needs are for a centralized, leader-dominated structure; but in less directive situations, leadership is chosen or arises that is more widely spread among the group members.

9. Psychological roles, consisting of sets of behaviors expected of the person, are distinct from theatrical roles.

10. In general, the more central the role is to the person, the more fixed will be the behavior associated with it.

11. The larger the context in which a role functions, the greater the likelihood that the context will generate different sets of expectations, some of them even conflicting, and therefore the more varied the norms that exert pressure on the individual.

12. Role conflict arises whenever expectancies are aroused that refer to different prescriptions for behavior.

In this Excursion, sexuality will be presented as a psychosocial phenomenon. The sex drive, unlike other biologically based drives, will be shown to have its focus on a felt lack outside the body. It will be shown that sexuality may have provided an important basis in evolution for variation and development of cognitive experience. We will then explore some relations between sexuality and the body, its development, and its cultural context.

In a discussion of sex differences, you will have the chance to see the distinction between male-female and masculine-feminine characteristics. Although anatomy significantly affects one's sexuality, you will see that a more comprehensive view is possible, in which a variety of psychosocial factors come together to form the whole of one's sexual experience and behavior.

"Sexual morality is exactly the same as the morality that should apply in any other human relationship."—Mary S. Calderone

Sex is for many persons the most complex and remarkable of experiences. It is also unique among biological phenomena. Fittingly, this book is almost bracketed by our two treatments of the topic of human sexuality—the treatment in Chapter 1, where we dealt with its genetic basis, and the treatment here, where we will carry the discussion, if only briefly, through the physiological, developmental, and cultural aspects of sexuality.

Our task in this Excursion will be to present an introduction to sexuality as experienced. We will be asking, "What is the normal experience of one's sexuality?" This question has not often been asked. Even investigators such as Sigmund Freud or Havelock Ellis, who boldly introduced the topic of sexual experience, dealt primarily with the abnormal. By contrast, we suggest that in the normal experience of one's sexuality we may find the data with which to develop a theory of sexuality that is appropriate to contemporary life situations.

Excursion V

Sex: a psychosocial phenomenon

Sex as drive

Sex is usually considered a drive, or a basic motive, on the order of such fundamental drives as hunger, thirst, and perhaps sleep, air, and self-preservation (see Chapter 4). All drives begin, as we know, with some lack in the organism. That is why they are also known as *tissue needs*. They arise because the organism develops a lack of something basic that it needs to keep it functioning. The behavior that results represents an attempt to obtain whatever is needed to fill the need, whether food or air or water.

Sexuality differs from other basic drives, however, in one important way. It is that sexual drive is not aroused because something is lacking within the body, as in the case of other basic drives, but because something is lacking outside the body. In regard to the sex drive, what is lacking is not something inside the body, but satisfaction. What is wanted is fulfillment, and it is always fulfillment in regard to a sexual object that is outside the body (Figure E5.1).

Fig. E5.1. Sometimes the sex drive in humans seems to be all pervasive.

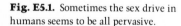

Sexuality and evolution

1. In evolution, sexuality is the basis for experiencing—perhaps even at the level of insects.

Very early in evolution, there arose the sexual differentiation into male and female that is now found in most species. Thus, from its beginning, sexuality as a drive was tied to the presence of two creatures to each other—their sexual drives could only be satisfied with each other.

A first advantage of this development is that much greater variation of progeny becomes possible when two different parents participate in reproducing. A second advantage is more significant—that mates can come together to reproduce only if they select one another. Their characteristics will determine what they see in each other and how they will go about the selection process. In this way, their characteristics come to play an important role in reproduction. With the linking of reproductive behavior to characteristics of individuals, the long evolutionary march had begun.

There is also a third advantage, although it is not usually recognized. If the evolution of a species is tied to processes of sexual selection, it is of great importance that the process requires two different individuals, for it then involves one creature perceiving another creature. This means that sexuality can function as a drive only to the degree that one member of the pair can perceive and attend to, perhaps even think about or want the other. These are the processes that form the elements of experiencing; and they are found in at least primitive form wherever the two sexes come together to mate.

The Swiss zoologist Portmann[1] has described in charming detail the mating process of dragonflies, which is carried out on the wing, with the two insects hooked together in tandem. In some species of dragonfly, the two remain hooked together while they alight on the stem of a waterlily and move rhythmically up and down so that the female can drop her eggs in the water. Occasionally another male, passing by and, seeing this mutually assisting behavior (each one of the pair guiding and timing the other), will be attracted to their movement and will begin to move in their rhythm on a nearby stem. Here we see all the processes of selective perception, attention, and motor identification that are required by their mating processes. The nervous systems capable of mastering and organizing these behavioral elements constitute a special contribution of sexuality to the evolutionary process.

At every level of evolutionary development, the basic drives affect perception, but in very different ways. Drives that are body centered, such as hunger and thirst, serve to "sharpen" existing perceptions. For example, cattle that are starved for calcium will develop greatly sensitized noses for sources of calcium, and can be seen to root up burial sites in order to get at bones. As laboratory studies have shown, rats will increase their sensitivity to a specific needed substance by a thousandfold when it is withheld from their diet.

The sexual drive, by contrast, does not only sharpen perceptions but directs them and can even distort them in the service of a desired object. The adage "Love is blind" applies to many other species than the human. The female rat, for example, develops a quite specific way of perceiving her pups during the nursing phase of her sexual cycle. She will rush out to retrieve any pup that strays more than a few feet from the nest. Yet her perceptual target here is not the pup, for under the influence of her maternal drive, she experiences any object of about the size and color of her pup as "to be retrieved." If the experimenter continually replaces the pups with others of smaller size, each time they grow too large, she will continue retrieving them for the ensuing six months. Her visual perception has not been sharpened to become more discriminating, but almost the reverse.

If sexuality is linked so closely to experience and its processes, then a theory of sexuality—particularly at the human level—ought to take account of sexual experience. Our only comprehensive sexual theory, that of Freud, did in fact attempt to do just this, although he ran afoul of a nineteenth-century biology with its notion of basic "instincts." As for the contemporary study of sex, in our post-Freudian era, the topic is apparently still being rediscovered.[2] The scientific study of sex in modern times dates only from the 1950s and is still only in the stage of gathering reliable data.[3]

Sexuality and the body

2. At the human level, and to a lesser degree among other animals, many bodily aspects of sexuality are tied to the individual's experience.

Sexuality is certainly the most elaborate form of patterned behavior exhibited by most species. Among many animals, it involves periodic bodily changes, elaborate courtship rituals, and complex mating procedures. It can involve extended activities such as selecting territories, building and defending nests, guarding eggs, and taking care of the young.

Much of this behavior appears to be under the direct control of hormones, yet it is not exclusively physiological. For example, even the production of hormones in many species is directly dependent on appropriate environmental stimulation; and this stimulation is not random but is tied through perception and meaning to the animal's experience. As an example, if male rats are reared entirely in the company of other males and never have the opportunity to see or smell a female, they will produce significantly less than the normal amount of the male hormone. Similarly, in some species of mammals, the female will not come into heat unless adult males are present. The experience, in its perceptual and meaningful aspects, is therefore essential in starting off a sequence whose subsequent stages may appear to be entirely biochemical.

Experience and anatomy. The central sexual achievement of the human child is the developing of what is called a *sexual identity* — that is, an organization of one's experience that is related to being one sex or the other. If my developed sexual identity is male, I will, first of all, know that I am male, and I will think of myself as male. My experience of myself as well as of other males and females will be organized around this knowing. It seems a straightforward achievement that ought to rest on a simple perception of one's own body: If I look at myself and see a male body, this ought to provide a sound enough basis for my sexual identity.

Yet there are many instances in which the individual's experience is not consistent with this simple perceptual directive. Experience does not always accord with anatomy. When the two conflict, the split may be so deep that it cannot be healed by an act of will or by some training or psychotherapy. Then we have the kind of case in which the individual may seek out a "sex-change" operation, a radical procedure for bringing the body into line with the ongoing experience. In other cases, a mixed picture is presented, perhaps with anatomical and hormonal characteristics not in agreement. If this happens, it is almost always the case that the person's developed sexual identity follows their lifetime of experience rather than the conformation of their anatomy. Those who have been reared as females, and who identify themselves as such, will "feel" female to themselves, regardless of what they can see or know about their bodies.[4]

But these are all exceptional cases. Normally, anatomy and experience work together, not at odds. And as they do, the body enters in a most important way into one's life of sexual experience. It enters because from a very early age children see their own bodies and use the perceptual data as a basis for what they know about themselves sexually. When they look at their own bodies, boys see a penis and girls do not. Now, we do not mean to revive here the error on which Freud's thought foundered. He insisted, against much evidence — and, indeed, against common sense — that because little girls did not see a male penis when they looked at themselves they would assume that they were lacking what they ought to have. They might even draw the conclusion that they had once had the penis but had lost it, perhaps as punishment. In any case (Freud concluded), they would be condemned to a lifetime of envy, of longing for the lost male organ, even of shame and a sense of being inferior.

Much of Freud's valuable thought in regard to the development of sexual identity was lost in the morass to which this curious "theory" led him — and we do not mean to repeat that here. Rather, we suggest simply that females know very well they have a sexual apparatus. But because it is not external, to be seen, their knowledge is necessarily based more on feeling and "bodily" knowing. In the case of males, knowledge of their own sex is based on seeing and "cognitive" knowing.

It is on this basis, we suggest, that from the very beginning the sexual identity of females is linked to the inner spaces of the body, to its feeling, its touching, and its experience of depth. But from the very beginning the sexual identity of the male is linked to externalizing, to knowing about, to the visual act, and to an apparatus that can be used in the external world. These two kinds of experiencing, tied to the nature of the body, prepare the two sexes for quite different kinds of sexual identity.

Sexuality and development

3. A developed sexual identity, making mature choices possible, results from a lifetime of experience.

As we noted at the start of Chapter 10, in discussing genetic and embryological differences between the sexes, increasing evidence suggests that the female, especially at the human level, is biologically more "sound" than the male.[5] With more responsive autonomic systems and greater resistance to the trauma of birth, females are better equipped for periodic physiological and hormonal "crises" such as menstruation, pregnancy, childbirth, and nursing. Even in the sexual act itself, it appears that it is vaginal contractions more than the movement of sperm cells that are responsible for the latter reaching the ovum.

Most important of all in regard to sexuality, the female capacity for sexual response is equal to or greater than that of the male. As the pioneering work of Masters and Johnson[6] has established, women are capable of repeated and variable sexual orgasms. By contrast, the male physiological capacity is more limited and restricted. Yet in practically all cultures, and as far back in recorded history as we can go, the male has been considered the stronger, and the male has been considered to have a sexual life of greater vigor and urgency. The contrast between the biological facts and the cultural status of the two sexes is so striking that Masters and Johnson suggest that it is no accident. The "psychosexual-social balance between the sexes that has been culturally established," they remark, may have been instituted specifically in order to "neutralize women's biophysical superiority."[7]

Many other supposed sex differences also disappear under careful examination; for example, in recent studies of male-female differences in response to visual pornography. With middle-class, presumably "liberated" subjects of both sexes, the expected differences (that this material appeals more to men than to women) are not found.[8]

On anatomy and destiny. In one of his most remarkable pronouncements, Freud said that in his view, "Anatomy is destiny." He meant by this that each person's life experiences were completely determined by whether the person was anatomically male or female. It was biology that completely determined both experience and behavior — with the further implication that if women were biologically inferior, that was unfortunate but, of course, unalterable.

We have pointed out a number of ways in which it might be said that Freud was right. In Chapter 10, in reviewing the findings of Maccoby and Jacklin, we noted that the only stable difference found between girls and boys was a difference in aggression. In humans, as in so many other species, male-male aggression is significantly more common during childhood development than female-female or female-male aggression, suggesting a hormonal basis for this culturally significant behavior. In this case, it might be said with some justification that anatomy is destiny. We have also suggested that, because boys see their own sexual organ and girls do not, this factual, anatomical difference may be an important basis for a lifetime of differences in sexual experience. Again, anatomy may in this instance be destiny. Finally, we suggested that, biologically, females are superior to males in many important autonomic and hormonal respects — and this too might (under the appropriate cultural conditions) give rise to a lifetime of different experiencing: one more instance of anatomy becoming destiny.

But we do not believe there are any other instances in which experience is completely determined by biology. As human history shows very clearly, sexual experience is relative to the culture in which it appears. Indeed, every society in history seems to have made use of the same discovery — that, of all the fundamental drives, sexuality is the most malleable, the one that can most easily and most radically and most completely be molded by the needs and demands of the culture.

Anatomy determines the male-female distinction, but it is culture, with all its demands and pressures, that gives rise to the distinction between masculine and feminine. The latter is the basis for the way that each person experiences him- or herself as a sexual being. In a sexually repressive culture, most persons will develop and maintain a sexual identity that is sharply limited to the cultural prescriptions of one sex. In more permissive cultures, sexual identities will be less clearly defined.

An "androgynous" identity. Jeanne H. Block is a research psychologist who has studied children in various cultures as part of a long-term investigation of how sexual identities are developed. She has suggested that the ideal may be a sexual identity that combines the best features of both sexes. If one is secure enough in the recognition of one's own gender, one might then be freed to act in ways not customarily associated with gender. This would lead to experience and behavior that she terms *androgynous,*° combining the traditionally feminine and masculine (Figure E5.2). Using a scale of personality development that was devised by Loevinger and her associates,[9] Block has traced the development of an androgynous sexual identity through its stages of growth.[10] What is described at each stage is not sexual behavior but rather aspects of experience: feelings, attitudes, self-perceptions, and personal traits.

Stage 1. The first two years of life. The sense of self is sexless, and the infant's task is simply to distinguish self from nonself.
Stage 2. With the ability to speak, children can say, "I am [one sex or the other]" — but behavior is not identifiable as unique to sex.
Stage 3. In the second and third years, a sense of independence is developed, gained through a "conflict of wills" with parental authority.
Stage 4. A sense of conformity now develops, and with it the first clear distinctions in sexual identity. Socialization encourages boys and girls to control different

Fig. E5.2. Two forms of androgyny.

androgyny. Having characteristics or elements that pertain to both sexes.

Table E5.1. Some examples of sexual customs considered normal in cultures other than our own.

The Chenchu people of India consider that it is dangerous to have sexual intercourse in the dark. A child conceived under such conditions, they believe, may be born blind.

Among the Jaluit of the Marshall Islands, men make sexual advances to women by rolling their eyes and pronouncing the names of their sexual organs. However, among the Goajiro of Colombia, a woman makes sexual advances to a man by attempting to trip him; if she succeeds, he must have sexual relations with her.

In the Toda culture of India, it is immoral for a man to begrudge the sexual favors of his wife to another man.

In the Siberian society of the Chukchee, a man who assumes a feminine dress and role is considered a powerful shaman.

On Ponape, in the Caroline Islands of the Pacific, all children are given formal instruction in sexual intercourse beginning with their fourth year.

The woman of the Apinaye tribe of north central Brazil during intercourse will bite off portions of her partner's eyebrows and noisily spit them out.

Source: Data from Ford and Beach, 1951.

emotions. This in turn is linked to the experience of "I am [one or the other sex]."

Stage 5. Sexual identity is now firmly linked to what is expected of children. During this period of transition and growth, the child experiences a wealth of new experiences and develops an "ideal self."

Stage 6. Block terms this the "autonomous" level, in early adolescence. Through the normal "conflicts" of this age, behavior comes to be moderated by way of a sense of duty, and individual values of one's sex role are worked out.

Stage 7. Through continuing growth, some individuals may now gain a more complex and "resilient" sexual identity, integrating masculine and feminine values within one's personal world of experience.

The chief problem in developing a mature sexuality is not simply to learn to act in one way rather than another but to be able to experience free and responsible choices to act one way or another. The adolescent boy (or man) who is limited sexually to a model of "making out," as a caricature of the young playboy, is not free, although he may think he is, but bound to a pattern of behavior that controls him. And the young woman who is limited, without knowing why, to an anxious defense of her innocence, is still as limited by cultural pressures as when she was a child. The real problem in adolescence may be, not to manage drives and needs, but to manage choices.

Sexuality and culture

It is hardly necessary to emphasize the profound influence of culture on the experience of sexuality. It is immediately evident in any consideration of cross-cultural variations. In one comprehensive survey, embracing more than a hundred human societies as well as some nonhuman species, Ford and Beach[11] demonstrated the almost endless variety of customs and habits that are considered natural, and even necessary, in regard to sex (see Table E5.1).

By contrast, the number of universal practices is very limited. Just about all societies forbid incest. Nearly all associate the sexual act with some degree of personal privacy. Most frown on adult masturbatory activity. But aside from these, it would be difficult to think of a custom or mode of behavior that is not somewhere permitted, even encouraged, in regard to sex. Within each social group, their own particular pattern of permission and denial is usually considered the only one that is morally acceptable. One conclusion to be drawn from the evidence concerning sexual custom and practice is that societies that maintain fewer strict rules seem to have a lower percentage of psychological disturbance in their young adults.[12]

4. Culture and the individual mutually interact to result in the experience of sexuality.

Culture influences the people in it, but not one-sidedly. People are not simply passive recipients of some vague, abstract cultural effect on them. Rather, what we call *culture* should be viewed as the effects that a society has on its members, coupled with the acts and expectations of the members themselves. As we can see by looking at some examples, people have as much influence on their culture as the culture has on them.

Victorian sexuality. The adjective *Victorian* is usually used to refer to the set of attitudes and behaviors of western Europe and America during the last half of the nineteenth century. It was a time of great industrial growth, of expansion, of aggressively mastering the material environment. And it was equally a time of sexual suppression in all spheres: in behavior, in expression, even in such experiences as thought and feeling and wish.

George Albee[13] has documented the relations in the Victorian middle class between sexual attitudes and social behavior. On the one hand, nearly absolute control over one's sexual urges was prescribed. On the other hand, all one's energies were to be organized in the form of work toward long-term goals. One saved, one did not spend; the verb *to spend* was the Victorian term for sexual orgasm. A key element in this set of prescriptions was the idea of privacy: It was the central and guiding idea pervading Victorian ideas about sexual matters.

We find many reminders of Victorian thought in today's culture. Not long ago a group of parents, in a small city in Minnesota, mounted a campaign against a program of sex education in their schools. Their central objection, as expressed by one leader of the group, was that such teaching would "take the privacy out of marriage." One of them stated it simply, "Now our kids know what a shut bedroom door means." As to when they would permit their children to be taught what happened behind closed bedroom doors, the group suggested that it should be when the girls started menstruating and the boys started shaving.

Primal scenery. Yet perhaps we should not be so quick to condemn these parents for what seems like a sexual attitude that is out of date. They did fail to make a necessary distinction between two kinds of privacy: There is a privacy that only covers up, forcing people (and especially children) to deny what they are afraid they already know, a privacy that consists of enforcing innocence and denying natural curiosity. That kind of privacy is as much an exercise in power as in morality. But a different kind of privacy is what all of us need and demand whenever we want our experience to be as full and rich as possible. We simply do not want to be interrupted, much less observed, during such special moments. This kind of privacy constitutes a legitimate need, and the parents should not apologize for insisting on it (Figure E5.3).

More important, however, is that the attitudes of these seemingly old-fashioned parents force us to examine our own experience in regard to the incident

Fig. E5.3. Should the door be closed, partly closed, or wide open?

that Freud called the *primal scene*© — the child's observation of the parents during an act of sexual intercourse. Again, Freud was mostly wrong in his views — for example, his curious belief that the child would spontaneously interpret this as an act of aggression. As any couple can testify who own a dog, the sexual intercourse of humans is not perceived by the pet as a fight but as a scene of either pleasure or love. Household pets will either ignore its occurrence or show a mild interest. They rarely get upset, as they would if observing a fight. However, Freud's insight was correct in leading him to suspect that in any case the primal scene was of central importance in the experience of both child and parents.

What Freud sensed was the complexity of the experience involved. For example, contemporary, liberal parents would like to do two contradictory things — to close the door so that their child will not see them during sexual intercourse, yet to encourage the child in the freedom to talk about adults who have sexual intercourse. One kind of privacy, the perceptual, is demanded. Another kind of privacy, the verbal, is refused. We can begin to understand this apparent contradiction if we make a distinction between two of our basic modes of experiencing, the bodily mode and the social mode. In my bodily existence, my experience is filled with what belongs to my body; therefore, whatever intrudes on my lived space is sensed as an invasion of my very body. This is the state that describes the person during the act of sexual intercourse: totally reduced, by personal choice, to a mode of bodily existence, a mode in which clothes are felt as an impediment, in which one gives up being reflective or sophisticated or adult or socialized, in which one willingly shares some ultimate in bodily intimacy.

Our social mode of existence, as we know, is quite different. In it we take on all the roles and masks that define us as social beings. And most of all, we talk to each other and to ourselves, and we talk about things. In contrast with the mode of bodily existence in which I feel, in my social existence I am involved mostly in knowing. As parents, we insist that in the bodily mode we not be invaded by another's perception but that in the social mode we share another's knowledge. Thus we will forbid the child to see us in our sexual acts but we will encourage the same child to talk about us as sexual beings.

The Minnesota parents who insisted that the primal scenery of their home be kept undefiled were not, then, as wrong as contemporary liberals might think. It is true that they choose to limit their social existence so as not to include sexuality; and in the modern world this may be a hopeless quest. But in their desire to maintain the "purity" of their modes of bodily existence they are asking no more than the rest of us do. They differ from more open-minded parents, not in their desire for greater privacy, but in the more rigid barriers they place between bodily and social, personal and public modes of existence.

Contemporary sexuality. In former years, the barrier between the personal and the public was so strict that what was on either side of the barrier was often quite opposite. In England's Victorian culture, a complete denial of sex at the public level was associated with a flourishing institution of literary pornography underground.[14] Today the scene appears to be much different. The commercial market reeks of sex that is suggested even if not fully revealed.[15]

One result appears to be a tension that is experienced between pressures from the culture and pressure arising from one's own needs and wants. Social influence is directed toward the physical and behavioral aspects of sex: A variety of acceptable contraceptive methods are provided, sexual activity in all its forms is freely discussed and described, and the new norm is one of relatively casual sexual behavior for the fun of it. As a result, there has been a marked increase in the openness and frequency of sexual relationships outside of marriage, particularly among persons who came of age following World War II.[16] But to a great degree

primal scene. A psychoanalytic term for a person's recollection (actual or fancied) of the first observation of a sex act. According to Freud, this has a great effect on personality formation.

these relationships are found to be based on felt needs for closeness and intimacy, even love. Whereas the public norms are that sex is fine as long as it is a mutually agreeable physical contact, the private norms appear to be that sex is fine if it involves a close personal relationship. The tension between the two sets of pressures is felt by many persons.

Experiencing sex

The changes in many aspects of sexuality that occurred following World War II were expressed, and probably influenced as well, by the pioneering surveys done by Alfred Kinsey and his colleagues at Indiana University.[17] They provided our first reliable data on the sexual practices of adult Americans—even though it was generally recognized that for various reasons their samples were not representative of the American population as a whole. A more serious criticism was that, in spite of their great value as sociological documents, their data were restricted to behavior. An equally important aspect of individual sexuality, the person's experience, was not treated at all. This is the aspect that we stress here, consistent with the viewpoint presented throughout this book.

On arousal and orgasm. In the sequence of sexuality, from its start to its completion, arousal is that opening part in which the person feels heightened, energized, directed, and organized toward a possible goal. Freud was the first to state clearly that arousal may occur in the experience of even very young children—a position for which he was condemned in many medical circles. However, he then made the mistake of adding that children of any age would strive to complete the sequence in the same manner as adults do—by aiming for the experience of orgasm. This is not true of children. In most cases, their sexual experience is restricted to the arousal phase—which may be what gives their behavior its appearance of innocence.

Just as in the case of other primary drives such as hunger, the higher the arousal, the more intense the subsequent experience of orgasm. Clinical data suggest, in addition, that the postorgasm state is also higher, with the person more awake and less sleepy, if arousal has been high and orgasm intense. In addition, if we undertake to explore the perceptual and attentional aspects of the arousal experience, we find that[18]

- If our arousal is in regard to the situation that we are in, a repetition of our experience is likely to lead to lessened arousal. But if our arousal is in regard to a specific person in the situation, repetition is likely to lead to heightened arousal.
- If our arousal target is the physical presence of another person, high arousal appears to be dependent on the other person's promise of acting in a way that is appealing or attractive to us.
- If during sexual activity we actively direct our attention, the experience will differ depending on what we choose as target. We may focus on the other person; if that person is appealing, arousal will be heightened. If we focus on ourselves or our own bodies, however, arousal will be lessened, and anxiety may result. If our attention during orgasm is directed toward our own bodies, the experience is likely to be one of numbness or lack of feeling—a complaint often made by persons who concentrate on their own sexual performance.

The role of the different senses in regard to sexual arousal remains unclear. The problem may be that our experiencing is not neatly divided into the familiar five senses and that both vision and touching have more in common in regard to sexual experience than we had thought. These two senses are similar to each other, and different from the other senses, in that they have two "sides," the active and the passive. We experience the two sides as seeing *versus* being seen or touching *versus* being touched. A major difference between the sexes, at least in Western cultures, may be that men are more turned on by seeing and touching, women by being seen and being touched—but this would require further study.

A more widespread difference between the sexes, as reported by women, is that women's preference is usually for arousal through a tender or loving contact first, followed by a genital, sexual contact. For men, the preference is often for the genital, sexual contact immediately. This difference is often experienced as well as described in terms of the different time that it takes the two sexes to become aroused—but it appears that the basic difference is in mode of arousal, which in turn influences speed of arousal (see Figure E5.4).

Much more of sexual experience needs to be studied in systematic fashion, but the area is only beginning to be explored from this viewpoint. There is evidence, for example, that in the sexual encounter people prefer some appropriate balance between concealing and revealing, between what is offered and what is held back, perhaps even between what is personal or private and what is mutual or shared. Like so many other aspects of sexuality, this is usually studied as a social phenomenon rather than, as we suggest in our title, a phenomenon that is psychosocial. Sexuality, like other important aspects of our lives, is a matter of both experience and behavior.

Fig. E5.4. For reasons that are both psychological and social, the sexual fantasies of the two sexes may differ very much.

Summary

1. The sex drive, as distinct from other basic biological drives, is aroused as a consequence of a felt lack that is *outside* the body.

2. Sexual arousal can either sharpen or distort perception of a desired object.

3. Sexual behavior is controlled by psychological and cultural as well as physiological processes.

4. In instances of a conflict between anatomically and hormonally determined characteristics, the person's developed sexual identity usually follows his or her lifetime of social behavior rather than the conformation of anatomy.

5. Because of anatomical differences in the genital organs, male sexual identity will be linked to the visible and the external, and female sexual identity to feeling and the internal.

6. The female capacity for sexual response appears to be biologically superior to that of the male, although cultural pressures often prevent its expression.

7. Anatomy largely determines the male-female distinction, but cultural influences largely determine the distinction between masculine and feminine.

8. Societies that maintain fewer strict rules related to sexual behavior appear to have a lower percentage of psychological disturbance in their young adults.

9. The desire for privacy during the sexual act appears to be a fusion of two kinds of needs and pressures, the personal and the public.

10. Public norms increasingly suggest that sexual activity is acceptable as long as it consists of mutually agreeable physical contact. Private norms, on the other hand, appear to demand a basis of close personal relationship.

In this book, we have tried to introduce beginning students to the achievements of psychology and to the significant thought and practice of today. But we also felt some obligation to give our readers some indication of what the field of psychology might be in the near future. We thought it would be presumptuous of us to venture such a prediction about the entire field of psychology. That, we reasoned, belongs more properly to individuals who are at the center of today's important developments.

To this end, we selected a representative group of distinguished psychologists around the world and invited them each to write a short message to our student readers. We asked them to outline what they saw as lacking in contemporary psychology and what they would like to see happen in psychology during the next ten years. For various reasons, not everyone we asked was able to accept our invitation. The ten contributions we received, which we think represent a fair sampling of leading figures in contemporary psychology, are presented on the following pages. We have added a brief statement to identify each contributor. The contributors, in alphabetical order, are

George W. Albee	Arnold A. Lazarus
Anne Anastasi	David C. McClelland
Hans J. Eysenck	Neal E. Miller
Donald O. Hebb	Jean Piaget
Ernest R. Hilgard	Carl R. Rogers

GEORGE W. ALBEE. Born in 1921 and educated at the University of Pittsburgh, Albee has been for two decades a major figure in contemporary American clinical psychology, particularly in its application to problems of social organization and the place of the individual in society. Currently professor of psychology at the University of Vermont, he has also served as president of the American Psychological Association (1969–1970).

Psychology ten years from now —George W. Albee

Epilogue

Psychology ten years from now

Status and power are seductive influences. Contemporary psychology is attracting bright young people into the field who are fascinated with the prospect of becoming psychotherapists, of the opportunity to "help people." The prospect of national health insurance and of reimbursement of fees to psychologists has significantly shaped our public relations activity. We seem so determined to be included that we are willing to compromise two important principles: (1) Persons suffering from emotional distress are really not sick and do not need illness-oriented treatment and (2) no mass distress afflicting humankind has ever been eliminated or controlled by attempts at treating each separate afflicted individual.

We must resist the temptation to become a therapy-oriented profession divorced from our scientific roots and from continuous scientific renewal. Psychology has been unique among the professions in having a close and continuing interaction with scientific research. To lose this integration with science would be to lose a major source of strength for the field.

I expect to see more bright young students attracted to the area of prevention of emotional disturbance. Everything we have learned in the past century suggests that prevention is far more effective than individual treatment in reducing or eliminating human distress. Research into prevention quickly leads to profound questions about the structure of society, about the sources of human distress, and to an examination of competency and coping skills. If psychology is truly to make a contribution to human welfare, I believe it will be in prevention.

ANNE ANASTASI. Born in 1908 and educated at Barnard College and Columbia University, Anastasi is currently professor and departmental chair of psychology at Fordham University. As teacher, author, consultant, and visiting professor, she has contributed importantly to systematizing the fields of test construction and measurement of human abilities. She was elected president of the American Psychological Association for the year 1971–1972, the first woman psychologist to be so honored since 1916.

Psychology ten years from now — Anne Anastasi

What I hope to see within the next decade is more factually based and theoretically sophisticated interpretations of test performance and of the causes of individual and group differences in behavior. I look for clarification of the operation of heredity and environment, with more attention to the actual mechanisms and chains of events whereby hereditary and environmental factors ultimately affect behavior. Closer contact and increasing collaboration of psychologists with geneticists, neurologists, and physiologists, among others, should help to bring this about. There should be more specific consideration of the modifiability of behavior, so that the behavioral effects of heredity are not regarded as implicitly permanent and immutable, nor the behavioral effects of environment as implicitly superficial and negligible. Both sets of conditions may influence behavior in a multiplicity of ways, with effects that range from basic, broad, and lasting to trivial, transitory, and narrowly limited.

Concurrently, I should like to see the interpretation and use of test scores more closely aligned with the growing understanding of the causes of individual differences. No test is designed to assess "innate" traits of ability or personality. In fact, to speak of traits in such terms is theoretically meaningless. Tests indicate where individuals are at the time and hence enable them to determine how to move forward in any direction along which they wish to develop. To proceed in the absence of such information is equivalent to trying to set a course on a journey without knowing where one is at the start. In the interests of both theoretical advances and societal goals, I should like to see these basic points more generally recognized by psychologists, regardless of their area of specialization, and more widely disseminated among the general public.

HANS J. EYSENCK. Born in Germany in 1916, Eysenck was educated there, in France, and in England, where he came to stay in the 1930s. He has spent a productive career as a clinical psychologist and a researcher on personality and on testing at the University of London, where he is now director of the Psychological Department of the University's Institute of Psychiatry. His work, consisting of more than thirty books and a number of widely used tests, has been concerned with the dimensions of personality and intelligence, with test construction, and with the application of psychology to politics and everyday life.

Psychology ten years from now — Hans J. Eysenck

No one can foresee the future, but it is possible to extrapolate from the recent past. The methods of behavior therapy, which originated and received their name only some fifteen years ago, have become very widely accepted for the treatment of neurotic disorders, behavior problems, classroom difficulties, criminal and psychotic behaviors, and many other psychological difficulties. I believe that in the next ten years these methods will completely oust psychotherapy and other non-scientific methods of treatment for what are essentially behavioral problems and will be very widely used and adapted to many other problem areas. My only fear is that this will develop into a bandwagon, with many people not properly qualified in learning theory and psychological experimental literature jumping on to it and advertising themselves as "behavior therapists" when in actual fact they are nothing but quacks. This situation obviously leads to the necessity for proper certification, and it is to be hoped that the next ten years will see advances in this direction also.

DONALD O. HEBB. A Canadian psychologist and educator, Hebb was born in 1904 and educated at McGill University and at Harvard University. His career in psychology has been concerned with the biological foundations of human and animal behavior, an area in which he has had a significant impact through his research and his popular textbooks. A former chancellor of McGill University, he was also elected president of the American Psychological Association, the only Canadian to receive this honor.

Psychology ten years from now — Donald O. Hebb

It seems likely to me that psychology in ten years' time will still be fragmented, with too little attention paid by biologically oriented psychologists to what is being done by the socially oriented, and vice versa; with no interaction between cognitivists and learning theorists, or not much; and so on, each specialized point of view or theoretical approach being sufficient unto itself, whereas our hope must lie in the integration of the special value of all those approaches, difficult as the integration must be in view of the complexity of the human mind. I hope however that some progress toward that goal will have been made. It seems to me also that the study of thought and consciousness is most likely to provide the key to the integration. It will not do so if the one who studies thought persists in a "black-box" approach — that is, refusing to make full use of what has been learned of the anatomy and physiology of the brain — or if the physiologically inclined student of the brain is unwilling to venture into the necessarily speculative analysis of larger patterns of brain function. Human thought is the crux of the problem of behavior, and no avenue of approach can we afford to neglect.

I believe these pious sentiments to be precisely true, if a sentiment may be said to be true.

ERNEST R. HILGARD. Born in 1904 and educated at Yale University, Hilgard has had a distinguished and varied career in teaching, writing, and research. He is senior author of one of the leading introductory textbooks in psychology, as well as of a number of other works on learning and hypnosis. Elected president of the American Psychological Association for the year 1948–1949, he is currently professor emeritus of psychology at Stanford University, where he continues his work on hypnosis and states of consciousness.

Psychology ten years from now — Ernest R. Hilgard

Psychology has grown rapidly and become widely accepted, so that it is now one of the leading majors in our colleges and universities. This is a mixed blessing for psychology as a science because it means that many students uninterested in accepting the discipline of science hope to find in psychology satisfaction through many of the things promised by contemporary cults: new powers of the mind, expanded consciousness, techniques for successful social living, creativity, and serenity. Psychology may indeed promise some of these things to those who are willing to work hard at it, but it has no secrets that will by magic unlock hidden sources of strength. Patient hard work is needed to deal with human problems, just as it is needed to solve serious and perplexing problems of science in any area.

Psychology has gone through a period of tool sharpening to prove that the methods of science are applicable to human behavior and subjective experience. It now has to be on guard lest its concern for sharp tools and precise methods may narrow its focus. The questions that students want psychology to answer are legitimate ones, and the test of psychology in the future is how soundly it will be able to answer them.

ARNOLD A. LAZARUS. A South African by birth (in 1932), Lazarus received his education at the University of Witwatersrand and came to the United States in the 1960s. He was a leading figure (with Joseph Wolpe) in the early development of methods of behavior therapy. Now professor and departmental chair of psychology at Rutgers University, he has written extensively on the theory of psychotherapy and on the applications of behavioral therapy, especially to sexual and marital problems.

Psychology ten years from now — Arnold A. Lazarus

Any science in its primitive stages of development (and psychology as a science is at a most elementary stage of growth) is characterized by rival factions, splinter groups, rigid adherents, loose-minded gurus, purists, integrationists, and an assortment of hard-nosed pragmatists and wooly-headed theorists. Over 300 separate systems of psychotherapy today have created their own popes, high priests, and a host of followers. But there has been some progress. For example, we have seen the beginnings of the end of psychoanalysis as the most lauded and respected form of therapy. In this regard, clinical psychology may be said to have taken its first stumbling footsteps.

Psychology is almost at the stage where it can start divesting itself of the fake, specious, and spurious ideologies that hinder its growth. The tendency for soft-hearted humanists ("Love, warmth and empathy conquer all!") to collide with hard-nosed behaviorists ("Keep outside of the black box and quantify everything in sight!") is starting to recede. The emergence of cognitive-behavioral amalgams is an encouraging trend. This paves the way for a truly scientific study of affect, sensation, imagery and cognition, and their interdependence, as well as their impact on overt behavior. In ten years from now, we should be able to begin to answer a crucial question: "Do our internal processes (for example, images, fantasies, thoughts, and feelings) follow the same 'laws of learning' as our overt behaviors?"

DAVID C. McCLELLAND. Born in 1917 and educated at Yale University, McClelland is now professor of psychology at Harvard University and on the faculty of its graduate school of education. His research and writing has been concerned with the relations among motivation, fantasy, individual development, and social change, and he has done important work on personality characteristics in cross-cultural contexts.

Psychology ten years from now — David C. McClelland

Psychology has made some progress in identifying the variables that influence how the organism processes information — in seeing, perceiving, learning, remembering, and adjusting. But it still has not reached anything like consensus on what "content" variables can best be utilized to bring some order out of the chaos of experience. In other words, we need to find out what attitudes, what motives, what memory systems are most important for explaining behavior. Factor analysis was supposed to be a shortcut to identifying such structures, but in my opinion it has simply failed to do the job in a convincing way. Psychology today is like chemistry before the invention of the periodic table, which made it possible to classify chemical components in a systematic way, which in turn permitted a better understanding of how those compounds functioned. Hopefully the next generation of psychologists will succeed in identifying the mental structures that organize behavior just as chemists succeeded in identifying the ways in which physical structures are organized. In fact, further knowledge of factors governing processes of perceiving, learning, and remembering is likely to be slowed down until we can discover how *what* is perceived or wanted or remembered modifies the process of responding.

NEAL E. MILLER. Born in 1909 and educated at Yale University, Miller's career has spanned the clinical and experimental areas of psychology. He has been a president of the American Psychological Association (1960–1961) and one of the very few psychologists to receive the National Medal of Science (1965), and is currently professor of psychology and head of the Laboratory in Physiological Psychology at Rockefeller University. His research contributions have centered on the physiological basis of human and animal learning and motivation, with a current emphasis on the phenomenon of biofeedback.

Psychology ten years from now — Neal E. Miller

The one thing that I can be most certain about is that psychology ten years from now will be different in a number of unexpected ways. Some rapidly developing areas will continue their growth, others will hit a plateau, while yet others, now in the doldrums or even not yet thought of, will get a sudden boost from new techniques, new ideas, and surprising discoveries. Anticipating such changes, the best thing that the student can do is to prepare himself for a lifetime of learning. He should learn a critical attitude and how to evaluate new evidence and hypotheses. He should try to gain an understanding of the process by which science develops, often in unexpected ways, and how the knowledge discovered by basic research sometimes leads to practical applications, which in turn may provide a point of departure for further basic research.

The boundaries between disciplines, which are artifacts of history, will continue to break down. The ties of psychology to both biological and social sciences will become stronger. Some of the most important new developments will occur on the boundaries between disciplines.

In an area in which I have been involved most recently, I shall venture a few short-range predictions. Instead of being related primarily to psychiatry, psychology will continue to develop ties to all of the fields of medicine. As physical diseases continue to be mastered, Behavioral Medicine will become increasingly important, first as a unification of diverse areas of research and eventually as a basis for certain types of prevention and therapy. Finally, as third-party payments by insurance companies and the government pay an increasing share of medical expenses, there will be an increasing demand for the rigorous evaluation of all therapeutic procedures, including behavioral ones.

JEAN PIAGET. Born in 1896 in Switzerland, Piaget began his career as a zoologist and teacher of philosophy. He became a professor of child psychology at the University of Geneva, and was made director of its bureau of educational science in 1929. Since then, through his researches on child development, he has become perhaps the most important world figure in child psychology. In more than a dozen books, he has explored such topics as morality, logic, judgment, time and space, intelligence, and other cognitive structures in infants and children. The result of his innovative research and extensive writing has been a comprehensive and historically important theory of human development.

Psychology ten years from now — Jean Piaget

The letter asking us for a few thoughts on "psychology in ten years" uses two formulations that are in no way equivalent: (1) what the disciplines of psychology promise us in the immediate future and (2) what we believe to be insufficient in today's psychology and what we expect from research in the next ten years. Now this is not the same, and for item 1 to coincide with item 2 one would have to be assured that psychologists to come will be "reasonable," which amounts to saying "will feel our own needs" (egocentrism of the authors). I will thus limit myself to item 2 by speaking of the only field I know: cognitive psychology.

In this respect, the first big gap in contemporary psychology, one that is of considerable importance, is the absence of a sufficient link between theories of intelligence and biological conceptions of adaptation, including interpretations of behavior for the most part hereditary (instincts). To be sure, there exists a "neuro-psychology," but it is not enough. Above all, the excuse of psychologists is that biology itself is still very far from the answers that we would need. Paul Weiss was able to write that molecular biology has thus far taught us "nothing" about development. Neo-Darwinism is in a state of crisis (see Temin's research on RNA, and so on). But a closer collaboration would be useful to both biology and psychology.

The second big gap is easier to fill, but it is far from being so: It is the insufficiency of collaborations between psychology and epistemology as a theory and history of the sciences. However, scientific thought is the finest example of the creative constructions that human intelligence has produced, and reciprocally, the psychogenesis of logical-mathematical structures is indispensable to the understanding of their nature. Nevertheless, authors who master the relations between these two types of study remain few.

In a word, the two kinds of progress to be expected in future years consist in completing our knowledge of the two extremes of cognitive psychology: its sources, which are biological, and its outcomes, which are epistemological.

CARL R. ROGERS. The originator of the client-centered approach in psychotherapy, Rogers was born in 1902 and received his education in theology and then in psychology at Columbia University. He has held various posts in child guidance clinics and as professor and research professor at a number of universities, was a president of the American Psychological Association in 1946–1947, and is currently a fellow of the Center for Studies of the Person at La Jolla, California. In his research, teaching, and writings, he has been perhaps the most significant influence for a humanistic approach in clinical psychology and in personality theory. Most recently, he has been one of the central figures in the study of encounter groups and their application to life changes.

Psychology ten years from now — Carl R. Rogers

To begin with, it should be noted that there is the field of psychology to which a great many people contribute and in which an even larger number of people are interested. Then there is the field of academic psychology, which is much narrower and a great deal more conservative. It often lags far behind the total field of psychology, slowly inching along as it digests the advances being made in the whole field of psychology.

What are the growing edges of the psychological field? One concerns itself with the biological and physiological aspects—biofeedback, the sharp functional differences between our right brains and left brains, the study of the effects of chemicals and drugs on human personality and behavior. Another leading edge, I believe, is the application of principles initially learned in psychotherapy to intensive small groups and to larger and larger bodies of people and to organizations. We are developing models for better communication among individuals, between family members, between members of different cultures. To me, this is a very exciting and promising development. An example is the coming ten-day workshop [at the Center for Studies of the Person] for 300 individuals from fifteen or more countries and cultures in which the staff will use their skills to endeavor to facilitate improved communication and understanding. Another way of stating all this is that this area of psychology will be reaching into organizational and governmental levels.

Another frontier is the psychic realm. There is now sufficient evidence to indicate that altered states of consciousness, telepathy, clairvoyance, out-of-the-body experiences, and other paranormal phenomena cannot be fully explained by the laws of psychology as we know them now. Adventurers in this field will be strongly criticized or ridiculed, but I believe we may be entering a whole new phase of psychological thought and knowledge, perhaps operating under laws as yet to be discovered.

For the student who does not let him- or herself be drowned in the sterility of much academic psychology, the whole field is full of excitement and promise, both for individuals and for society.

Chapter notes

But first, this message . . .

1. Smith (1945), p. 35.
2. Bender (1950), p. 135.
3. Gallup (1970).
4. Amsterdam (1972).
5. Bertrand (1969).
6. Altmann (1967), p. 353.
7. Jourard (1971). For a review of the literature on this topic, see Cozby (1973).
8. Wolff (1943).
9. Clark and Clark (1958).
10. Coopersmith (1967).
11. Rogers (1970).
12. Thigpen and Cleckley (1957).
13. Schreiber (1973).
14. Wilde (1974), p. 224.
15. Agee (1969), p. 14.

Chapter 1. Genetics and inheritance

1. For an introductory survey, see McClearn and De Fries (1973).
2. Jarvik, Klodin, and Matsuyama (1973).
3. Borgaonkar and Shah (1974).
4. Breland and Breland (1961), p. 682.

5. Lockard (1971), p. 172.
6. Kettlewell (1965).
7. Williams (1976).
8. Hess (1959).
9. Cullen (1957).
10. Lehrman (1955).
11. An authoritative recent summary is given by McKusick and Ruddle (1977).
12. Money (1965); Money and Eberhardt (1972).
13. Beach (1969).

Chapter 2. The human body

1. Smith (1945), p. v.
2. Thomas, Chess, and Birch (1968). This study is brought up to date in Thomas and Chess (1977).
3. This is discussed in Cannon (1932).
4. Luria (1966), p. 18.
5. Keleman (1975), p. 82.
6. Lefties who insist on their rights will be interested in a shop catering to their needs: The Left Hand, 140 West 22nd St., New York, NY 10011.
7. For a review of the experimental research on these questions, see Shontz (1969).
8. Maccoby and Jacklin (1974).

Chapter 3. Making sense: the five sensory systems

1. This important distinction was first made by Gibson (1966).
2. Went (1968).
3. Geldard (1953), pp. 189–190.
4. Amoore, Johnston, and Rubin (1964).
5. Zeigler (1975).
6. Landis and Hunt (1939).
7. McGill (1960).
8. Von Békésy (1960).
9. Wever and Bray (1930).
10. Rock and Victor (1964).
11. Gregory (1973), p. 50.
12. Metzger (1930), p. 13.
13. Lashley (1930).
14. Lettvin, Maturana, McCulloch, and Pitts (1959).
15. Hubel and Wiesel (1962, 1965).
16. Arend (1973).

Chapter 4. Wanting: the story of basic motives

1. Thurber (1942), p. 84.
2. For a history of modern concepts of motivation, see Bolles (1967), chap. 2.
3. Cannon and Washburn (1912); Cannon (1929).
4. Wyrwicka and Dobrzecka (1960).
5. The answer is given a few paragraphs ahead.
6. For a review of this material, see Fiske and Maddi (1961), and for a more technical discussion see Eisenberger (1972).

7. Bowlby (1961).
8. Fromm (1941, 1955).
9. Maslow (1970).
10. For a full exposition, see Bolles (1967).
11. Garcia, Clarke, and Hankins (1973).
12. Hendry (1972).
13. McClelland and Atkinson (1948).
14. Schacter (1971a, 1971b).
15. Nisbett (1968).

Excursion 1. the feelings: pleasure and pain

1. Mountcastle (1974).
2. Olds (1956, 1958); Olds and Milner (1954); Olds and Olds (1965).
3. A fine discussion of these studies can be found in Wooldridge (1963).
4. Melzack and Wall (1965).
5. Beecher (1946); Van den Berg (1974), p. 222.
6. Reich (1971).
7. Petrie (1967).
8. Barrell and Price (1975).
9. Anand, Chhina, and Singh (1961).
10. Cuddon (1968); also, see the discussion in Bakan (1968).
11. Freud ([1920] 1967).
12. Keyes (1974).

Excursion 2. the feelings: varieties of emotion

1. Darwin ([1859] 1890).
2. For a recent account, see Sokolov (1963).
3. Fuster (1958).
4. Selye (1973, 1976).
5. Brady, Porter, Conrad, and Mason (1958).
6. Sawrey and Weisz (1956).
7. Seligman (1968).
7a. Barrell and Neimeyer (1975).
8. For systematic reviews of theories of emotion, see Arnold (1968); Solomon (1976).
9. Some groups, such as the Cheyenne Indians, do, however, deliberately display "opposite" expressions as part of their training procedures.
10. Duffy (1962); Lacey (1967).
11. Paige (1973).
12. James (1950).
13. Cannon described his experimental work in an article (1927) and described his own theory of emotions in a later book (1929).
14. Schacter and Singer (1962).
15. Miller (1948).
16. Research on anxiety is reviewed in Spielberger (1972). Major theories of anxiety are discussed in Fischer (1970).
17. Spitz (1946).
18. Seligman (1975).
19. Lorenz (1966).

20. Barker, Dembo, and Lewin (1941); Dollard, Doob, Miller, Mowrer, and Sears (1939).
21. Bandura (1973); the research is summarized in Geen (1972).

Chapter 5. Secondary motives: the story of needs and values

1. Quoted in United Press dispatch, March 11, 1974.
2. Maslow (1970).
3. Pepper (1973); Neill (1960, 1972).
4. Petrie (1967).
5. These studies are reported in full in Roethlisberger and Dickson ([1939] 1950). For a "radical critique" of their conclusions, see Carey (1967). For an excellent discussion of some of the experimental problems, see Sommer (1968).
6. Schacter (1959).
7. Crowne and Marlowe (1964).
8. McClelland, Clark, Roby, and Atkinson (1949).
9. Atkinson (1957, 1964); McClelland (1961); Feather (1967).
10. McClelland and Winter (1969).
11. Maehr (1974).
12. Sinha (1973).
13. Lesser, Krawitz, and Packard (1963).
14. Horner (1968, 1971).
15. Hoppe (1931).
16. Cohen (1964); Cohen and Christiansen (1970).
17. Meyer, quoted in Heckhauser (1968).
18. Deci (1975).
19. White (1959).
20. Abe (1964).
21. Neuringer (1969).
22. Keynes (1936).
23. Katona (1960, 1967).
24. Friedman and Rosenman (1974). For a discussion of some other consequences of competition, see Beecher and Beecher (1966).
25. Maslow (1968).
26. Michotte (1963).
27. Heider (1944).
28. Heider (1946).
29. Festinger (1964).
30. Festinger, Riecken, and Schacter (1956).

Chapter 6. Perception and attention: the creating of meaning

1. Boffey (1974); Nietzke (1974).
2. Ware and Williams (1975).
3. Sokolov and Vinogradora (1975).
4. Sheahan (1973) describes a testing program for infants, based on this method.
5. Spong, Haider, and Lindsley (1965).
6. Cherry (1953).
7. Treisman (1964, 1969).
8. Neisser (1967).
9. Zillig (1928).
10. Kilpatrick (1952).
11. Wittreich (1952).
12. Schafer and Murphy (1943). For a critique, see Jackson (1954).
13. McClelland and Atkinson (1948).
14. Held and Hein (1963).
15. Lashley and Russell (1934).
16. Ball and Tronick (1971).
17. Walk and Gibson (1961). Walk (1968) has shown that this behavior in human infants is not dependent on the use of two eyes.
18. Almost all the known cases are collected in Von Senden (1960).
19. Gregory and Wallace (1963).
20. Stevens (1962).
21. Russell (1976).
22. Geldard (1968).
23. Garner (1970).
24. Flavell and Draguns (1957).
25. Wald (1964).
26. Hurvich and Jameson (1957).
27. De Valoris and Jacobs (1968).
28. Katz (1935).
29. Arnheim (1974).
30. Pritchard, Heron, and Hebb (1960). For a full discussion, see Cornsweet (1970) and Arend (1973).
31. Gregory (1973).

Chapter 7. Learning: the new and the old

1. Fleer (1972)
2. A number of books are available that cover the field of learning. On an introductory level, see Adams (1976); for a more advanced treatment, see Rachlin (1976). An excellent presentation of an "information" approach to learning theory is given by Restle (1975).
3. Babkin (1968).
4. Herrnstein (1969).
5. Pavlov ([1927] 1960).
6. Thorndike (1898).
7. Skinner (1938).
8. Ferster and Skinner (1957); Skinner (1969).
9. Skinner (1971, 1976).
10. Tinbergen (1951).
11. Lorenz (1965).
12. Garcia and Koelling (1966).
13. Mowrer (1947, 1960).
14. H. D. Kimmel (1974).
15. Green and Green (1973–1974).
16. Skinner (1971).
17. Garcia, Kovner, and Green (1970).
18. Rescorla (1967, 1972).
19. Rescorla (1966).
20. Restle (1975), pp. 52–54.
21. Lockard (1963).
22. Seligman (1968).
23. Seligman, Maier, and Geer (1968).
24. Seligman (1970, 1975).

25. Studies on locus of control are reviewed in Phares (1973) and in Lefcourt (1966).
26. Tolman (1948).
27. Levine and Fasnacht (1974).
28. Miller and Dollard (1941).
29. Rotter (1966); Rotter, Chance, and Phares (1972).
30. Bandura (1971); Bandura and Walters (1963).

Chapter 8. Remembering: the old and the new

1. Ebbinghaus ([1885] 1964).
2. McCrary and Hunter (1953).
3. Haber (1969).
4. Stromeyer and Psotka (1970). These studies are reported and discussed in Stromeyer (1970) and In Julesz (1971).
5. McGaugh (1970).
6. Penfield (1959).
7. Jenkins and Dallenbach (1924).
8. Studies of proactive inhibition are reviewed in Underwood (1957).
9. Reported in Smirnov (1973). An excellent discussion of this work is given in a review by Estes (1974).
10. Botwinick (1970).
11. Atkinson and Shifrin (1971).
12. Luria (1968).
13. Brown and McNeill (1966).
14. Babich, Jacobson, Bubash, and Jacobson (1965).
15. McConnell, Shigehisa, and Salive (1970).
16. Frank, Stein, and Rosen (1970).
17. Bartz (1968), p. 2.
18. This famous article is reprinted in Lashley (1960).
19. Bartlett (1932).
20. Hyde and Jenkins (1973).
21. Straus (1962).
22. Tulving and Thomson (1973), p. 370.
24. Estes (1974), p. 182.
25. Jenkins (1974); Sachs (1967).
26. Overton (1972).
27. Aristotle ([300 B.C.] 1808).

Chapter 9. Consciousness: normal and altered states of mind

1. James (1929), pp. 378–379.
2. Aubert and White (1959).
3. Ornstein (1977).
4. Tart (1969). See also the summary in Hilgard (1969); earlier work by King (1963); Huxley (1954).
5. Stoyva and Kamiya (1971).
6. Barrell (1967).
7. Zung and Wilson (1961).
8. Kleitman (1963).
9. A first report was in Dement and Kleitman (1957a). See also Webb and Agnew (1973).
10. Aserinsky and Kleitman (1953).
11. Dement (1965).

12. Dement and Kleitman (1957b).
13. Foulkes (1966); Dement (1965).
14. For a complete review, see Hartmann (1973).
15. Dement (1960).
16. Othmer, Hayden, and Segelbaum (1969).
17. Van de Castle (1971), p. 3.
18. Aserinsky and Kleitman (1955).
19. Freud ([1900] 1953).
20. Stewart (1969).
21. Greenleaf (1973).
22. Stewart (1954).
23. Weil (1973).
24. Tart (1970).
25. Van den Berg (1974), pp. 70–71, 75.
26. The literature on hypnosis is vast. See Hilgard (1965) on hypnotic susceptibility; see Hilgard (1968) for a general review.
27. Vingoe (1973).
28. Halliday and Mason (1964).
29. Sarbin and Andersen (1967).
30. Barber (1964). His work is summarized in Barber (1970).
31. Hilgard (1973).
32. Chapman, Goodell, and Wolff (1959).
33. Pattie (1941).
34. Dudley, Holmes, Martin, and Ripley (1966).
35. Hilgard (1975).
36. Belo (1960).
37. Wenger and Bagchi (1961); Wenger, Bagchi, and Anand (1961).
38. Nowlis and Kamiya (1970).
39. Maslach, Marshall, and Zimbardo (1972).
40. Pelletier (1974).
41. Tart (1969).
42. Das and Gastaut (1955).

Excursion 3. About time

1. Bakan (1970), p. 596. However, there has recently been a revival of interest: See Fraser, Haber, and Müller (1972).
2. Tart (1970).
3. Piaget (1971).
4. Barrell (1974).
5. These studies are reviewed in Fraisse (1963).
6. Miller and Selfridge (1950).
7. This is discussed at length in Ornstein (1970).
8. Aaronson (1966).
9. Cohen (1958), p. 106.
10. Farber (1953).
11. Gurdjieff (1975).
12. Fraisse (1963), p. 49.
13. Jenkins (1950).
14. The credit for the first report should be split among a number of investigators: Black (1950, 1951); Lee (1951); Fairbanks and Jaeger (1951).
15. Kalmus, Denes, and Fry (1955).
16. Smith, McCrary, and Smith (1960).
17. Malécot, Johnston, and Kizziar (1972).
18. Hoagland (1933, 1943).

19. It is reviewed and summarized in Luce (1971, 1973).
20. Brown, Hastings, and Palmer (1970).
21. Siffre (1975).
22. Miles, Raynal, and Wilson (1977).
23. Salk (1973).
24. Thurber (1960).
25. Yaker, Osmond, and Cheek (1972).
26. Barrell and Barrell (1976).

Chapter 10. Growing up: from birth to puberty

1. Money and Eberhardt (1972); Childs (1965).
2. Sherman (1971), p. 4; Kagan and Moss (1962).
3. Gesell (1940).
4. The original study was by Knobloch, Rider, Harper, and Pasamanick (1956). The followup study was by Harper, Fischer, and Rider (1959).
5. Libenfeld, Pasamanick, and Rogers (1955).
6. The evidence is surveyed in Wiener (1962).
7. Robinson and Robinson (1965).
8. Carmichael (1926).
9. Gesell (1940); Bower (1974), chaps. 2, 4, 5, 7.
10. Ames (1944).
11. A. Freud (1944).
12. Clarke and Clarke (1977).
13. Kagan and Klein (1973).
14. Wolff (1968).
15. Fantz (1963, 1965).
16. Polak, Emde, and Spitz (1964).
17. Ribble (1965).
18. Mitchell (1974).
19. Fuller (1967).
20. Eichenwald and Fry (1969).
21. Bowlby (1966), p. 59.
22. Spitz and Wolff (1946).
23. Polak, Emde, and Spitz (1964), fig. 2.
24. Scott, Ferguson, Jenkins, and Cutter (1955).
25. Bayley (1965).
26. Maccoby and Jacklin (1974).
27. Hartup (1974).
28. For a review of this topic, see Sommer (1969).
29. Patterson, Littmen, and Bricker (1967).
30. Gallup (1977).
31. Tasch (1952).
32. McCarthy (1930).
33. Jersild and Ritzman (1938).
34. Stack (1974).
35. Block (1973), p. 512.
36. Barry, Bacon, and Child (1957).
37. Gesell (1940).
38. Zimiles and Konstadt (1962).
39. O'Malley and Eisenberg (1973); Rie (1975).
40. Block (1973); Maccoby (1966).
41. Piaget (1932).
42. Loevinger (1976).
43. Kohlberg (1969, 1973).
44. Hartshorne and May (1928).

Chapter 11. Individual differences in ability

1. Kretschmer (1970).
2. Sheldon, Stevens, and Tucker ([1940] 1970); Sheldon (1954).
3. Sheldon and Stevens (1942).
4. Ramul (1960, 1963).
5. Spearman (1904, 1927).
6. Thurstone (1938).
7. Guilford (1966).
8. Wolf (1964).
9. For a complete review, see Peterson (1925).
10. Thompson and Magaret (1947).
11. Wechsler (1955).
12. Carver (1974).
13. Hutt and Gibby (1976).
14. Mercer (1973).
15. Wolfensberger, Nirje, Olshansky, Perske, and Roos (1972).
16. Terman, Baldwin, and Bronson (1925).
17. Hollingworth (1942).
18. Cattell (1963).
19. Vernon (1975).
20. Berg (1970).
21. McClelland (1973), p. 7.
22. Goddard (1925).
23. For a discussion of this point, see Chomsky (1972a). The literature on a wide range of black–white comparisons of psychological factors is reviewed in Dreger and Miller (1968).
24. Jensen (1969).
25. Jensen's original paper plus the major criticisms and discussions of it have been collected in a separate volume (Jensen and others, 1969).
26. Kamin (1974). For a discussion, see Loehlin, Lindzey, and Spuhler (1974).
27. Burt (1955).
28. The controversy is reviewed in Wade (1976).
29. Scarr and Weinberg (1976).
30. Vernon (1975), p. 94.
31. Cole, Guy, Glick, and Sharp (1971).

Chapter 12. Communication and language

1. Searle (1969, 1972).
2. Von Frisch (1954). The recent work is summarized in Zajonc (1972).
3. B. F. Stokes, of Bay Area Rapid Transit, San Francisco; quoted in *San Francisco Chronicle*, March 21, 1973.
4. Lieberman (1975).
5. Slobin (1972).
6. Skinner (1957).
7. The best starting point in regard to Chomsky's views is Chomsky (1972b); a complete but more advanced treatment is in Chomsky (1965).
8. Suppes (1974).
9. Kaplan and Kaplan (1970).

10. Bloom (1970).
11. Brown (1973), p. 99.
12. Baratz and Shuey (1969), p. 94.
13. For further discussion and details, see Dillard (1972); Labov (1973).
14. Lieberman (1975). Evidence countering this is given in Limber (1977).
15. Kellogg and Kellogg (1933).
16. Hayes and Hayes (1951).
17. Fouts (1972); Gardner and Gardner (in press).
18. Fouts (1975); Zuckerman (1977).
19. Gardner and Gardner (in press), p. 53.
20. Brown (1970).
21. Gardner and Gardner (in press), p. 59.
22. Gardner and Gardner (1974), pp. 20–21.
23. Premack (1971); Premack and Premack (1972).
24. Rumbaugh, Gill, and Von Glasensfeld (1973).
25. Osgood, Suci, and Tannenbaum (1957); Osgood (1962).
26. Schaller (1965), p. 132, 133.
27. Darwin ([1872] 1890), p. 380.
28. Straus (1951), p. 440.
29. Mehrabian (1972).
30. Ekman (1972).

Chapter 13. Personality: the consistency of personal history

1. Wilde (1974), p. 58.
2. Forer (1949).
3. Hartshorne and May (1928).
4. Barker (1966).
5. Mischel (1973), p. 258.
6. Heider (1958) refers to these as "naive" theories of personality.
7. Mischel (1973), p. 275, table 1; Bern and Allen (1974).
8. Cattell (1946).
9. Cattell (1957).
10. Cattell (1965).
11. Maehr (1974).
12. Sinha (1973).
13. Duijker and Frijda (1960); Martindale (1967).
14. Inkeles and Levinson (1954).
15. For a survey of the major theories, see Hall and Lindzey (1970).
16. Sheldon and Stevens (1942).
17. The "official" (and most complete) biography of Freud is in three volumes by Ernest Jones (1953, 1955, 1957). A one-volume condensation of this work, which leaves out the technical material, has been edited by Marcus and Trilling (Jones, 1963). Freud's complete writings, exclusive of his correspondence, have been collected in twenty-four volumes, under the title *Standard Edition of the Complete Psychological Works of Sigmund Freud*, edited by James Strachey (1953–1974).
18. Rycroft (1975), p. 26.

19. Jung ([1916] 1968) gives a summary of his psychological "theory." His autobiography is given in Jung (1961).
20. Escalona and Heider (1959).
21. Thomas, Chess, and Birch (1970).
22. Bettelheim (1960).
23. Allport (1955, 1961).
24. Rorschach (1942).
25. Dahlstrom and Welsh (1960); Dahlstrom, Welsh, and Dahlstrom (1972).

Chapter 14. The life span: changes in personal history

1. Campbell (1956).
2. Erikson (1959); Roazen (1976).
3. Erikson (1959), p. 100.
4. Erikson (1968, 1958, 1969).
5. Newman and Newman (1975), p. 380.
6. Based on Block (1971), pp. 32–36.
7. Schaie (1965, 1973).
8. Emmerich (1966); Wohlwill (1970).
9. Jones, Bayley, MacFarlane, and Honzik (1971).
10. Maas and Kuypers (1974).
11. For a review of theories of aging, see Comfort (1964).
12. Birren (1974), p. 808.
13. Friedman and Rosenman (1974).
14. Abrahams (1972).
15. Selye (1973, 1976).
16. Szafran (1968).
17. Granick and Patterson (1971).
18. Palmore (1970). A more recent report is Palmore (1974).
19. Palmore (1970), p. 417.
20. Palmore (1970).
21. Schonfield (1974).
22. King (1973).
23. Riley and Foner (1968).
24. Newman and Newman (1975).
25. Neugarten (1964)
26. Quoted in Schonfield (1974), p. 796.
27. Kastenbaum and Durkee (1964).
28. D. C. Kimmel (1974), pp. 11–14.
29. Eisdorfer (1972).
30. Simmons (1945).
31. Shanas, Townsend, Wedderburn, Friis, Milhøj, and Stehouwer (1968).
32. Troll (1971).
33. Schaie (1974), p. 806.
34. Compare with the discussion in Wohlwill (1970).

Excursion 4. Death and dying

1. Riegel and Riegel (1972).
2. Keleman (1974).
3. Kübler-Ross (1969).
4. Farberow and Shneidman (1961).
5. Levy (1973).
6. Elliott (1940).

7. Schmidt (1928).

8. Grof and Halifax (1977).

9. Castaneda (1972).

Chapter 15. Getting along: adjustment and deviance

1. Quoted in Krafft-Ebing ([1886] 1965), pp. 85–86.

2. This account is taken from Parry (1975), pp. 216–223.

3. Temerlin (1970).

4. Wolpe (1971), p. 341.

5. For his final word on the subject, see Freud ([1926] 1959).

6. For a summary of various theories, see Fischer (1970).

7. The best-known general measure is Taylor (1953). More recent ones are Husek and Alexander (1963); Endler, Hunt and Rosenstein (1962).

8. Sarason (1960); Alpert and Huber (1960).

9. Compare with Paul (1966); Watson and Friend (1969).

10. Jacobsen (1938).

11. Comfort (1972).

12. Friedman and Rosenman (1974).

13. Lacey (1967).

14. Compiled from Goldfried and Sprafkin (1974), pp. 21–22; and from Bandura (1968).

15. Simpson (1973).

16. Freud ([1926] 1959).

17. Reich (1969).

18. Shapiro (1965).

19. Freud ([1917] 1957b).

20. Klein (1952).

21. Seligman (1975).

22. Van den Berg (1974).

23. Whalen and Henker (1976).

24. Clements and Peters (1962).

25. Lambert, Windmiller, Sandoval, and Moore (1976).

26. This view is expressed in Schrag and Divoky (1975).

27. Shepherd, Oppenheim, and Mitchell (1971).

28. For example, Escalona and Heider (1959).

29. Harrington (1972).

30. Glenn (1967).

31. Harrington (1972), pp. 40–44.

32. Schlumberg (1972), p. 567.

Chapter 16. Getting along: psychosis

1. For a sampling of the extensive literature on the experience of psychosis, see Kaplan (1964); Sommer and Osmond (1960, 1961); Adams (1971).

2. Mischel and Mischel (1977), p. 397.

3. Brenner (1973).

4. Milton and Wahler (1973), p. 6.

5. Fried (1964).

6. Neihardt (1961); Silverman (1967).

7. Raush and Raush (1968).

8. Baynes (1971), p. 495.

9. Opton (1975), p. 7.

10. Goffman (1961), pp. 1–124.

11. Rosenthal (1963).

12. Hoffer and Osmond (1974).

13. For a first-person account of such a case, see Vonnegut (1975).

14. Mendel and Rapport (1969).

15. Taken from Cerletti's account (1956) in Sackler, Sackler, Sackler, and Marti-Ibañez (1956), pp. 93–94.

16. Bateson, Jackson, Haley, and Weakland (1956); Weakland (1960).

17. Haley (1963), pp. 108–109.

18. Laing and Esterson (1970).

19. Haley (1965).

20. Schiff (1966).

21. Goffman (1961); Braginsky, Braginsky, and Ring (1969); Farina (1972).

22. Braginsky and Braginsky (1967).

23. Opler (1956).

24. Ong (1967), p. 134.

25. Draguns and Phillips (1972), p. 13.

26. Phillips (1968).

27. Szasz (1961).

28. Foucault (1965).

29. Grob (1966).

30. Hollingshead and Redlich (1958).

31. Myers, Bean, and Pepper (1965).

32. Agel (1971).

33. Beit-Hallahmi (1974), p. 125.

34. Caplan and Nelson (1973), p. 210.

35. Rosenhan (1973).

36. Neisser (1973).

37. Rosenhan (1973), p. 250.

Chapter 17. Psychotherapy

1. Breuer and Freud ([1895] 1955).

2. A summary of her life and career is given by Grant (1974); her biography is given by Freeman (1972).

3. The original description of the case of Anna O. is in Breuer and Freud ([1895] 1955), pp. 21–47. Freud's own summary is in a lecture he gave at Clark University in 1909 ([1909] 1957, pp. 9–16). A full discussion of the case is in Ellenberger (1970), pp. 480–484.

4. Breuer and Freud ([1895] 1955), p. 63.

5. Rogers (1955), pp. 267–268.

6. Ansbacher and Ansbacher (1956).

7. Thompson (1950).

8. Horney (1950).

9. Rogers (1951).

10. Rogers (1957).

11. Rogers (1970).

12. Wolpe (1969).

13. Fuller (1949).

14. Lovaas (1977).

15. Bandura (1969).

16. London (1972).

17. Goldfried and Davison (1976).
18. Ayllon and Azrin (1968).
19. Lazarus (1971), p. 350.
20. The definitive biography of Reich is Boadella (1975). A brief and surprisingly sympathetic account is by Reich's second wife, Ilse Ollendorf Reich (1969).
21. The full story of this strange trial is told in Greenfield (1974).
22. Reich (1969).
23. Lowen (1975).
24. Reich (1967), p. 271.
25. Rolf (1977).
26. Perls (1969b) is his autobiography. A popular, sympathetic account of his life is Shepard (1975).
27. Perls (1969a, 1973).
28. Lakin (1972).

Chapter 18. Social psychology: awareness and effect of others

1. Genet (1962), p. 19.
2. This evidence is reviewed in Zajonc (1972).
3. Chen (1937).
4. Zajonc (1965).
5. Cottrell (1972).
6. Festinger (1954).
7. Schacter (1959).
8. Gerard and Rabbie (1961).
9. Ring, Lipinski, and Braginsky (1965).
10. Heider (1958).
11. Ross, Amabile, and Steinmetz (1977).
12. Jones and Nisbett (1972).
13. Jones and Davis (1965).
14. Kelley (1967).
15. Sarnoff (1960).
16. Berschied, Dion, Walster, and Walster (1971).
17. E. E. Jones (1973).
18. Kerckhoff and Davis (1962).
19. Zajonc (1968).
20. Festinger, Schacter, and Back (1950).
21. Rubin (1973).
22. Adorno, Frenkel-Brunswik, Levinson, and Sanford (1950). For a more recent study, see Wilkinson (1972).
23. Fishbein and Ajzen (1975).
24. La Piere (1934).
25. Kutner, Wilkins, and Yarrow (1952).
26. Wilner, Walkley, and Cook (1952).
27. Kelman (1958). See Kiesler (1971) for experiments on these issues.
28. Hovland, Janis, and Kelley (1953, 1966).
29. Hovland (1959).
30. Bauer (1964), p. 327.

Chapter 19. Social psychology: awareness and effect of groups

1. White and Lippitt (1950).
2. Morrison (1974).
3. Meade (1967).
4. Asch (1951, 1956, 1958).
5. Crutchfield (1955).
6. Tuddenham and McBride (1959).
7. Latané and Darley (1970).
8. Reported in Latané and Darley (1969), pp. 258–259.
9. Piliavin, Rodin, and Piliavin (1969).
10. Latané and Rodin (1969).
11. Schwartz (1974).
12. Clark and Word (1974).
13. Bandura, Underwood, and Fromson (1975).
14. Milgram (1963).
15. Milgram (1974).
16. This is spelled out in detail in Combs, Richards, and Richards (1976).
17. This is the title of an excellent biography of Lewin by Marrow (1969).
18. Compare with Rice (1965); Bion (1961).
19. Bradford, Gibb, and Benne (1964).
20. Newcomb (1958). This work is reviewed, and additional studies reported, in Newcomb (1961).
21. Rogers (1967).
22. Rioch (1970).
23. Leavitt (1951).
24. Bavelas, Hastorf, Gross, and Kite (1965).
25. Sommer (1969).
26. Sommer (1974).
27. Cowan, Egleson, and Hentoff (1974).
28. Katz (1952).
29. Fiedler (1967).
30. Biddle and Thomas (1966), p. 29.
31. Bettelheim (1943).
32. Sarbin (1954).
33. Goffman (1959, 1967).

Excursion 5. Sex: a psychosocial phenomenon

1. Portmann (1964).
2. Krich (1964).
3. For a readable summary of existing facts and theory, see Katchadourian (1974).
4. Money (1965); Money and Eberhardt (1972).
5. Montagu (1974).
6. Masters and Johnson (1966).
7. Masters and Johnson (1970), p. 220.
8. Commission on Obscenity and Pornography (1968): studies by Mann, Sidman, and Starr (1968), Kutschinsky (1968).
9. Loevinger (1976); Loevinger and Wessler (1970).
10. Block (1973).
11. Ford and Beach (1951).
12. Mead (1961).
13. Albee (1977).
14. Marcus (1964).
15. This is fully discussed in Winick (1968).
16. Hunt (1974).
17. Kinsey, Martin, and Pomeroy (1948); Kinsey, Martin, Pomeroy, and Gebhard (1953).
18. Barrell (1974).

Aaronson, B. S. Behavior and the place names of time. *American journal of hypnosis: Clinical, experimental, theoretical*, 1966, 9, 1–17.

Abe, K. *The woman in the dunes.* (E. Dale, trans.). New York: Knopf, 1964.

Abrahams, J. P. Psychomotor performance and change in cardiac rate in subjects behaviorally predisposed to coronary heart disease. Unpublished doctoral dissertation, University of Southern California, 1972.

Abse, D. W. *Hysteria and related mental disorders: An approach to psychological medicine.* Bristol, England: Wright, 1966.

Adams, J. A. *Learning and memory: An introduction.* Homewood, Ill.: Dorsey, 1976.

Adams, J. K. *Secrets of the trade.* New York: Viking, 1971.

Adorno, T. W., Frenkel-Brunswik, E., Levinson, D. J., and Sanford, R. N. *The authoritarian personality.* New York: Harper & Row, 1950.

Agee, J. *A death in the family.* New York: Bantam, 1969.

Agel, J. (ed.). *The radical therapist.* New York: Ballantine Books, 1971.

Albee, G. W. The Protestant ethic, sex, and psychotherapy. *American psychologist*, 1977, 32, 150–161.

Alexander, F. *Psychosomatic medicine: Its principles and applications.* New York: Norton, 1950.

Allport, G. W. *Becoming.* New Haven, Conn.: Yale University Press, 1955.

Allport, G. W. *Pattern and growth in personality.* New York: Holt, Rinehart and Winston, 1961.

Alpert, R., and Haber, R. N. Anxiety in academic achievement situations. *Journal of abnormal and social psychology*, 1960, 61, 207–215.

Altmann, S. A. The structure of primate social communication. In S. A. Altmann (ed.), *Social communication among primates.* Chicago: University of Chicago Press, 1967, 325–362.

References

Ames, L. B. Early individual differences in visual and motor behavior patterns: A comparative study of two normal infants by the method of cinemanalysis. *Journal of genetic psychology*, 1944, *65*, 219–226.

Amoore, J. E., Johnston, J. W., Jr., and Rubin, M. The stereochemical theory of odor. *Scientific American*, 1964, *210*, 42–49.

Amsterdam, B. Mirror self-image reactions before age two. *Developmental psychology*, 1972, *5*, 297–305.

Anand, B. K., Chhina, G. S., and Singh, B. Some aspects of electroencephalographic studies in yogis. *Electroencephalography and clinical neurophysiology*, 1961, *13*, 452–456.

Ansbacher, H. L., and Ansbacher, R. R. *The individual psychology of Alfred Adler*. New York: Basic Books, 1956.

Arend, L. S., Jr. Spatial differential and integral operations in human vision: Implications of stabilized retinal image fading. *Psychological review*, 1973, *80*, 374–395.

Aristotle. "On memory and reminiscence." In T. Taylor (ed. and trans.), *The treatises of Aristotle on the soul*. London: Wilks, 1808, 165–177. (Originally written 300 B.C.)

Arnheim, R. *Art and visual perception: A psychology of the creative eye*. Berkeley: University of California Press, 1974.

Arnold, M. B. (ed.). *The nature of emotion: Selected readings*. Baltimore: Penguin Books, 1968.

Asch, S. E. Effects of group pressure upon the modification and distortion of judgments. In H. Guetzkow (ed.), *Groups, leadership, and men*. Pittsburgh: Carnegie University Press, 1951.

Asch, S. E. Studies of independence and conformity: A minority of one against a unanimous majority. *Psychological monographs*, 1956, *70*, Whole No. 416.

Asch, S. E. Effects of group pressure upon modification and distortion of judgments. In E. E. Maccoby, T. M. Newcomb, and E. L. Hartley (eds.), *Readings in social psychology*. (3rd ed.). New York: Holt, Rinehart and Winston, 1958.

Aserinsky, E., and Kleitman, N. Regularly occurring periods of eye motility, and concomitant phenomena, during sleep. *Science*, 1953, *118*, 273–274.

Aserinsky, E., and Kleitman, N. Two types of ocular motility occurring in sleep. *Journal of applied physiology*, 1955, *8*, 1–10.

Atkinson, J. W. Motivational determinants of risk-taking behavior. *Psychological review*, 1957, *64*, 359–372.

Atkinson, J. W. *An introduction to motivation*. New York: Van Nostrand, 1964.

Atkinson, R. C., and Shifrin, R. M. The control of short-term memory. *Scientific American*, 1971, *224*, 82–90.

Aubert, V., and White, H. Sleep: A sociological interpretation. Part 1: *Acta Sociologica*, 1959, *4*, 46–54.

Ayllon, T., and Azrin, N. H. *The token economy*. New York: Appleton-Century-Crofts, 1968.

Babich, F. R., Jacobson, A. L., Bubash, S., and Jacobson, A. Transfer of a response to naive rats by injection of ribonucleic acid extracted from trained rats. *Science*, 1965, *149*, 656.

Babkin, B. P. *Pavlov: A biography*. Chicago: University of Chicago Press, 1968.

Badia, P., and Culbertson, S. The relative aversiveness of signalled vs. unsignalled escapable and inescapable shock. *Journal of the experimental analysis of behavior*, 1972, *17*, 463–471.

Bakan, D. *Disease, pain, and sacrifice*. Chicago: University of Chicago Press, 1968.

Bakan, P. Time: Recaptured and prefigured. [Review of J. E. Orme, *Time experience and behavior*.]. *Contemporary psychology*, 1970, *15*, 595–596.

Ball, W., and Tronick, E. Infant responses to impending collision: optical and real. *Science*, 1971, *171*, 818–820.

Bandura, A. A social learning interpretation of psychological dysfunctions. In P. London and D. Rosenhan (eds.), *Foundations of abnormal psychology*. New York: Holt, Rinehart and Winston, 1968.

Bandura, A. *Principles of behavior modification*. New York: Holt, Rinehart and Winston, 1969.

Bandura, A. *Social learning theory*. Morristown, N.J.: General Learning Press, 1971.

Bandura, A. *Aggression: A social learning analysis*. Englewood Cliffs, N.J.: Prentice-Hall, 1973.

Bandura, A., Ross, D., and Ross, S. A. Imitation of film-mediated aggressive models. *Journal of abnormal and social psychology*, 1963, *66*, 3–11.

Bandura, A., Underwood, B., and Fromson, M. E. Disinhibition of aggression through diffusion of responsibility and dehumanization of victims. *Journal of research in personality*, 1975, *9*, 253–269.

Bandura, A., and Walters, R. H. *Social learning and personality development*. New York: Holt, Rinehart and Winston, 1963.

Baratz, J. C., and Shuy, R. W. (eds.). *Teaching black children to read*. Washington, D.C.: Center for Applied Linguistics, 1969.

Barber, T. X. "Hypnosis" as a causal variable in present-day psychology: A critical analysis. *Psychological reports*, 1964, *14*, 839–842.

Barber, T. X. *LSD, marijuana, yoga, and hypnosis*. Chicago: Aldine, 1970.

Barker, R. G. *The stream of behavior*. New York: Appleton-Century-Crofts, 1966.

Barker, R. G., Dembo, T., and Lewin, K. Frustration and regression: An experiment with young children. *University of Iowa Studies in Child Welfare*, 1941, *18*, No. 1.

Barrell, J. J. "Modulation" of pain and suffering by the central nervous system: A review of the literature. Unpublished master's thesis, University of California at Davis, 1967.

Barrell, J. J. Subjective estimation of sleep duration. Unpublished pilot study, Department of Psychology, University of Florida, 1974.

Barrell, J. J. Sexual arousal in the objectifying attitude.

Review of existential psychology and psychiatry, 1974, *13,* 98–105.

Barrell, J. J., and Barrell, J. E. How we can control time: An experiential model. *Journal of pastoral counseling,* 1976, *11,* 42–53.

Barrell, J. J., and Neimeyer, R. A mathematical formula for the psychological control of suffering. *The journal of pastoral counseling,* 1975, *(10)1,* 60–67.

Barrell, J. J., and Price, D. The perception of first and second pain as a function of psychological set. *Perception and psychophysics,* 1975, *17,* 163–166.

Barry, H., Bacon, M. K., and Child, E. L. A cross-cultural survey of some sex differences in socialization. *Journal of abnormal and social psychology,* 1957, *55,* 327–332.

Bartlett, F. C. *Remembering.* New York: Cambridge University Press, 1932.

Bartz, W. H. Memory. In J. Vernon (ed.), *Introduction to psychology: A self-selection textbook.* Dubuque, Iowa: Brown, 1968.

Bateson, G., Jackson, D. D., Haley, J., and Weakland, J. H. Toward a theory of schizophrenia. *Behavioral science,* 1956, *1,* 251–264.

Bauer, R. A. The obstinate audience: The influence process from the point of view of social communication. *American psychologist,* 1964, *19,* 319–328.

Bavelas, A., Hastorf, A. H., Gross, A. E., and Kite, W. R. Experiments on the alteration of group structure. *Journal of experimental social psychology,* 1965, *1,* 55–70.

Bayley, N. Comparisons of mental and motor test scores for ages 1–15 months by sex, birth order, race, geographical location, and education of parents. *Child development,* 1965, *36,* 379–411.

Baynes, T. E., Jr. Continuing conjectural concepts concerning civil commitment criteria. *American psychologist,* 1971, *26,* 485–495.

Beach, F. A. Locks and beagles. *American psychologist,* 1969, *24,* 971–989.

Beecher, H. K. Pain in men wounded in battle. *Annals of surgery,* 1946, *123,* 96–105.

Beecher, W., and Beecher, M. *Beyond success and failure.* New York: Pocket Books, 1966.

Beit-Hallahmi, B. Salvation and its vicissitudes: Clinical psychology and political values. *American psychologist,* 1974, *29,* 124–129.

Belo, J. *The trance in Bali.* New York: Columbia University Press, 1960.

Bem, D. J., and Allen, A. On predicting some of the people some of the time: The search for cross-situational consistencies in behavior. *Psychological review,* 1974, *81,* 506–520.

Bender, L. Anxiety in disturbed children. In P. H. Hoch and J. Zubin (eds.), *Anxiety.* New York: Grune & Stratton, 1950.

Berg, I. *Education and jobs: The great training robbery.* New York: Praeger, 1970.

Berlyne, D. E. Curiosity and exploration. *Science,* 1966, *153,* 25–33.

Berscheid, E., Dion, K., Walster, E., and Walster, G. W. Physical attractiveness and dating choice: A test of the matching hypothesis. *Journal of experimental social psychology,* 1971, *7,* 173–179.

Bertrand, M. The behavioral repertoire of the stumptail macaque: A descriptive and comparative study. *Biblioteca primatologica* (Basel), 1969, *11,* 1–123.

Bettelheim, B. Individual and mass behavior in extreme situations. *Journal of abnormal and social psychology,* 1943, *38,* 417–452.

Bettelheim, B. *The informed heart.* New York: Free Press, 1960.

Biddle, B. J., and Thomas, E. J. *Role theory: Concepts and research.* New York: Wiley, 1966.

Bierbrauer, G. A. Attribution and perspective: Effects of time, set, and role on interpersonal inference. Unpublished doctoral dissertation, Stanford, 1973.

Bion, W. R. *Experiences in groups, and other papers.* New York: Basic Books, 1961.

Birren, J. E. Translations in gerontology — From lab to life: Psychopathology and speed of response. *American psychologist,* 1974, *29,* 808–815.

Black, J. W. The effect of room characteristics upon vocal intensity and rate. *Journal of the acoustical society of America,* 1950, *21,* 174–176.

Black, J. W. The effect of delayed side-tone upon vocal rate and intensity. *Journal of speech and hearing disorders,* 1951, *16,* 56–60.

Block, J. *Lives through time.* Berkeley, Bancroft, 1971.

Block, J. H. Conceptions of sex role: Some cross-cultural and longitudinal perspectives. *American psychologist,* 1973, *28,* 512–526.

Bloom, L. *Language development: Form and function in emerging grammars.* Cambridge, MIT. 1970.

Boadella, D. *Wilhelm Reich: The evolution of his work.* New York: Dell, 1975.

Boffey, P. M. Return of Dr. Fox. *Chronicle of higher education,* 1974, *9,* 3.

Bolles, R. C. *Theory of motivation.* New York: Harper & Row, 1967.

Borgaonkar, D. S., and Shah, S. A. The XYY chromosome male — or syndrome. *Progress in medical genetics,* 1974, *10,* 135–222.

Botwinick, J. Geropsychology. In P. H. Mussen and M. R. Rosenzweig (eds.), *Annual review of psychology.* Palo Alto, Calif.: Annual Reviews, 1970.

Bower, T. G. R. *Development in infancy.* San Francisco: Freeman, 1974.

Bowlby, J. Separation anxiety: A critical review of the literature. *Journal of child psychology and psychiatry,* 1961, *1,* 251–269.

Bowlby, J. *Maternal care and mental health.* New York: Schocken, 1966.

Bradford, L. P., Gibb, J. R., and Benne, K. D. *T-group theory and laboratory method.* New York: Wiley, 1964.

Brady, J. V., Porter, R. W., Conrad, D. G., and Mason, J. W. Avoidance behavior and the development of gastroduodenal ulcers. *Journal of the experimental analysis of behavior,* 1958, *1,* 69–73.

Braginsky, B., and Braginsky, D. Schizophrenic patients

in the psychiatric interview: An experimental study of their effectiveness at manipulation. *Journal of consulting psychology*, 1967, *21*, 543–547.

Braginsky, B. M., Braginsky, D. D., and Ring, K. *Methods of madness: The mental hospital as a last resort.* New York: Holt, Rinehart and Winston, 1969.

Breland, K., and Breland, M. The misbehavior of organisms. *American psychologist*, 1961, *16*, 681–684.

Brenner, M. H. *Mental illness and the economy.* Cambridge, Mass.: Harvard University Press, 1973.

Breuer, J., and Freud, S. Studies on hysteria. In J. Strachey (ed.), *Standard edition of the complete psychological works of Sigmund Freud.* Vol. 2. London: Hogarth Press, 1955. (Originally published 1895.)

Brown, F. A., Jr., Hastings, J. W., and Palmer, J. D. *The biological clock: Two views.* New York: Academic Press, 1970.

Brown, R. The first sentences of child and chimpanzee. In R. Brown (ed.), *Selected psycholinguistic papers.* New York: Macmillan, 1970.

Brown, R. Development of the first language in the human species. *American psychologist*, 1973, *28*, 97–106.

Brown, R. W., and McNeill, B. The "tip-of-the-tongue" phenomenon. *Journal of verbal learning and verbal behavior*, 1966, *5*, 325–337.

Burt, C. L. The evidence for the concept of intelligence. *British journal of educational psychology*, 1955, *25*, 158–177.

Campbell, J. *The hero with a thousand faces.* New York: Meridian Books, 1956.

Cannon, W. B. The James-Lange theory of emotions: A critical examination and an alternative theory. *American journal of psychology*, 1927, *39*, 106–124.

Cannon, W. B. *Bodily changes in pain, hunger, fear and rage.* (2nd ed.). New York: Appleton-Century-Crofts, 1929.

Cannon, W. B. *The wisdom of the body.* New York: Norton, 1932.

Cannon, W. B., and Washburn, A. L. An explanation of hunger. *American journal of physiology*, 1912, *29*, 441–454.

Caplan, N., and Nelson, S. D. On being useful: The nature and consequences of psychological research on social problems. *American psychologist*, 1973, *28*, 199–211.

Carey, A. The Hawthorne studies: A radical critique. *American sociological review*, 1967, *32*, 403–416.

Carmichael, L. The development of behavior in vertebrates experimentally removed from the influence of external stimulation. *Psychological review*, 1926, *33*, 51–58.

Carver, R. P. Two dimensions of tests—Psychometric and edumetric. *American psychologist*, 1974, *29*, 512–518.

Castaneda, C. *Journey to Ixtlan.* New York: Simon & Schuster, 1972.

Cattell, R. B. *Description and measurement of personality.* Yonkers-on-Hudson, N.Y.: World, 1946.

Cattell, R. B. *Personality and motivation structure and measurement.* Yonkers-on-Hudson, N.Y.: World, 1957.

Cattell, R. B. Theory of fluid and crystallized intelligence: A critical experiment. *Journal of educational psychology*, 1963, *54*, 1–22.

Cattell, R. B. *The scientific analysis of personality.* Baltimore: Penguin, 1965.

Cerletti, U. Electroshock therapy. In A. M. Sackler, M. D. Sackler, R. R. Sackler, and F. Marti-Ibañez (eds.), *The great physiodynamic therapies in psychiatry: An historical reappraisal.* New York: Hoeber and Harper & Row, 1956, 91–120.

Chapman, L. F., Goodell, H., and Wolff, H. G. Augmentation of the inflammatory reaction by activity of the central nervous system. *AMA archives of neurology*, 1959, *1*, 113–128.

Chen, S. C. Social modification of activity of ants in nest building. *Physiological zoology*, 1937, *10*, 420–436.

Cherry, E. C. Some experiments on the recognition of speech, with one and two ears. *Journal of the acoustical society of America*, 1953, *25*, 975–979.

Childs, B. Genetic origins of some sex differences among human beings. *Pediatrics*, 1965, *35*, 798–812.

Chomsky, N. *Aspects of the theory of syntax.* Cambridge, Mass.: MIT Press, 1965.

Chomsky, N. *Language and mind.* (2nd ed.). New York: Harcourt Brace Jovanovich, 1972a.

Chomsky, N. IQ tests: Building blocks for the new class system. *Ramparts*, 1972b, *11* (July), 24–30.

Clark, K. B., and Clark, M. P. Racial identification and preference in Negro children. In E. E. Maccoby, T. M. Newcomb, and E. L. Hartley (eds.), *Readings in social psychology.* New York: Holt, Rinehart and Winston, 1958.

Clark, R. D., and Word, L. E. Where is the apathetic bystander? Situational characteristics of the emergency. *Journal of personality and social psychology*, 1974, *29*, 279–287.

Clarke, A. M., and Clarke, A. D. B. (eds.). *Early experience: Myth and evidence.* New York: Free Press, 1977.

Clements, S., and Peters, J. Minimal brain dysfunction in the school-age child. *Archives of general psychiatry*, 1962, *6*, 185–197.

Cohen, J. *Humanistic psychology.* London: Allen & Unwin, 1958.

Cohen, J. *Behaviour in uncertainty and its social implications.* New York: Basic Books, 1964.

Cohen, J., and Christiansen, I. *Information and choice.* Edinburgh, Scotland: Oliver and Boyle, 1970.

Cole, M., Guy, J., Glick, J. A., and Sharp, D. W. *The cultural context of learning and thinking.* New York: Basic Books, 1971.

Combs, A. W., Richards, A. C., and Richards, F. *Perceptual psychology: A humanistic approach to the study of persons.* New York: Harper & Row, 1976.

Comfort, A. *Ageing: The biology of senescence.* New

York: Holt, Rinehart and Winston, 1964.

Comfort, A. (ed.). *The joy of sex: A Cordon Bleu guide to lovemaking*. New York: Crown, 1972.

Commission on Obscenity and Pornography. *Technical Report*. Vol. 8. Washington, D.C.: U.S. Government Printing Office, 1971.

Coopersmith, S. *The antecedents of self-esteem*. San Francisco: Freeman, 1967.

Cornsweet, T. N. *Visual perception*. New York: Academic Press, 1970.

Cotterman, C. W., and Snyder, L. H. Tests of simple Mendelian inheritance in randomly collected data of one and two generations. *Journal of the American Statistical Association*, 1939, *34*, 511–523.

Cottrell, N. B. Social facilitation. In C. G. McClintock (ed.), *Experimental social psychology*. New York: Holt, Rinehart and Winston, 1972.

Cowan, P., Egleson, N., and Hentoff, N. *State secrets*. New York: Holt, Rinehart and Winston, 1974.

Cozby, P. C. Self-disclosure: A literature review. *Psychological bulletin*, 1973, *79*, 73–91.

Crowne, D., and Marlowe, D. *The approval motive: Studies in evaluative dependence*. New York: Wiley, 1964.

Crutchfield, R. S. Conformity and character. *American psychologist*, 1955, *10*, 191–198.

Cuddon, E. The relief of pain by laying on of hands. *International journal of parapsychology*, 1968, *10*, 85–92.

Cullen, E. Adaptations in the kittiwake to cliff-nesting. *Ibis*, 1957, *99*, 275–302.

Dahlstrom, W. G., and Welsh, G. S. *An MMPI Handbook*. Minneapolis: University of Minnesota Press, 1960.

Dahlstrom, W. G., Welsh, G. S., and Dahlstrom, L. E. *An MMPI Handbook*. Vol. 1: *Clinical interpretation*. Minneapolis: University of Minnesota Press, 1972.

Darwin, C. *The expression of the emotions in man and animals*. (2nd ed.). London: Murray, 1890. (Originally published in 1872.)

Das, N. M., and Gastaut, H. Variations in the electrical activity of the brain, heart, and skeletal system during yogic meditation and ecstasy. International Federated Societies for EEG and Clinical Neurophysiology, *Journal supplement*, 1955, No. 6.

Dean, R. *Views*. Dimpsfield, England: Dragon's Dream, 1975.

Deci, E. L. *Intrinsic motivation*. New York: Plenum Press, 1975.

Dement, W. C. The effect of dream deprivation. *Science*, 1960, *131*, 1705–1707.

Dement, W. C. An essay on dreams: The role of physiology in understanding their nature. In *New directions in psychology*. Vol. 2. New York: Holt, Rinehart and Winston, 1965, 135–257.

Dement, W. C., and Kleitman, N. Cyclic variations in EEG during sleep and their relation to eye movements, body motility, and dreaming. *Electroencephalography and clinical neurophysiology*, 1957a, *9*, 673–690.

Dement, W., and Kleitman, N. Relationship of eye movements during sleep to dream activity; objective method for study of dreaming. *Journal of experimental psychology*, 1957b, *53*, 339–346.

De Valoris, R. L., and Jacobs, G. H. Primate color vision. *Science*, 1968, *162*, 533–540.

Dillard, J. L. *Black English: Its history and usage in the U.S.* New York: Random House, 1972.

Dollard, J., Doob, L., Miller, N., Mowrer, O. H., and Sears, R. R. *Frustration and aggression*. New Haven, Conn.: Yale University Press, 1939.

Draguns, J. G., and Phillips, L. *Culture and psychopathology: The quest for a relationship*. Morristown, N.J.: General Learning Press, 1972.

Dreger, R. M., and Miller, K. S. Comparative psychological studies of Negroes and whites in the United States: 1959–1965. *Psychological bulletin: Monograph supplement*, 1968, *70*(2), pp. 58.

Dudley, D., Holmes, T., Martin, C., and Ripley, H. Hypnotically induced facsimile of pain. *Archives of general psychiatry*, 1966, *15*, 198–204.

Duffy, E. *Activation and behavior*. New York: Wiley, 1962.

Duijker, H. C. J., and Frijda, N. H. *National character and national stereotypes*. Amsterdam: North Holland Publishing, 1960.

Ebbinghaus, H. *Memory: A contribution to experimental psychology*. New York: Dover, 1964. (Originally published 1885.)

Eichenwald, H. F., and Fry, P. G. Nutrition and learning. *Science*, 1969, *163*, 644–648.

Eisdorfer, C. Adaptation to loss of work. In F. Carp (ed.), *Retirement*. New York: Behavioral Publications, 1972.

Eisenberger, R. Explanation of rewards that do not reduce tissue needs. *Psychological bulletin*, 1972, *77*, 319–339.

Ekman, P. Universals and cultural differences in facial expressions of emotion. In J. K. Cole (ed.), *Nebraska symposium on motivation. Vol. 19: Theory and research on motivation*. Lincoln: University of Nebraska Press, 1971.

Ellenberger, H. F. *The discovery of the unconscious: The history and evolution of dynamic psychiatry*. New York: Basic Books, 1970.

Elliott, R. G., with Beatty, A. R. *Agent of death: The memoirs of an executioner*. New York: Dutton, 1940.

Emmerich, W. Stability and change in early personality development. *Young children*, 1966, *21*, 233–243.

Endler, N. S., Hunt, J. M., and Rosenstein, A. J. An S–R inventory of anxiousness. *Psychological monographs*, 1962, *76*, Whole No. 17, pp. 1–33.

Erikson, E. H. *Young man Luther*. New York: Norton, 1958.

Erikson, E. H. Growth and crises of the healthy personality. *Psychological issues*, 1959, *1*, 50–100.

Erikson, E. H. *Identity: Youth and crisis.* New York: Norton, 1968.

Erikson, E. H. *Gandhi's truth: On the origins of militant nonviolence.* New York: Norton, 1969.

Erlenmeyer-Kimling, L., and Jarvik, L. F. Genetics and intelligence: A review. *Science*, 1963, *142*, 1477–1479.

Escalona, S. K., and Heider, G. *Prediction and outcome: A study in child development.* New York: Basic Books, 1959.

Estes, W. K. Memory — East and West. [Review of A. A. Smirnov, *Problems of the psychology of memory*.] *Contemporary psychology*, 1974, *19*, 179–182.

Fairbanks, G., and Jaeger, R. A device for continuously variable time delay of headset monitoring during magnetic recording of speech. *Journal of speech and hearing disorders*, 1951, *16*, 162–164.

Fantz, R. L. Pattern vision in newborn infants. *Science*, 1963, *140*, 296–297.

Fantz, R. L. Visual perception from birth as shown by pattern selectivity. *Annals of the New York Academy of Science*, 1965, *118*, 793–814.

Farber, M. L. Time perspective and feeling-tone: A study in the perception of the days. *Journal of psychology*, 1953, *35*, 253–257.

Farberow, N. L., and Shneidman, E. S. *The cry for help.* New York: McGraw-Hill, 1961.

Farina, A. *Schizophrenia.* Morristown, N.J.: General Learning Press, 1972.

Feather, N. Valence of outcome and expectation of success in relation to task difficulty and perceived locus of control. *Journal of personality and social psychology*, 1967, *7*, 372–386.

Ferster, C. B., and Skinner, B. F. *Schedules of reinforcement.* New York: Appleton-Century-Crofts, 1957.

Festinger, L. A theory of social comparison processes. *Human relations*, 1954, *7*, 117–140.

Festinger, L. *Conflict, decision, and dissonance.* Stanford, Calif.: Stanford University Press, 1964.

Festinger, L., Riecken, H. W., Jr., and Schacter, S. *When prophecy fails.* Minneapolis: University of Minnesota Press, 1956.

Festinger, L., Schacter, S., and Back, K. W. *Social pressures in informal groups: A study of human factors in housing.* New York: Harper & Row, 1950.

Fiedler, F. *A theory of leadership effectiveness.* New York: McGraw-Hill, 1967.

Fischer, W. F. *Theories of anxiety.* New York: Harper & Row, 1970.

Fishbein, M., and Ajzen, I. *Belief, attitude, intention, and behavior: An introduction to theory and research.* Reading, Mass.: Addison-Wesley, 1975.

Fiske, D. W., and Maddi, S. R. (eds.). *Functions of varied experience.* Homewood, Ill.: Dorsey, 1961.

Flavell, J. H., and Draguns, J. G. Microgenetic approach to perception and thought. *Psychological bulletin*,

1957, *54*, 197–217.

Fleer, R. Some behavioral observations on the ant with special reference to habit reversal learning. Unpublished doctoral dissertation, State University of New York at Stony Brook, 1972.

Ford, C. S., and Beach, F. A. *Patterns of sexual behavior.* New York: Harper & Row, 1951.

Ford, P. K. (ed. and trans.). *The poetry of Llywarch Hen.* Berkeley: University of California Press, 1974.

Forer, B. R. The fallacy of personal validation: A classroom demonstration of gullibility. *Journal of abnormal and social psychology*, 1949, *44*, 118–123.

Foucault, M. *Madness and civilization.* New York: Mentor books, 1965.

Foulkes, D. *The psychology of sleep.* New York: Scribner's, 1966.

Fouts, R. S. Use of guidance in teaching sign language to a chimpanzee *(Pan Troglodytes). Journal of comparative and physiological psychology*, 1972, *80*, 515–522.

Fouts, R. S. Acquisition and testing of gestural signs in four young chimpanzees. *Science*, 1975, *180*, 978–980.

Fraisse, P. *The psychology of time.* New York: Harper & Row, 1963.

Frank, B., Stein, D. G., and Rosen, J. Interanimal "memory" transfer: Results from brain and liver homogenates. *Science*, 1970, *169*, 399–402.

Fraser, J. T., Haber, F. C., and Müller, G. H. (eds.). *The study of time.* New York: Springer Verlag, 1972.

Freeman, L. *The story of Anna O.: The woman who led Freud to psychoanalysis.* New York: Walker, 1972.

Freud, A. *War and children.* New York: International Universities Press, 1944.

Freud, S. The interpretation of dreams. In J. Strachey (ed. and trans.), *The standard edition of the complete psychological works of Sigmund Freud.* Vols. 4, 5. London: Hogarth Press, 1953. (Originally published 1900.)

Freud, S. Five lectures on psychoanalysis. Lecture 1. In J. Strachey (ed. and trans.), *The standard edition of the complete psychological works of Sigmund Freud.* Vol. 11. London: Hogarth Press, 1957a, pp. 9–16. (Originally published 1909.)

Freud, S. Mourning and melancholia. In J. Strachey (ed. and trans.), *The standard edition of the complete psychological works of Sigmund Freud.* Vol. 14. London: Hogarth Press, 1957b, pp. 243–258. (Originally published 1917.)

Freud, S. Inhibition, symptom, and anxiety. In J. Strachey (ed. and trans.), *The standard edition of the complete psychological works of Sigmund Freud.* Vol. 20. London: Hogarth Press, 1959. (Originally published 1926.)

Freud, S. *Beyond the pleasure principle.* New York: Bantam Books, 1967. (Originally published 1920.)

Fried, M. Effects of social change on mental health. *American journal of orthopsychiatry*, 1964, *34*, 3–28.

Friedman, M., and Rosenman, R. H. *Type A behavior*

and your heart. New York: Knopf, 1974.

Friedrich, O. *Going crazy: An inquiry into madness in our time.* New York: Simon & Schuster, 1975.

Fromm, E. *Escape from freedom.* New York: Holt, Rinehart and Winston, 1941.

Fromm, E. *The sane society.* New York: Holt, Rinehart and Winston, 1955.

Fuller, J. L. Experiential deprivation and later behavior. *Science,* 1967, *158,* 1645–1652.

Fuller, P. R. Operant conditioning of a vegetative human organism. *American journal of psychology,* 1949, *62,* 587–590.

Fuster, J. M. Effects of stimulation of brain stem on tachistoscopic perception. *Science,* 1958, *127,* 150.

Gallup, G. G. Chimpanzees: Self-recognition. *Science,* 1970, *167,* 86–87.

Gallup, G. G. Self-recognition in primates: A comparative approach to the bidirectional properties of consciousness. *American psychologist,* 1977, *32,* 329–338.

Garcia, J., Clarke, J. C., and Hankins, W. G. Natural responses to scheduled rewards. In P. P. G. Bateson, and P. H. Klopfer (eds.), *Perspectives in ethology.* New York: Plenum Press, 1973, pp. 1–41.

Garcia, J., and Koelling, R. A. Relation of cue to consequence in avoidance learning. *Psychonomic science,* 1966, *4,* 123–124.

Garcia, J., Kovner, R., and Green, K. F. Cue properties vs. palatability of flavors in avoidance learning. *Psychonomic science,* 1970, *20,* 313–314.

Gardner, B. T., and Gardner, R. A. Comparing the early utterances of child and chimpanzee. In A. Pick (ed.), *Minnesota symposium on child psychology.* Vol. 8. Minneapolis: University of Minnesota Press, 1974, pp. 3–24.

Gardner, B. T., and Gardner, R. A. Evidence for sentence constituents in the early utterances of child and chimpanzee. *Journal of experimental psychology: General,* 1975, *104,* 244–267.

Gardner, R. A., and Gardner, B. T. Comparative psychology and language acquisition. In K. Salzinger and F. Denmark (eds.), *Psychology: The state of the art,* in press.

Garner, W. R. Good patterns have few alternatives. *American scientist,* 1970, *58,* 34–42.

Geen, R. G. *Aggression.* Morristown, N.J.: General Learning Press, 1972.

Geldard, F. A. *The human senses.* New York: Wiley, 1953.

Geldard, F. A. Pattern perception by the skin. In D. Kenshalo (ed.), *The skin senses.* Springfield, Ill.: Thomas, 1968.

Genet, J. *The balcony.* (rev. ed.). London: Faber and Faber, 1962.

Gerard, H. B., and Rabbie, J. Fear and social comparisons. *Journal of abnormal and social psychology,* 1961, *62,* 586–592.

Gesell, A., and associates. *The first five years of life.* New York: Harper & Row, 1940.

Gibson, J. J. *The senses considered as perceptual systems.* Boston: Houghton Mifflin, 1966.

Glenn, M. L. The psychopath: Hero of our age. *The Village Voice,* September 14, 1967, pp. 24, 28–29.

Glickstein, M., Chevalier, J. A., Korchin, S. J., Basowitz, H., Sabshin, M., Hamburg, D. A., and Grinker, R. R. Temporal heart rate patterns in anxious patients. *AMA archives of neurology and psychiatry,* 1957, *78,* 101–106.

Goddard, H. H. *The Kallikak family: A study in the heredity of feeblemindedness.* New York: Macmillan, 1925.

Goffman, E. *The presentation of self in everyday life.* New York: Doubleday Anchor, 1959.

Goffman, E. *Asylums.* New York: Doubleday Anchor, 1961.

Goffman, E. *Interaction ritual: Essays on face-to-face behavior.* New York: Doubleday Anchor, 1967.

Goldfried, M. R., and Davison, G. C. *Clinical behavior therapy.* New York: Holt, Rinehart and Winston, 1976.

Goldfried, M. R., and Sprafkin, J. N. *Behavioral personality assessment.* Morristown, N.J.: General Learning Press, 1974.

Granick, S., and Patterson, R. D. (eds.). *Human aging. Part 2: An eleven-year followup biomedical and behavioral study.* Rockville, Md.: Section on Mental Health of the Aging, National Institute of Mental Health, U.S. Department of Health, Education, and Welfare, 1971.

Grant, A. Bertha Pappenheim: Alias Anna O. *Ms.* Magazine, 1974, *3,* 118–120.

Green, E. E., and Green, A. M. Regulating our mind–body processes. *Fields within fields,* 1973–1974 (Winter), No. 10, 16–24.

Greenfield, J. *Wilhelm Reich versus the U.S.A.* New York: Norton, 1974.

Greenleaf, E. Senoi dream groups. *Psychotherapy: theory, research, and practice,* 1973, *10,* 218–222.

Gregory, R. L. *Eye and brain: The psychology of seeing.* (2nd ed.). New York: McGraw-Hill, 1973.

Gregory, R. L., and Wallace, J. G. Recovery from early blindness: A case study. *Experimental Society monograph no. 2.* Cambridge, England: Cambridge University, 1963.

Grob, G. N. The state mental hospital in mid-nineteenth-century America. *American psychologist,* 1966, *21,* 510–523.

Grof, S., and Halifax, J. *The human encounter with death.* New York: Dutton, 1977.

Guilford, J. P. Intelligence: 1965 model. *American psychologist,* 1966, *21,* 20–26.

Gurdjieff, G. *Views from the real world.* New York: Dutton, 1975.

Haber, R. N. Eidetic images. *Scientific American,* 1969, *220,* 36–44.

Haley, J. *Strategies of psychotherapy.* New York: Grune

502

References

& Stratton, 1963.

Haley, J. The art of being schizophrenic. *Voices*, 1965, *1*, 133–147.

Hall, C. S., and Lindzey, G. *Theories of personality.* (2nd ed.). New York: Wiley, 1970.

Halliday, A. M., and Mason, A. A. The effect of hyponotic anesthesia on cortical responses. *Journal of neurology, neurosurgery, and psychiatry*, 1964, *27*, 300–312.

Harlow, H. F. The nature of love. *American psychologist*, 1958, *13*, 673–685.

Harper, P. A., Fischer, L. K., and Rider, R. V. Neurological and intellectual status of prematures at three to five years of age. *Journal of pediatrics*, 1959, *55*, 679–690.

Harrington, A. *Psychopaths.* New York: Simon & Schuster, 1972.

Hartmann, E. L. *The functions of sleep.* New Haven, Conn.: Yale University Press, 1973.

Hartshorne, H., and May, M. A. *Studies in the nature of character.* Vol. 1: *Studies in deceit.* New York: Macmillan, 1928.

Hartup, W. H. Aggression in childhood: Developmental perspectives. *American psychologist*, 1974, *29*, 336–341.

Hauser, R. M. Socioeconomic background and differential returns to education. In L. C. Solomon and P. J. Taubman (eds.), *Does college matter?* New York: Academic Press, 1973.

Hayes, K. J., and Hayes, C. The intellectual development of a home-raised chimpanzee. *Proceedings of the American Philosophical Society*, 1951, *95*, 105–109.

Heckhauser, H. Achievement motive research: Current problems and some contributions toward a general theory of motivation. In W. J. Arnold (ed.), *Nebraska symposium on motivation, 1968.* Lincoln: University of Nebraska Press, 1968, pp. 103–174.

Heider, F. Social perception and phenomenal causality. *Psychological review*, 1944, *51*, 358–374.

Heider, F. Attitudes and cognitive organization. *Journal of psychology*, 1946, *21*, 107–112.

Heider, F. *The psychology of interpersonal relations.* New York: Wiley, 1958.

Held, R., and Hein, A. Movement-produced stimulation in the development of visually guided behavior. *Journal of comparative and physiological psychology*, 1963, *56*, 872–876.

Hendry, D. P. Reinforcing value of information: Fixed-ratio schedules. In D. P. Hendry (ed.), *Conditioned reinforcement.* Homewood, Ill.: Dorsey, 1972.

Herrnstein, R. J. Method and theory in the study of avoidance. *Psychological review.* 1969, *76*, 49–69.

Hess, E. H. Imprinting. *Science*, 1959, *130*, 133–141.

Hilgard, E. R. *Hypnotic susceptibility.* New York: Harcourt Brace Jovanovich, 1965.

Hilgard, E. R. *The experience of hypnosis.* New York: Harcourt Brace Jovanovich, 1968.

Hilgard, E. R. Altered states of awareness. *Journal of nervous and mental diseases*, 1969, *149*, 68–78.

Hilgard, E. R. A neodissociation interpretation of pain reduction in hypnosis. *Psychological review*, 1973, *80*, 396–411.

Hilgard, E. R. The alleviation of pain by hypnosis. *Pain*, 1975, *1*, 213–231.

Hoagland, H. The physiological control of judgments of duration: Evidence for a chemical clock. *Journal of general psychology*, 1933, *9*, 267–287.

Hoagland, H. The chemistry of time. *Scientific monthly*, 1943, *56*, 56–61.

Hockett, C. F. Logical considerations in the study of animal communication. In W. E. Lanyon and W. N. Tavolga, (eds.), *Animal sounds and communication.* Washington, D.C.: American Institute of Biological Sciences, 1960.

Hoffer, A., and Osmond, H. *How to live with schizophrenia.* New York: Universal Books, 1974.

Hollingshead, A. B., and Redlich, F. C. *Social class and mental illness.* New York: Wiley, 1958.

Hollingworth, L. S. *Children above 180 IQ, Stanford-Binet: Origin and development.* Yonkers-on-Hudson, N.Y.: World, 1942.

Hoppe, F. Erfolg und Misserfolg. *Psychologische Forschung*, 1931, *14*, 1–62.

Horner, M. Sex differences in achievement motivation and performance in competitive and non-competitive situations. Unpublished doctoral dissertation, University of Michigan, 1968.

Horner, M. S. The psychological significance of success in competitive achievement situations: A threat as well as a promise. In H. I. Day, D. E. Berlyne, and D. E. Hunt (eds.), *Intrinsic motivation: A new direction in education.* New York: Holt, Rinehart and Winston, 1971.

Horney, K. *Neurosis and human growth: The struggle toward self-realization.* New York: Norton, 1950.

Hovland, C. I. Reconciling conflicting results derived from experimental and survey studies of attitude change. *American psychologist*, 1959, *14*, 8–17.

Hovland, C. I., Janis, I., and Kelley, H. *Communication and persuasion.* New Haven, Conn.: Yale University Press, 1953.

Hovland, C. I., Janis, I. L., and Kelley, H. H. A summary of experimental studies of opinion change. In M. Jahoda and N. Warren (eds.), *Attitudes.* Baltimore: Penguin Books, 1966.

Hubel, D. H., and Wiesel, T. N. Receptive fields, binocular interaction and functional architecture in the cat's visual cortex. *Journal of physiology* (London), 1962, *160*, 106–154.

Hubel, D. H., and Wiesel, T. N. Receptive fields and functional architecture in two non-striate visual areas (18 and 19) of the cat. *Journal of neurophysiology*, 1965, *28*, 229–289.

Hunt, M. M. *Sexual behavior in the 1970s.* Chicago: Playboy Press, 1974.

Hurvich, L. M., and Jameson, D. An opponent-process theory of color vision. *Psychological Review*, 1957, *64*, 384–404.

Husek, T., and Alexander, S. The effectiveness of the anxiety differential in examination stress situations. *Educational and psychological measurement*, 1963, *23*, 309–318.

Hutt, M. L., and Gibby, R. G. *The mentally retarded child: Development, education, and treatment.* (3rd ed.). Boston: Allyn & Bacon, 1976.

Huxley, A. *The doors of perception.* New York: Harper & Row, 1954.

Hyde, T. S., and Jenkins, J. J. Recall for words as a function of semantic, graphic, and syntactic orienting tasks. *Journal of verbal learning and verbal behavior*, 1973, *12*, 471–480.

Inkeles, A., and Levinson, D. J. National character: The study of modal personality and sociocultural systems. In G. Lindzey (ed.), *Handbook of social psychology.* Vol. 2. Cambridge, Mass.: Addison-Wesley, 1954, pp. 977–1020.

Irwin, F. W., and Newland, E. A genetic study of the naming of visual figures. *Journal of psychology*, 1940, *9*, 3–16.

Jackson, D. N. A further examination of the role of autism in a visual figure–ground relationship. *Journal of psychology*, 1954, *38*, 339–357.

Jacobsen, E. *Progressive relaxation.* Chicago: University of Chicago Press, 1938.

James, W. *The varieties of religious experience.* New York: Modern Library, 1929.

James, W. *The principles of psychology.* (2 vols.). New York: Dover, 1950.

Jarvik, L. F., Klodin, V., and Matsuyama, S. S. Human aggression and the extra Y chromosome: Fact or fancy? *American psychologist*, 1973, *28*, 674–682.

Jenkins, J. G., and Dallenbach, K. M. Obliviscence during sleep and waking. *American journal of psychology*, 1924, *35*, 605–612.

Jenkins, J. J. Remember that old theory of memory? Well, forget it! *American psychologist*, 1974, *29*, 785–795.

Jenkins, W. O. A temporal gradient of derived reinforcement. *American journal of psychology*, 1950, *63*, 237–243.

Jensen, A. R. How much can we boost IQ and scholastic achievement? *Harvard educational review*, 1969, *39* (Winter), 1–123.

Jensen, A. R., and others. *Environment, heredity, and intelligence. Harvard educational review*, Reprint Series, No. 2. Cambridge, Mass.: Harvard Educational Review, 1969, pp. 246.

Jersild, A. T., and Ritzman, R. Aspects of language development: The growth of loquacity and vocabulary. *Child development*, 1938, *9*, 243–259.

Jones, E. *The life and work of Sigmund Freud.* (3 vols.). New York: Basic Books, 1953, 1955, 1957.

Jones, E. *The life and work of Sigmund Freud.* (Ed. and abridged by L. Trilling and S. Marcus.) New York: Doubleday Anchor, 1963.

Jones, E. E. Flattery will get you somewhere: Styles and uses of ingratiation. In E. Aronson (ed.), *Readings about the social animal.* San Francisco: Freeman, 1973.

Jones, E. E., and Davis, K. E. From acts to dispositions: The attribution process in person perception. In L. Berkowitz (ed.), *Advances in experimental social psychology.* Vol. 2. New York: Academic Press, 1965.

Jones, E. E., and Nisbett, R. E. The actor and the observer: Divergent perceptions of the causes of behavior. In E. E. Jones et al. (eds.), *Attribution: Perceiving the causes of behavior.* Morristown, N.J.: General Learning Corporation, 1972.

Jones, M. C., Bayley, N., MacFarlane, J. W., and Honzik, M. P. (eds.). *The course of human development.* Waltham, Mass.: Xerox College Publishing, 1971.

Jourard, S. M. *The transparent self.* (2nd ed.). New York: Van Nostrand Reinhold, 1971.

Julesz, B. *Foundations of Cyclopean perception.* Chicago: University of Chicago Press, 1971.

Jung, C. G. *Memories, dreams, reflections.* (Ed. A. Jaffe, Trans. R. Winston and C. Winston.). New York: Random House, 1961.

Jung, C. G. *Analytical psychology: Its theory and practice.* (Trans. R. C. Hull). New York: Pantheon, 1968. (Originally published 1961.)

Kagan, J., and Klein, R. E. Cross-cultural perspectives on early development. *American psychologist*, 1973, *28*, 947–961.

Kagan, J., and Moss, H. *Birth to maturity: A study in psychological development.* New York: Wiley, 1962.

Kalmus, H., Denes, P., and Fry, D. B. Effect of delayed acoustic feed-back on some non-vocal activities. *Nature*, 1955, *175*, 1078.

Kamin, L. *The science and politics of IQ.* Potomac, Md.: Lawrence Erlbaum Associates, 1974.

Kaplan, B. (ed.). *The inner world of mental illness.* New York: Harper & Row, 1964.

Kaplan, E. L., and Kaplan, G. A. Is there such a thing as a prelinguistic child? In J. Eliot (ed.), *Human development and cognitive processes.* New York: Holt, Rinehart and Winston, 1970.

Kastenbaum, R. K., and Durkee, N. Young people view old age. In R. K. Kastenbaum (ed.), *New thoughts on old age.* New York: Springer, 1964, pp. 237–249.

Katchadourian, H. *Human sexuality: Sense and nonsense.* San Francisco: Freeman, 1974.

Katona, G. *The powerful consumer: Psychological studies of the American economy.* New York: McGraw-Hill, 1960.

Katona, G. What is consumer psychology? *American psychologist*, 1967, *22*, 219–226.

Katz, D. Group morale and individual motivation. In J. E. Hulett and R. Stagner (eds.), *Problems in social psychology.* Urbana: University of Illinois Press, 1952.

Katz, D. *The world of colour*. London: Kegan Paul, Trench, Trubner, 1935.

Keleman, S. *Living your dying*. New York: Random House, 1974.

Keleman, S. *Your body speaks its mind*. New York: Simon & Schuster, 1975.

Kelley, H. H. Attribution theory in social psychology. In D. Levine (ed.), *Nebraska symposium on motivation*. Vol. 15. Lincoln: University of Nebraska Press, 1967.

Kellogg, W. N., and Kellogg, L. A. *The ape and the child*. New York: McGraw-Hill, 1933.

Kelman, H. C. Compliance, identification, and internalization: Three processes of attitude change. *Journal of conflict resolution*, 1958, *2*, 51–60.

Kerckhoff, A. C., and Davis, K. E. Value consensus and need complementarity in mate selection. *American sociological review*, 1962, *27*, 295–303.

Kettlewell, H. B. D. Insect survival and selection for pattern. *Science*, 1965, *148*, 1290–1296.

Keyes, K., Jr. *Handbook to higher consciousness*. Berkeley, Calif.: Living Love Center, 1974.

Keynes, J. M. *The general theory of employment, interest, and money*. London: Macmillan, 1936.

Kiesler, C. *The psychology of commitment: Experiments linking behavior to belief*. New York: Academic Press, 1971.

Kilpatrick. F. P. (ed.). *Human behavior from the transactional point of view*. Hanover, N.H.: Institute for Associated Research, 1952.

Kimmel, D. C. *Adulthood and aging*. New York: Wiley, 1974.

Kimmel, H. D. Instrumental conditioning of autonomically mediated responses in human beings. *American psychologist*, 1974, *29*, 325–335.

King, C. *The states of human consciousness*. New Hyde Park, N.Y.: University Books, 1963.

King, S. H. *Five lives at Harvard: Personality changes during college*. Cambridge, Mass.: Harvard University Press, 1973.

Kinsey, A. C., Martin, C. E., and Pomeroy, W. B. *Sexual behavior in the human male*. Philadelphia: Saunders, 1948.

Kinsey, A. C., Martin, C. E., Pomeroy, W. B., and Gebhard, P. H. *Sexual behavior in the human female*. Philadelphia: Saunders, 1953.

Klein, M. *Developments in psychoanalysis*. London: Hogarth Press, 1952.

Klein, M. *Narrative of a child analysis*. New York: Delta, 1975.

Kleitman, N. *Sleep and wakefulness*. Chicago: University of Chicago Press, 1963.

Knobloch, H., Rider, R. V., Harper, P., and Pasamanick, B. Neuropsychiatric sequelae of prematurity. *Journal of the American Medical Association*, 1956, *161*, 581–585.

Kohlberg, L. Stage and sequence: The cognitive–developmental approach to socialization. In D. A. Goslin (ed.), *Handbook of socialization theory and research*. Chicago: Rand-McNally, 1969.

Kohlberg, L. Implications of developmental psychology for education: Examples from moral development. *Educational psychologist*, 1973, *10*, 2–14.

Krafft-Ebing, R. von. *Psychopathia sexualis*. New York: Putnam's, 1965. (Originally published 1886.)

Kretschmer, E. *Physique and character*. (2nd ed.). New York: Cooper Square, 1970.

Krich, A. (ed.). *The sexual revolution*. Vol. 1: *Pioneer writings on sex*. New York: Delta, 1964.

Kübler-Ross, E. *On death and dying*. New York: Macmillan, 1969.

Kurtz, R., and Prestera, H. *The body reveals*. New York: Harper & Row, 1976.

Kutchinsky, B. The effect of pornography: A pilot experiment on perception, behavior, and attitudes. In Commission on Obscenity and Pornography, *Technical report*. Vol. 8. Washington, D.C.: U.S. Government Printing Office, 1968.

Kutner, B., Wilkins, C., and Yarrow, P. R. Verbal attitudes and overt behavior involving racial prejudice. *Journal of abnormal and social psychology*, 1952, *47*, 649–652.

Labov, W. *Language in the inner city: Studies in the black English vernacular*. Philadelphia: University of Pennsylvania Press, 1973.

Lacey, J. I. Somatic response patterning and stress: Some revisions of activation theory. In M. H. Appley and R. Trumbull (eds.), *Psychological stress*. New York: Appleton-Century-Crofts, 1967.

Laing, R. D. *Knots*. New York: Pantheon, 1970.

Laing, R. D., and Esterson, A. *Sanity, madness and the family*. (2nd ed.). London: Tavistock, 1970.

Lakin, M. *Experiential groups: The uses of interpersonal encounter, psychotherapy groups, and sensitivity training*. Morristown, N.J.: General Learning Press, 1972.

Lambert, N. M., Windmiller, M., Sandoval, J., and Moore, B. Hyperactive children and the efficacy of psychoactive drugs as a treatment intervention. *American journal of orthopsychiatry*, 1976, *46*, 335–352.

Landis, C., and Hunt, W. A. *The startle pattern*. New York: Farrar and Rinehart, 1939.

La Piere, R. T. Attitudes versus actions. *Social forces*, 1934, *13*, 230–237.

Lashley, K. S. The mechanism of vision. Part 1: A method for rapid analysis of pattern-vision in the rat. *Journal of genetic psychology*, 1930, *37*, 453–460.

Lashley, K. S. *The neuropsychology of Lashley: Selected papers*. New York: McGraw-Hill, 1960.

Lashley, K. S., and Russell, J. T. The mechanism of vision. Part 11: A preliminary test of innate organization. *Journal of genetic psychology*, 1934, *45*, 136–144.

Latané, B., and Darley, J. M. Bystander "apathy." *American scientist*, 1969, *57*, 244–268.

Latané, B., and Darley, J. M. *The unresponsive by-*

stander: Why doesn't he help?* New York: Appleton-Century-Crofts, 1970.

Latané, B., and Rodin, J. A lady in distress: Inhibiting effects of friends and strangers on bystander intervention. *Journal of experimental social psychology*, 1969, *5*, 189–202.

Lazarus, A. A. Where do behavior therapists take their troubles? *Psychological reports*, 1971, *28*, 349–350.

Leavitt, H. J. Some effects of certain communication patterns on group performance. *Journal of abnormal and social psychology*, 1951, *46*, 38–50.

Lee, B. S. Artificial stutter. *Journal of speech and hearing disorders*, 1951, *16*, 53–55.

Lefcourt, H. M. Internal versus external control of reinforcement: A review. *Psychological bulletin*, 1966, *65*, 206–220.

Lehrman, D. S. The physiological basis of parental feeding behavior in the ring dove *(Streptopelia risoria)*. *Behaviour*, 1955, *7*, 241–286.

Lehrman, D. S. The reproductive behavior of ring doves. *Scientific American*, 1964, *211*, 48–54.

Lesser, G. S., Krawitz, R., and Packard, R. Experimental arousal of achievement motivation in adolescent girls. *Journal of abnormal and social psychology*, 1963, *66*, 59–66.

Lettvin, J. Y., Maturana, H. R., McCulloch, W. S., and Pitts, W. H. What the frog's eye tells the frog's brain. *Proceedings of the Institute of Radio Engineers*, 1959, *47*, 1940–1951.

Levine, F. M., and Fasnacht, G. Token rewards may lead to token learning. *American psychologist*, 1974, *29*, 816–820.

Levy, B. *Legacy of death*. Englewood Cliffs, N.J.: Prentice-Hall, 1973.

Libenfeld, A. M., Pasamanick, B., and Rogers, M. Relationship between pregnancy experience and the development of certain neuropsychiatric disorders in childhood. *American journal of public health*, 1955, *45*, 637–664.

Lieberman, P. *On the origins of language: An introduction to the evolution of human speech*. New York: Macmillan, 1975.

Limber, J. Language in child and chimp? *American psychologist*, 1977, *32*, 280–295.

Lockard, J. S. Choice of a warning signal or no warning signal in an unavoidable shock situation. *Journal of comparative and physiological psychology*, 1963, *56*, 526–530.

Lockard, R. B. Reflections on the fall of comparative psychology: Is there a message for us all? *American psychologist*, 1971, *26*, 168–179.

Loehlin, J. C., Lindzey, G., and Spuhler, J. N. *Race differences in intelligence*. San Francisco: Freeman, 1974.

Loevinger, J. *Ego development: Conceptions and theories*. San Francisco: Jossey-Bass, 1976.

Loevinger, J., and Wessler, R. *Measuring ego development*. Vol. 1. San Francisco: Jossey-Bass, 1970.

London, P. The end of ideology in behavior modification. *American psychologist*, 1972, *27*, 913–920.

Lorenz, K. L. *Evolution and modification of behavior*. Chicago: University of Chicago Press, 1965.

Lorenz, K. L. *On aggression*. New York: Harcourt Brace Jovanovich, 1966.

Lovaas, O. I. *The autistic child: Language development through behavior modification*. New York: Irvington, 1977.

Lowen, A. *The betrayal of the body*. New York: Macmillan, 1967.

Lowen, A. *Bioenergetics*. New York: Coward, McCann & Geoghegan, 1975.

Luce, G. G. *Biological rhythms in human and animal physiology*. New York: Dover, 1971.

Luce, G. G. *Body time*. New York: Bantam, 1973.

Luria, A. R. *Human brain and psychological processes*. New York: Harper & Row, 1966.

Luria, A. R. *The mind of a mnemonist*. New York: Basic Books, 1968.

Maas, H., and Kuypers, J. *From thirty to seventy*. San Francisco: Jossey-Bass, 1974.

McCarthy, D. Language development of the preschool child. *Institute of Child Welfare monograph*, no. 4. Minneapolis: University of Minnesota Press, 1930.

Mach, E. *The analysis of sensations*. Jena: Fischer Verlag, 1897.

McClearn, G. E., and De Fries, J. C. *Introduction to behavioral genetics*. San Francisco: Freeman, 1973.

McClelland, D. C. *The achieving society*. New York: Van Nostrand, 1961.

McClelland, D. C. Testing for competence rather than for "intelligence." *American psychologist*, 1973, *28*, 1–14.

McClelland, D. C., and Atkinson, J. W. The projective expression of needs. Part 1: The effect of different intensities of hunger drive on perception. *Journal of psychology*, 1948, *25*, 205–232.

McClelland, D. C., and Winter, D. G. *Motivating economic achievement*. New York: Free Press, 1969.

McClelland, D. C., Clark, R. A., Roby, T. B., and Atkinson, J. W. The effect of need for achievement on thematic apperception. *Journal of experimental psychology*, 1949, *37*, 242–255.

Maccoby, E. E. (ed.). *The development of sex differences*. Stanford, Calif.: Stanford University Press, 1966.

Maccoby, E. E., and Jacklin, C. N. *The psychology of sex role differences*. Palo Alto, Calif.: Stanford University Press, 1974.

McConnell, J. V., Shigehisa, T., and Salive, H. Attempts to transfer approach and avoidance responses by RNA injections in rats. In K. H. Pribram and D. E. Broadbent (eds.), *Biology of memory*. New York: Academic Press, 1970, pp. 129–159.

McCrary, J. W., Jr., and Hunter, W. S. Serial position curves in verbal learning. *Science*, 1953, *117*, 131–134.

McGaugh, J. L. Time-dependent processes in memory

storage. In J. L. McGaugh and M. J. Herz (eds.), *Controversial issues in consolidation of the memory trace.* Chicago: Aldine, 1970.

McGill, T. E. A review of hearing in amphibians and reptiles. *Psychological bulletin,* 1960, *57,* 165–168.

McKusick, V. A., and Ruddle, F. H. The status of the gene map of the human chromosomes. *Science,* 1977, *196,* 390–405.

McWhirter, N., and McWhirter, R. *Guinness book of world records.* New York: Bantam, 1963.

Maehr, M. L. Culture and achievement motivation. *American psychologist,* 1974, *29,* 887–896.

Malécot, A., Johnston, R. and Kizziar, P.-A. Syllabic rate and utterance length in French. *Phonetica,* 1972, *26,* 235–251.

Mann, J., Sidman, J., and Starr, S. Effects of erotic films on sexual behavior of married couples. In Commission on Obscenity and Pornography, *Technical Report.* Vol. 8. Washington, D.C.: U.S. Government Printing Office, 1968.

Marcus, S. *The other Victorians.* New York: Basic Books, 1964.

Marrow, A. *The practical theorist: The life and work of Kurt Lewin.* New York: Basic Books, 1969.

Martindale, D. A. (ed.). National character in the perspective of the social sciences. *The annals of the American Academy of Political and Social Science,* 1967, whole Vol. *370.*

Maslach, C., Marshall, G., and Zimbardo, P. Hypnotic control of peripheral skin temperature: A case report. *Psychophysiology,* 1972, *9,* 600–605.

Maslow, A. H. *Toward a psychology of being.* (2nd ed.). Princeton: Van Nostrand, 1968.

Maslow, A. H. *Motivation and personality.* (2nd ed.). New York: Harper & Row, 1970.

Masters, W. H., and Johnson, V. E. *Human sexual response.* Boston: Little, Brown, 1966.

Masters, W. H., and Johnson, V. E. *Human sexual inadequacy.* Boston: Little, Brown, 1970.

Matarazzo, J. D. *Wechsler's measurement and appraisal of adult intelligence.* (5th ed.). Baltimore: Williams & Wilkins, 1972.

Mead, M. *Coming of age in Samoa.* New York: Morrow, 1961.

Meade, R. D. An experimental study of leadership in India. *Journal of social psychology,* 1967, *72,* 35–43.

Mehrabian, A. *Nonverbal communication.* Chicago: Aldine, 1972.

Melzack, R., and Wall, P. O. Pain mechanisms: a new theory. *Science,* 1965, *150,* 971–979.

Mendel, W. M., and Rapport, S. Determinants of the decision for psychiatric hospitalization. *Archives of general psychiatry,* 1969, *20,* 321–328.

Mendels, J. *Concepts of depression.* New York: Wiley, 1970.

Mercer, J. R. *Labeling the mentally retarded: Clinical and social perspectives on mental retardation.*

Berkeley: University of California Press, 1973.

Metzger, W. Optische Untersuchungen am Ganzfeld, Teil 2: Zur Phänomenologie des homogenen Ganzfelds. *Psychologische Forschung,* 1930, *13,* 6–29.

Michotte, A. *The perception of causality.* London: Methuen, 1963.

Miles, E. M., Raynal, D. M., and Wilson, M. A. Blind man living in normal society has circadian rhythms of 24.9 hours. *Science,* 1977, *198,* 421–423.

Milgram, S. Behavioral study of obedience. *Journal of abnormal and social psychology,* 1963, *67,* 371–378.

Milgram, S. *Obedience to authority.* New York: Harper & Row, 1974.

Miller, G., and Selfridge, J. Verbal context and the recall of meaningful material. *American journal of psychology,* 1950, *63,* 176–185.

Miller, N. E. Studies of fear as an acquirable drive. Part 1: Fear as motivation and fear-reduction as reinforcement in the learning of new responses. *Journal of experimental psychology,* 1948, *38,* 89–101.

Miller, N. E., and Dollard, J. *Social learning and imitation.* New Haven, Conn.: Yale University Press, 1941.

Milton, O., and Wahler, R. G. *Behavior disorders. Perspectives and trends.* (3rd ed.). Philadelphia: Lippincott, 1973.

Mischel, W. Toward a cognitive social learning reconceptualization of personality. *Psychological review,* 1973, *80,* 252–283.

Mischel, W., and Mischel, H. N. *Essentials of psychology.* New York: Random House, 1977.

Mitchell, G. Syndromes resulting from social isolation. Part 2: Primates. In J. H. Cullen (ed.), *Experimental behaviour: A basis for the study of mental disturbance.* Dublin: Irish University Press, 1974, pp. 216–223.

Money, J. Psychosexual differentiation. In J. Money (ed.), *Sex research: New developments.* New York: Holt, Rinehart and Winston, 1965, pp. 3–23.

Money, J., and Eberhardt, A. A. *Man and woman, boy and girl: The differentiation and dimorphism of gender identity from conception to maturity.* Baltimore: Johns Hopkins University Press, 1972.

Montagu, A. *The natural superiority of women.* (rev. ed.). New York: Collier, 1974.

Morrison, T. L. Control as an aspect of group leadership: A review of research. *Journal of education,* 1974, *156,* 38–64.

Mountcastle, V. B. *Medical physiology.* St. Louis: Mosby, 1974.

Mowrer, O. H. On the dual nature of learning—A reinterpretation of "conditioning" and "problem-solving." *Harvard educational review,* 1947, *17,* 102–148.

Mowrer, O. H. *Learning theory and behavior.* New York: Wiley, 1960.

Rogers, C. R. Persons or science? A philosophical question. *American psychologist*, 1955, *10*, 267–278.

Rogers, C. R. The necessary and sufficient conditions of therapeutic personality change. *Journal of consulting psychology*, 1957, *21*, 95–103.

Rogers, C. R. The process of the basic encounter group. In J. F. T. Bugental (ed.), *The challenge of humanistic psychology*. New York: McGraw-Hill, 1967.

Rogers, C. R. *On becoming a person: A therapist's view of psychotherapy*. Boston: Houghton Mifflin, 1970.

Rolf, I. *Rolfing: The structural integration of human beings*. New York: Viking, 1977.

Rorschach, H. *Psychodiagnostics*. (4th ed.). Bern: Verlag Hans Huber, 1942.

Rosenhan, D. L. On being sane in insane places. *Science*, 1973, *179*, 250–258.

Rosenthal, D. (ed.). *The Genain quadruplets: A case study and theoretical analysis of heredity and environment in schizophrenia*. New York: Basic Books, 1963.

Ross, L., Amabile, T., and Steinmetz, J. Social roles, social control, and biases in social-perception processes. *Journal of personality and social psychology*, 1977, *35*, 485–494.

Rotter, J. B. Generalized expectancies for internal versus external control of reinforcement. *Psychological monographs*, 1966, *80*, Whole No. 609.

Rotter, J. B., Chance, J. E., and Phares, E. J. *Applications of a social learning theory of personality*. New York: Holt, Rinehart and Winston, 1972.

Rubin, Z. Measurement of romantic love. *Journal of personality and social psychology*, 1970, *16*, 265–273.

Rubin, Z. *Liking and loving: An invitation to social psychology*. New York: Holt, Rinehart and Winston, 1973.

Rumbaugh, D. M., Gill, T. V., and Von Glasensfeld, E. Reading and sentence completion by a chimpanzee. *Science*, 1973, *182*, 731–733.

Russell, M. J. Human olfactory communication. *Nature*, 1976, *260*, 520–522.

Rycroft, C. Freud and the imagination. *New York Review of Books*, 1975, *22* (5), 26–30.

Sachs, J. S. Recognition memory for syntactic and semantic aspects of connected discourse. *Perception and psychophysics*, 1967, *2*, 441.

Salk, L. The role of the heartbeat in the relations between mother and infant. *Scientific American*, 1973, *228*, 24–29.

Sarason, S. B. *Anxiety in elementary school children*. New York: Wiley, 1960.

Sarbin, T. R. Role theory. In G. Lindzey (ed.), *Handbook of social psychology*. Vol. 1. Cambridge, Mass.: Addison-Wesley, 1954, pp. 223–258.

Sarbin, T. R., and Andersen, M. L. Role-theoretical analysis of hypnotic behavior. In J. E. Gordon (ed.), *Handbook of clinical and experimental hypnosis*. New York: Macmillan, 1967, pp. 319–324.

Sarnoff, I. Psychoanalytic theory and social attitudes. *Public opinion quarterly*, 1960, *24*, 251–279.

Sawrey, W. L., and Weisz, J. D. An experimental method of producing gastric ulcers: Role of psychological factors in the production of gastric ulcers in the rat. *Journal of comparative and physiological psychology*, 1956, *49*, 457–461.

Scarr, S., and Weinberg, R. A. IQ test performance of black children adopted by white families. *American psychologist*, 1976, *31*, 726–739.

Schacter, S. *The psychology of affiliation*. Palo Alto, Calif.: Stanford University Press, 1959.

Schacter, S. *Emotion, obesity, and crime*. New York: Academic Press, 1971a.

Schacter, S. Some extraordinary facts about obese humans and rats. *American psychologist*, 1971b, *26*, 129–144.

Schacter, S., and Singer, J. E. Cognitive, social, and physiological determinants of emotional state. *Psychological review*, 1962, *69*, 379–399.

Schafer, R., and Murphy, G. The role of autism in visual figure–ground relationship. *Journal of experimental psychology*, 1943, *32*, 335–343.

Schaie, K. W. A general model for the study of developmental problems. *Psychological bulletin*, 1965, *64*, 92–107.

Schaie, K. W. Methodological problems in descriptive developmental research on adulthood and aging. In J. R. Nesselroade and H. W. Reese (eds.), *Lifespan developmental psychology: Methodological issues*. New York: Academic Press, 1973.

Schaie, K. W. Translations in gerontology—From lab to life: Intellectual functioning. *American psychologist*, 1974, *29*, 802–807.

Schaller, G. *The year of the gorilla*. New York: Ballantine Books, 1965.

Scheerer, M., and Lyons, J. Line drawings as responses to word meanings. *Journal of personality*, 1957, *25*, 251–273.

Schiff, T. S. *Being mentally ill: A sociological theory*. Chicago: Aldine, 1966.

Schlumberg, H. C. Challenge of human service programs for psychologists. *American psychologist*, 1972, *27*, 566–573.

Schmidt, Master F. *A hangman's diary*. (Ed. A. Keller.) London: Allan, 1928.

Schonfield, D. Translations in gerontology—From lab to life: Utilizing information. *American psychologist*, 1974, *29*, 796–801.

Schrag, P., and Divoky, D. *The myth of the hyperactive child*. New York: Pantheon, 1975.

Schreiber, F. R. *Sybil*. Chicago: Regnery, 1973.

Schwartz, S. H. Awareness of interpersonal consequences, responsibility denial, and volunteering. *Journal of personality and social psychology*, 1974, *30*, 57–63.

Scott, R. B., Ferguson, A. D., Jenkins, M. E., and Cutter, F. F. Growth and development of Negro infants. Part 5: Neuromuscular patterns of behavior during the first year of life. *Pediatrics*, 1955, *16*, 24–30.

Searle, J. R. *Speech acts: An essay in the philosophy of language.* Cambridge, England: Cambridge University Press, 1969.

Searle, J. R. Chomsky's revolution in linguistics. *New York Review of Books,* June 29, 1972, pp. 16–24.

Sechehaye, M. *Autobiography of a schizophrenic girl.* New York: Grune & Stratton, 1951.

Seligman, M. E. P. Chronic fear produced by unpredictable electric shock. *Journal of comparative and physiological psychology,* 1968, *66,* 402–411.

Seligman, M. E. P. On the generality of the laws of learning. *Psychological review,* 1970, *77,* 406–418.

Seligman, M. E. P. *Helplessness—on depression, development, and death.* San Francisco: Freeman, 1975.

Seligman, M. E. P., Maier, S. F., and Geer, J. H. Alleviation of learned helplessness in the dog. *Journal of abnormal psychology,* 1968, *73,* 256–262.

Selye, H. The evolution of the stress concept. *American scientist,* 1973, *61,* 692–699.

Selye, H. *The stress of life.* (rev. ed.). New York: McGraw-Hill, 1976.

Shanas, E., Townsend, P., Wedderburn, D., Friis, H., Milhøj, P., and Stehouwer, J. *Old people in three industrial societies.* Chicago: Aldine, 1968.

Shapiro, D. *Neurotic styles.* New York: Basic Books, 1965.

Sheahan, M. Can Your baby hear? *Menninger perspective,* 1973, *4,* 11–13.

Sheldon, W. H. *Atlas of men.* New York: Harper & Row, 1954.

Sheldon, W. H., and Stevens, S. S. *The varieties of temperament.* New York: Harper & Row, 1942.

Sheldon, W. H., Stevens, S. S., and Tucker, W. B. *The varieties of human physique.* Darien, Conn.: Hafner, 1970. (Originally published 1940.)

Shepherd, M. *Fritz.* New York: Dutton, 1975.

Shepherd, M., Oppenheim, B., and Mitchell, S. *Childhood behavior and mental health.* New York: Grune & Stratton, 1971.

Sherman, J. A. *On the psychology of women: A survey of empirical studies.* Springfield, Ill.: Thomas, 1971.

Shneidman, E. S., Farberow, N. L, and Litman, R. E. *The psychology of suicide.* New York: Aronson, 1970.

Shontz, F. C. *Perceptual and cognitive aspects of body experience.* New York: Academic Press, 1969.

Siffre, N. Six months alone in a cave. *National geographic,* 1975, *147,* 426–435.

Silverman, J. Shamans and schizophrenia. *American anthropologist,* 1967, *69,* 21–32.

Simmons, L. *The role of the aged in primitive society.* New Haven, Conn.: Yale University Press, 1945.

Simpson, T. Male hair length is a doctrinal issue. *The Texas coach,* May 1973, pp. 7–8.

Sinha, D. Psychology and the problems of developing countries: A general overview. *International review of applied psychology,* 1973, *22,* 5–26.

Skinner, B. F. *The behavior of organisms.* New York: Appleton-Century-Crofts, 1938.

Skinner, B. F. *Verbal behavior.* New York: Appleton-Century-Crofts, 1957.

Skinner, B. F. *Contingencies of reinforcement: A theoretical analysis.* New York: Appleton-Century-Crofts, 1969.

Skinner, B. F. *Beyond freedom and dignity.* New York: Knopf, 1971.

Skinner, B. F. *Walden Two.* New York: Macmillan, 1976.

Slobin, D. I. Children and language: They learn the same way all around the world. *Psychology today,* 1972, *6,* 71–76.

Smirnov, A. A. *Problems of the psychology of memory.* New York: Plenum Press, 1973.

Smith, L. P. *All trivia.* New York: Harcourt Brace Jovanovich, 1945.

Smith, W. M., McCrary, J. W., and Smith, K. U. Delayed visual feedback and behavior. *Science,* 1960, *132,* 1013–1014.

Sokolov, E. N. *Perception and the conditioned reflex.* New York: Macmillan, 1963.

Sokolov, E. N., and Vinogradora, O. S. (eds.). *Neuronal mechanisms of the orienting reflex.* New York: Halsted Press, 1975.

Solomon, R. C. *The passions: The myth and nature of human emotion.* New York: Doubleday Anchor, 1976.

Sommer, R. Hawthorne dogma. *Psychological bulletin,* 1968, *70,* 592–595.

Sommer, R. *Personal space: The behavioral basis of design.* Englewood Cliffs, N.J.: Prentice-Hall, 1969.

Sommer, R. *Tight spaces: Hard architecture and how to humanize it.* Englewood Cliffs, N.J.: Prentice-Hall, 1974.

Sommer, R., and Osmond, H. Autobiographies of former mental patients. *The journal of mental science,* 1960, *106,* 648–662.

Sommer, R., and Osmond, H. Autobiographies of former mental patients, *The journal of mental science,* 1961, *107,* 1030–1032.

Spearman, C. "General intelligence" objectively determined and measured. *American journal of psychology,* 1904, *15,* 201–293.

Spearman, C. E. *The abilities of man, their nature and measurement.* New York: Macmillan, 1927.

Spielberger, C. D. (ed.). *Anxiety: Current trends in theory and research.* New York: Academic Press, 1972.

Spitz, R. Anaclitic depression. *Psychoanalytic study of the child,* 1946, *2,* 313–341.

Spitz, R. A., and Wolf, K. M. The smiling response: A contribution to the ontogenesis of social relations. *Genetic psychology monographs,* 1946, *34,* 57–125.

Spong, P., Haider, M., and Lindsley, D. R. Selective attentiveness and cortical evoked responses to visual and auditory stimuli. *Science,* 1965, *148,* 395–397.

Stack, C. B. *All our kin: Strategies for survival in a black community.* New York: Harper & Row, 1974.

Stevens, S. S. The surprising simplicity of sensory metrics. *American psychologist*, 1962, *17*, 29–39.

Stewart, K. Mental hygiene and world peace. *Mental hygiene*, 1954, *38*, 387–403.

Stewart, K. Dream theory in Malaya. In C. T. Tart (ed.), *Altered states of consciousness*. New York: Wiley, 1969, pp. 159–167.

Stoyva, J., and Kamiya, J. Electrophysiological studies of dreaming as the prototype of a new strategy in the study of consciousness. In J. Kamiya and others (eds.), *Biofeedback and self-control*. Chicago: Aldine, 1971, pp. 775–788.

Straus, E. W. On obsession: A clinical and methodological study. *Nervous and mental disease monographs*, No. 73, 1948.

Straus, E. W. Rheoscopic studies of expression. Methodology of approach. *American journal of psychiatry*, 1951, *168*, 439–443.

Straus, E. W. On memory traces. *Tijdschrift voor philosophie*, 1962, *24*, 1–32.

Stromeyer, C. F. Eidetikers. *Psychology today*, 1970, *4*, 76–80.

Stromeyer, C. F., and Psotka, J. The detailed texture of eidetic images. *Nature*, 1970, *225*, 346–349.

Suppes, P. The semantics of children's language. *American psychologist*, 1974, *29*, 103–114.

Szafran, J. Psychophysiological studies of aging in pilots. In G. A. Talland (ed.), *Human aging and behavior*. New York: Academic Press, 1968.

Szasz, T. *The myth of mental illness*. New York: Hoeber, 1961.

Tart, C. T. (ed.). *Altered states of consciousness*. New York: Wiley, 1969.

Tart, C. T. Waking from sleep at a preselected time. *Journal of the American Society of Psychosomatic Dentistry and Medicine*, 1970, *17*, 3–16.

Tasch, R. J. The role of the father in the family. *Journal of experimental education*, 1952, *20*, 319–361.

Taylor, J. A. A personality scale of manifest anxiety. *Journal of abnormal and social psychology*, 1953, *48*, 285–290.

Temerlin, M. K. Diagnostic bias in community mental health. *Community mental health journal*, 1970, *6*, 110–117.

Terman, L. M., Baldwin, B. T., and Bronson, E. *Genetic studies of genius*. Vol. 1: *Mental and physical traits of a thousand gifted children*. Palo Alto, Calif.: Stanford University Press, 1925.

Thigpen, C. H., and Cleckley, H. A. *The three faces of Eve*. New York: McGraw-Hill, 1957.

Thomas, A., and Chess, S. *Temperament and development*. New York: Brunner/Mazel, 1977.

Thomas, A., Chess, S., and Birch, H. G. *Temperament and behavior disorders in children*. New York: New York University Press, 1968.

Thomas, A., Chess, S., and Birch, H. G. The origin of personality. In R. C. Atkinson (ed.), *Contemporary psychology: Readings from* Scientific American. San Francisco: Freeman, 1970.

Thompson, C. *Psychoanalysis: Evolution and development*. New York: Hermitage House, 1950.

Thompson, C. W., and Margaret, A. Differential test responses of normals and mental defectives. *Journal of abnormal and social psychology*, 1947, *42*, 285–293.

Thorndike, E. L. *Animal intelligence*. New York: Macmillan, 1898.

Thurber, J. Interview with a lemming. In J. Thurber, *My world—and welcome to it*. New York: Harcourt Brace Jovanovich, 1942, pp. 82–84.

Thurber, J. Spreading "you know." *New Yorker*, 1960, *36*, 23.

Thurstone, L. L. *Primary mental abilities*. Chicago: University of Chicago Press, 1938.

Tinbergen, N. *The study of instinct*. Oxford, England: Clarendon Press, 1951.

Tinbergen, N. The evolution of behavior in gulls. *Scientific American*, 1960, *203*, 118–130.

Tolman, E. C. Cognitive maps in rats and men. *Psychological review*, 1948, *55*, 189–208.

Treisman, A. M. Monitoring and storing of irrelevant messages in selective attention. *Journal of verbal learning and verbal behavior*, 1964, *3*, 449–459.

Treisman, A. M. Strategies and models of selective attention. *Psychological review*, 1969, *76*, 282–299.

Troll, L. E. The family of later life: A decade review. *Journal of marriage and the family*, 1971, *33*, 263–290.

Tucker, D. The superhuman Soviet. *San Francisco Examiner*, May 30, 1976, Travel Section, p. 1.

Tuddenham, R. D., and McBride, P. D. The yielding experiment from the subject's point of view. *Journal of personality*, 1959, *27*, 259–271.

Tulving, E., and Thomson, D. M. Encoding specificity and retrieval processes in episodic memory. *Psychological review*, 1973, *80*, 352–373.

Underwood, B. J. Interference and forgetting. *Psychological review*, 1957, *64*, 49–60.

Van de Castle, R. L. *The psychology of dreaming*. Morristown, N.J.: General Learning Press, 1971.

Van den Berg, J. H. *Divided existence and complex society*. Pittsburgh: Duquesne University Press, 1974.

Veith, I. (trans.). *The yellow emperor's classic of internal medicine*. Berkeley: University of California Press, 1949.

Vernon, P. E. Recent attacks on the concept of intelligence. *International review of applied psychology*, 1975, *24*, 93–97.

Vingoe, F. J. Comparison of the Harvard Group Scale of hypnotic susceptibility, Form A, and the group alert trance scale in a university population. *International journal of clinical and experimental hypnosis*, 1973, *21*, 169–178.

Von Békésy, G. *Experiments in hearing*. New York: McGraw-Hill, 1960.

Von Frisch, K. *The dancing bees.* London: Methuen, 1954.

Vonnegut, M. *The Eden express.* New York: Praeger, 1975.

Von Senden, M. *Space and sight.* New York: Free Press, 1960.

Wade, N. IQ and heredity—Suspicion of fraud beclouds classic experiments. *Science,* 1976, *194,* 916–919.

Wald, G. The receptors of human color vision. *Science,* 1964, *145,* 1007–1017.

Walk, R. D. Monocular compared to binocular depth perception in human infants. *Science,* 1968, *162,* 473–475.

Walk, R. D., and Gibson, E. J. A comparative and analytical study of visual depth perception. *Psychological monographs,* 1961, *75,* Whole No. 519.

Ware, J. E., Jr., and Williams, R. G. The Dr. Fox effect: A study of lecturer effectiveness and ratings of instruction. *Journal of medical education,* 1975, *50,* 149–156.

Watson, D., and Friend, R. Measurement of social-evaluative anxiety. *Journal of consulting and clinical psychology,* 1969, *33,* 448–457.

Watson, D. J. *The double helix: A personal account of the discovery of the structure of DNA.* New York: Atheneum, 1968.

Weakland, J. H. The double-bind hypothesis of schizophrenia and three-party interaction. In D. D. Jackson (ed.), *The etiology of schizophrenia.* New York: Basic Books, 1960.

Webb, W. B., and Agnew, H. W. *Sleep and dreams.* Dubuque, Iowa: Brown, 1973.

Wechsler, D. *Manual for the Wechsler Adult Intelligence Scale.* New York: Psychological Corporation, 1955.

Weil, A. *The natural mind: A new way of looking at drugs and the higher consciousness.* Boston: Houghton Mifflin, 1973.

Weisman, A. *On dying and denying.* New York: Behavioral Publications, 1972.

Welford, A. T. Psychomotor performance. In J. E. Birren (ed.), *Handbook of aging and the individual.* Chicago: University of Chicago Press, 1959.

Wenger, M. A., and Bagchi, B. K. Studies of autonomic functions in practitioners of yoga in India. *Behavioral science,* 1961, *6,* 312–323.

Wenger, M. A., Bagchi, B. K., and Anand, D. Experiments in India on "voluntary" control of the heart and pulse. *Circulation,* 1961, *24,* 1319–1325.

Went, F. W. The size of man. *American scientist,* 1968, *56,* 400–413.

Wever, E. G., and Bray, C. W. The nature of acoustic response: The relation between sound frequency and frequency of impulses in the auditory nerve. *Journal of experimental psychology,* 1930, *13,* 373–387.

Whalen, C., and Henker, B. Psychostimulants and children: A review and analysis. *Psychological bulletin,* 1976, *83,* 1113–1130.

White, R. K., and Lippitt, R. O. *Autocracy and democracy.* New York: Harper & Row, 1950.

White, R. W. Motivation reconsidered: the concept of competence. *Psychological review,* 1959, *66,* 297–333.

Wiener, G. Psychologic correlates of premature birth: A review. *Journal of nervous and mental disease,* 1962, *134,* 129–144.

Wilde, O. *The picture of Dorian Gray.* London: Oxford University Press, 1974.

Wilkinson, R. *The broken rebel: A study in culture, politics, and authoritarian character.* New York: Harper & Row, 1972.

Williams, M[argery]. *The velveteen rabbit, or How toys become real.* New York: Avon, 1975.

Williams, M[oyra]. *Horse psychology.* (rev. ed.). London: Allen, 1976.

Wilner, D. M., Walkley, R. P., and Cook, S. W. Residential proximity and intergroup relations in public housing projects. *Journal of social issues,* 1952, *8,* 45–69.

Winick, C. E. *The new people: Desexualization in American life.* New York: Pegasus, 1968.

Wittreich, W. J. The Honi phenomenon: A case of selective perceptual distortion. *Journal of abnormal and social psychology,* 1952, *47,* 705–712.

Wohlwill, J. F. The age variable in psychological research. *Psychological review,* 1970, *77,* 49–64.

Wolf, T. H. Alfred Binet: A time of crisis. *American psychologist,* 1964, *19,* 762–771.

Wolfensberger, W., Nirje, B., Olshansky, S., Perske, R., and Roos, P. *The principles of normalization in human services.* Toronto: National Institute of Mental Retardation, 1972.

Wolff, P. H. The serial organization of sucking in the young infant. *Pediatrics,* 1968, *42,* 943–956.

Wolff, W. *The expression of personality.* New York: Harper & Row, 1943.

Wolpe, J. *The practice of behavior therapy.* New York: Pergamon Press, 1969.

Wolpe, J. The behavioristic conception of neurosis: A reply to two critics. *Psychological review,* 1971, *78,* 341–343.

Wooldridge, D. E. *The machinery of the brain.* New York: McGraw-Hill, 1963.

Wyrwricka, W., and Dobrzecka, C. Relationship between feeding and satiation centers of the hypothalamus. *Science,* 1960, *132,* 805–806.

Yaker, H., Osmond, H., and Cheek, F. *The future of time.* New York: Doubleday Anchor, 1972.

Zajonc, R. B. Social facilitation. *Science,* 1965, *149,* 269–274.

Zajonc, R. B. Attitudinal effects of mere exposure. *Journal of personality and social psychology* (Monograph Supplement), 1968, *9,* No. 2.

Zajonc, R. B. *Animal social behavior*. Morristown, N.J.: General Learning Press, 1972.

Zeigler, H. P. Oral satisfaction and obesity: The sensual feel of food. *Psychology today*, 1975, *9*, 62–66.

Zillig, M. Einstellung und Aussage. *Zeitschrift für Psychologie*, 1928, *106*, 58–106.

Zimiles, H., and Konstadt, N. Orthography and authority: A study of cognitive interaction. *Psychological reports*, 1962, *10*, 623–626.

Zuckerman, E. You talkin' to me? Teaching apes to speak their mind. *Rolling stone*, June 16, 1977, No. 241, pp. 45–51.

Zung, W. K., and Wilson, W. T. Response to auditory stiumulation during sleep. *Archives of general psychiatry*, 1961, *4*, 548–552.

Credits

Message: Fig. 2, Washington Star Syndicate. Fig. 4, from S. M. Jourard, *The Transparent Self* (revised edition), New York, D. Van Nostrand Company, 1971, by permission. Fig. 1.3, Roger Dean. Fig. 1.4, Figure 3, J. Garcia, J. C. Clarke, and W. G. Hankins, "Natural Responses to Scheduled Rewards," from P. P. G. Bateson and P. H. Klopfer, *Perspectives in Ethology* (New York: Plenum Press, 1973). Fig. 1.5, Peter N. Witt. Fig. 1.6, from Daniel S. Lehrman, "The Reproductive Behavior of Ring Doves," Copyright © 1964 by Scientific American, Inc. All rights reserved. Fig. 1.7, from *Sex Research: New Developments*, edited by John Money. Copyright © 1965 by Holt, Rinehart and Winston, Inc. Reprinted by permission of Holt, Rinehart and Winston. Fig. 1.8, Frank A. Beach, "Locks and Beagles," *American Psychologist*, 1969, *24*, 977 (fig. 5). Copyright 1969 by the American Psychological Association. Reprinted by permission. Fig. 1.9, Susan Lohwasser.

Chapter 2: Fig. 2.1, Jules Feiffer. Fig. 2.2, University of California Press. Fig. 2.3, International News Photo (UPI). Fig. 2.7, Walter Chandoha; Susan Lohwasser. Fig. 2.9, The Metropolitan Museum of Art, Gift of Thomas Ryan, 1910.

Chapter 3: Fig. 3.1, NASA. Fig. 3.2, Susan Lohwasser. Fig. 3.3, Compix, United Press International. Fig. 3.4, Harry F. Harlow, "The Nature of Love," *American Psychologist*, 1958, *13*, 676–678 (fig. 6). Copyright 1958 by the American Psychological Association. Reprinted by permission. Fig. 3.6, *Punch* Magazine and Toronto Sun Syndicate. Fig. 3.7, Susan Lohwasser.

Chapter 4: Fig. 4.4, R. Valentine Atkinson; Galen A. Rowell. Fig. 4.8, Susan Lohwasser. Fig. 4.9, Stanley Schachter, "Some Extraordinary Facts About Obese Humans and Rats," *American Psychologist*, 1971, *26*, 135 (table 5). Copyright 1971 by the American Psychological Association. Reprinted by permission.

514

Glossary and subject index

Children (continued)
self-concepts of, 5–6
self-consciousness of, 6
self-esteem of, 9
sex differences in, 45
sexual identity and, 470, 472
sexuality in, 476
testing of, 227
time experience in, 214
wanting in, 119
See also Development
Chimpanzees:
communication in, 292–96
self-concepts and, 5–6
"Chromosomal error," 18–19
Chromosome, 16, 18, 26–27. The chainlike structures found in all body cells, that carry the genes, which are the genetic determiners that are transmitted from parent to child.
Chronological age (CA), 265
Circadian rhythm, 221. A recurring biological rhythm of events that is approximately twenty-four hours long.
Circulatory system:
aging and, 336
competition and, 121–22
Classical conditioning, 153, 156, 158. Learning in which a stimulus paired with a desired or meaningful stimulus becomes a substitution for the meaningful stimulus itself. Pavlov, the originator of the concept, paired the sound of a bell with food, and his dogs learned to respond by salivating to just the bell ringing.
Classical genetics, 18
Classroom seating patterns, 459
Client-centered therapy, 413–16. A form of humanistic, nondirective therapy developed by Rogers and based on the theory that people can work out their problems in a supportive atmosphere.
Cliques, 248
Clock time, 214, 216, 217
Clothing, national character, 310
Cluster analysis, 308
Cochlea, 59. The coiled, shell-shaped bone cavity of the inner ear containing the hearing receptors.
"Cocktail party phenomenon," 130. The phenomenon by which one registers stimuli to which one is not directly attending until something makes it important to notice the stimulus.
Cognition:
abnormalities in, 369
emotions and, 102
learning and, 160–66

Cognition (continued)
in NREM sleep, 201
Cognitive ability, 232
Cognitive approach to learning theory, 161
Cognitive balance, 124–25
Cognitive "conditions," 305–06
Cognitive development, 248
Cognitive dissonance, 124–25. Festinger's principle that when an individual has beliefs or actions that conflict or disagree with one another, a state of tension is present. One therefore acts to reduce this dissonance through changes in thought or behavior.
Cognitive elements, learning and, 163
Cognitive learning, 188–90
"Cognitive maps," 163–64
Cognitive psychology, 484
Cognitive-situation theory, 305–06
Cohesion, 51–52. Hanging together in some way or being mutually attractive. The term is used in reference to social groups, learning theory, and perceptual phenomena.
Cohort, 330. In developmental studies, a group whose members are similar in some measurable way.
Cohort effect, 330–332
Colitis, 371
Collective unconscious, 316. Jung's concept of the universal unconscious that is the "pool" from which all people draw.
Color blindness, 26, 229
Color perception, 135, 142
Commitment, to mental hospitals, 388–89
Common sense, psychology of, 435
Communes, child rearing in, 245
Communication, 280–301, 443–44, 459, 485
Communications media, 436–37
Communication skills, 242–43, 248
Community health clinics, 381
Comparison:
as a motive, 121
social, 432–33
Competence, 118. The ability or skill that enables one to interact effectively with one's environment.
Competition, 121–22, 430–31
Competitive sports, 121
Complexity, of patterns, 141
Compliance, 443
Compulsive, obsessive-, character, 375
Concentration camps, 447, 462–63
Concrete operations, 236, 248. Piaget's third stage of

Concrete operations (continued)
cognitive development (from seven to eleven years) in which the child develops a cognitive system that organizes the events of the external world into a logical structure.
Conditioned response. *See* CR
Conditioned suppression, 159
Conditioning, 149–57
Conditioning:
aging and, 338
in psychotherapy, 417
social, 110
Cone, 62. Photosensitive receptors found in the retina of the eye, predominantly around the fovea. They are responsible for both chromatic (color) and achromatic (without color) vision.
Conflicts:
cognitive, 124–25
of motives, 116
Confluence, 424
Conforming personality, 447–50
Conformist level, moral development, 251
Conformity, 450–52. Behaving according to social norms; being influenced by group pressure.
Confusion, role, 327
Connotative meaning, 297–98. The meaning beyond the denotative meaning; the emotional meaning of a symbol or concept.
Conscientious level, moral development, 251
Consciousness, 192–224
altered states of, 192–211, 313, 421
research in, 481
Conservation, 248. Piaget's term for the ability of the child to distinguish that the amount of a substance is not changed—that it is conserved—even when it is placed in a different container or setting that makes it appear different.
Consistency:
as a motive, 123–25
of personality, 302–11, 317, 321–22
Consumer motivation, 119–20
Contact-comfort motivational system, 70
Contact system, 52–54
See also Touch system
Context:
language development and, 290–91
memory traces and, 185
perception and, 142
Contextualist theory of memory, 188
Contiguity, 158–60. The occurrence of stimulus-

Contiguity (continued)
response elements close together in time in order for the learning process to be facilitated.
Contraception, 475
Control group, 366. The group, in an experiment, which is similar in all respects to the experimental group except that it is not exposed to the independent variable that is being studied.
Conversion hysteria, 370. A neurotic reaction in which psychological conflict is converted to bodily symptoms. The person then shows illnesses that have no physical basis.
Convulsions, 42
Coronary heart disease, 121–22
Cortex, 55. Also called *gray matter* of the brain. A rind of tissue consisting of neurons and connectors covering the cerebrum. It is thought to be active in conscious experiences and higher mental processes.
attention and, 130
hemispheres of, 157
memory storage and, 184
vision and, 63
Cortical evoked response, or *cortical evoked potential*, 130. The term for neural impulses that have been evoked by a stimulus and are then recorded as electrical potential in the brain.
Counseling, 10
Countertransference, 409. A reversal of transference; a process whereby the therapist develops personal feelings about the client derived from the analyst's own earlier life experiences.
CR (conditioned response), 149, 150, 152, 154
Crawling, 239
Creativity, 328
perception and, 131
repression and, 193
social facilitation and, 432
work and, 119
Criminals, 18, 380
Crises, life, 327–28, 329
Criterion, 8. The level of performance at which learning is defined as being completed for a certain task.
"Critical alternatives," 327
Cropmilk, ring doves', 25–26
Cross-sectional study, 330. A research method in the study of the continuity of behavior in which behavior characteristics are sampled at different ages.
Cross-sequential study, 332. A method of developmental

Housing projects, 442
Humanistic psychology, 72, 122, 411. A contemporary branch of psychology in which Maslow and others accent the positive features of humans. Maslow's psychology takes human life as it is, with all its potentials and aspirations toward personal growth and self-actualization.
Human service networks, 381
Hunger:
    as a drive, 65, 67–69, 73–74, 110, 125
    obesity and, 79–80
    as wanting, 76–77, 82
Hunger pains, 69
Hurtfulness, 455–56
Hydrocephalus, 268. An excess of fluid in the brain, causing enlargement of the head and wasting away of the brain.
Hydrocortisone, 349
Hyperactivity, 112, 217, 249, 377–78, 379. Also hyperkinesis. Intense, restless activity in children, accompanied often by an inability to concentrate or complete a task.
Hyperkinesis, 249, 377–78, 379
Hypnosis, 194, 195, 206–09, 377
Hypnosis:
    altered consciousness and, 193
    as an anesthetic, 89
    in psychotherapy, 406–07
Hypnotizability scale, 208
Hypochondriasis, 412. A neurosis in which an individual is excessively concerned with physical wellbeing.
Hypothalamus, 43, 69, 88. A region of the forebrain that plays an important role for regulation of temperature, thirst, sex, sleep, hunger, emotion, and endocrine gland functions.
Hypothalamus:
    aging and, 334
    emotional arousal and, 97, 98
    pain and, 97
Hysteria, 407. A form of neurosis in which mental conflicts have been converted into physical symptoms such as paralysis or tics.
Hysterical character, 375
Hysterical neurosis, 369. A psychological disorder characterized by physical symptoms (such as paralysis) or loss of sensory functions (such as amnesia).

Id, 313. In Freud's theory of personality, the reservoir of impulses that seek immediate gratification of primitive needs.

Identical twins, 275–77, 391
Identification (in development), 245–46. The process of learning social roles in childhood by copying or imitating the behavior of others, particularly adults.
Identification (in Freudian theory), 314, 443. A defense mechanism that involves taking on the characteristics of an admired person.
Identity, 327. *See also* Self; Sexual identity
Ignorance, pluralistic, 432
Iliad (Homer), 216
Illness:
    psychosis as, 398–404
    work and, 342
Illumination:
    and efficiency, 112–13
    intensity of, 62–63
Images:
    development of, 240
    in Jung's personality theory, 315–17
    projected, 143–44
Imitation, 238–39, 245
Immortality, attitudes toward, 357–58
Immune system, 334–35
Impasse, 423. Difficulty without a solution, or a situation from which there is no escape. Perls' term for the "stuck point" in therapy.
Impatience, 214
Implicit set, 196. The beliefs and attitudes with which a subject enters in an experiment or new project.
Implosive layer, 423
Impression management, 396. A social skill (studied in hospitalized mental patients) enabling one to influence how one is perceived by others.
Imprinting, 24, 291. Relatively fixed learning that occurs within a critical period of development in response to a stimulus and is later difficult to modify.
Impulse abnormalities, 370–71
Impulsive level of moral development, 251
Inappropriate behavior, 305
Incentive theory, 73. A theory of motivation that stresses the importance of rewards or threats in determining behavior. It is opposed to the theory that internal drives instigate activity.
Incest taboo, 30
Income:
    discretionary, 120
    experience and, 271
Independence, 241, 424, 425
Individual differences, 255–79, 480

Individuality. *See* Self
Individual psychology, 411. Adler's school of psychoanalytic thought and therapy.
Induced states of consciousness, 205–10
Industrialized nations, n Ach and, 115
Industry vs. inferiority, 327
Infancy, repertoire of cries in, 290
Infant development, 228–35
Infantile amnesia, 189–90. The normal forgetting of early child experiences, particularly of the first three years of life.
Infant-mother relations, 234–35
Infection, resistance to, 229
Inferiority, vs. industry, 327
Influence, 296
Information approach to motivation, 74–75
Information explosion, 1
Information processing:
    aging and, 334, 335
    attitudes and, 440
    by central nervous system, 42
    conditioning and, 158, 159–60
    drives and, 65
    in groups, 459
    by infants, 233
    memory traces and, 186
    through perception, 129–31
    personality and, 317
    sensory, 87
    vision and, 60–62
Information processing theory of memory, 188
Inhalation, 40
Inheritance, 15–31, 480. *See also* Heredity
Inhibitions, to learning 175–76
Initiation rites, 204
Initiative, 327
Inner ear, 59
Insanity, 384. *See also* Psychoses
Inside view, 4
    learning and, 161
    of motivation, 76, 125
    of personality consistency, 321–23
    recognition and, 173
    self-concept and, 5–6, 8–9
    of sleep, 197
    to social facilitation, 431, 434
    of time experience, 215
Instinct, 21. A complex, inborn pattern of behavior that is supposed to be unlearned and common to all members within a species.
Instrumental behavior, 68. Often referred to as *operant behavior*. Behavior that generally accomplishes a purpose, such as the satisfaction of a need.
Instrumental conditioning, 151–56
Integration, 442
Integrity vs. despair, 328

Intellectualization; or isolation, 314. A defense mechanism in which one detaches oneself from an emotionally threatening situation by handling it in abstract or intellectual terms.
Intelligence:
    aging and, 262–63, 338
    development of, 330
    environment and, 273, 275–77
    genetic factors in, 18, 264, 272, 273–78
    "practical," 236
    testing of, 261–78, 332–33
Intelligence quotient (IQ), 265. A measurement of intelligence obtained by dividing the person's mental age (determined by a standardized test) by the chronological age and multiplying by 100. An IQ of 100, is by definition average.
Intelligence tests, 261–78, 332–33
Interference theory, 175, 181. In learning, the theory that forgetting is caused by interference from other material.
Internal clock, 220–21. The hypothetical mechanism that regulates cyclic variations in the body's physiological systems.
Internalization, 443
Internal models, 238, 240
International Social Science Council, 310
Interpersonal attraction, 436–39
Interpersonal relations, 449–50
Interpretation, 412. In psychoanalysis, the analyst making the patient aware of resistances, as well as explaining symbolism.
Interpretation of Dreams, The (Freud), 204
Intimacy vs. isolation, 328
Intoxication, and, memory, 188
Intractable pain, 87. Pain that is difficult to treat or alleviate.
Intraversion, 317. The psychological type Jung classified as inward and withdrawn.
Intrinsic motivation, 117, 125. A type of personal motivation based on behaving for the sake of doing rather than for an external reward to be gained.
Introjection, 424
Inventions, dreams and, 203
Involuntary hospitalization, 388–89
Involuntary vs. voluntary behavior, 156–57
Inward turning, 339, 340
Irregular verbs, 289

Isolation, 113, 193, 232
  in monkeys, 234–35
  peer presence and, 430
  suicide and, 354
  See also Intellectualization

James-Lange theory, 102–03
"Jet lag " 220–21
Jews:
  attitudes towards, 442
  killing of, 447
Jokes, 313
Joy, 94
Judgment, 132

Kansas City study of
    personality, 340
Kibbutz, 245. A collective farm
    community in Israel.
Kinesthetic perception, 142–43.
    Sensing or perceiving one's
    own muscles.
Kinsey reports, 346
Knowledge, "perfect," 287
Korsakoff's syndrome, 178. A
    chronic brain syndrome
    characterized by severe
    disorientation, confusion,
    and loss of immediate
    memory. It is found in some
    cases of chronic alcoholism.

Laboratory animals. *See* entries
    for individual animals
Laboratory learning, 149–69
Laissez-faire leadership, 449, 459
Language, 283–301
Language:
  architecture and, 311
  development of, 243–44
  pacing of, 219
"Language culture," 295
Late bloomers, 344–45
Latency period, 34, 247, 315. A
    psychoanalytic term used to
    refer to the middle
    childhood years
    (approximately six to twelve
    years old), a period during
    which some sexual and
    aggressive impulses are
    subdued, and the child
    reaches out to the
    environment.
Laughing, 85–86
Law of effect, 151. Thorndike's
    principle that the outcome
    of an activity will determine
    whether it is learned or
    repeated. He postulated that
    reward would tend to
    increase learning and
    discomfort would tend to
    inhibit learning.
Layers of neurotic personality,
    423
Leadership, 460–61
Leaderless groups, 456
Learned helplessness, 104, 161,
    376. A feeling of
    helplessness an organism
    has, because of prior

Learned helplessness (continued)
    experiences, when it realizes
    that it cannot change a
    situation to avoid hurt. It is
    often manifested as
    depression in humans.
Learning, 148–66
  aging and, 338
  anxiety and, 104
  body vs. cognitive, 189–90
  expectations and, 161–63, 165
  forgetting and, 175–76
  of habits, 148
  inhibitions to, 175–76
  intoxication and, 188
  memory and, 173–74, 189
  modeling and, 165–66
  motivation and, 75, 76
  perception and, 133–35
  of secondary motives, 110
  sex differences in, 237
  social facilitation and, 431, 432
  of speech, 286–92
  survival, 291–92
Learning theory, 156, 158, 417
  cognitive approach to, 161
  psychosis and, 395
  See also Social learning theory
Left-handedness, 44
Leisure, 342
Lens, 335
Leptosome, 257. Kretschmer's
    term for a slim body build.
    In his view, people with this
    build are often intraverted,
    tend to daydream, and lack
    rapport with their
    environment.
Level of aspiration, 117. The level
    at which an individual sets
    goals.
Library seating patterns, 459
Life crises, 327–28, 339
Life span, 325–47
Liked/disliked girls experiment,
    132
Liking, 437–39
Liking Scale, 438–39
Line drawings, perception of, 141
Linguistics, 280, 286
Listening, dichotic, 130
Literate vs. preliterate cultures,
    396–97
"Little words," 288
Locus of control, 163. Rotter's
    term for where the
    individual places causation
    and life consequences.
    Persons with an *internal
    locus* see causation as part of
    their own destiny. Persons
    with an *external locus* are
    more apt to look outside of
    themselves for causation.
Longitudinal study, 329–30, 331.
    A research method in the
    study of development in
    which a person's behavior is
    observed over a long period
    of time.
Long-term memory (LTM), 178–
    79. The component of the

Long-term memory (continued)
    memory's storage system
    characterized by its relative
    permanence.
Loops, behavioral, 429
Loving Scale, 438–39
LSD-25, 21, 358
LTM (long-term memory), 178–
    79
Lucy, the chimpanzee, 296
Lung capacity, 229
Lying, 7, 284

MA (mental age), 262, 264–65
Madness, 384. *See also* Psychoses
Mainstreaming, 269
Malaria, 220
Manic-depressive, 257, 387, 397.
    A psychotic reaction
    described by mood swings,
    from excessive elation and
    euphoria in the manic state,
    to severe depression and
    despondency in the
    depressive state.
Mantras, 209–10
Mapping:
  brain, 88
  cognitive, 163–64
  gene, 27
Marijuana, 206
Marxist critique of psychological
    theory, 402
Masculinity, 246, 250
Masochism, 371, 373. The sexual
    gratification a person
    receives from pain, whether
    self-inflicted or inflicted by
    another person.
Mass action, 184
Massage, 410
Masturbation, 371, 473
Maternal deprivation, 53–54
Mating, 30–31, 468
  behavioral loops and, 429
  communication and, 281
Matrix, person behavior, 462
Maturation, 231, 251–52, 326,
    424. The completion,
    through heredity and
    environment, of
    developmental growth
    processes in the body. Also,
    the actual growing process.
Maturational view of language,
    287–88, 291
MBD (minimal brain
    dysfunction), 377
Mean, 260. The arithmetic
    average, found by dividing
    the sum of a group of scores
    by the number of items.
Meaning:
  creation and, 127–47
  need for, 111
  as secondary motivation, 121–
    25
Measurement, of individual
    differences, 255–59
Media, and attitude study, 436–
    37

Medical model, for psychoses,
    398–404, 416
Meditation, 92, 194, 210, 410. A
    process of conscious
    concentration on
    something—object, idea, or
    feeling—for an extended
    period of time. The goal is
    often to achieve an altered
    state of consciousness.
Megavitamin therapy, 392
Membership groups, 457
Memory, 168–91
Memory chunks, 179
Memory loss, 336
"Memory systems," 179–81
Memory trace, 173, 174–76, 185–
    87, 290–91. *See also* Engram.
    A physical representation of
    memory on tissue in the
    brain. Also called *engram*.
Men:
  n Ach and, 116
  self-disclosure and, 7
Mendelian (classical) genetics, 18
Menstrual blues, 101–02
Menstruation, 44, 101, 221
Mental abilities, primary, 261
Mental age (MA), 262, 264–65. A
    score developed by Binet and
    Simon for intelligence
    testing. If the test is
    representative of, and
    standardized to, a certain age
    group, children of a certain
    age should have the same
    mental age.
"Mental defectives," 272
Mental Deficiency Act (England),
    268
Mental energy, 261
Mental hospitals, 385–87, 388–
    90, 399–400, 402–03
Mental illness, 385–87, 388–90,
    398–401. *See also* Neuroses;
    Psychoses
Mental retardation, 268–69, 270
Mental retardation:
  anxiety and, 368
  genotype and, 18
Mesomorph, 311
Mesomorphy, 257. Sheldon's
    classification of an athletic
    body type, marked by a
    prominent bone and muscle
    structure.
Messages:
  in context, 285
  subordination of, 130–31
Metabolism, 35. The continual
    physical and chemical
    processes going on within a
    living organism. Some of
    these processes build up food
    into protoplasm, and some
    break down protoplasm into
    simpler units and waste,
    releasing energy.
Metaneed, 110. Maslow's needs,
    beyond the basic ones, that
    he believes must be filled if
    one is to become a

Operant conditioning, 152, 156. *See also* Instrumental conditioning. A type of behavior conditioning in which a subject learns to make a particular response in order to secure positive reinforcement or avoid negative reinforcement.

Operant therapy, 416, 417. A form of behavioral therapy in which the therapist tries to eliminate the elements in the client's background and environment that are causing the problem and also to provide positive reward for learning appropriate behavior.

Opiate, 392. Opium and its derivatives, morphine, heroin, and codeine. More generally, a sedative drug.

Oral stage, 34, 240, 247, 313–14

Oral stance, 80–81

Orderliness, neurotic, 369

Organic psychosis, 387–88. A severe mental disorder caused by some physiological problem, such as disease, drugs, or injury.

Organization of perception, 140–44

Orgasm, 87, 471, 474, 476–77

Orienting reaction, 98, 129. The physiological reaction that allows an organism to pay attention to a novel stimulus. It includes changes in viscera, muscles, and brain waves, increasing the organism's sensitivity and preparing it for action.

Orientation, 74–75. Attention focused on something in the environment.

Orgone energy, 420. Reich's term for the cosmic force that underlies all matter and energy in the universe.

Outer ear, 58

Outside view 3, 4
self-concepts and, 6
self-reports and, 8–9
of sleep, 197
social facilitation and, 434
of time experience, 215

Ova, 15

Oval window, 58–59. The oval opening between the middle and inner ear through which sound vibrations pass.

Ovariectomy, 29

Ovaries, 28, 69

Overcontrol, 327

Overcrowding, 430

Overeating, 78–81

Overlearning, 179, 188, 335. A method of improving memory that involves extra practice after the basic mastery is completed.

Oysters, shell-opening rhythms of, 221

Pacing, 218–19, 339

Pain, 86–94
hypnosis and, 207–08
hypothalamus and, 97
voluntary control of, 209

"Paradoxical sleep," 200

Paralysis, 37

Paranoid character, 375

Paranormal phenomena, 485

Parasympathetic nervous system, 43. A subdivision of the autonomic nervous system that is active in the restful state of the organism. It is primarily concerned with the recuperative, restorative, and nutritive functions of the body.

Parenting, and sex differences, 234

Partial reinforcement, 153, 162

Past tense, 289–90

Peak experience, 122–23. Maslow's term for a rare moment of self-actualization. This experience is one of happiness and fulfillment characterized by a state of being in which the individual feels at one with the world.

Pecking behavior, 134, 143

Peer presence, 430–31

Peer socialization, 244

Penguins, Antarctic, 24

Penis, 28, 470

Perception, 127–47
attitudes and, 444–45
development of, 235–36
selective, 282
vs. sensing, 47
sexuality and, 469

"Perfect knowledge," 287

Persona, 317. Jung's term for the mask of social conformity each person wears.

Personal control, 163

Personal freedom, 111, 345

Personal fulfillment, 328

Personal history, 194, 325–47

Personality, 302–24
attitudes and, 440
authoritarian, 448
breathing and, 40
conforming, 447–50
conformity and, 451
dreams and, 204–05
multiple, 10, 376–77
neurotic, 369
sexual identity and, 472
time sense and, 213
See also Character; Self

Personality problems, 411–12

Personality styles, 340

Personality tests, 303, 306–11, 318–21, 332

Personality theories, 411
Freud's, 204, 312–15
Jung's, 315–17
person-centered, 311, 317
Rogers', 9–10

Personality trait, 308–11. A fairly constant and measurable characteristic of a personality that gives the person's acts his or her own "color."

Personal responsibility, 454

Personal space, 238, 246, 459. The term for the physical proximity people will allow others before feeling uncomfortable or stressed. It varies from place to place and from situation to situation.

Personal time, 213

Person-behavior matrix, 462

Person-centered approach to personality, 311, 317

Persuasion, 442–44

Phallic stage, 34, 247, 315

Phasic (activity), 203. A sleeping condition in which phases of marked autonomic activity occur.

Phenotype, 16, 17, 19. In genetics, the observable characteristics of an organism, such as hair color or intelligence. It is distinct from the *genotype*, which is not displayed.

Phi phenomenon, 144. The apparent movement of light from one place to another when, in fact, two stationary lights are being flashed on and off in succession.

Phobia, 373, 416. An exaggerated and unrealistic fear of something.

Phoneme, 287. The smallest and most basic unit of sound in a given language.

Physical contact, responses to, 48

Pictures, perceiving, 243. *See also* Line drawing

Pili, the chimpanzee, 294

Pituitary gland, 28, 97. An endocrine gland located beneath the hypothalamus that secretes hormones that control growth and activates other endocrine glands.

Placebo, 208. An inactive substance substituted for a drug and given to the subjects of a control group in an experiment.

Plants, gravity system of, 51

Pleasure, 86–94
developmental stages, 241
hypothalamus and, 97

Pleasure centers, 88–89

Pleasure principle, 92

Pluralistic ignorance, 432. A situation in which

Pluralistic ignorance (continued) individuals each are unaware that other persons feel or behave in the same way as themselves.

Polaroid glass, 143

Polaroid (Land) camera, 143

Politics, leadership in, 460, 461

Polls, public opinion, 120

Population:
aging of, 341
psychotic, 385–86, 393

Pornography, 471

Porpoises, 60

Posthypnotic suggestion, 207

Postpartum depression, 376. Symptoms of depression often brought on after giving birth and lasting from about two to six weeks. Physical exhaustion, hormone changes, and personality conflicts seem to be probable causes.

Posture:
muscles and, 38–39
upright, 242

Poverty:
mental retardation and, 269
old people, 341

Power law, 136

Power sense, 241

"Practical intelligence," 236

Prediction:
conditioning and, 92
pleasure and, 92
stress and, 99
testing and, 271

Prejudice, 375, 440, 441

Premature birth, 229–31

Prenatal development, 15, 228–31

Preschool development, 244–47, 327

Prevention, 354–55, 479–80

Primal scene, 475. A psychoanalytic term for a person's recollection (actual or fancied) of the first observation of a sex act. According to Freud, this has a great effect on personality formation.

Primary group, 458. A small group, such as family or friends, with which a person has had frequent, informal, and significant contact.

Primary mental abilities, 261. The abilities identified as making up general intelligence. These relatively independent abilities include verbal, numerical, perceptual, and spatial reasoning.

Primary motivation, 65–83, 110, 122. A term for the primary motives based on physical conditions that drive an individual to action. Also called *physiological motives.*

Primary reinforcer, 151, 164. The

79 80 81 10 9 8 7 6 5 4 3 2 1